Fünf Monate in Berlin

Schriftenreihe des Landesarchivs Berlin

Herausgegeben von Uwe Schaper

Band 18

Fünf Monate in Berlin

Briefe von Edgar N. Johnson aus dem Jahre 1946

Herausgegeben und bearbeitet
von
Werner Breunig und Jürgen Wetzel

DE GRUYTER
OLDENBOURG

ISBN 978-3-486-73566-6
e-ISBN 978-3-486-85698-9

Bibliografische Information der Deutschen Nationalbibliothek
Die Deutsche Nationalbibliothek verzeichnet diese Publikation in der Deutschen Nationalbibliografie; detaillierte bibliografische Daten sind im Internet über http://dnb.dnb.de abrufbar.

Library of Congress Cataloging-in-Publication Data
A CIP catalog record for this book has been applied for at the Library of Congress.

© 2014 Oldenbourg Wissenschaftsverlag GmbH
Rosenheimer Straße 143, 81671 München, Deutschland
www.degruyter.com
Ein Unternehmen von De Gruyter

Titelbild: Edgar N. Johnson (rechts) und sein Executive Officer Elliott W. Schryver, München, Juli 1945 (The University of Chicago Library, Special Collections Research Center, Chicago, Illinois, USA, Edgar N. Johnson Papers).
Druck und Bindung: Memminger MedienCentrum Druckerei und Verlags-AG, Memmingen

Gedruckt in Deutschland
Dieses Papier ist alterungsbeständig nach DIN/ISO 9706

Inhalt

Vorbemerkung..	1
Werner Breunig Edgar N. Johnson – eine biografische Skizze........................	5
Jürgen Wetzel "Winning the Peace"...	43
Dokumentenverzeichnis..	57
Dokumente...	63
Bildanhang...	363
Abkürzungsverzeichnis...	427
Quellen- und Literaturverzeichnis	435
Personenregister	451

Vorbemerkung

Edgar N. Johnson, Professor für europäische Geschichte an der University of Nebraska, kam Anfang März 1946 in die Viermächtestadt Berlin, um wichtige Aufgaben für die amerikanische Militärregierung zu übernehmen. Von General Lucius D. Clay, dem stellvertretenden Militärgouverneur, zum Special Assistant ernannt, wurde er gleichzeitig als politischer Berater des amerikanischen Stadtkommandanten von Berlin eingesetzt. Über seine fünf Monate in der alten Reichshauptstadt, seine Begegnungen mit besatzungspolitischen Akteuren und deutschen Persönlichkeiten aus Politik und Kultur, seine Beobachtungen, Gedanken und Einsichten geben die Briefe an Ehefrau Emily und ein von ihm nach seinem Deutschlandaufenthalt verfasster Bericht detailliert Auskunft. Diese Aufzeichnungen eröffnen uns ein vielschichtiges Panorama von Besatzungsalltag und politischem Wiederaufbau in Berlin 1946.

Zum Abdruck gebracht werden nicht nur die zwischen dem 7. März und 15. Juli 1946 aus Berlin geschriebenen Briefe (Dok. 15-75), die den größten Teil der Dokumente ausmachen, sondern auch die zuvor, zwischen dem 12. Februar und 5. März 1946, auf dem Weg nach Berlin in Washington, D. C., und New York, an Bord der „George W. Goethals" sowie in Le Havre und Paris verfassten Schreiben (Dok. 1-14), ferner die Briefe, die Johnson während seiner Reise durch die amerikanische Besatzungszone, zwischen dem 21. Juli und 1. August 1946, in Butzbach, Stuttgart und München (Dok. 76-79) und am Ende seines Deutschlandaufenthalts, am 7. und 9. August 1946, in Bremerhaven (Dok. 80-82) zu Papier brachte. Bis auf seine an die beiden kleinen Söhne und an den Vater gerichteten Zeilen (Dok. 60 und Dok. 69) gingen die Mitteilungen an die Ehefrau in Lincoln im US-Bundesstaat Nebraska. Den Dokumententeil beschließt der nicht datierte Report "Five Months in Berlin" (Dok. 83), den Johnson offensichtlich kurz nach seiner Heimkehr schrieb, im Rückblick auf das Erlebte. Möglicherweise griff er bei der Abfassung, mit der er vielleicht schon während der Rückreise auf See begonnen hatte, auf die Briefe zurück, die er seiner Frau geschrieben hatte. Es ist nicht auszuschließen, dass er ursprünglich beabsichtigte, seinen Bericht zu veröffentlichen.

Unter dem Titel "Five Months in Berlin" hielt Johnson im Herbst 1946 auch mehrere Vorträge, unter anderem vor Mitgliedern der American Library Association und dem University of Nebraska Faculty Women's Club.

Johnsons Aufzeichnungen wurden in dessen „Studierhütte" auf dem 1951 erworbenen Feriengrundstück in den Rocky Mountains, in Allenspark im US-Bundesstaat Colorado, in einem alten Überseekoffer gefunden. "I had never expected to see these published when I found them"[1], so Johnsons Schwiegertochter Candice E. Johnson. "The trunk had been used by Edgar in Austria and Berlin and contained the letters all inside the original envelopes, tied in bundles with string."[2]

---

[1] Candice E. Johnson in einer E-Mail an Werner Breunig vom 4. Mai 2007.
[2] Candice E. Johnson in einer E-Mail an Werner Breunig vom 24. Mai 2010.

Die Briefe wurden 2005 der University of Chicago Library, Special Collections Research Center, übergeben, wo sie einen Bestandteil des Nachlasses von Edgar N. Johnson, der Edgar N. Johnson Papers,[3] bilden.[4] Auch der Bericht "Five Months in Berlin" gehört zu dem in Chicago verwahrten Nachlass.[5]

Während der Bericht maschinenschriftlich abgefasst ist, sind die Briefe handgeschrieben. Obwohl Johnson eine schwierige Handschrift hatte und es große Mühe bereitet, "to read his terrible handwriting"[6], ist es den Bearbeitern gelungen, eine lückenlose Transkription zu erstellen.

Die Texte sind in der Originalsprache belassen worden, um die Authentizität zu wahren. Sie werden hier weitgehend unverändert und ungekürzt wiedergegeben. Lediglich in zwei Ausnahmefällen sind aus privaten Rücksichten geringfügige Auslassungen vorgenommen worden; diese werden durch [...] gekennzeichnet und im wissenschaftlichen Kommentar erläutert. Die falsche Schreibweise von Eigennamen (zum Beispiel „Drum" statt „Glum" oder „Ullbrecht" statt „Ulbricht") ist nicht korrigiert worden, die richtige Schreibweise findet sich im Kommentar. Abkürzungen wie „Em." für „Emily" sind in eckigen Klammern aufgelöst. Unterstrichene Wörter werden kursiv wiedergegeben.

Die Kommentierung der hier abgedruckten Dokumente fußt auf der Auswertung von Materialien aus Privatbesitz (vor allem der im Besitz von Johnsons Sohn Thomas R. Johnson und dessen Ehefrau Candice E. Johnson in Denver, Colorado, USA, verbliebenen, nicht in der University of Chicago Library befindlichen Unterlagen aus dem Nachlass Edgar N. Johnson) und zahlreicher Bestände in- und ausländischer Archive sowie auf Gesprächen mit Zeitzeugen und Auskünften von Institutionen und Personen. Berücksichtigt wurden auch die Briefe, die Ehefrau Emily an Edgar N. Johnson geschrieben hatte und die von Candice E. und Thomas R. Johnson verwahrt werden. Hilfreich bei der Kommentierung waren ferner die im Archiv des Instituts für Zeitgeschichte in München und im Bundesarchiv in Koblenz zur Verfügung stehenden Mikrofiche-Bestände der OMGUS-Akten (OMGUS = Office of Military Government for Germany [US]) sowie die Mikrofiche-Bestände der OMGBS-Akten (OMGBS = Office of Military Government, Berlin Sector) im Landesarchiv Berlin. Ausgewertet wurden auch Protokolle der OMGUS-Stabskonferenzen, die im Archiv des Instituts für Zeitgeschichte in München als Protokollkopien vorhanden sind, und Protokolle der Sitzungen des Local Government Committee, Allied Kommandatura Berlin, die in The National Archives, Kew, Richmond, Surrey, Großbritannien, im Bestand "Allied Kommandatura: Directives, Minutes and Papers" ausfindig gemacht wurden. Erwähnenswert sind schließlich die Unterlagen aus dem Nachlass Louis Glaser, die sich im Besitz von Anthony J. Glaser, Bethesda, Maryland, USA, befinden, und die Lieutenant Colonel Harold Hays MBE Collection im Imperial War Museum Duxford, Cambridgeshire, Großbritannien. Glaser leitete die Civil Administration Branch der

---

[3] Siehe University of Chicago Library, Guide to the Edgar N. Johnson Papers 1930–1966, http://www.lib.uchicago.edu/e/scrc/findingaids/view.php?eadid=ICU.SPCL.ENJOHNSON (letzter Zugriff am 2. September 2013).
[4] Box 1, Folder 8–10; Box 2, Folder 1.
[5] Box 2, Folder 13.
[6] Candice E. Johnson in einer E-Mail an Werner Breunig vom 4. Mai 2007.

amerikanischen Militärregierung für Berlin und war der amerikanische, Hays der britische Vertreter im Local Government Committee, Allied Kommandatura Berlin. Mit beiden arbeitete Johnson zusammen.

Neben Besatzungsangehörigen und deutschen Persönlichkeiten aus Politik und Kultur finden in den Briefen zahlreiche Freunde und Bekannte aus gemeinsamen Zeiten beim Office of Strategic Services (OSS), dem Nachrichtendienst, für den Johnson von 1943 bis 1945 in Washington, D. C., und Europa gearbeitet hatte, Erwähnung, außerdem Kollegen von der University of Nebraska und Verwandte in der Heimat. Zu allen Personen, die in den Aufzeichnungen genannt werden, hält der Kommentarteil biografische Informationen bereit.

Bislang fand Johnson keinerlei Beachtung in der Berlin-Literatur. In der 1990 erschienenen Quellenedition „Die Entstehung der Verfassung von Berlin" taucht sein Name in sechs Dokumenten alliierter Herkunft auf, die mit zwei Themen zu tun haben: mit der Suche nach einem Termin erster Berliner Nachkriegswahlen und mit der Schaffung einer provisorischen Berliner Verfassung.[7] Im 1987 publizierten Tagebuch des Darmstädter Regierungspräsidenten Ludwig Bergsträsser aus den Jahren 1945 bis 1948 wird eine Begegnung festgehalten, die dieser am 26. Juli 1946 in Darmstadt mit Johnson hatte.[8] Die Wochenzeitung "OMGUS Observer" berichtet am 12. Juli 1946 ausführlich über einen Vortrag, den Edgar N. Johnson vor den Damen des American Women's Club of Berlin hielt.[9] Für eine deutsche Ausgabe von Benjamin Franklins Autobiografie schrieb Johnson in Berlin das Vorwort; das Buch erschien noch 1946 im Karl H. Henssel Verlag, Berlin.[10] In Auszügen wurde das Vorwort in der amerikanisch lizenzierten Berliner Zeitschrift „Horizont. Halbmonatsschrift für junge Menschen" abgedruckt.[11]

Johnson veröffentlichte nach seiner Tätigkeit für die amerikanische Militärregierung nichts über seine gewonnenen Eindrücke und Einsichten, während er nach seinem OSS-Einsatz in Österreich einen Aufsatz unter dem Titel "The American Occupation of Austria"[12] publiziert hatte.

Allen Personen und Institutionen, die uns bei der Suche nach Quellen bzw. bei Einzelfragen der Kommentierung geholfen haben, möchten wir herzlich danken. Unser Dank gilt vor allem Edgar N. Johnsons Sohn Thomas R. Johnson, PhD, Senior Research Associate, und dessen Ehefrau, Candice E. Johnson, MD, PhD, Professor of Pediatrics, aus Denver, Colorado, USA, mit deren Einverständnis diese Veröffentlichung möglich wurde und die stets bereitwillig

---

[7] Siehe Die Entstehung der Verfassung von Berlin. Eine Dokumentation, im Auftrag des Präsidenten des Abgeordnetenhauses von Berlin hrsg. von Hans J. Reichhardt unter Mitarbeit von Werner Breunig/Josephine Gabler, 2 Bde., Berlin und New York 1990, S. 296f., 299, 301, 308 und 336.

[8] Siehe Ludwig Bergsträsser, Befreiung, Besatzung, Neubeginn. Tagebuch des Darmstädter Regierungspräsidenten 1945-1948, hrsg. von Walter Mühlhausen (= Biographische Quellen zur deutschen Geschichte nach 1945, Bd. 5), München 1987, S. 149f.

[9] Siehe "Shun Nazis", Wives Told At Women's Club Meeting, in: OMGUS Observer vom 12. Juli 1946, S. 2.

[10] Siehe Benjamin Franklin. Sein Leben von ihm selbst erzählt, Berlin 1946.

[11] Siehe Benjamin Franklin und die deutsche Jugend, in: Horizont, 20. Heft, 1. Jg., 1. September 1946, S. 19.

[12] In: Nebraska History, Vol. 26, 1945, S. 201-210.

Auskünfte erteilt sowie Materialien zur Verfügung gestellt haben. Auch für ein anregendes Gespräch in Berlin sei ihnen gedankt. Professor DDr. Oliver Rathkolb vom Institut für Zeitgeschichte der Universität Wien möchten wir dafür danken, dass er uns auf die Tätigkeit von Edgar N. Johnson für die amerikanische Militärregierung in Deutschland aufmerksam gemacht und uns dessen Berlin-Briefe zu einem Zeitpunkt, als sie noch nicht der University of Chicago Library übergeben waren, zur Verfügung gestellt hat. Unseren Dank sprechen wir auch dem Direktor des Landesarchivs Berlin, Professor Dr. Uwe Schaper, aus, der uns geduldig unterstützt und die Aufnahme der Edition in die Schriftenreihe des Landesarchivs Berlin ermöglicht hat.

Berlin, im März 2014   Werner Breunig und Jürgen Wetzel

Werner Breunig
Edgar N. Johnson – eine biografische Skizze

Edgar Nathaniel Johnson kam Anfang März 1946 ins zerbombte Berlin. Wer war dieser ernst und angespannt wirkende Amerikaner, der als Mitarbeiter von General Lucius D. Clay wichtige Aufgaben im Nachkriegsdeutschland übernehmen sollte? Welche Stationen lagen hinter ihm, welche vor ihm? Im Folgenden soll sein Lebensweg, der 1901 begann und 1969 endete, umrissen und dabei auch seine Zeit in der Viermächtestadt Berlin festgehalten werden.

Geboren wurde Edgar N. Johnson am 4. April 1901 als Sohn schwedischstämmiger Eltern in Chicago im US-Bundesstaat Illinois. Sein Vater, Frank E. Johnson, eigentl. Johanson, hatte Schweden, wo er mit elf Geschwistern aufgewachsen war, als junger Mann verlassen, wohl aufgrund materieller Not. 1898 wurde er in den USA eingebürgert. Die Mutter, Mabel A. Johnson, geb. Walstrom, war in Chicago als Tochter von aus Schweden emigrierten Eltern zur Welt gekommen. Edgar hatte einen älteren Bruder, der im Kindesalter starb. Zwei jüngere Geschwister, ein Bruder und eine Schwester, wurden 1904 bzw. 1911 geboren. Die Familie zog aus der großen Einwanderermetropole am Michigansee weg, als der Vater Arbeit als Klavierbauer in einer Fabrik in Holly, Michigan, und schließlich in La Porte, Indiana, fand. In der Kleinstadt La Porte, unweit von Chicago, verbrachten die Eltern einen Großteil ihres Lebens.

Edgar besuchte zunächst in Holly und dann in La Porte die Grundschule, absolvierte die staatliche La Porte High School und begann im Herbst 1918 in seiner Geburtsstadt Chicago ein Studium. An der privaten University of Chicago belegte er als Hauptfach Geschichte, daneben Politikwissenschaft, Wirtschaftswissenschaft und Französisch. Um Geld für die Finanzierung seines Studiums zu verdienen, betätigte er sich als Pianist bei Stummfilmvorführungen. Ebenso wie sein Vater war er ein versierter Klavierspieler, und die Liebe zur Musik sollte ihn lebenslang begleiten. "Loved music, and relaxed by playing the piano, which he did very well – mostly 19th century classical music, often Baroque."[1]

1922 schloss Johnson sein Undergraduate-Studium an der University of Chicago ab und erwarb den Bachelor of Philosophy (PhB), "with honorable mention and special honors for work in history"[2]. Anschließend, von September 1922 bis Juni 1924, sammelte er erste Berufserfahrungen: Als Instructor in History unterrichtete er europäische Geschichte an der angesehenen Culver Military Academy[3], einer Privatschule in Culver, Indiana, etwa eine Fahrtstunde

---

[1] Eugene N. Anderson Jr. in einer E-Mail an Werner Breunig vom 17. Juli 2007.
[2] Schreiben von Edgar N. Johnson an Charles Henry Oldfather, Chairman des Department of History der University of Nebraska in Lincoln, Nebraska, vom 13. Mai 1931, in: University of Nebraska-Lincoln (UNL) Libraries, Archives & Special Collections, Lincoln, Nebraska, USA, Biographical File of Edgar N. Johnson, RG/52-01, Box 134.
[3] Gegründet 1894 von Henry H. Culver "for the purpose of thoroughly preparing young men for the best colleges, scientific schools and businesses of America". Zit. nach http://www.culver.org/about-culver/introduction/history-a-traditions/overview (letzter Zugriff am 28. August 2013).

von seiner Heimatstadt La Porte entfernt. Sommers unterrichtete er in einem Schulcamp.

Culver war für Johnson nur eine kurze Zwischenstation. Im Herbst 1924 kehrte er an die Universität Chicago zurück, um ein Graduate-Studium der mittelalterlichen und neuzeitlichen europäischen Geschichte aufzunehmen. Sein Hauptinteresse galt dem Mittelalter, das ihn seit der Lektüre von Henry Adams' faszinierendem Werk "Mont-Saint-Michel and Chartres" fesselte. Drei Studienjahre verbrachte er als Graduate-Student an der University of Chicago. Stipendien halfen ihm, sein Studium zu finanzieren: "During the last two of these years I held fellowships from the department."[4] Zu seinen Lehrern zählten Godfrey Davies, Walter L. Dorn, Carl F. Huth Jr., Einar Joranson, Ferdinand Schevill, Bernadotte E. Schmitt und James W. Thompson. Sein wichtigster Lehrer war Thompson, ein Experte für mittelalterliche und frühneuzeitliche europäische Geschichte (insbesondere für das Heilige Römische Reich und Frankreich), der später – ab 1932 – an der University of California, Berkeley, lehrte und 1937 gemeinsam mit Johnson ein voluminöses Werk veröffentlichte: James Westfall Thompson/Edgar Nathaniel Johnson, An Introduction to Medieval Europe 300–1500, New York 1937. Es handelte sich um Johnsons völlige Neubearbeitung eines früheren Buches von Thompson.

Im Sommer 1927 verließ Johnson seinen Studienort Chicago, "for a fourteen months stay of travel and study in Europe"[5], ausgestattet mit einem Stipendium der in Berlin ansässigen Alexander von Humboldt-Stiftung[6]. Im Wintersemester 1927/1928 studierte er an der Ludwig-Maximilians-Universität München – "to which I did not become wholly attached"[7] – mittelalterliche Geschichte.[8] Reisen führten ihn quer durch Europa: "Time away from Munich I spent in travel in England, France, Germany, Czecho-Slovakia, Austria, Hungary, Italy and Switzerland."[9]

Begleitet wurde er von seinem Freund John D. Bickford, ein promovierter Altphilologe, Absolvent der Princeton University und seit 1920 Lehrer an der

---

[4] Schreiben von Edgar N. Johnson an Charles Henry Oldfather, Chairman des Department of History der University of Nebraska in Lincoln, Nebraska, vom 13. Mai 1931, in: UNL Libraries, Archives & Special Collections, Biographical File of Edgar N. Johnson, RG/52-01, Box 134.

[5] Ebd.

[6] Zu der 1925 eingerichteten Humboldt-Stiftung siehe Holger Impekoven, Die Alexander von Humboldt-Stiftung und das Ausländerstudium in Deutschland 1925–1945. Von der „geräuschlosen Propaganda" zur Ausbildung der „geistigen Wehr" des „Neuen Europa" (= Internationale Beziehungen. Theorie und Geschichte, Bd. 9), Göttingen 2013.

[7] So Edgar N. Johnson später in einem Schreiben aus Salzburg an Ehefrau Emily vom 8. Juli 1945, in: The University of Chicago (UChicago) Library, Special Collections Research Center, Chicago, Illinois, USA, Edgar N. Johnson Papers.

[8] Nach telefonischer Auskunft von Holger Impekoven (siehe Anm. 6) vom 16. Oktober 2013 war Johnson im Wintersemester 1927/1928 einer von vier US-Amerikanern, die mit finanzieller Unterstützung der Humboldt-Stiftung in Deutschland studierten.

[9] Edgar N. Johnson, Curriculum Vitae, undatiert [ca. 1963], S. 1, in: UChicago Library, Special Collections Research Center, Edgar N. Johnson Papers.

Culver Military Academy, wo auch Johnson unterrichtet hatte.[10] Im März 1927 war ihr gemeinsam verfasster Aufsatz "The Contemplated Anglo-German Alliance: 1890-1901"[11] erschienen – "the offshoot of one of Professor Schmitt's seminars, which I worked out with a friend of mine"[12], so Johnson. Bickford unterrichtete nach seiner Rückkehr aus Europa an der renommierten und exklusiven Hotchkiss School in Lakeville, Connecticut, neben Latein auch Deutsch. 1934 heiratete er die rund 20 Jahre jüngere Mildred H. Johnson, die Schwester seines Freundes Edgar N. Johnson. Zwei Jahre später starb Bickford im Alter von nur 45 Jahren – ein schmerzvoller Verlust für seine Frau und für seinen Schwager. "Mildred left to spend a year at the Sorbonne in Paris to study French and became profoundly depressed, losting 20 pounds weight before she returned."[13]

In München besuchte Johnson Vorlesungen oder Übungen der Professoren Heinrich Günter, Paul Joachimsen, Paul Lehmann, Hermann Oncken und anderen. Lehrveranstaltungen wie „Die deutsche Kaiserzeit. Das Mittelalter" von Günter, „Luther, Zwingli, Calvin" von Joachimsen, „Einleitung in die lateinische Philologie des Mittelalters" oder „Kritische Übungen des Seminars für lateinische Philologie des Mittelalters" des Altphilologen Lehmann dürften sein Interesse gefunden haben.[14]

Während seines Studienaufenthalts in München wohnte Johnson in der Hohenstaufenstraße 10/II,[15] in einer unweit der Universität gelegenen Gästepension, die von Anna Engelhorn betrieben wurde, einer aus Straßburg im Elsass stammenden, als Kunstmalerin ausgebildeten Frau. Deren Vater, August Winnecke, hatte als Professor für Astronomie an der Universität Straßburg und Direktor der dortigen Sternwarte gewirkt. Ihr Ehemann, Kommerzienrat Karl Engelhorn, ein früherer Bankdirektor, war erst im August 1927 verstorben. Von ihrem Enkelsohn Wolfgang Oppenheimer wird sie als „immer jovial, menschenfreundlich, stark verbunden mit ihrer Verwandtschaft – aber auch mit der Politik"[16] beschrieben. Mit dieser herzlichen, heiteren, lebensbejahenden und geistreichen Frau[17] führten Johnson und Bickford noch Jahre später einen regen Briefwechsel; auch in der NS-Zeit existierten die Kontakte zu Anna Engel-

---

[10] Nach telefonischer Auskunft von Holger Impekoven (siehe Anm. 6) vom 16. Oktober 2013 war Bickford kein Humboldt-Stipendiat.
[11] In: Political Science Quarterly, Vol. 42, No. 1 (März 1927), S. 1-57.
[12] Schreiben von Edgar N. Johnson an Charles Henry Oldfather, Chairman des Department of History der University of Nebraska in Lincoln, Nebraska, vom 13. Mai 1931, in: UNL Libraries, Archives & Special Collections, Biographical File of Edgar N. Johnson, RG/52-01, Box 134.
[13] Candice E. Johnson in einer E-Mail an Werner Breunig vom 1. Juni 2010.
[14] Siehe Ludwig-Maximilians-Universität München. Verzeichnis der Vorlesungen Winter-Halbjahr 1927/28, München 1927, S. 26 und 29.
[15] Siehe Personenstand der Ludwig-Maximilians-Universität München. Winter-Halbjahr 1927/28, München 1928, S. 116.
[16] Schreiben von Wolfgang Oppenheimer an Werner Breunig vom 10. Januar 2012.
[17] „Hinter ihrer Heiterkeit, Toleranz und Lebensbejahung stand ein geprüfter, innerlich gefestigter Glaube. Ihr glückliches Naturell erlaubte es ihr, wenn ich recht urteile, immer das Positive im Leben zu erkennen und darauf hinzuweisen." Erinnerungen von Marcus Löw-Suter, S. 61, Privatbesitz Dieter Loew, Basel, Schweiz.

horn, die eine dezidierte Gegnerin des nationalsozialistischen Regimes war,[18] fort.[19]

Im Herbst 1928 kehrte Johnson an die University of Chicago zurück und lehrte bis Juni 1931 als Instructor im dortigen Department of History, gleichzeitig arbeitete er an seiner Dissertation. "My work here" – so Johnson 1931 – "has been with the freshmen survey course in the history of civilization. For two years the instructors gave this course individually. For this year we have been working with Professor Arthur P. Scott. I have also given two courses in the Down Town College for Professor Huth, one on the Middle Ages, and the other on the Absolute Monarchy in the seventeenth and eighteenth centuries."[20]

Ende 1931 erwarb Johnson an der University of Chicago den Doctor of Philosophy (PhD) mit seiner Dissertation "The Secular Activities of the German Episcopate 919-1024". Der Historiker Karl Jordan, Mitarbeiter der Monumenta Germaniae Historica in Berlin, besprach die Arbeit in der „Deutschen Literaturzeitung". Sie „ist aus der Schule von I. W. Thompson hervorgegangen, der durch seine verschiedenen Arbeiten der letzten Jahre die amerikanischen Historiker in besonderem Maße auf die mittelalterliche deutsche Geschichte hingewiesen hat"[21], so Jordan. „Aus dem großen Fragenkreis, den Thompson in seinem 1928

---

[18] „Schon als Anhängerin der Anthroposophie, aber auch nach ihrer Eigenart lehnte Tante Aenne den aufkommenden Nationalsozialismus ab und unterstützte alle Bemühungen, um die Opfer dieser Bewegung zu retten." Erinnerungen von Marcus Löw-Suter, S. 61, Privatbesitz Dieter Loew, Basel, Schweiz.

[19] Im Oktober 1933 berichtet sie in einem Schreiben an ihre „lieben guten Freunde", dass sie „unserem deutschen Gefängnis u. Narrenhaus einmal für 3 Wochen entronnen" sei und sich in der Schweiz am Lago Maggiore aufhalte, wo ihre Stieftochter Clara, die mit dem deutsch-jüdischen Industriellen Clemens Oppenheimer verheiratet war, mit ihrer aus Deutschland übergesiedelten Familie lebte. Schreiben aus Ascona vom 27. Oktober 1933, in: Unterlagen aus dem Nachlass Edgar N. Johnson, Privatbesitz Candice E. und Thomas R. Johnson, Denver, Colorado, USA. „Wissen Sie", so Engelhorn, „was wir zum Scherz in D[eutschland] sagen? Es gibt nur noch 2 Sorten Deutsche 1. Statthalter u. 2. Maulhalter u. den Maulaufreisser u. Propagandachef Goebbels nennen wir ‚Wotans Mickymaus' od. den nachgedunkelten Schrumpfgermanen. So entlasten wir uns durch weitergegebene Bon mots um nicht an aufgesammeltem Verdruss zu zerplatzen." Ebd. Über ihren Enkelsohn Wolfgang Oppenheimer, der später als Wirtschaftswissenschaftler, Historiker und Autor hervortrat, schreibt sie: „Welch ein bezauberndes hochbegabtes Kind, das nicht wert sein soll deutscher Staatsbürger zu sein, dem man den Stempel der Minderwertigkeit aufprägen will!" Ebd. Im Januar 1935 teilt sie mit, „ungemein gelitten" zu haben „unter den Umwälzungen der letzten 2½ Jahre". Schreiben aus Basel vom 5. Januar 1935, in: Unterlagen aus dem Nachlass Edgar N. Johnson, Privatbesitz Candice E. und Thomas R. Johnson, Denver, Colorado, USA. „Die Eingriffe in die Universitäten, die Erziehung, die Kirchen sind finsteres Mittelalter, das Vorgehen gegen die Juden eine Kulturschande. Nicht leicht sich seines eigenen Volkes so bitter schämen zu müssen." Ebd.

[20] Schreiben von Edgar N. Johnson an Charles Henry Oldfather, Chairman des Department of History der University of Nebraska in Lincoln, Nebraska, vom 13. Mai 1931, in: UNL Libraries, Archives & Special Collections, Biographical File of Edgar N. Johnson, RG/52-01, Box 134.

[21] Karl Jordan, Rezension von: Edgar Nathaniel Johnson, The Secular Activities of the German Episcopate 919-1024, Lincoln, Nebraska, 1932, in: Deutsche Literaturzeitung, 1933, Heft 50, Sp. 2378-2380, hier Sp. 2378.

erschienenen Buche Feudal Germany behandelt hat, greift J[ohnson] ein einzelnes Problem, die Stellung des Episkopats im Staate der Ottonen, heraus und ist bestrebt, ihm eine vielseitige Darstellung zu widmen."²² Die „im allgemeinen klar und übersichtlich geschriebene" Arbeit würde „dem amerikanischen Leser ein umfassendes und im wesentlichen zutreffendes Bild von der eigenartigen Stellung des deutschen Episkopats zur Zeit der sächsischen Kaiser"²³ geben.

"I had meanwhile been invited to join the staff of the University of Nebraska beginning with the fall semester of 1931."²⁴ Im Mai 1931 schrieb Johnson an Professor Charles Henry Oldfather, Chairman des Department of History der staatlichen University of Nebraska in Lincoln, der Hauptstadt des Bundesstaats Nebraska: "I need not say, perhaps, that I am very happy over the opportunity of coming to Lincoln, and that I anticipate eagerly my work there, and work forward to becoming acquainted."²⁵ Er dankte Oldfather "for your offer to keep an eye open for a place for me to live. I am obliged to live quite modestly – a place to sleep, to work and for breathe is about all that I need."²⁶

Johnson war 30 Jahre alt, als er die Millionenstadt Chicago verließ und sich in das vergleichsweise kleine, damals keine 80 000 Einwohner zählende Lincoln, Nebraska, begab. Seine Tätigkeit an der dortigen Universität begann im September 1931. Zunächst war er Instructor, ab 1932 Assistant Professor of History, 1935 erfolgte die Beförderung zum Associate Professor, und schließlich erhielt er 1942 den Rang eines Full Professor. 1943 beschreibt er seine Aufgaben wie folgt: "Teaching classes, both undergraduate and graduate in European History, supervising graduate research in mediaeval History and serving on University Committees".²⁷ Ausführlich schildert er später in einem Lebenslauf seine Tätigkeit an der University of Nebraska: "During these years I always taught in the elementary course in European history, and in fact, always enjoyed working with good freshmen. In addition I always taught regularly a year's course in mediaeval history and irregularly a similar course in Reformation. But under the stimulus of Ferdinand Schevill's emphasis at Chicago I early substituted for the course on the Reformation, first, a year's course for advanced undergraduates and graduates on mediaeval civilization, and then a two years' course which I labelled, perhaps rather ambitiously, the History of Western Culture. This course spends the first year on the ancient and medieval periods (including the Renaissance) and its second year on the period from about 1600 to date. It aims to be what it is called, a history of western culture, culture being defined in historical rather than anthropological terms as the discipline of thought and the

---

22   Ebd.
23   Ebd., hier Sp. 2380.
24   Edgar N. Johnson, Curriculum Vitae, undatiert [ca. 1963], S. 1, in: UChicago Library, Special Collections Research Center, Edgar N. Johnson Papers.
25   Schreiben von Edgar N. Johnson an Charles Henry Oldfather, Chairman des Department of History der University of Nebraska in Lincoln, Nebraska, vom 13. Mai 1931, in: UNL Libraries, Archives & Special Collections, Biographical File of Edgar N. Johnson, RG/52-01, Box 134.
26   Ebd.
27   Application for Federal Employment vom 30. Januar 1943, S. 2, in: National Archives and Records Administration (NARA), College Park, Maryland, USA, Record Group 226 (Records of the Office of Strategic Services), Personalakte Dr. Edgar N. Johnson.

arts. As World War II approached the course developed into a history of the western tradition. [...] I have found the course on the History of Western Culture to be, perhaps my most useful teaching, for it has served to aid advanced undergraduate and graduate students to integrate their historical and other studies."[28]

Johnson gehörte der 1884 gegründeten American Historical Association an. Außerdem war er ein frühes Mitglied der Mediaeval Academy of America, "one of the first members of the Academy, which was founded in 1925"[29], und fungierte von 1946 bis 1949 als Councillor.[30] Später gehörte er auch der 1954 ins Leben gerufenen Renaissance Society of America an.

Ca. 1934 lernte er die aus Beatrice, Nebraska, stammende Emily L. Floyd kennen, seine spätere Ehefrau. Sie studierte seit 1931 an der University of Nebraska und besuchte seine Lehrveranstaltungen. Im Juni 1935 erwarb sie den Bachelor of Arts (AB) in Englisch und Geschichte. Ihre Wiege hatte auf einer Farm in Goodland, Kansas, gestanden. Dort war sie am 20. November 1910 als das älteste von elf Kindern geboren worden.

Die beiden heirateten am 14. Juli 1936 in La Porte, Indiana, wo Edgar N. Johnsons Eltern lebten. Genau zehn Jahre später, am 14. Juli 1946, schreibt Johnson aus Berlin: "This is the day 10 years ago. 10 full and precious years."[31] Dass sie eine glückliche Ehe führten, darauf deuten auch diese Worte Emilys hin: "I wish we had met and been married long before we did."[32] Ein Freund der Familie: "He [Edgar N. Johnson] had a close and wonderful marriage. His wife Emily was a really intelligent and totally delightful and charming lady. In those days, women stayed home and raised kids, and she put up with that pretty well. She was an outstanding cook."[33]

Aus der Ehe gingen zwei Söhne hervor. Im September 1939 wurde in Lincoln John F. Johnson geboren, im Juli 1944 kam in Washington, D. C., Thomas R. Johnson zur Welt.

Für ein Semester, von September 1939 bis Februar 1940, lehrte Johnson als Gastprofessor an der staatlichen University of Wisconsin in Madison, Wisconsin, wo er für den beurlaubten Historiker Gaines Post einsprang. Seine Aufgabe: "Teaching classes in European History, both graduate and undergraduate"[34].

---

[28] Edgar N. Johnson, Curriculum Vitae, undatiert [ca. 1963], S. 1f., in: UChicago Library, Special Collections Research Center, Edgar N. Johnson Papers.
[29] Lisa F. Davis, Acting Executive Director, Medieval Academy of America, in einer E-Mail an Werner Breunig vom 29. Mai 2013.
[30] Johnson wurde im April 1946 zum Mitglied des Council gewählt. Siehe Historical News, in: The American Historical Review, Vol. 51, No. 4 (Juli 1946), S. 788–804, hier S. 794f.; The Mediaeval Academy of America. Proceedings of the Twenty-first Annual Meeting of the Corporation 1946, in: Speculum, Vol. 21, No. 3 (Juli 1946), S. 362–375, hier S. 362.
[31] Dok. 74.
[32] Emily L. Johnson in einem Schreiben an Ehemann Edgar vom 15. Mai 1946, in: Unterlagen aus dem Nachlass Edgar N. Johnson, Privatbesitz Candice E. und Thomas R. Johnson, Denver, Colorado, USA.
[33] Eugene N. Anderson Jr. in einer E-Mail an Werner Breunig vom 17. Juli 2007.
[34] Application for Federal Employment vom 30. Januar 1943, S. 3, in: NARA, Record Group 226 (Records of the Office of Strategic Services), Personalakte Dr. Edgar N. Johnson.

Ab dem 20. Februar 1943 war Johnson von der Universität freigestellt, "for duration of war"³⁵, um für das Office of Strategic Services (OSS) in Washington, D. C., zu arbeiten, einem 1942 eingerichteten und 1945 wieder aufgelösten amerikanischen Nachrichtendienst. Die weitaus größte Abteilung dieser Behörde war die Research and Analysis Branch, in der vorrangig interdisziplinäre Regionalstudien erstellt wurden, die der Feindaufklärung bzw. der Besatzungsplanung dienten. Johnson sollte als Research Analyst in der Central European Section dieser Forschungsabteilung arbeiten. Vieles sprach dafür, ihn in dieser Sektion einzusetzen: "Dr. Edgar Johnson, Professor of History at the University of Nebraska, is one of the ablest students of German affairs among the members of the American Historical Association. Although he acquired his present reputation largely through his scholarly publications in medieval German history, he is without doubt one of the best-informed students of contemporary Germany in the Middle West. [...] Dr. Johnson is without doubt one of the ablest American students in the field of Medieval German history. He has published a number of brilliant monographs in this field, all of which were reviewed with warm enthusiasm. Notwithstanding his reputation as a medievalist, his keen interest in the internal development of Germany under the Nazi regime has borne fruit in a number of excellent articles. In addition to his training in historical method, Dr. Johnson is a close student of the social sciences. He is a reflective, thorough scholar with an unusual capacity for work. His scholarly background and present equipment offer the promise that he will become one of the most useful members of the Central European Section."³⁶

Die Tätigkeit dieses ausgewiesenen Wissenschaftlers, der die deutsche Sprache beherrschte³⁷ und gute Kenntnisse von Deutschland und den Deutschen hatte, für die Mitteleuropasektion der Forschungsabteilung "Research and Analysis" in Washington, D. C., begann am 22. Februar 1943. Am selben Tag kam der in die USA emigrierte deutsche Jurist und Politikwissenschaftler Franz L. Neumann, der sich mit seinem Buch „Behemoth", einer Strukturanalyse des „Dritten Reiches", einen Namen als scharfsinniger Analytiker des Nationalsozialismus gemacht hatte, zur Central European Section. "A refugee by the name of Franz Neumann (he has written a book on Germany called Behemoth – considered the best) came in on the same day with me"³⁸, teilt Johnson seiner Frau mit.

---

35 Bulletin of the University of Nebraska, 31. August 1945, S. 42, in: UNL Libraries, Archives & Special Collections, Bulletins & Catalogs (University, General), RG/00-07.
36 Robert H. Alcorn, Office of Strategic Services, in einem Vermerk vom 21. Dezember 1942, Subject: Dr. Edgar Johnson and Miss Ethel P. Ross, Anhang, in: NARA, Record Group 226 (Records of the Office of Strategic Services), Personalakte Dr. Edgar N. Johnson.
37 Johnson verfügte über Fremdsprachenkenntnisse in Deutsch, Französisch, Italienisch und Latein. Deutsch und Französisch konnte er nach eigenen Angaben sehr gut lesen, ausreichend sprechen und gut verstehen, Italienisch konnte er ausreichend und Latein gut lesen. Siehe Application for Federal Employment vom 30. Januar 1943, S. 2, in: NARA, Record Group 226 (Records of the Office of Strategic Services), Personalakte Dr. Edgar N. Johnson.
38 Schreiben von Edgar N. Johnson aus Washington, D. C., an Ehefrau Emily vom 24. Februar 1943, in: Unterlagen aus dem Nachlass Edgar N. Johnson, Privatbesitz Candice E. und Thomas R. Johnson, Denver, Colorado, USA.

Die Mitteleuropasektion, in der amerikanische und exilierte Wissenschaftler zusammenarbeiteten und Johnson ebenso wie Franz L. Neumann oder die Emigranten Felix Gilbert, Hajo Holborn und Herbert Marcuse zu einer intellektuellen Elite von historisch-politischen Deutschlandkennern gehörte, unterstand zunächst dem Historiker Walter L. Dorn, Experte für preußische Geschichte im 18. Jahrhundert, im Mittleren Westen der USA geborener Sohn einer deutsch-amerikanischen Pastorenfamilie, den Johnson von der University of Chicago her bereits kannte. Seiner organisatorischen Aufgabe als Sektionsleiter zeigte sich Dorn nicht gewachsen.[39] "Dorn is a washout as an administrator, and as long as he is chief nothing serious will be done"[40], stellt Johnson schnell fest. "[...] I shall get a desk in the Congressional Library. You can't work in the Office with Dorn around."[41] Dieser wurde schließlich nach Großbritannien versetzt und in Washington von seinem bisherigen Stellvertreter abgelöst, dem Historiker Eugene N. Anderson, gleichfalls Fachmann für deutsche Geschichte, der ebenso wie Dorn in Deutschland geforscht hatte und mit Johnson eng befreundet war.

"It was tentatively decided today that I shall specialize on the German Church and Churches, which would be up my alley a bit and would interest me"[42], teilt Johnson zu Beginn seiner Verwendung als Research Analyst seiner Frau mit. Er befasste sich zunächst mit den Kirchen und war dann für Österreich-Studien zuständig. "In OSS I was associated, first, with the work on Germany and then on Austria. In the former capacity I was responsible for the final edition of the *Handbook on the German Church* and the *Military Government Guide on the German Church*."[43] Ein „Österreichproblem" gab es bis zur Moskauer Deklaration vom 1. November 1943, in der die Alliierten erstmals die Wiedererrichtung eines selbstständigen Österreichs in seinen Grenzen vor 1938 in Aussicht stellten, nur im Gesamtverband des Deutschen Reiches, gesonderte Österreichplanungen gab es bis dahin keine.[44]

In einer Beurteilung vom November 1943 wurde ihm bescheinigt, einer der befähigsten Mitarbeiter der Central European Section zu sein: "Mr. Johnson has proved to be one of the ablest members of the Section and has written some of

---

[39] Siehe Walter L. Dorn, Inspektionsreisen in der US-Zone. Notizen, Denkschriften und Erinnerungen aus dem Nachlaß übersetzt und hrsg. von Lutz Niethammer (= Schriftenreihe der Vierteljahrshefte für Zeitgeschichte, Nr. 26), Stuttgart 1973, S. 11; Ernst C. Stiefel/Frank Mecklenburg, Deutsche Juristen im amerikanischen Exil (1933–1950), Tübingen 1991, S. 152.

[40] Schreiben von Edgar N. Johnson aus Washington, D. C., an Ehefrau Emily vom 24. Februar 1943, in: Unterlagen aus dem Nachlass Edgar N. Johnson, Privatbesitz Candice E. und Thomas R. Johnson, Denver, Colorado, USA.

[41] Ebd.

[42] Ebd.

[43] Edgar N. Johnson, Curriculum Vitae, undatiert [ca. 1963], S. 2, in: UChicago Library, Special Collections Research Center, Edgar N. Johnson Papers.

[44] Siehe Oliver Rathkolb, Professorenpläne für Österreichs Zukunft. Nachkriegsfragen im Diskurs der Forschungsabteilung Research and Analysis, in: Geheimdienstkrieg gegen Deutschland. Subversion, Propaganda und politische Planungen des amerikanischen Geheimdienstes im Zweiten Weltkrieg, hrsg. von Jürgen Heideking/Christof Mauch (Sammlung Vandenhoeck), Göttingen 1993, S. 166–181, hier S. 167 und 169.

our most important reports. He is a mature scholar, the author of several books and has more than carried his share of the intellectual leadership of the Section. He is responsible for the coverage of Church questions and is serving as the general director of the studies on Austria. In this capacity he assists in planning and in criticising the work of a number of other persons in the Section."[45]

Der aus Österreich stammende Lorenz Eitner, der 1944 zur Central European Section kam, beschreibt Edgar N. Johnson als „kurzsichtigen, sehr ernsten Mann mit vornübergebeugten Schultern, der sich sein Wissen über Österreich aus zweiter Hand angeeignet hatte, durch fleißiges Studieren"[46]. Dass Johnson „sich ganz offensichtlich unter den Neumanns & Marcuses nicht wohl fühlte (und wahrscheinlich auch nicht sonderlich ernst genommen wurde)"[47], wie Eitner vermerkt, dürfte ein falscher Eindruck sein, der durch seine unaufdringliche, zurückhaltende, bescheidene, sich nicht in den Mittelpunkt drängende und ernste Art entstanden sein könnte. Johnson war keine Primadonna.

Nach seinem Weggang aus Lincoln und dem Beginn seiner Tätigkeit für das OSS blieb Johnson nicht lange von seiner Familie getrennt. Bereits im März 1943 kamen seine Frau Emily und Sohn John nach, um mit ihm in Washington, D. C, zu wohnen. Das 1941 erworbene Haus in Lincoln wurde vermietet. Sohn Thomas, auch Timmy oder Tim genannt, kam im Juli 1944 in der US-Hauptstadt zur Welt. Allerdings war Johnson zu diesem Zeitpunkt schon nicht mehr in der OSS-Zentrale tätig, sondern in der Londoner Außenstelle der Research and Analysis Branch als Leiter der Austrian Section: "In June 1944 I went to London as the Chief of the Austrian Section of the Research and Analysis Branch and was there until the spring of 1945 working closely with military government and state department officials who were preparing to go to Austria. In the spring of 1945, before leaving for Italy, I worked at the American Embassy preparing material for Mr. Philip [E.] Mosely to use in some of his negotiations with Mr. [Fedor Tarasovič] Gusev over the division of Vienna among the Allies."[48] Johnson „schien in London der Hauptansprechpartner in Österreichfragen gewesen zu sein"[49].[50]

---

[45] Personnel Action Request vom 24. November 1943, in: NARA, Record Group 226 (Records of the Office of Strategic Services), Personalakte Dr. Edgar N. Johnson.
[46] Schreiben von Lorenz Eitner an Oliver Rathkolb vom 14. Juni 1985, zit. nach Oliver Rathkolb, Professorenpläne für Österreichs Zukunft. Nachkriegsfragen im Diskurs der Forschungsabteilung Research and Analysis, in: Geheimdienstkrieg gegen Deutschland. Subversion, Propaganda und politische Planungen des amerikanischen Geheimdienstes im Zweiten Weltkrieg, hrsg. von Jürgen Heideking/Christof Mauch (Sammlung Vandenhoeck), Göttingen 1993, S. 166–181, hier S. 168.
[47] Ebd.
[48] Edgar N. Johnson, Curriculum Vitae, undatiert [ca. 1963], S. 2, in: UChicago Library, Special Collections Research Center, Edgar N. Johnson Papers.
[49] Oliver Rathkolb, Professorenpläne für Österreichs Zukunft. Nachkriegsfragen im Diskurs der Forschungsabteilung Research and Analysis, in: Geheimdienstkrieg gegen Deutschland. Subversion, Propaganda und politische Planungen des amerikanischen Geheimdienstes im Zweiten Weltkrieg, hrsg. von Jürgen Heideking/Christof Mauch (Sammlung Vandenhoeck), Göttingen 1993, S. 166–181, hier S. 169.
[50] Siehe Oliver Rathkolb (Hrsg.), Gesellschaft und Politik am Beginn der Zweiten Republik. Vertrauliche Berichte der US-Militäradministration aus Österreich 1945 in englischer Originalfassung, Wien, Köln und Graz 1985, S. 13f.

Nach dem Tod seiner 68-jährigen Mutter kehrte Johnson Anfang 1945 für zwei Monate in die USA zurück.

Im April 1945 ging es von London nach Caserta in Süditalien, "where various task forces for Austria were located"[51]. An den 8. Mai 1945, den "Victory-in-Europe day", erinnert sich Johnson ein Jahr später wie folgt: "A year ago – on the first V-E day I was in Caserta. I still of course remember the great relief of that day. It was finally over. I remember the delicious quality of the Italian spring day. OSS gave a party in the garden of the hunting lodge belonging to the present crown prince of Italy."[52]

Nach Kriegsende, im Mai 1945, kam Johnson nach Österreich, wo er bis November 1945 blieb. "In Austria, after the cessation of hostilities, as the chief still of the Austrian section of the Research and Analysis Branch of OSS, I was associated with the restoration of governments in the Länder of Salzburg and Linz, and in Vienna got to know the members of the [Karl] Renner government fairly well and helped American officials in their contacts with this government. At this period also I worked closely with Ambassador [John G.] Erhardt and was privileged to help rectify mistakes of military government in Linz."[53]

Im Juli 1945 nutzte Johnson die Gelegenheit, von Salzburg aus einen Abstecher nach München zu unternehmen, in die amerikanische Besatzungszone Deutschlands, um mit eigenen Augen zu sehen, was mit seiner alten Studienstadt geschehen war. "Munich is only the empty shell of a dead city"[54], stellt er fest. "That is a slight exaggeration, of course, there are people about."[55] Die Zerstörung deutscher Städte durch den Luftkrieg, "no matter what the justification, is hard to take"[56].

Johnson suchte in München auch die Hohenstaufenstraße 10 auf. Das Haus, in dem er einst im zweiten Stock bei Anna Engelhorn logiert hatte, war ausgebombt und präsentierte sich als Hülle ohne Inhalt. "I was a bit sobered – after all this was home for about six months and home with a very sweet and liberal person."[57] "And here many evenings were spent listening to Lieder by Germany's Brahms and Schubert, Strauss and Wolff"[58], erinnert er sich. Jetzt wurde ihm hier ein recht eigenartiges und fast unheimlich anmutendes Musikerlebnis geboten, als inmitten der stillen Trümmerlandschaft die Klänge von Ludwig van Beethovens Mondscheinsonate ertönten: "The whole area, except for one house is a shell. In that house someone was playing a piano – the Moonlight Sonata, a little uncanny."[59]

---

[51] Edgar N. Johnson, Curriculum Vitae, undatiert [ca. 1963], S. 2, in: UChicago Library, Special Collections Research Center, Edgar N. Johnson Papers.
[52] Dok. 45.
[53] Edgar N. Johnson, Curriculum Vitae, undatiert [ca. 1963], S. 2f., in: UChicago Library, Special Collections Research Center, Edgar N. Johnson Papers.
[54] Edgar N. Johnson in einem Schreiben aus Salzburg an Ehefrau Emily vom 8. Juli 1945, in: UChicago Library, Special Collections Research Center, Edgar N. Johnson Papers.
[55] Ebd.
[56] Ebd.
[57] Ebd.
[58] Ebd.
[59] Ebd.

Als Johnson im November 1945, nach Beendigung seiner Aufgaben in Österreich, Deutschland bereiste, führte ihn der Weg zunächst erneut nach München. Quer durch die amerikanische Besatzungszone ging es dann über Augsburg, Ulm, Nürnberg, Schweinfurt, Bamberg, Würzburg und Aschaffenburg – der Blick des Mediävisten fiel auch auf mehr oder weniger stark beschädigte historische Bauten wie die Fuggerei in Augsburg, das Ulmer Münster oder die Nürnberger Burg – nach Wiesbaden, wo das OSS Germany seinen Sitz hatte. Von Wiesbaden aus bot sich ein kleiner Ausflug auf die andere Rheinseite nach Mainz, das in der französischen Besatzungszone lag, an. Bei der Besichtigung des Mainzer Doms, "one of my favorite churches in Germany"[60], im Zweiten Weltkrieg von Bomben getroffen, wurden Erinnerungen an die in den 1920er-Jahren unternommene Studienreise wach: "When I last saw it, it was a warm sunny day, not the cold grey day it has been today and for some days. And I saw the church, built in red sandstone glow with a late afternoon light. I tried to capture that experience in a passage in the book. It wouldn't have been right today to have had that effect. For a glowing cathedral would have been out of place in desolate Mainz."[61]

In Frankfurt am Main gab es ein Wiedersehen mit Walter L. Dorn. "He has had the opportunity to play much the same rôle in the American zone in Germany as we played in Austria."[62] "The professors (Drs. as they are known to the military) have not done so bad in this war"[63], meint Johnson.

Ein weiteres Reiseziel war Berlin, die von den vier alliierten Mächten besetzte alte Reichshauptstadt. Der Anblick der vom Krieg schwer gezeichneten Spreemetropole dürfte Johnson genauso erschüttert haben wie das Bild der anderen zerstörten deutschen Städte. Aus den vorliegenden Schreiben geht nicht hervor, ob er sich zum allerersten Mal in Berlin aufhielt oder schon einmal während seines Studienaufenthalts in Europa 1927/1928 an die Spree gekommen war. Briefe oder ein Tagebuch aus dieser Zeit sind nicht erhalten geblieben. "We have no letters or other information regarding Edgar's graduate student days in Germany, unfortunately"[64], so Thomas R. Johnson.

Nach seiner Deutschlandreise – in mehrfacher Hinsicht "a dreary trip", "dreary because of the devastation, dreary because of the general hopelessness, and dreary because of the rainy weather"[65] – flog Johnson in die USA zurück und konnte Weihnachten im Kreise seiner geliebten Familie verbringen.

---

[60] Edgar N. Johnson in einem Schreiben aus Wiesbaden an Ehefrau Emily vom 7. November 1945, in: UChicago Library, Special Collections Research Center, Edgar N. Johnson Papers.
[61] Ebd.
[62] Edgar N. Johnson in einem Schreiben aus Berlin an Ehefrau Emily vom 10. November 1945, in: UChicago Library, Special Collections Research Center, Edgar N. Johnson Papers.
[63] Ebd.
[64] Thomas R. Johnson in einer E-Mail an Werner Breunig vom 14. Juni 2013.
[65] Edgar N. Johnson in einem Schreiben aus Berlin an Ehefrau Emily vom 10. November 1945, in: UChicago Library, Special Collections Research Center, Edgar N. Johnson Papers.

Die in Österreich gewonnenen Eindrücke und Einsichten publizierte er in der Vierteljahreszeitschrift "Nebraska History".[66]

Für seine OSS-Tätigkeit in Europa – "for services from June 1944 to September 1945"[67] – erhielt Johnson später die hohe zivile Auszeichnung "Medal of Freedom".

Im Februar 1946 brach Johnson erneut nach Europa auf, um in Deutschland, wo die USA als eine von vier Besatzungsmächten bestrebt waren, „ehrlich dem deutschen Volk zu helfen, seinen Weg in die internationale Gemeinschaft zurückzufinden"[68], für die amerikanische Militärregierung, das Office of Military Government for Germany (US), kurz OMGUS genannt, tätig zu werden. Er zählte sich zu den Zivilisten, "who are going over to help solve the German problem"[69]. Nach seinem erfolgreichen Einsatz in Österreich, ebenso wie Deutschland von den vier alliierten Mächten besetzt und kontrolliert, sollte Johnson als War Department Employee im Stab von General Lucius D. Clay, dem stellvertretenden Militärgouverneur und Commanding General von OMGUS, arbeiten und als Leiter des wichtigen Regional Government Coordinating Office (RGCO) in Stuttgart fungieren. Diese Behörde, mit deren Aufbau James K. Pollock, Professor für Politikwissenschaft an der University of Michigan, im Oktober 1945 begonnen hatte,[70] diente als Koordinierungsorgan zwischen der amerikanischen Militärregierung und dem deutschen Länderrat der US-Zone.[71] Sie war eine der wichtigsten Dienststellen innerhalb des Besatzungsmechanismus und bot direkte Kontaktmöglichkeiten zu Clay, dessen Mitarbeitern und den Direktoren der Militärregierungen der Länder.[72]

Von Reisebeginn im Februar 1946 bis zum Ende seiner Tätigkeit in Deutschland im August 1946 schrieb Johnson lange, tagebuchartige Briefe an seine Frau, die somit alles nach- bzw. miterleben konnte. Ausführlich, detailfreudig, unmittelbar und ungeschminkt berichtet er von seinen täglichen Erlebnissen, seiner

---

[66] Siehe Edgar N. Johnson, The American Occupation of Austria, in: Nebraska History, Vol. 26, 1945, S. 201–210.

[67] Mitteilung des Adjutant General, Department of War, an den Director, Strategic Services Unit, vom 31. Juli 1946, in: Unterlagen aus dem Nachlass Edgar N. Johnson, Privatbesitz Candice E. und Thomas R. Johnson, Denver, Colorado, USA.

[68] Edgar N. Johnson, Vorwort, in: Benjamin Franklin. Sein Leben von ihm selbst erzählt, Berlin 1946, S. 5–10, hier S. 6.

[69] Dok. 9.

[70] Siehe James K. Pollock, Besatzung und Staatsaufbau nach 1945. Occupation Diary and Private Correspondence 1945–1948, hrsg. von Ingrid Krüger-Bulcke (= Biographische Quellen zur deutschen Geschichte nach 1945, Bd. 14), München 1994.

[71] Siehe Josef Henke/Klaus Oldenhage, Office of Military Government for Germany (U. S.), in: OMGUS-Handbuch. Die amerikanische Militärregierung in Deutschland 1945–1949, hrsg. von Christoph Weisz (= Quellen und Darstellungen zur Zeitgeschichte, Bd. 35), München 1994, S. 1–142, hier S. 122f.

[72] Vgl. Conrad F. Latour/Thilo Vogelsang, Okkupation und Wiederaufbau. Die Tätigkeit der Militärregierung in der amerikanischen Besatzungszone Deutschlands 1944–1947 (Studien zur Zeitgeschichte), Stuttgart 1973, S. 123f.; Josef Henke/Klaus Oldenhage, Office of Military Government for Germany (U. S.), in: OMGUS-Handbuch. Die amerikanische Militärregierung in Deutschland 1945–1949, hrsg. von Christoph Weisz (= Quellen und Darstellungen zur Zeitgeschichte, Bd. 35), München 1994, S. 1–142, hier S. 43.

Arbeit, seinen Aufgaben, vom Alltag, von Besprechungen, Sitzungen, Begegnungen mit besatzungspolitischen Akteuren sowie deutschen Persönlichkeiten aus Politik und Kultur. Beachtung verdienen seine Beurteilungen von Personen, seine kritischen Bemerkungen zur Besatzungspolitik, seine Meinungen, Ansichten und Anmerkungen zu Deutschland, den Deutschen, den Alliierten, zu den Lebensverhältnissen, zur Stimmung und Atmosphäre in Deutschland. Seine Personenbeschreibungen zeugen von einer ausgeprägten Beobachtungsgabe. Da er kein Tagebuch führte, zeichnete er das Erlebte ausschließlich in diesen Briefen auf. Zum einen hatte er die Absicht, seine Frau und Partnerin auf dem Laufenden zu halten, möglichst über alles zu informieren, an allem teilhaben zu lassen und mit ihr in geistigen Austausch zu treten. Zum anderen ging es ihm darum, seine Erlebnisse, Beobachtungen, Gedanken und Einsichten festzuhalten, um später eine Grundlage für Veröffentlichungen oder Vorträge zu haben. Uns gewähren die unter dem Eindruck des unmittelbar Erlebten niedergeschriebenen, nicht für die Öffentlichkeit bestimmten Briefe neue, tiefe Einblicke in Besatzung und politischen Wiederaufbau in der Viermächtestadt Berlin 1946.

Als seine Reise begann, fühlte sich Johnson an sein Gastsemester 1939/1940 an der University of Wisconsin erinnert, damals hatte er mit Depressionen zu kämpfen: "Generally speaking I am still low and begin to wonder if perhaps what I am doing now is not going to be something like another Wisconsin semester."[73] Von Anfang an machte ihm eine gewisse psychische Labilität zu schaffen, stellte er den Sinn seines Unternehmens in Frage, belastete ihn die Trennung von Emily und den "sweet boys".

Da Johnson nicht wie ursprünglich geplant mit dem Flugzeug nach Europa befördert werden konnte und die Abreise mit einem Transportschiff der US Army, der „George W. Goethals", erst nach Tagen erfolgte, traf er verspätet, am 7. März 1946, in Berlin ein. Dort kam er zunächst in der ehemaligen Dienstvilla des Generaldirektors der Kaiser-Wilhelm-Gesellschaft zur Förderung der Wissenschaften unter, in der Ihnestraße 14 (heute Brümmerstraße 74) in dem von Bomben weitgehend verschont gebliebenen Ortsteil Dahlem: "[...] they treated me as a VIP and put me, not in the ordinary hotel but in a room in a very nice house reserved for special guests."[74]

Die inmitten der Sowjetzone liegende alliierte Viersektorenstadt war Sitz der OMGUS-Zentrale und sollte für Johnson eigentlich nur eine kurze Zwischenstation sein, vor seiner Weiterreise nach Stuttgart, wo sich das RGCO befand. In Berlin wurde ihm aber schnell klar: Pollock würde das RGCO möglicherweise noch bis zu dessen Rückkehr in die USA im Sommer 1946 leiten und nicht wie ursprünglich geplant als Clays politischer Berater an die Spree kommen. Johnson war natürlich sehr enttäuscht, und als er ein erstes Gespräch mit Clay führte, schlug dieser ihm vor, "that for the next few weeks I should spend my time getting acquainted with the international and military government set-up here in Berlin and in the zone preparatory to whatever I shall be doing after that date"[75]. "What would be Pollock's fate he had not yet decided, i. e., whether

---

[73] Dok. 1.
[74] Dok. 15.
[75] Dok. 16.

he was to be permanently here or remain in Stuttgart and I was led to believe that if it were Stuttgart I could be here in some advisory capacity to him, and if Pollock were to come here then I should be in Stuttgart."[76]

Johnson sollte sich erst einmal orientieren ("along the highways and by-ways of OMGUS"[77]), sich sowohl mit der Militärregierung als auch mit den Viermächtegremien vertraut machen, sich in Berlin und in der US-Zone auf kommende Aufgaben vorbereiten. Der Civil Administration Branch der Internal Affairs and Communications Division, OMGUS,[78] zugeteilt und von General Charles K. Gailey, dem Leiter dieser Branch, persönlich betreut, nahm er fortan an Sitzungen und Besprechungen, auch auf Viermächteebene, teil, unter anderem an den regelmäßig stattfindenden, dem Informationsaustausch zwischen Clay und seinem Beraterstab dienenden OMGUS-Stabskonferenzen[79], erstmals am 9. März 1946: "After the various people had reported Clay made a very nice introductory speech concerning me, referring to my previous acquaintance with Germany and my experience with OSS and then asked all those present to extend to me every courtesy possible in order to aid me in getting acquainted with the set-up here in Berlin. He then asked me to stand up. This certainly was extremely decent and helpful of him to do."[80] Clay machte auf ihn einen guten Eindruck: "I must say he makes a good impression, conducting the meeting with good sense, efficiency, authority and good humor and breaking into the reports with sharp questions, and rigorous comments."[81] Und später, nach einem Partygespräch mit dem Dreisternegeneral über die KPD und die Zukunft Amerikas in Deutschland, hält Johnson fest: "He has a terribly good head."[82]

Als definitiv feststand, dass Pollock bis zu seiner Rückkehr in die Vereinigten Staaten in Stuttgart bleiben würde, ernannte Clay den Professor aus Nebraska zu seinem Sonderberater ("Special Assistant"[83]) und stellte ihm am Sitz von OMGUS in Berlin-Dahlem ein Büro bereit. "I am to spend some time each week in this office keeping acquainted with the affairs of Omgus and I am to be permitted to see necessary documents to keep me in touch."[84] Außerdem wurde

---

[76] Ebd.
[77] Dok. 83.
[78] Die Civil Administration Branch hatte folgende Zuständigkeiten: „Vereinbarung von Vier-Mächte-Abkommen zur Dezentralisierung der politischen Strukturen in Deutschland, Wiedererrichtung demokratischer Verhältnisse in der kommunalen Selbstverwaltung, Überwachung der politischen Parteien, Vorbereitung zentraler Verwaltungseinrichtungen, Angleichung und Koordinierung der Politik und Verwaltung auf Länderebene sowie Überwachung der Reform des Öffentlichen Dienstes". Josef Henke/Klaus Oldenhage, Office of Military Government for Germany (U. S.), in: OMGUS-Handbuch. Die amerikanische Militärregierung in Deutschland 1945–1949, hrsg. von Christoph Weisz (= Quellen und Darstellungen zur Zeitgeschichte, Bd. 35), München 1994, S. 1–142, hier S. 110.
[79] Siehe Bernd Steger, General Clays Stabskonferenzen und die Organisation der amerikanischen Militärregierung in Deutschland. Die „Clay-Minutes" als historische Quelle, in: Vierteljahrshefte für Zeitgeschichte, 27. Jg. 1979, S. 113–130.
[80] Dok. 17.
[81] Ebd.
[82] Dok. 55.
[83] Dok. 25.
[84] Ebd.

Johnson auf unbestimmte Zeit an den Commanding General, US Headquarters Berlin District, und amerikanischen Stadtkommandanten von Berlin, General Ray W. Barker, „ausgeliehen", "on a temporary basis"[85], um als dessen politischer Berater zu fungieren. Interesse an dieser Tätigkeit hatte auch Walter L. Dorn gezeigt, der aber dann zu Clays Sonderberater für die Beziehungen zwischen den Military Government Detachments und den deutschen regionalen Dienststellen und kurze Zeit später zu Clays Personal Adviser on Denazification unter Beibehaltung seiner bisherigen Pflichten ernannt wurde, Jobs, für die auch Johnson im Gespräch gewesen war. Barker stand Dorns "red leanings"[86] misstrauisch gegenüber und war deshalb froh, Johnson gewonnen zu haben, der sein hochgeschätzter Ratgeber wurde.

Barker war ein politisch denkender Kopf, der nicht in allen Fragen mit Clay übereinstimmte. Und er war durch ein Rückenleiden gesundheitlich angeschlagen.[87] Ende April/Anfang Mai 1946 wurde er von General Frank A. Keating abgelöst. Dieser war ein politisch ziemlich desinteressierter Organisationsmensch. Johnson empfand Barkers Weggang als Verlust. "It will be a worthy task to do what I can to help the new General"[88], schreibt er seiner Frau. "But somehow or another I have become personally devoted to Barker in the little time that I have been permitted to work for him, and I don't like to see him go. He is one of the few in high places here who does have any principles."[89] Über den „neuen" General schreibt Johnson: "The new general is quite unpolitical, though not, I take it, without intelligence. I am told he is something of a hot headed Irishman."[90] Aber diese Einschätzungen bzw. Befürchtungen hielten Johnson nicht davon ab, seinen Berlin-Job fortzuführen und auch für Barkers Nachfolger beratend tätig zu sein. Dieser machte übrigens unter Clay Karriere. Als Clay im März 1947 Militärgouverneur wurde, übernahm Keating die Funktion des stellvertretenden Militärgouverneurs und damit des Commanding General, OMGUS.

Den Berlin-Job hielt Johnson für interessant und wichtig, schließlich war die unter der Hoheit der vier Alliierten stehende alte Reichshauptstadt "a center of importance, what is done here has significance for all of Germany and certainly it is an indication of what we stand for to all the world"[91]. Als Berater des amerikanischen Stadtkommandanten hatte er ein Büro am Sitz der amerikanischen Militärregierung für Berlin (Office of Military Government, Berlin District [OMGBD]) in Berlin-Steglitz. Zunächst kümmerte er sich um den Aufbau einer neuen Civil Administration Branch, OMGBD,[92] der er zugeteilt wurde.

---

[85] Dok. 41.
[86] Dok. 33.
[87] "Because of a bad back, he sat at meetings in a padded chair, with a big green pillow behind him, but always started to squirm in acute discomfort after the first half hour." Frank Howley, Berlin Command, New York 1950, S. 109.
[88] Dok. 39.
[89] Ebd.
[90] Dok. 41.
[91] Dok. 34.
[92] "On the 25th of January a Civil Administration Branch was organized and started operations. On the 4th of April it was officially activated with terms of reference approved by the Commanding General". Civil Administration. Six Months Report

Vor dem Hintergrund der von der sowjetischen Besatzungsmacht betriebenen Vereinigung von KPD und SPD zu einer Sozialistischen Einheitspartei begleitete Johnson den Aufbau einer neuen Berliner SPD durch jene Sozialdemokraten, die der erzwungenen Parteienfusion in Berlin Widerstand entgegensetzten.[93] Während in der Sowjetzone nicht frei über die Zukunft der sozialdemokratischen Parteiorganisation entschieden werden konnte, die Mehrheit des SPD-Zentralausschusses sich dem Druck beugte und den Weg des Zusammenschlusses mit der KPD ging, konnte in der Viermächtestadt eine parteiinterne Urabstimmung über die geplante Vereinigung von den Gegnern eines Zusammengehens durchgesetzt werden. Diese Mitgliederbefragung war allerdings nur in den amerikanisch, britisch und französisch besetzten Sektoren möglich. Dort votierten 82,6 Prozent der abstimmenden SPD-Mitglieder gegen „den sofortigen Zusammenschluß beider Arbeiterparteien"[94].

Johnson war davon überzeugt, dass der Zusammenschluss nicht freiwillig erfolgte und dass die Kommunisten – "whom I am coming to hate here, not because of their program, but because of their dirty, tricky, methods"[95] – in der neuen Partei den Ton angeben würden. Den oppositionellen Sozialdemokraten, die sich den Einheitsparolen der KPD widersetzten und nach der Berliner Urabstimmung eine eigene Parteiorganisation aufbauten, Politikern wie Otto Suhr, der geschäftsführender Generalsekretär der neuen SPD wurde, "a very able fellow"[96], galt seine Sympathie, und er wünschte sich, dass die amerikanische Militärregierung die Distanz zu diesen Kräften durchbrechen, ihnen Verständnis entgegenbringen und sie aktiv unterstützen würde. "These are the people we ought to be supporting because they stand for the kind of democratic decency which we stand for. But we are doing nothing to support them. We won't even let them have a newspaper yet."[97] Scharf kritisiert er die von der amerikanischen Militärregierung eingenommene neutrale und passive Haltung, die die Sowjets, deren Dominanz man nicht energisch entgegentrat, in dem Glauben bestärkten musste, in Berlin wie in ihrer Zone handeln und eine Sonderentwicklung der Viermächtestadt gegenüber der sie umgebenden Zone vereiteln

---

4 January–3 July 1946, in: Office of Military Government U. S. Berlin District (Hrsg.), Six Months Report 4 January–3 July 1946, Berlin 1946, S. 40–43, hier S. 41. "Matters which have been of primary interest to the Civil Administration Branch and which it has handled or helped to handle are: (a) the SPD referendum of 31 March, (b) establishment of civil rights free from political interference in U. S. Sector, (c) recognition of the SPD, (e) a new constitution for Berlin, (f) plans for city-wide elections." Digest of Reports 4 January–3 July 1946, in: ebd., S. 17–22, hier S. 19.

[93] Zur Fusion von SPD und KPD zur SED und zum Aufbau einer eigenen sozialdemokratischen Parteiorganisation durch die Vereinigungsgegner siehe Werner Breunig, Berlin 1945/46. Vom Kriegsende bis zum parlamentarischen Neubeginn, in: „Berlin kommt wieder". Die Nachkriegsjahre 1945/46 (= Ausstellungskataloge des Landesarchivs Berlin, 16), Berlin 2005, S. 7–43, hier S. 24–26.

[94] Stimmzettel zur parteiinternen Urabstimmung über die Einheitsfrage am 31. März 1946, in: Landesarchiv Berlin (LAB), F Rep. 280 (Quellensammlung zur Berliner Zeitgeschichte [LAZ-Sammlung]), Nr. 1226.

[95] Dok. 39.

[96] Dok. 56.

[97] Dok. 39. Die Zeitung „Der Sozialdemokrat. Organ der Sozialdemokratie Groß-Berlin" erschien erst ab dem 3. Juni 1946, und zwar unter britischer Lizenz.

zu können: "Don't we care whether the real democrats have a chance here or not? Why did we fight this war? As I remember it was for the American way of life or at least it had something to do about democracy? If we don't care about democracy in Europe then we'd better get the hell out of here and turn the place over to the Communists and the Soviets, and if we do we had better organize ourselves in some positive way and make a display, and a protest. As it is we are permitting Russia to run away with the game here."[98] Johnson machte sich berechtigte Sorgen und war der Meinung, "it might be best for not only Germany but for our relations with the Russians if we come out for a policy of straight democratic socialism, supporting the Social Democrats"[99].

Clay hingegen bestand auf absolute politische Neutralität,[100] eine Unterstützung der rebellischen Sozialdemokraten lehnte er ab.[101] Am Tag vor der Urabstimmung hatte er, bestärkt von seinem Verbindungsmann zum State Department, Robert D. Murphy, Political Adviser for Germany, auf einer Stabskonferenz die Ansicht vertreten, dass der SPD-Zentralausschuss "was within its rights in urging a sabotage of the referendum"[102] – für Johnson ein inakzeptabler Standpunkt. "Later I learned", lässt er seine Frau wissen, "that Clay would have been ready to forbid the referendum which would have raised an uproar at home. If Clay is supposed to be kept politically wise by Murphy then Murphy has failed in his job so far. I intend, pardon the presumption, to take upon myself, with a little help, the job of making Clay politically informed."[103]

Nach dem Zusammenschluss von KPD und SPD war die SED in Berlin zunächst nur im sowjetisch besetzten Ostsektor anerkannt, die von den Vereinigungsgegnern neu konstituierte SPD lediglich in den Westsektoren. Erst Ende Mai 1946 ließen die Stadtkommandanten sowohl die SED als auch die SPD in allen vier Sektoren zu – "upon my initiative"[104], so Johnson, der sich für diese Kompromisslösung stark gemacht hatte. Entscheidend war für ihn, dass die aus der Urabstimmung hervorgegangene SPD künftig in der ganzen Stadt als politische Gegenkraft zur SED tätig sein konnte.

Weitere wichtige Aufgaben fand Johnson in einem Fachausschuss der als oberstes politisches Organ der Stadt fungierenden Alliierten Kommandantur Berlin, dem Local Government Committee[105], an dessen Sitzungen er als zu-

---

[98] Dok. 39.
[99] Dok. 36.
[100] Vgl. John H. Backer, Die deutschen Jahre des Generals Clay. Der Weg zur Bundesrepublik 1945–1949, München 1983, S. 174f.
[101] Vgl. Harold Hurwitz, Die Eintracht der Siegermächte und die Orientierungsnot der Deutschen 1945–1946 (= Demokratie und Antikommunismus in Berlin nach 1945, Bd. III), Köln 1984, S. 117.
[102] Dok. 30.
[103] Ebd.
[104] Dok. 55.
[105] Dieser Ausschuss beschäftigte sich mit "all governmental affairs and enterprises (such as the constitution of Berlin and the census of Berlin), all political matters, and the broad list which would be included under the term 'local government'". Civil Administration. Six Months Report 4 January–3 July 1946, in: Office of Military Government U. S. Berlin District (Hrsg.), Six Months Report 4 January–3 July 1946, Berlin 1946, S. 40–43, hier S. 41.

sätzliches amerikanisches Mitglied teilnahm, neben Lieutenant Colonel Louis Glaser, der die Civil Administration Branch des OMGBD leitete.[106] Das Local Government Committee beschäftigte sich mit der Frage erster Berliner Nachkriegskommunalwahlen, deren baldige Abhaltung von den Amerikanern, in deren Zone bereits im Januar 1946 Wahlen in den kleineren Gemeinden stattgefunden hatten, vehement gefordert wurde. Die Sowjets widersetzten sich zunächst der Festlegung eines Wahltermins, erst nach der Fusion von KPD und SPD zur SED und der Einigung auf Zulassung von SED und neuer SPD als Gesamtberliner Parteien stimmten sie auf Kontrollratsebene der baldigen Durchführung von Stadtverordnetenwahlen – im Oktober 1946 – zu, in der Erwartung, dass die Wählerbasis der SPD mehrheitlich zur SED wechseln würde.[107] Das Local Government Committee arbeitete dann unter Berücksichtigung deutscher Vorarbeiten eine vorläufige Berliner Verfassung aus, auf deren Grundlage die Wahlen durchgeführt werden sollten, und fungierte somit als verfassunggebendes Gremium. Da Johnson, der mit großem Eifer und Interesse an die Verfassungsarbeit heranging, die deutsche Sprache beherrschte, konnte er mit dem vom Magistrat vorgelegten deutschsprachigen Verfassungstext arbeiten. Colonel Glaser hingegen "knows no word of German, and the draft of the Constitution as submitted by the City Government is of course not in English. There is an English translation but it is pretty frightful and no one could make much sense of it. This is a good example of what could happen if there were no-one around who could handle the German in some fashion."[108]

Der britische Vertreter im Local Government Committee, Major Harold Hays, erinnert sich später an den Kollegen Johnson als "a most charming man"[109]. Wie Hays berichtet, setzte sich Johnson bei den Beratungen in dem Viermächtegremium unter anderem dafür ein, nicht nur die Anzahl der Magistratsabteilungen in der Verfassung festzulegen, "but the type and functions of each. He did in fact produce a list of 18 Departments, fully named, and he only

---

[106] Die Zusammenarbeit zwischen Johnson und Glaser in der Civil Administration Branch verlief nicht reibungsfrei. "I think", so Johnson, "that Col. Glaser would be only too glad to get rid of me, since my position as political advisor to the Commanding General sort of cramps his style. He is moreover a jealous and ambitious person, an advertising man, who takes, I think a certain amount of pleasure in shoving people about." Dok. 47.

[107] Zu den Auseinandersetzungen um den Termin erster Wahlen siehe Werner Breunig, Verfassunggebung in Berlin 1945-1950 (= Beiträge zur Politischen Wissenschaft, Bd. 58), Berlin 1990, S. 174-183.

[108] Dok. 64. Später, als der endgültige Verfassungstext vorlag, vermerkte OMGBD-Direktor Frank L. Howley: "The official language of the constitution is German and I am informed that the German is much more accurate und correct than either the English or Russian translations; much of the work of the Committee having been done in the original German because of the reference material being in German, the recommendations of the Magistrat being in German and the need for speed." OMGBD, Interoffice Memo Slip, 20. August 1946, Subject: Constitution for Greater Berlin, in: LAB, B Rep. 036-01 (Office of Military Government, Berlin Sector [OMGBS]), 4/136-1/9.

[109] Erinnerungen von Harold Hays, Chapter 10: Berlin Constitution 1946, S. 148, in: Imperial War Museum (IWM) Duxford, Cambridgeshire, Großbritannien, Lieutenant Colonel Harold Hays MBE Collection.

withdrew it on the urgent representation of the British and Soviet Representatives, who claimed that such was an infringement of the democratic rights of the elected Assembly, and that any alteration proposed in future would bring in its train an amendment to the Constitution itself!"[110] In dem endgültigen Verfassungstext heißt es dann lediglich, dass die Zahl der Abteilungen 18 nicht übersteigen dürfe. Zwar blieb der Vorschlag, die Magistratsabteilungen namentlich aufzulisten, erfolglos, aber dieses Beispiel macht die engagierte Mitarbeit Johnsons bei der Formulierung einer Berliner Verfassung deutlich.

Deutsche Verfassungsexperten, mit denen Johnson sich austauschte, waren der frühere Generalsekretär bzw. -direktor der Kaiser-Wilhelm-Gesellschaft zur Förderung der Wissenschaften, Friedrich Glum, damals Berater der amerikanischen Militärregierung in Verfassungs- und Verwaltungsfragen, und vor allem der kommissarische Stadtkämmerer Friedrich Haas, ein Verwaltungs- und Verfassungsfachmann, der der CDU angehörte und an der Schaffung des Magistratsentwurfs maßgeblich beteiligt gewesen war.

Das Local Government Committee stand bei seinen Verfassungsarbeiten unter einem enormen Zeitdruck, da die Abhaltung der Wahlen zum festgesetzten Termin nicht gefährdet, ein Aufschub des Urnengangs verhindert werden sollte. Gerade die Amerikaner waren aus Sorge um die Durchführung der Oktoberwahlen daran interessiert, die Arbeiten zügig abschließen und der deutschen Seite rechtzeitig eine Verfassung – "a valid instrument under which elections could be held"[111] – übermitteln zu können. Trotz unterschiedlicher Konzeptionen, mit denen die vier Mächte an die gemeinsame Aufgabe herangingen,[112] gelang es ihnen nicht zuletzt aufgrund des Zeitdrucks und der daraus resultierenden Kompromissbereitschaft und Atmosphäre des "good will", sich auf einen Verfassungstext zu einigen. Johnson schreibt später über die erfolgreiche alliierte Zusammenarbeit im Local Government Committee: "The necessity for meeting in long sessions at frequent intervals soon broke down whatever official character there was to these meetings. The members of the Committee became friends. As meeting after meeting passed and every difficulty was settled, it became clear that no difficulty was to be too great; the Committee would come out with an agreed report."[113]

Nirgendwo sonst in Deutschland wurde eine Verfassung von allen vier Besatzungsmächten gemeinsam geschaffen, ein beispielloser Verfassunggebungsprozess. Die Einigung, die erzielt werden konnte, zeigt, dass es 1946 immer noch kooperative Verhaltensweisen gab, die den Anzeichen einer beginnenden Ost-West-Konfrontation gegenüberstanden.

In einem Dankschreiben der Stadtkommandanten an die Mitarbeiter des Local Government Committee – auch Johnson wird im Briefkopf genannt – heißt es unter anderem: "The Commandants of the Allied Kommandatura

---

[110] Ebd.
[111] Civil Administration. Six Months Report 4 January–3 July 1946, in: Office of Military Government U. S. Berlin District (Hrsg.), Six Months Report 4 January–3 July 1946, Berlin 1946, S. 40–43, hier S. 41.
[112] Siehe Werner Breunig, Verfassunggebung in Berlin 1945–1950 (= Beiträge zur Politischen Wissenschaft, Bd. 58), Berlin 1990, S. 186–189.
[113] Dok. 83.

Berlin are aware of the long, arduous hours that the Local Government Committee has labored in formulating and drafting the Constitution of the City of Berlin and the instructions to the Magistrat concerning the 'Electoral Procedure of Berlin'. The members of the Local Government Committee have given unstintingly of their time, and have drawn deeply upon their professional knowledge and experience to complete this important and difficult task assigned them by the Commandants."[114]

Die Vorläufige Verfassung von Groß-Berlin[115], diese amerikanisch-britisch-französisch-sowjetische Gemeinschaftsarbeit, ermöglichte die Durchführung von Stadtverordnetenwahlen im Oktober 1946 und die Bildung eines neuen, demokratisch legitimierten Magistrats, der die von der sowjetischen Besatzungsmacht im Mai 1945 eingesetzte Stadtregierung ersetzte,[116] sodass die aus der kurzzeitigen sowjetischen Alleinherrschaft in Berlin herrührende Vorherrschaft der SED gebrochen werden konnte.[117]

Seit der Übernahme der Beratertätigkeit für General Barker wohnte Johnson im Wannsee Hotel/Wannsee Officers' Club, Am Sandwerder 17/19, wo sich ihm ein grandioser Ausblick auf den Großen Wannsee bot. "[…] there may be a good chance here to sit quietly once in awhile, and reflect about the meaning of what is going on here"[118], so Johnson, als er hier Ende März 1946, veranlasst durch Barker, einzog. "I need lots of time to think. Now I have a good place to do it."[119] Die alte Villa am östlichen Seeufer, in der Johnson über eine hübsche Wohnung verfügte, lag wenige Gehminuten von Barkers Residenz Am Sandwerder 27 entfernt, "only a few steps from General Barker and he has asked me to drop down in the evenings whenever I please"[120].

Seit 25 Jahren kümmerte sich der Gärtner Albert Redmann um die große Gartenanlage des Anwesens Am Sandwerder 17/19, und von ihm erfuhr Johnson einiges über die Geschichte des Hauses. Redmann kannte es seit jenen Tagen, als hier der belgisch-britische Botaniker und Geograf Marcel Hardy, nach dem Ersten Weltkrieg Mitglied der alliierten Reparationskommission in Berlin, gewohnt hatte. Später zog der jüdische Bankier Hans Arnhold ein. Dieser muss-

---

114 Schreiben vom 31. August 1946, in: Unterlagen aus dem Nachlass Louis Glaser, Privatbesitz Anthony J. Glaser, Bethesda, Maryland, USA.
115 Groß-Berlin wurde durch die Verfassung die amtliche Bezeichnung für Berlin.
116 Zum ernannten Magistrat siehe Die Sitzungsprotokolle des Magistrats der Stadt Berlin 1945/46. Teil I: 1945, bearb. und eingel. von Dieter Hanauske (= Schriftenreihe des Landesarchivs Berlin, Bd. 2/I), Berlin 1995; Die Sitzungsprotokolle des Magistrats der Stadt Berlin 1945/46. Teil II: 1946, bearb. und eingel. von Dieter Hanauske (= Schriftenreihe des Landesarchivs Berlin, Bd. 2/II), Berlin 1999.
117 Ausführlich zur Entstehung der Vorläufigen Verfassung von Groß-Berlin siehe Werner Breunig, Verfassunggebung in Berlin 1945–1950 (= Beiträge zur Politischen Wissenschaft, Bd. 58), Berlin 1990, S. 154–235. Siehe auch den Bericht des sowjetischen Oberstleutnants Alexandr Michailowitsch Sosulja vom 18. Juni 1946 zur Vorbereitung der Berliner Kommunalwahlen und zur Verfassungsfrage, in: Die UdSSR und die deutsche Frage 1941–1948. Dokumente aus dem Archiv für Außenpolitik der Russischen Föderation, bearb. und hrsg. von Jochen P. Laufer/Georgij P. Kynin unter Mitarbeit von Viktor Knoll, Bd. 2: 9. Mai 1945 bis 3. Oktober 1946, Berlin 2004, Dok. 142.
118 Dok. 31.
119 Dok. 32.
120 Dok. 33.

te 1938 emigrieren. Es folgte der NS-Politiker Walther Funk, Reichswirtschaftsminister und Reichsbankpräsident, "who now" – so Johnson – "occupies quarters of an entirely different character at Nürnberg"[121]. Nach dem Zweiten Weltkrieg requirierten die Amerikaner das Anwesen. Und Redmann, alle Wechsel überdauernd, züchtete weiterhin emsig seine Blumen und sein Gemüse: "His gardening has brought him through the crises all right – Englishman – Jew – Nazi – Americans, and he goes on growing his flowers and his vegetables."[122] Es lässt sich sagen, dass Gärtner "like bureaucrats have a nice ability to survive all regimes"[123].

Seit 1998 ist in der Villa am Wannsee The American Academy in Berlin, Hans Arnhold Center, untergebracht, ein Kulturinstitut, das der Verständigung und dem geistigen Austausch zwischen Deutschland und den USA dient.

Trotz seines prallen Terminkalenders fand Johnson noch Zeit, um das Vorwort für eine deutsche Ausgabe von Benjamin Franklins Autobiografie zu schreiben, worum ihn der junge Berliner Verleger Karl Heinz Henssel gebeten hatte. Als der Text fertig war, zeigte sich Johnson hochzufrieden mit seinem Arbeitsergebnis: "If you will pardon, I shall say that I don't think it's bad"[124], schreibt er seiner Frau. "Indeed I think that it is perhaps the best thing I have ever written. Properly understood there is much of myself in it, the meaning of the war for me, the experience in Austria, and especially the experience here, which I think, the intelligent German can catch, all these things rising up through Franklin's text and catching hold of certain phrases and sentences which seem to have particular meaning for this sad Berlin of June 1946."[125] Das Buch mit Johnsons Vorwort erschien noch 1946 im Karl H. Henssel Verlag, Berlin.[126] In einer Besprechung heißt es: „Das Vorwort von Edgar N. Johnson stellt die Verbindung zwischen diesem Dokument eines vergangenen Jahrhunderts und unserer heutigen Welt her, indem es, menschenwürdig erhaben über jegliche Parteilichkeit oder pharisäisches Erziehenwollen, eine deutsche Aufgabe zwischen Ost und West als immanent annimmt und das Franklin'sche Ethos als Anliegen der ganzen heutigen Menschheit sieht."[127] In Auszügen wurde das Vorwort in der amerikanisch lizenzierten Berliner Zeitschrift „Horizont. Halbmonatsschrift für junge Menschen" veröffentlicht, unter der Überschrift „Benjamin Franklin und die deutsche Jugend".[128]

Zeit nahm sich Johnson auch für einen Vortrag am 9. Juli 1946 im Harnack House vor den Damen des American Women's Club of Berlin, denen er wertvolle Ratschläge und Anregungen für ihren Aufenthalt in Deutschland gab. "The ladies seemed to like the speech and asked for copies. I referred to you at

---

[121] Dok. 83.
[122] Dok. 47.
[123] Dok. 83.
[124] Dok. 64.
[125] Ebd.
[126] Siehe Benjamin Franklin. Sein Leben von ihm selbst erzählt, Berlin 1946.
[127] Ursula Seyffarth, Rezension von: Benjamin Franklin. Sein Leben von ihm selbst erzählt, Berlin 1946, in: Welt und Wort. Literarische Monatsschrift, November 1946, S. 188.
[128] Siehe Horizont, 20. Heft, 1. Jg., 1. September 1946, S. 19.

the beginning and at the end"[129], teilt er seiner Frau mit. Ausführlich berichtet die Wochenzeitung "OMGUS Observer" unter der Überschrift "'Shun Nazis', Wives Told At Women's Club Meeting": "American families should have no toleration for Nazi-Germans, no matter how cultured or charming they seem to be, stated Dr. E. N. Johnson, Special Assistant to the Commanding General, Headquarters, B[erlin] D[istrict] at the second meeting of the American Women's Club of Berlin, Tuesday, when he discussed the responsibilities of American women in occupation. 'But Germans who conspicuously fought and resisted the influence of distorted Nazi minds should be fought and resisted the influence of [sic!] build their country along democratic lines,' he pointed out. 'The American women should reach out to German women like Helen Weber who are now trying to organize healthy political parties in a wholesome German government, or to persons like Gunther Weisenborn, who after imprisonment in concentration camps for underground activities against the Nazis, is still trying to direct the people away from the hypnotic influence of Nazism.' As Berlin is the nerve center of the world, Dr. Johnson said that what happened here would have lasting influence on the world of tomorrow. Therefore it is up to American women, who other women of the world are closely watching, to study international situations and keep abreast of world problems, particularly those to which they are so close. As the American families are apt to lose their sense of value and timing because of their comfortable communities, he advised them not to isolate themselves from the German people and their problems. 'The coming of American wives and families to Europe,' Dr. Johnson said, 'is but a further extension of America into Europe, a further representation of the best that America stands for in a Germany which has sore need for it. Your coming, in fact, amounts to the introduction into Germany of another American institution, the American home.'"[130] Johnsons Rede war die erste in einer Vortragsreihe "on occupation problems"[131].

Entspannung und Zerstreuung fand Johnson bei abendlichen Zusammenkünften ("just a drink, a smoke, and some salted nuts"[132]), auch im exklusiven Lakeside Club für hohe Offiziere, "the top personnel in Omgus"[133], beim Segeln auf dem Wannsee und vor allem in der Musik, die ihm so viel bedeutete. In seinen Briefen berichtet er von musikalischen Erlebnissen in der Deutschen Staatsoper im Admiralspalast oder unvergesslichen Abenden mit "my cellist friend"[134] Max Baldner, der mit dem Zernick-Quartett spielte und Lehrer für Cello an der Hochschule für Musik der Stadt Berlin war.

Ehefrau Emilys mühselige Suche nach einem neuen Klavier für den musikalisch talentierten Sohn John, in dem der ehrgeizige Vater ein Piano-Wunderkind

---

[129] Dok. 72.
[130] "Shun Nazi", Wives Told At Women's Club Meeting, in: OMGUS Observer vom 12. Juli 1946, S. 2.
[131] Ebd.
[132] Einladung zu einer Zusammenkunft am 5. Juli 1946, in: Unterlagen aus dem Nachlass Edgar N. Johnson, Privatbesitz Candice E. und Thomas R. Johnson, Denver, Colorado, USA.
[133] Dok. 17.
[134] Dok. 55.

sah, ist ein Dauerthema in der Korrespondenz. Emily in einem Schreiben an ihren Mann: "My hunting for pianos is even more amusing than your working on a constitution for Berlin!"[135] Dass Musik einen hohen Stellenwert in der Familie einnahm, zeigt auch die Aussage der Babysitterin für John und Thomas: "They [die Johnsons] had a nice record player and an interesting collection of records. I discovered a taste for Schubert's string quintets there (after putting the kids to bed)."[136]

In einem Schreiben vom 29. Juni 1946 an seinen Vater gibt Johnson eine knappe, anschauliche Zusammenfassung seiner Erlebnisse und Tätigkeiten: "I have been a little disappointed in coming back here. As Norman [Edgar N. Johnsons Bruder] may have told you, the job I thought I was going to get wasn't ready for me when I came because of the long time it took for me to get back here. Consequently I was sent down to Berlin to become the political adviser of the Commanding General of the troops in the Berlin area. This work has been interesting and important enough, and I have not felt that my time was wasted. During the first part of it there was a nasty political fight going on here between the Communists and the Socialists. The Communists, with the support of Russia, wanted the Socialists to join with them in a united workers' party, and the Socialists wanted to retain their independence. The Socialists lost out in the Russian zone, but in Berlin, with the help of the British, French, and ourselves they managed to preserve their independence. I had something to do with this and for this I am glad. Since that time we have been busy trying to get ready for elections in Berlin in October. This has meant preparing a constitution for the city and preparing for the machinery of elections. In another week or so this work should be done."[137]

General Clay ging davon aus, dass Johnson den Stuttgart-Job nach dem Ausscheiden von Pollock im August 1946 übernehmen würde. Aber es kam anders. Die Trennung von der Familie fiel Johnson überaus schwer.[138] Zwar hätte er seine Lieben nachholen können, aber seine Frau konnte sich nicht dazu durchringen, mit den Kindern nach Europa zu kommen. Deshalb war Johnson fest entschlossen, seine Tätigkeit für die amerikanische Militärregierung zu beenden und zu seiner Familie und an seine Alma Mater zurückzukehren. Ein Kollege gab ihm zu verstehen, "that he thought it very strange and absurd that I should be abandoning my position here, which was of considerable importance, to return to the academic life of Nebraska. Here I would be associated with the making of history rather than the teaching of it. He insisted that if I stayed on here for a few more years, I could accumulate enough money to carry us over an interim period until I could get an academic position which would be worthy

---

[135] Emily L. Johnson in einem Schreiben an Ehemann Edgar vom 26. Juni 1946, in: Unterlagen aus dem Nachlass Edgar N. Johnson, Privatbesitz Candice E. und Thomas R. Johnson, Denver, Colorado, USA.
[136] Alison E. Gass in einer E-Mail an Werner Breunig vom 10. Januar 2010.
[137] Dok. 69.
[138] "I was so lonesome yesterday I could have wept, and I am almost in the same state today – a lovely Easter Sunday. Lonesome of course for my sweet wife and for my boys", so Johnson in einem seiner Schreiben an die Ehefrau. Dok. 39.

of my experience in the past few years."[139] Zweifellos reizte ihn die Möglichkeit, sich dem Wiederaufbau Deutschlands zu widmen und den Verlauf der Geschichte mitzugestalten, aber das Bedürfnis, bei seiner über allem stehenden Familie, die ihm eine unentbehrliche Stütze im Leben war, zu sein, ließ das verlockende Angebot in den Hintergrund treten. Die Gelegenheit, eine herausragende, lukrative Position in der amerikanischen Militärregierung einzunehmen, wurde nicht genutzt. "It is something of a temptation to stay on here", schreibt er seinem Vater, "but Emily does not want to come over with the children, and I am not sure that I want to abandon the university for work of this kind inasmuch as there is really no guarantee of how long it will last. I shall have to take a huge salary cut, which, with the inflation imminent in America will make things a bit difficult but I have made up my mind. I couldn't stay over here another year in any case without my family."[140]

Es fiel Johnson nicht leicht, Clay von seinen Rückzugsplänen in Kenntnis zu setzen, schließlich verlor dieser mit ihm einen seiner "chief professional assistants"[141]. Anfang Juli 1946 teilte er dem General seine Entscheidung brieflich mit. Gleichzeitig informierte er General Keating, der mit einem netten Dankschreiben antwortete. "I do not know what I would have done without your help"[142], so der Stadtkommandant. "That is saying too much", meint Johnson in einem Schreiben an seine Frau, "but I am glad he feels that I have not been utterly useless."[143]

Vor seiner Rückkehr in die Vereinigten Staaten brach Johnson am 20. Juli 1946 mit seinem Chauffeur Artur Sanow zu einer von Clay genehmigten, bestens vorbereiteten Reise durch die amerikanische Besatzungszone Deutschlands auf, nach Groß-Hessen, Württemberg-Baden und Bayern, "to study political conditions in the zone"[144]. Ein dicht gedrängtes Programm sollte ihm interessante Einblicke vermitteln. Aber schnell kamen ihm Zweifel am Sinn seiner Zonentour, die ursprünglich der Orientierung vor Beginn seiner eigentlichen Tätigkeit für die Militärregierung dienen sollte: "My work is really over and the uncertainty of our future in Germany makes it seems pointless to consider how much positive good we can do here. The Germans, I am sure, are itching for us to leave in order to get control themselves."[145]

Über Kassel und Butzbach ging es zunächst nach Wiesbaden, wo er Gast des Chefs der Militärregierung für Groß-Hessen, Colonel James R. Newman, ein promovierter Erziehungswissenschaftler, war. In Darmstadt besuchte Johnson ein amerikanisches Internierungslager, das CI Camp 91, eine von Stacheldraht-

---

[139] Dok. 67.
[140] Dok. 69.
[141] Dok. 71.
[142] Schreiben von General Frank A. Keating an Edgar N. Johnson vom 5. Juli 1946, in: Unterlagen aus dem Nachlass Edgar N. Johnson, Privatbesitz Candice E. und Thomas R. Johnson, Denver, Colorado, USA.
[143] Dok. 72.
[144] OMGUS, Office of the Commanding General, Subject: Orders, 18. Juli 1946, in: Unterlagen aus dem Nachlass Edgar N. Johnson, Privatbesitz Candice E. und Thomas R. Johnson, Denver, Colorado, USA.
[145] Dok. 77.

zaun und Wachtürmen umgebene Zeltstadt, "where 17,000 Nazis considered dangerous enough to be put away are kept"[146]. Er berichtet von den Bemühungen um menschenwürdige Lebensbedingungen im Lager: "They have organized a university within the camp and there are all sorts of workshops, and artists' ateliers busy doing things, I am afraid, for American officers. There is a theatre and an orchestra. Indeed they played the Egmont Overture for me."[147] Aber "I hardly know what to think"[148], denn: "I learned that these people were being fed 1700 calories a day which is a good deal more than the average German gets. And one man at a machine who was doing especially hard work was getting a ration of 2500 calories which is more than the heavy workers ration in Germany."[149] Dies sorgte für Unmut auch bei der Bevölkerung.[150] Aber ausgemergelte Lagerinsassen, die an KZ-Häftlinge erinnern, sollte es nicht geben.

Unerwähnt bleibt in Johnsons Aufzeichnungen der Besuch, den er am 26. Juli 1946 dem Darmstädter Regierungspräsidenten Ludwig Bergsträsser, sozialdemokratisches Mitglied der Verfassungberatenden Landesversammlung Groß-Hessen, abstattete.[151] In dessen Tagebuch liest man: „Gegen Mittag kam [Major William R.] Sheehan mit Professor Edgar N. Johnson, der bald in die Staaten zurückkehrt und dort gegen die Illusionisten und für die Entwicklung der deutschen Zustände auch in der Öffentlichkeit wirken will. Er besucht jetzt drei Wochen die amerikanische Zone, um sich im einzelnen zu informieren. Langes, sehr interessantes Gespräch. Er stellte vielerlei Fragen und war erstaunt, wie ich ihm sagte, es sei doch eine Dummheit, daß uns nicht von drüben Bücher geschickt werden dürften. Schließlich sähe ich den Grund nicht ein, warum wir nur Briefe privaten Inhalts hinüberschicken dürften. Wenn ich z.B. über politische Dinge nach drüben schreiben wolle, müsse ich Sheehan bitten, diese weiterzugeben, und könne das nicht direkt tun. Er fragte auch nach den Möglichkeiten der demokratischen Weiterentwicklung und vielen anderen Dingen. Ich betonte die wirtschaftliche Notwendigkeit, auch das Hereinkommen von Rohstoffen für unseren Export, verwies auf die Offenbacher Industrie."[152] Bergsträsser wurde von Johnson über die Zusammenarbeit in der Alliierten Kommandantur informiert: „Er hat in der Internationalen Kommandantur in Berlin

---

[146] Dok. 77.
[147] Ebd.
[148] Ebd.
[149] Ebd. Das Thema hatte Johnson schon zu einem früheren Zeitpunkt beschäftigt; nach der OMGUS-Stabskonferenz vom 25. Mai 1946 schreibt er seiner Frau: "It came out in Clay's meeting this morning that the camps for civilian internees (these are mostly Nazis put away for safe keeping) are much better fed than the ordinary German civilian. So if you don't mind your loss of freedom you can be better fed." Dok. 52.
[150] Siehe http://www.fr-online.de/zeitgeschichte/internierungslager-mit-eigener-zeitung-und-universitaet,1477344,2802516.html (letzter Zugriff am 28. August 2013).
[151] Von der Begegnung zwischen Johnson und Bergsträsser zeugt eine Visitenkarte, die der Regierungspräsident seinem amerikanischen Gast überreichte. Sie findet sich in: Unterlagen aus dem Nachlass Edgar N. Johnson, Privatbesitz Candice E. und Thomas R. Johnson, Denver, Colorado, USA.
[152] Ludwig Bergsträsser, Befreiung, Besatzung, Neubeginn. Tagebuch des Darmstädter Regierungspräsidenten 1945-1948, hrsg. von Walter Mühlhausen (= Biographische Quellen zur deutschen Geschichte nach 1945, Bd. 5), München 1987, S. 149f.

gearbeitet und erzählte, wie umständlich es sei, schon der Sprache wegen. Sie hätten allein über die Frage des Eides und das Wort ‚unparteiisch', das die Russen krampfhaft als ‚unpolitisch' auffassen wollten, zwei Stunden diskutiert."[153] Weiter heißt es in Bergsträssers Tagebuchnotiz: „Meiner Meinung, daß Austausch von Professoren und Studenten, auch Lehrern im großen Maßstab geschehen müsse, stimmte er sehr zu. Als ich im Gespräch sagte, ich wäre noch nie in den Staaten gewesen, sagte er, das müsse arrangiert werden, daß ich bald einmal hinüberkomme. Er betonte sehr stark die Bedeutung der Denazifizierung für die öffentliche Meinung in USA."[154]

In Stuttgart, Hauptstadt des Landes Württemberg-Baden, war Johnson Gast des Chefs der Militärregierung für Württemberg-Baden, Colonel William W. Dawson, im Zivilleben Rechtsprofessor. Dieser sollte bald als Nachfolger von James K. Pollock RGCO-Direktor werden und somit das Amt übernehmen, das Johnson hätte bekleiden können.[155]

"This is a lovely spot, and it would have been pleasant to be here"[156], stellt Johnson in Stuttgart fest. Um einen flüchtigen Eindruck "of the job I was to have"[157] zu bekommen, besuchte er Pollock in der Villa Reitzenstein, dem früheren Amtssitz des württembergischen Ministerpräsidenten, wo das RGCO und der Länderrat untergebracht waren. "I can see that he is a very difficult person – capable, to be sure, but a little of a stuffed shirt. At least he treated me rather coldly and off-hand, leaving me to be impressed with his importance. Yet at the same time he was polite, has invited me to dinner today"[158], so Johnson über den scheidenden RGCO-Direktor.

Erinnerungen an seine in den 1920er-Jahren durchgeführte Studienreise konnte Johnson auffrischen, als er das in der französischen Besatzungszone gelegene Kloster Bebenhausen bei Tübingen besuchte, eine der schönsten und besterhaltenen mittelalterlichen Klosteranlagen Deutschlands, "a wonderful Cistercian abbey"[159].

Auch die im Zweiten Weltkrieg verschont gebliebene Universitätsstadt Heidelberg stand auf Johnsons Reiseliste, "to see some of the professors there"[160]. In seinen Unterlagen[161] findet sich eine Auflistung mit den Namen einiger Personen, die er dort aufgesucht haben könnte, Repräsentanten des intellektuellen Lebens: Fritz Ernst, Historiker und Prorektor der Universität Heidelberg, Adolf Rausch, Gewerkschafter und SPD-Stadtrat, Dolf Sternberger, Herausgeber der Monatsschrift „Die Wandlung", Alfred Weber, Nationalökonom und Soziologe,

---

[153] Ebd., S. 150.
[154] Ebd.
[155] Wenige Monate nach der Amtsübernahme, im Februar 1947, verstarb Dawson. Direktor war dann, bis zur Auflösung des RGCO im Jahre 1948, Colonel Charles D. Winning.
[156] Dok. 78.
[157] Dok. 73.
[158] Dok. 78.
[159] Ebd.
[160] Ebd.
[161] Unterlagen aus dem Nachlass Edgar N. Johnson, Privatbesitz Candice E. und Thomas R. Johnson, Denver, Colorado, USA.

sowie dessen Schwägerin Marianne Weber, Witwe von Max Weber, Nationalökonom und Soziologe.

In Nürnberg, der einstigen „Stadt der Reichsparteitage", wohnte Johnson dem Hauptkriegsverbrecherprozess vor dem Internationalen Militärgerichtshof als Beobachter bei. Die Männer auf der Anklagebank beschreibt er als "a horrible looking bunch"[162]. "Except for a few they seemed to be all in a fairly cheerful state of mind, and munched bread during the hearing."[163]

Seine Reiseroute führte ihn schließlich nach München, wo er unter anderem mit dem Ministerpräsidenten des Landes Bayern, dem SPD-Politiker Wilhelm Hoegner, und dem Landesvorsitzenden der CSU, Josef Müller, sprechen konnte. Außerdem besuchte er seine frühere Pensionswirtin Anna Engelhorn, die er zuletzt im November 1945 gesehen hatte. "The nicest thing about the trip was, I guess, the couple visits to Frau Engelhorn."[164] "[…] she still has sharp intelligence, good humor, and is certainly one of the best if not really the best German, I have ever met."[165] Ihr Haus und die Einrichtung waren von den Amerikanern requiriert worden, "as part of the so-called American Military Communities which are established here in the zone: blocks of barbed-wire surrounded houses. The Germans don't react well to this separation."[166] Das Thema beschäftigte ihn sehr. In einer OMGUS-Stabsbesprechung hatte Johnson von Protesten in Stuttgart erfahren, wo die Bewohner des Stadtteils Sonnenberg ihre Häuser für die Familien von Besatzungsangehörigen räumen sollten. "We have never tried to distinguish between Nazis and non-Nazis in the requisition of dwelling space, a hot issue in this country where rooms are at premium."[167] Über die Wohnsituation der Amerikaner in Berlin schreibt er später: "Nobody from the lowliest to the high could complain about quarters. We had simply taken over the best available, and could not be bothered much about the political histories of those we obliged to get out."[168]

Johnsons Reiseplanung sah vor, auch "some of the so-called church heroes"[169], über die er als Research Analyst beim OSS geschrieben hatte, zu sehen und dem Münchner Erzbischof Michael Kardinal von Faulhaber einen Besuch abzustatten. Ob es zu einer Zusammenkunft mit diesem profilierten Vertreter des deutschen Episkopats kam, geht aus den Briefen nicht hervor. Fest steht, dass Johnson von der Kirche, "that church which I once thought was going to be such a great help in bringing back Germany to its feet"[170], enttäuscht war – von einer Kirche, "which doesn't want to get rid of its Nazi clergy"[171] und deren „Helden" "do not happen to be at the moment, the heroes I thought they were going to be"[172].

---

[162] Dok. 79.
[163] Ebd.
[164] Dok. 80.
[165] Ebd.
[166] Dok. 79.
[167] Dok. 26.
[168] Dok. 83.
[169] Dok. 75.
[170] Dok. 74.
[171] Dok. 52.
[172] Dok. 75.

General Walter J. Muller, der Chef der Militärregierung für Bayern, "paid no attention to me, nor any of his henchmen, and the people on his M[ilitary] G[overnment] staff whom I could find in their offices were a little condescending or else a little dead"[173].

Ein Abstecher führte Johnson ins pittoreske, durch seine Passionsspiele berühmte Oberammergau, wo er im Gästehaus der European Theater Intelligence School[174] unterkam. "I have thought how nice it would be to come here some summer, perhaps, when the Passion Play is on, which it will certainly be again, and spend part of the summer here, and part in Austria."[175]

Bei der Reiseplanung hatte Johnson auch eine Fahrt nach Wien in Betracht gezogen: "I suppose I ought to try to go to Vienna again, and catch up with the situation there."[176] Der Abstecher fiel dann allerdings dem Zeitmangel zum Opfer.

Nach Beendigung seiner rund zweiwöchigen Tour durch die Zone kehrte Johnson am 4. August 1946 nach Berlin zurück. Zwei Tage später verließ er die Stadt endgültig. Mit der Eisenbahn ging es nach Bremerhaven, von wo aus er erst nach ein paar Tagen mit dem Schiff die Heimreise über den Atlantik antreten konnte. Seine Vorfreude auf erholsame Ferien mit seiner Familie in den Bergen von Colorado, vor dem Wiederbeginn seiner Tätigkeit an der Universität, war groß. Ende August zu Hause in Lincoln angekommen, konnte er endlich wieder seine Lieben, ohne die er in Deutschland nicht länger hatte bleiben wollen, in die Arme schließen.

Johnson kehrte nie wieder nach Deutschland zurück. Wahrscheinlich hätte er erneut für OMGUS tätig werden können, denn qualifiziertes Personal war rar, und vor der Abreise aus Deutschland hatte ihm Donald R. Heath, der aus der Diplomatie kommende Director of Political Affairs, vorgeschlagen, "that if I found the life of the University to be a little too much to take, I should write him here at Berlin with the idea of coming into the service of the State Department here. I think he meant it."[177] Und auch die Leute der Education and Religious Affairs Branch hatten ihr Interesse bekundet: "[...] the Education people would be glad to take me on for an important job if I wished to come back here."[178] Dass ihm die Tätigkeit an der Universität und vor allem seine Familie wichtiger waren, geht unmissverständlich aus einem Schreiben an Ehefrau Emily hervor, in dem er über seine Zeit nach der Rückkehr ins heimatliche Lincoln nachdenkt: "I think when I get there I shall want, despite all my talk about trying to get into politics to do nothing much more than stay at home and

---

[173] Dok. 80.
[174] Zu deren Lehrkörper gehörte der spätere US-Außenminister und Friedensnobelpreisträger Henry Kissinger. 1923 im fränkischen Fürth geboren und 1938 mit seiner Familie in die USA emigriert, hatte ihn der Zweite Weltkrieg nach Deutschland zurückgebracht.
[175] Schreiben aus Oberammergau an Ehefrau Emily vom 1. August 1946, in: Unterlagen aus dem Nachlass Edgar N. Johnson, Privatbesitz Candice E. und Thomas R. Johnson, Denver, Colorado, USA. Das nicht unterzeichnete Schreiben wurde von Johnson verlegt und nie abgesandt.
[176] Dok. 72.
[177] Dok. 75.
[178] Ebd.

tend to my classes. Staying at home will mean cultivating you, cultivating the boys, and I suppose the garden. We have lost over two years, and you are always rightly reminding me of how really little time there is left. It is rather futile to think that I shall ever be able to do anything much outside of the rôle of teacher, and there is much still that I have to make up for. May be the time is coming with the boys getting a little older when you will get a better break, and when we can share more fully than we have ever shared, and cultivate more than we have ever cultivated a larger intellectual life. I have always in mind too being adequate for the boys. All this is enough without worrying about others promotions and salaries."[179]

Der politische Bazillus, den Johnson hier anspricht ("trying to get into politics"), hatte sich offensichtlich nur für kurze Zeit in ihm eingenistet. Die Idee, in die Politik zu gehen, um isolationistischen Tendenzen entgegenzutreten und seine Landsleute von der Notwendigkeit des amerikanischen Engagements, der aktiven Gestaltung Nachkriegsdeutschlands und Europas bzw. davon zu überzeugen, "that the peace, having not yet been won, was as vital to win as the war"[180], kam ihm, als sich im Juni 1946 in Nebraska der republikanische Senator und Isolationist Hugh A. Butler gegen Dwight P. Griswold, der dem internationalistischen Flügel der Republikanischen Partei angehörte, durchsetzen konnte und erneut als Kandidat für den US-Senat nominiert wurde. "I wonder if the Nebraskans realize the extent to which this is world news, and how much the Europeans will seek in it a confirmation of their notion that we are certain to abandon them again"[181], so Johnson zu dieser Entscheidung in Nebraska. "I propose to offer my services to the Democratic Party of Nebraska to campaign against Butler for as much as they want to use me."[182] Wäre Johnson als Politiker geeignet gewesen? "[...] sometimes I think I could let go my academic reserve and get down to basic sentiments which might have a popular emotional appeal."[183] Zu einem Einstieg in die Politik konnte er sich aber nicht durchringen. "To my knowledge", teilt Thomas R. Johnson mit, "he never tried to get into politics, although, as you might imagine, he voted for Democrats most of the time and was most likely a registered Democrat although I have no proof of that. The closest he came I think was helping to put together and contributing to the essay collection 'Freedom and the University', from the Cornell University Press, which was a response to the Joseph McCarthy-inspired investigations into liberal/left academicians."[184]

Es ist festzuhalten, dass der Universitätsprofessor aus Nebraska, ein hochintelligenter, vielseitig interessierter und einsetzbarer, tüchtiger Mann, in den wenigen Monaten, die er im besetzten Nachkriegsberlin verbrachte, einen kleinen, aber bedeutsamen Beitrag zum politischen Wiederaufbau, zur Schaffung eines demokratischen Fundaments leistete. Er beschäftigte sich unter anderem mit der Urabstimmung unter den Berliner SPD-Mitgliedern über die Frage der

---

[179] Dok. 65.
[180] Dok. 83.
[181] Dok. 62.
[182] Dok. 64.
[183] Ebd.
[184] E-Mail von Thomas R. Johnson an Werner Breunig vom 18. Oktober 2013.

Vereinigung von Kommunisten und Sozialdemokraten, mit der Anerkennung der von den Fusionsgegnern neu konstituierten SPD in allen vier Sektoren, mit der Planung von ersten Nachkriegskommunalwahlen und mit der Vorläufigen Verfassung von Groß-Berlin, zu deren Vätern er aufgrund seiner aktiven Beteiligung an den Beratungen im Local Government Committee der Alliierten Kommandantur zählt.

Ausgewiesene Deutschlandexperten aus der akademischen Welt der USA waren für OMGUS unverzichtbar. Zu ihnen gehörte Johnson ebenso wie beispielsweise die Erziehungswissenschaftler Richard T. Alexander und John W. Taylor, die bei der Education and Religious Affairs Branch, Internal Affairs and Communications Division, beschäftigt waren. Taylor, 1930/1931 Englischlehrer am Kaiser-Friedrich-Realgymnasium in Berlin-Neukölln, Verfasser einer Dissertation über "Youth Welfare in Germany", hatte nach 1945 seinen früheren akademischen Lehrer Alexander, Professor of Education am Teachers College der Columbia University in New York City und anerkannter Experte für das deutsche Bildungswesen, gebeten, als Mitarbeiter der Militärregierung nach Deutschland zu kommen. Johnson lernte beide in Berlin kennen und dachte zeitweise an eine Mitarbeit in der Education and Religious Affairs Branch. Es gab viele anspruchsvolle Jobs, für die geeignete Leute fehlten, und Franz L. Neumann erkannte richtig, "that there ought to be more Edgar Johnsons in Germany"[185].

Für seine geleistete Arbeit erntete Johnson Dankbarkeit und Lob. Dr. Johnson habe großartige Arbeit für den Berlin District geleistet, so der Chef von OMGBD, Colonel Frank L. Howley.[186] Im Entwurf eines Dankschreibens von General Lucius D. Clay an den Chancellor der University of Nebraska heißt es: "I wanted to thank you for what you and the University of Nebraska have done to help me and my Military Government officers by letting us have the invaluable services of Doctor Johnson for so long. I believe he has been on sabbatical leave from the University over three and a half years."[187] Johnsons Mitarbeit an der Vorläufigen Verfassung von Groß-Berlin wird hier besonders herausgestellt: "During the past five months he has been my personal advisor on political matters in Berlin and has been largely responsible for the temporary constitution for the City of Berlin which has just been approved by the Allied Control Authority for Germany and which previously had been approved by the Berlin Allied Kommandatura. The preparation of this constitution called for a most thorough knowledge of German political history and a deep knowledge of practical constitutional law. In order to draw up the constitution with the unanimous approval and assistance of his Russian, British and French colleagues, Doctor Johnson displayed extraordinary tact and persuasion."[188]

---

[185] Schreiben von Franz L. Neumann an Edgar N. Johnson vom 17. Mai 1946, in: UChicago Library, Special Collections Research Center, Edgar N. Johnson Papers.
[186] Vgl. OMGBD, Interoffice Memo Slip, 7. August 1946, Subject: Commendation for Dr. Edgar N. Johnson, in: LAB, B Rep. 036-01 (Office of Military Government, Berlin Sector [OMGBS]), 4/135-2/14.
[187] Entwurf eines Schreibens von General Lucius D. Clay an den Chancellor der University of Nebraska, Reuben G. Gustavson, vom 8. August 1946, in: LAB, B Rep. 036-01 (Office of Military Government, Berlin Sector [OMGBS]), 4/135-2/14.
[188] Ebd.

An Johnson schreibt Clay: "It was unfortunate that delays over which we had no control brought you back to Germany too late for the assignment with the Landerrat. However, it did make you available as the adviser to Berlin Military Government at a time when the political structure of the city was in grave difficulty. Your contribution can be measured by the fact that prior to your departure, the four Allied Governments had agreed on a democratic city charter and a free election. I shall ever be grateful to you for the spirit in which you undertook a changed assignment and to your insistence on a liberal and democratic philosophy of city government which will mean even more to Berlin and Germany in the future."[189] Und weiter heißt es in dem Schreiben: "We miss you at our staff meetings. However, we also hope you will have an occasional pang of regret that you are not still with us. In any event, if liberalism can become a reality in Germany, it will grow from the foundation which you helped so much to place."[190]

Nach Beendigung seiner Tätigkeit für die amerikanische Militärregierung verarbeitete Johnson das Erlebte in einem Bericht über seine Zeit in Berlin: "Five Months in Berlin"[191]. Unter diesem Titel hielt er im Herbst 1946 auch mehrere Vorträge, beispielsweise am 8. November vor Mitgliedern der American Library Association,[192] und führte somit seinen Landsleuten die Bedeutung der amerikanischen Präsenz in Berlin und Deutschland vor Augen.

Am 20. Oktober 1946 wurden in ganz Berlin freie Stadtverordnetenwahlen abgehalten, aus denen die SPD als klarer Sieger hervorging und die von der sowjetischen Besatzungsmacht favorisierte SED eine schwere Niederlage hinnehmen musste. Am selben Tag trat die Vorläufige Verfassung von Groß-Berlin in Kraft. Rund fünf Wochen später, am 26. November 1946, schlugen die für zwei Jahre gewählten Stadtverordneten ein neues Kapitel in der Berliner Nachkriegsgeschichte auf und begannen mit der parlamentarischen Arbeit.[193] An der Vorbereitung dieser herausragenden Ereignisse im politischen Leben Berlins war Johnson maßgeblich beteiligt gewesen. Als sie stattfanden, war er längst in die Vereinigten Staaten zurückgekehrt. "All the excitement without waiting for the event."[194]

In Berlin hatte Johnson freundschaftliche Kontakte zu dem kommissarischen Stadtkämmerer Friedrich Haas – "he is the kind of German upon whom Germany will have to rebuild"[195] – unterhalten[196] und mit ihm verfassungsrecht-

---

[189] Schreiben von General Lucius D. Clay an Edgar N. Johnson vom 12. September 1946, in: UChicago Library, Special Collections Research Center, Edgar N. Johnson Papers.
[190] Ebd.
[191] Dok. 83.
[192] Siehe Nebraska State Journal vom 9. November 1946, S. 2.
[193] Siehe Werner Breunig, Der parlamentarische Neubeginn. Die Konstituierung der Stadtverordnetenversammlung von Groß-Berlin am 26. November 1946, in: Berlin in Geschichte und Gegenwart. Jahrbuch des Landesarchivs Berlin 2011, S. 213-235.
[194] Dok. 54.
[195] Dok. 74.
[196] Es ist erwähnenswert, dass Johnson Haas und dessen Ehefrau Charlotte nach einem gemeinsamen Opernbesuch zum Essen in den Wannsee Officers' Club mitnahm: "I brought them out here for dinner and they stayed until after twelve – the first Germans, I imagine, who have been entertained in this expensive club." Ebd.

liche Fragen erörtert. Ende Dezember 1946 bedankte sich Haas, inzwischen Leiter der Finanzabteilung im neuen Magistrat, schriftlich bei Johnson „für Ihre werten Zeilen, die ich im Oktober erhalten habe"[197], und unterrichtete den Professor im fernen Nebraska über die weitere Entwicklung in Berlin, die ihn brennend interessiert haben dürfte: „Die vorläufige Verfassung, an der Sie so großen Anteil hatten, ist am 13. August 1946 veröffentlicht und am Wahltag, am 20. Oktober, in Kraft getreten. Inzwischen ist der neue Magistrat gewählt und hat zum größten Teil seine Tätigkeit aufgenommen. Der Wechsel vom alten, von den Besatzungsmächten eingesetzten, zum neuen, von den Bürgern gewählten, war nicht einfach. Wir befinden uns zur Zeit noch im Übergangsstadium."[198] Wie eng und freundschaftlich Haas und Johnson in Berliner Tagen zusammengearbeitet hatten, davon zeugen folgende Zeilen: „Augenblicklich benutze ich die Tage um Weihnachten und Neujahr, um den Ihnen angekündigten Kommentar zur vorläufigen Verfassung zu schreiben. Ich hoffe, mit dem Entwurf Mitte Januar fertig zu sein. Sobald er gedruckt ist, werde ich Ihnen ein Stück zugehen lassen. Daß ich bei der Erläuterung der vorläufigen Verfassung beinahe bei jedem Wort an unsere freundliche und offene Aussprache denke, brauche ich wohl nicht besonders zu betonen. Die Stunden und Tage unseres Kennenlernens und Zusammenarbeitens für eine größere, in die Zukunft weisende gemeinsame Sache bleiben mir unvergessen."[199]

Auch mit seinem früheren Chauffeur Artur Sanow hielt Johnson Kontakt, versorgte den Berliner in trostloser Zeit mit CARE-Paketen.[200]

Krieg und Besetzung hatten Johnson über seine Aufgaben als Historiker hinausgeführt. Nach dreieinhalbjähriger Abwesenheit und Tätigkeit auf internationaler Bühne kehrte er im Herbst 1946 an die University of Nebraska zurück und betrat wieder die kleine, enge Welt des dortigen Department of History. War dies noch die rechte Wirkungsstätte für ihn? Er hatte seine Zweifel. "I shall not be perfectly happy in University work again, at least to begin with"[201], so Johnson in einem seiner Schreiben aus Berlin.

Das Department of History war auf der Suche nach einem neuen Chairman, nachdem Charles Henry Oldfather um die Entbindung von seinem Amt gebeten hatte. Schon in Berlin hatte Johnson sich Gedanken über die Nachfolge gemacht. "I am not anxious for it since it would be only extra administrative and personal problems pain, having to do with raises and promotions. [...] But should I refuse it, if it comes my way? Ben Franklin said he would never ask

---

[197] Schreiben von Friedrich Haas an Edgar N. Johnson vom 30. Dezember 1946, in: UChicago Library, Special Collections Research Center, Edgar N. Johnson Papers.
[198] Ebd.
[199] Ebd.
[200] Siehe Bestätigung des Empfangs eines CARE-Pakets vom 10. Januar 1948, in: Unterlagen aus dem Nachlass Edgar N. Johnson, Privatbesitz Candice E. und Thomas R. Johnson, Denver, Colorado, USA.
[201] Dok. 39.
[202] "[...] I had read or heard of some Public Man, who made it a Rule never to ask for an Office, and never to refuse one when offer'd to him. I approve, says I, of his Rule, and will practise it with a small Addition; I shall never *ask*, never *refuse*, nor ever *resign* an Office." Benjamin Franklin, The Autobiography, with an introduction by Daniel Aaron, New York 1990, S. 109. In der deutschen Übertragung von Berthold Auer-

for, never refuse, and never resign from an office."[202]"[203] Diesen Rat Benjamin Franklins befolgend, übernahm Johnson im Herbst 1946 das Amt des temporary Chairman. Wahrscheinlich bekleidete er den Posten nur ein Jahr lang.

Seine Kenntnisse und Erfahrungen, die er in den Kriegsjahren gewonnen hatte, wusste Johnson in Lehre und Veröffentlichungen anzuwenden. "My experience in the war years has colored a good deal of my subsequent teaching and writing. How it has colored a mediaeval theme could be seen in my essay, *The Background of the University Tradition* in 'Freedom and the University' (Cornell University Press, 1950)."[204]

Es war für Johnson eine große Freude, dass er seinen guten Freund, den Historiker Eugene N. Anderson, der seit der Auflösung des OSS in den Diensten des State Department stand, an die University of Nebraska holen konnte. Und Anderson, der sich im Außenministerium nicht wohlfühlte, war überaus glücklich, dass er dem Ministerium den Rücken kehren, wieder eine universitäre Position bekleiden und sich der Wissenschaft widmen konnte. „Ich wollte unabhängig sein, wollte niemandem zu Diensten sein"[205], so äußert er sich später. Die State-Department-Leute mochte er nicht so recht, „sie waren zu bürokratisch für mich, zu Hierarchie-orientiert"[206]. "He left in 1947 with infinite relief and delight to go to U[niversity] [of] N[ebraska]"[207], erinnert sich sein Sohn, Eugene N. Anderson Jr.

Anderson, der sich als Historiker vor allem mit deutscher Geschichte des 19. und 20. Jahrhunderts beschäftigte, hatte 1924/1925 an der Universität Berlin studiert, wurde an der University of Chicago promoviert, war nach einem Forschungsaufenthalt in Deutschland Professor of Modern European History an der University of Chicago, wirkte dann an der American University, lehrte 1939 als Gastprofessor an der University of Nebraska, leitete ab 1943 beim OSS die Central European Section der Research and Analysis Branch und war somit Johnsons Vorgesetzter. Eugene N. Anderson Jr. erinnert sich an seinen Vater und an Edgar N. Johnson: "He [Johnson] was my father's lifelong best friend, and our families were very close."[208] Johnson und Anderson "could talk shop

---

bach, revidiert von Heinz Förster, heißt es: „[...] ich habe von einem Manne in öffentlicher Stellung gehört oder gelesen, der es sich zur Regel gemacht hatte, sich niemals um ein Amt zu bewerben, aber auch niemals eines auszuschlagen, wenn es ihm angeboten wurde. ‚Ich pflichte dieser Regel bei und werde sie, nur mit einem kleinen Zusatz, befolgen', sagte ich; ‚ich werde mich nie um ein Amt *bewerben*, nie eins *ablehnen*, aber auch nie eins *aufgeben*. [...]'" Benjamin Franklin, Autobiographie, mit einem Nachwort von Klaus Harpprecht (= Beck'sche Reihe, 1510), 2. Auflage, München 2010, S. 155.

[203] Dok. 65.
[204] Edgar N. Johnson, Curriculum Vitae, undatiert [ca. 1963], S. 3, in: UChicago Library, Special Collections Research Center, Edgar N. Johnson Papers.
[205] Interview mit Prof. Eugene N. Anderson am 10. Dezember 1983 in Santa Barbara/Californien, in: Zur Archäologie der Demokratie in Deutschland, Bd. 2: Analysen von politischen Emigranten im amerikanischen Außenministerium 1946–1949, hrsg. von Alfons Söllner, Frankfurt am Main 1986, S. 22–34, hier S. 32.
[206] Ebd., hier S. 31f.
[207] Eugene N. Anderson Jr. in einer E-Mail an Werner Breunig vom 30. Juli 2007.
[208] Eugene N. Anderson Jr. in einer E-Mail an Werner Breunig vom 23. Juni 2007.

for hours and hours, and my father", so Eugene N. Anderson Jr., "got a lot of stimulation – my father was also tense and bright but more quiet, less adventurous – he needed Edgar and Edgar's strong opinions and mercilessly sharp mind to get him going. Edgar I think got some benefit from my father's quietness and philosophical attitude toward the world. Edgar kept up on current events and the world in general more than my father did, and was always great to talk to about most anything. Both of them were compulsive workers, though, so finding a chance to talk with them was always pretty difficult."[209]

Während Anderson 1955, in der McCarthy-Ära, nach Anschuldigungen der American Legion an die University of California, Los Angeles, wechselte, blieb Johnson noch bis 1958 in Lincoln. Über dessen Tätigkeit an der University of Nebraska schreibt Robert E. Knoll in seinem Buch "Prairie University. A History of the University of Nebraska": "In the Department of History, Edgar N. Johnson attracted a circle of admirers almost in spite of himself. Concerned with the largest intellectual questions, he offered a two-year course in the history of Western civilization in which he asked students to ponder the rise of rational liberalism from ancient times through the Enlightenment down to modern 'scientism', one of his words. He did not pretend to be unbiased and thought that history revealed the eternal truths of civil rights. Cultural relativism was not for him. After Harley Burr Alexander left the campus, Johnson was sometimes referred to as the intellectual conscience of the University. A very intense man, rather indifferent to his appearance, he talked to freshmen as though they were his intellectual equals and to advanced students as though they were as passionately committed to the intellectual life as he was. In devoting himself to his grand ideas, he did not always seem aware of the individual students to whom he lectured, but they did not mind. He opened doors to worlds they had not known existed, and he changed the lives of some. Edgar Johnson was a synthesizer, a writer of textbooks, and a generalist."[210] Offensichtlich genoss er eine besondere Wertschätzung bei seinen Studenten. Donald J. Ziegler schreibt im Vorwort seiner 1958 veröffentlichten, auf seiner Dissertation basierenden Studie "Prelude to Democracy. A Study of Proportional Representation and the Heritage of Weimar Germany 1871-1920", er sei Edgar N. Johnson zu Dank verpflichtet "for an approach to history which emphasizes the goodness and the rationality of man"[211].

Im Studienjahr 1956/1957 lehrte Johnson als Gastprofessor am Washington Square College der privaten New York University, wo er für den Mediävisten Wallace K. Ferguson einsprang. Ehefrau Emily und die Kinder waren schon 1953 nach New York City gekommen, um Sohn John den Besuch der berühmten Juilliard School of Music zu ermöglichen. Emily studierte in der Stadt an der Ostküste an einer pädagogischen Hochschule und unterrichtete dann an der Barnard School for Boys.

---

[209] Eugene N. Anderson Jr. in einer E-Mail an Werner Breunig vom 17. Juli 2007.
[210] Robert E. Knoll, Prairie University. A History of the University of Nebraska, Lincoln, Nebraska, 1995, S. 87.
[211] Donald J. Ziegler, Prelude to Democracy. A Study of Proportional Representation and the Heritage of Weimar Germany 1871-1920 (= University of Nebraska Studies, New Series No. 20), Lincoln, Nebraska, 1958, S. VII.

In New York könnte es ein Wiedersehen mit einem alten Bekannten aus Berliner Zeiten gegeben haben: Frank L. Howley, 1946 OMGBD-Direktor und stellvertretender amerikanischer Stadtkommandant von Berlin, fungierte mittlerweile als Vice Chancellor for University Development an der New York University. Ihn hatte Johnson zu jenen Besatzern gezählt, "who are out to make this show a pleasure and an adventure for themselves"[212].

Möglicherweise wären Edgar N. und Emily L. Johnson gerne dauerhaft im weltstädtischen New York geblieben. Thomas R. Johnson: "I don't know whether they wished to move to N[ew] Y[ork] C[ity] permanently or not, though I am sure they felt much more culturally attuned to that city than to Lincoln Nebraska. I suspect, but do not know for sure, that Edgar was negotiating for a new job in several places at that time; perhaps New York University was one."[213]

Eine Fortsetzung seiner Tätigkeit an der New York University war allerdings nicht möglich, da ein weiterer Mediävist – neben Wallace K. Ferguson – nicht benötigt wurde. In einem Schreiben des Leiters des Historischen Instituts, Bayrd Still, an Edgar N. Johnson vom 18. Juni 1957 heißt es: "You fitted into the Department with remarkable ease and unobtrusiveness and helped us admirably in filling the gap left by Wally Ferguson's departure. I know that a number of us enjoyed you and your wife so much as to wish we had a place for another medievalist at N[ew] Y[ork] U[niversity]. Unfortunately, our needs do not seem to point in that direction at the moment."[214]

Nach dem Studienjahr 1956/1957 kehrten die Johnsons wieder zurück nach Lincoln, ins ländlich geprägte, konservative Nebraska. Sohn John, der im September 1957 18 Jahre alt wurde, setzte seine Ausbildung an der Juilliard School in New York fort und war im Studienjahr 1957/1958 ein Schüler der russisch-amerikanischen Pianistin Rosina Lhévinne. Die erhoffte große Pianistenkarriere sollte ihm allerdings versagt bleiben.

Wiederholt hatte Edgar N. Johnson in der Vergangenheit Angebote anderer Hochschulen ausgeschlagen, aus welchen Gründen auch immer. "I remained in Lincoln, thinking it wise to decline invitations to come to Scripps College, the University of Southern California, and Ohio State University (chairmanship)."[215] Nach dem Weggang seines ihm eng verbundenen Freundes und Kollegen Eugene N. Anderson und der Zeit in New York mit seinem kulturellen und intellektuellen Angebot schien ihn aber nichts mehr in der nach Abraham Lincoln benannten Präriestadt zu halten. 1958 verließ er die University of Nebraska, an der er fast drei Jahrzehnte lang gelehrt hatte, und wechselte an die Brandeis University in Waltham bei Boston, der Hauptstadt des US-Bundesstaats Massachusetts – "wanted to be back in a city with a lot of intellectual activity, as well as a more professionally good placement"[216]. An der kleinen Privatuniversität,

---

[212] Dok. 46.
[213] Thomas R. Johnson in einer E-Mail an Werner Breunig vom 24. April 2013.
[214] Zit. nach Claire A. Wolford, Graduate Assistant, New York University Archives, E-Mail an Werner Breunig vom 11. April 2013.
[215] Edgar N. Johnson, Curriculum Vitae, undatiert [ca. 1963], S. 1, in: UChicago Library, Special Collections Research Center, Edgar N. Johnson Papers.
[216] Eugene N. Anderson Jr. in einer E-Mail an Werner Breunig vom 3. Juli 2007.

1948 von jüdischen Migranten gegründet, sollte er über Jahre hinweg – bis April 1963 – Chairman des Department of History sein. Zu seinen Kollegen in Brandeis gehörte Herbert Marcuse, Professor of Politics and Philosophy, mit dem er beim History of Ideas Program zusammenarbeitete und den er bereits aus seiner Zeit beim OSS kannte. Für das Programm der Ideengeschichte bestritt Johnson Lehrveranstaltungen wie "Intellectual History of the Twelfth and Thirteenth Centuries"[217] oder "The Thought of the Latin Fathers of the Church"[218].

Zu Johnsons Studentinnen und Studenten in Brandeis zählte die aus Griechenland stammende Angeliki Laiou. 1961/1962 wohnte sie bei den Johnsons in Newton bei Boston und Thomas R. Johnson bei den Laious in Athen. Durch diesen Familientausch kam Edgar N. Johnson 1962 erstmals seit 1946 wieder nach Europa, als er gemeinsam mit seiner Frau Emily und Angeliki Laiou nach Griechenland reiste. Thomas R. Johnson: "I stayed with Angeliki's family (parents, brother and grandmother) from September, 1961 until about June, 1962 in Athens. Angeliki stayed with my parents in Newton, Massachusetts for the same period. Edgar, Emily and Angeliki came to Greece at the end of my stay and Emily, Edgar and I traveled around a bit after that."[219] Es sollte Edgar N. Johnsons letzter Europaaufenthalt sein. Einen Abstecher nach Deutschland unternahm er nicht.

Angeliki Laiou war später, ab 1981, Professorin für byzantinische Geschichte an der Harvard University und galt als "one of the world's leading historians of the Byzantine empire – the successor of the Roman empire in the Middle East – and of the Crusades"[220]. Zeitweise leitete sie das History Department der Harvard University, war Mitglied des griechischen Parlaments und stellvertretende griechische Außenministerin.

Emily L. Johnson setzte in Massachusetts ihre in New York begonnene pädagogische Tätigkeit fort und leitete die Charles River School in Dover bei Boston.

Brandeis war nicht Edgar N. Johnsons letzte berufliche Station. Am Ende seiner Laufbahn hatte er eine Professur an der staatlichen University of Massachusetts in Amherst im Westen des US-Bundesstaats Massachusetts inne. Seine Tätigkeit an dieser Universität begann im September 1965. 1968/1969 hielt er am Regis College, einem privaten römisch-katholischen Frauencollege in Weston, Massachusetts, ein "Colloquium in Intellectual History"[221] ab. Im Frühjahr 1969 trat er in den Ruhestand.

Emily L. Johnson, "an innovative and progressive educator"[222], gründete 1967 in Amherst "The Common School", "an independent elementary school that inculcated a love of learning and a respect for different cultures and learning

---

[217] Brandeis University Bulletin, 1958–1959, S. 129.
[218] Brandeis University Bulletin, 1963–1964, S. 132.
[219] Thomas R. Johnson in einer E-Mail an Werner Breunig vom 24. April 2013.
[220] http://history.fas.harvard.edu/news/?p=258 (letzter Zugriff am 28. August 2013).
[221] E-Mail von Sister Mary Rita Grady, Archivist, Regis College Archives, an Werner Breunig vom 25. April 2013.
[222] http://vimeo.com/12266425 (letzter Zugriff am 28. August 2013).

styles among its students"[223]. Diese Schule "became a vibrant community of learners that thrives today. Over 100 students from ages 3 to 12, take part in joyful learning, based on Emily Johnson's earliest ideas about educating children."[224]

Einige Monate nach seinem Eintritt in den Ruhestand, an Silvester 1969, starb Edgar N. Johnson mit 68 Jahren im Cooley Dickinson Hospital in Amhersts Nachbarstadt Northampton an einem Herzinfarkt. Seine Asche wurde auf dem 1951 erworbenen, am Rande des Rocky Mountain National Park gelegenen Feriengrundstück in Allenspark, Colorado, wohin er sich, wann immer möglich, gerne begeben hatte, verstreut. Noch heute steht dort seine „Studierhütte", in die der Gelehrte sich oft zum Arbeiten zurückgezogen hatte und in der sich später in einem alten Überseekoffer die an seine geliebte und verehrte Frau adressierten Briefe fanden.

Emily L. Johnson leitete noch bis 1975 die von ihr gegründete Schule in Amherst. Sie zog 1981 dauerhaft nach Allenspark, blieb in Kontakt mit der Common School und starb 74-jährig am 10. September 1985 in Boulder, Colorado.

2005 übergab Thomas R. Johnson den schriftlichen Nachlass seines Vaters, auch die 1946 in Berlin verfassten Briefe, der University of Chicago, an der Edgar N. Johnson studiert, seine Lehrtätigkeit begonnen und seinen Doktortitel erworben hatte.

---

[223] Ebd. (letzter Zugriff am 28. August 2013).
[224] Ebd. (letzter Zugriff am 28. August 2013).

Jürgen Wetzel
"Winning the Peace"

Edgar N. Johnson kam Anfang März 1946 in eine Stadt der Ruinen und des menschlichen Elends. Schlecht gekleidete, hungernde Menschen hausten in zerstörten Gebäuden und kämpften um das nackte Überleben. Nicht einmal die an den Straßenrändern beigesetzten Toten waren zu diesem Zeitpunkt umgebettet worden. Nach diesen ersten Eindrücken war es für Johnson zweifelhaft, ob Deutschland jemals wieder aus den Ruinen auferstehen könnte.

Der Gegensatz zu den wohlgenährten, in abgeschirmten Wohnquartieren lebenden amerikanischen Besatzern konnte nicht größer sein. Diese Kontraste und die in der Stadt spürbaren politischen Spannungen haben ihn so berührt, dass er seine Eindrücke und Beobachtungen, für deren ausführliche Aufzeichnung die Zeit fehlte, tagebuchartig analysierend und kommentierend fast täglich seiner Frau Emily in langen Briefen anvertraute. "I am sorry to omit details because if I don't write them to you they will escape me forever"[1], schreibt er entschuldigend seiner Frau. "[...] I am keeping no journal, no diary. Only my letters to you contain a chronicle of what is happening to me."[2] Möglicherweise hatte er die Absicht, die Briefe später als Grundlage für einen historischen Diskurs zu verwenden, wie er es bereits mit seinen österreichischen Erfahrungen in "The American Occupation of Austria"[3] getan hatte. Er war sich der Brisanz seiner Mitteilungen bewusst, bat seine Frau um Diskretion und hoffte, dass seine Briefe nicht zensiert würden. Die vertraulichen Informationen sollten auch im Bekanntenkreis nicht weitergegeben werden: "Please do not use these details in conversation"[4], damit sie nicht in die Presse gelangten. Denn das hätte, wie er befürchtete, den Verlust seines Berliner Jobs bedeuten können, und seine Vorgesetzten wollte er nicht enttäuschen: "I must be absolutely loyal."[5]

Johnson war ursprünglich für die Leitung des Verbindungsbüros zwischen dem Länderrat und der amerikanischen Militärregierung in Stuttgart als "Regional Military Governor"[6] vorgesehen. Der damalige Chef, James K. Pollock, sollte im Austausch als politischer Berater in die Militärregierung nach Berlin wechseln. Johnson wollte dann eventuell bis zum Herbst 1947 in Deutschland bleiben und stellte Überlegungen an, seine Familie, seine Frau und seine beiden kleinen Söhne, von denen er ungern getrennt war, nach Europa – wegen der unsicheren Lage in Deutschland eventuell in die Schweiz – nachkommen zu lassen.[7] Eine Begegnung mit Pollock Anfang März in Berlin verlief jedoch recht kühl, und es stellte sich schnell heraus, dass Pollock den Posten in Stutt-

---

[1] Dok. 28.
[2] Dok. 67.
[3] In: Nebraska History, Vol. 26, 1945, S. 201–210.
[4] Dok. 27.
[5] Dok. 26.
[6] Dok. 41.
[7] Siehe Dok. 23 und Dok. 43.

gart nicht vor Ende des Sommers räumen würde. Über diese Reorganisationsmaßnahme war Johnson zunächst nicht unterrichtet worden.⁸ Die „zweite Geige" aber wollte er in Stuttgart nicht spielen und bis zum August nicht in Berlin ausharren, da auch seine Frau Emily keinerlei Bereitschaft erkennen ließ, mit den Söhnen nach Europa zu kommen.⁹ Das war für ihn eine herbe Enttäuschung, zumal sich nun eine längere Hängepartie über seine Verwendung in Berlin anschloss: "[...] it is a little hard on me. If I had known that I wasn't going to have the Stuttgart job, than I shouldn't have returned here."¹⁰ Der stellvertretende Militärgouverneur, General Lucius D. Clay, riet ihm, sich erst einmal umzusehen und sich über die Strukturen der Militärregierung zu informieren.¹¹ Es dauerte dann einige Zeit, bis die schwerfällige Militäradministration, mit der er schon vor seiner Abreise aus Amerika schlechte Erfahrungen gemacht hatte, ihm schließlich eine Position als "Special Assistant to the Deputy Military Governor" und ein Büro nahe dem von Clay und gegenüber dem von Botschafter Robert D. Murphy, dem Political Adviser for Germany, zuwies.¹² In dieser Position nahm er an den von Clay geleiteten Stabskonferenzen, an Abteilungsbesprechungen und an Viermächtesitzungen der Alliierten Kontrollratsbehörde teil. Zu den Tagesordnungspunkten zählten u. a. Demilitarisierung, Demontagen der Industrie, die Ernährungssituation, Entnazifizierungsmaßnahmen, die Polizeireform, die Zwangsvereinigung von KPD und SPD zur SED und die Wahlen in Berlin.¹³

Johnson empfand die Atmosphäre in der OMGUS-Zentrale zunächst sehr hektisch und unübersichtlich. Er lernte aber schnell, wie das Besatzungsregime funktionierte, und musste feststellen, dass die Handelnden oft genug gegen "principles of American democracy"¹⁴ verstießen. "I am just a little bit dizzy. I have attended so many meetings today; met and seen so many generals that I'm not quite sure where I am what I am or who I am"¹⁵, schreibt er seiner Frau. Nicht frei von Eitelkeit, fühlte er sich aber geschmeichelt, als VIP behandelt und sich in der Umgebung hoher Militärs und Diplomaten bewegen zu können. Trotz seiner unbefriedigenden Stellung entwickelte sich zu General Clay, den er bewunderte, ein vertrauensvolles Verhältnis, das durch gegenseitigen Respekt gekennzeichnet war. Da ihn aber diese Stellung auch nach Auffassung von Clay nicht ausfüllen konnte, wurde er auf Wunsch des amerikanischen Stadtkommandanten, General Ray W. Barker, an die für Berlin zuständige Militärregierung „ausgeliehen".¹⁶

Als "Political Adviser to the Commanding General" wurde er der Civil Administration Branch zugeteilt. Von General Barker, "an altogether decent and

---

8   Siehe Dok. 15, Dok. 16, Dok. 24, Dok. 43, Dok. 47 und Dok. 78.
9   Siehe Dok. 49 und Dok. 69.
10 Dok. 24.
11 Siehe Dok. 16 und Dok. 17.
12 Siehe Dok. 25 und Dok. 74.
13 Siehe Dok. 16, Dok. 17, Dok. 19, Dok. 27, Dok. 50, Dok. 52, Dok. 54, Dok. 55, Dok. 67 und Dok. 74.
14 Dok. 17.
15 Ebd.
16 Siehe Dok. 24.

interesting fellow"[17], war er beeindruckt. Die Sympathien waren auf beiden Seiten. Barker schätzte Johnsons Rat ebenso wie Clay, und es entwickelte sich zwischen ihnen ebenfalls ein enges Vertrauensverhältnis: "My early impressions of him are confirmed. He is a man definitely worth working for"[18], schreibt Johnson. Dagegen blieb das Verhältnis zum Chef der Branch, Lieutenant Colonel Louis Glaser, sowie zu dem Direktor der Berliner Militärregierung, Colonel Frank L. Howley, distanziert kühl, obwohl er Glaser in die Sitzungen des Local Government Committee der Alliierten Kommandantur begleitete und ihn dort mehrmals vertreten konnte. Beide Männer waren nach Johnsons Meinung arrogant, ehrgeizig und ambitioniert. Sie sahen in ihrem Job nur Vergnügen und Abenteuer; und er hatte das Gefühl, Glaser wollte ihn so schnell wie möglich wieder los werden.[19]

Für die Beratertätigkeit hatte Johnson die besten Voraussetzungen. Im Gegensatz zu Glaser und Howley besaß er sehr gute Deutsch- und Deutschlandkenntnisse, hatte 1927/28 als Stipendiat der Alexander von Humboldt-Stiftung bei den renommierten Professoren Paul Lehmann und Hermann Oncken in München studiert und war selbst seit den 30er-Jahren als Professor für europäische Geschichte an der Universität Nebraska in Lincoln tätig. Als Historiker besaß er einen geschulten Blick für die politischen Umwälzungen in Europa nach dem Zweiten Weltkrieg, die sich in Berlin fokussierten. Praktische Erfahrungen für seine Berliner Tätigkeit konnte er seit 1943 als Research Analyst im Office of Strategic Services in Washington, D. C., London, Caserta und unmittelbar nach dem Krieg in Österreich sammeln.

In Berlin war Johnson zunächst in einem Haus in der Ihnestraße untergebracht und zog Ende März auf Vermittlung von General Barker in das sogenannte Wannsee Hotel/Wannsee Officers' Club Am Sandwerder um, in eine repräsentative Villa des ehemaligen NS-Reichswirtschaftsministers Walther Funk. Das Haus befand sich unmittelbar am Ufer des Großen Wannsees, und Johnson genoss den wunderbaren Ausblick, den beginnenden Frühling und die Sportmöglichkeiten, vor allem mit Segeln. Im Wannsee Hotel wohnten ranghohe Amerikaner in eleganten und komfortablen Quartieren.[20]

Für seine Arbeit bezog er ein "splendiferous"[21] Büro in der Zentrale von Berlin District in Steglitz. Es standen ihm nun eine deutsche Sekretärin sowie ein Auto mit einem deutschen Chauffeur zur Verfügung. Johnson sollte im Auftrag von Barker ein "political reporting office"[22] aufbauen. Auch wenn Clay darin nur "small potatoes"[23] sah, hellte sich nach den Enttäuschungen der vergangenen Wochen seine Stimmung auf. "Actually I think the job is going to be an interesting one"[24], schreibt er erleichtert seiner Frau. Bei seiner Einführung

---

[17] Dok. 25.
[18] Dok. 28; siehe auch Dok. 33.
[19] Siehe Dok. 40, Dok. 46, Dok. 47, Dok. 52, Dok. 53, Dok. 64, Dok. 67, Dok. 71 und Dok. 80.
[20] Siehe Dok. 31, Dok. 33, Dok. 36, Dok. 37, Dok. 41, Dok. 45 und Dok. 56.
[21] Dok. 25 und Dok. 28.
[22] Dok. 20.
[23] Ebd.
[24] Dok. 25.

meinte Barker, die Tätigkeit der Militärregierung in Berlin sei „Politik und Erziehung". Endlich konnte er nützliche Arbeit verrichten, mit den Deutschen in Kontakt treten, was ihm besonders am Herzen lag, und sie zurück auf den Weg zur Demokratie begleiten.

Zunächst beauftragte ihn der General, Kommandanturberatungen vorzubereiten, und nahm ihn zu den Sitzungen selbst mit, die ihn faszinierten. Die brisanten Verhandlungen und die Beobachtung der Akteure gaben ihm das Gefühl, im Zentrum des politischen Geschehens in Berlin angekommen zu sein. Er lernte, wie die "international machinery" funktionierte: "These international meetings are fun"[25] und "highly exciting"[26], schreibt er begeistert. Es erstaunte ihn, dass bei dem Wirrwarr von vielen Teilnehmern, mehreren Sekretärinnen, den schwerfälligen Übersetzungen in zwei andere Sprachen eine Verständigung überhaupt möglich war und dass sogar Übereinkünfte erzielt werden konnten. Besonders faszinierten ihn die Gelage mit "lots of liquor, lots of food"[27].

Der Ost-West-Konflikt in der alliierten Stadt erlebte kurz nach Johnsons Ankunft seine erste größere Belastungsprobe. Die Situation in Berlin sei "particularly hot"[28], schreibt er seiner Frau, denn die von den Sowjets beeinflussten Kommunisten in der Sowjetzone und Berlin forcierten im Frühjahr 1946 den Zusammenschluss mit den Sozialdemokraten zu einer "new left-wing, workers' Unity Party"[29]. Wenn diese Fusion gelänge, meint Johnson, habe es möglicherweise große politische Auswirkungen auf die Zukunft Deutschlands. Die Sowjets versprachen sich von dieser Maßnahme einen größeren Einfluss auch auf ganz Berlin und hofften, ihrem Ziel näher zu kommen, die Westalliierten aus Berlin zu verdrängen und die Stadt ihrem Machtbereich einzuverleiben. Viele Sozialdemokraten wehrten sich gegen eine Vereinigung und gegen die Dominanz der Kommunisten. Sie hatten unter dem Naziregime schwer gelitten und wollten sich nicht von der einen Diktatur in die nächste zwingen lassen. Johnson sah in der Lösung dieses Konflikts eine zentrale Aufgabe der amerikanischen Politik und vermittelte General Barker Informationen, Analysen und Lösungsvorschläge, die der Stadtkommandant in den Kommandanturverhandlungen und in seinen Ansprachen nutzte. Als der Zentralausschuss der SPD eine freie Abstimmung über die Vereinigung sabotieren wollte, schaltete sich Johnson direkt ein: "This made me mad", schreibt er, "and I went to Barker with the suggestion that he write a letter to the Central Committee reminding them that he wanted a free expression of opinion on the matter to be held and that he also release a statement to the press expressing his point of view. He agreed (he is a man of principle) and let me write the letter and the release."[30] Tatsächlich erschien die von Johnson entworfene Pressemitteilung am 30. März in den Berliner Zeitungen, und am 31. März fand die Urabstimmung, allerdings nur in den Westsektoren, statt, in der die überwiegende Mehrheit der SPD-Mitglieder die

---

[25] Dok. 28.
[26] Dok. 25.
[27] Ebd.
[28] Dok. 20.
[29] Ebd.
[30] Dok. 30; siehe auch Dok. 69.

Vereinigung ablehnte.[31] In langen Verhandlungen in den alliierten Gremien, die Johnson engagiert miterlebte, einigten sich die Besatzungsmächte schließlich auf einen auch von Johnson vorgeschlagenen Kompromiss: "I had written out a statement of our policy for the last meeting which was circulated among all the Commandants. It proposed simply that both parties be recognized."[32] Beide Parteien, SED und SPD, sollten in ganz Berlin gleichberechtigt agieren können, in der sowjetischen Zone herrschte allerdings nun allein die Einheitspartei. Im Vorfeld dieser Auseinandersetzungen besuchte Johnson Parteiveranstaltungen und sprach mit deutschen Politikern. Er traf den Sozialdemokraten Otto Grotewohl, der den Willen seiner Partei hintertrieb und als Opportunist sich den Kommunisten andiente. "I didn't like the look in his eye", schreibt er nach einer Begegnung im Mai und fügt hinzu: "But he was hardly a man in whom you could really put your trust."[33]

Gegenüber den sowjetischen Initiativen vermisste Johnson positive Akzente der amerikanischen Politik. Ihn beschlich das Gefühl, dass die amerikanischen Autoritäten in Washington keine vorausschauende Strategie entwickelten, um der sowjetischen Aggression zu begegnen. Offenbar hatten sie seiner Meinung nach keine rechte Vorstellung von der dringend benötigten Hilfe für Deutschland, um das Land vor dem kommunistischen Einfluss zu schützen und den Frieden zu sichern. Selbst "the best Americans", so erscheint es Johnson, "were not that interested in winning the peace"[34].

Johnsons wichtigste Aufgabe war die Arbeit im Local Government Committee der Alliierten Kommandantur. Er half mit, in Berlin ein parlamentarisches Regime zu installieren. Das hieß: eine Verfassung zu erarbeiten und Wahlen für die Stadtverordnetenversammlung vorzubereiten, um schließlich einen demokratisch legitimierten Magistrat bilden zu können. Das bedeutete vor allem intensive Viermächteverhandlungen. Durch die vertrauensvolle Zusammenarbeit mit General Barker erhielt Johnson die Gelegenheit, ihn vor den Sitzungen der Stadtkommandanten in allen Berliner Angelegenheiten intensiv zu beraten. Am 27. April schreibt er: "I think I reported on the last meeting when I had carefully prepared statements for General Barker to present at the previous meeting on such important subjects as elections in Berlin, the recognition of the anti-merger Social Democrats, and the supervision of political activities in the city of Berlin."[35] Und an einer anderen Stelle des Briefes heißt es: "I had briefed him"[36].

Anfang Mai 1946 quittierte General Barker den Dienst, vielleicht aus gesundheitlichen Gründen, wahrscheinlich aber, weil er "a line somewhat different

---

[31] Siehe Berlin. Kampf um Freiheit und Selbstverwaltung 1945–1946, hrsg. im Auftrage des Senats von Berlin (= Schriftenreihe zur Berliner Zeitgeschichte, Bd. 1), 2., erg. und erw. Auflage, Berlin 1961, S. 401, Nr. 97, und 404, Nr. 105.
[32] Dok. 40; siehe auch Dok. 31, Dok. 32, Dok. 33, Dok. 37, Dok. 38, Dok. 55, Dok. 71 und Dok. 83.
[33] Dok. 52.
[34] Dok. 83; siehe auch Dok. 39.
[35] Dok. 40.
[36] Ebd.; siehe auch Dok. 29, Dok. 49, Dok. 55, Dok. 67 und Dok. 83.

from Clay"[37] verfolgte. "There is also the fact that he and Clay do not see eye to eye on all matters"[38], erläutert Johnson die Differenzen zwischen Clay und Barker. Er bedauert sehr den Weggang des Stadtkommandanten und meint: "He has been a fine person to come to know, and I regret very much his going."[39] Barker wurde durch General Frank A. Keating ersetzt, der keinerlei Kenntnisse von den Verhältnissen in Berlin hatte und nach Johnsons Meinung "quite unpolitical"[40] und "quite innocent of politics"[41] war. Zu ihm entwickelte Johnson kein enges Beraterverhältnis. Das war eine weitere Enttäuschung für ihn. Da auch seine Frau mit den Kindern nicht nach Europa kommen wollte, verfestigte sich bei ihm die Auffassung, nicht auf das Freiwerden der Stelle in Stuttgart zu warten, sondern im August – wie ursprünglich vorgesehen – nach Lincoln zurückzukehren. "If you don't want to come here, I shall be in Lincoln in the Fall."[42] Es seien zwar patriotische Gründe, in Berlin zu bleiben, meinte er, andererseits sei es ohne ausfüllende Aufgaben reine Verschwendung von Steuergeldern, wenn er noch länger in Berlin bliebe.[43] Bei all seinen Karrierehoffnungen in der Militärregierung stand die Familie stets im Mittelpunkt seiner Gefühlswelt. Er fühlte sich einsam. Immer wieder übermannte ihn die Sehnsucht nach seiner Frau und seinen Söhnen im fernen Nebraska. "I can't stand being alone. It is not good for me."[44] Ihnen opferte er leichten Herzens die Aussicht auf eine herausragende Stellung in der Militärregierung. Es fiel ihm aber schwer, General Clay von seinen Absichten zu unterrichten, und er zögerte die Aussprache immer wieder hinaus, denn Clay rechnete damit, dass Johnson im Sommer Pollock nachfolgen würde.[45] An dem Stuttgart-Job hatten ihn ursprünglich die Gestaltungsmöglichkeiten und die Bezahlung gereizt; denn mit dem Geld hätte er seinen Lebensstandard in Amerika heben und sich beruflich verbessern können. Aber ein weiteres Jahr wollte er ohne seine Familie nicht in Deutschland bleiben, und er befürchtete, damit auch seine Wurzeln in Lincoln zu kappen. Andererseits scheute er die Rückkehr in das Intrigengewirr des Universitätsbetriebes und stellte resignierend fest, dass die Aussicht, in Lincoln zu lehren, für ihn genauso unbefriedigend sei wie in Berlin zu bleiben: "In some ways I hate to enter this small world again, and I think perhaps I shouldn't"[46], stellt er unentschlossen fest. Ein Kollege in Berlin, schreibt er seiner Frau, hielt seine Entscheidung für absurd, seine Position in Deutschland aufzugeben und wieder zum akademischen Leben zurückzukehren: "Here I would be associated with the making of history rather than the teaching of it."[47]

[37] Dok. 28.
[38] Dok. 33.
[39] Dok. 41.
[40] Ebd.
[41] Dok. 53.
[42] Dok. 47.
[43] Siehe Dok. 44, Dok. 56, Dok. 59 und Dok. 63.
[44] Dok. 47; siehe auch Dok. 42 und Dok. 69.
[45] Siehe Dok. 41, Dok. 43, Dok. 44, Dok. 53, Dok. 58 und Dok. 63.
[46] Dok. 65; siehe auch Dok. 41, Dok. 42, Dok. 43, Dok. 44, Dok. 53, Dok. 63 und Dok. 67.
[47] Dok. 67.

Seine Enttäuschungen und seine Rückkehrplanungen bedeuteten aber nicht, dass er nicht weiterhin mit wachem Verstand die amerikanische und die alliierte Politik in Berlin beobachtete und analysierte. Besonders engagierte er sich bei der Erarbeitung einer vorläufigen Verfassung für Berlin im Local Government Committee der Alliierten Kommandantur und meint zu den Problemen in Berlin: "The important decisions depend upon so many factors that the historian cannot ever hope to get at from the documents."[48] Seine Briefe haben deshalb einen besonderen Quellenwert, weil sie neben den Mitteilungen über die politische Entwicklung in Berlin, die weitgehend bekannt sind, Stimmungen in der Stadt einfangen sowie das Verhalten der Menschen und der politischen Akteure beleuchten.

So empfand er die amerikanische Besatzungspolitik gegenüber den Deutschen, die sich nicht schuldig gemacht hatten, als zu hart. Die meisten Amerikaner waren unausgebildet und für ihre Aufgaben nicht vorbereitet. Sie hatten schon wegen der mangelnden Sprachkenntnisse keine Kontakte zu den Deutschen und überhaupt kein Verständnis für deren Situation. In der rigorosen amerikanischen Entnazifizierungspolitik beklagte er viele Ungerechtigkeiten und musste sogar in Clays Stabskonferenz zur Kenntnis nehmen, dass die Naziinternierten in den Camps besser ernährt würden als die unbelasteten Deutschen.[49] Die Deutschen aber brauchten Zuversicht: "These Germans need some ray of hope"[50], denn ihre derzeitige Lage sei hoffnungslos. Sie seien unterernährt, wirkten psychisch erschöpft, seien schäbig gekleidet, und bettelnde Kinder irrten durch die von Ruinen gesäumten Straßen. "But politics must have a future."[51] "Did we really, under the circumstances, have anything positive to offer this people?"[52], fragt Johnson.

Im Gegensatz zu den meisten Amerikanern suchte er den Kontakt mit den Menschen. Er nahm extra Unterricht, um sein Deutsch zu verbessern.[53] Man müsse mit den Deutschen deutsch reden, um sich besser mit ihnen verständigen zu können. In seinen Begegnungen aber beklagten sie ihr Elend, und er erfuhr viel Selbstmitleid. Die Deutschen ignorierten, dass sie selbst für ihre Lage verantwortlich waren. Viele täten so, als habe es das Naziregime nicht gegeben. Er vermisste das Eingeständnis, dass die Deutschen den Krieg angefangen hätten und dass die Welttragödie von Berlin ausgegangen sei. Keiner seiner Gesprächspartner empfand Scham, dass die Deutschen für unbeschreibliche Verbrechen verantwortlich waren. Viele, so stellte Johnson fest, würden am liebsten vor den Konsquenzen fliehen: "A great majority of Germans, I think, would now like to emigrate, if only they had some place to go. Having ruined their own country they would now like to escape the consequences of that ruin."[54] Nach diesen Erfahrungen befürchtet er eine lange Okkupation: "I am afraid this has to be a very long occupation, and that we have to make very long range plans. These

---

[48] Dok. 40.
[49] Siehe Dok. 52 und Dok. 77.
[50] Dok. 21.
[51] Ebd.
[52] Dok. 83; siehe auch Dok. 21, Dok. 36 und Dok. 42.
[53] Siehe Dok. 40 und Dok. 49.
[54] Dok. 66; siehe auch Dok. 18, Dok. 22, Dok. 50 und Dok. 76.

people have literally to be re-educated over a long period by themselves but under our direction."[55]

Ebenso kritisch aber ging Johnson mit der amerikanischen Politik und der amerikanischen Besatzung ins Gericht. Vor Ort sah er die amerikanische Militärregierung durch schlimmsten Bürokratismus behindert. Der Befehlsweg von der Spitze herunter zu den Besatzungssoldaten sei zu lang und deshalb ineffektiv.[56] Viele Amerikaner in Berlin agierten ohne die erforderlichen Erfahrungen und die notwendige Intelligenz. Er sah Opportunisten und Abenteurer am Werk, darunter "husky-throated, hard-faced women"[57], die sich mit der Zigarettenwährung in Schwarzmarktgeschäften schamlos bereicherten. Zu Hause waren viele Besatzungssoldaten nichts, in Berlin aber Könige, und sie wollten ihre privilegierte Stellung in Deutschland so lange wie möglich behalten. "I believe the atmosphere is becoming more corrupt – corrupt in the sense of creating a privileged conqueror-class which is interested in nothing much more than what they can get out of it."[58] Besonders scharf verurteilte er die Übergriffe amerikanischer GIs auf die deutsche Bevölkerung, deren Untaten nicht in die Presse gelangen und nicht geahndet würden. "I don't suppose", kommentiert er diese Vorgänge, "that any historian, or other person can quite comprehend it all."[59] Fern von den in Ruinen hausenden Berlinern, die sich allmählich an das Leben in der kaputten Stadt zu gewöhnen schienen, lebten die Besatzer in unnatürlicher Atmosphäre in eleganten Villen in Dahlem, Wannsee und Zehlendorf. In Frankfurt am Main, so berichtet er, sprach man von den abgeschirmten amerikanischen Wohnquartieren sogar vom "Ghetto of the Pharisees"[60]. Die Amerikaner ließen sich von deutschen Hausangestellten, Gärtnern und Chauffeuren bedienen. Kontakte zu den Deutschen fanden nur auf dieser Ebene statt. Viele Amerikaner schienen nur ihrem Vergnügen nachzugehen. Eine Party jagte die andere, und ständig traf man sie mit einer Flasche Brandy unter dem Arm. Ja, er sah einige Besatzer durch den sie umgebenden Luxus verwöhnt als "a new group of American colonial governors"[61]. Besonders verachtenswert fand er vor allem die Lebensmittelverschwendung, von denen die Deutschen nicht einmal die Brosamen von den Tischen der Herren erhielten. Sie waren auch nicht bereit, ihren Überfluss mit Waisen und Kranken zu teilen.[62] Scharf kritisierte er auch die Reduzierung der Kalorien durch die britischen und französischen Besatzungsmächte: "You can't preach democracy on empty stomachs"[63]. Und er hoffte, dass die Amerikaner diesem Beispiel nicht folgen würden, denn: "It would be disastrous for the slow progress we have made here, and fatal to whatever trust the Germans put in us."[64]

---

55 Dok. 49.
56 Siehe Dok. 56.
57 Dok. 83; siehe auch Dok. 49.
58 Dok. 51; siehe auch Dok. 21, Dok. 49 und Dok. 67.
59 Dok. 56; siehe auch Dok. 67.
60 Dok. 79 und Dok. 83.
61 Dok. 83; siehe auch Dok. 49.
62 Siehe Dok. 27, Dok. 33, Dok. 56 und Dok. 83.
63 Dok. 23.
64 Ebd.; siehe auch Dok. 26.

Eine Begegnung im Haus von Dr. Max Rheinstein, dem deutsch-amerikanischen Juristen in der Legal Divison der Militärregierung, berührte ihn sehr. Die Amerikaner hatten die repräsentative Villa in Dahlem beschlagnahmt, während der Besitzer, der Cellist Max Baldner, mit seinen vier Kindern und seiner Frau, wegen deren jüdischer Herkunft die ganze Familie unter den Nazis gelitten hatte, in einem benachbarten zerbombten Haus leben musste. Baldner gab für die Besatzer ein Cellosolokonzert: "How would you like to be a guest of your conquerors in your own house"[65], fragt er beschämt seine Frau. Er war entsetzt, dass die amerikanische Militärregierung selbst ehemalige KZ-Häftlinge aus ihren Häusern vertrieben: "It is true that concentration camp people have had to get out to make room for the conquerors."[66]

Johnson, der aus einer musikalischen Familie stammte, nahm in Berlin jede Gelegenheit wahr, um Konzerte und Opernaufführungen zu besuchen. Die Berichte über die Aufführungen nehmen einen breiten Raum in seiner Berichterstattung ein, ebenso sein großes Interesse an der musikalischen Erziehung seines Sohnes John.[67]

Trotz der Zerstörungen war Berlin nach Johnsons Auffassung nicht nur die wichtigste Stadt Deutschlands, sondern Europas: "There could be no doubt that this city was still the most important in Germany [...]. From the point of view of what was going on here, it was even the most important city in Europe. From the point of view of the struggle between East and West it was one of the most fascinating, if discouraging, focal points in the world."[68] Dort, so sah er voraus, würde sich das Schicksal des Kontinents entscheiden. Zwar war die Euphorie unter den Alliierten über den gemeinsamen Sieg über das NS-Regime längst verflogen, dennoch hielten die Amerikaner an der engen Waffenbrüderschaft mit den Sowjets fest. Während die militärische Führung weiterhin an der partnerschaftlichen Kooperation mit den Sowjets über die Behandlung der Deutschen und Deutschlands glaubten, sah Johnson längst viele Zeichen, die auf Spannungen unter den Alliierten und auf den beginnenden Kalten Krieg deuteten. "You remember when I came here I said that our relations with the Soviets were gradually getting worse. They have continued to go in that direction"[69], meint er im Juni. Die Sowjets würden alles tun, um die amerikanische Politik in einem schlechten Licht erscheinen zu lassen. Und er hörte von einem Gerücht, dass "five Russian armies being concentrated in the Russian zone from the Czech border to Stettin, so powerful that, if anything were to happen they could sweep the rest of the western powers out of Germany and not be stopped until they reacted the Atlantic and the Spanish border"[70]. Bereits im April schreibt er: "I find myself taking on an ever stronger anti-Russian stand here."[71] Er spricht bereits von Berlin als "an international island in the Russian sea"[72]. Er

---

[65] Dok. 25; siehe auch Dok. 21, Dok. 34, Dok. 55 und Dok. 83.
[66] Dok. 52.
[67] Siehe Dok. 36, Dok. 38, Dok. 59, Dok. 66, Dok. 71 und Dok. 72.
[68] Dok. 83.
[69] Dok. 58; siehe auch Dok. 44 und Dok. 61.
[70] Dok. 63; siehe auch Dok. 52.
[71] Dok. 38.
[72] Dok. 83.

beklagte einerseits die Orientierungslosigkeit der amerikanischen Politik und sah andererseits als Konsequenz, wie die Sowjets darauf hinarbeiteten, die Westmächte aus der Stadt zu drängen, um ganz Berlin ihrer Besatzungszone einverleiben zu können.

Für dieses Ziel hatten die Sowjets in Berlin bereits die Weichen gestellt: ein von den Kommunisten dominierter Magistrat, eine Polizeiverwaltung, die ihre Instruktionen aus Moskau empfing, Parteien, Gewerkschaften, Jugend- und Frauenorganisationen, in denen "Russian trained Communists"[73] die Fäden zogen. Johnson traf einige dieser Personen, unter anderem Walter Ulbricht, die für ihn "agents of Russian policy"[74] waren. Karl Maron war seiner Meinung nach der eigentliche Lenker der Magistratspolitik. Wilhelm Pieck charkterisierte er als "empty-headed Communist leader", und Ulbricht war für ihn ein "unscrupulous and clever demagogue"[75]: "They are like the Nazis now and want to forget the past."[76] Hinzu kam die kommunistische Beherrschung des größten Teils der Presse und des Rundfunks. Alle Bestrebungen in den Parteien und Verbänden hatten – ob freiwillig oder durch Zwang – nur das eine Ziel: Einfluss und Macht zu gewinnen. Es gab Privilegien für die, die mitmachten, und Deportationen oder sogar Todesstrafen für die, die sich dieser Politik widersetzten. "This was the system that was crowding in on quadripartite Berlin from the Russian zone and the Russian sector. Could it be stopped? Could it be modified? Could East and West really come together in the city?"[77], fragt Johnson zweifelnd.

Die Westmächte durchschauten zunächst diese Strategie der Sowjets nicht, sondern hatten in der ersten Sitzung der Alliierten Kommandantur am 11. Juli 1945 mit Befehl Nr. 1 alle von den Sowjets nach der Kapitulation erlassenen Anordnungen für Berlin gebilligt. Die amerikanische Militärregierung kam auch im weiteren Verlauf in den Kommandantursitzungen den sowjetischen Wünschen weit entgegen, um ein Klima der freundschaftlichen Zusammenarbeit zu erhalten und Geschlossenheit gegenüber der deutschen Bevölkerung zu demonstrieren. So konnten die Sowjets Schritt für Schritt ihre Positionen ausbauen. Wäre es unter diesen Umständen nach Meinung von Johnson nicht Aufgabe der Amerikaner gewesen, Gegenmaßnahmen zu treffen? Stattdessen reduzierten sie ihr Personal in der Militärregierung so drastisch, "that it was neither possible to keep close watch on the *Magistrat*, or to keep in close enough contact with what was going on in the American sector of Berlin"[78].

Trotz der sowjetischen Aggressionspolitik war die offizielle Linie der Vereinigten Staaten in allen innerdeutschen Angelegenheiten weiterhin strikte Neutralität. Darüber ist Johnson äußerst erbost und fragt: "And where do we stand in this fight? Neutral! What does the liberal tradition of American democracy mean to these people? Nothing. [...] What are we doing to present the American picture in a positive light? Nothing. Don't we care whether the real democrats have a chance here or not? Why did we fight this war? As I remem-

---

[73] Dok. 58.
[74] Dok. 83.
[75] Ebd.
[76] Dok. 58; siehe auch Dok. 61 und Dok. 83.
[77] Dok. 83; siehe auch Dok. 61, Dok. 62 und Dok. 71.
[78] Dok. 83.

ber it was for the American way of life or at least it had something to do about democracy? If we don't care about democracy in Europe then we'd better get the hell out of here and turn the place over to the Communists and the Soviets"[79]. Diese Politik war nach Johnsons Auffassung "political indifference"[80], kurzsichtig und gefährlich. Die Amerikaner müssten ihre Neutralität aufgeben und in Berlin Politiker wie den geschäftsführenden Generalsekretär der Berliner Sozialdemokratischen Partei, Otto Suhr, und den kommissarischen Stadtkämmerer Friedrich Haas, mit denen Johnson auch privat verkehrte, fördern und unterstützen. Sie hatten sich den sowjetischen Pressionen widersetzt, und mit Persönlichkeiten wie Haas und Suhr könnten die Amerikaner ein demokratisches Deutschland gestalten. "These were the kind of Germans we wanted to support, the kind in whose hands a future Germany ought to be."[81]

Eine Perspektive für die Stadt sah Johnson in den von amerikanischer Seite geforderten freien Kommunalwahlen, um die kommunistische Dominanz des von den Sowjets eingesetzten Magistrats zu beseitigen. Voraussetzung für freie Wahlen war die Erarbeitung einer vorläufigen Verfassung. Daran beteiligte er sich im Local Government Committee der Alliierten Kommandantur. Nach langen Verhandlungen stimmten die Sowjets schließlich der Durchführung von freien Wahlen in der Hoffnung zu, durch die Vereinigung von KPD und SPD eine für die Kommunisten günstige Ausgangsposition gewonnen zu haben: "They know what Berlin means to Germany, and they want a victory of the new Communist dominated SED when elections are held in Berlin."[82] Die Amerikaner dagegen hofften, durch die Wahlen den sowjetischen Einfluss auf den Magistrat zurückdrängen zu können, den sowjetischen Druck abzumildern und eine demokratische Entwicklung in Berlin zu ermöglichen. In Berlin sah Johnson im Übrigen das zukünftige Zentrum für die demokratische Erneuerung Deutschlands. Hierbei hoffte er auf die Unterstützung der Kirchen, um den Deutschen moralisch wieder auf die Füße zu helfen.[83]

Neben der politischen Weichenstellung erschien ihm in der ideologischen Auseinandersetzung mit den Sowjets sehr wichtig, die Berliner für den "American way of life" zu gewinnen: "We need books about America, and people who can speak to Germans in German about America. We need to introduce into the educational system a breath of the fresh air present in our schools and universities, into the German press some of the virtues of our press (and there are some) and into German political life some of the tolerance, the give and take which we do have. This it seems to me is what the Germans need now. They don't need Communism at the moment, certainly, if they need it at all"[84], schreibt er seiner Frau.

Johnson, der sich selbst als einer von Clays "chief professional assistants"[85] sah, war enttäuscht über seine Verwendung in der amerikanischen Militärregie-

---

[79] Dok. 39.
[80] Dok. 83.
[81] Ebd.; siehe auch Dok. 40, Dok. 56 und Dok. 74.
[82] Dok. 40; siehe auch Dok. 64, Dok. 68, Dok. 69, Dok. 70, Dok. 74 und Dok. 83.
[83] Siehe Dok. 74 und Dok. 68.
[84] Dok. 40.
[85] Dok. 71.

rung und fühlte sich nicht ausgefüllt. Gerne hätte er "the rebirth of Germany"[86] erlebt, meint aber: "I shall leave here with regret because there is much to do but I have never thought that my decision to leave is unwise."[87] Seit Mai hatte er sich verstärkt mit seinem zukünftigen Leben in Lincoln beschäftigt. Er diskutierte in der Korrespondenz detaillierte Urlaubspläne mit seiner Familie wie auch über die Personalpolitik und seine Rolle an der Universität von Nebraska.[88] Die offizielle Mitteilung über seinen Rückkehrbeschluss zögerte er aber immer noch hinaus. Anfang Juli rang er sich endlich durch, Clay und Keating über seine Pläne zu unterrichten und Clay um das Privileg zu bitten, seinen Deutschlandaufenthalt mit einer Reise durch die amerikanische Zone zu beschließen. Clay, der ihn nicht gerne gehen sah, gewährte ihm diese Bitte.[89]

Während seiner 16-tägigen Fahrt im Dienstwagen mit Chauffeur durch Groß-Hessen, Württemberg-Baden und Bayern traf er hochrangige Offiziere der regionalen Militärregierungen. In seinem Bericht über den Besuch in der Villa Reitzenstein in Stuttgart ist das Bedauern zu spüren, dort nicht – wie ursprünglich erhofft – zu residieren. Und über Pollock fiel dementsprechend sein Urteil recht negativ aus: "He has the most palatial and colonial office I have yet seen in Germany."[90] Ein kurzer Aufenthalt in Nürnberg ermöglichte ihm, an Verhandlungen des Nürnberger Kriegsverbrechertribunals teilzunehmen. Sie bestärkten ihn in der Abscheu vor den Nazigrößen.[91] In München schließlich, der letzten Station auf seiner Reise durch die amerikanische Zone, begegnete er auch deutschen Persönlichkeiten, unter anderem Ministerpräsident Wilhelm Hoegner sowie einigen Ministern seiner Regierung, und gewann interessante Einblicke in die Situation in der amerikanischen Zone. Vor seiner Abreise von Bremerhaven machte er bei der Organisation seiner Rückreise noch einmal schlechte Erfahrungen mit der Militärbürokratie und verließ schließlich erleichtert Deutschland.

Einige Wochen nach seinem Einsatz zog Johnson in dem Report "Five Months in Berlin" eine Bilanz der amerikanischen Besatzungspolitik und der Situation in der Viermächtestadt Berlin. Er war überzeugt, dass die Okkupation Deutschlands das wichtigste Unternehmen war, welches die Vereinigten Staaten jenseits ihrer Grenzen jemals unternommen hatten. Die Amerikaner sollten noch mindestens zehn Jahre die Kontrolle über die Deutschen behalten und sich nicht wie nach dem Ersten Weltkrieg vorzeitig zurückziehen. Aber, so bilanziert er: "[...] we can do a still better job in Germany."[92] Seiner Meinung nach müssten die Deutschen gewonnen werden für den "American capitalism and English socialism, both associated with certain democratic liberties"[93]. Und bereits im April schreibt er: "[...] we need here a positive policy which will go as far as is possible to the left but still proclaims and implements the few things

---

[86] Dok. 74.
[87] Dok. 73.
[88] Siehe Dok. 49, Dok. 52, Dok. 60 und Dok. 62.
[89] Siehe Dok. 70.
[90] Dok. 78.
[91] Siehe Dok. 79.
[92] Dok. 83.
[93] Ebd.

we are able to stand for."[94] Positive Ansätze der amerikanischen Politik sah Johnson in der Entnazifizierung und der Re-education, in der Durchführung freier Wahlen und der verstärkten Heranziehung von unbelasteten Deutschen an der politischen Gestaltung in der amerikanischen Zone: "In our own sphere of action, that is in our zones, I think much more could have been done if we had begun to collaborate immediately with those Germans and Austrians whom we could trust. [...] In Berlin we have not really done it yet in our sector."[95] Die Einsetzung des Länderrates in Stuttgart schien ihm der richtige Weg zur demokratischen Erneuerung Deutschlands zu sein. Andererseits aber schien ihm die amerikanische Politik noch zu unfertig, ohne zukunftsweisende Perspektiven und vor allem zu nachgiebig gegenüber der sowjetischen Herausforderung in Berlin und Deutschland. Die Amerikaner hätten zwar den Krieg gewonnen, und er kam nach Deutschland, "to assist in winning the peace"[96]. Aber konnte unter den derzeitigen Umständen, so seine Bedenken, der Frieden tatsächlich in Deutschland und Europa gewonnen werden?

---

[94] Dok. 40.
[95] Dok. 45.
[96] Dok. 83.

Dokumentenverzeichnis

Nr.	Dokument	Ort	Datum	Seite
1	Schreiben an die Ehefrau	Washington, D. C., Genes Büro	12. Februar 1946	63
2	Schreiben an die Ehefrau	Washington, D. C., The Roger Smith, Pennsylvania Avenue at 18th Street, N. W.	13. Februar 1946	66
3	Schreiben an die Ehefrau	Washington, D. C.	15. Februar 1946 (vormittags)	71
4	Schreiben an die Ehefrau	Washington (16), D. C., 412 Baltimore Avenue	15. Februar 1946	73
5	Schreiben an die Ehefrau	Washington (16), D. C., 412 Baltimore Avenue	17. Februar 1946	76
6	Schreiben an die Ehefrau	New York, Hotel Pennsylvania	18. Februar 1946	79
7	Schreiben an die Ehefrau	New York # 19, Hotel Knickerbocker, 120 West 45th Street	19. Februar 1946	81
8	Schreiben an die Ehefrau	New York # 19, Hotel Knickerbocker, 120 West 45th Street	20. Februar 1946	83
9	Schreiben an die Ehefrau	An Bord der „George W. Goethals"	22. Februar 1946	85
10	Schreiben an die Ehefrau	An Bord der „George W. Goethals"	27. Februar 1946	90
11	Schreiben an die Ehefrau	An Bord der „George W. Goethals"	28. Februar 1946	92
12	Schreiben an die Ehefrau	An Bord der „George W. Goethals"	1. März 1946	95
13	Schreiben an die Ehefrau	Le Havre	5. März 1946	96
14	Schreiben an die Ehefrau	Paris	5. März 1946	100
15	Schreiben an die Ehefrau	Berlin, Ihnestraße 14	7. März 1946	102

Nr.	Dokument	Ort	Datum	Seite
16	Schreiben an die Ehefrau	Berlin, Ihnestraße 14	8. März 1946	107
17	Schreiben an die Ehefrau	Berlin, Ihnestraße 14	9. März 1946	110
18	Schreiben an die Ehefrau	Berlin, Ihnestraße 14	11. März 1946	116
19	Schreiben an die Ehefrau	Berlin, Ihnestraße 14	12. März 1946	118
20	Schreiben an die Ehefrau	Berlin, Ihnestraße 14	14. März 1946	121
21	Schreiben an die Ehefrau	Berlin, Ihnestraße 14	16. März 1946	128
22	Schreiben an die Ehefrau	Berlin, Ihnestraße 14	17. März 1946	133
23	Schreiben an die Ehefrau	Berlin, Ihnestraße 14	18. März 1946	137
24	Schreiben an die Ehefrau	Berlin, Ihnestraße 14	19. März 1946	140
25	Schreiben an die Ehefrau	Berlin, Ihnestraße 14	22. März 1946	143
26	Schreiben an die Ehefrau	Berlin, Ihnestraße 14	23. März 1946	148
27	Schreiben an die Ehefrau	Berlin, Ihnestraße 14	24. März 1946	151
28	Schreiben an die Ehefrau	Berlin, Ihnestraße 14	26. März 1946	155
29	Schreiben an die Ehefrau	Berlin, Ihnestraße 14	27. März 1946	159
30	Schreiben an die Ehefrau	Berlin, Ihnestraße 14	30. März 1946	161
31	Schreiben an die Ehefrau	Berlin, Wannsee Hotel, Am Sandwerder 17/19	31. März 1946	164
32	Schreiben an die Ehefrau	Berlin, Wannsee Hotel, Am Sandwerder 17/19	2. April 1946	165
33	Schreiben an die Ehefrau	Berlin, Wannsee Hotel, Am Sandwerder 17/19	6. April 1946	166

Dokumentenverzeichnis 59

Nr.	Dokument	Ort	Datum	Seite
34	Schreiben an die Ehefrau	Berlin, Wannsee Hotel, Am Sandwerder 17/19	8. April 1946	173
35	Schreiben an die Ehefrau	Berlin, Wannsee Hotel, Am Sandwerder 17/19	12. April 1946	175
36	Schreiben an die Ehefrau	Berlin, Wannsee Hotel, Am Sandwerder 17/19	14. April 1946	177
37	Schreiben an die Ehefrau	Berlin, Wannsee Hotel, Am Sandwerder 17/19	15. April 1946	180
38	Schreiben an die Ehefrau	Berlin, Wannsee Hotel, Am Sandwerder 17/19	18. April 1946	183
39	Schreiben an die Ehefrau	Berlin, Wannsee Hotel, Am Sandwerder 17/19	21. April 1946	188
40	Schreiben an die Ehefrau	Berlin, Wannsee Hotel, Am Sandwerder 17/19	27. April 1946	193
41	Schreiben an die Ehefrau	Berlin	30. April 1946	199
42	Schreiben an die Ehefrau	Berlin	1. Mai 1946	203
43	Schreiben an die Ehefrau	Berlin	5. Mai 1946	205
44	Schreiben an die Ehefrau	Berlin	6. Mai 1946	207
45	Schreiben an die Ehefrau	Berlin	8. Mai 1946	211
46	Schreiben an die Ehefrau	Berlin	9. Mai 1946	214
47	Schreiben an die Ehefrau	Berlin, Wannsee Hotel, Am Sandwerder 17/19	11. Mai 1946	216
48	Schreiben an die Ehefrau	Berlin	14. Mai 1946	220
49	Schreiben an die Ehefrau	Berlin, Wannsee Officers' Club, Am Sandwerder 17/19	19. Mai 1946	222
50	Schreiben an die Ehefrau	Berlin, Wannsee Officers' Club, Am Sandwerder 17/19	20. Mai 1946	232
51	Schreiben an die Ehefrau	Berlin	23. Mai 1946	236

Nr.	Dokument	Ort	Datum	Seite
52	Schreiben an die Ehefrau	Berlin, Wannsee	25. Mai 1946	237
53	Schreiben an die Ehefrau	Berlin, Wannsee Officers' Club, Am Sandwerder 17/19	27. Mai 1946	244
54	Schreiben an die Ehefrau	Berlin, Wannsee Officers' Club, Am Sandwerder 17/19	28. Mai 1946	246
55	Schreiben an die Ehefrau	Berlin, Wannsee Officers' Club, Am Sandwerder 17/19	31. Mai 1946	248
56	Schreiben an die Ehefrau	Berlin, Wannsee Officers' Club, Am Sandwerder 17/19	2. Juni 1946	253
57	Schreiben an die Ehefrau	Berlin	3. Juni 1946	256
58	Schreiben an die Ehefrau	Berlin	5. Juni 1946	257
59	Schreiben an die Ehefrau	Berlin	9. Juni 1946	261
60	Schreiben an die Söhne	Berlin	9. Juni 1946	265
61	Schreiben an die Ehefrau	Berlin	13. Juni 1946	265
62	Schreiben an die Ehefrau	Berlin	15. Juni 1946	268
63	Schreiben an die Ehefrau	Berlin	17. Juni 1946	272
64	Schreiben an die Ehefrau	Berlin	18. Juni 1946	276
65	Schreiben an die Ehefrau	Berlin	19. Juni 1946	278
66	Schreiben an die Ehefrau	Berlin	23. Juni 1946	281
67	Schreiben an die Ehefrau	Berlin, Wannsee Officers' Club, Am Sandwerder 17/19	26. Juni 1946	284
68	Schreiben an die Ehefrau	Berlin, Wannsee Officers' Club, Am Sandwerder 17/19	29. Juni 1946	290
69	Schreiben an den Vater	Berlin, Wannsee Officers' Club, Am Sandwerder 17/19	29. Juni 1946	295

Nr.	Dokument	Ort	Datum	Seite
70	Schreiben an die Ehefrau	Berlin	2. Juli 1946	296
71	Schreiben an die Ehefrau	Berlin, Wannsee Officers' Club, Am Sandwerder 17/19	7. Juli 1946	297
72	Schreiben an die Ehefrau	Berlin, Wannsee Officers' Club, Am Sandwerder 17/19	9. Juli 1946	302
73	Schreiben an die Ehefrau	Berlin, Wannsee Officers' Club, Am Sandwerder 17/19	12. Juli 1946	305
74	Schreiben an die Ehefrau	Berlin, Wannsee Officers' Club, Am Sandwerder 17/19	14. Juli 1946	307
75	Schreiben an die Ehefrau	Berlin, Wannsee Officers' Club, Am Sandwerder 17/19	15. Juli 1946	311
76	Schreiben an die Ehefrau	Butzbach, Groß-Hessen, Officers' Club – vormals Deutsches Haus	21. Juli 1946	314
77	Schreiben an die Ehefrau	Stuttgart	26. Juli 1946	318
78	Schreiben an die Ehefrau	Stuttgart	28. Juli 1946	320
79	Schreiben an die Ehefrau	München	1. August 1946	322
80	Schreiben an die Ehefrau	Bremerhaven	7. August 1946	325
81	Schreiben an die Ehefrau	Bremerhaven	9. August 1946	330
82	Schreiben an die Ehefrau	Bremerhaven	9. August 1946	333
83	Bericht "Five Months in Berlin"	o. O.	o. D.	334

Dokumente

Dok. 1
Schreiben an die Ehefrau
Washington, D. C., Genes[1] Büro[2], 12. Februar 1946

Dear Sweetheart and the boys:

I am going down to a store or two to get some things that I couldn't get yesterday in the officers' shop at the Pentagon[3]. Gene tells me that they don't open until about 9:30 and accordingly I am up here in his office awaiting their opening time.

Nothing much happened yesterday. The lady whom I was supposed to see was surprised and somewhat annoyed that I had arrived a day early but I explained that they don't work in Omaha[4] on Saturday and Sunday and accordingly could not get me here on time with a departure on Monday[5]. Then she gave me my passport with visas for Britain and France. The passport is valid until May only which strikes me as strange – this suspicious state department. Then with instructions on how to get my picture taken for a new AGO[6] card she bade me make an appearance on Wednesday[7] morning before 9:30. At this

---

[1] Eugene N. Anderson (1900–1984), amerikanischer Historiker, 1924/1925 Studium an der Universität Berlin, 1928 PhD, University of Chicago, 1930/1931 Forschungsaufenthalt in Deutschland (Social Sciences Research Fellowship), 1932–1936 Professor of Modern European History, University of Chicago, 1936–1941 American University, 1941/1942 Research Assistant, Office of Coordinator of Information, 1942–1945 Assistant Chief/Chief, Central European Section, Research and Analysis Branch, OSS, 1945–1947 Department of State, 1947–1955 University of Nebraska, in der McCarthy-Ära Anschuldigungen der American Legion, 1955–1968 University of California, Los Angeles, anschließend bis 1970 University of California, Santa Barbara. Edgar N. Johnson war zeitlebens mit Eugene N. Anderson befreundet. Andersons Sohn, Eugene N. Anderson Jr. (siehe Dok. 4, Anm. 30), schreibt in einer E-Mail an Werner Breunig vom 17. Juli 2007: "He [Johnson] and my father could talk shop for hours and hours, and my father got a lot of stimulation – my father was also tense and bright but more quiet, less adventurous – he needed Edgar and Edgar's strong opinions and mercilessly sharp mind to get him going. Edgar I think got some benefit from my father's quietness and philosophical attitude toward the world. Edgar kept up on current events and the world in general more than my father did, and was always great to talk to about most anything. Both of them were compulsive workers, though, so finding a chance to talk with them was always pretty difficult."

[2] Im Department of State, wo Anderson als Acting Assistant Chief, Area Division V – Occupied Areas, tätig war.

[3] Das auf einem fünfeckigen Grundriss errichtete Gebäude des Department of War in Arlington im US-Bundesstaat Virginia an der Grenze zu Washington, D. C.

[4] Stadt im US-Bundesstaat Nebraska, nordöstlich von Johnsons Wohnort Lincoln.

[5] 11. Februar 1946.

[6] Adjutant General's Office.

[7] 13. Februar 1946.

time I shall get my AGO card and my orders. Then I think everything will be done except going to airport headquarters. And how long after this before getting away I don't know.

After this exciting experience I went to the Officers' Uniform store and bought instead of another coat such as I have, a short dress battle jacket as the one I left at home but made of the same material as my present coat. For an overcoat I bought one of the combination affairs – combination topcoat, raincoat and overcoat somewhat like the beltless one I have at present only with a belt and all wool. The lining snaps instead of buttons in. Then a pair of trousers. I need now only some gloves and a scarf and some insignia. The overcoat will be very useful after this is all over.

I had lunch with Franz[8] who had nothing much to say and went over to the old headquarters in OSS[9] to see if my things had come from Vienna[10]. As a

---

[8] Franz L. Neumann (1900-1954), deutsch-amerikanischer Jurist und Politikwissenschaftler, geboren in Kattowitz, Deutschland, 1923 Dr. jur., Universität Frankfurt am Main, bis 1933 Rechtsanwalt mit Schwerpunkt Arbeitsrecht in Sozietät mit Ernst Fraenkel (1898-1975) in Berlin und Dozent an der Deutschen Hochschule für Politik, 1932/1933 Syndikus der SPD, 1933 Emigration nach England, 1936 PhD, London School of Economics and Political Science, 1936 Übersiedlung in die USA, bis 1942 Mitarbeiter des Institute for Social Research, Columbia University, 1942/1943 Consultant, Board of Economic Warfare, 1943 US-Staatsbürgerschaft, 1943-1945 Research Analyst, Research and Analysis Branch, OSS, 1946 Chief, German Research Section, Office of Research and Intelligence, Department of State, ab 1948 Professor of Government, Columbia University, 1952 Verleihung der Ehrendoktorwürde der Freien Universität Berlin. Franz L. Neumann und Edgar N. Johnson hatten sich in der Central European Section, Research and Analysis Branch, OSS, kennengelernt.

[9] Office of Strategic Services, ein 1942 eingerichteter und 1945 wieder aufgelöster amerikanischer Nachrichtendienst, dessen Hauptquartier sich in 25th and E Streets, N. W., Washington, D. C., befand. Die weitaus größte Abteilung dieser Behörde war die Research and Analysis Branch, in der vorrangig interdisziplinäre Regionalstudien erstellt wurden, die der Feindaufklärung bzw. der Besatzungsplanung dienten. Nach Auflösung des OSS wurden die operativen Abteilungen als Vorläufer der Central Intelligence Agency (CIA) in das Department of War und die Forschungs- und Analyseabteilung in das Department of State eingegliedert. Edgar N. Johnson hatte 1943-1945 als Research Analyst für die Central European Section, Research and Analysis Branch, OSS, gearbeitet. „In dieser Sektion arbeiteten mehrere hochqualifizierte, aus Deutschland und anderen Ländern Mitteleuropas emigrierte Akademiker und Beamte, darunter Franz Leopold Neumann [siehe Anm. 8], Herbert Marcuse, Otto Kirchheimer und Oscar Weigert, ein früherer Ministerialdirektor aus dem Reichsarbeitsministerium. Louis Wiesner [siehe Dok. 8, Anm. 11], der im November 1943 vom Council on Foreign Relations zur Central European Section kam und mit der Sammlung und Auswertung von Informationen über sozialdemokratische und gewerkschaftliche Exil- und Widerstandsgruppen beauftragt wurde, erinnert sich an diese Sektion als '*strongly* pro-social democratic, which you might expect from Franz Neumann, Herbert Marcuse, and so on'." Michael Fichter, Besatzungsmacht und Gewerkschaften. Zur Entwicklung und Anwendung der US-Gewerkschaftspolitik in Deutschland 1944-1948 (= Schriften des Zentralinstituts für sozialwissenschaftliche Forschung der Freien Universität Berlin, Bd. 40), Opladen 1982, S. 61. Zum OSS siehe Zur Archäologie der Demokratie in Deutschland. Analysen politischer Emigranten im amerikanischen Geheimdienst, Bd. 1: 1943-1945, hrsg. von Alfons Söllner, Frankfurt am Main 1982; Bradley F. Smith, The Shadow Warriors. O. S. S. and the

matter of fact they have but how to get them home is a question. The section is over-crowded with Germans home from the wars – I mean people like Felix[11] and Len[12] for example who are going through much the same experience as I have being going through with respect to their colleagues and reaction to the present scene. They do not seem to have much to do and the great source of the bureaucracy – the New York Times[13] was much in evidence. I'll write more about this later. And more about the other things that have happened since I left you.[14]

Generally speaking I am still low and begin to wonder if perhaps what I am doing now is not going to be something like another Wisconsin semester.[15] Not

---

Origins of the C. I. A., New York 1983; Zur Archäologie der Demokratie in Deutschland, Bd. 2: Analysen von politischen Emigranten im amerikanischen Außenministerium 1946-1949, hrsg. von Alfons Söllner, Frankfurt am Main 1986; Robin W. Winks, Cloak & Gown. Scholars in the Secret War 1939-1961, New York 1987; Barry M. Katz, Foreign Intelligence. Research and Analysis in the Office of Strategic Services 1942-1945, Cambridge und London 1989; George C. Chalou (Hrsg.), The Secrets War. The Office of Strategic Services in World War II, Washington, D. C., 1992; Petra Marquardt-Bigman, Amerikanische Geheimdienstanalysen über Deutschland 1942-1949 (= Studien zur Zeitgeschichte, Bd. 45), München 1995; Christof Mauch, Schattenkrieg gegen Hitler. Das Dritte Reich im Visier der amerikanischen Geheimdienste 1941-1945, Stuttgart 1999.

[10] Johnson war Ende 1945, "when OSS in Austria disbanded", in die USA zurückgekehrt. Edgar N. Johnson, Curriculum Vitae, undatiert [ca. 1963], S. 3, in: The University of Chicago (UChicago) Library, Special Collections Research Center, Chicago, Illinois, USA, Edgar N. Johnson Papers.

[11] Felix Gilbert (1905-1991), deutsch-amerikanischer Historiker, geboren in Baden-Baden, Deutschland, Schüler von Friedrich Meinecke (1862-1954), 1930 Dr. phil, Universität Berlin, 1936 Emigration in die USA, 1939-1943 Institute for Advanced Study, 1943 US-Staatsbürgerschaft, 1943-1946 Research Analyst, Central European Section, Research and Analysis Branch, OSS, and Department of State, 1946-1962 Bryn Mawr College (ab 1947 Professor), 1962-1975 Institute for Advanced Study, 1980 Verleihung der Ehrendoktorwürde der Freien Universität Berlin, 1981 Aufnahme in den Orden Pour le mérite für Wissenschaften und Künste. Foto mit Gilbert im Bildanhang, Abb. 10.

[12] Gemeint sein könnte Leonard Krieger (1918-1990), amerikanischer Historiker, 1942 MA und 1949 PhD, Yale University, Research Analyst, Central European Section, Research and Analysis Branch, OSS, lehrte 1946-1962 an der Yale University (zunächst als Instructor, ab 1950 als Professor), 1962-1969 University of Chicago, 1969-1972 Columbia University, ab 1972 University of Chicago. Felix Gilbert und Leonard Krieger hatten 1945 im besetzten Deutschland Feldforschungen betrieben. Siehe Tim B. Müller, Die gelehrten Krieger und die Rockefeller-Revolution. Intellektuelle zwischen Geheimdienst, Neuer Linken und dem Entwurf einer neuen Ideengeschichte, in: Geschichte und Gesellschaft, Heft 2007/33,2, S. 198-227, hier S. 220. Siehe auch Felix Gilbert, Lehrjahre im alten Europa. Erinnerungen 1905-1945, Berlin 1989, S. 205-230.

[13] Amerikanische Tageszeitung.

[14] Johnson hatte sich wohl am 8. Februar 1946 von seiner Ehefrau verabschiedet. Siehe Dok. 2, Anm. 33.

[15] Johnson fühlte sich an seine Depressionen erinnert, unter denen er gelitten hatte, als er von September 1939 bis Februar 1940 an der University of Wisconsin in Madison, der Hauptstadt des US-Bundesstaats Wisconsin, als Gastprofessor für den beurlaubten Historiker Gaines Post (1902-1987) einsprang. Zur Gastprofessur siehe Uni-

in detail I mean but only bad judgement. I send my love, and all of it to my sweet Emily and to the boys.[16] Edgar

Dok. 2
Schreiben an die Ehefrau
Washington, D. C., The Roger Smith[1], Pennsylvania Avenue at 18th Street, N. W., 13. Februar 1946

Dearest Emily and my boys:

This is the hotel in which the War Department reserved a room for me. I cancelled it last night inasmuch as I went out to Polly's[2] last night. I shall cancel it again tonight for I shall return there for what is I hope my last night in Washington. It has, however, been a discouraging morning. I went to my Mrs. Chatham in the Overseas Branch of the War Department hoping to get final papers and to be sent to the Air Transport Command. I got my orders and this completed all my papers but I got the news also that there were no planes available, and that I should have to go by boat – a liberty ship[3]. I did not want to let this go without further protest and so I went up to General Hilldring's[4] office, to the Colonel Chard[5] who got results before, and wrote me the decent letter. There was nothing he could do but turn me over to Major Smith, General Clay's[6] liaison officer with whom I talked over the phone from Lincoln[7], a boy-

---

versity of Wisconsin-Madison (UW-Madison) Archives, Madison, Wisconsin, USA, Department of History, Faculty Personnel Files, Series 7/16/3/1 Box 10.

[16] Eugene N. Anderson Jr. (siehe Dok. 4, Anm. 30) schreibt in einer E-Mail an Werner Breunig vom 17. Juli 2007: "He [Johnson] had a close and wonderful marriage. His wife Emily was a really intelligent and totally delightful and charming lady. In those days, women stayed home and raised kids, and she put up with that pretty well. She was an outstanding cook. Edgar was pretty strict with his sons."

[1] Hotel, 1912 als Hotel Powhatan eröffnet, 1975 abgerissen.
[2] Pauline R. Anderson, geb. Relyea (1903–1985), Ehefrau von Eugene N. Anderson (siehe Dok. 1, Anm. 1), den sie während ihres Studienaufenthalts in Deutschland kennengelernt hatte, amerikanische Historikerin, 1937 PhD, Bryn Mawr College. Das Ehepaar wohnte in Washington, D. C.
[3] Frachtschiffstyp.
[4] John H. Hilldring (1895–1974), Major General, 1943–1946 Director, Civil Affairs Division, Department of War, 1945 Member of US Delegation, Berlin Conference, April 1946–1947 Assistant Secretary of State for Occupied Areas.
[5] Robert H. Chard (1906–1958), Colonel, 1929 Absolvent der United States Military Academy, 1945 Personnel Officer, USGCC, 1945–1947 Executive Officer, Civil Affairs Division, Department of War.
[6] Lucius D. Clay (1897–1978), Lieutenant General, 1918 Absolvent der United States Military Academy, 1945–1947 Deputy Military Governor, Germany (US), Commanding General, USGCC/OMGUS, 1947–1949 Military Governor, Germany (US), Commander-in-Chief, European Command, 1953 Verleihung der Ehrendoktorwürde der Freien Universität Berlin, 1961/1962 persönlicher Sonderbeauftragter von US-Präsident John F. Kennedy (1917–1963) für Berlin-Fragen, 1962 Ernennung zum Ehrenbürger von Berlin. Fotos mit Clay im Bildanhang, Abb. 21 und Abb. 24.

ish blond major whose present position is understandable. As I came into his office there were people – one described to me as an adviser to General Clay – whose flight had been cancelled yesterday. There was nothing to do. Various explanations were offered. Planes had been taken off. There was a back-log of three or four hundred people waiting to get out of Washington, and they just had to stop taking on more until they could up. The Mamas had been so anxious to have their boys out of the army that, while there were plenty of planes and crews there were not sufficient ground crews to take care of them. Not much point in trying to find out the reason. Certainly it can't be for lack of planes. About the only people who can get away are those with a 1 priority – and this is, I suppose reserved for generals. A colonel in Col. Chard's office said he was trying to get back to Germany. He had a 3 priority which is my priority and said he didn't expect to get away until the 25th. Major Smith said the air delay would take months to clear up. All 2-3-4 priorities have been cancelled. The Colonel in Col. Chard's office said you had to be a cabinet member in order to get a 2. So there you are. My orders are being amended. I get the amended orders tomorrow at 1 or 1:30 pm. I go to New York tomorrow afternoon or evening. I go to Captain Rosenzweig to make arrangements to get a boat.[8] He was on this job when I left in June 1944[9]. When a boat will take me I haven't the slightest idea. I am discouraged. It is hard to get to work. I suppose I ought to cable Walter Dorn[10]. It would be amusing if the job[11] were already filled when I got there.

---

[7] Hauptstadt des US-Bundesstaats Nebraska, wo Johnson mit seiner Familie wohnte und an der Universität lehrte.

[8] Um per Schiff nach Europa zu kommen, wollte Johnson sich zum US Army's New York Port of Embarkation begeben, den er bereits durch seine Überfahrt nach Europa im Jahre 1944 kannte.

[9] "In June 1944 I went to London as the Chief of the Austrian Section of the Research and Analysis Branch [siehe Dok. 1, Anm. 9] and was there until the spring of 1945 working closely with military government and state department officials who were preparing to go to Austria." Edgar N. Johnson, Curriculum Vitae, undatiert [ca. 1963], S. 2, in: UChicago Library, Special Collections Research Center, Edgar N. Johnson Papers.

[10] Walter L. Dorn (1894–1961), amerikanischer Historiker, Sohn einer deutsch-amerikanischen Pastorenfamilie in Illinois, 1917 BD, Concordia Seminary, ab 1923 Instructor, University of Chicago, 1925 PhD, University of Chicago, ab 1927 zweijähriges Stipendium, Forschungsaufenthalte in London und Berlin, anschließend Professor, University of Wisconsin, ab 1931 Ohio State University, 1942/1943 Chief, Central European Section, Research and Analysis Branch, OSS, Ausbilder an den Schulen für Militärregierungsoffiziere in Shrivenham und Manchester, Großbritannien, 1945 Berater der Militärregierungen im Rheinland, in Sachsen und in Bremen, 1945/1946 Personal Adviser von Clarence L. Adcock (siehe Dok. 14, Anm. 9), ab April 1946 Special Adviser for German Civil Administration und ab Juni 1946 zusätzlich Personal Adviser on Denazification von Lucius D. Clay (siehe Anm. 6), ab 1947 wieder Ohio State University, 1957–1961 Columbia University. Dorn war in den 1920er-Jahren ein Lehrer Johnsons an der University of Chicago gewesen. Außerdem kannten sie sich aus gemeinsamen OSS-Tagen. Foto von Dorn im Bildanhang, Abb. 23.

[11] Johnson ging davon aus, dass er die Leitung des Regional Government Coordinating Office (RGCO), OMGUS, in Stuttgart übernehmen würde. Das RGCO, mit dessen

I went to Harold's[12] and Marguerite's[13] last night for dinner and stayed on into the evening. Marguerite's Mother[14] is there. Harold and I got there first after shopping for some meat. Marguerite came later, tired after a hard day's work but with a new and to her unsatisfactory hair-do. She is much grayer. I find her magnificent. After much conversation about you and John[15] and Timmy[16], and they are much devoted to you all, we got on to the prospects of peace and had a very gloomy conversation. I was astounded to find that she assures, as you assure, that there is going to be war, and that it will be the horrible end of everything. She has a new job in the Navy[17] and is working harder than ever and very tired and anxious to get out. We finally got on to the topic of Harold's return.[18] You must not repeat anything I say about this. Harold asked me not to say anything. He is writing Henry[19] over the weekend, and after you have heard

Aufbau James K. Pollock (siehe Dok. 15, Anm. 6) im Oktober 1945 begonnen hatte, diente der amerikanischen Militärregierung als koordinierende Dienststelle in allen Fragen, die mehr als ein deutsches Land in der US-Zone betrafen. Es beriet und überwachte den Länderrat der amerikanischen Besatzungszone, in dem die Regierungschefs der Länder zusammenarbeiteten, um eine gewisse Einheitlichkeit der deutschen Verwaltungstätigkeit oberhalb der Landesebene zu sichern. Siehe Josef Henke/Klaus Oldenhage, Office of Military Government for Germany (U. S.), in: OMGUS-Handbuch. Die amerikanische Militärregierung in Deutschland 1945-1949, hrsg. von Christoph Weisz (= Quellen und Darstellungen zur Zeitgeschichte, Bd. 35), München 1994, S. 1-142, hier S. 122f.

12 Harold C. Vedeler (1903-2007), Patenonkel von Thomas R. Johnson (siehe Anm. 16), amerikanischer Historiker, 1933 PhD, University of Wisconsin, 1934-1941 Professor, University of Idaho, Southern Branch (heute Idaho State University), 1941-1943 University of Nebraska, 1943-1965 Department of State, zuletzt Director, Office of Eastern European Affairs.

13 Marguerite D. Vedeler, geb. Drew (1898-1988), Ehefrau von Harold C. Vedeler, Patentante von Thomas R. Johnson (siehe Anm. 16), 1920 BA (Englisch und Politikwissenschaft), Swarthmore College, 1922/1923 Studium der Politikwissenschaft an der Stanford University, 1935/1936 Dean of Women, University of Idaho, Southern Branch (heute Idaho State University), 1943-1946 Navy WAVES, Washington, D. C.

14 Marian P. Drew, geb. Pendleton (geb. 1872), "who worked in 'textile crafts'". E-Mail von Will Treece, Friends Historical Library Intern, Swarthmore College, an Werner Breunig vom 6. Juli 2009.

15 Johnsons Sohn John F. Johnson (geb. 1939), der später Musiker wurde. Siehe Bildanhang, Abb. 3 und Abb. 4.

16 Johnsons Sohn Thomas R. Johnson (geb. 1944), der später Molekularbiologe wurde. Siehe Bildanhang, Abb. 3.

17 "Mrs. Vedeler, a Nebraskan, served during World War II as officer in charge of the first Waves' barracks in Washington and later as women's representative at the Washington Navy Yard." Dorothea Pattee, Mrs. Floberg's at the Helm for Navy Ball, in: The Washington Post vom 13. April 1952, S. 5S. "In 1943, Mrs. Vedeler came to Washington as an officer in the Navy WAVES. She was the women's representative at the Naval Gun Factory. She left the service in 1946 as a lieutenant commander." Marguerite Drew Vedeler. Teacher and Navy Veteran, in: The Washington Post vom 7. September 1988, S. B7 (Obituaries).

18 Gemeint ist die Rückkehr an die University of Nebraska, wo Vedeler bis zu seiner Beurlaubung 1943 gelehrt hatte.

19 Charles Henry Oldfather (1887-1954), amerikanischer Historiker, studierte unter anderem an der Universität München (1911/1912), 1922 PhD, University of Wisconsin,

that he has written you can talk. The upshot of the matter is that he isn't going to return. Henry offered him the same financial inducements as he did to me, i. e., his raise of last year plus yearly raises since his departure. No increase in rank. But he doesn't ask for anything. He said to me that to take an increase in rank would be to violate University standards for such promotions. He was not entitled to it and would not have it. He said it was simply the importance of the work he was now doing. It is also I imagine partly Rudy's[20] return.[21] It is just possible that this return will always keep the department from getting good people. I had an explanation of why perhaps Rudy is returning from Francis Williamson[22] in the State Department. When it came time to appoint a chief army historian, the job was offered to someone else in Rudy's group (one Greenfield[23] from the U. of C.[24]) and not to Rudy. I thought this would be Harold's decision. For he is doing very important work. When I came into the State Department yesterday he was working on the preliminary draft of a treaty of peace with a country in which I recently spent a considerable amount of time.[25] Nothing could be more important than this. He will take over the Austrian desk when Francis Williamson journeys soon to the Continent.[26] He has already done very important work. His chief thinks very highly of him. He will be con-

1912–1914 Teacher, Syrian Protestant College, Beirut, 1914–1916 Professor of Classics, Hanover College, 1916–1926 Professor of Greek and Ancient History, Wabash College, ab 1926 Professor of Ancient History, University of Nebraska, 1929–1946 Chairman, Department of History, 1932–1952 Dean, College of Arts and Sciences.

[20] Rudolph A. Winnacker (1904–1985), amerikanischer Historiker, geboren in Deutschland, kam 1919 in die USA, 1933 PhD, Harvard University, 1936–1941 Professor, University of Nebraska, 1941/1942 Office of Coordinator of Information, 1942–1945 Research Analyst, OSS, 1945–1949 Historical Division, Department of War (ab 1947 Department of the Army), 1949–1973 Chiefhistorian, Office of the Secretary of Defense.

[21] Rudolph A. Winnacker war 1941 von der University of Nebraska "for service to the government in Washington" beurlaubt worden, und Harold C. Vedeler trat als Visiting Professor of European History an seine Stelle. Historical News, in: The American Historical Review, Vol. 47, No. 2 (Januar 1942), S. 442–458, hier S. 457.

[22] Francis T. Williamson (1907–1964), amerikanischer Historiker, 1935 PhD, Johns Hopkins University, 1930–1937 Instructor in History, Johns Hopkins University, 1937–1943 College of the City of New York, 1943/1944 Research Analyst, OSS, ab 1944 Department of State.

[23] Kent R. Greenfield (1893–1967), amerikanischer Historiker, 1915 PhD, Johns Hopkins University, 1920–1930 Professor of History, Yale University, ab 1930 Professor of Modern European History and Chairman, History Department, Johns Hopkins University, ab 1942 Assistant to the Historical Officer in the Army Ground Forces, 1946–1958 Chief Historian of the Department of War/Department of the Army. "Kent Roberts Greenfield, formerly of Johns Hopkins University, has been made chief historian of the War Department. He will direct the writing of the Army's 120-volume history of World War II and on September 1 will become professional adviser to a special staff section which, with the aid of teams of officers and men working in actual battle zones, has been collecting material for the work since early in the war." Historical News, in: The American Historical Review, Vol. 51, No. 4 (Juli 1946), S. 788–804, hier S. 799.

[24] University of Chicago. Greenfield kam von der Johns Hopkins University.

[25] Gemeint ist der Entwurf eines Friedensvertrages mit Österreich. Vedeler war beim Department of State als Country Specialist, Division of Territorial Studies, tätig.

[26] Williamson ging 1947 nach Wien, als US delegate, Four Power Commission.

stantly promoted and become more and more important. They would as a matter of fact have to come back to Lincoln. But they worry about finding a place to live among other things. In any case they won't be there and it is a very great loss. Now we know one person who is coming back and one person who is not coming back. I have mentioned the matter to Gene[27] but I don't think he will be much interested, and I shall mention it to Paul Sweet[28], who may be interested, though I wonder how he will care to contend with the boy who always intended to come back to the department.

I'll write about my own feelings about coming back later since I must rush off to an appointment. I will only say that after talking with the Vedelers[29] last night I think I ought to try, what with this new job, to make myself eligible for a job as important as Harold's.

Your lovely letter of Sunday[30] and John's Valentine[31] arrived yesterday.[32] Tell John I have bought him a big balloon for a valentine. I bought it from a man on the street. It is supposed to be an army weather balloon and the man I bought it from (a street vendor) suggested that to fill it one could use the exhaust of the vacuum cleaner. I'll send it when I get the time. I'm sorry you didn't get a cab home.[33] I don't yet feel equal to writing about the beautiful stay at home but I shall get over my depression at leaving, a depression that has stayed with me. Your very wonderful last paragraph is a start at recovery.[34] I will only say now that I love you and love you, that in the months to come I shall exert myself to the utmost to be worthy of what you write me, and to make possible a future for us that may be better than what we have had. I shall write John about the Valentine. Kiss him for me and tell him his Father loves him. Kiss the baby[35] for me too. And my darling beloved, let me kiss you too. Edgar

---

[27] Eugene N. Anderson. Siehe Dok. 1, Anm. 1. Anderson hatte im Sommer 1939 als Gastprofessor an der University of Nebraska gelehrt.

[28] Paul R. Sweet (1907–2003), amerikanischer Historiker, studierte unter anderem an den Universitäten Göttingen (1929/1930) und München (1930), 1934 PhD, University of Wisconsin, lehrte 1934–1936 am Birmingham-Southern College, 1936–1943 Bates College, Professor, 1943–1945 Research and Analysis Branch, OSS (ab April 1945 Stellvertreter Edgar N. Johnsons im Team, das für Österreich zuständig war), zeitweise (Mai 1944–März 1945) Intelligence Officer, Psychological Warfare Division, 12th Army Group, 1946/1947 University of Chicago, 1947 Colby College, ab 1948 Department of State, 1959–1963 US-Botschaft in Bonn, 1963–1967 Generalkonsul in Stuttgart, lehrte anschließend an der Michigan State University.

[29] Harold C. Vedeler und Marguerite D. Vedeler, geb. Drew. Siehe Anm. 12 und 13.

[30] 10. Februar 1946.

[31] John F. Johnsons Valentinsgruß an den Vater zum Valentinstag am 14. Februar 1946, Brief mit Poststempel vom 10. Februar 1946.

[32] Die Briefe, adressiert an Eugene N. Andersons Adresse in Washington, D. C., gehören zu den Unterlagen aus dem Nachlass Edgar N. Johnson, Privatbesitz Candice E. und Thomas R. Johnson, Denver, Colorado, USA.

[33] Johnsons Ehefrau hatte geschrieben: "There was no cab when I got out of the station Friday." Am 8. Februar 1946 hatte sie demnach Edgar N. Johnson auf dem Bahnhof in Lincoln, Nebraska, verabschiedet.

[34] Unter anderem hatte sie geschrieben: "I want to tell you I love you above all else in this world or any world."

[35] Sohn Thomas. Siehe Anm. 16.

Dok. 3
Schreiben an die Ehefrau
Washington, D. C., 15. Februar 1946 (vormittags)

Dearest Sweetheart and my boys –

I am afraid I am getting even more unmilitary for my job. I seem to have lost the green fountain pen, trying to put it into the shirt behind a military blouse was too much. I don't like to lose it for it has written many *important* things – important at least to me. I find now that one shoe has one kind of a lace and the other another and this is rather conspicuous. And I notice that my glasses are beginning to droop. The other of the pieces that goes over the ear is wobbly.

If I have to wait much longer for transportation I shall be completely demilitarized – the way a good German is now supposed to be. When I went yesterday for my *amended* orders – amended to send me by water[1] I waited for hours (1:30 to 4:30) and when a batch came up mine was not among them. So they will perhaps be ready today. If so I shall go on to New York today and try to arrange to see Sin[2] and Hajo[3] over the week-end[4]. I have been summoned to the POE (Port of Embarkation)[5] for Monday[6]. It will perhaps be just as inexpensive to go to the Armstrongs[7] at Providence[8] and drop off at New Haven[9] as it would be to stay in New York. Besides it seems unreasonable to ask them to come to New York if I am free. But how long after being summoned to the POE does one have to wait before venturing out on the wide, deep and I suppose strong Atlantic?

I did change my reservation in Chicago on Saturday[10] morning, until 10 in the evening and left for Milwaukee[11] on a 9:15 train. I went straight to Dad's[12] room

---

[1] Siehe Dok. 2.
[2] Sinclair W. Armstrong (1897–1959), amerikanischer Historiker, unterrichtete 1923–1928 an der St. George's School, Newport, Rhode Island, kam 1930 als Dozent an die Brown University, 1935 PhD, University of Wisconsin, ab 1935 Professor, Brown University, 1941/1942 Office of Coordinator of Information, 1942–1945 OSS/Office of Military Government in Washington, D. C., London und Deutschland.
[3] Hajo Holborn (1902–1969), deutsch-amerikanischer Historiker, geboren in Charlottenburg, Deutschland, Schüler von Friedrich Meinecke (siehe Dok. 1, Anm. 11), 1924 Dr. phil., Universität Berlin, 1926–1931 Privatdozent, Universität Heidelberg, 1931–1933 Professor, Deutsche Hochschule für Politik, 1933 Privatdozent, Universität Berlin, 1933 Emigration nach England, 1934 in die USA, 1934–1943 Professor, Yale University, 1940 US-Staatsbürgerschaft, 1943–1945 Research and Analysis Branch, OSS, 1945–1969 Yale University, 1947–1949, Consultant, Department of State, 1967 Verleihung der Ehrendoktorwürde der Freien Universität Berlin, ab 1967 President, American Historical Association.
[4] 16./17. Februar 1946.
[5] US Army's New York Port of Embarkation.
[6] 18. Februar 1946.
[7] Sinclair W. Armstrong und seine Ehefrau Mary H. Armstrong, geb. Hallock (1898–1958).
[8] Hauptstadt des US-Bundesstaats Rhode Island, wo Sinclair W. Armstrong als Geschichtsprofessor an der Brown University lehrte.
[9] Hafenstadt im US-Bundesstaat Connecticut.
[10] 9. Februar 1946.
[11] Stadt im US-Bundesstaat Wisconsin.

after not finding him at the music store and found him there. I think he looked somewhat better than in December but he has been the victim of a series of colds and complains about burning sensations in two fingers of his right hand and up his right arm. He has been looking for work but has found nothing that he thought he could do and has therefore remained unemployed. He has tried to spend his time writing these marches. Norman[13] says there has been no difficulty of any kind because at least in part there is no opportunity. Norman keeps the money on a weekly ration. He goes to Norman's on Sundays when he wishes. He did not come to Lincoln[14] because he hoped to get a job, was doing some negotiating over unemployment insurance, and I think, under prompting by Norman, did not want to disturb things while I was at home[15]. But he wanted to come and still would like to come. I brought up the question of their being difficulties over his weakness and this, he assured me would not arise. He looks forward to the possibility of being useful especially with the yard and garden and with the kids. He said he would write you. I said I would write you about the whole matter, and that if we agreed again that he should come you would write and set a date for his arrival and he would arrive on that date. Norman spoke of taking him to Billings[16] for a complete check-over, and this could be done, either before he came to Lincoln or en route. Lucille[17], of course, urges you to think the matter over very carefully before you decide to let him come and urges it in a very unpleasant manner. In general I think I should like to try it. He may prove to be of considerable help to you in taking care of the yard and garden, in staying with Timmy[18] while you are out on errands, and in general making it possible for you to get out while he stays with the children. Certainly his life in Milwaukee is desolate at present. Maybe you should wait before actually deciding until I have word about the possibility of your coming to Germany. For if you are to come it would be complicating for you to have to set up arrangements in Lincoln for him while you are away. But if you do not come maybe we could try having him there and see how it works. If not then something else has to be tried. It might be a good idea, until I am back, for Norman

---

12   Frank E. Johnson, eigentl. Johanson (1872–1949), Edgar N. Johnsons Vater, Klavierbauer, geboren in Varola Sköfde, Schweden, 1891 in die USA eingewandert, 1898 US-Staatsbürgerschaft, lebte in Chicago, Illinois, arbeitete dann in einer Klavierfabrik in Holly, Michigan, und schließlich in La Porte, Indiana, ein versierter Klavierspieler. "He lived most of his life in LaPorte, Indiana as an 'action finisher in a piano factory' and was an accomplished pianist, as was Edgar. He never attended college and could barely write in English." Candice E. Johnson in einer E-Mail an Werner Breunig vom 1. Juni 2010.
13   Norman D. Johnson (1904–1964), Edgar N. Johnsons Bruder, war zunächst in Kansas City, Missouri, als Manager of Bonds tätig, dann als Businessman bei Allis-Chalmers Manufacturing Company, Milwaukee, Wisconsin.
14   Hauptstadt des US-Bundesstaats Nebraska, wo Johnson mit seiner Familie wohnte und an der Universität lehrte.
15   Johnson war Ende 1945/Anfang 1946, nach seiner Rückkehr aus Europa, bei seiner Familie in Lincoln gewesen.
16   Gemeint sein könnte das Billings Hospital der University of Chicago.
17   Lucille Johnson, Norman D. Johnsons Ehefrau.
18   Sohn Thomas. Siehe Dok. 2, Anm. 16.

to continue to manage his finances from Milwaukee. But I'm sure he is a dear sweet person and by no means hopeless or useless and we should be glad I think for having tried a solution.

I stayed with him until after lunch and then went over to Norman's for a call with him. I found that I had very little to say to Norman and Lucille, I don't believe that relationship can ever improve. On the contrary it will grow worse. I left on a 4 o'clock train for Chicago, and this I will tell you about in my next.

Good-bye to my sweet beloved. I dare not think too much or in too vivid detail about you and John[19] and Timmy[20]. I must try to postpone my yearning for you. I have already had twinges of it. But I love you, love you and send you all a sweet kiss – my sweetest. Edgar

Dok. 4
Schreiben an die Ehefrau
Washington (16), D. C., 412 Baltimore Avenue[1], 15. Februar 1946

Dearest Emily –

I'll try to catch up a little with the news while remaining in the clutches of the bureaucracy. I learn now that the difficulty is that the amended orders (to enable travel by sea) have been so amended that payment could not be made (per diems) for the delay in Washington. I did not notice this but someone else did. The result has been a conflict between overseas branch and the Finance branch of the war department as to how the orders are to be ordered in order to make payment possible. This conflict was not resolved until today, the result being (I have just learned by telephone) that the orders won't be ready until Monday[2] morning at 11 o'clock and I am to pick them up by 12. I should have been willing to risk the non-payment in order to avoid this further delay since by imposing upon Polly[3] the way I am. I am not spending much money. But there was not much I could do about it, and of course they don't work on Saturday here either. I wish I were back in Lincoln[4] teaching rather than doing this waiting around. There is no good reason why I shouldn't have been in Lincoln all this time. I suppose now that because of this delay I shall miss the appointment at the POE[5] and have to take the following ship. I wonder what delays are to be met in Europe. I have already thought that it would be best to go from Le Havre[6] to

---

[19] Sohn John. Siehe Dok. 2, Anm. 15.
[20] Sohn Thomas. Siehe Dok. 2, Anm. 16.

[1] Hier wohnten Eugene N. Anderson (siehe Dok. 1, Anm. 1), dessen Ehefrau Pauline R. Anderson, geb. Relyea (siehe Dok. 2, Anm. 2) und Sohn Eugene N. Anderson Jr. (siehe Anm. 30).
[2] 18. Februar 1946.
[3] Pauline R. Anderson, geb. Relyea. Siehe Dok. 2, Anm. 2.
[4] Hauptstadt des US-Bundesstaats Nebraska, wo Johnson mit seiner Familie wohnte und an der Universität lehrte.
[5] US Army's New York Port of Embarkation.
[6] Französische Hafenstadt an der Atlantikküste.

Paris to Frankfurt[7] to Walter Dorn[8] in order to get at the heart of the matter. Maybe they can get me transportation to Berlin. Perhaps one can become hardened to this kind of thing.

I think I abandoned Milwaukee[9] at 4:00 pm on last Saturday[10] for Chicago.[11] I finally got a taxi out to Mildred's[12] traveling with a noisy GI[13] just returned from Germany and a blind man who was trying to get vicarious war experiences. Mildred had had Aunt Hannah[14] come out to help her with the supper. She spoke appreciatively of the dress and Mildred did likewise about their Christmas box from us. Mildred looks well and not too tired. She is still a bit large from the pregnancy. William Williams[15] is a charming baby. He was sleeping most of the time I was there but Mildred took him up and laid him on the bed and he awoke and smiled and kicked ingratiatingly. David Henry[16] is also a beautiful and smart and apparently healthy child. He does not walk yet but crawls all over and stands and will walk at almost any time. I did not hear him talk. He made friends with me. David[17] is devoted to him and David Jr.[18] is undoubtedly very very affectionate, the result they think of the terrible things he has been through. […][19] Kirsten[20] is still very active, very independent and certainly clever. Her dress fitted. She paid little attention to me.

David is not going to teach during the Spring Quarter (April May June) but will teach during the Summer Quarter.[21] If by any chance you are to come over to Germany during April they might want to have our house for that period. I mentioned this but I did not talk about it. I suppose they would not feel free to leave their Chicago doctor unless it could be assured that Hancock[22] could han-

[7] Frankfurt am Main, Stadt im Land Groß-Hessen in der amerikanischen Besatzungszone Deutschlands.
[8] Siehe Dok. 2, Anm. 10.
[9] Stadt im US-Bundesstaat Wisconsin.
[10] 9. Februar 1946.
[11] Siehe Dok. 3.
[12] Mildred H. Williams, geb. Johnson, verw. Bickford (1911-2009), Edgar N. Johnsons Schwester, Lehrerin für Latein und Französisch.
[13] Government Issue, ugs. für amerikanischer Soldat.
[14] Hannah Walstrom (1870-1959), Schwester von Edgar N. Johnsons Mutter (siehe Dok. 46, Anm. 13), lebte in Chicago, Illinois.
[15] William G. Williams (geb. 1945), Sohn von David G. Williams (siehe Anm. 17) und Mildred H. Williams.
[16] David H. Williams (geb. 1944), Sohn von David G. Williams (siehe Anm. 17) und Mildred H. Williams.
[17] David G. Williams (1907-1987), Ehemann von Mildred H. Williams, amerikanischer Philologe, lehrte 1945-1973 an der University of Chicago, Department of English Language and Literature, Professor, 1957-1960 Chairman, Division of the Humanities, 1977-1981 Assistant Dean of Students in the College.
[18] David H. Williams.
[19] Weggelassen wurden Johnsons Ausführungen zur Krankheitsgeschichte von David H. Williams.
[20] Kirsten D. Williams, später verh. Kaiser (1942-1994), Tochter von David G. Williams und Mildred H. Williams.
[21] David G. Williams lehrte an der University of Chicago, Department of English Language and Literature. Siehe Anm. 17.
[22] Wahrscheinlich Dr. Ernest W. Hancock (1894-1954), Kinderarzt in Lincoln, Nebraska.

dle the case. We talked about the piano some. It is clear that we owe them 20 dollars for storage on the piano, and that all further storage until they bring it to Chicago, if they do, must be paid by us. This I said. They are a little uncertain about bringing it to Chicago since David has a piano at his home which he thinks is better although it would cost more to bring it to Chicago. They are also uncertain about bringing Dad's[23] piano to Chicago because of the cost of moving it about in case they move. There are too many pianos between us. But I think we should offer to pay the storage until they decide which if any piano they want to bring to Chicago. If they decide none for the present, we ought to stop paying storage on the piano in La Porte[24] and have it brought to Lincoln where we can also store it or use it. I am not sure but that if Dad fixed the touch it would be in better shape than the Steinway[25], which is no great improvement over what we had. I perhaps get a little more friendly with David Sr.[26] who took me to the Englewood station[27] for the 10:15 Pennsylvania[28]. David and Mildred have stopped smoking. It was a dreary ride to Washington. I went first to the Vedelers[29] and was given dinner, whereupon I went, before Gene[30] got to bed to the Andersons[31]. About the reactions to Washington I shall have to write later.

Dearest I hope that this venture is not going to turn out as it has begun, as it is so far I would be much better teaching in Lincoln and home with you and the boys. There I would have some meaning and use. Here I have none and what I am to have is doubtful. I cannot write easily about the stay at home. It had a dream-like quality even more intensified than that which we ordinarily comment on. It seems that everything I read mentions this quality about existence. I was aware too many times, although I believe I did not comment on it, about this danger of taking this beautiful family for granted. I hope I did not seem to do so. I sometimes feel I am not adequate enough for this richness it contains of course I have always felt this about you, that I could not match your spirit, your quick intelligence, your lovely humanity, your sweet sensitivity and your gaiety. I know the ways in which I was really inadequate. You are always I think too good to me. No matter how beautiful and lovely the boys, and who can say that there are better boys, the times when we were alone were best, whether at the

---

[23] Frank E. Johnson. Siehe Dok. 3, Anm. 12.
[24] Stadt im US-Bundesstaat Indiana, wo Edgar N. Johnson die High School besucht hatte und seine Eltern einen Großteil ihres Lebens verbrachten.
[25] Gemeint ist ein Klavier von Steinway & Sons. Die Firma wurde von Heinrich Engelhard Steinweg, ab 1854: Henry E. Steinway (1797-1871), geboren in Wolfshagen im Harz, Deutschland, und seinen Söhnen 1853 in New York gegründet.
[26] David G. Williams.
[27] Bahnhof in Chicago.
[28] Pennsylvania Railroad.
[29] Harold C. Vedeler und Marguerite D. Vedeler, geb. Drew. Siehe Dok. 2, Anm. 12 und 13.
[30] Eugene N. Anderson Jr. (geb. 1941), Sohn von Eugene N. Anderson (siehe Dok. 1, Anm. 1) und Pauline R. Anderson, geb. Relyea (siehe Dok. 2, Anm. 2), wurde später Professor of Anthropology, University of California, Riverside.
[31] Eugene N. Anderson (siehe Dok. 1, Anm. 1), Pauline R. Anderson, geb. Relyea (siehe Dok. 2, Anm. 2) und Sohn Eugene N. Anderson Jr.

breakfast table, or in the living room before a fire, or out together, or in each others arms. At these times I can never exhaust your grace and love and resourcefulness. I guess it all comes down to saying I love you, and worship you, that I am utterly and most willingly dependent upon you and that I can think of nothing better to do than to be at your mercy, to do what you want me to do. It is too good a love that lets us be so easily separated, but if it turns out as we expect, we shall not be sorry. It is only worth it if when we see each other again I shall have earned the right to have been away by the things I have done. I shall try to be worthy of you, try to merit your pride in me, fulfill your hope and increase your joy. Dearest Emily if it is within me I shall not fail you, and may be when I come back I shall be a little bigger and better person and a little more worthy of my precious wife and our children.

I suppose you are not writing here any more on the theory that I have departed. My present orders say that until I have a permanent APO[32] address, I should use as a temporary address

New Arrivals Section
25th Base Post Office
APO 800. c/o PM, NY, NY.

Letters addressed here will be forwarded to my permanent APO when I notify this office.

Bye-bye my sweet one. Kiss the boys for me and have them kiss you for me.
Edgar

Dok. 5
Schreiben an die Ehefrau
Washington (16), D. C., 412 Baltimore Avenue[1], 17. Februar 1946

Dearest Em[ily] and the boys –

It is a quiet and warmish afternoon here. Gene[2] is napping. Polly[3] is reading to Genie[4]. I want to catch up on correspondence with you with the new pen[5].

We went for a walk this morning first with Genie (i. e. Gene and I). He fell and cut his hand slightly and set up a terrific yell which he continued until we brought him home. [...][6]

Gene and I took a subsequent walk through nice Maryland[7] woods in the neighbourhood. It was rather extensive. He talking for the most part about the evils of the bureaucracy and about his own frustration in not being able to get anything accomplished. He wants to get back to teaching but the right job does

---

[32] Army Post Office.

[1] Siehe Dok. 4, Anm. 1.
[2] Eugene N. Anderson. Siehe Dok. 1, Anm. 1.
[3] Pauline R. Anderson, geb. Relyea. Siehe Dok. 2, Anm. 2.
[4] Eugene N. Anderson Jr. Siehe Dok. 4, Anm. 30.
[5] Siehe Dok. 3.
[6] Weggelassen wurden Johnsons Ausführungen über Erziehungsprobleme.
[7] US-Bundesstaat bei Washington, D. C.

not come along.[8] I'll mention him to Henry[9] for Harold's[10] place[11] but I don't believe he's interested. There would be a big salary cut in his case. He is not interested in Rudy[12] and I don't believe the University interests him much. Polly I think is also a little concerned about being confined so much. She devotes hours and hours to Genie.

When I first came here I was much discouraged with what I saw of the bureaucracy – especially in the successor agency to OSS[13] whose fate is still somewhat in doubt, and the thought of returning to it was repugnant. What I have heard of the administrative chaos in the State Department, from others than Gene, is enough to confirm me in the decision I made before I came back – not to go into it. Harold V[edeler] on the contrary is content because, in some way, he gets assigned important work to do, and what he does filters up to the top and gets initialed and ultimately acted upon. But he himself can be critical enough. No policy seems to be made at high levels in sufficient time ahead to make possible comment at lower levels. Policy is first shaped at lower levels and gets established as it goes the rounds to the top. By that time it is watered down into something that is often unspecific – the expression of an attitude not a policy. I got a good example of it earlier in the week from John Howe[14], whom I knew at the University of Chicago[15] and who has been here since September as an assistant to Benton[16], an assistant secretary of state for informational and

---

[8] In einem Interview, das im Jahre 1983 mit Anderson durchgeführt wurde, sagte dieser, dass er nicht in das State Department hineingepasst habe. „Ich wollte unabhängig sein, wollte niemandem zu Diensten sein." Die State-Department-Leute mochte er nicht so recht, „sie waren zu bürokratisch für mich, zu Hierarchie-orientiert". „[...] wenn man in der amerikanischen Bürokratie zurecht kommen wollte, dann mußte man ein ganz bestimmter Charakter sein, man mußte aufpassen, mußte seine Worte genau überlegen, mußte sich zu schnell anpassen. Im State Department ging es ehrgeizig zu, man wollte schnell nach oben kommen." Interview mit Prof. Eugene N. Anderson am 10. Dezember 1983 in Santa Barbara/Kalifornien, in: Zur Archäologie der Demokratie in Deutschland, Bd. 2: Analysen von politischen Emigranten im amerikanischen Außenministerium 1946-1949, hrsg. von Alfons Söllner, Frankfurt am Main 1986, S. 22-34, hier S. 31 f.
[9] Charles Henry Oldfather. Siehe Dok. 2, Anm. 19.
[10] Harold C. Vedeler. Siehe Dok. 2, Anm. 12.
[11] Harold C. Vedeler wollte nicht an die University of Nebraska zurückkehren. Siehe Dok. 2.
[12] Rudolph A. Winnacker. Siehe Dok. 2, Anm. 20.
[13] Office of Strategic Services. Siehe Dok. 1, Anm. 9. OSS war mit Wirkung vom 1. Oktober 1945 aufgelöst worden, die Funktionen wurden zwischen dem Department of War und dem Department of State aufgeteilt.
[14] John P. Howe (1905-1967), 1927 PhD, University of Chicago, 1927-1938 Press Relations Officer at University, 1938-1945 Assistant to Vice President and Executive Secretary of Radio Office, University of Chicago, ab Oktober 1945 Special Assistant to Assistant Secretary of State for Public Affairs, Department of State.
[15] 1890 gegründete Universität in Chicago, Illinois.
[16] William B. Benton (1900-1973), 1921 BA, Yale University, 1921-1929 advertising business, 1927-1945 Vice President, University of Chicago, 1929-1936 founder and president of advertising agency, 1945-1947 Assistant Secretary of State for Public Affairs, Department of State, 1949-1953 Senator des US-Bundesstaats Connecticut.

cultural affairs. John was attending a meeting with Benton and Byrnes[17] late on Saturday afternoon. At the meeting Byrnes received a memo from the White House[18] asking for a draft on what the president[19] should say in his Navy Day speech[20] on international affairs and the control of atomic energy. After Byrnes read it he passed it on to Benton who read it and passed it on to Howe to prepare without any further instructions. Howe worked all Saturday night on a draft, the atomic energy part of which being based on what he learned from professors at the University of Chicago. Benton saw this draft on Sunday and said it would not do. What the president wanted was some vague and generalized statement for public consumption. John had this ready by Monday and it was actually used by the president, as John said, "who in the hell makes American policy".

One gets no better impression of the president's stature here than in Lincoln[21]. The manner in which he handled the Ickes[22] resignation is pretty terrible. Clearly he should have kept Ickes and dropped Pauley[23] both of which he could have done and not gotten into this mess.

So I must say that my present mood is not to enter this scene. Yet all the reasons for good people going into it are as valid as ever. But good people who do not have infinite patience, and a desire to meet with and manipulate with the people who get things done should not go into the government. I could acquire infinite patience but I am not much of an administrator or a manipulator and I am not very good at making the sounds of the important people. Continued frustration is no mood under which to live a satisfactory life. I am impressed more and more too with the necessity for ceasing to follow the will of the wisps of professional governmental advancement which is involved with continuous uncertainty. Our old plans are very good if they include as they did a piano and the mountains. I shall therefore not think much about or hope for a change

[17] James F. Byrnes (1879–1972), amerikanischer Jurist und Politiker (Demokratische Partei), 1911–1925 Mitglied des Repräsentantenhauses, 1930–1941 Senator, 1941/1942 Richter am obersten Bundesgericht der USA, 1943–1945 Direktor des Amtes für Kriegsmobilisierung, 1945–1947 Außenminister der USA, 1951–1955 Gouverneur des US-Bundesstaats South Carolina.
[18] Sitz des Präsidenten der USA.
[19] Harry S. Truman (1884–1972), 1945–1953 33. Präsident der USA.
[20] Rede des Präsidenten der USA zum amerikanischen Flottentag am 27. Oktober 1945. Siehe Keesing's Archiv der Gegenwart, XV. Jg., 1945, S. 498 G. Der Flottentag war der Geburtstag von Theodore Roosevelt (1858–1919), 1901–1909 26. Präsident der USA.
[21] Hauptstadt des US-Bundesstaats Nebraska, wo Johnson mit seiner Familie wohnte und an der Universität lehrte.
[22] Harold L. Ickes (1874–1952), ab 1933 Innenminister der USA, Februar 1946 Rücktritt.
[23] Edwin W. Pauley (1903–1981), amerikanischer Geschäftsmann, 1945–1947 US-Vertreter in der alliierten Reparationskommission im Rang eines Botschafters. US-Präsident Truman ernannte ihn zum Unterstaatssekretär für die Marine. Daraufhin trat Innenminister Ickes im Februar 1946 zurück, griff auf einer Pressekonferenz den Präsidenten scharf an und kritisierte die Ernennung Pauleys, dem er Bevorzugung privater Ölinteressen vorwarf, sowie die Auswahl der übrigen Ratgeber Trumans. Siehe Keesing's Archiv der Gegenwart, XVI. Jg., 1946, S. 649 G. Truman zog im März 1946 die Ernennung Pauleys auf dessen eigenes Verlangen zurück. Siehe ebd., S. 679 A.

from the University in general. If something specific comes up we shall have to consider it. But I am not going to court anything at this point at least.

I am enclosing 1, a clipping Marguerite V[edeler][24] gave me. It made her furious and 2, the application sheet for this new insurance policy. The policy is not good after you leave the government service but you may take out its equivalent at regular rates. I think we should take it out while I am away and transfer it when I come back. I haven't enough surplus cash to pay the initial fee here so I am asking you to do it.

It is clear I think that you will have to cash enough bonds not only to pay the 1944 income tax but also to provide yourself with some cash to keep going and possibly to send me some cash. When you will get the check covering my accumulated leave is uncertain. At the War Department they told me that allotments are made by the Personnel Officer in Berlin. Whether the action I took in Omaha[25] on this matter is really enough I don't know, and at the present rate I don't know when I shall get to Berlin. I have actually less cash now than I thought I would have, and how it will be when I am permanently stationed I don't know. I hope to make what I have do until I receive a check but I may have to cable from Germany for money. I won't bother you until I am in desperate circumstances. Also will you send that khaki battle jacket to me as soon as I give you a permanent address. I find it can be worn with these green pants, and I should have brought it along.

Tomorrow I suppose I shall be on my way. I miss your letters. I send to you and John and Timmy all my love and a heap of endearments. Edgar

Dok. 6
Schreiben an die Ehefrau
New York, Hotel Pennsylvania[1], 18. Februar 1946

Dearest beloved –

For a good deal of the time on the way from Washington to here[2] my mind has been on you, and on the essential senselessness of my leaving you and the boys. Unlike the trains before Christmas this one (I left Washington at 5 p. m.) had practically no military people on it. Except for my uniform I saw only one other army and one naval uniform, an officer back from Japan who commended on the excellent job MacArthur[3] is doing and on the general subservience of

---

[24] Siehe Dok. 2, Anm. 13.
[25] Stadt im US-Bundesstaat Nebraska, nordöstlich von Johnsons Wohnort Lincoln.

[1] Hotel in New York City/Manhattan, 7th Avenue, 32nd to 33rd Streets. Als es 1919 eröffnet wurde, war es mit 2200 Zimmern das größte Hotel der Welt. Siehe The New York Times vom 25. Januar 1919, S. 9.
[2] New York City.
[3] Douglas MacArthur (1880–1964), General of the Army, 1945–1951 Commander in Chief, Allied Forces of Occupation, Japan.

the Japs. The rest were Washington bureaucrats going up to New York for a day or so. You could tell them and you wondered how the government gets along as well as it does.

My thoughts of you were of an intimate character. I could not help thinking of those times together when we were free to be quite one. I thought of the things we did which we had not done before and I wondered why we had not done them before. I thought of your loving receptivity and of your responses and I wondered if there were men who could have sweeter and more endearing wives than I. I wondered if you thought upon these occasions with the same intense longing as I and with the same joyful satisfaction. Sometimes they are well right perfect; sometimes they are quite perfect and sometimes you are obliged to put up with what you should not have to put up with. At all times you are wonderfully kind and exciting to me even though your return is not equivalent. You never act as if you were censorious no matter what has happened and I never think to wonder if the residue left with you is really as you make it out to be, so genuine and good all your reactions are. This part of our marriage has been less than perfect but in spite of the imperfections the actual desire to be together under these conditions has increased for me, and with it, the desire to try to make more of it than we have ever succeeded in making. And there will be time and occasions. I wish tonight that we were sitting alone together in the living room in front of a fire. I wish that we were about to lose each other in the warmth of emotion that comes with the taste of your soft lips and the feeling of your breast. I wish I were about to take you to the bed-room where I might watch the lovely body emerge from the clothes. I wish that I were to feel that body on my body from head to toe. No years of marriage can ever temper completely or assuage this longing. My darling beloved. I love you, love you deeply, love all of you with all of me.

We are to report to the POE[4] tomorrow morning. It is rumored that we sail tomorrow night, but this seems far too soon. It would be some compensation for all this waiting, though the boy sharing my room has been waiting since January 28th and has been taken off a plane. Polly[5] loaded me up with things to take to hungry Germans – particularly the old mother of a friend[6] who just received notice after years that her mother was alive, ill and very hungry. This woman lost her father on the last day of the war – a Russian bomb.

Good-night my sweet beloved. I shall have to go on thinking about you until I fall asleep. Edgar

---

[4] US Army's New York Port of Embarkation.
[5] Pauline R. Anderson, geb. Relyea. Siehe Dok. 2, Anm. 2.
[6] Hier ist Pollys Freundin Katharina Posner, geb. Melchior, gesch. Bungert (siehe Dok. 22, Anm. 3) gemeint, deren Mutter (siehe Dok. 22, Anm. 9) in Berlin lebte. Siehe Dok. 23.

Dok. 7
Schreiben an die Ehefrau
New York # 19, Hotel Knickerbocker[1], 120 West 45th Street, 19. Februar 1946

Dearest Sweetheart:

We were thrown out of the Pennsylvania Hotel[2] this morning on the theory that we had promised to stay only for the night. But they did help us to get a room in this place. I am rooming with an innocent young man from South Dakota[3] since no single rooms are available. I ran into him at the Pentagon building[4] as he was getting a railroad ticket. I was relieved to find that he is only a clerk-stenographer, who, having been dismissed from the army in December is now out to see the world. He is amazed to find that the taxi-drivers expect tips. I suppose they don't do that in Fargo[5] or wherever Mr. Case is from.

We went out to the POE[6] this morning. The cab driver was as innocent of New York as I was of Boston[7] when we first hit it. After driving around in all directions, and almost crossing the Queensborough and Brooklyn bridges[8], after questioning many cab and taxi drivers he finally gave up in despair and acknowledged us how we'd better get into another cab. The second driver spent his time berating the first, wondering how a driver could take anyone any place if he didn't know where he was going. It happened to be the same place that I went in June 1944[9] when I went for OSS[10]. The difference in atmosphere is great however and expressive of the changed attitude of the work now to be done. Then of course we were in the midst of war and everything was enveloped with the sense of security. I remember though that I called you from here as I must do before leaving here. We were then taken of well. Now we are left to shift for ourselves. Then the offices at the port were manned by GI's[11]. Now, except for Captain Rosenzweig[12] they are manned by pretty girls, and it is even possible to see why the Captain hasn't moved on or been promoted. Then there was a group of young eager people courting the danger of the submarine. Now, in so far as I can tell, there is a group of people who know little of the world they are going to, do not look eager, on the contrary rather dull. There is one person who seems to be something of a big shot. I saw him in Washington where Major Smith[13]

---

1 1925 eröffnetes Hotel in New York City/Manhattan, das über 400 Zimmer verfügte.
2 Siehe Dok. 6, Anm. 1.
3 US-Bundesstaat.
4 Siehe Dok. 1, Anm. 3.
5 Stadt im US-Bundesstaat North Dakota.
6 US Army's New York Port of Embarkation.
7 Hauptstadt des US-Bundesstaats Massachusetts.
8 Brücken, die den East River in New York City überspannen. Die im Jahre 1909 eröffnete Queensboro Bridge verbindet die Stadtbezirke Queens und Manhattan, die 1883 vollendete Brooklyn Bridge Brooklyn und Manhattan.
9 Siehe Dok. 2, Anm. 9.
10 Office of Strategic Services. Siehe Dok. 1, Anm. 9.
11 Government Issues, ugs. für amerikanische Soldaten.
12 Siehe Dok. 2.
13 Siehe Dok. 2.

told me he was an adviser to Clay[14] who had been pulled off a plane.[15] I noticed he was a CAF 14[16]. We are to sail on Thursday[17], if present plans go through on the Goethals[18], the one ship Major Smith in Washington told me to avoid if possible. May be he doesn't know anything about it. There is accordingly nothing very exciting about it. I filled out blanks, got another typhus inoculation and one for smallpox.[19] So that helps my mood.

I also have contracted a heavy cold which descended on me this morning. But the voyage will clear that up I imagine. There is much to do here. Katharine Cornell[20] opens in Antigone[21] tonight and there are many other interesting plays but my stock of cash is running too low what with New York expenses. I shouldn't go any places tonight in any case. Tomorrow however I may try to get a seat for Evans'[22] version of Hamlet[23]. We call tomorrow at 11 for final instruc-

[14] Siehe Dok. 2, Anm. 6.
[15] Siehe Dok. 2.
[16] Beschäftigter der Klasse 14 des Clerical, Administrative, and Fiscal Service.
[17] 21. Februar 1946.
[18] USAT George W. Goethals, Transportschiff der US Army seit 1942, benannt nach George W. Goethals (1858-1928), dem Chefingenieur des Panamakanals. Im "Dictionary of American Naval Fighting Ships" des "Naval Historical Center" heißt es: "During World War II *George W. Goethals* operated as an Army transport out of New York, Boston, and Gulf Coast ports to ports in North Africa, France, and the United Kingdom. After the war, she continued transatlantic runs carrying military dependents between the United States and Europe." http://www.history.navy.mil/danfs/g4/george_w_goethals.htm (letzter Zugriff am 30. Januar 2013). Siehe Roland W. Charles, Troopships of World War II, with a foreword by Major General Edmond H. Leavey, Washington, D. C., 1947, S. 31. Foto des Schiffes im Bildanhang, Abb. 12.
[19] Siehe Immunization Register, 1944-1946, in: Unterlagen aus dem Nachlass Edgar N. Johnson, Privatbesitz Candice E. und Thomas R. Johnson, Denver, Colorado, USA; Bildanhang, Abb. 6.
[20] Katharine Cornell (1893-1974), amerikanische Schauspielerin, Broadwaylegende, war mit dem Regisseur Guthrie McClintic (1893-1961) verheiratet.
[21] Antigone, Drama von Jean Anouilh (1910-1987) nach Sophokles (497/496 v. Chr.-406/405 v. Chr.), übersetzt und bearbeitet von Lewis Galantiere (1893-1977), wurde vom 18. Februar bis 4. Mai 1946 im Cort Theatre in New York City/Manhattan, 48th Street East of Broadway, aufgeführt. Siehe Sam Zolotow, "Antigone" Opens at Cort Tonight. Katharine Cornell, Sir Cedric Hardwicke to Star in Modern Dress Version of Classic, in: The New York Times vom 18. Februar 1946, S. 17; Lewis Nichols, The Play, in: The New York Times vom 19. Februar 1946, S. 21; http://www.ibdb.com/production.php?id=1773 (letzter Zugriff am 30. Januar 2013).
[22] Maurice Evans (1901-1989), britisch-amerikanischer Schauspieler, geboren in Dorchester, Dorset, England, kam 1935 in die USA, wurde dort einer der bekanntesten Shakespeare-Interpreten, 1941 US-Staatsbürgerschaft, war während des Zweiten Weltkriegs für eine Army Entertainment Section zuständig, arbeitete auch für Film und Fernsehen, spielte unter anderem in dem Science-Fiction-Film „Planet der Affen" (1968) und in der Fortsetzung „Rückkehr zum Planet der Affen" (1970) mit.
[23] Gemeint ist eine verkürzte Version der Tragödie „Hamlet" von William Shakespeare (1564-1616), auch als „G. I. Hamlet" bekannt. Sie wurde während des Zweiten Weltkriegs vor Soldaten aufgeführt und war vom 13. Dezember 1945 bis 8. April 1946 im Columbus Circle Theatre in New York City/Manhattan, Broadway at 59th Street, zu sehen. "Some of the members of the company served with Major Evans in the Pacific and over twenty were ex-service men." http://www.ibdb.com/production.php?id=1751

tions and if I feel up to it I might try to do some aht[24] at the Museum of Modern Art[25] or the Museum of the Pennsylvania Coal baron[26].

I hope it doesn't continue as drab as this or I shall be a very very homesick little boy. The fact that I don't know when I shall be able to get news from you does not help. I love you, my dearest Emily, and that and your love will keep me going. Kiss the boys for me, and I kiss you. Edgar

Dok. 8
Schreiben an die Ehefrau
New York # 19, Hotel Knickerbocker[1], 120 West 45th Street, 20. Februar 1946[2]

Dearest Emily and my sweet boys –

I am trying to call you by long distance, but the "toll" line seems to be busy. Evidently the services for this small hotel is unlike that for the Pennsylvania[3] for there when I called you upon my return there was no difficulty. There will be some contrast in the moods of these calls but I am eager to hear your voice.

We are leaving tomorrow. At least we have been given a clearance ship and a customs declaration and told to report at the ship's side tomorrow between 11 and 12 a. m. This means I suppose that the ship will actually get off tomorrow – the first of what Captain Rosenzweig[4] intimated would be from 6 to 10 days, meaning of course ten days. The Goethals[5] is an old, slow, tired ship I am told from which too much cannot be expected.[6] Ten days from tomorrow and it will

(letzter Zugriff am 30. Januar 2013). Siehe Sam Zolotow, Modern "Hamlet" Arriving Tonight. Maurice Evans Returning in GI Version of Shakespeare Play – Mike Todd the Producer, in: The New York Times vom 13. Dezember 1945, S. 33; Lewis Nichols, The Play, in: The New York Times vom 14. Dezember 1945, S. 25.

[24] Gemeint ist „art". Johnson macht sich hier offensichtlich über das gebildete amerikanische Bürgertum lustig, das „art" wie „aht" ausspricht.

[25] MoMA, Museum in New York City/Manhattan, 11 West 53rd Street, das sich der Kunst von den 1880er-Jahren (Impressionisten) bis zur Gegenwart widmet. 1929 gegründet, zog es 1939 in den Neubau an der 53rd Street, der inzwischen mehrmals erweitert wurde. Siehe http://www.moma.org/ (letzter Zugriff am 30. Januar 2013).

[26] Gemeint ist der Kohle- und Stahlmagnat Henry C. Frick (1849-1919) aus Pittsburgh, Pennsylvania, der sich 1913/1914 in New York City/Manhattan, an der Ecke 5th Avenue und 70th Street, ein Stadtpalais hatte errichten lassen, in dem er seine kostbare Kunstsammlung unterbrachte. Nach Fricks Tod lebte seine Witwe weiter hier, erst nach ihrem Tod im Jahre 1931 begann die Umgestaltung des Wohnpalais zum Museum, das 1935 eröffnet wurde. Die Frick Collection wartet mit hochkarätiger europäischer Kunst des 14. bis 19. Jahrhunderts auf. Siehe http://www.frick.org/ (letzter Zugriff am 30. Januar 2013).

1 Siehe Dok. 7, Anm. 1.
2 Siehe Bildanhang, Abb. 11.
3 Hotel Pennsylvania. Siehe Dok. 6, Anm. 1.
4 Siehe Dok. 2 und Dok. 7.
5 USAT George W. Goethals. Siehe Dok. 7, Anm. 18.
6 Möglicherweise Verwechslung mit SS General G. W. Goethals bzw. USS General G. W. Goethals (1919). "*General G. W. Goethals*, a 4707 gross ton passenger-cargo ship,

be already March, and before I get settled in my job I am sure that a full month will have passed since I left you and the boys. As you know I am to go first to Berlin. How one gets transported there I do not know. It will perhaps be best to go by way of Frankfurt[7]. Gene[8] and Polly[9] gave me the names of people to see in Berlin together with food packages. I shall try to see Marshall Knappen[10] and Louis Wiesner[11]. Jimmy Riddleberger[12] in the State Department wanted me to see Ambassador Murphy[13] and his assistants, Jacob Beam[14] and Donald Health[15]. He promised to write ahead introducing me. But I don't know what

was built at Hamburg, Germany, in 1911 as the German commercial steamer *Grunewald*. Later becoming a U. S. flag merchantman, she was taken over by the Navy in March 1919 and placed in commission as USS *General G. W. Goethals* (ID # 1443). As a troop transport assigned to the Cruiser and Transport Force, she was employed carrying U. S. service personnel home from France and taking cargo to Europe. The ship made three round-trip trans-Atlantic voyages for these purposes between April and August 1919, then carried supplies from the East Coast to the Gulf Coast, Caribbean and Panama. Decommissioned upon her return to New York in mid-September 1919, *General G. W. Goethals* was returned to her owner, the Panama Railroad Steamship Company." http://www.history.navy.mil/photos/sh-civil/civsh-g/gen-goet.htm (letzter Zugriff am 30. Januar 2013).

[7] Frankfurt am Main, Stadt im Land Groß-Hessen in der amerikanischen Besatzungszone Deutschlands.
[8] Eugene N. Anderson. Siehe Dok. 1, Anm. 1.
[9] Pauline R. Anderson, geb. Relyea. Siehe Dok. 2, Anm. 2.
[10] Marshall M. Knappen (1901–1966), Major, amerikanischer Theologe, Historiker und Politikwissenschaftler, PhD, Cornell University, vorübergehend Pastor der First Congregational Church Redfield im US-Bundesstaat South Dakota, 1931 Professor of History, University of Chicago, 1939–1942 Professor of History and Political Science, Michigan State College, 1945/1946 Chief, Religious Section, Education and Religious Affairs Branch, Internal Affairs and Communications Division, OMGUS, nahm 1947 wieder seine Tätigkeit als Professor of History and Political Science am Michigan State College auf, ab 1948 Professor of Political Science, University of Michigan, ab 1960 University of Delaware.
[11] Louis A. Wiesner (1916–2002), amerikanischer Foreign Service Officer, 1938 MA, Harvard University, 1939–1942 Assistant and Teaching Fellow, Harvard University, 1942/1943 Research Secretary, Council on Foreign Relations, 1943/1944 Research Analyst, OSS, 1944–1975 Department of State, bis 1949 Labor Affairs Attaché, Office of Political Affairs, Political Adviser (POLAD).
[12] James W. Riddleberger (1904–1982), amerikanischer Diplomat, 1944–1947 Chief, Division of Central European Affairs, Department of State, 1947–1949 Director of Political Affairs, OMGUS, Stellvertreter von Botschafter Robert D. Murphy.
[13] Robert D. Murphy (1894–1978), amerikanischer Diplomat, 1921–1924 Vice-Consul, München, 1944–1949 Ambassador, Political Adviser for Germany, 1949–1952 Ambassador, Belgien, 1952/1953 Japan, 1959 Under Secretary of State for Political Affairs. Foto von Murphy im Bildanhang, Abb. 22.
[14] Jacob D. Beam (1908–1993), amerikanischer Diplomat, 1929 BA, Princeton University, ab 1931 Foreign Service, 1934–1940 Third Secretary, Berlin, 1944–1947 Foreign Service Officer, Staff of Political Adviser for Germany, 1947–1949 Chief, Division of Central European Affairs, Department of State, 1957–1961 Ambassador, Polen, 1966–1969 Tschechoslowakei, 1969–1973 Sowjetunion.
[15] Donald R. Heath (1894–1981), amerikanischer Diplomat, 1937–1941 First Secretary, Berlin, 1945–1947 Director of Political Affairs, Office of the Deputy Military Governor, OMGUS, 1947–1950 Minister, Bulgarien, 1952 Ambassador, Kambodscha, 1952–1955 Vietnam, 1955–1957 Libanon, 1958–1961 Saudi-Arabien.

the transportation situation in Berlin will be, and whether I can see these people.

I am still low. Mrs. Roosevelt's[16] statement in today's paper,[17] after her brief trip to Germany,[18] that there is a dearth of good people for important jobs offers some encouragement but I need more than that at the present moment.[19] I wish I had had more sense about judging what would happen to me when once I got to Washington. Being cut off from you and the children so suddenly with only one letter[20] has become something of a trial. And after tomorrow I shall not be able to write a letter that can be mailed immediately for at least ten days. I shall, however, write a chronicle of the trip on the boat which I do not at all look forward to. But certainly it will be weeks yet before I get a word from you.

I love you my sweet darling, you and our precious sons. I am still determined to make what I can of this assignment but it will be difficult. I love you honey and beg of you to write a few letters to the temporary address I sent since I am sure they will come to me at some time. Here suddenly a whole month has disappeared from our lives. Kiss John and Timmy for me and let me tell you again, I love you and I love you. My lovely and sweetest wife. Edgar

Dok. 9
Schreiben an die Ehefrau
An Bord der „George W. Goethals"[1], 22. Februar 1946

Dearest Sweetheart –

I can begin to give you a chronology of this trip but unless there is more paper about I shall run out before the ten days are over. You will remember this

---

[16] Anna Eleanor Roosevelt (1884-1962), amerikanische Delegierte bei den Vereinten Nationen, Witwe von Franklin D. Roosevelt (1882-1945), 1933-1945 32. Präsident der USA.

[17] Eleanor Roosevelt schrieb von 1935 bis kurz vor ihrem Tod 1962 die Kolumne "My Day", die sechs Mal pro Woche in vielen amerikanischen Tageszeitungen erschien.

[18] Zu Eleanor Roosevelts Deutschland-Besuch siehe Eleanor Roosevelts deutsche Impressionen. Tagebuchblätter der Witwe des großen Präsidenten der Vereinigten Staaten, in: Die Neue Zeitung vom 18. Februar 1946, S. 2.

[19] In Eleanor Roosevelts Zeitungskolumne "My Day" vom 20. Februar 1946 heißt es: "[…] we need really able people to take over the key positions as the main military establishment shifts responsibility to a civilian administration. I'm told that these key people are hard to find and I'm not surprised, because it means a real sacrifice for the period of time one gives to this job. Yet the job has to be done for our own as well as the interests of the people of Europe." http://www.gwu.edu/~erpapers/myday/displaydoc.cfm?_y=1946&_f=md000267 (letzter Zugriff am 30. Januar 2013).

[20] Emily L. Johnsons Brief vom 10. Februar 1946, in: Unterlagen aus dem Nachlass Edgar N. Johnson, Privatbesitz Candice E. und Thomas R. Johnson, Denver, Colorado, USA.

[1] Siehe Dok. 7, Anm. 18.

paper. It came from you and it was used for the most part in the place to which I first went when I left you.

The boat is not so bad as it was painted by Major Smith[2] who must be used to great luxury or is not a very responsible reporter. It is about a 13 000 ton ship, and therefore not so large, about the size of the Montnairn[3], a Canadian ship I came back on in the late summer of 1928[4]. It has begun to roll and will continue to roll all the way across but I don't expect it will get me. I did not think we would have state-rooms, but rather all be drawn together in one large room. Instead there is a large roomy cabin with eight bunks in it, four lower and four upper. I have one of the uppers. There are springs, and clean sheets and blankets. I have just discovered a shelf in the dresses to pull out and write on. There are lamps and lockers and two toilet-baths for the 6 of us in the cabin. Everything is kept in marvelous order and cleanliness by the steward. The dining room is unpretentious. It must seat over a hundred people. Meals are served at 7:30, 11:30 and 4:30, and there are not, as on larger liners in peace time in between snacks. A 4:30 dinner is a little early but I imagine union conditions make it necessary. It might work better if you were anyplace except a boat. How would you like to be through dinner at 5:30. It would give you a long evening. The long evenings on this boat would be pretty dull without something to read. The food is excellent. Yesterday (I won't give you the menu every day) there was flounder for lunch, and chicken for supper and this morning there were bacon and eggs. So one will gain weight on the trip.

The ship moves very silently, so silently in fact that I did not know immediately that it was leaving the harbor. Yet I got out in time to see the tip of Manhattan[5] before we slipped into the narrows. There is something to be said for a ship over and against a plane. I went out on deck after breakfast this morning. The sun was shining brightly. The water a deep navy blue with white caps, the air brisk but not too cold and after all here was the marvel of 13 000 tons moving through the water at 18 knots an hour and seeming to go very fast. We have a deck to walk upon but it is cluttered with all kinds of naval equipment. There is no decent lounging room. This 13 000 tons of steel is carrying very few people some 200 crew perhaps and may be a hundred passengers[6] what else it is carrying I do not know. Some say 1000 tons of ballast. I saw partly filling the lounging room a great deal of baby equipment including swell high chairs, toilet seats, playpens, Mennen's oil. I wondered whether these could be meant for European children and then was informed that they were for the British wives of our GI's[7]. This is a sweet thought, however, and I doubt if any other nation would

---

[2] Siehe Dok. 2 und Dok. 7.
[3] SS Montnairn, Dampfschiff der Canadian Pacific Line. Siehe http://www.norwayherit age.com/p_ship.asp?sh=mont6 (letzter Zugriff am 30. Januar 2013).
[4] Gemeint ist Johnsons Rückkehr nach seinem Studienaufenthalt in Europa 1927/1928.
[5] Stadtbezirk von New York City.
[6] Eine Passagierliste liegt nicht vor. "Passenger lists were not considered permanent historical records", heißt es in einem Schreiben der National Archives and Records Administration (NARA), College Park, Maryland, USA, an Werner Breunig vom 21. Dezember 2010.
[7] Government Issues, ugs. für amerikanische Soldaten.

be foresighted and considerate enough (except it be the English themselves) to do a thing like this.

In the cabin are two people I'll try to describe a little more fully later. A Mr. Anderson[8], a road building expert (WPA[9]) and a Mr. Hoover[10], professor of economics at Mills College, California[11]. There is also a Czech boy from Pilsen[12] and of the others one a southerner and the other as yet without form. At lunch yesterday there sat across from me the wife of the assistant military attaché in Berne[13] who was going to Switzerland to join her husband[14]. She had a child about three[15] along and her Mother[16]. She said they were going to live in a hotel at first. No other wives are aboard I think[17] though I have been told that the highest ranking officers in Germany are already bringing their wives over. There are of course the usual number of coca-cola people[18] on board and a further scattering of professors, some of them refugees, with whom I have not yet become acquainted.

22 February, after dinner.

It must be all of 5:15 p. m. and dinner has been eaten. I don't believe I'll eat lunches. It's too much for this lazy life. There are a few corrections to the above gathered from a member of the crew. The ship is 12 000 instead of 13 000. It is coming back on the diaper run as they call it. It has no supplies of any kind for Europe which amazes me. It is of course a transport ship but why, when there is supposed to be a great shipping shortage, and there are no troops aboard, it can't be used to carry something to needy Europeans, I don't understand. As it

---

[8] William J. Anderson (1887–1958), amerikanischer Bauingenieur, 1910 BE, Union College, 1946–1948 Highway Consultant, Road Branch, Transport Division, OMGUS, ab 1950 Consulting Engineer, private Engineering practice, West Hartford, Connecticut.

[9] Die 1935 im Zuge des New Deal geschaffene Works Progress Administration (später Works Projects Administration) war als Arbeitsbeschaffungsbehörde für die Arbeitslosen während der Great Depression konzipiert.

[10] Glenn E. Hoover (1888–1961), amerikanischer Wirtschaftswissenschaftler, LLD, University of Washington, Promotion an der Universität Straßburg, war zunächst Professor of Economics and Political Science, University of Oregon, anschließend bis 1953 Mills College, 1946/1947 Finance Division, OMGUS.

[11] College in Oakland, California.

[12] Stadt in der Tschechoslowakei (heute Tschechien).

[13] Hauptstadt der Schweiz.

[14] Wahrscheinlich Davis O. Harrington (1913–1984), Lieutenant Colonel, 1935 BA, Yale University, 1935–1940 Banker, 1941–1949 US Army, ab November 1945 Assistant Military Attaché, Bern, verheiratet mit Margaret M. Harrington, geb. Mercer (1910–1990).

[15] Davis O. und Margaret M. Harringtons Kind, Nancy L. Harrington (geb. 1943), war knapp drei Jahre alt. Siehe D. O. Harringtons Have Child, in: The New York Times vom 10. Mai 1943, S. 14.

[16] Margaret V. Mercer, geb. McGarr (gest. 1955), Witwe von James Sidney (Sid) Mercer (1881–1945), amerikanischer Sportjournalist.

[17] An Bord befand sich auch Mrs. Wynona C. Schuyler (siehe Dok. 12, Anm. 7).

[18] Johnson benutzte den Begriff "coca-cola-people" für Rassisten aus den Südstaaten der USA. Hierzu Candice E. Johnson in einer E-Mail an Werner Breunig vom 16. Dezember 2007: "Edgar hated any person who was prejudiced against other races or religions, and he certainly met plenty of them on the ship."

is this is pretty expensive passage. A whole ship and a crew of 170 to carry something like a hundred civilians to work in Germany. I suppose it's a question of bureaucracy. It is impossible to route goods to this ship since it ordinarily does not carry supplies. It is rolling much more now.

The civilians who are going over to help solve the German problem are not a very encouraging lot. I include myself within this characterization. These are a mild oldish looking lot who, I am sure, will not do better than the military in executing American policy. Indeed I think they will do worse. I haven't come across any yet who pretend to know any German. It has not been set up as a requirement. They are just average, well-meaning, conscientious Americans without any particular knowledge of the German scene, and not knowing, in many cases what they are going to do. They are just going to report to Berlin. I think in most cases they are those who did not get in on the first call of the war agencies and who still feel a sense of responsibility for the American mission abroad and who at least want a little foreign experience. From any acquaintance with them I should not think they were of the stuff to keep the Germans in hand once the military are withdrawn. We just do not have experience of that kind. If once we succeed a setting up a satisfactory German administration it will be necessary to recruit a small body of very well trained controllers who know the German language and who know what to look after, otherwise we may loose our battle again.

These men are very easy to get acquainted with. (It is beginning to roll pretty badly now. I don't know which is worse this or turbulence. This reminds me of your mention of turbulence when I left Lincoln[19], and I knew what you were thinking). In fact getting acquainted is a kind of American rite which when properly initiated you are expected by any other American to go through with almost upon demand. You learn as much about a fellow American in this way as you would from a European in months of acquaintance. Take the Scotchman Mr. W[illia]m Anderson who sleeps in a lower bunk across from me in cabin 113. We got down to business last evening (the first evening out) and there was some continuation today. I know something about his grandfather who settled in northern New York[20], something about a great uncle who moved to Kansas[21], but more about his Father[22] and Mother[23]. His Father was a road contractor who used to bring over Italians from Sicily[24] and Calabria[25], move them to Albany[26] and deal with them, not according to name, but according to the number tied around their necks. They were treated, I gather, much like the Mexican sugar beet workers about whom that article in *Accent*[27] had to do. They were

---

[19] Hauptstadt des US-Bundesstaats Nebraska, wo Johnson mit seiner Familie wohnte und an der Universität lehrte.
[20] US-Bundesstaat.
[21] US-Bundesstaat.
[22] James Anderson (1858–1941), amerikanischer Straßenbauunternehmer.
[23] Julia F. Anderson, geb. Fitzgerald (1860–1931).
[24] Italienische Insel im Mittelmeer.
[25] Der äußerste Süden des italienischen Festlands.
[26] Hauptstadt des US-Bundesstaats New York.
[27] Gilbert Neiman, Lazarus Laughs, in: Accent. A Quarterly of New Literature, Vol. 6, No. 1 (Herbst 1945), S. 13–22.

our slave labor at the turn of the century or a little later. The father wanted him soon to be a learned contractor and sent him off to Union College[28] in Schenectady[29] to study civil engineering[30]. There he played Varsity football, and did well in school, being duly impressed with the hero of the Union College faculty at that time, a protégé of General Electric[31] one *Steimetz*[32] of whom you may have heard. Mr. Anderson graduated from college in 1910 and went first into his Father's business[33], helped to build the New York subways after the last war[34], and has now landed in the bureaucracy as an expert on road building[35]. While supervising road-building in Kentucky[36] he found his wife[37] who I gather is about 10 years or so his junior. He married her[38] when she was 23 and they tried for 15 years to have children. Her trouble was fibrous tumors but she was determined to have a child in spite of them and succeeded when she was 38 in giving birth to a fine boy[39] and afterwards had the nasty series of many sized tumors removed. The boy is now seven. I have seen all the pictures. I have heard of a great many of "Jimmy's"[40] virtues. I have even had to assure Mr. Anderson that I didn't think children of 6 or 7 nowadays are any smarter than they were when we were that age. He is inclined to think that his boy proves it. They have built a house in Hartford Connecticut.[41] I know how much it cost and how much the lot cost, and I am led to understand what a superior house it is because Mr. Anderson designed and built it. He wants his boy to go to Union College and to be a contractor or a civil engineer.[42] He teaches him how to play contractor. He is to play on the Varsity and be a thoroughly

[28] 1795 gegründetes College.
[29] Stadt im US-Bundesstaat New York.
[30] Studienbeginn 1906.
[31] Die 1892 gegründete General Electric Company hatte ihren Hauptsitz in Schenectady.
[32] Charles P. Steinmetz (1865–1923), deutsch-amerikanischer Mathematiker und Elektroingenieur, geboren in Breslau, Deutschland, Studium an der Universität Breslau, 1889 Emigration in die USA, war bei der General Electric Company beschäftigt und lehrte Electrical Engineering am Union College.
[33] James Anderson & Sons.
[34] Gemeint ist der Erste Weltkrieg (1914–1918).
[35] Seit 1944 war Anderson bei der US Public Roads Administration, Washington, D. C., beschäftigt.
[36] US-Bundesstaat. Anderson war 1920–1922 in Kentucky als Bauingenieur im öffentlichen Dienst tätig gewesen.
[37] Edith B. Anderson, geb. Bottorff (1899–1994).
[38] Am 12. Juni 1923.
[39] James E. Anderson (geb. 1938), amerikanischer Chemiker, 1960 BS, Union College, Research Chemist, Ford Motor Company. Lebte mit seinen Eltern in Berlin, als sein Vater dort bei OMGUS beschäftigt war: "My father lived by himself in Berlin for approximately 1 year before my mother & I joined him. The 3 of us lived in Berlin for about 1 year." E-Mail von James E. Anderson an Werner Breunig vom 24. Februar 2013. "I attended the American grade school in Berlin-Dahlem." E-Mail von James E. Anderson an Werner Breunig vom 30. Mai 2008.
[40] Gemeint ist Andersons Sohn James.
[41] Anderson kam aus West Hartford, einer Stadt im Hartford County im US-Bundesstaat Connecticut, 479 South Main Street.
[42] Andersons Sohn besuchte später tatsächlich das Union College. Siehe Anm. 39.

"normal" young boy. Mrs. Anderson is a D. A. R.[43] and the boy attends the activities of the C. A. R. (Children of the American Revolution[44]) a new organization to me.[45]

Dok. 10
Schreiben an die Ehefrau
An Bord der „George W. Goethals"[1], 27. Februar 1946

Dearest Emily –

Dinner is over and it is about 5 o' clock. At the table a southerner (Georgia[2]) remarked: "That's one thing I like about Joe Lewis[3]. He's a nigger; he knows it and doesn't try to get out of his place." There are too many southerners aboard. One, who I understand is cracked since he enjoys nothing more than to repeat over and over again his war experiences, is a cocoa-cola expert. When I first went over in June 1944[4] there were cocoa-cola experts on board. Did I tell you the story told by one of them that the founder of the C-C Company[5] once took aboard his yacht a lady named Dubauchee[6]. In a fit of the grand passion this

---

[43] Daughters of the American Revolution, eine Vereinigung von Nachfahren der Veteranen des amerikanischen Unabhängigkeitskriegs (1775–1783), die Patriotismus und Geschichtsbewusstsein fördern will. "The National Society Daughters of the American Revolution was founded on October 11, 1890, during a time that was marked by a revival in patriotism and intense interest in the beginnings of the United States of America. Women felt the desire to express their patriotic feelings and were frustrated by their exclusion from men's organizations formed to perpetuate the memory of ancestors who fought to make this country free and independent. As a result, a group of pioneering women in the nation's capital formed their own organization and the Daughters of the American Revolution has carried the torch of patriotism ever since." http://www.dar.org/natsociety/history.cfm (letzter Zugriff am 30. Januar 2013).

[44] Eine patriotische Vereinigung, 1895 von der Kinderbuchautorin Harriett M. Lothrop, geb. Stone (1844–1924) als Kinder- und Jugendlichenverband der Daughters of the American Revolution ins Leben gerufen.

[45] Johnson verzichtete auf eine Schlussformel, weil er die an Bord geschriebenen Briefe gesammelt abschicken wollte.

[1] Siehe Dok. 7, Anm. 18.
[2] US-Bundesstaat.
[3] Gemeint ist Joe Louis, eigentl. Joseph Louis Barrow (1914–1981), amerikanischer Profiboxer, 1937–1949 Boxweltmeister im Schwergewicht, 1942–1945 US Army, wurde als positives Gegenbeispiel zu dem früheren schwarzen Boxweltmeister Jack Johnson (1878–1946) aufgebaut, um Anfeindungen des „weißen Amerika" zu vermeiden. "[...] his behavior was dignified and friendly at all times. He thereby avoided antagonizing white people, as the earlier heavyweight champion Jack Johnson had [...]." Luckett V. Davis, Louis, Joe, in: American National Biography, Bd. 13, New York und Oxford 1999, S. 942–944, hier S. 944.
[4] Siehe Dok. 2, Anm. 9.
[5] Gründer der Coca-Cola Company war Asa G. Candler (1851–1929), 1916–1919 Bürgermeister von Atlanta, Georgia.
[6] Onezima de Bouchel, "member of an old Louisiana family, and New Orleans society leader". The Atlanta Constitution vom 18. Februar 1923, S. 1.

president Chandler[7] bit off one of the nipples on Madame Dubauchee's breasts. She sued the old rake in a Georgia court,[8] and to convince the jury she hauled out her breast and exhibited the oral mutilation. There is a conspiracy among the southerners aboard this boat to show that every colored unit in the army disgraced itself. We ought to take a trip through the south some summer. It could give us a better picture of this land of ours. My picture at present is a little jaded.

This morning I got up and closed the door of our cabin to shut out the noise of the radio. This left the cabin quite dark. One of the southerners in our cabin awoke later with a start and a yell. He had been drinking considerably yesterday, and thought for a moment when he could not see anything upon awakening, that he had been blinded by the liquor he had consumed. This in fact was why I didn't write yesterday. Our cabin was the scene of a pretty continuous party from about three o' clock on. The room I usually escape to has been closed in order to prepare it for a nursery on the return trip. The other so-called lounge cannot be used as a writing place. To watch the younger generation amuse itself is very discouraging. One of the ladies at the party yesterday was a young girl from Wisconsin[9] with a husky, whiskey throat who I imagine has drunk more liquor than any of the men in the cabin. She said she was the daughter of a tavern owner in Wisconsin. Her friend at the party was only a little more impressive. What is done is to go up on deck after liquor enough has been consumed for necking. Now from another gentleman in the cabin it was learned that the whiskey belle and her partner suffered from pyrhoea[10] (I can't spell it) and that the gentleman who wished to kiss these girls ought to know what they were about. He wouldn't touch them. And the little Czech boy in the cabin who had kissed one of them last week wondered how long it took for pyrhoea to break out. There must be much that goes on in a boat. We had physical examinations before we left port to check up on shots and contagious diseases. They insisted I have two more shots (the smallpox has taken).[11] But we have to have another physical examination before we get off the boat.

When I tried to escape the party by going upstairs to the so-called lounge I was again discouraged to see how they were amusing themselves. In so far as I could see there were few if any people reading. Nor were there any conversations going on. It was mostly cards. Some adults were playing dominoes. A group were avidly bent on putting together a large jig-saw puzzle. The young

---

[7] Asa G. Candler. Siehe Anm. 5.
[8] De Bouchel verklagte Candler wegen Bruchs des Eheversprechens und verlangte eine finanzielle Entschädigung in Höhe von 500 000 US-Dollar. Am 5. Februar 1924 wurde ein Urteil zugunsten von Candler gefällt. Siehe The New York Times vom 11. Oktober 1922, S. 1 und 7, vom 12. Oktober 1922, S. 1f., vom 13. Oktober 1922, S. 18, vom 14. Oktober 1922, S. 13, vom 15. Oktober 1922, S. 25, vom 27. Oktober 1922, S. 8, vom 18. Februar 1923, S. 1, vom 13. März 1923, S. 3, vom 21. Juni 1923, S. 19, vom 31. Januar 1924, S. 6, vom 1. Februar 1924, S. 3, vom 2. Februar 1924, S. 3, vom 3. Februar 1924, S. 22, vom 5. Februar 1924, S. 11, vom 6. Februar 1924, S. 21. Siehe auch Kathryn W. Kemp, God's Capitalist. Asa Candler of Coca-Cola, Macon, Georgia, 2002, S. 253–272.
[9] US-Bundesstaat.
[10] Gemeint ist wahrscheinlich „gonorrhoea" (Gonorrhö).
[11] Siehe Dok. 7 und Dok. 7, Anm. 19.

people do not seem to talk to each other. They sit, listen to radio, yip through a popular song, pass a wise crack – nothing else. Then they go on deck for a little loving – something like a night-cap. I wonder if they are as empty headed as they seem. Mr. Anderson[12] was also horrified by it all (I learn that he is 58[13]) and said that the cause and remedy for it all was the family. And indeed of these young people are typical it is the obligation of some of us who feel some responsibility in the matter to have more children. I am not trying to engage in propaganda. Yet in addition to the problem of the German youth who are empty-headed and evil by indoctrinated there is also the problem of American youth who are empty-headed and aimless.[14]

Dok. 11
Schreiben an die Ehefrau
An Bord der „George W. Goethals"[1], 28. Februar 1946

My sweet darling –

The end of a month. I did not think I should be returning in three months.[2] I sometimes wonder if you have changed your mind to any degree about my returning. You have never said anything. Tomorrow is the last day of the voyage. The gulls have rejoined us and there are poking schooners in some number. Breton I suppose. We disembark at Le Havre[3] on Saturday[4] morning, I understand. I suppose they will get us off to Paris by Sunday[5] but what happens from then on nobody seems to know.

I wrote a letter to Henry[6] yesterday about a successor to Harold V[edeler][7].[8] I suggested they try to get Gene Anderson[9] or Paul Sweet[10]. I don't think Gene really wants to come out our way but I do think there is a possibility of getting Paul if they act quickly. I also mentioned, without going into any detail that I was not particularly happy about R[udy]'s[11] coming back.[12] I thought I ought to say this much to confirm Henry's suspicions. I took a strong stand, too, against

---

12   Siehe Dok. 9, Anm. 8.
13   Geboren am 14. August 1887.
14   Johnson verzichtete auf eine Schlussformel. Siehe Dok. 9, Anm. 45.

1   Siehe Dok. 7, Anm. 18.
2   Johnson war Ende November 1945 aus Europa in die USA zurückgekehrt, drei Monate später kam er nach Europa zurück.
3   Französische Hafenstadt an der Atlantikküste.
4   2. März 1946.
5   3. März 1946.
6   Charles Henry Oldfather. Siehe Dok. 2, Anm. 19.
7   Siehe Dok. 2, Anm. 12.
8   Vedeler wollte nicht an die University of Nebraska zurückkehren. Siehe Dok. 2.
9   Eugene N. Anderson. Siehe Dok. 1, Anm. 1.
10   Siehe Dok. 2, Anm. 28.
11   Rudolph A. Winnacker. Siehe Dok. 2, Anm. 20.
12   Johnson ging davon aus, dass Winnacker an die University of Nebraska zurückkehren wollte. Siehe Dok. 2.

introducing Ginzburg[13] into the department as a teacher of Russian history, saying that I did not think the history department ought to become the graveyard of a dying classicism. It was a good letter, however, and I don't think Henry will mind my being frank. He has much to answer for as a result of some of the decisions he has made as dean. You know, when I stop to think of it, he has not one outstanding accomplishment to his credit. Oh yes, Senning[14] was demoted and Ray[15] made chairman of the English department.

I finished the desultory Antic Hay[16] and was almost ready to shriek when I finished. There is not one half way decent person in the book except the old father architect who does finally do a good deed at the very end of the novel. Madame Myra Viveash[17] was so thoroughly bored throughout the book that I don't believe I can ever use the word bore again or have any patience with anyone who is bored. There is a riot of fornication and adultery of various kinds and degrees. It is a thoroughly rotten society he depicts, and I hope we are not descending to the same. Huxley wields a clever and sophisticated pen, and from these depths it is not surprising that he has swung to Indian theosophy. I should like now to read Ends and Means[18] (wasn't that the title?) to see how he made the swing. There are some foreshadowings of Point Counter Point[19] in the literary critic Mr. Mercaptan[20], and in the artist Lypiatt[21]. There is one passage of considerable satisfaction on advertising – the American brand. But, on the whole, the book leaves nothing but a bad taste in one's mouth.

This is getting to be a very tedious voyage. Everyone is feeling it and if it lasted much longer there would be an outburst of drunkenness, fornication or simply irritability.

Dr. Rheinstein[22] told me today that American authorities in Berlin had arrested the assistant Bürgermeister[23] and some of his entourage for a minor and

[13] Michael S. Ginsburg (1902–1982), amerikanischer Altphilologe, 1924 LLD, Universität Petrograd, 1929 DLitt, Universität Paris, lehrte ab 1931 an der University of Nebraska, 1943–1947 beurlaubt, 1945–1947 Chief, Internal Political Section, USSR Division, Office of Research and Intelligence, Department of State, 1947–1966 Professor, Indiana University, Director, Department of Slavic Studies.
[14] John P. Senning (1884–1954), amerikanischer Politikwissenschaftler, 1924 PhD, University of Illinois, 1916–1952 Professor, University of Nebraska, zeitweise Chairman, Department of Political Science.
[15] Ray W. Frantz (1898–1976), amerikanischer Neuphilologe, 1930 PhD, University of Chicago, ab 1929 University of Nebraska, Professor of English (Chairman of Department).
[16] Roman (deutsch „Narrenreigen") aus dem Jahre 1923 von Aldous Huxley (1894–1963), englischer Schriftsteller, der von 1937 bis zu seinem Tod in den USA lebte.
[17] Romanfigur in Antic Hay.
[18] Philosophische Schrift von Aldous Huxley aus dem Jahre 1937.
[19] Roman von Aldous Huxley aus dem Jahre 1928 (deutsch „Kontrapunkt des Lebens").
[20] Romanfigur in Antic Hay.
[21] Casimir Lypiatt, Romanfigur in Antic Hay.
[22] Max Rheinstein (1899–1977), deutsch-amerikanischer Jurist, geboren in Bad Kreuznach, Deutschland, 1924 Dr. jur., Universität München, 1925 zweites juristisches Examen, ab 1926 Bibliothekar und Forschungsassistent, Kaiser-Wilhelm-Institut für ausländisches und internationales Privatrecht, Berlin, ab 1928 Mitglied der SPD, 1932/1933 Privatdozent, Universität Berlin, kam 1933 mit einem Stipendium der

unwarranted offense and actually mistreated them. He referred also to the fact that the M[ilitary] G[overnment] authorities in Bavaria[24] have refused to let the recent pastoral letter of the Catholic bishops of Germany[25] circulate because 1) the bishops demanded the return of their denominational schools when they were in no position to demand anything and 2) the bishops ventured opinions on marriage and divorce which were uncalled for, there being an international rather than a German institution.[26] He also mentioned our M[ilitary] G[overnment] officers summoning Minister President Höggner[27] of Bavaria to their offices five and six times a day and keeping him waiting for long stretches at a time. We don't know how to treat the people whom we have asked to cooperate with us. General Truscott[28], (he has taken Patton's[29] place) has issued an order commanding American troops in his area to respect the German authorities. There seems to be room for Americans with a bit of sense.

I think much of you beloved, much more than you suspect. I send you all my love to you and our sweet boys. Edgar

Rockefeller-Stiftung in die USA, blieb 1935 nach Ablauf des Stipendiums in den USA, 1935–1968 Professor, University of Chicago, 1940 US-Staatsbürgerschaft, 1945–1947 Mitarbeiter der Legal Division, OMGUS.

[23] Gemeint sein könnte ein Stellvertreter des Oberbürgermeisters oder ein stellvertretender Bezirksbürgermeister.

[24] Land in der amerikanischen Besatzungszone Deutschlands.

[25] Gemeint ist der Fuldaer Hirtenbrief vom 23. August 1945, der erste gemeinsame Hirtenbrief der deutschen katholischen Bischöfe nach dem Krieg. Abgedruckt in: Hirtenbriefe und Ansprachen zu Gesellschaft und Politik 1945–1949, bearb. von Wolfgang Löhr (= Dokumente deutscher Bischöfe, Bd. I), Würzburg 1985, S. 40–45.

[26] Der Chief Publications Officer in Bayern hatte die Abänderung des Fuldaer Hirtenbriefs in drei Passagen verlangt. Dies verursachte einen ernsthaften Konflikt mit Michael Kardinal von Faulhaber (1869–1952), Erzbischof von München und Freising, der auf einer vollständigen, unzensierten Veröffentlichung des Hirtenbriefs bestand. Erst durch die Intervention eines Religious-Affairs-Officers von OMGUS konnte der Hirtenbrief schließlich in ganz Bayern am Sonntag vor Weihnachten verlesen werden. Siehe Bernhard Lehmann, Katholische Kirche und Besatzungsmacht in Bayern 1945–1949 im Spiegel der OMGUS-Akten (= Miscellanea Bavarica Monacensia. Dissertationen zur Bayerischen Landes- und Münchner Stadtgeschichte, Bd. 153), München 1994, S. 166. Zu den inhaltlichen Aspekten, um die es bei der verlangten Abänderung des Fuldaer Hirtenbriefs ging, siehe ebd., S. 419, Anm. 67. Marshall Knappen (siehe Dok. 8, Anm. 10) berichtet in seinem Buch "And call it peace", Chicago 1947, S. 103, von "the unfortunate effort of an information control officer at Munich to censor the pastoral letter adopted by the Fulda Conference".

[27] Wilhelm Hoegner (1887–1980), deutscher Politiker (SPD), 1911 Dr. jur., 1930–1933 MdR, 1933 Emigration nach Österreich, 1934 in die Schweiz, 1945/1946 und 1954–1957 Ministerpräsident des Landes Bayern, 1961/1962 MdB.

[28] Lucian K. Truscott Jr. (1895–1965), Lieutenant General, 1945/1946 Commanding General 3rd Army and Eastern Military District of the US Occupation Zone of Germany.

[29] George S. Patton Jr. (1885–1945), General, 1909 Absolvent der United States Military Academy, 1944/1945 Commanding General 3rd Army, 1945 Commanding General, Eastern Military District of the US Occupation Zone of Germany. Patton war von seinem Kommando über die 3. Armee und den Eastern Military District abgelöst worden, nachdem er im September 1945 den Eindruck erweckt hatte, er stelle die Nationalsozialisten mit den Republikanern und Demokraten in den USA auf eine Stufe.

Dok. 12
Schreiben an die Ehefrau
An Bord der „George W. Goethals"[1], 1. März 1946

Dearest Emily –

This is the last long evening aboard this ship. Inasmuch as they are painting the exterior of the ship for the benefit of the war brides (who, I understand now) are to be French instead of English, we are practically restricted to these dull cabins where much unwanted conversation is forced on one. The conversation last evening centered around the number of hours that would have to be worked abroad, and the rate of pay for over-time.

I have been thinking the last couple of days, since thinking is so cheap, what are the things we must aim to accomplish, before we reach the stage where it is impossible to accomplish anything. The chief ones seem to me to be:

1. Security for you in case of my death.
2. Proper education for the boys[2] until the time when they are able to take care of themselves.
3. A piano for John[3].
4. A place in the mountains where we can spend our summers.[4]
5. A trip around the world with the boys when they are old enough to profit by it.

4 and 5 are I suppose unnecessary but who will deny that they are very desirable?

If I ask how this is to be accomplished I cannot say whether best in Lincoln[5] or elsewhere but I have the feeling that to get it all it will have to planned for, worked hard for and saved for. With one we have made a beginning with the new additional insurance which we will continue. But it will have to be increased by that much again if you are to be adequately secure for in the normal course of events you will live at least ten more years than I. For 2. I imagine we should already be beginning to build up as much surplus as we can, though there is every reason to believe that the boys can do much to help themselves. We are agreed that 3 should be the result of the surplus which comes out of my being in the government. If I do not go into a job when there is higher remuneration than at Nebraska[6], then at Nebraska I shall have to spend some time in writing some textbooks which will take much time and effort. But it would be nice to plan and achieve 4 and 5. Is there anything wrong with this honey? It

---

[1] Siehe Dok. 7, Anm. 18.
[2] Gemeint sind die Söhne John und Thomas. Siehe Dok. 2, Anm. 15 und 16.
[3] Sohn John. Siehe Dok. 2, Anm. 15.
[4] Die Johnsons erwarben 1951 ein Grundstück mit Ferienhütte in Allenspark im US-Bundesstaat Colorado, am östlichen Rand des Rocky Mountain National Park und am Fuße des Longs Peak (siehe Dok. 67, Anm. 52). Sie kauften es Ellen D. Raysor, geb. Koopman (1898-1995) und Thomas M. Raysor (1895-1974), Professor für Englisch an der University of Nebraska, ab.
[5] Hauptstadt des US-Bundesstaats Nebraska, wo Johnson mit seiner Familie wohnte und an der Universität lehrte.
[6] Gemeint ist die University of Nebraska.

ought to be possible to figure it out in monetary terms and to calculate the amount we shall have to be saving in the coming years.

I love you very much sweetheart and I am very lonesome for you and the boys. I am prepared to be for many months to come. I noticed in the ship's bulletin today that a certain Mrs. Schuyler[7] and her son[8] are on board, bound for Bucharest[9] where General Schuyler[10] is the American member of the control council[11].[12] So the wives and children are beginning to move over. I shall make inquiry as soon as I can. It would be tempting to promise to stay over here just in order to bring you and the children over. Much travel in Europe and German could be learned in this time. But we should have to be certain about what to do afterwards. We shall have to be careful not to be tempted by money alone. Sometimes I think that that is what I am doing. Yet that is not fair.

Goodnight my sweet and lovely Emily and good-night to my boys. I love you all very very much. I shall do my best. Without you this voyage, as indeed all other times would have been much more desultory. When I think of you I am happy. I know what I have to come back to. Edgar

Dok. 13
Schreiben an die Ehefrau
Le Havre[1], 5. März 1946

Dearest and beloved –

It has been too dispiriting to write the last couple days. Soon after I left I began to get into the attitude of the GI[2] that there is no point in concerning yourself about anything, simply let the army do it. I'm pretty well confirmed in this

[7] Wynona C. Schuyler, geb. Coykendall (1902–1981).
[8] Philip V. R. Schuyler (geb. 1932).
[9] Hauptstadt Rumäniens.
[10] Cortlandt V. R. Schuyler (1900–1993), Brigadier General, 1922 Absolvent der United States Military Academy, 1944–1947 US Military Chief, Allied Control Command Romania, 1953–1959 Chief of Staff, Supreme Headquarters Allied Powers Europe.
[11] Alliierte Kontrollkommission für Rumänien, bestand aus Vertretern der Sowjetunion, USA und Großbritanniens, "was to control the process of fulfilling the terms of the cease-fire". http://ww2.debello.ca/balkans/transylvania/index.html (letzter Zugriff am 30. Januar 2013).
[12] Philip V. R. Schuyler, der 13 Jahre alt war, als er mit seiner Mutter zu einem 15-monatigen Aufenthalt nach Europa reiste, schreibt in einer E-Mail an Werner Breunig vom 8. Februar 2008: "My mother, Wynona Coykendall Schuyler, and I traveled to Europe aboard the 'George W. Goethals' in the spring of 1946, to join my father in Romania. We were among the first – possibly *the* first – family dependents to join American service personnel in Europe after the war." Die Schiffsreise war natürlich ein großes Abenteuer für den 13-jährigen Jungen, "especially as I was the only youngster aboard [...]. I spent much time on the crossing chatting with members of the crew and was able to learn much about the Merchant Marine (the ship was a U. S. Army vessel but it was operated by the U. S. Merchant Marine)." E-Mail vom 6. März 2008.

[1] Französische Hafenstadt an der Atlantikküste.
[2] Government Issue, ugs. für amerikanischer Soldat.

attitude now. In its destruction of initiative the Army is really a vicious institution.

We arrived in the bay of Le Havre on Saturday[3] night expecting to disembark on Sunday[4] morning fairly well pleased with the voyage, which, after all, had not been unpleasant if exceeding tedious, days passing out of your life almost unaccounted for. I had begun to read a collection of short stories, "Seven Gothic Tales" by one Sak Dinesèn[5], a pseudonym. It was a stormy day and the sea was rough. Later on in the day we learned that s. e.[6] England and France had had storms more severe than for a long time. We learned after breakfast that we would not disembark that day. The reasons? The same reasons for the cancellation of the flight from Washington. Nobody seemed to know or if they did they didn't inform us. This is bad psychology, keeping people uninformed and leads to the speedy propagation of rumors. It was too rough for the pilot to get on board, there was no space for our ship in the harbor, a tanker was sunk across the harbor's entrance, Le Havre was on fire, since no-body worked on Sunday, we wouldn't be able to get off on Sunday! Monday[7] was a French holiday so we wouldn't get off then. You can imagine the effect of this. We spent a dull and listless day wondering about our fate, rocking up and down, to and fro at anchor.

As a matter of fact we did get off early yesterday afternoon. There was a sunk tanker just outside the harbor, and Le Havre, if not burning was badly destroyed. None of the regular piers was functioning. The center of the town was a waste-land dominated by huge piles of bricks which the French are using for re-building. There is some re-building going on. Everyone expected, of course, that it would be known that we are coming and that ships would be taken to get us on our way quickly.

Instead, after disembarking at a temporary pier, we were taken in trucks to one of these embarkation camps for GI's – Home Run[8], supposedly a camp for

[3] 2. März 1946.
[4] 3. März 1946.
[5] Karen Blixen, geb. Dinesen, eigentl. Baronin Karen von Blixen-Finecke, Pseudonym Isak Dinesen (1885–1962), dänische Schriftstellerin. Mit "Seven Gothic Tales" (deutsch „Die Sintflut von Norderney und andere seltsame Geschichten" bzw. „Sieben phantastische Geschichten"), in den USA erstmals 1934 erschienen, wurde sie auf einen Schlag berühmt.
[6] Southeast.
[7] 4. März 1946.
[8] Benannt nach der amerikanischen Zigarettenmarke "Home Run" (Hersteller: Liggett & Myers Tobacco Co., Durham, North Carolina). "Once France had been liberated, the U. S. Army established a series of camps just outside of the harbor city of Le Havre. Each was named after a popular American cigarette of the period, primarily for security reasons: Lucky Strike, Old Gold, Philip Morris, Twenty Grand, and Chesterfield, among others. In 1944–45, the camps were essentially depots for new arrivals bound for the front lines bordering the West Wall (the 'Siegfried Line'). These replacements were desperately needed to bring the American divisions being bloodied in places like the Hürtgen Forest, the Saar, and, later, the Bulge. After V-E day, they were transformed into way stations for men returning home. Like the cigarettes they were named after, they were a pleasant diversion from war no matter how short-lived, though the men who spent time there going in either direction certainly cursed them at the time." The Cigarette Camps. The U. S. Army Camps in the Le Havre Area, http://www.skylighters.org/special/cigcamps/ (letzter Zugriff am 30. Januar 2013).

élite and top-priority people on the way home. In the harbor as we came away were several ships loaded with GI's and on the way off the pier dozens of trucks drew up carrying hundreds upon hundreds of GI's who rushed for the boats. That there were people coming back to this place after the war, these people could not understand. May be as a GI said in our cell last night it was because "this working for the government is a swell racket". I wondered how they would find the USA they were coming back to, whether they would find jobs, and whether they would be lost.

At the camp we put through the same routine as anyone else. We had first to go for blankets, and then be assigned to a bunk in one of the long cone like cells into which this old fort is divided. The fort I understand was built sometime in the early 19th century. Maybe there were a hundred 2 decker beds in the cell. It was pretty dirty. Latrines and washing facilities were a considerable distance away. It was a return to war conditions and for civilians who had not been through it somewhat discouraging. Indeed I don't think that the Army can attract many first class civilians to its service under these conditions.

I tried to get permission to telephone Frankfurt[9] but couldn't. There was nothing-to-do but sit and wait until we were told to get on a train for Paris. The big shots on board the boat had gotten off to Paris yesterday – the Lt. Cols. and Cols. The Military attaché[10] from Bern[11] had driven up from Switzerland to get his wife but the roads were so bad that he was going back with them by train.[12] Why couldn't we get off too? Why did we have to wait more than 24 hours? Wasn't there more than one train a day from Le Havre to Paris? No one seemed to know or if so there was no one who thought it worthwhile to tell us. It was just that way – thrown again into the huge mill of transporting people. Maybe completely totalitarian society is like this or may be it's only bureaucracy or may be only the army – I don't know.

After fixing my bed for the night, three blankets over 2 straw mattresses, I went out to the ramparts of this port and got a good view of this harbor with the Seine[13] flowing into the Atlantic at one side of it. The Nazis had heavily refortified it – concrete pill-boxes and gun emplacements at the corners and concrete passage-ways just beneath the top of the ramparts themselves. After this it was about time to go to eat. We are not allowed in the officers' mess being civilians and obliged to pay for our meals (25 cents). But the food was decent enough. A much dissipated-looking, boggy-eyed WAC[14] (sergeant) sat in front of me and ate in a listless fashion. It was estimated by one lady on the boat that about 30 % of the women on board were pregnant as a result of their experiences on the voyage.

---

[9] Frankfurt am Main, Stadt im Land Groß-Hessen in der amerikanischen Besatzungszone Deutschlands.
[10] Siehe Dok. 9, Anm. 14.
[11] Hauptstadt der Schweiz.
[12] Siehe Dok. 9.
[13] Fluss, der bei Le Havre in den Ärmelkanal mündet.
[14] Member of the Women's Army Corps (weibliche Hilfskraft des US-Heeres). Siehe Wacs Mark Fourth Year, in: OMGUS Observer vom 17. Mai 1946, S. 3.

After dinner I retreated to what is called the Day-Room supplied with music by an orchestra of German PW's[15]. The camp is kept up by them. Their barracks are alongside of the camps within a brushed wire enclosure. A watch-tower looks after them. The PW camp is next to the cemetery of Le Havre, perhaps a symbolic place for it. The Day-Room was full of GI's, most of them very pale and dirty who were going to Paris on a night train. They had a radio full blast. The library in the Day-Room was especially good and I pulled out T. H. Benton's[16] Account of America[17], which had not been signed out before and got a few chapters of it read before returning to the cell. Good reading, hard on the "parvenu" spirit of the middle-west which crowds out aesthetic expression. But Benton must be a very difficult man and some of the compromises he made to get along in the world were indeed very shady and he tosses them off very easily. The GI's left for their Paris train and went to the cell.

Sleeping in one of the beds was a thirteen-year old boy – pale-dirty, ragged and with one eye. It was said that he lost his eye on D-day[18]. Nobody seemed to know who his parents were – some said they were Danish; some said the father was English. In any case he did not know anything about his parents. Possibly they were foreign workers brought by the Germans to work in France. He had been with American soldiers since the landing in Normandy and they said had fought the whole war with them. His buddies left by boat yesterday. He was being cared for by a sailor who was going to try to get him aboard a boat today and take him to New York where he is supposed to have an uncle. It is uncertain whether he can get aboard. He seems to live on cookies and candy-bars. Why he isn't in the hands of responsible people and being taken care of, I don't know. The Red Cross evidently doesn't want to take him over. How many of these orphans are astray in Europe!

We were kept from going to sleep by a conversation of GI's which made me pretty sick. It is no longer amusing to hear God-damn, fucking, cock-sucker, and son-of-a-bitch interlarded into a conversation as every other word. There is much for youth-leaders in America to do. Finally I got to sleep on my medieval mattress.

On boat the last day there was a grand half-hour listening to C. Franck's Violin and Piano Sonata[19]. But it was turned off for something else. Later I heard a Bach[20] Prelude and Fugue being played. It was turned off for something else.

In one of the stories in "Seven Gothic Tales" there is the sentence: "I believe that this feeling of safety and perfect freedom must be what happily married people mean when they talk about [the] two being one."[21] I am very grateful in

---

15   Prisoners of War, Kriegsgefangene.
16   Thomas H. Benton (1782–1858), amerikanischer Politiker und Autor.
17   Gemeint sein könnte das 1854–1856 erschienene Werk "Thirty years' view. Or A history of the working of the American Government for thirty years, from 1820 to 1850".
18   Am 6. Juni 1944, als die Landung alliierter Truppen in der Normandie begann.
19   Sonate für Violine und Klavier (1886) von César Franck (1822–1890), französischer Komponist und Organist deutsch-belgischer Abstammung.
20   Johann Sebastian Bach (1685–1750), deutscher Komponist des Barock.
21   The Old Chevalier, in: Isak Dinesen, Seven Gothic Tales (Penguin Modern Classics), London u. a. 1988, S. 52–74, hier S. 67f. In der deutschen Übertragung von Thyra Dohrenburg heißt es: „Ich glaube, dies eigentümliche Gefühl von selbstverständlicher Sicherheit und Freiheit ist es, von dem glückliche Eheleute sprechen, wenn sie

these moments, as at all times, for this feeling of safety and perfect freedom. I know quite what is meant. It keeps me balanced here. But I keep wondering why I left you and the children to come back here. Maybe the GI who shouted to us yesterday as he made for the boat "You're crazy to come back here" was right. I love you, love you my sweet beloved. Kiss the boys for me. Edgar

Dok. 14
Schreiben an die Ehefrau
Paris, 5. März 1946

Dearest Emily:

I am sitting in compartment 19/20 of car 3782 of the equivalent of a pullman car (Schlafwagen)[1] which is leaving for Frankfurt[2] at 5:32, if these details interest you. It is, as a matter of fact my first experience with a European pullman car. When John[3] and I were in Europe we always planned to get to a town in order to put up for the night.[4] They are not as well planned as ours. The car is divided into compartments for two, although I notice that, in case adjoining compartments should desire to get together there are means to join. You can see how desirable this might be for some persons under some circumstances. The hot water is supplied from a little coal stove for each car at the end. The cars are heated by means of little steam radiators. There are upper and lower bunks and the two occupiers face in the same direction. There is a lavatory, a mirror, a little writing stand and an ashtray. There is plenty of room for baggage in this particular the planning is better than for an ordinary pullman of ours. I am lucky to be in this pullman and on this train. I take it it is because of my rating since there were some of our party who did not get on the train at all and

den Ausdruck gebrauchen, zwei seien eines." Der alte, wandernde Ritter, in: Tania Blixen, Sieben phantastische Geschichten, Stuttgart 1979, S. 73–100, hier S. 91 f.

[1] Gemeint ist ein Eisenbahnwagen, der nach Bauart der Pullman Palace Car Company hergestellt wurde.
[2] Frankfurt am Main, Stadt im Land Groß-Hessen in der amerikanischen Besatzungszone Deutschlands.
[3] John D. Bickford (1890–1936), amerikanischer Altphilologe und Lehrer, 1914 MA und 1921 PhD, Princeton University, 1914–1917 Instructor, Phillips Exeter Academy, Exeter, New Hampshire, 1920–1927 Culver Military Academy, Culver, Indiana, ab 1928 The Hotchkiss School, Lakeville, Connecticut. Johnson und Bickford hatten 1927 gemeinsam den Aufsatz "The Contemplated Anglo-German Alliance: 1890–1901" veröffentlicht, in: Political Science Quarterly, Vol. 42, No. 1 (März 1927), S. 1–57. 1934 heiratete Bickford Johnsons Schwester Mildred H. Johnson (siehe Dok. 4, Anm. 12).
[4] Bickford und Johnson hatten 1927/1928 an der Universität München studiert und Europa bereist. "Time away from Munich I spent in travel in England, France, Germany, Czecho-Slovakia, Austria, Hungary, Italy and Switzerland", so Edgar N. Johnson, Curriculum Vitae, undatiert [ca. 1963], S. 1, in: UChicago Library, Special Collections Research Center, Edgar N. Johnson Papers.
[5] Control Council. Gemeint ist hier wahrscheinlich die amerikanische Militärregierung für Deutschland, sonst die Alliierte Kontrollbehörde (Allied Control Authority) für Deutschland, die oberste Viermächtebesatzungsbehörde für alle Deutschland als

others, one a new addition to the legal section of the CC[5] (Rosenwald[6]) who had to sit in a chair. (The train is moving now). There were plenty of military about, majors and up, and I heard a major say that he got accommodations only because there was a cancellation. With the human being so rank conscious there are really small chances for real democracy. The man who is in this compartment with me sighed with relief when he entered and remarked "It's certainly good not to be classified with the cattle." He has unfortunately caught a cold in his kidneys, and begged for the lower berth when he entered on account of urination. I found a pot in the compartment which he immediately proceeded to use. But he managed to get some on the floor and some on a piece of his baggage. The offending part of the baggage is now turned to the wall. This reminds me to report, while on the same subject that the cells in which we were billeted in camp Home Run[7] were a long distance from the toilet, so long that a journey outside to a neighboring building was necessary. In order to avoid this one GI[8] or one sailor (I cannot believe it was one of our party) actually defecated in his bed, it was discovered in the morning. This was the thing the Viennese were so furious about concerning the habits of the Russians.

The subject of rank may require new significance in the theatre, I mean military theatre. It is reported by those who come from Germany that the army has just got out an order ordering civilians to take from their clothes all braids and brass buttons that are to be found on a regular officer's uniform. If they try to enter officers' clubs without having done this they are refused entrance. The same is true I suppose for officers' messes also. If this is true I can't imagine it will last. I can't imagine an easier way to wreck an administration than to create a distinction between the officer and civilian class. (6th March – Frankfurt) I'll finish this at length later + mail what I have written, I am leaving for Berlin at 4.35. The people I want to see are there. I had lunch with General Adcock[9] this noon. Among other topics of conversation I learned that the above in re civilian uniform is correct. If I had brought my civilian clothes, I could have worn them.

    Ganzes betreffenden Angelegenheiten, deren oberste Spitze der Kontrollrat (Control Council) war, der aus den vier Militärgouverneuren bestand, die zugleich die Oberbefehlshaber der alliierten Besatzungstruppen waren. Siehe Gunther Mai, Der Alliierte Kontrollrat in Deutschland 1945-1948. Alliierte Einheit – deutsche Teilung? (= Quellen und Darstellungen zur Zeitgeschichte, Bd. 37), München 1995; ders., Alliierter Kontrollrat, in: Deutschland unter alliierter Besatzung 1945-1949/55, hrsg. von Wolfgang Benz, Berlin 1999, S. 229-234.

[6] Henry (Heinz) M. Rosenwald (1905-1978), deutsch-amerikanischer Jurist, geboren in Nürnberg, Deutschland, 1930 Dr. jur., Universität Erlangen, Rechtsanwalt in Nürnberg, büßte 1933 seine 1932 verliehene Zulassung ein, 1934 Emigration nach Italien, nach erneutem Jurastudium mit anschließender Promotion Rechtsanwalt in Mailand, 1939 USA, dort neuerliches Jurastudium mit Abschluss 1943, arbeitete in Anwaltskanzlei, 1946/1947 für die US-Militärregierung in Berlin tätig, ab 1948 in einem US-Patentanwaltsbüro, bei einer Bank und in der Rechtsabteilung eines Lebensmittelkonzerns beschäftigt.

[7] Camp Home Run in Le Havre. Siehe Dok. 13, Anm. 8.

[8] Government Issue, ugs. für amerikanischer Soldat.

[9] Clarence L. Adcock (1895-1967), Major General, Oktober 1945-März 1946 Chief, OMGUSZ, ab April 1946 Assistant Deputy Military Governor for Operations and Deputy to the Commanding General, OMGUS, 1947-1949 US Chairman, Bipartite Control Office (BICO), Frankfurt am Main.

The General took pains to inform me of the change though I hope he was not embarrassed to take me to lunch with a quasi-military uniform.

I am sort of hoping there will be mail in Berlin in case the 25th Base Post Office[10] is in Berlin.[11] In any case I love you very much – dear Sweetheart. Kiss the boys for me, I'll go over now + write some on the train. Edgar

Dok. 15
Schreiben an die Ehefrau
Berlin, Ihnestraße 14[1], 7. März 1946

Dearest Emily –

I didn't write on the train last night because I was obliged to talk with a military government officer from Karlsruhe[2] (Borter) who is working in Public Welfare. It was not exciting conversation. The boy grew up in Chicago, has a high school education, went to New York and got into welfare work, and then into the regular army from which he transferred to military government. He had a broad New York accent – dees for this, etc., and he has acquired a violent dislike for the German character mixed with a certain amount of sympathy for the actual sufferings of the German people which he is afraid to show because he thinks the Germans interpret sympathy as a sign of weakness and he doesn't want to be weak. What he really wants to do is to go back to Pensacola[3] Florida, where he was for a couple of years and where people are friendly and there is good fishing. He finds it hard to make friends in New York.

---

[10] Siehe Dok. 4.
[11] Das 25. Base Post Office befand sich nicht in Berlin, sondern in Würzburg im Land Bayern in der amerikanischen Besatzungszone Deutschlands.

[1] Die ehemalige Dienstvilla des Generaldirektors der Kaiser-Wilhelm-Gesellschaft zur Förderung der Wissenschaften in der Ihnestraße 14 (heute Brümmerstraße 74), Berlin-Dahlem, war Edgar N. Johnsons erste Unterkunft in Berlin. Er hatte hier ein Zimmer, das er bis zu seinem Umzug in das Wannsee Hotel (siehe Dok. 25, Anm. 9) Ende März 1946 bewohnte. Die Generaldirektorenvilla war im Sommer 1925 nach Plänen des Münchener Architekten Carl Sattler (1877–1966) errichtet worden und wurde bis 1938 von Friedrich Glum (siehe Dok. 66, Anm. 20) bewohnt, der das Haus nach seinem von den Nationalsozialisten erzwungenen Ausscheiden aus dem Amt des Generaldirektors verlassen musste. Anschließend bezog es sein Nachfolger Ernst Telschow (1889–1988), der hier bis zur Übersiedlung der Generalverwaltung nach Göttingen im Jahre 1945 wohnte. Heute beherbergt das Haus Mitarbeiter aus verschiedenen Max-Planck-Instituten. Siehe Eckart Henning/Marion Kazemi, Dahlem – Domäne der Wissenschaft. Ein Spaziergang zu den Berliner Instituten der Kaiser-Wilhelm-/Max-Planck-Gesellschaft im „deutschen Oxford" (= Veröffentlichungen aus dem Archiv der Max-Planck-Gesellschaft, Bd. 16/I), 4., erw. und aktualisierte Auflage, Berlin 2009, S. 68–70. Foto der Villa im Bildanhang, Abb. 42.
[2] Stadt im Land Württemberg-Baden in der amerikanischen Besatzungszone Deutschlands.
[3] Stadt im US-Bundesstaat Florida.
[4] Frankfurt am Main, Stadt im Land Groß-Hessen in der amerikanischen Besatzungszone Deutschlands.

At Frankfurt[4] yesterday I found that Walter Dorn[5] was in Berlin, and that Dr. J. K. Pollock[6] was in Berlin. General Adcock[7] invited me to lunch as I mentioned[8] and there was sherry before lunch. I detected nothing particularly wrong in the atmosphere. The General seemed to assume that I would be going to Stuttgart[9] to take the job that I was offered, spoke of the elegant quarters that Dr. Pollock had set up in Stuttgart and that I would inherit, etc., etc., talked a good deal about the importance of this Länderrat[10] until I was rather perked up.[11] It was going to be as I believed or had been led to believe that it was going to be.

This feeling of coming to do an important job was built up today in the way I was treated by the officials who get you processed. I went to the visitors' bureau for various kinds of cards and passes; I went to the personnel office where I was treated as a VIP (very important person). I learned however that I cannot receive more than 10,000 dollars in government employ. I also learned that the allotment slip I made out in Omaha[12] was inadequately filled out.[13] They cabled from here a cancellation of it and made out a new one. I am alloting to you 600 a month, and keeping $ 116.92 for myself. This is based on the following:

Base pay			673.08	
25 % differential[14]			96.15	($1/_{13}$ of 10,000 – 8750).
			769.23	You will get your first
From which is				allotment around April 15th.
substracted:				Thereafter soon after the
	13.85	Quarters		1st of the month.
	38.46	Retirement		
	$ 52.31			
			52.31	
			$ 716.92	

[5] Siehe Dok. 2, Anm. 10.
[6] James K. Pollock (1898–1968), amerikanischer Politikwissenschaftler, 1925 PhD, Harvard University, lehrte ab 1925 an der University of Michigan (ab 1934 als Full Professor), 1945–Januar 1946 Chief, Civil Administration Branch, Internal Affairs and Communications Division, OMGUS, 1945–August 1946 Leiter des RGCO, OMGUS, April 1946 förmlich zum Direktor des RGCO bestellt, lehrte anschließend wieder an der University of Michigan (bis 1968), wiederholt Berater für OMGUS bzw. den United States High Commissioner for Germany, 1955–1958 President, International Political Science Association. Siehe Bildanhang, Abb. 20 und Abb. 21.
[7] Siehe Dok. 14, Anm. 9.
[8] Siehe Dok. 14.
[9] Hauptstadt des Landes Württemberg-Baden in der amerikanischen Besatzungszone Deutschlands.
[10] Im Oktober 1945 war in Stuttgart der Länderrat errichtet worden, in dem die Regierungschefs der Länder der amerikanischen Besatzungszone Deutschlands zusammenarbeiteten, um eine gewisse Einheitlichkeit der deutschen Verwaltungstätigkeit oberhalb der Länderebene zu sichern. Siehe Sebastian Lamm, Länderrat (US-Zone), in: Deutschland unter alliierter Besatzung 1945–1949/55, hrsg. von Wolfgang Benz, Berlin 1999, S. 281–283.
[11] Siehe Dok. 2, Anm. 11. Pollock wurde im April 1946 förmlich zum Direktor des RGCO bestellt und übte das Amt bis August 1946 aus.
[12] Stadt im US-Bundesstaat Nebraska, nordöstlich von Johnsons Wohnort Lincoln.
[13] Siehe Dok. 5.
[14] Auslandszulage.

When I went to the billeting office they treated me as a VIP and put me, not in the ordinary hotel but in a room in a very nice house[15] reserved for special guests. This was the result of some telephone calls.

I met Walter Dorn and Dr. J. K. Pollock on the way back from lunch at the Harnack House[16]. Walter seemed glad to see me but I thought I detected a bit of coldness in Dr. Pollock. I said I wanted to see them both and Pollock said he was going back to Stuttgart on Saturday[17]. This did not seem too strange to me, although I wondered a bit. Pollock and I in Stuttgart? It could only be that he would be there for a short time until I got initiated into my job.

After going to my billet and getting cleaned up, a bath with plenty of warm water, I set out to find General Clay[18]. I was told to go to a Colonel Heastie[19] who turned out to be General Millburn's[20] (Chief of Staff) secretary. The Colonel was out but the General was in and I asked to see him. He was very friendly and said that General Clay would certainly want to see me but that he was for the moment in a meeting of the Coordination Committee[21]. We went to Clay's office and I got an appointment for 9:30 tomorrow morning. Walter Dorn has an appointment for 9:00 from what Millburn said to me I became a little more worried. Pollock was going back to Stuttgart. He was going home during the summer. Certainly there must be some overlapping of work at Stuttgart. I could

---

[15] Ihnestraße 14. Siehe Anm. 1.
[16] Ihnestraße 16, Berlin-Dahlem, wenige Schritte von Edgar N. Johnsons Unterkunft, Ihnestraße 14 (siehe Anm. 1), entfernt. Das von dem Münchener Architekten Carl Sattler (siehe Anm. 1) entworfene, am 7. Mai 1929 eingeweihte Harnack-Haus, benannt nach dem protestantischen Theologen und Kirchenhistoriker Adolf von Harnack (1851-1930), erster Präsident der 1911 in Berlin gegründeten Kaiser-Wilhelm-Gesellschaft zur Förderung der Wissenschaften, hatte der Kaiser-Wilhelm-Gesellschaft als Vortrags- und Begegnungszentrum sowie als Gästehaus für Wissenschaftler aus aller Welt gedient. Nach dem Zweiten Weltkrieg wurde das von den Amerikanern requirierte Haus unter anderem als Offizierskasino genutzt. Im Kino des Hauses sah Johnson am 8. März 1946 den Film "The Story of G. I. Joe". Siehe Dok. 16 und Dok. 16, Anm. 37. Am 9. Juli 1946 hielt Johnson im Harnack House einen Vortrag vor dem American Women's Club of Berlin. Siehe Dok. 72, Anm. 2. Das Haus steht heute der Max-Planck-Gesellschaft zur Förderung der Wissenschaften als Stätte der Begegnung der Wissenschaft und als internationales Gästehaus wieder zur Verfügung. Siehe Eckart Henning/Marion Kazemi, Dahlem – Domäne der Wissenschaft. Ein Spaziergang zu den Berliner Instituten der Kaiser-Wilhelm-/Max-Planck-Gesellschaft im „deutschen Oxford" (= Veröffentlichungen aus dem Archiv der Max-Planck-Gesellschaft, Bd. 16/I), 4., erw. und aktualisierte Auflage, Berlin 2009, S. 57-67. Foto des Hauses im Bildanhang, Abb. 41.
[17] 9. März 1946.
[18] Siehe Dok. 2, Anm. 6.
[19] Charles F. Heasty Jr. (1917-2010), Lieutenant Colonel, Executive Officer to the Staff Secretary, Office of the Deputy Military Governor, OMGUS, 1947 Acting Secretary General, OMGUS.
[20] Bryan L. Milburn (1896-1991), Brigadier General, 1945/1946 Chief of Staff, OMGUS, dann Director, Administrative Services and Headquarters Commandant, OMGUS.
[21] Das Koordinierungskomitee der Alliierten Kontrollbehörde, der obersten Viermächtebesatzungsbehörde für alle Deutschland als Ganzes betreffenden Angelegenheiten (siehe Dok. 14, Anm. 5), setzte sich aus den vier stellvertretenden Militärgouverneuren zusammen.

be inducted into the office. But certainly General Clay would be anxious to see me.

I went over to see Marshall Knappen[22], and soon learned the full story and why Dr. Pollock and Dr. Dorn are in Berlin. These people here seem to have been completely mystified about the delay in my coming but they have known that I was coming. Pollock has been running the Stuttgart office and has built up a kind of empire there. His job as political adviser to General Clay has fallen through because of some reorganization and a cut in expenditures: *Nobody here has bothered to inform me of this.* He has been content to take orders from a General Dailey[23] who is now heading the Civil Affairs Division[24] under which the Stuttgart office comes. But a shift is taking place. General Dailey is moving up. He is either taking the place of a General Eccles[25] who is Clay's deputy or going to Washington to take General Hilldring's[26] place (General Hilldring is going to the state department as the head of a division of occupied areas[27] – (more reorganization for Gene[28]). Now Mr. Pollock doesn't want to take orders from the civilian (formerly a General – Parkman[29]) who is taking General

---

[22] Siehe Dok. 8, Anm. 10.
[23] Charles K. Gailey Jr. (1901–1966), Brigadier General, 1920 Absolvent der United States Military Academy, Januar–April 1946 Chief, Civil Administration Branch, Internal Affairs and Communications Division, OMGUS, April–Oktober 1946 Director, Public Relations, OMGUS, Oktober 1946–1949 Chief of Staff, OMGUS, 1959–1961 Commanding General, Military District of Washington. Siehe Bildanhang, Abb. 24.
[24] Gemeint ist die Civil Administration Branch, Internal Affairs and Communications Division, OMGUS. Sie hatte folgende Zuständigkeiten: „Vereinbarung von Vier-Mächte-Abkommen zur Dezentralisierung der politischen Strukturen in Deutschland, Wiedererrichtung demokratischer Verhältnisse in der kommunalen Selbstverwaltung, Überwachung der politischen Parteien, Vorbereitung zentraler Verwaltungseinrichtungen, Angleichung und Koordinierung der Politik und Verwaltung auf Länderebene sowie Überwachung der Reform des Öffentlichen Dienstes". Josef Henke/Klaus Oldenhage, Office of Military Government for Germany (U. S.), in: OMGUS-Handbuch. Die amerikanische Militärregierung in Deutschland 1945–1949, hrsg. von Christoph Weisz (= Quellen und Darstellungen zur Zeitgeschichte, Bd. 35), München 1994, S. 1–142, hier S. 110.
[25] Oliver P. Echols (1892–1954), Major General, Juli 1945–April 1946 Assistant Deputy Military Governor, Germany (US), 1946/1947 Director, Civil Affairs Division, Department of War.
[26] Siehe Dok. 2, Anm. 4.
[27] Area Division V – Occupied Areas.
[28] Eugene N. Anderson (siehe Dok. 1, Anm. 1) war in der Area Division V – Occupied Areas als Acting Assistant Chief tätig.
[29] Henry C. Parkman (1894–1958), amerikanischer Jurist und Politiker (Republikanische Partei), 1916 MA, Harvard University, ab 1924 als Rechtsanwalt tätig, 1926–1929 Mitglied des Stadtparlaments von Boston, 1929–1936 Mitglied des Senats von Massachusetts, 1940 Kandidat für den US-Senat, 1945 Brigadier General, Civil Affairs Division, War Department, ab April 1946 Director, Civil Administration Division, OMGUS, 1947 Governmental Affairs Adviser to the Commander-in-Chief, European Command, and US Military Governor in Germany, 1949/50 US Delegate on the International Ruhr Authority, anschließend Chief, ECA Mission to France, 1953–1955 Assistant US High Commissioner for Germany.

Dailey's place[30]. He is up here suggesting to General Clay that he will continue in Stuttgart if he can be responsible to Clay and not to Parkman.[31] Dr. Dorn is in Berlin because General Adcock, who wants to go home he told me is coming to Berlin. They are amalgamating the Frankfurt with the Berlin group[32] and here General Adcock will not play the rôle he has hitherto played[33] and it is questionable whether he needs a political adviser here[34]. General Clay no longer has Pollock but only Murphy[35]. So Walter may be out of a job and looking at Stuttgart.

Where does this leave me? I don't know what Clay will say to me tomorrow. If Pollock is going to stay in Stuttgart then I do not have my job. I doubt very much whether I want to play second fiddle to him in the same office. There cannot be room for two of us there. I haven't thought the matter through and can't because I don't know what Clay's proposition is. There are in any case, many jobs available here. I can get a good one from M[arshall] Knappen (Religion and Education). There are others for which I can shop around. I could even go to Austria, I suppose. Or I could come home. I only know now I shall speak rather strongly tomorrow to Clay about being kept uninformed, left in the lurch. I may have to write an article for the Nation[36] on how the generals treat their civilian appointees. Don't concern yourself until you hear how it comes out. But it looks as if I'm being let down on Stuttgart.

All my love to you and the boys. I should never have left you. Edgar

---

[30] Parkman trat als Leiter der Civil Administration Branch Gaileys Nachfolge an. Im April 1946 erhielt Civil Administration den Status einer Abteilung, und Parkman wurde Direktor der Civil Administration Division.

[31] Pollock wurde dann im April 1946 förmlich zum Direktor des RGCO bestellt und war dem Militärgouverneur bzw. seinem Stellvertreter, Clay, unmittelbar verantwortlich.

[32] Das von Adcock geleitete OMGUSZ (Office of Military Government [US Zone]) in Frankfurt am Main, das die Aufgabe hatte, die von OMGUS (siehe Dok. 17, Anm. 45) in Berlin beschlossene Politik in der amerikanischen Besatzungszone Deutschlands auszuführen, wurde zum 1. April 1946 aufgelöst, und die Aufgaben gingen, von geringfügigen Ausnahmen abgesehen, auf OMGUS über. Siehe Josef Henke/Klaus Oldenhage, Office of Military Government for Germany (U. S.), in: OMGUS-Handbuch. Die amerikanische Militärregierung in Deutschland 1945-1949, hrsg. von Christoph Weisz (= Quellen und Darstellungen zur Zeitgeschichte, Bd. 35), München 1994, S. 1-142, hier S. 28 und 36.

[33] Ab April 1946 war Adcock Assistant Deputy Military Governor for Operations and Deputy to the Commanding General, OMGUS.

[34] Dorn war in Frankfurt am Main Adcocks Personal Adviser. Siehe Walter L. Dorn, Inspektionsreisen in der US-Zone. Notizen, Denkschriften und Erinnerungen aus dem Nachlaß übersetzt und hrsg. von Lutz Niethammer (= Schriftenreihe der Vierteljahrshefte für Zeitgeschichte, Nr. 26), Stuttgart 1973, S. 12f.

[35] Siehe Dok. 8, Anm. 13.

[36] The Nation, eine als linksliberal geltende amerikanische Wochenzeitschrift aus New York, begründet 1865.

Dok. 16
Schreiben an die Ehefrau
Berlin, Ihnestraße 14[1], 8. März 1946

Dearest and beloved –

One month ago I left for Omaha[2] and then came back to Lincoln[3] again to be with you a few hours. You came with me to the train.[4] Since that time I have had one letter[5] from you and have heard your sweet voice over the telephone. I heard my dear John's[6] voice too. A month ago you came back and found him tearful, fearful that a car had struck you down. I haven't had time to discover as yet whether the 25th Base Post Office[7] is in Berlin or not.[8] There will be mail for me there. But it looks as if I may miss mail for many months to come according to present plans.

I saw General Clay[9] this morning for a few minutes and I must say he was very nice, very considerate and very kind. He proposed that for the next few weeks I should spend my time getting acquainted with the international and military government set-up here in Berlin and in the zone preparatory to whatever I shall be doing after that date. To that end he proposed that I should attend the meetings of his staff[10] beginning at 11:30 tomorrow at which time I am to meet the directors of the divisions and they are to be told to put myself at my services. He also spoke of my attending some meetings of the Coordinating Committee (the subordinate Committee of the Control Council[11] itself composed of the Deputies of the Commanders-in-Chief)[12] and even of the Control Council itself. After familiarizing myself with the situation here I am to go throughout the zone and become acquainted with set-ups in the Länder, including I take it Stuttgart[13].

---

[1] Siehe Dok. 15, Anm. 1.
[2] Stadt im US-Bundesstaat Nebraska, nordöstlich von Johnsons Wohnort Lincoln.
[3] Hauptstadt des US-Bundesstaats Nebraska, wo Johnson mit seiner Familie wohnte und an der Universität lehrte.
[4] Siehe Dok. 2, Anm. 33.
[5] Emily L. Johnsons Brief vom 10. Februar 1946, in: Unterlagen aus dem Nachlass Edgar N. Johnson, Privatbesitz Candice E. und Thomas R. Johnson, Denver, Colorado, USA.
[6] Johnsons Sohn John. Siehe Dok. 2, Anm. 15.
[7] Siehe Dok. 4.
[8] Siehe Dok. 14, Anm. 11.
[9] Siehe Dok. 2, Anm. 6.
[10] Zu den OMGUS-Stabskonferenzen, die jeden Samstag am Sitz von OMGUS in der Kronprinzenallee (heute Clayallee), Berlin-Dahlem, stattfanden und dem Informationsaustausch zwischen Clay und seinem Beraterstab dienten, siehe Bernd Steger, General Clays Stabskonferenzen und die Organisation der amerikanischen Militärregierung in Deutschland. Die „Clay-Minutes" als historische Quelle, in: Vierteljahrshefte für Zeitgeschichte, 27. Jg. 1979, S. 113–130.
[11] Der Control Council war das oberste Organ der Alliierten Kontrollbehörde (Allied Control Authority) und bestand aus den vier Militärgouverneuren. Siehe Dok. 14, Anm. 5.
[12] Siehe Dok. 15, Anm. 21.
[13] Hauptstadt des Landes Württemberg-Baden in der amerikanischen Besatzungszone Deutschlands.

Frankfurt[14] will soon be almost out of the picture.[15] At the end of that time I am to report to him again and then what my task will be will be made clear. I said I was a little disturbed about the change in the picture but he insisted that there was no fundamental change. What would be Pollock's[16] fate he had not yet decided, i. e., whether he was to be permanently here or remain in Stuttgart and I was led to believe that if it were Stuttgart I could be here in some advisory capacity to him, and if Pollock were to come here then I should be in Stuttgart. I mentioned keeping in mind that I might want to go back in the fall and he said that that would be kept in mind. He spoke of Pollock's first wanting to go home in May and then in the summer. He also spoke of his splendid work in Stuttgart and of how he had worked himself into his job[17], and that there was nothing to be done for the time being but to continue his work there. That is quite understandable. He then called General Milburn[18] and told him to introduce me to General Gailey[19] who is the chief of the Civil Affairs Branch of the Internal Affairs and Communications Division[20] who was then to take care of me. I met General Gailey in General Milburn's Office after lunch (the General comes from Georgia[21])[22]. He then took me over to his building and set me up with an office and a secretary and something to read. It was amusing to see the old bureaucratic procedure in order. An administrative officer (female) cleaned the desk, desk top, blotters, paper, pencils, clips, ink, in basket, out basket and before I left in the afternoon things were going into the in-basket. I don't have much use yet for a secretary. Clay mentioned that I was to have transportation. Milburn came along and gave somebody orders about a car. Gailey mentioned a car. Well I don't see that I need a car but I am supposed to take it while I can get it and before I get swallowed into the huge bureaucracy that is here. I shall only have it in any case for a couple of weeks while I am here.

There was nothing to do of course to consent to General Clay's proposals. I saw Walter Dorn[23] at lunch and Mr. Pollock late in the afternoon. Walter confirmed the picture of flux that Marshal[l] Knappen[24] presented last night.[25] He is being washed out with the closing of the Frankfurt office[26] and doesn't know

---

14   Frankfurt am Main, Stadt im Land Groß-Hessen in der amerikanischen Besatzungszone Deutschlands.
15   Johnson spricht hier die Auflösung von OMGUSZ in Frankfurt am Main an. Siehe Dok. 15, Anm. 32.
16   Siehe Dok. 15, Anm. 6.
17   Als Leiter des RGCO, OMGUS. Siehe Dok. 2, Anm. 11.
18   Siehe Dok. 15, Anm. 20.
19   Siehe Dok. 15, Anm. 23.
20   Gemeint ist die Civil Administration Branch, Internal Affairs and Communications Division, OMGUS. Siehe Dok. 15, Anm. 24.
21   US-Bundesstaat.
22   Gailey wurde in Conyers, Georgia, geboren, "a small deeply segregated town about 30 miles from Atlanta (now a sizeable 'bedroom' suburb)" (Gaileys Tochter Christine W. Gailey in einer E-Mail an Werner Breunig vom 26. Oktober 2009).
23   Siehe Dok. 2, Anm. 10.
24   Siehe Dok. 8, Anm. 10.
25   Siehe Dok. 15.
26   Johnson spricht hier die Auflösung von OMGUSZ in Frankfurt am Main an. Siehe Dok. 15, Anm. 32.

quite what is going to happen to him. He thinks that may be he will be doing the same thing for Clay as he is now doing for Adcock[27], and he hinted that he may get the present position of Gailey should Gailey move to another position. Walter is much tied up with himself and his future prospects. But he urged me to be patient and to see what comes out after the preliminary period of learning and flux is over. He said that there at the moment only three people with a direct relationship to Clay – Pollock, himself and I and that under no circumstances should I release this position for something that will closet me in a division or branch. I think Pollock is all right. He was a little careful with me, seemed to be suspicious that I had had no actual experiences with military government as such, though I tried to correct him a little on this point. He is extremely proud of his part in the Länderrat[28], and of the manner in which it appreciates his efforts and of course does not intend to let anyone interfere with his part unless he is given definite instructions by Clay. But he said that in the present confusion he did not know whether Clay would want him to come up here or stay down there. In this he confirmed what Clay said. He also welcomed me to Stuttgart when it would be time for me to come and expressed the desire to become better acquainted. It is generally agreed that he is a powerful figure with Clay whom he regards highly and I shall do my best to get along with him.

He made a remark which I think is possibly correct that Clay gives people time to prove themselves and then decides what they shall do. That I take it is the position I now am in, and I shall do my best.

I had dinner with Louis Wiesner[29]. Poor kid. In Washington their first child was born dead.[30] He brought his wife[31] to London[32] but she has now gone home and gone to *Reno*[33].[34] She wants to settle down in a teaching position. He is now in the foreign service and wants to make that his career.[35] He is pretty badly broken up.

---

[27] Siehe Dok. 14, Anm. 9.
[28] Siehe Dok. 15, Anm. 10.
[29] Siehe Dok. 8, Anm. 11.
[30] Louis A. Wiesner hatte 1943/1944 in Washington für das OSS gearbeitet, zuvor, 1942/1943, in New York für den Council on Foreign Relations.
[31] Wahrscheinlich Jean H. Wiesner, geb. Hagen.
[32] Louis A. Wiesner hatte sich Ende 1944 als Foreign Service Officer nach London begeben, "to join Ambassador Murphy's [siehe Dok. 8, Anm. 13] mission at Bushy Park, England, which was on the grounds of Hampton Court Palace. I was assigned to be the assistant labor attaché in Ambassador Murphy's mission". Interview mit Louis A. Wiesner vom 5. Juni 1981, S. 2, in: Landesarchiv Berlin (LAB), F Rep. 037 (Sammlung Amerikanische Behörden in Berlin), Nr. 99.
[33] Stadt im US-Bundesstaat Nevada.
[34] Anscheinend wurde die Ehe im „Scheidungsparadies" Reno geschieden. Siehe die Bekanntgabe von Scheidungen in: Nevada State Journal vom 23. März 1946, S. 8 ("Jean Wiesner from Louis Wiesner"); Reno Evening Gazette vom 25. März 1946, S. 11 ("Jean Hagen Wiesner from Louis Arnold Wiesner"). Louis A. Wiesner heiratete dann 1950 Elizabeth Q. Phenix.
[35] "Now, in September of 1944 while I was still at OSS, I was taken into the Foreign Service of the United States and then became an employee of the State Department." Interview mit Louis A. Wiesner vom 5. Juni 1981, S. 2, in: LAB, F Rep. 037 (Sammlung Amerikanische Behörden in Berlin), Nr. 99.

I saw GI[36] Joe[37] at the movies in Harnackhouse[38] tonight. Very excellent. When the captain died a boy broke out sobbing behind us and had to leave the room.

I love my Sweetheart and my boys. I imagine this is going to be a good challenge here and I shall do my best to meet it. Goodnight dearest one – Edgar

Dok. 17
Schreiben an die Ehefrau
Berlin, Ihnestraße 14[1], 9. März 1946

Dearest beloved:

I am just a little bit dizzy. I have attended so many meetings today; met and seen so many generals that I'm not quite sure where I am what I am or who I am. I understand now a little more completely what it means to have one's head turned by the prospect of power and influence and association with the right people. But you don't have to worry about me. I think the best qualifications for people who are engaged in this sort of work are those which make it possible to look on the scene quite objectively without being moved at all by stars

---

[36] Government Issue, ugs. für amerikanischer Soldat.
[37] Gemeint ist der amerikanische Film "The Story of G. I. Joe" (deutscher Titel: „Schlachtgewitter am Monte Cassino") von William A. Wellman (1896-1975) aus dem Jahre 1945. Burgess Meredith (1908-1997) spielt den amerikanischen Kriegsberichterstatter Ernie Pyle, der gemeinsam mit einer Infanteriekompanie während des Zweiten Weltkriegs die Schlachtfelder von Nordafrika und Italien bereist, und Robert Mitchum (1917-1997) verkörpert Lieutenant/Captain Bill Walker, der bei einem Sturmangriff auf die deutschen Linien getötet wird. "Mud, monotony and the grueling life of the infantryman are well depicted In *The Story of GI Joe* [...]. Burgess Meredith, portraying a sincere and unassuming Ernie Pyle, follows C Company of the 18th Infantry through the African and Italian campaigns. The story revolves around the siege and subsequent capitulation of historic Cassino. While Combat Infantry Badges are still to be seen these days in OMGUS, this film should serve to impress on newcomers the loftiness of the ideals for which so much was sacrificed. The captain of C Company says to Ernie, 'I know ... I know its not my fault they get killed, but I feel like a murderer. I can't stand to look at them anymore. If only some good could be made to come from all this energy, and all these men.' A bitter sort of humor is injected into the movie with situations similar to those Bill Mauldin illustrated in his 'Up Front' cartoons. No attempt is made to glorify or to glamorize the real heroes of this war. The men fight, freeze, go beserk, die and 'wolf' in an unexalted 'there's a war to be won' manner. If you've never been in combat, *The Story of GI Joe* will undoubtedly give you a truer concept of what it's like than you have received from any previous Hollywood attempt. If you have been in combat, you may feel the film falls short in many of the real and often galling details. Where else but in Hollywood would every Doughboy in the midst of battle wear a raincoat?" "Life of GI Joe" is Films' Best Tribute to Doughs, in: The Grooper vom 2. März 1946, S. 2. Siehe Das Jahr 1945 und das Kino, Berlin 1995, S. 173.
[38] Siehe Dok. 15, Anm. 16.

[1] Siehe Dok. 15, Anm. 1.

on the shoulders, villas on the lakeside or exclusive clubs, and who are capable of asking simply what is being done here for the American people, and for the principles of American democracy.

I have been more or less taken in tow today by General Gailey[2], (I think it's perhaps two stars)[3] who is head of the Civil Administration Branch of the Division of Internal Affairs and Communications[4]. The General is from Georgia[5] (as I learn is General Clay[6])[7] and he is a regular officer, indeed a West Point Graduate[8]. He strikes me as a simple, decent and altogether likeable individual who has no particular pretensions with respect to his own intellectual abilities but who is accustomed to exercise authority. He said rather simply today in re Nebraska – Biff Jones[9] and Dana X Bible[10] (that is how the University of Nebraska[11] is identified) that he just loved football and it turned out as we discussed why he loved football that it was not so much the actual game but the environment of the game. I have always said that football was to be enjoyed because it afforded the spectators the occasion to go on an emotional drunk. And he added after he had enumerated the features outside of the game itself that it gave oldish men a day of escape back into the days when they were kids, well that must be very true and it is human, and I sort of liked the general for the remark.

He invited me to lunch after the meetings of the morning. We were whisked out to his house in his car and with his own driver. It is on the westernest edge of the American zone in Berlin, on an island in the Swansee[12], one of the large lakes on the outskirts of Berlin.[13] It was a swell place. The large living room

---

[2] Siehe Dok. 15, Anm. 23.
[3] Gailey war damals ein Brigadier General (ein Stern).
[4] Siehe Dok. 15, Anm. 24.
[5] US-Bundesstaat. Siehe Dok. 16, Anm. 22.
[6] Siehe Dok. 2, Anm. 6.
[7] Clay kam aus Marietta, Georgia.
[8] Gailey hatte die United States Military Academy in West Point, New York, 1920 absolviert.
[9] Lawrence McC. (Biff) Jones (1895–1980), amerikanischer College Football Head Coach, 1937–1941 University of Nebraska.
[10] Dana X. Bible (1891–1980), amerikanischer College Football Head Coach, 1929–1936 University of Nebraska, Vorgänger von Lawrence McC. (Biff) Jones.
[11] 1869 gegründete Universität in Lincoln, Nebraska.
[12] Gemeint ist der Große Wannsee, eine Ausbuchtung der Havel (siehe Dok. 74, Anm. 24) im Südwesten Berlins.
[13] Gailey wohnte auf der mit Villen bebauten Insel Schwanenwerder, die in der Havel am Ausgang des Großen Wannsees liegt und zum Berliner Verwaltungsbezirk Zehlendorf, Ortsteil Wannsee, gehörte. Später wohnte er hier mit seiner Familie, und zwar in demselben Haus, so die Auskunft seines ältesten Sohnes, Charles K. Gailey III (siehe Anm. 18), in einer E-Mail an Werner Breunig vom 2. November 2009. In einer E-Mail vom 26. Oktober 2009 schreibt Charles K. Gailey III: "We lived […] in the house on the west side that had a huge thatched roof. We had a beautiful view of the water." Und Gaileys 1950 geborene Tochter Christine W. Gailey teilt in einer E-Mail vom 25. Oktober 2009 mit, dass das Haus einem "film maker" gehört habe. Offensichtlich handelte es sich um das reetgedeckte Landhaus Inselstraße 36, das 1939 erbaut worden war (Architekt: Jürgen Schweitzer [1907–1996], Bauherr: der

(beamed) was covered with oriental rugs (I imagine it was some important Nazis' place and it is OK with me to see these generals occupy houses the Nazis were thrown out of)[14]. Two large plate glass windows looked out over the lake, on one side of which the high British officials live.[15] The room was simply but elegantly furnished. A large fire-place dominated one end and the German servants had a fire crackling when we came in and kept it crackling. There was a piano in the room and books (English, French and classical German authors including Joyce[16] and Proust[17] which I don't believe the General reads). In one corner was a large white vase filled with magnificent branches of pussy willows, four and five feet in length. Smaller vases of the same were on other tables. There was also a small vase of snow-drops, and some tulips. It is tulip time here (re-forced plants). There are in most offices and I asked my secretary (!) who has nothing to do to get some for my office. It was a simple lunch (soup and fresh fruit and coffee) and the general and I got along very well. At least he invited me to come out and stay with him when my tenure at this place is over. He liked to talk, he said, and would like to thresh over some problems. I think I'll do it. I can't imagine a nicer place to stay. There may be a chance for some walks. The General knows everybody around here and can help me to get properly and thoroughly indoctrinated into the place. I think to put it professionally that to have won the General's confidences to this extent is not so bad for a two days' presence. And I mean to make friends with him. His family is coming over in August and he has two boys[18], younger even than ours[19].[20] There are so many people who are old (he must be in his 50's[21]) and who have young children. He laughs easily and heartily and does not appear pretentious. But in meetings with his subordinates he speaks with authority.

Schauspieler und Regisseur Carl Ludwig Duisberg, Pseudonym Achaz [1889–1958], Sohn des Chemikers und Industriellen Carl Duisberg [1861–1935]). Siehe Janin Reif/ Horst Schumacher/Lothar Uebel, Schwanenwerder. Ein Inselparadies in Berlin, Berlin 2000, S. 234–237. Duisberg war mit seiner Familie ab dem 3. Juni 1940 auf Schwanenwerder gemeldet. Siehe Meldekarten Carl Ludwig Duisberg, in: LAB, B Rep. 021 (Einwohnermeldeamt Berlin).

[14] Nach 1933 waren unter anderen Joseph Goebbels (1897–1945), Adolf Hitlers (siehe Dok. 22, Anm. 19) Leibarzt Theodor Morell (1886–1948) und Albert Speer (1905–1981) auf die Insel gezogen. Siehe hierzu Georg Schertz, Schwanenwerder. Eine Insel im Spiegelbild der Geschichte, in: Berlin in Geschichte und Gegenwart. Jahrbuch des Landesarchivs Berlin 2005, S. 209–223, insbesondere S. 214f.

[15] Der Blick fiel auf das westliche Wannseeufer, auf von britischen Besatzungsoffizieren bewohnte Villen in Kladow, einem Ortsteil im Berliner Verwaltungsbezirk Spandau (britischer Sektor von Berlin).

[16] James Joyce (1882–1941), irischer Schriftsteller.

[17] Marcel Proust (1871–1922), französischer Schriftsteller.

[18] Charles K. Gailey III (geb. 1942) und John Bruce Gailey (geb. 1943). Ein dritter Sohn, Timothy H. Gailey, kam erst im April 1946 zur Welt.

[19] Johnsons Söhne John und Thomas wurden 1939 bzw. 1944 geboren. Siehe Dok. 2, Anm. 15 und 16.

[20] Gaileys Frau, Margaret A. Gailey, geb. Pearsall (1913–1981), und die drei Söhne kamen im November oder Dezember 1946 nach Berlin. So die Auskunft von Charles K. Gailey III in einer E-Mail an Werner Breunig vom 26. Oktober 2009.

[21] Gailey, geboren am 14. Mai 1901, war 44 Jahre alt.

The first meeting I attended was that of the staff of General Stayer[22] (who is a Public Health man and was active in our last occupation of Germany[23]) and who is head of the Division of Internal Affairs and Communications[24]. I found Marshal[l] Knappen[25] and Taylor[26] (Education – whom I have mentioned)[27] attending the meeting and went to sit by them, but General Gailey insisted that I came over to sit by him. I was introduced to most of the colonels who were present and listened to their reports for the week. They were not particularly exciting but it gave you a good idea of how the Divisions work. It was reported that the Religion and Education people are a little perturbed to find GI's[28] and Fräuleins on the davenports in their offices when they come in to work in the evening. The GI's use showers on their floor and run around naked in the evenings to the consternation of the German women who are cleaning up the place.

At 11:30 I went to General Clay's weekly staff meeting[29] with General Gailey. It is held in a big room next to General Clay's office[30]. I have never seen so much brass together in one place. They sat around four huge tables arranged in a square. There must have been from 60 to 75 top ranking officers. On each side of this square were two small tables at one of which sat the members of the secretariat and at the other Mr. Pollock[31], a naval officer of some kind and I. The officers at the main tables were the heads of the offices and the Divisions and some heads of Branches. Clay was flanked by Milburn[32] his Chief of Staff and Echols[33], his Deputy who is supposed to be leaving. Mr. (Ambassador) Murphy[34] sat next to General Echols. Around the table were people I had heard of since OSS[35] days or had just recently met: General Draper[36] (Industry – he is

---

[22] Morrison C. Stayer (1882–1969), Major General, 1945/1946 Chief, Public Health and Welfare Branch, Internal Affairs and Communications Division, OMGUS.
[23] 1919–1921 Chief Health Officer, American Occupation Forces Germany.
[24] Direktor der Internal Affairs and Communications Division, OMGUS, war damals Frank C. Meade (siehe Dok. 20, Anm. 53).
[25] Siehe Dok. 8, Anm. 10.
[26] John W. Taylor (1906–2001), Lieutenant Colonel, amerikanischer Erziehungswissenschaftler, 1930/1931 Englischlehrer, Kaiser-Friedrich-Realgymnasium, Berlin-Neukölln, 1936 PhD, Teachers College, Columbia University, 1945/1946 Chief, Education Section, Education and Religious Affairs Branch, Internal Affairs and Communications Division, OMGUS, Mai 1946–1947 Chief, Education and Religious Affairs Branch, Internal Affairs and Communications Division, OMGUS, 1947–1950 President, University of Louisville, 1952/1953 Acting Director General, UNESCO.
[27] Siehe Dok. 15.
[28] Government Issues, ugs. für amerikanische Soldaten.
[29] Siehe Protokoll der OMGUS-Stabskonferenz am 9. März 1946, in: Archiv des Instituts für Zeitgeschichte (IfZ), München, OMGUS – Staff Conferences (Protokollkopien), Fg 12/3.
[30] In der Kronprinzenallee (heute Clayallee), Berlin-Dahlem.
[31] Siehe Dok. 15, Anm. 6.
[32] Siehe Dok. 15, Anm. 20.
[33] Siehe Dok. 15, Anm. 25.
[34] Siehe Dok. 8, Anm. 13.
[35] Office of Strategic Services. Siehe Dok. 1, Anm. 9.
[36] William H. Draper Jr. (1894–1974), Brigadier General, ab 1945 Director, Economics Division, OMGUS, 1947 Economics Adviser, Office of the Commander-in-Chief,

often in the New York Times[37]), General McClure[38] (Information Control – press-films-radio), General Stayer, General McSherry[39] (Manpower), General Conrad[40] (Intelligence) and a host of other officers including some naval people. Clay goes around the table asking for a report, calling some of the people by their first names, including Murphy. I must say he makes a good impression, conducting the meeting with good sense, efficiency, authority and good humor and breaking into the reports with sharp questions, and rigorous comments. When General Conrad reported that the Germans were conducting themselves with more independence, meaning this as something bad, Clay interrupted to suggest that it might on the contrary be something good that we should rejoice that there is evidence that the Germans were discarding their abject submissiveness and conducting themselves like men. He also used the terms "bad Germans" and "good Germans". After the various people had reported Clay made a very nice introductory speech concerning me, referring to my previous acquaintance with Germany and my experience with OSS and then asked all those present to extend to me every courtesy possible in order to aid me in getting acquainted with the set-up here in Berlin. He then asked me to stand up. This certainly was extremely decent and helpful of him to do. After this Pollock made a short report and the meeting was over. This was a new experience to me, to see the results of what I suppose is the work of thousands of people here for a week summarized in the form of short oral reports to McNarney's[41] Deputy. I don't really believe I was at the meeting and was presented to them.

(There was a meeting here with the Civil Administration Branch[42])

I went back to my office after lunch and was called in the afternoon by a Colonel of the Office of Administrative Service[43] asking me if I wanted to join a club[44] of the top personnel in Omgus (Office of Military Government U. S.)[45].

European Command (EUCOM), 1947-1949 Under Secretary of the Army, 1952/1953 US Member, NATO Council, Paris.

[37] Siehe unter anderem Kathleen McLaughlin, Allies Asked to Pool Food To Avert Crisis in Germany, in: The New York Times vom 1. März 1946, S. 1 und 8.

[38] Robert A. McClure (1897-1957), Brigadier General, 1944/1945 Director, Psychological Warfare Division, SHAEF, 1945 Director, Office of Information, USGCC, 1945/1946 Director, Office of Information Control Services, Office of the Deputy Military Governor, OMGUS, 1947 Director, Information Control Division, OMGUS.

[39] Frank J. McSherry (1892-1977), Brigadier General, 1945/1946 Director, Manpower Division, OMGUS.

[40] G. Bryan Conrad (1898-1976), Brigadier General, 1945/1946 Director, Office of the Director of Intelligence, OMGUS.

[41] Joseph T. McNarney (1893-1972), General, 1945-1947 Commanding General, US Forces in the European Theater, Commander-in-Chief, US Forces of Occupation in Germany, Military Governor, Germany (US).

[42] Civil Administration Branch der Internal Affairs and Communications Division, OMGUS. Siehe Dok. 15, Anm. 24.

[43] Gemeint ist das Office of the Director of Administrative Services, Office of the Deputy Military Governor, OMGUS.

[44] Gemeint ist der exklusive Lakeside Club für hohe Offiziere.

[45] Das am 1. Oktober 1945 unter Leitung von Lucius D. Clay (siehe Dok. 2, Anm. 6) eingesetzte OMGUS (Office of Military Government for Germany [US]) war die oberste politische Instanz im amerikanisch besetzten Teil Deutschlands. In der Alliierten Kontrollbehörde (siehe Dok. 14, Anm. 5) in Berlin stellte es gemeinsam mit den anderen

General Millburn[46] had referred to this previously. I said yes, and the Colonel said he would send over a membership card and literature. In due time a WAC[47] sergeant delivered the stuff. I found out that the initiation fee was twenty-five dollars and the dues 2.50 a month. I found out that the club was limited to 75 of the "top personnel" (the by-laws) of Omgus but I notice that my membership card is 79. The Club house is on the shores of the Wannsee[48] and they are opening formally tomorrow night with a buffet supper and dance. I shall go tomorrow, and attend once in a while thereafter. I can see well enough into the situation here to see that it is important for me to do this.

It is going to be interesting enough for the next five or six weeks, and I am going to make the most of it. There is no doubt of the wisdom of my decision of staying with Clay until I see just exactly what is going to happen to me. By that time if they have not formed an unfavorable impression of me, I ought to be put in a position of some importance and influence where I can make good.

I love you my sweet angel and my boys. I think we'd better use this APO[49] as a permanent address until further notice. I'll cable it and this will be confirmation. I shall be here about two weeks more and then out in the zone for about a month. They can hold mail for me here or else send it out into the zone. Possibly I can get some from the temporary address (I haven't been able to find out where 25th Base Post Office[50] is[51]) before I leave here. The address is:

Office of Military Government for Germany (U. S.)
Internal Affairs and Communications Division
APO # 742[52]
c/o PM, N. Y., N. Y.

I hope it won't continue to be as hectic as this has been but I am sure it is going to be a very very busy time. There is a tremendous shortage of personnel here. But in so far as I can see excellent work is being done in the implementation of the policy so far announced. What I have heard does not lead one to suspect that the Russians are impossible in international negotiations. But they are undoubtedly pulling fast ones in politics.

I love you my sweet one and I shall be so happy when my first word comes from you. Goodnight – beloved. Edgar

> drei Militärregierungen die oberste Viermächtebesatzungsbehörde für alle Deutschland als Ganzes betreffenden Angelegenheiten. Seinen Sitz hatte OMGUS in der Kronprinzenallee (heute Clayallee), Berlin-Dahlem, auf dem Gelände des NS-Luftgaukommandos III. Siehe Josef Henke/Klaus Oldenhage, Office of Military Government for Germany (U. S.), in: OMGUS-Handbuch. Die amerikanische Militärregierung in Deutschland 1945-1949, hrsg. von Christoph Weisz (= Quellen und Darstellungen zur Zeitgeschichte, Bd. 35), München 1994, S. 1–142. Siehe Foto im Bildanhang, Abb. 39.
> 46 Bryan L. Milburn. Siehe Dok. 15, Anm. 20.
> 47 Women's Army Corps. Siehe Dok. 13, Anm. 14.
> 48 Gemeint ist der Große Wannsee, eine Ausbuchtung der Havel (siehe Dok. 74, Anm. 24) im Südwesten Berlins.
> 49 Army Post Office.
> 50 Siehe Dok. 4.
> 51 Siehe Dok. 14, Anm. 11.
> 52 Berlin-Dahlem, Kronprinzenallee (heute Clayallee).

Dok. 18
Schreiben an die Ehefrau
Berlin, Ihnestraße 14[1], 11. März 1946

Dearest and beloved:

I am a little cheerful tonight because I learned that the 25th Base Post Office, APO[2] 800[3] is located at Würzburg[4] and that brings the possibility of my getting a letter from you in a few days. I wrote them yesterday giving them my new APO address. It shouldn't take long for this to get to Würzburg nor for letters to be returned here. Maybe there will be more than one. You should be hearing from me from here about the same time.

I called on some friends of Gene's[5] yesterday afternoon where he stayed in 1930 when he met Polly[6].[7] I was ushered into a bedroom on the top floor of the house which was unheated. One daughter of the family is employed by Omgus (Office of Military Government US)[8] only an office or so from me. Then I was invited by the daughter down to the one heated room in the house for afternoon coffee. There were twelve people in the room. Another daughter and her four children who had fled the Russian zone and were on their way to the British zone to live in the country. 2 of the children had whooping cough. But they and the two others were fat, and even red-cheeked, and the baby, not much younger than Timmy[9] (the sweet kid) was drinking milk from a bottle when I came in. I was surprised at what I was served even as I always am when Germans or Austrians entertain. The coffee was quite potable and there was plenty of it. There was, in some abundance, toasted white bread, good black bread and a tasteless fruit tart. The kids had marmalade and sugar on their bread. I was even offered a glass of schnaps. But I refused and of course did not eat much of their stuff.

The conversation, however, I could not stomach very well. There was much self-pity, much complaint, much of the usual anti-Russian talk, and no admission that Germany had started a war, exploited most of Europe, and lost the war. It was as if there had been no Nazi regime. The old Mother, in good shape indeed, said that the world had suffered some Judgment of God, some stroke of Fate, but not that the German nation had spawned the Nazis. She said no guilt could be assessed and referred somewhat caustically to the repetition of the old dispute after the war of 1918 as to war guilt.

I went to the opening of the Lakeside Club.[10] The motor pool sent over a staff car which is more than OSS[11] ever did, though I must not forget my blue

---

[1] Siehe Dok. 15, Anm. 1.
[2] Army Post Office.
[3] Siehe Dok. 4.
[4] Stadt im Land Bayern in der amerikanischen Besatzungszone Deutschlands.
[5] Eugene N. Anderson. Siehe Dok. 1, Anm. 1.
[6] Pauline R. Anderson. Siehe Dok. 2, Anm. 2.
[7] Eugene N. Anderson hatte seine Ehefrau Pauline während eines Forschungsaufenthalts 1930/1931 in Deutschland kennengelernt.
[8] Siehe Dok. 17, Anm. 45.
[9] Johnsons Sohn Thomas, der damals 20 Monate alt war. Siehe Dok. 2, Anm. 16.
[10] Der Club wurde am 10. März 1946 eröffnet. Siehe Dok. 17.
[11] Office of Strategic Services. Siehe Dok. 1, Anm. 9.

Plymouth[12]. The driver was a POW[13] whose home is in Saarbrücken[14], a simple and rather dumb person who was glad to be working for the Americans, and glad an American car ran like a Mercedes[15]. He was also beware of MP's[16]. The place on the shore of Wannsee[17] is a swanky one, the former home, it was said, of Brigitte Helm[18], a movie actress and mistress of a German industrialist[19].[20] General Gailey[21] was there, and took me in hand a bit, General Clay[22] shook hands and introduced me to Ambassador Murphy[23] who remarked that he noticed me at the staff meeting[24]. I met a few others. There was a bar with a plenteous assortment of liquors including whiskies which are not ordinary here. There was a sumptuous buffet dinner – everything. There was entertainment, a ballet dancer, an acrobat, and what was introduced as a "favorite of General

12 Limousine des amerikanischen Automobilherstellers Plymouth, die Johnson 1945 in Österreich zur Verfügung gestellt worden war.
13 Prisoner of War.
14 Deutsche Stadt im Saargebiet, das zur französischen Besatzungszone Deutschlands gehörte, 1947 ausgegliedert, der Kompetenz der Alliierten Kontrollbehörde entzogen und wirtschaftlich an Frankreich angegliedert wurde.
15 Deutsche Automarke.
16 Military Police officers.
17 Gemeint ist der Große Wannsee, eine Ausbuchtung der Havel (siehe Dok. 74, Anm. 24) im Südwesten Berlins.
18 Brigitte Helm, eigentl. Schittenhelm, verh. Kunheim, gesch. Weißbach (1908–1996), deutsche Filmschauspielerin, wurde durch die weibliche Haupt- bzw. Doppelrolle der Maria und des Roboters in dem Stummfilm „Metropolis" (1927) von Fritz Lang (1890–1976) über Nacht berühmt, war „für ein Jahrzehnt der Inbegriff einer enigmatischen Leinwanddiva und dämonischen Verführerin" (Kay Weniger, Das große Personenlexikon des Films, Dritter Bd.: F–H, Berlin 2001, S. 628).
19 Brigitte Helm war ab 1935 in zweiter Ehe mit dem Kaufmann Dr. phil. Hugo Kunheim (1902–1986), der die Kohlengroßhandlung „Caesar Wollheim" führte, verheiratet.
20 Der Lakeside Club befand sich Am Großen Wannsee 2/4 im Berliner Verwaltungsbezirk Zehlendorf, Ortsteil Wannsee, wo Brigitte Helm nach der Heirat mit Dr. Hugo Kunheim gewohnt hatte. Siehe Berliner Adreßbuch, 1936–1943: Dr. phil. Hugo Kunheim; Meldekarte Brigitte Kunheim, geb. Schittenhelm, in: LAB, B Rep. 021 (Einwohnermeldeamt Berlin). "A house that most Americans know is the very modernistic Lion House, so called because of the almost life-sized bronze lion on the front porch. This house was owned formerly by a famous German movie actress, Brigitte Helm. It was taken over for the Officers Lake-Side Club and is now the home of one of OMGUS General's." Viviane W. Adams, Wannsee, in: OMGUS Observer vom 28. Juni 1946, S. 4 f. und 8, hier S. 8. Das zweigeschossige Haus mit Flachdach war 1932/1933 erbaut worden (Architekt: Moritz Ernst Lesser [1882–1958]). Siehe Ingo Krüger, Landhäuser und Villen in Berlin & Potsdam. Nr. 3: Großer Wannsee, Colonie Alsen, Villa Liebermann, Bremen 2005, S. 14 f. „[…] das Haus existiert noch, da bin ich mal hingefahren. Das haben wir ungefähr 1943 verlassen, da wurden die Bombenangriffe zu heftig, und unser Vater wollte uns aus Berlin raus haben", so Pieter Kunheim (1936–2007), Brigitte Helms Sohn, in einem Gespräch im Jahre 2003. Daniel Semler, Brigitte Helm. Der Vamp des deutschen Films, München 2008, S. 214. Foto des Hauses im Bildanhang, Abb. 59.
21 Siehe Dok. 15, Anm. 23.
22 Siehe Dok. 2, Anm. 6.
23 Siehe Dok. 8, Anm. 13.
24 Gemeint ist die OMGUS-Stabskonferenz vom 9. März 1946. Siehe Dok. 17.

Eisenhower's[25]" a good looking and competent accordian player. There was also an orchestra and dancing. The officers had their secretaries along for the most part. But I was alone and did not know many people and left early. I don't imagine I shall use the Lakeside Club much.

Goodnight to my sweet Emily and to my sweet boys. I love them intensely.
Edgar

Dok. 19
Schreiben an die Ehefrau
Berlin, Ihnestraße 14[1], 12. März 1946

Dearest, my dearest Emily:

Today has been an interesting day. You have heard me comment on the difficulty of 4 powers speaking three different languages ever getting anything done. Today I had a chance of witnessing the difficulty. General Gailey[2] took me to a meeting of the Allied Commission on Civil Administration[3].[4] This is a quadripartite committee on the Branch level. The branches are sub-divisions of the Divisions. My branch at present is the Civil Administration Branch[5]. My division is the Internal Affairs and Communications Division (IA + C). The quadripartite committee of the corresponding divisions is called a Directorate, and the directorate of my division is accordingly the Directorate of Internal Affairs and Communications (DIAC).[6] The Branch Committees report to the Division Committees. They have, as well, Sub-Committees and so-called working parties under them. The Directorates report to the Coordinating Committee (com-

---

[25] Dwight D. Eisenhower (1890-1969), General of the Army, 1944/1945 Commander-in-Chief, Supreme Headquarters Allied Expeditionary Force, Commanding General, US Forces, European Theater, 1945 Commander-in-Chief, US Forces of Occupation in Germany, Military Governor, Germany (US), 1945-1948 Chief of Staff, US Army, 1949-1952 Supreme Allied Commander Europe (NATO), 1953-1961 34. Präsident der USA.

[1] Siehe Dok. 15, Anm. 1.
[2] Siehe Dok. 15, Anm. 23.
[3] Civil Administration Committee, Directorate of Internal Affairs and Communications, Allied Control Authority.
[4] Siehe Protokoll der 22. Sitzung des Civil Administration Committee, Directorate of Internal Affairs and Communications, Allied Control Authority, am 12. März 1946, DIAC/CAC/M (46) 7, englischsprachige Fassung, in: Archiv des IfZ, OMGUS-Akten (Mikrofiche-Reproduktion), 2/124-3/2-4.
[5] Civil Administration Branch der Internal Affairs and Communications Division, OMGUS. Siehe Dok. 15, Anm. 24.
[6] Der Leiter der Internal Affairs and Communications Division, OMGUS, vertrat die USA im Directorate of Internal Affairs and Communications, Allied Control Authority. Siehe Josef Henke/Klaus Oldenhage, Office of Military Government for Germany (U. S.), in: OMGUS-Handbuch. Die amerikanische Militärregierung in Deutschland 1945-1949, hrsg. von Christoph Weisz (= Quellen und Darstellungen zur Zeitgeschichte, Bd. 35), München 1994, S. 30.

posed of the Deputies of the Commanding Generals)[7] and the Coordinating Committee reports to the Control Council[8] itself.

All these meetings are held in the building of the German Supreme Court[9] which is decorated with the four Allied flags, and is about five miles from the Headquarters of Omgus[10]. The meeting was held in a conference room (135)[11] outside of which German workmen were making furious pounding noises. A Russian lieutenant leaned out the windows and shouted at them to stop, and they did of course. The chairmanship of the meetings of the Allied Control Authority (ACA) are this month in the hands of the Russians. They change every month. The Russian presiding officer (Shkvarin)[12] was a Colonel and played a minor part in the discussions. His deputy was a civilian (Soldatin?[13]) who was not too well dressed, had on a dirty collar and an ill-fitting tie. The Colonel picked his teeth with a toothpick after lunch. To the right of Soldatin was the French interpreter of the Soviet Delegation. To the left of Shkvarin was the English interpreter of the Soviet Delegation. But the English interpreter was not up to her job and most of the Russian-English interpretation was made by the American interpreter who did both our Russian and French interpretation and played a good share in the negotiations because the Russians trusted him and were somewhat embarrased by the poor quality of their own English interpreter. There were in addition two Russian secretaries, one a woman, rather shabbily dressed, and the other a rather smart and good looking lieutenant. There was in addition a Russian expert. The French delegation was headed by a

---

[7] Siehe Dok. 15, Anm. 21.
[8] Siehe Dok. 16, Anm. 11.
[9] Das 1913 errichtete Gebäude für das Preußische Kammergericht am Kleistpark in Berlin-Schöneberg, seit 1945 Sitz der Alliierten Kontrollbehörde für Deutschland (siehe Dok. 14, Anm. 5). In dem Plenarsitzungssaal waren nach dem 20. Juli 1944 vor dem sogenannten Volksgerichtshof und dessen oberstem Richter, Roland Freisler (1893-1945), die berüchtigten Schauprozesse gegen die an dem missglückten Staatsstreich gegen Adolf Hitler (siehe Dok. 22, Anm. 19) beteiligten Widerstandskämpfer inszeniert worden. Am 18. Oktober 1945 konstituierte sich dort der für den Prozess gegen die Hauptkriegsverbrecher eingerichtete Internationale Militärgerichtshof. In dieser ersten Sitzung überreichten die Ankläger die Anklageschrift. Das Verfahren wurde dann in Nürnberg weitergeführt. Nachdem die Tätigkeit der Alliierten Kontrollbehörde 1948 zum Erliegen gekommen war, wurde das Gebäude noch von der Alliierten Luftsicherheitszentrale genutzt. Heute befindet sich das Gebäude wieder im Besitz der Justiz. Foto des Gebäudes im Bildanhang, Abb. 36.
[10] Siehe Dok. 17, Anm. 45.
[11] Ulrich Wimmer, Richter am Kammergericht, in einer E-Mail an Werner Breunig vom 6. November 2012: „[...] nach Auskunft des hiesigen Hausmeisters, der seinerzeit das Gebäude von den Alliierten übernommen hatte, ist die Numerierung der Räume unverändert geblieben. Der Saal 135 [...] wird heute als Sitzungssaal für Zivilprozesse genutzt. Die Alliierten hatten darin die Luftsicherheitszentrale platziert (Berlin Air Safety Center – BASC), von dem aus der Flugbetrieb über der Stadt sowie in den Luftkorridoren kontrolliert wurde."
[12] Alexei Iwanowitsch Schkwarin (geb. 1905), sowjetischer Major, 1945-1947 Stellvertreter des Chefs der Verwaltung für Innere Angelegenheiten, SMAD.
[13] Laut Protokoll: Soldatov. Gemeint ist möglicherweise W. G. Soldatow, 1947 Chef der Unterabteilung für die Verfolgung und Verhaftung von Kriegsverbrechern in den Westzonen der Verwaltung für Innere Angelegenheiten, SMAD.

M[onsieur] Mauleon, a bureaucrat, either a prefect or sub-prefect[14]. He had with him a capable Russian interpreter (female), a deputy (M[onsieur] Fontaine), an English interpreter (male) but the French did not bother with secretaries. The English delegation was headed by a fine looking civilian (Mr. Inghram[15]), a deputy (Col. Hall), a capable Russian, and French interpreter (both female) and an officer secretary (male). We had for our chief General Gailey, who was assisted by an acting deputy (Dr. Wells[16]). We had one interpreter, the above-mentioned Russian-French interpreter (Lt. Forrest), a representative of our Secretariat (Col. Rosengren[17]) and a secretary (Miss Kramer). When the Russian chairman spoke, he had to speak sentence by sentence. Each sentence was translated first into English (when the Russian lady could manage it) and then into French. When the French chief spoke, his interpreters translated into Russian and English. When the British and Americans spoke their words, sentence by sentence, were translated into French and Russian. It is incredible that there is any understanding at all.

There were three matters up for discussion: (1) the general conditions under which future elections were to be conducted in Germany; (2) the establishment of a Sub-Committee to settle civil service problems and (3) the resolution of certain questions which had to do with the forthcoming German census.

The first question took about two hours to settle. It was settled not by agreeing on the conditions under which future elections are to be held but by turning over the question to a special working party to write up in detail, the second question was more easily dispatched because there was no substance to discuss, only the formality of a committee. The discussion on point 3 was interesting to me because it shows the great disadvantage of language as a means of understanding. On the census questionnaires which are to be submitted information is wanted on the citizenship of those at present in Germany, and on the nationality of those at present in Germany. Could you explain the differences between citizenship and nationality in English? The Russians are supposed to want information as nationality because they feel there are still here a number of persons whom the Germans deported from Russia. These they want back in Russia. The German word for citizenship is Staatsangehörigkeit. They have essentially two words for nationality. Nationalität and Volkszugehörigkeit. The Russians wanted to use Volkszugehörigkeit for nationality since it is a well established word. But the French, English and Americans did not want to use it because the Nazis gave a definite legal meaning to the word which involved

---

[14] Laut Protokoll: Prefect.
[15] William Harold Ingrams (1897–1973), britischer Kolonialbeamter, 1945–1947 Assistant Secretary, Allied Control Commission for Germany (British Element).
[16] Roger H. Wells (1894–1994), amerikanischer Politikwissenschaftler, 1923 PhD, Harvard University, lehrte 1923–1963 als Professor am Bryn Mawr College, 1927/1928 Guggenheim Fellow in Deutschland, 1946/1947 Civil Administration Division, OMGUS, Deputy Director, 1951–1953 Chief, Historical Division, HICOG, 1963–1968 Visiting Professor, Mac Murray College.
[17] Roswell P. Rosengren (1902–1988), Lieutenant Colonel, 1927 LLB, University of Buffalo Law School, 1946 Chief, Civil Service Branch, Civil Administration Division, OMGUS.

denying Germans with Jewish grandparents German nationality. Question 7 in the census sheet is to concern citizenship and Question 8 nationality. How make this distinction clear to the person (simple and ignorant) who has to fill out the blank. After prolonged discussion they agreed. The translation of the German equivalent for the French, English and Russian words for nationality was to be left up to German linguistic experts only it was forbidden that they come to the conclusion that Volkszugehörigkeit was to be used. You can get cynical about this dispute over the meaning of words while industry is at a stand-still and people are going hungry and living crowded in ruins. But if there is going to be any community of action in the 4 zones (not that these decisions really secure it) then these questions have to be discussed and agreed upon.

The questions were not of such serious political import that humanity was left out of the meeting. During it all the Russians knew what they wanted but were conciliatory. The French were clear definite and to the point but no less insistent upon their point of view. The British were quite human and civilized perhaps the most well balanced of the lot. We were not too greatly interested, but were not going to let anything be put over on us. But we sort of stole the show with our interpreter upon whom everyone came to rely.

The world could easily be run by simple men of this good will. I was attracted to them all, but especially to the French and the British. But the poor human race, trying to solve its problems by this antiquated method, antiquated in so far as language is concerned. How the world needs a universal language, and how long it will take it to get it. I could have wept at some moments. General Gailey admitted that he was discussing the use of German words, the meaning of which he did not really understand. And so we heard Staatszugehörigkeit and Volksangehörigkeit as well as Volkszugehörigkeit and Staatsangehörigkeit. Every American should understand the difficulty of these negotiations.

I hope it continues as interesting as this for the next four or five weeks. If so it will have been worth returning here.

Goodnight my sweet ones, I love my Em[ily] and John and Tim. Edgar

Dok. 20
Schreiben an die Ehefrau
Berlin, Ihnestraße 14[1], 14. März 1946

Dearest beloved –

I arrived a week ago today.[2] Five weeks have I been away from you, my darling, and my sweet boys. No letter has come but it won't be long now.

There has been a slight development with respect to what I am going to do. Yesterday morning I set out to make the acquaintance of the State Department people. I went to Mr. Murphy's[3] office, but learned that he was out of town and

---

[1] Siehe Dok. 15, Anm. 1.
[2] Am 7. März 1946 war Johnson in Berlin eingetroffen.
[3] Siehe Dok. 8, Anm. 13.

accordingly made an appointment with his secretary, a Mr. Bush[4], who is going to call me when the ambassador returns. All very elegant in Mr. Murphy's surroundings. A large vase with forsythia in it in the reception room. Then I went down to make an appointment to see Mr. Don Heath[5], the director of the political office, whom Harold Vedeler[6] asked me to see. The appointment was for three in the afternoon. Then I went to see Louis Wiesner[7], whom I have spoken of,[8] and who is a labor officer on the political staff here. Louis asked me my opinion of Walter Dorn[9], and I couldn't do else but speak favorably of Walter Dorn. He asked because the State Department people have been asked by General Barker[10], who is the U. S. representative on the Kommandatura[11] (the quadripartite administration for the city of Berlin) to suggest a person who could act as a political adviser and organize a political reporting office for him. The political situation in Berlin is particularly hot at the moment because the Communists[12] are trying to force an amalgamation with the Social Democrats[13]

---

[4] Henry C. S. Bush (geb. 1900), ab 1926 Clerk, Department of State, ab 1931 Berlin, ab 1945 Attaché, Office of US Political Adviser on German Affairs, Administrative Officer.

[5] Donald R. Heath. Siehe Dok. 8, Anm. 15.

[6] Siehe Dok. 2, Anm. 12.

[7] Siehe Dok. 8, Anm. 11.

[8] Siehe Dok. 16.

[9] Siehe Dok. 2, Anm. 10.

[10] Ray W. Barker (1889–1974), Major General, 1945–Mai 1946 Commanding General, US Headquarters Berlin District, US Commandant, Allied Kommandatura Berlin, 1947–1960 Superintendent, Manlius School. Siehe Bildanhang, Abb. 25, Abb. 26, Abb. 29, Abb. 30 und Abb. 31.

[11] Die Alliierte Kommandantur (Allied Kommandatura) Berlin hatte sich am 11. Juli 1945, nach der Ankunft der Westmächte in Berlin, am Sitz der sowjetischen Militärregierung (Luisenstraße 56, Berlin-Mitte) als oberstes politisches Organ der Stadt konstituiert. An der Spitze der Kommandantur, die ihren Sitz in dem Gebäude des Verbandes der öffentlichen Feuerversicherungsanstalten in Berlin-Dahlem, Kaiserswerther Straße 16/18 (heute Präsidialamt der Freien Universität Berlin), einrichtete, standen die vier Stadtkommandanten, die Befugnisse an ihre Stellvertreter übertragen konnten. Die über ein ständiges Sekretariat verfügenden Stabschefs der Kommandantur bereiteten die Tagesordnungen und die Sitzungen der Kommandanten und ihrer Stellvertreter vor, übermittelten dem Magistrat die alliierten Anordnungen in Form von Befehlen und klärten die täglichen Fragen. Schließlich gab es Fachkomitees. Auf allen Ebenen der Kommandantur wechselte der Vorsitz in zunächst 15-tägigem, dann monatlichem Turnus. Die Alliierte Kommandantur, um die sich die Militärregierungen der einzelnen Sektoren gruppierten, unterstand der Alliierten Kontrollbehörde für Deutschland. Siehe Dok. 14, Anm. 5. Foto des Gebäudes der Alliierten Kommandantur Berlin im Bildanhang, Abb. 37.

[12] Am 11. Juni 1945 war die Kommunistische Partei Deutschlands (KPD) als erste Partei mit einem (Wieder-)Gründungsaufruf an die Öffentlichkeit getreten. Siehe Berlin. Quellen und Dokumente 1945–1951, hrsg. im Auftrage des Senats von Berlin, bearb. durch Hans J. Reichhardt/Hanns U. Treutler/Albrecht Lampe (= Schriftenreihe zur Berliner Zeitgeschichte, Bd. 4/1. Halbbd.), Berlin 1964, Nr. 469.

[13] Die Sozialdemokratische Partei Deutschlands (SPD) hatte am 15. Juni 1945 ihren (Wieder-)Gründungsaufruf veröffentlicht. Siehe Berlin. Quellen und Dokumente 1945–1951, hrsg. im Auftrage des Senats von Berlin, bearb. durch Hans J. Reichhardt/

into a new left-wing, workers' Unity Party (Einheitspartei).[14] The fusion has already been noted in the Soviet Zone[15] and the Communists are now apparently trying to push it for Berlin. If they succeed the fusion has all sorts of political implications for the political future not only of German parties but possibly also of the future German state. We don't at least want the matter to be forced, or to have the resultant fusion party, if it is to be formed, dominated by a minority of Communists. There is a certain tension here between the Russians and us over the administration of the city. The Russians have arrested some judges in our area,[16] and we have just arrested some 12 Communists in the area for putting the interests of the Communists party before the orders of military government[17]. I know Walter Dorn was interested in this job when he was up here last because he stayed with General Barker and Colonel Howley[18] and brought the matter up to Clay[19]. But Clay advised him not to take it saying that in comparison with other things that he might do, it was small potatoes. So Dorn I guess dropped the matter.

Louis Wiesner who is interested in being in the new political office, said that he was about to go into Heath's office and was going to recommend me strongly as the State Department's appointee. When I went to see Mr. Heath, who seems to be a terribly nice guy, smooth and affable and elegant, he called in two other members of it[20] staff to meet me, a Mr. Muccio[21], whom I met at the

---

Hanns U. Treutler/Albrecht Lampe (= Schriftenreihe zur Berliner Zeitgeschichte, Bd. 4/1. Halbbd.), Berlin 1964, Nr. 470.

[14] Die KPD forderte seit Herbst 1945 einen schnellen Zusammenschluss mit der SPD, den sie nach Kriegsende zunächst abgelehnt hatte. Durch eine massive Einheitskampagne der KPD und repressive Maßnahmen der sowjetischen Besatzungsmacht gegen sozialdemokratische Fusionsgegner, die bis hin zu Verhaftungen reichten, wurde auf die SPD ein massiver Druck ausgeübt.

[15] In der Sowjetzone konnten die Sozialdemokraten nicht frei über die Zukunft ihrer Parteiorganisation entscheiden. Am 11. Februar 1946 hatte die Mehrheit des SPD-Zentralausschusses der mehr und mehr erzwungenen Vereinigung zugestimmt.

[16] Zu der Verhaftung von Richtern im amerikanischen und britischen Sektor Berlins siehe Berlin. Kampf um Freiheit und Selbstverwaltung 1945-1946, hrsg. im Auftrage des Senats von Berlin (= Schriftenreihe zur Berliner Zeitgeschichte, Bd. 1), 2., erg. und erw. Auflage, Berlin 1961, S. 335, Nr. 69 a, und 371, Nr. 79.

[17] Siehe ebd., S. 380, Nr. 24 a; Die Sitzungsprotokolle des Magistrats der Stadt Berlin 1945/46. Teil II: 1946, bearb. und eingel. von Dieter Hanauske (= Schriftenreihe des Landesarchivs Berlin, Bd. 2/II), Berlin 1999, Dok. 74, S. 258-260.

[18] Frank L. Howley (1903-1993), Colonel, amerikanischer Werbefachmann, 1925 BCS, New York University, 1937-1940 President, Frank Howley Advertising Co., Philadelphia, ab 1940 US Army, 1945-1947 US Deputy Commandant, Allied Kommandatura Berlin, 1945-1949 Director, OMGBD/OMGBS, 1947-1949 US Commandant, Allied Kommandatura Berlin, 1949 Beförderung zum Brigadier General, ab 1952 Vice Chancellor/Vice President for University Development, New York University, 1954 Verleihung der Ehrendoktorwürde (Dr. med. h. c.) der Freien Universität Berlin, ab 1962 Vice President, New York University, 1965-1967 Special Assistant to the President, New York University. Foto im Bildanhang, Abb. 32.

[19] Siehe Dok. 2, Anm. 6.

[20] Richtig: his.

[21] John J. Muccio (1900-1989), amerikanischer Diplomat, geboren in Italien, 1921 US-Staatsbürgerschaft, ab 1921 Department of State, 1924 Vice Consul, Hamburg, 1945/1946 Chief, Political Branch and Denazification Branch, Office of the Director

Lakeside Club[22], and a Mr. Steere[23], who is responsible, among other things, for Kommandatura matters. Both, I think, have had much experience in Germany. I was flattered by being told that my work in Austria was well known to them and after some discussion the question was put to me of whether I would be interested in this job and would talk with General Barker. I indicated, of course, that my fate was really in General Clay's hands but that I certainly would be interested in meeting Gen. Barker. Accordingly I was asked to come over to Mr. Steere's office this afternoon to meet the General, who put the question directly to me. I repeated that I was obligated for the time being to carry out General Clay's instructions about orienting myself here and in the zone, that I did not know what exactly Clay had in mind for me when this was over. The General decided accordingly that he must go to see Clay immediately and left to do so, after talking about how he was going to meet the problem of the misconduct of American troops stationed here in Berlin. I left Mr. Steeres's office for my own. Mr. Steere called later to say that General Barker had reported that Clay was sympathetic to his request for my service, if only for a short time but that he would have to talk the matter over with me and would give Barker an answer by Monday[24]. I suppose I shall hear from Clay tomorrow. It can do no harm to have Clay asked by another general for my services (there are so many generals). If he really has nothing especial in mind for me, this will force him to make up his mind. If he says that I should go ahead (his hesitation with Barker indicated that he is at present uncertain) I shall know that he is willing that I do a job which he told Walter Dorn was "small potatoes". I should not mind because this would be a good, and interesting and important job and I could watch the intimate workings of international machinery on a small scale where something has to be done and can be done and is, of course, being done. I should like to go on with this orientation that Clay has ordered, particularly in the zone, because I should learn much but it is not necessary to do for this Berlin job. If Clay says go ahead, I think then I should have to decide between this job and one which Taylor[25] and Knappen[26] would like to have me take in their division[27]. I suppose too Gailey[28] would offer me a job. There are evidently many good jobs here and no available good people to take them. And it is

of Political Affairs, Office of the Deputy Military Governor, OMGUS, 1949–1952 Botschafter in Südkorea.
[22] Siehe Dok. 17 und Dok. 18.
[23] Loyd V. Steere (1898–1985), amerikanischer Agrarwirtschaftsexperte und Diplomat, 1923 MBA, Harvard University, ab 1923 Bureau of Agricultural Economics, Department of Agriculture, ab 1926 Assistant Agricultural Commissioner, Berlin Office of the Department of Agriculture, ab 1929 Agricultural Commissioner/Attaché, Berlin, ab 1939 Agricultural Attaché, London, 1945/1946 Chief, Economics Branch, Office of the Director of Political Affairs, Office of the Deputy Military Governor, OMGUS.
[24] 18. März 1946.
[25] Siehe Dok. 17, Anm. 26.
[26] Siehe Dok. 8, Anm. 10.
[27] Gemeint ist die Education and Religious Affairs Branch, Internal Affairs and Communications Division, OMGUS.
[28] Siehe Dok. 15, Anm. 23.

interesting again to find that Gen. Barker needs the services of an R + A-OSS[29] just as Mr. Erhardt[30] needed them, and needs them badly.

I had luncheon yesterday with a Captain Biel[31] who is a German refugee here in the Civil Administration Branch[32], who knows the boys in the Central European Section[33], and who is interested in going into the Berlin show,[34] whether he is the right kind of German refugee, I don't know yet. But I doubt it.

General Gailey had me to dinner at his Villa[35] last night. There were drinks beforehand (a choice of Scotch, Rye or Martinis), champagne with dinner and brandy afterwards. Invited also were Mr. Fahy[36], the head of the Legal Division

---

[29] Mitarbeiter der Research and Analysis Branch, Office of Strategic Services. Siehe Dok. 1, Anm. 9.

[30] John G. Erhardt (1889-1951), amerikanischer Diplomat, ab 1919 Department of State, 1933-1937 Consul General, Hamburg, 1939-1941 Consul General and 1st Secretary, London, 1945/1946 Political Adviser to Commanding General, United States Forces Austria (USFA)/High Commissioner, Austria (US), 1946-1950 Gesandter in Österreich, 1950/1951 Botschafter in Südafrika.

[31] Ulrich E. Biel, urspr. Bielschowsky (1907-1996), Captain, deutsch-amerikanischer Jurist, geboren in Charlottenburg, Deutschland, 1933 Entlassung aus dem juristischen Vorbereitungsdienst aus rassischen Gründen, 1934 Dr. jur., Universität Bonn, 1934 Emigration in die USA, 1934-1942 Tätigkeit in der amerikanischen Privatwirtschaft (im internationalen Investment- und Exportfinanzierungsgeschäft), 1940 US-Staatsbürgerschaft, 1942-1946 US Army, 1945 mit der US Army nach Deutschland zurückgekehrt, 1946-1949 Chief, Political Affairs Section, Civil Administration Branch/Civil Administration and Political Affairs Branch, OMGBD/OMGBS, 1946-1952 im amerikanischen Staatsdienst, zunächst beim Department of War/Department of Defense, ab 1949 im Foreign Service des Department of State, 1949-1951 US Land Observer für Niedersachsen, Hannover, anschließend Mitarbeiter des amerikanischen Hohen Kommissars in Deutschland, 1952 Assessorexamen, ab 1953 Rechtsanwalt in Berlin, 1954 wieder deutsche Staatsbürgerschaft, 1965 CDU, 1967 Bestellung zum Notar, 1971-1979 Mitglied des Abgeordnetenhauses von Berlin, ab 1975 Alterspräsident, 1977 Ernst-Reuter-Plakette, ab 1984 Vorsitzender der Vereinigung ehemaliger Mitglieder des Abgeordnetenhauses von Berlin e.V., 1987 Großes Bundesverdienstkreuz mit Stern. Anthony J. Glaser (siehe Dok. 59, Anm. 6), Sohn von Louis Glaser (siehe Dok. 28, Anm. 4), in einer E-Mail an Werner Breunig vom 23. Oktober 2012 über Biel: "He was a nice man but really tough if you had information that he wanted; he could talk it out of you. Since my father had an 'intelligence' job, in addition to his regular military government job, Dr. Biel was a very important asset."

[32] Civil Administration Branch der Internal Affairs and Communications Division, OMGUS. Siehe Dok. 15, Anm. 24.

[33] Central European Section, Research and Analysis Branch, OSS.

[34] Biel wurde Leiter der Political Affairs Section, Civil Administration Branch, OMGBD. Er „sollte in Berlin Politiker auswählen, mit denen die Amerikaner zusammenarbeiten konnten". Martin Otto, Ulrich Biel (1907-1996) – graue Eminenz der (West-)Berliner Politik. Eine erste biografische Annäherung, in: Berlin in Geschichte und Gegenwart. Jahrbuch des Landesarchivs Berlin 2011, S. 285-304, hier S. 293.

[35] Auf der Insel Schwanenwerder, Inselstraße 36. Siehe Dok. 17, Anm. 13.

[36] Charles H. Fahy (1892-1979), amerikanischer Jurist, 1914 LLB, Georgetown University Law School, 1941-1945 Solicitor General, Department of Justice, 1945-Mai 1946 Legal Adviser and Director, Legal Division, OMGUS, 1946/1947 Legal Adviser, State Department, 1949-1967 Judge of the United States Court of Appeals for the District of Columbia Circuit.

and a former Solicitor General of the United States, Judge Madden[37], a former judge of the Washington D. C. court of appeals (the same job, I think, that Thurman Arnold[38] now has. There was much talk of Arnold), Mr. Walter Lichtenstein[39], a former vice-president of the First National Bank of Chicago and a very close friend of James W. Thompson[40] and Carl Frederick Huth[41] and a Col. MacLean[42], a product of the Yale Law School[43] and a special assistant to General Clay. The talk was mostly shop by those who know all of what is going on and it centered about the poor press which military government was getting in the United States. The lady who takes care of General Gailey's house is a Ph. D. from the University of Berlin[44].[45] But it was well to meet these people. They all were good substantial American types who spoke about belonging to the fraternity here.

[37] J. Warren Madden (1890–1972), amerikanischer Jurist, 1941–1945 und 1946–1961 Judge of the United States Court of Claims, 1945–Mai 1946 Associate Director, Legal Division, OMGUS, Mai/Juni 1946 Legal Adviser and Director, Legal Division, OMGUS.

[38] Thurman W. Arnold (1891–1969), amerikanischer Jurist, 1943–1945 Judge of the United States Court of Appeals for the District of Columbia Circuit.

[39] Walter Lichtenstein (1880–1964), amerikanischer Historiker, geboren in Braunschweig, Deutschland, kam im Alter von zwei Jahren mit seiner Familie in die USA, 1907 PhD, Harvard University, 1908–1918 Head Librarian, Northwestern University Library, 1918–1945 First National Bank of Chicago, Vice President, 1945–1947 Chief, Financial Institutions Branch, Finance Division, OMGUS.

[40] James W. Thompson (1869–1941), amerikanischer Historiker, 1895 PhD, University of Chicago, Professor, University of Chicago, 1932–1939 University of California, Berkeley. Thompson war in den 1920er-Jahren Johnsons "principal teacher" (Edgar N. Johnson, Curriculum Vitae, undatiert [ca. 1963], S. 1, in: UChicago Library, Special Collections Research Center, Edgar N. Johnson Papers) an der University of Chicago. Gemeinsam mit Johnson veröffentlichte er 1937 eine Neubearbeitung seiner 1931 erschienenen "History of the Middle Ages 300–1500": James Westfall Thompson/Edgar Nathaniel Johnson, An Introduction to Medieval Europe 300–1500, New York 1937.

[41] Carl F. Huth Jr. (geb. 1883), amerikanischer Historiker, 1905 MA, University of Wisconsin, 1909/1910 Lecturer, Columbia University, 1910–1948 University of Chicago (ab 1914 Professor of Ancient History). Huth war in den 1920er-Jahren ein Lehrer Johnsons an der University of Chicago.

[42] Donald H. McLean Jr. (1910–1984), Lieutenant Colonel, amerikanischer Jurist, 1935 LLB, Yale Law School, Civil Affairs Division, Department of War, 1945–1948 Special Assistant to Lucius D. Clay (siehe Dok. 2, Anm. 6), dann legal office of Socony-Vacuum Oil.

[43] Die 1843 gegründete Yale Law School ist die juristische Fakultät der Yale University in New Haven im US-Bundesstaat Connecticut.

[44] 1810 gegründete, am 29. Januar 1946 feierlich wiedereröffnete Universität.

[45] Vermutlich handelte es sich um einen Scherz. Die Frau, die sich gemeinsam mit ihrem Ehemann um das Haus kümmerte, war eine beeindruckende Persönlichkeit, besaß aber keinen Doktortitel. Es handelte sich um Helene Heller, geb. Fischer (1896–1984), ihr Ehemann war der Gärtner Erich Heller (1894–1957). Sie waren seit 1923 auf Schwanenwerder, Inselstraße 30, gemeldet. Siehe Meldekarte Erich Heller, in: LAB, B Rep. 021 (Einwohnermeldeamt Berlin). Timothy H. Gailey (siehe Dok. 17, Anm. 18) in einer E-Mail an Werner Breunig vom 29. Juli 2011: "[…] I clearly recall Frau and Herr Heller who took care of us and the wonderful thatched-roof house."

I had lunch today with General McClure[46], head of Information Control[47] and some of the members of his staff. McClure formerly had Paul Sweet[48] and Saul Padover[49] working for him,[50] said he had heard of me before and certainly remembered Paul. I learned of the present status of Furtwängler[51] who is now in Berlin, and who certainly was not much of a Nazi and of the possible advantages of having control of the paper supply for the press, periodicals, etc. (of course I learned this in Austria where the Russians controlled it in Vienna, to the advantage, the SD's[52] said of the Communists). The talk was mostly political and some colonel asked if he could come over to see me. General Gailey took me into to see General Meade[53] this afternoon who is the head of the IA + C[54] Division. He proceeded to tell me of some things that I might do for him during my trip through the zone, mostly political and interesting in their way and requiring knowledge that I shall have to get a hold of en passant. I have tried to read much these last few days and prepare to meet the other heads of the divisions.

But there are too many generals and colonels and this life so far is just a little bit hectic. I want it to settle down. And I could take a bit of the quiet and comfort and blessed happiness that exists at 3268[55]. There is enough comfort here (too much) but not enough quiet and happiness. I love you my dearest Emily and my sweetest of all boys. I shall be relieved when news comes. Goodnight my beloved. Edgar

    Dass die Eheleute Heller sich um Gaileys Haus gekümmert hatten, wurde bestätigt durch deren Sohn, Aribert Heller, in einem Telefongespräch mit Werner Breunig am 5. Januar 2010.
[46] Siehe Dok. 17, Anm. 38.
[47] Office of Information Control Services, Office of the Deputy Military Governor, OMGUS.
[48] Siehe Dok. 2, Anm. 28.
[49] Saul K. Padover (1905–1981), amerikanischer Historiker und Politikwissenschaftler, geboren in Wien, Österreich, kam 1920 mit seinen Eltern in die USA, 1932 PhD, University of Chicago, 1938–1944 Department of the Interior, 1944 Political Analyst, Federal Communications Commission, 1944 Research and Analysis Branch, OSS, 1944–1946 Intelligence Officer, Psychological Warfare Division, 12th Army Group, lehrte ab 1949 Politikwissenschaft an der New School for Social Research.
[50] McClure hatte die Psychological Warfare Division, SHAEF, geleitet, als Sweet und Padover für die Psychological Warfare Division, 12th Army Group, tätig waren.
[51] Wilhelm Furtwängler (1886–1954), deutscher Dirigent und Komponist, ab 1922 Chefdirigent des Berliner Philharmonischen Orchesters, erhielt 1945 Dirigierverbot, konnte die Berliner Philharmoniker erst nach seiner Entnazifizierung 1947 wieder dirigieren, übernahm 1952 erneut als Chefdirgent die Leitung des Orchesters.
[52] Social Democrats.
[53] Frank C. Meade (1896–1978), Brigadier General, 1945/1946 Director, Internal Affairs and Communications Division, OMGUS.
[54] Internal Affairs and Communications.
[55] 3268 South 31st Street, Lincoln (2), Nebraska, USA, wo die Johnsons seit November 1941 wohnten.

Dok. 21
Schreiben an die Ehefrau
Berlin, Ihnestraße 14[1], 16. März 1946

Dear Sweetheart –

My second Saturday[2] here gone and five weeks away from you. Nothing has come from the 25th Base Post Office[3] of Wurzburg[4].[5] Certainly something will come next week. I confess to being lonesome. When I came to my room tonight I stopped to play a bit on the piano.[6] But I could only think of John[7], his sweet remark the last lesson[8] I took him to about wanting to do well for me because it was the last time, of the piano we are going to have some time, of our house, of you and so I came upstairs.

I think the second staff meeting[9] I attended this morning has left me a little chilled. There is so little that is happening here that is actually encouraging looked at from the fundamental aspects of the situation. Our GI's[10] are not behaving very well. The ordinary civilian help (US) does not have very high standards – they deal a great deal in the Black Market[11] and are still talking about overtime. Of course there are exceptions. I ran into two very strange creatures at my table last night – ex-munition worker Wacs[12] who are now civilians, who are comparatively ignorant, who find this something of a lark and who are determined to stay here just as long as they can possibly stay.

This mind I guess has been growing. Yesterday evening I spent the evening with Dr. Max Rheinstein[13] whom I met on the boat[14]. He says there is no one

---

[1] Siehe Dok. 15, Anm. 1.
[2] 16. März 1946.
[3] Siehe Dok. 4.
[4] Würzburg, Stadt im Land Bayern in der amerikanischen Besatzungszone Deutschlands.
[5] Siehe Dok. 18.
[6] Eugene N. Anderson Jr. (siehe Dok. 4, Anm. 30) schreibt in einer E-Mail an Werner Breunig vom 17. Juli 2007 über Edgar N. Johnson: "Loved music, and relaxed by playing the piano, which he did very well – mostly 19th century classical music, often Baroque." Und in einer E-Mail von Candice E. Johnson an Werner Breunig vom 1. Juni 2010 heißt es: "Edgar did play piano in silent movie theaters, to accompany the movies!!"
[7] Johnsons Sohn John. Siehe Dok. 2, Anm. 15.
[8] Johns letzte Klavierstunde vor der Abreise seines Vaters nach Europa.
[9] Siehe Protokoll der OMGUS-Stabskonferenz am 16. März 1946, in: Archiv des IfZ, OMGUS – Staff Conferences (Protokollkopien), Fg 12/3.
[10] Government Issues, ugs. für amerikanische Soldaten.
[11] Da die Versorgungslage der Bevölkerung sehr schlecht war, Lebensmittel und Güter des täglichen Bedarfs nur gegen Lebensmittelmarken und in geringen Mengen legal in Geschäften erhältlich waren, entwickelte sich ein illegaler „Schwarzmarkt", der ein wichtiger Faktor des alltäglichen Überlebens wurde, zumal die Zuteilung der auf den Lebensmittelkarten ausgewiesenen Rationen oftmals nicht gesichert war. Siehe Werner Bührer, Schwarzer Markt, in: Deutschland unter alliierter Besatzung 1945–1949/55, hrsg. von Wolfgang Benz, Berlin 1999, S. 365f.
[12] Members of the Women's Army Corps. Siehe Dok. 13, Anm. 14.
[13] Siehe Dok. 11, Anm. 22.
[14] Gemeint ist USAT George W. Goethals, das Schiff, mit dem Johnson und Rheinstein nach Europa gekommen waren. Siehe Dok. 7, Anm. 18, und Dok. 11.

he has met here who is not working under a complete frustration (except me). When I came in he was talking with a German who in earlier days had been a prominent international lawyer in Berlin with clients such as Standard Oil, etc. He became a party[15] member and is now employed as a badge guard. This is what is known as proletarianization. In Frankfurt[16] the German who drove me to the station complained of what he had lost during the war. Dr. Rheinstein lives in the house[17] of a distinguished German cellist[18] who was a member of the Klinger Quartet[19] – evidently a famous quartet.[20] He has a Jewish Wife[21]. He was outcast by the Nazis though his wife had enough for them to live on.[22]

---

[15] Gemeint ist die Nationalsozialistische Deutsche Arbeiterpartei (NSDAP).

[16] Frankfurt am Main, Stadt im Land Groß-Hessen in der amerikanischen Besatzungszone Deutschlands.

[17] Podbielskiallee 65, Berlin-Dahlem. Das Haus gehört heute zur Botschaft der Islamischen Republik Iran und beherbergt die Iranische Schule. Foto im Bildanhang, Abb. 56.

[18] Gemeint ist Max Baldner (1887–1946), 1945/1946 Lehrer für Cello an der Hochschule für Musik der Stadt Berlin. Siehe Bildanhang, Abb. 57 und Abb. 58.

[19] Klingler-Quartett, 1905 von dem deutschen Violinvirtuosen Karl Klingler (1879–1971) gegründet, 1936 aufgelöst, zählte zu den international renommierten Streichquartetten, war besonders um die späten Streichquartette Ludwig van Beethovens (siehe Dok. 37, Anm. 29) und das Werk Arnold Schönbergs (1874–1951) bemüht. Baldner wurde nach eigenen Angaben 1914 Mitglied des Quartetts und gehörte ihm bis 1926/1927 an. Siehe Persönlicher Fragebogen Max Baldner, in: LAB, C Rep. 120 (Magistrat von Berlin, Abteilung Volksbildung), Nr. 88, Bl. 23–25, hier Bl. 24; Lebenslauf Max Baldner, in: ebd., Bl. 21 f., hier Bl. 21.

[20] Rheinstein bewohnte das Haus nicht allein. Thomas Baldner (siehe Anm. 24) in einer E-Mail an Werner Breunig vom 20. September 2010: „Da haben noch andere Offiziere der Militärregierung im Hause Podbielskiallee 65 gewohnt. Prof. Rheinstein war aber wohl derjenige, der von den Gesellschaftsräumen des Hauses in größerem Stil Gebrauch gemacht hat. Er erfand ein Zusammentreffen von amerikanischen und deutschen jungen Leuten am Sonntagnachmittag, bei dem sehr anspruchsvoll und sinnvoll über die grundlegenden Aspekte eines geistigen deutschen Wiedererwachens diskutiert wurde. Das waren für uns Jungens Feststunden. Ich habe dort, sozusagen als Fremder im eigenen Haus, meine besten Freunde dieser so aufregenden Zeit gewonnen. Max Rheinstein sei dafür heute noch großer Dank." Friedrich Glum, Zwischen Wissenschaft, Wirtschaft und Politik. Erlebtes und Erdachtes in vier Reichen, Bonn 1964, S. 571 f.: „Er [Rheinstein] nahm sich in geradezu vorbildlicher Weise der Deutschen an. Man hatte ihm die Villa des Cellisten Baldner in Dahlem zugewiesen. Dort hielt er gewissermaßen offenes Haus für Studenten und Studentinnen und andere junge Leute, die er auch mit Amerikanern zusammenbrachte."

[21] Charlotte Baldner, geb. Lindemann (1901–1996). Ihr Vater, der Kaufmann Leopold Lindemann (1862–1923), war Vorstandsmitglied der – 1929 mit der Rudolph Karstadt AG, Hamburg, verschmolzenen – Lindemann & Co. AG, Berlin, gewesen. Siehe LAB, A Rep. 342-02 (Amtsgericht Charlottenburg – Handelsregister), Nr. 12170.

[22] „Da meine Frau Jüdin ist, wurde ich aus der ‚Reichskulturkammer' ausgeschlossen und mir überhaupt jedwede Tätigkeit auf kulturellem Gebiete untersagt. Meine Anstellung als Lehrer einer Ausbildungsklasse an der Staatlichen Hochschule für Musik, zu der ich von Herrn Professor Schünemann als Nachfolger Feuermanns vorgeschlagen war, scheiterte aus dem oben angeführten Grunde. Eine Leidenszeit ohne Gleichen begann für mich und meine Familie. Wir verloren den grössten Teil unseres Vermögens, meine Kinder wurden aus dem Gymnasium verwiesen und ich selber noch im November 1944 als Zwangsarbeiter in ein Lager nach Leuna deportiert. Von dort kehrte ich

We took over his house, and then threw them out of the house.[23] They are now living with their children[24] in the cellar of a ruined house[25]. The man has been in a concentration camp.[26] The officer who threw them out came to the ruins some days afterwards and offered to sell the wife 20 cans of powdered milk for the children at the Black Market price of 15 dollars (150 Occupation Marks[27]) a

    schwer geschädigt an Leib und Seele nach Berlin zurück." Lebenslauf Max Baldner, in: LAB, C Rep. 120 (Magistrat von Berlin, Abteilung Volksbildung), Nr. 88, Bl. 21f.

[23] Thomas Baldner (siehe Anm. 24) berichtet in einer E-Mail an Werner Breunig vom 21. September 2010, dass das Haus „von einem Requirierungs-Kommando in Beschlag gelegt" wurde, „das unter Führung eines Captains zwei Tage nach Eintreffen der Amerikaner in Berlin in Windeseile das Haus sozusagen stürmte und uns anwies, es in zwei Stunden zu räumen. Alle Vorhaltungen meines Vaters, der fließend Englisch sprach, bezüglich NS-Opfer etc. nutzten nichts. Wir mussten heraus. Das Satyrspiel zu dieser Aktion folgte ein paar Tage später, als es mir gelang, einen der Flügel mittels eines Pferdewagens aus dem Hause zu ‚klauen' und in unser anderes Domizil zu schaffen."

[24] Die Zwillinge Monika und Thomas Baldner (geb. 1928) und die Zwillinge Angelika und Lutz Baldner (geb. 1931). Thomas lebt heute in den USA, Lutz in Argentinien, Angelika und Monika wohnen in Deutschland.

[25] Podbielskiallee 57, Berlin-Dahlem. Siehe Persönlicher Fragebogen Max Baldner, in: LAB, C Rep. 120 (Magistrat von Berlin, Abteilung Volksbildung), Nr. 88, Bl. 23–25, hier Bl. 23. In dem Haus hatte früher der Kaufmann Ernst von Morgen (1893–1963) mit seiner Familie gewohnt. Siehe Berliner Adreßbuch, 1938–1943: Podbielskiallee 57; Meldekarte Ernst von Morgen, in: LAB, B Rep. 021 (Einwohnermeldeamt Berlin). Im Jahre 1943 verließ die Ehefrau, Margarethe von Morgen, geb. Gräfin von Schlitz gen. von Görtz (1909–1994), mit den Kindern Berlin. Siehe Meldekarte Margarethe von Morgen, geb. Gräfin von Schlitz gen. von Görtz, in: LAB, B Rep. 021 (Einwohnermeldeamt Berlin). Wie Thomas Baldner sich in einem Telefongespräch mit Werner Breunig am 29. April 2009 erinnern konnte, hatte die Familie Baldner die letzten Kriegstage in dem verlassenen Haus Nr. 57, das über einen Luftschutzkeller verfügte, verbracht. Nach der Vertreibung aus Haus Nr. 65 durch die Amerikaner lebte die Familie dauerhaft in Haus Nr. 57. Auch die guten Englischkenntnisse Max Baldners und der Hinweis auf die Verfolgung der Familie durch die Nationalsozialisten hatten nicht verhindern können, aus dem eigenen Haus vertrieben zu werden. Angela Wepper, Tochter von Ernst von Morgen, äußerte in einem Telefongespräch mit Werner Breunig am 18. Juni 2009 die Vermutung, die Nutzung des leerstehenden Hauses sei mit ihrem Vater vereinbart worden.

[26] Max Baldner, der sich einer Trennung von seiner jüdischen Ehefrau verweigert hatte, war im November 1944 von der Gestapo als Zwangsarbeiter in ein Lager nach Leuna verschickt worden. Wegen Krankheit wurde er im Dezember 1944 entlassen. Siehe Persönlicher Fragebogen Max Baldner, in: LAB, C Rep. 120 (Magistrat von Berlin, Abteilung Volksbildung), Nr. 88, Bl. 23–25, hier Bl. 24. „Der Druck und die Unsicherheit des Daseins steigerte sich besonders in den Kriegsjahren bis zur Unerträglichkeit und gipfelte in meiner zwangsweisen Deportierung in ein Lager nach Leuna, wo ich die allerschwerste und niedrigste Arbeit verrichten musste und hinter Stacheldraht und unter ständiger Bewachung eine Art von Konzentrationslagerdasein führte. Dies war die berüchtigte ‚Aktion Mitte' veranlasst durch die Gestapo und getarnt durch die O. T. Sie erfasste all die Männer, die allen Drohungen zum Trotz, ihren jüdischen Frauen die Treue gehalten hatten. Ich erkrankte dort schwer und musste entlassen werden." Ebd., hier Bl. 25 (Beilage).

[27] Mark der Alliierten Militärbehörde, auch „Besatzungsmark" genannt. Siehe Befehl der Allied Kommandatura Berlin Nr. BK/Ord. (45) 2 vom 9. August 1945 über die Geltung des von der Alliierten Militärbehörde in Umlauf gesetzten Papiergeldes als

can.²⁸ One of the boys who came over on the boat left many of his cigarettes on the Paris Black Market and the day after his arrival here was displaying a diamond ring which he had acquired on the Black Market here. There was nothing strange in his attitude. He just took it for granted that you were a fool if you didn't take advantage of the situation. Rheinstein is going home when his present job is completed. We were lamenting the lack of anything positive in our policy, the lack of anything generous or kindly in our treatment of those Germans who are not in any sense guilty. The kids and the concentration camp victims. The sight of the Germans themselves is depressing. These are an abject, beaten bunch in appearance, sort of slinking and slouching around here at Headquarters carrying their food trays around at noon (they are fed from a central building). The kids are loafing and begging though rather piteously. I must begin to carry things around in my pockets. I was down in the center of town today and streets were empty with only a few shabbily dressed people around and the utterly depressing ruins on every hand which one wonders how they are ever going to rebuild.

I went to a political meeting this afternoon held by delegates of the Berlin section of the Conservative Party (the Christian Democratic Union²⁹).³⁰ This is slightly encouraging. I don't see how they can bear to do much political thinking and organization in view of the very uncertain future. But politics must have a future. I found the speech of the main speaker³¹ moving in spots. This party is composed of some remnants of the old Center (Catholic) Party³² and some evangelical elements. When the speaker referred to the fact that indeed the religious groups were the only ones who really fought the Nazis he got cheers.³³

    gesetzliches Zahlungsmittel für alle Arten von Markschulden in der Stadt Berlin, in: LAB, F Rep. 280 (Quellensammlung zur Berliner Zeitgeschichte [LAZ-Sammlung]), Nr. 1267.
28 Thomas Baldner berichtet in einer E-Mail an Werner Breunig vom 20. September 2010 von einem Mann, der „im Mittelstock des Hauses [Podbielskiallee 65] wohnte" und „Schwarzhandel in großem Stil betrieb. Zeitweise war das Wohnzimmer ein reines Warenlager, das nach und nach auf den Schwarzen Markt am Tiergarten wanderte. Leider hat der Mann auch Diebstahl betrieben an Wertgegenständen des Hauses."
29 Die Christlich-Demokratische Union Deutschlands (CDU) war am 26. Juni 1945 mit einem Gründungsaufruf an die Öffentlichkeit getreten. Siehe Berlin. Quellen und Dokumente 1945–1951, hrsg. im Auftrage des Senats von Berlin, bearb. durch Hans J. Reichhardt/Hanns U. Treutler/Albrecht Lampe (= Schriftenreihe zur Berliner Zeitgeschichte, Bd. 4/1. Halbbd.), Berlin 1964, Nr. 471.
30 Am 16./17. März 1946 fand der erste Parteitag des Landesverbands Groß-Berlin der CDU im Parteihaus in der Jägerstraße im Berliner Verwaltungsbezirk Mitte statt. Siehe Berlin. Kampf um Freiheit und Selbstverwaltung 1945–1946, hrsg. im Auftrage des Senats von Berlin (= Schriftenreihe zur Berliner Zeitgeschichte, Bd. 1), 2., erg. und erw. Auflage, Berlin 1961, S. 389, Nr. 53.
31 Im Mittelpunkt des ersten Verhandlungstags stand ein Vortrag von Ernst Lemmer (1898–1970), des 2. Vorsitzenden der CDU in der sowjetischen Besatzungszone.
32 Die 1870 gegründete Deutsche Zentrumspartei, genannt nach ihren Plätzen im Reichstag, war bis 1933 der wichtigste Repräsentant des politischen Katholizismus in Deutschland.
33 Lemmer in seinem Vortrag: „[...] dass es wenige Stellen in der Nazizeit gegeben hat, an denen mit so viel Mut gegen die Barbarei des Rassenwahns und des Nationalsozialismus Widerstand geleistet wurde, wie auf den Kanzeln der christlichen Kirche.

These Germans were proud that they could cite some resistance. I thought of the "God-damned Luther[34] language" in my guide[35]. The speaker took some cracks also at the Poles who are unable to make usable the waste land now being left by the evacuated Germans of Poland.[36] These Germans need some ray of hope. It is not in their immediate situation. That give it to themselves in trying to hope that Germany will again be a united state, somehow or another a more socialized state, that there will be peace, that Germany will gain the respect again of the world. There was talk about the ten commandments, about the fusion of morals and politics. There is no point in taking this all as insincere. It is pathetic. And sitting up at the front of the meeting was a Russian officer whom the speaker also was trying to please. One wonders if it isn't worth trying real Christianity on these people or at least tempering our present policy with a little bit of it. Don Heath[37] was also present at the meeting.

Clay[38] has not called me about the Berlin job so I gather he is not seriously interested in my going to General Barker[39].

Tell Wilma Peterson[40] I had lunch with Virginia Pettit[41] yesterday. She is none too happy in her job but is, nonetheless, cheerful about getting something better.

(Beifall)" Vortrag des Parteivorsitzenden Ernst Lemmer auf dem Landesparteitag am 16. März in Berlin, S. 14, in: Archiv für Christlich-Demokratische Politik (ACDP) der Konrad-Adenauer-Stiftung, Sankt Augustin, Landesverband Berlin, 03-012-032/1.

[34] Martin Luther (1483–1546), deutscher Reformator.
[35] In Johnsons Lebenslauf heißt es: "In 1943 I was granted a leave of absence from the University to join the staff of the Office of Strategic Service (Central European Division of the Research and Analysis Branch). In OSS I was associated, first, with the work on Germany and then on Austria. In the former capacity I was responsible for the final edition of the *Handbook on the German Church* and the *Military Government Guide on the German Church*." Edgar N. Johnson, Curriculum Vitae, undatiert [ca. 1963], S. 2, in: UChicago Library, Special Collections Research Center, Edgar N. Johnson Papers. Petra Marquardt-Bigman, Amerikanische Geheimdienstanalysen über Deutschland 1942–1949 (= Studien zur Zeitgeschichte, Bd. 45), München 1995, S. 288, erwähnt einen von Johnson ausgearbeiteten Civil Affairs Guide "The Protestant and the Catholic Churches in Germany", War Department Pamphlet No. 31-120.
[36] Ernst Lemmer sagte: „Zur Ueberwindung der Ernährungsschwierigkeiten bei uns und in aller Welt gehört freilich auch, und das darf ich ohne missverstanden zu werden, aussprechen, dass es nicht nur in Deutschland, sondern in ganz Europa keine Zone, kein Gebiet geben darf, in dem nicht menschliche Anstrengungen sich zeigen, das Letzte auf dem Boden für die Sicherung des täglichen Brotes der Menschen herauszuholen. (Zurufe: Schlesien!) Da denken wir an verschiedene Räume unseres Kontinents, sie mögen zur Zeit verwaltet werden von wem es auch sei, ihre nationale Zukunft mag sich entwickeln wie es nur sei; aber unvollstellbar ist, dass es fruchtbaren Boden auf diesem Kontinent geben darf, der einer Wüste gleich brach liegt, wenn es gilt, das Letzte auf den Kräften des Bodens herauszuholen. (Starker Beifall)" Vortrag des Parteivorsitzenden Ernst Lemmer auf dem Landesparteitag am 16. März in Berlin, S. 10f., in: ACDP, Landesverband Berlin, 03-012-032/1.
[37] Donald R. Heath. Siehe Dok. 8, Anm. 15.
[38] Siehe Dok. 2, Anm. 6.
[39] Siehe Dok. 20, Anm. 10.
[40] Wahrscheinlich eine in Lincoln, Nebraska, lebende Bekannte.
[41] Virginia M. Pettit, später verh. Loomis (geb. 1922) aus Lincoln, Nebraska, Februar 1946–1947 "a stenographer with the State Department attached to the Berlin Office Military Government of the United States (OMGUS)". E-Mail von Kelly Loomis,

I suppose I'll feel better when I get something specific to do. I shall be leaving for the zone by the end of the week if the Berlin thing doesn't eventuate.

Your love for me and mine for you alone give sense to the word. Goodnight my precious Emily and my boys. Edgar

Dok. 22
Schreiben an die Ehefrau
Berlin, Ihnestraße 14[1], 17. März 1946

My lovely Sweetheart and my boys:

It has been an interesting day, and from it I have learned, I think, much, much that will be of further use, much that helps one to come to basic points of view. On the day I left Washington, Polly[2] received a telephone call from a German refugee friend whom she had helped, a certain Frau Posener[3], who is the wife of a distinguished German archivist[4], who was employed by the Government Archives in Washington[5], but who, because of the interference of Congress[6], had to give up his job, and is now the Acting Dean of the Graduate School of American University[7].[8] She has just learned the whereabouts of her Mother in Berlin, and Polly therefore gave me as much foodstuffs as I wanted to carry for this

    Schwiegertochter von Virginia P. Loomis, an Werner Breunig vom 14. Juni 2012. Im November 1946 heiratete Virginia M. Pettit in Berlin John J. Loomis (1921-1995): "Miss Virginia Pettit of Political Affairs will become the bride of John J. Loomis of the Motor Battalion Saturday, November 16th at 3 p. m., in the Nikolassee church, 1 Kirche Weg, with Chaplain Marvin E. Utter performing the ceremony." Four Weddings Held At OMGUS This Week, in: Berlin Observer vom 15. November 1946, S. 2.

[1] Siehe Dok. 15, Anm. 1.
[2] Pauline R. Anderson. Siehe Dok. 2, Anm. 2.
[3] Katharina Posner, geb. Melchior, gesch. Bungert (1898-1979), 1918/1919 und 1925-1928 Kanzleigehilfin am Preußischen Geheimen Staatsarchiv, Berlin-Dahlem, 1939 Emigration in die USA.
[4] Ernst Posner (1892-1980), deutsch-amerikanischer Historiker und Archivar, geboren in Berlin, Deutschland, 1920 Dr. phil., Universität Berlin, 1922-1935 Staatsarchivrat am Preußischen Geheimen Staatsarchiv, Berlin-Dahlem, 1930-1935 Dozent, Institut für Geschichtswissenschaft und Archivwissenschaftliche Fortbildung, Berlin-Dahlem, 1936 Zwangspensionierung, 1939 Emigration über Schweden in die USA, 1942-1961 Leiter der Archivkurse des Nationalarchivs in Washington, D. C., 1944 US-Staatsbürgerschaft, 1945-1961 Professor of History and Archival Administration, American University, Berater der amerikanischen Militärregierung beim Aufbau des deutschen Archivwesens, 1954 Begründer und Leiter des Instituts für Records Management, 1955/1956 Präsident der Society of American Archivists.
[5] Gemeint sind die 1934 errichteten National Archives of the United States mit Sitz in Washington, D. C.
[6] Die Legislative der USA, setzt sich aus dem Senat und dem Repräsentantenhaus zusammen.
[7] 1893 gegründete Universität in Washington, D. C.
[8] Eugene N. Anderson (siehe Dok. 1, Anm. 1) und Pauline R. Anderson hatten Ernst und Katharina Posner bei ihrer Emigration in die USA geholfen und unterhielten freundschaftliche Beziehungen. Siehe Wolfgang A. Mommsen, Ernst Posner, Mittler

Mother whose name is Frau Melchior[9]. This morning, about ten o'clock, I started out to find her. She lives in Wannsee[10], the westernmost part of our zone of occupation in Berlin. She was living in a house which had been pretty thoroughly ruined by bombs which fell in the neighborhood. I was invited to wait in the dining room for her. At the table was a family who had fled the Russians from the East and were now settled in Berlin. I was interested in what they were eating because I have been told by the Germans here that there were no potatoes to be had. But these people had plenty of potatoes to eat for lunch and along with them they were eating what was in so far as I could see was a meat (hamburger) concoction, which supplied also plenty of gravy. The family I did not like because they started to complain to me about the manner in which they had to live. In fact the lady who dominated the scene struck an elevated tone, referred to the menschenunwürdig (inhumane) character of their dwelling; indeed she compared it with a concentration camp. I was almost moved to a very angry speech. Here was a woman accusing me, an American, of subjecting Germans to concentration camp conditions without giving a thought to what the Germans had created for other peoples. I think the Germans are fundamentally hopeless. You can't tell them that they are responsible for anything. Frau Melchior is in fact living in very shabby and unsatisfactory conditions but she is alive, and healthy and cheerful and is now beginning to have the support of Americans who have been set on her trail. There are hundreds of thousands of young Americans who are dead to make this possible for her. I brought her foodstuffs from Washington which Polly had given me, and I added to these some of the supplies which I have accumulated since coming here. But I was given to believe that this was no more than was to be expected. The Americans exist in order to administer unto the Germans who now suffer more than anyone else in this world if we are to believe their story. There are of course fundamentally tragic undertones to this general situation. There were at the table to which I referred above, two children. Their Mother had committed suicide in Posen[11] when the Russians approached, and the father's whereabouts were unknown. They had accordingly been taken over by an aunt. But their future is as secure as, under the circumstances it can be, and we can hardly be responsible for mothers and fathers without courage who have fallen for the Nazi Russian propaganda. Under American auspices Frau Melchior will soon move to better quarters[12] and await her transportation to the United States to join her chil-

zwischen deutschem und amerikanischem Archivwesen. Zu seinem 75. Geburtstag, in: Der Archivar, Jg. 20, 1967, Heft 3, Sp. 217-230; Eugene N. Anderson Papers, Collection 2074, Box 2, Folder 2-5, in: University of California, Los Angeles (UCLA), Charles E. Young Research Library, Department of Special Collections, Los Angeles, California, USA.

[9] Hedwig Melchior, geb. Krüger (geb. 1870).
[10] Ortsteil im Berliner Verwaltungsbezirk Zehlendorf.
[11] Posen, heute Hauptstadt der gleichnamigen Woiwotschaft in Polen, war am 23. Februar 1945 durch sowjetische Truppen erobert worden. Im September 1939 hatte die deutsche Wehrmacht Posen besetzt, die Stadt wurde Hauptstadt des Reichsgaus Wartheland.
[12] Laut Meldekarte war Hedwig Melchior ab 1. April 1946 in der Spanischen Allee 110 im Berliner Verwaltungsbezirk Zehlendorf gemeldet. Siehe Meldekarte Hedwig Melchior, geb. Krüger, in: LAB, B Rep. 021 (Einwohnermeldeamt Berlin).

dren[13]. She has it much better than the American soldiers who are buried on German soil. I was much annoyed when a young lady who accompanied Frau Melchior and myself on a visit to the quarters which she will soon occupy (now occupied by American GI's[14] of the 209th Division) suggested that of course the few broken windows in the house would be repaired by us before the old lady moved in. These windows have not been repaired in order to make the occupation of American GI's more comfortable and healthful. I don't see why they should be repaired for an old lady in excellent condition whose daughter abandoned her in order to come to the comfortable United States. This young lady expected as a matter of course that we would do more for Germans than we would do for GI's.

I hope we don't become in the U. S. the victims of another crusade of German self-pity and appeal for sympathy. They have much to learn here in order to become convinced that they are not a people whom it is the privilege of the world to exalt above all others. I saw thousands of Germans today. I could not tell what they were thinking, and indeed it is better for my state of mind that I do not know. But I can tell you how these thousands of Germans were dressed and how they looked. Their clothes are a little bit worn, slightly shabby, but they are good and will be good for years to come. The women have on, for the most party, fur coats or fur-decorated coats and the men have on good substantial warm cloth coats. The women's stockings are silk or rayon and I saw no mended ones. The children are well and warmly dressed. These people are not starving. They must have plenty of reserves. They have none of the ashen look which the Viennese had when I first came to Vienna in August[15]. In fact I took particular note of color in the cheeks, and I'll swear that for the most part, they all, old and young alike, had color in their cheeks, more indeed than you and I have. They were all out hunting wood and bringing it back in wagon loads and on their backs. But they all have at least one warm room, and a stove and wood enough and with this it is possible to get along. Who in the hell are these Germans anyway who have brought untold misery upon the world and murdered many millions of their own compatriots as well who expect that the Allies have come to occupy this land in order to prepare for the criminal Germans a situation which is better than that of anyone else in Europe. I want to be fair but I don't want to be the victim of a sympathy campaign. If the Germans don't suffer a bit they won't know what the last 16 years have been all about. I helped some women onto the subway with their little wagons of wood. But they seemed to think that this was to be expected of me. They didn't say thank you. I opened the door of the subway for another lady. She looked at me with slight contempt and did not deign to say thank you.

I ran into a slightly different atmosphere this afternoon when I went to call on some friends of Franz's[16] for whom I brought a heavy package all the way from Washington. They did not seem to be aware of what I had done. At least

---

[13] Im Februar 1947 meldete sich Hedwig Melchior nach Arlington im US-Bundesstaat Virginia ab. Siehe ebd.
[14] Government Issues, ugs. für amerikanische Soldaten.
[15] Johnson war am 7. August 1945 nach Wien gekommen.
[16] Franz L. Neumann. Siehe Dok. 1, Anm. 8.

they did not go out of their way to say thank-you. But there was one woman present who caught my sympathy. She was a Frau Leber[17]. Her husband[18] was a Social Democrat who was involved in the conspiracy of 20 July against Hitler's[19] life.[20] He was caught and brought before the Volksgericht[21] (the people's court) which is now the Control Council's headquarters[22]. Her husband was given an official defender. His defense she said, consisted of one sentence: "I know this man has committed a serious crime, and I hope the court will bring out a verdict corresponding to the seriousness of the crime." The man was sentenced to death and Frau Leber is now a widow, prominent in Social Democratic circles, left with two children[23]. What she could not understand, and I agree with her fully, is that, after happenings like this a man like Göring[24] is permitted to take the stand and spew his rot for days on end, and thus awaken all the dormant sentiments of the Nazis lurking in the German Hintergrund. I too wish that we could shoot these guys and have an end of their criminal and offensive talk.

I shall finish my work here this week and be off to the zone. I think too I shall go out and stay with General Gailey[25] tomorrow night. My best use, here, as I see it, is to deal with Germans for the Americans. They have little contact and little understanding. And I think I prefer to be out in the zone. Berlin is interesting politically, and especially at the present moment, when the Commu-

---

[17] Annedore Leber, geb. Rosenthal (1904–1968), deutsche Politikerin (SPD), Jurastudium an der Universität München, Lehre als Schneiderin, 1927 SPD, 1945/1946 Mitglied des Frauensekretariats im Zentralausschuss der SPD, ab 1946 Lizenzträgerin des „Telegraf", einer SPD-nahen, britisch lizenzierten Zeitung, 1946-1951 Mitglied der Stadtverordnetenversammlung von Groß-Berlin, 1963–1967 Mitglied des Abgeordnetenhauses von Berlin.

[18] Julius Leber (1891–1945), deutscher Politiker (SPD), Gewerkschaftler, Widerstandskämpfer gegen den Nationalsozialismus, 1912 SPD, 1920 Dr. rer. pol., Universität Freiburg im Breisgau, 1921–1933 Mitglied der Lübecker Bürgerschaft, 1924–1933 MdR, 1944 Verurteilung zum Tode durch den Volksgerichtshof, 1945 Hinrichtung in Berlin-Plötzensee.

[19] Adolf Hitler (1889–1945), NS-Politiker, ab 1921 Vorsitzender der NSDAP, 1933 Ernennung zum Reichskanzler, 1934–1945 „Führer und Reichskanzler", errichtete in Deutschland die nationalsozialistische Diktatur.

[20] Am 20. Juli 1944 waren das Attentat von deutschen Widerstandskämpfern auf Adolf Hitler und der versuchte Staatsstreich gegen das NS-Regime gescheitert.

[21] Der Volksgerichtshof war 1934 als Sondergericht zur Aburteilung von Hoch- und Landesverrat gegen den NS-Staat in Berlin eingerichtet worden und wurde 1936 ein ordentliches Gericht.

[22] Die Alliierte Kontrollbehörde für Deutschland hatte ihren Sitz im Gebäude des ehemaligen Berliner Kammergerichts in Berlin-Schöneberg. Siehe Dok. 14, Anm. 5.

[23] Katharina Leber, ab 1950 verh. Heinemann, später verh. Christiansen (1929–2008) und Matthias Leber (1931–1963).

[24] Hermann Göring (1893–1946), NS-Politiker, 1932 Wahl zum Reichstagspräsidenten, 1933 Ernennung zum Ministerpräsidenten von Preußen, 1935 Übernahme des Oberbefehls über die Luftwaffe, erhielt 1940 den für ihn geschaffenen militärischen Dienstgrad „Reichsmarschall des Großdeutschen Reiches", 1946 vom Internationalen Militärgerichtshof in Nürnberg als Hauptkriegsverbrecher zum Tode verurteilt, entzog sich der Vollstreckung durch Selbstmord.

[25] Siehe Dok. 15, Anm. 23.

nists are trying to force the Socialists into a United Socialist Workers' Party, but it is an ugly city, and rampant with the essential decadence of the metropolis and I prefer to be out where it is possible to look a peasant in the face, and to walk in the shade of a pleasant forest adjoining a nicer valley. I find, so far, that the Germans are a tremendously uninteresting people, not worth the sacrifice we have made to liberate them. And I don't believe they have much to offer the world. They will return to their old ways quickly, and expect us to help them to them. May be the Communists can cure them of this but I doubt it.

Good-night, my beloved, I am sorry to seem so hard-boiled. But I did fill several children's hands with chocolate today and other people's with food-stuffs and cigarettes. I love you and my boys, above all, humans that I know are to be trusted. Edgar

Dok. 23
Schreiben an die Ehefrau
Berlin, Ihnestraße 14[1], 18. März 1946[2]

Dearest Sweetheart –

No letter, still, today. I sent you a cable with my address and with a little ultimate word. Love. I hope you will feel all that went into the word even though the manner of its transmission is just a bit mechanical. I shall soon have to look up the manner and the circumstances under which one may use the international telephone.

You may have wondered why I have not mentioned the possibility of your coming over here. It is because the situation is as I suspected. No one who does not promise to stay at least one year has a chance of bringing his family over and I am told that even in this the military has the advantage over the civilians. Nor do I think that you would be particularly happy in Berlin. Life here for dependents is going to be something like life in a missionary compound in a foreign land. There will not be, I think, any serious discomforts. The quarters will be adequate. I heard of plans today to move out bachelor officers from apartments and houses to "bachelor quarters", so that these facilities will be available to dependents. There will be plenty of food from the army commissary, good medical care from army doctors, and I read today of plans to bring over American teachers to teach American children in American schools in Berlin. It is permitted also to bring over American cars. I suppose, when I get finally settled that I shall be permitted an army car. In general, however, I think, that we shall be confined, American families, I mean, to the environs of Berlin. There are then the advantages of what is going on in Berlin. There is the musical and artistic life of a large city. There may be some chance to get acquainted with the families of our Allies, though all this depends upon language facilities. I don't believe there is going to be any difficulty about disease or unrest. But, in

---

[1] Siehe Dok. 15, Anm. 1.
[2] Im Briefkopf heißt es: "Monday, 17 March 1946". Nicht der 17., sondern der 18. März 1946 war ein Montag.

any case, I am not going to be able to bring you over here if I am to come home in the Fall.

There remains the possibility of bringing you over someplace else. I talked with a man at dinner who has his wife and two children in a small inn in Sussex, England. This costs him about 400 dollars a month and all expenses, of course, he has to bear. He can't get to see them very often. The advantage is chiefly their being able to live in England, though I should think that living in an inn in Sussex for an extended period of time might have its limitation. Then there is Switzerland, which, indeed, could be much more exciting. That would cost, I understand, even less. It might not cost more that it costs for you to live with the kids[3] in Lincoln[4]. Transportation expenses would then amount to a payment for the privilege of living in Switzerland for awhile. Other countries are, I think rather out of the question (I am thinking of Denmark) as the Scandinavian countries, because of the difficulty of making arrangements and of my ever getting there. Until I know where I am to be settled I don't think there is much point in our discussing the question further. But if I land in Stuttgart[5] then I believe it is worth contemplating your coming there. It is possible that one could find a lovely out of the way spot in the mountains where you and the kids would be quite delighted, and I could get there once in a while and we could go home together. I think that you should get something out of this foreign migration of mine by way of European experience. But we can't discuss it very practically until we know what it will cost, and that we can't very well know until, if I get to Stuttgart, I can get to Switzerland and make some inquiries.

I had an interview with Ambassador Murphy[6] at noon. I must say he was very cordial and evidently had received some kind of a letter from Jimmy Riddleberger[7] concerning me, for he professed to know about me and what I had done. The interview was unsatisfactory in so far as it was constantly interrupted by telephone, and then finally General Clay[8] appeared and showed the Ambassador a telegram. I was not made to feel as if I should leave the room. In fact I was drawn a bit into the discussion of the telegram without being shown its contents. I could surmise its contents but I don't believe I am free to reveal my surmise. I'll tell you if I am subsequently confirmed by events. In any event my surmise was not encouraging. The Ambassador indicated that he would wish to see me later at some greater length before I go off on my trip. I have been invited for Wednesday[9] to a dinner at Don Heath's[10] at which Murphy may be present. In any case I seem to have gotten off to a good start in so far as the State Department people are concerned. And I am not sorry if General Clay

---

[3] Gemeint sind die Söhne John und Thomas. Siehe Dok. 2, Anm. 15 und 16.
[4] Hauptstadt des US-Bundesstaats Nebraska, wo Johnson mit seiner Familie wohnte und an der Universität lehrte.
[5] Hauptstadt des Landes Württemberg-Baden in der amerikanischen Besatzungszone Deutschlands.
[6] Siehe Dok. 8, Anm. 13.
[7] James W. Riddleberger. Siehe Dok. 8, Anm. 12.
[8] Siehe Dok. 2, Anm. 6.
[9] 20. März 1946.
[10] Donald R. Heath. Siehe Dok. 8, Anm. 15.

has appeals for my help now from General Barker[11], and then sees me later in Ambassador Murphy's office.

I also had a good talk today with Mr. Fahy[12], whom, I believe, I have already mentioned,[13] the head of the legal division, a shrewd and genial southerner. It was about the mechanics of the legal division for the most part and therefore not especially revealing. I did learn however that the French opposition to the establishment of a central German administration goes so far that they will not even consent to talking about the setting up of a German Central Patent Office. The practice of the legal division is to bring over special experts (on prisons, patents, e. g.) from the U. S. to head the administrative branches here. Tomorrow I am to see the Head of the Manpower Division and this should prove more interesting.[14] I leave at the end of the week for about a month's trip through the zone. It ought to be Spring now in the South. After that I hope to get something definite to do.

I have the feeling now that things are going to turn out all right in so far as the importance of what I am to do is concerned. But the future here of all our work depends upon the uncertainty of the food situation. The British, as you know, have cut their rations to something over a thousand, a virtually starvation ration.[15] I read in a German paper today that the French have cut their ration to well below 1000 calories.[16] This is disastrous. You can't preach democracy on empty stomachs, and you can't exemplify democracy by cutting rations. The Germans won't be much interested in the right to elect their own officials if they are starving while filling in the ballot. I only hope that we don't have to reduce the rations in our zone.[17] It would be disastrous for the slow progress we have made here, and fatal to whatever trust the Germans put in us. I hope you will preach the gospel at home of the necessity of keeping up our present minimum ration here in order to achieve even a minimum political victory. If necessary to heal this spot of Europe we have to feed our former enemies before our friends even if Americans have to tighten their belts slightly to do it. In my report of yesterday[18] I think I exaggerated to the extent that the people whom one sees on the streets are those who are healthy enough to be on the streets. I

---

[11] Siehe Dok. 20, Anm. 10.
[12] Siehe Dok. 20, Anm. 36.
[13] Siehe Dok. 19.
[14] Siehe Dok. 24.
[15] In der britischen Besatzungszone waren die Rationen für normale Verbraucher auf 1014 Kalorien täglich gekürzt worden. Siehe Der Tagesspiegel vom 28. Februar 1946, S. 2; Berliner Zeitung vom 1. März 1946, [S. 1].
[16] In der französischen Besatzungszone wurde die Brotration von 270 Gramm täglich auf 200 Gramm herabgesetzt. Damit betrug die Gesamtzuteilung weniger als 1000 Kalorien täglich, die geringste Zuteilung in den vier Zonen. Siehe Der Tagesspiegel vom 16. März 1946, S. 2; Berliner Zeitung vom 17. März 1946, [S. 1].
[17] Am 29. März 1946 setzte der stellvertretende US-Militärgouverneur Lucius D. Clay (siehe Dok. 2, Anm. 6) die Ministerpräsidenten von Bayern, Groß-Hessen und Württemberg-Baden davon in Kenntnis, "that the present daily scale of 1550 calories for the normal consumer in the American Zone would be cut to 1275 calories, effective April 1". Food Ration Cut To 1275 Calories, in: The Grooper vom 30. März 1946, S. 1.
[18] Siehe Dok. 22.

understand there are plenty of people here who are strong enough only to remain in bed from day to day. How true this actually is I don't know. Perhaps for some old people.

This is not an attractive world over here. As it becomes less attractive more Americans will be going home. Those here now and those who stay are to be given credit for sticking out a pretty hopeless job.

I kiss you my sweet Emily, and my dear John and Thomas. How I long for news. It must come soon. I love you with all of me. Edgar

Dok. 24
Schreiben an die Ehefrau
Berlin, Ihnestraße 14[1], 19. März 1946

My sweet beloved one:

I am a little discouraged tonight over the future here – my personal future I mean. I started out the day nicely with a conference with Mr. Werts[2], the head of the Manpower (Labor) Division who appears to be a good American liberal. He let me attend a meeting of Labor officers from the field who were discussing the problem of trade union organization in the zone, and this was interesting, and even moving – good Americans trying to do the best job they know how.

When I got back to the office I was told that General Clay[3] was about to call me. He did and asked me to come right over. We talked generally for about fifteen minutes about the difficulties inherent in the general situation here especially with the threatened reduction in our calorie rations[4]. He even read to me the telegram which McNarney[5] sent to the War Department yesterday about this threat.[6] It was the telegram which he and Murphy[7] discussed yesterday in

---

[1] Siehe Dok. 15, Anm. 1.
[2] Leo R. Werts (1905–1989), 1945/1946 Deputy Director, Manpower Division, OMGUS, Juni 1946–1949 Director, 1949/1950 Associate Director, Office International Labor Affairs, Department of Labor, 1950–1953 Deputy Executive Director, Defense Manpower Administration.
[3] Siehe Dok. 2, Anm. 6.
[4] Siehe Dok. 23.
[5] Siehe Dok. 17, Anm. 41.
[6] Clay erwähnt das Telegramm in seinen Erinnerungen: „Im März waren die Anzeichen der Not unverkennbar. Ich fühlte mich veranlaßt, General McNarney nahezulegen, General Eisenhower [siehe Dok. 18, Anm. 25] durch ein Kabel persönlich um seine Unterstützung dafür zu bitten, daß geholfen wurde. Wir hatten den Deutschen versprochen, für genügend Lebensmittel zu sorgen, um die ihnen zugebilligte Ration aufrecht zu erhalten. In seinem Telegramm wies McNarney darauf hin, daß mit der verkürzten Ration das Existenzminimum nicht mehr gesichert sei; Krankheit und Unterernährung seien unvermeidlich, die Arbeitsleistung der Bevölkerung werde rapid absinken. Wir konnten nicht erwarten, Demokratie bei Hungerrationen zu entwickeln; wir konnten nicht einmal Krankheiten und Unzufriedenheit aufhalten." Lucius D. Clay, Entscheidung in Deutschland, Frankfurt am Main 1950, S. 297. Siehe Wolfgang Krieger, General Lucius D. Clay und die amerikanische Deutschlandpoli-

Murphy's office when I was there.[8] Then finally he came to the main point of what I was going to do.

The just of it is that the Stuttgart[9] job[10] is out until Pollock[11] goes home which is I believe towards the end of the summer, and that is when I want to go home. He explained quite decently what I understand perfectly – it is nobody's fault except the bureaucracy's in Washington – that because of the protracted delay in my return here (about which they did nothing) he had to send Pollock down to Stuttgart, and that, because Pollock had built up, and grown into and come to love, the job, he could hardly summon him to Berlin, and send me down there. I can understand this. I shouldn't like to be treated this way either – only it is a little hard on me. If I had known that I wasn't going to have the Stuttgart job, than I shouldn't have returned here. I should be in Lincoln[12] with the people I love best of all. He then went on to bring up the job with Colonel Barker[13] which I have mentioned in a previous letter[14], and asked me what I thought about it. I told him that it was a question of alternatives. He then went on to speak of his plans to use Walter Dorn[15] and myself as special assistants to him for the purpose of constant travelling through the zone, in order to keep an oversight over what is going on both in M[ilitary] G[overnment] and German circles – something like Charlemagne's[16] missi

---

tik 1945–1949 (= Forschungen und Quellen zur Zeitgeschichte, Bd. 10), Stuttgart 1987, S. 169.
[7] Siehe Dok. 8, Anm. 13.
[8] Siehe Dok. 23.
[9] Hauptstadt des Landes Württemberg-Baden in der amerikanischen Besatzungszone Deutschlands.
[10] Die Leitung des RGCO in Stuttgart. Siehe Dok. 2, Anm. 11.
[11] Siehe Dok. 15, Anm. 6.
[12] Hauptstadt des US-Bundesstaats Nebraska, wo Johnson mit seiner Familie wohnte und an der Universität lehrte.
[13] Siehe Dok. 20, Anm. 10.
[14] Siehe Dok. 20.
[15] Siehe Dok. 2, Anm. 10.
[16] Karl der Große (wahrscheinlich 747–814), stammte aus dem Geschlecht der Arnulfinger, das später nach ihm Karolinger genannt wurde, ab 768 König der Franken, ab 774 auch König der Langobarden, ab 800 römischer Kaiser.
[17] Die Königsboten, die von Karl entsandt wurden, um die als Stellvertreter des Königs eingesetzten Grafen zu überwachen. Hierzu James Westfall Thompson/Edgar Nathaniel Johnson, An Introduction to Medieval Europe 300–1500, New York 1937, Kapitel 9 ("The Frankish State under the Carolingians"), S. 251 f.: "To supervise the counts and check their frequent abuses of power Charles created a new official, the *missus dominicus*, or royal messenger. The empire was divided into districts, each consisting of a number of counties, over which the *missi*, usually two, a layman and a bishop or abbot, made yearly circuits. They were intended also to serve as a direct link between the people and the emperor, to whom they submitted regular reports. In his *General Capitulary about the Missi*, of 802, Charles ordered them 'to investigate and to report to him any inequality or injustice that might appear in the law as then constituted … to inquire diligently into every case where any man complained that he had been dealt with unjustly by anyone, and in the fear of God to render justice to all, to the holy churches of God, to the poor, to widows and orphans and to the whole people; … they are not to be hindered in the doing of justice by the flattery or bribery of anyone, by their partiality for their own friends or by the fear of

dominici[17] if you remember.[18] He said he planned to get out an order to this effect and to establish us, as special assistants in offices close to him. He explained that Colonel Barker only wanted to borrow me for a period of six or eight weeks, and that he thought that during this time I should only have to spend about three or four days a week on the Berlin job. Since I am over here there is not much point in my getting on my high horse and deciding to come home immediately. I said I was only interested in my greatest utility and that I thought I could be of most use in dealing with Germans and trying to further our democratic aims. He accordingly asked me to get in touch with General Barker as soon as possible and talk over the job with him. Accordingly I have made arrangements to see him tomorrow, and I shall go over the details of the job with him. The only alternative I have is to go with Taylor[19] and Knappen's[20] crowd.[21] I shall make my real decision tomorrow. The Berlin job, according to those I talk with here is an interesting and relatively important job. It involves setting up a democratic government for Berlin,[22] elections, a constitution for the city, etc. To do this involves quadripartite negotiations which ought to be interesting too. Berlin is a kind of small Germany. It involves also becoming acquainted with the political leaders of Berlin, and Berlin is, at the moment, the political center of this potential democratic state.

The inspection of the zone job is also an interesting one. Somewhat along my OSS[23] line. It is the sort of thing which Walter Dorn is now doing for General Adcock[24], and which he will continue to do for Clay when once he moves up here from Frankfurt[25]. This will involve my working with Walter Dorn. But Walter Dorn, I am afraid, can't be worked with. He is a little of a prima donna. Therefore we should either have to divide the Länder between us or I should

    powerful men.' The *missi* held their own courts, and supervised the administration of the counts and their subordinates, of the bishops and abbots, and of the officers of the royal domain. They were even given the authority in extreme cases to remove for cause royal officials. They were protected by a triple wergild, and armed resistance to them was punishable by death. When loyal and honest the *missi* were an effective aid to efficient centralized administration. But from the beginning Charles feared that they too might become identified with local interests, and provided that their circuits be changed every year, to prevent collusion between *missi* and counts."

[18] Dorn wurde dann im April 1946 zum Sonderberater Clays für die Beziehungen zwischen den Military Government Detachments und den deutschen regionalen Dienststellen ernannt. Siehe Josef Henke/Klaus Oldenhage, Office of Military Government for Germany (U. S.), in: OMGUS-Handbuch. Die amerikanische Militärregierung in Deutschland 1945-1949, hrsg. von Christoph Weisz (= Quellen und Darstellungen zur Zeitgeschichte, Bd. 35), München 1994, S. 1–142, hier S. 45.

[19] Siehe Dok. 17, Anm. 26.

[20] Siehe Dok. 8, Anm. 10.

[21] Gemeint ist eine Tätigkeit in der Education and Religious Affairs Branch, Internal Affairs and Communications Division, OMGUS. Siehe Dok. 15 und Dok. 20.

[22] Der erste Berliner Nachkriegsmagistrat war von der sowjetischen Besatzungsmacht eingesetzt worden, hatte also keine demokratische Legitimation.

[23] Office of Strategic Services. Siehe Dok. 1, Anm. 9.

[24] Siehe Dok. 14, Anm. 9.

[25] Frankfurt am Main, Stadt im Land Groß-Hessen in der amerikanischen Besatzungszone Deutschlands.

have to work for Walter, which I did not come back here to do. This may be reason for my preserving a certain amount of independence by taking up the Berlin job.

I was also planning to leave for the zone on Friday[26]. General Gailey[27] made special arrangements at Frankfurt for me to have a car with which to make the trip. It is now possible that I shall have to give this up, or at least make only a short trip. Anyway I want to go to Frankfurt and talk with Walter Dorn. It will depend upon my interview with Colonel Barker tomorrow.

And so this is an unsatisfactory and shifting world. Clay is all right I think. He is hardly to blame and understands the importance of having some satisfactory civilians around. I shall always be well treated by him. But I didn't come here to be well treated by Clay but to do a job. Yet I can't pick up and go home like a child. I can learn something by staying on the spot.

A letter from you would help. I heard today that there are endless delays in getting mail from one city to another in Germany, and I remember how long it took to get things from Munich[28] to Salzburg[29]. Now that you have my cable I can at least hope for something in ten days or so, provided I am at that time in Berlin. I guess I don't really like change when I personally am involved. It's all right in the past.

I love you, my sweetest, and think of you in many, most intimate ways. I kiss you and the sweet little lads of ours[30]. Edgar

Dok. 25
Schreiben an die Ehefrau
Berlin, Ihnestraße 14[1], 22. März 1946[2]

Dearest beloved:

I have been kept from writing you for a couple of nights by 2 engagements and the necessity of making arrangements to get settled in my new job. For the Stuttgart job is out for the time being as I learned after another conference with General Clay[3] – as I perhaps told you.[4] He has now made me a Special Assistant of his. I am to have an office near his across from Ambassador Mur-

---

[26] 22. März 1946.
[27] Siehe Dok. 15, Anm. 23.
[28] München, Hauptstadt des Landes Bayern in der amerikanischen Besatzungszone Deutschlands.
[29] Stadt in der amerikanischen Besatzungszone Österreichs, Sitz des US-Oberkommandos.
[30] Gemeint sind die Söhne John und Thomas. Siehe Dok. 2, Anm. 15 und 16.

[1] Siehe Dok. 15, Anm. 1.
[2] Im Briefkopf heißt es: "21 March 1946 Friday". Nicht der 21., sondern der 22. März 1946 war ein Freitag.
[3] Siehe Dok. 2, Anm. 6.
[4] Siehe Dok. 24.
[5] Siehe Dok. 8, Anm. 13.
[6] Siehe Dok. 17, Anm. 45.

phy's[5]. I am to spend some time each week in this office keeping acquainted with the affairs of Omgus[6] and I am to be permitted to see necessary documents to keep me in touch. I shall try to insist upon an impressive list. For the next 40 days or as long thereafter as is necessary I am to be loaned to General Barker[7], the Commanding General and Chief of M[ilitary] G[overnment] in the Berlin area. Yesterday I spent mostly with General Barker, an altogether decent and interesting fellow, teetotaler and non-smoker who knows what he is about. He told me that M[ilitary] G[overnment] in Berlin consists now of politics and education – the mechanics of sewers, lighting etc. can now be taken care of by the Germans. I am going to live in some quarters on the Wannsee[8] (the big lake bordering on our section). We went out together to see what is now called the Wannsee Hotel[9] (formerly the home of Minister of Economics Funk[10], now a War Criminal in Nuremberg[11]). There are wonderful apartments in it overlooking the lake – where there would be swimming and boat. If I don't live there I shall probably live next door in what General Barker told me are equally fine apartments in a large house.[12] This will be a place where I can

[7] Siehe Dok. 20, Anm. 10.
[8] Gemeint ist der Große Wannsee, eine Ausbuchtung der Havel (siehe Dok. 74, Anm. 24) im Südwesten Berlins.
[9] Das Wannsee Hotel bzw. der Wannsee Officers' Club befand sich Am Sandwerder 17/19 (vor 1933: Friedrich-Karl-Straße 24) im Berliner Verwaltungsbezirk Zehlendorf, Ortsteil Wannsee, am Ostufer des Großen Wannsees. 1886/1887 war hier ein von dem Architekten Johannes Otzen (1839–1911) entworfenes Landhaus für den Chemiker Franz Oppenheim (1852–1929) errichtet worden. Siehe Berlin und seine Bauten, bearb. und hrsg. vom Architekten-Verein zu Berlin und der Vereinigung Berliner Architekten, III. Bd.: Privatbauten, Berlin 1896, S. 172 und 175. Später gehörte das Haus dem jüdischen Bankier Hans Arnhold (siehe Dok. 47, Anm. 7), der in der NS-Zeit mit seiner Familie emigrieren musste. Anschließend zog hier NS-Reichswirtschaftsminister Walther Funk (siehe Anm. 10) ein. Nach dem Zweiten Weltkrieg wurde das seit seiner Errichtung mehrfach umgebaute Haus von den Amerikanern genutzt. "The two top floors of the Wannsee Officers Club are reserved for VIPs; the spacious rooms on the main floor are for dining, lounging and dancing. From the wide Italian terrace the view of the lake and the wooded surrounding far below is magnificent." Viviane W. Adams, Wannsee, in: OMGUS Observer vom 28. Juni 1946, S. 4f. und 8, hier S. 5. "Wannsee-Outdoor Rec Center" nannten die Amerikaner das Anwesen später. Seit 1998 hat hier die American Academy in Berlin, Hans Arnhold Center, ihren Sitz. Diese Institution dient der Verständigung und dem geistigen Austausch zwischen Deutschland und den USA. Fotos des Gebäudes im Bildanhang, Abb. 43 und Abb. 46; Blick von der Terrasse auf den Großen Wannsee: Abb. 47.
[10] Walther Funk (1890–1960), deutscher Wirtschaftsjournalist und NS-Politiker, 1932/1933 MdR, ab 1938 Reichswirtschaftsminister, ab 1939 zugleich Reichsbankpräsident, im Oktober 1946 vom Internationalen Militärgerichtshof in Nürnberg als Hauptkriegsverbrecher zu lebenslanger Haft verurteilt, 1957 vorzeitige Haftentlassung aus gesundheitlichen Gründen.
[11] Nürnberg, Stadt im Land Bayern in der amerikanischen Besatzungszone Deutschlands.
[12] Gemeint ist das benachbarte Anwesen Am Sandwerder 21/23, das als Erweiterung des Wannsee Officers' Club fungieren sollte: "Next door to the officers club at 23 Am Sanderwerder Strasse is the home of Heinrich Schicht, who was president of the German Sunlight Soap Co. The beautiful rooms with heavily carved doors imported from Italy, rich colored brocade silk walls, and mirrored Hollywood style, ornate

entertain Germans or anyone else I please, and I think I might as well take advantage of decent quarters. In general the Americans here of any rank live in very elegant and comfortable quarters. I am to have a car at my disposition finally, when I get settled. I am to have what is to be some kind of a splendiferous office in the Berlin District (BD) headquarters of Military Government[13], suitable to one who acts in an advisory capacity to a General, etc. etc. Actually I think the job is going to be an interesting one, and I shall be able to do it well I think and get along with the few people who will be helping with it. The Colonel who is now doing it is a good friend of Walter Dorn[14], and Sinclair Armstrong[15] and I learn, after spending a couple hours with him tonight, a very human, intelligent and earnest fellow. He has a grand Steinway piano[16] in his quarters. General Barker took me to lunch yesterday with his regular military staff in a wonderful house the library of which has some original medieval manuscripts. There I met a former student whose name I have forgotten but who is here the secretary[17] of the Chief of Staff[18] to Barker. I met a sergeant the other day who is a former student also. The general let me attend his briefing for the Kommandatura[19] (the 4 Allied Generals governing Berlin) meeting[20] today. He was bitter about the English into which most of the documents was cast. (Russian English which others hesitate to change because the Russians might fear that something is up). He is now reading Krutch's[21] life of

bathrooms are now being renovated to serve as an Annex to the Wannsee Officers Club. This house will be run as billets for transient officers." Viviane W. Adams, Wannsee, in: OMGUS Observer vom 28. Juni 1946, S. 4f. und 8, hier S. 5. Das Wohnhaus, in dem Johann Heinrich Schicht (1912-1944), Sunlicht Gesellschaft AG, gewohnt hatte, war 1906/1907 nach Entwürfen des Architekten Friedrich Kristeller (geb. 1860) für den Bankier Adolph Schwabacher errichtet worden. Siehe Gartendenkmale in Berlin: Privatgärten, bearb. von Katrin Lesser, mit einer Einführung von Klaus-Henning von Krosigk und Beiträgen von Josef Batzhuber et al. (= Beiträge zur Denkmalpflege in Berlin, 21), Petersberg 2005, S. 206f.

[13] Gemeint ist das Office of Military Government, Berlin District (OMGBD), das seinen Sitz in dem Gebäude der Deutschen Forschungsgemeinschaft in der Grunewaldstraße 35 im Berliner Verwaltungsbezirk Steglitz hatte. Auch benachbarte Gebäude in der Brentano- und der Kaiser-Wilhelm-Straße (heute: Schmidt-Ott-Straße) wurden von OMGBD genutzt. Foto des Gebäudes in der Grunewaldstraße im Bildanhang, Abb. 40.
[14] Siehe Dok. 2, Anm. 10.
[15] Siehe Dok. 3, Anm. 2.
[16] Siehe Dok. 4, Anm. 25.
[17] Es handelte sich um Robert E. Grovert (1921-2003), 1st Lieutenant, Absolvent der University of Nebraska, wurde nach seinem Einsatz in Berlin Air Force Fighter Pilot, war Air Attache an der Botschaft der USA in der Bundesrepublik Deutschland, Bonn.
[18] Elmer E. Barnes (1895-1986), Colonel, 1918 Absolvent der United States Military Academy, 1946 Chief of Staff, Headquarters Berlin District, US Army. Fotos mit Barnes im Bildanhang, Abb. 29 und Abb. 30.
[19] Siehe Dok. 20, Anm. 11.
[20] 8. Sitzung der Stadtkommandanten am 22. März 1946. Siehe Protokoll dieser Sitzung, BKC/M (46) 8, englischsprachige Fassung, in: LAB, B Rep. 036-01 (Office of Military Government, Berlin Sector [OMGBS]), 11/148-1/10.
[21] Joseph W. Krutch (1893-1970), amerikanischer Schriftsteller.

Sam Johnson[22] and is well acquainted with Lords and Ladies, and important Frenchmen. I went to the Kommandatura meeting this morning, and it was for me highly exciting, fascinating, mostful depressing. I wish all Americans could attend a meeting of this kind to see how the international machinery works on a small scale, and how delicate it is, so delicate that a slightly impatient or tactless remark would bring it crashing to the ground. I took elaborate notes on it and will write you a full account the first opportunity I get. The Russians were in the chair (General Smirnov[23]) and taking full advantage of the situation. I imagine I shall be participating in some of the meetings considering political matters in the Kommandatura (participating and not attending). I shall also get in on some social gatherings when our Allies are present. I imagine I shall even have to do some entertaining myself. You could let yourself in for a merry round here.

I went to Don Heath's[24] on Wednesday[25]. He had together what I suppose he regards as relatively less important people. I met Col. Howley[26], Barker's Deputy for Military Government who is my military boss but whom, Barker told me I have the privilege of going over the head of. There was Col. Durand[27] (a mediaeval colleague) who is in charge of the OSS[28] unit here. There was a Mr. King[29], formerly British Consul at Paris whose solution for the GI[30] situation is – give them coffee and sugar and they will sit in cafes and talk about politics without doing anything about it. I protested the simplicity of this. There was Mr. Steere[31], under Don Heath, and his very attractive wife[32] (arrived a month ago), a colonel in the Wacs[33], and who knows Mabel Lee[34] of the U[niversity] of

---

[22] Gemeint ist Krutchs Biografie über den englischen Gelehrten, Lexikografen, Schriftsteller, Dichter und Kritiker Samuel Johnson (1709–1784), die 1944 in New York erschienen war.
[23] Dmitri Iwanowitsch Smirnow (1901–1975), sowjetischer Generalleutnant, ab 1920 in der Roten Armee, 1936 Absolvent der Frunse-Militärakademie, 1945–April 1946 Chef der Garnison des sowjetischen Sektors von Berlin und sowjetischer Stadtkommandant, Alliierte Kommandantur Berlin.
[24] Donald R. Heath. Siehe Dok. 8, Anm. 15.
[25] 20. März 1946.
[26] Siehe Dok. 20, Anm. 18.
[27] Dana B. Durand (1904–1982), Lieutenant Colonel, amerikanischer Historiker, 1935 PhD, Harvard University (Dissertation: The Origins of German Cartography in the Fifteenth Century), Assistant Professor of History and Literature, Harvard University, 1941/1942 Associate Professor, Mount Holyoke College, OSS-Mitarbeiter, 1947–1964 CIA-Mitarbeiter.
[28] Office of Strategic Services. Siehe Dok. 1, Anm. 9.
[29] Alfred Hazell King (1896–1956), britischer Diplomat, 1944 Consul, Paris, ab 1945 Consul General for British Zone of Germany, ab 1948 Counsellor and Consul General, Kairo, ab 1952 Counsellor and Consul General, Buenos Aires.
[30] Government Issue, ugs. für amerikanischer Soldat.
[31] Siehe Dok. 20, Anm. 23.
[32] Anna W. Steere, geb. Walker, verw. Wilson (1909–1999), Lieutenant Colonel, amerikanische Lehrerin, 1938 MA, Claremont Colleges, Lehrerin, Beverly Hills High School, Beverly Hills, California, ab 1942 Women's Army Auxiliary Corps/Women's Army Corps, 1943–1945 Staff Director of the Women's Army Corps in the European Theater of Operations.
[33] Women's Army Corps. Siehe Dok. 13, Anm. 14.

N[ebraska] very very well.[35] There was an attractive young British Major – the political division. Lots of secretaries, lots of liquor, lots of food. Entertainment in the abundant Statement Department manner.

Yesterday evening was something different. Max Rheinstein[36] had Americans and some Germans together in his house[37]. Among them was a Max Bandler[38], a distinguished German cellist, and a pupil of Casals[39]. He played in a former Klinger Quartet[40] here and was ostracised by the Nazis because of a Jewish wife[41].[42] Now he happens to own the house Rheinstein now occupies. He was thrown out by former American occupants together with his family (wife, 2 pairs of twins[43] and another child[44]) and obliged to move into one room of a bombed house[45] next door. How would you like to be a guest of your conquerors in your own house. He was excellent about it. He complained to me that the hairs of his bow are wearing out and there are no hairs for the bow of a cello here. Would you make a special effort to get from the Lincoln[46] music stores some hairs for the stringing of a cello bow. Get enough for a few stringings and send them to me as soon as possible. I told him about John[47] and he is going to investigate for me the possibilities of getting some music for him here.

I turned down parties at the Lakeside Club[48] for tonight and tomorrow. You can see that it is so far interesting here. I wonder for how long? I love you my dearest, am still craving to hear from you, and send you and my boys sweet kisses and caresses. Edgar

[34] Mabel Lee (1886–1985), amerikanische Leibeserzieherin, 1908 BSc, Coe College, 1924–1952 an der University of Nebraska tätig, Professor of Physical Education for Women, Chairman of Department, gehörte dem zivilen Beirat des Women's Army Corps an.
[35] Loyd V. Steere und Anna W. Wilson hatten am 26. Januar 1946 in einer Kirche in Bad Nauheim im Land Groß-Hessen in der amerikanischen Besatzungszone Deutschlands geheiratet. Siehe Leader in the Wac Bride in Germany. Lieut. Col. Anna W. Wilson Is Wed to Lloyd V. Steere of Military Government Staff, in: The New York Times vom 27. Januar 1946, S. 38.
[36] Siehe Dok. 11, Anm. 22.
[37] Podbielskiallee 65. Siehe Dok. 21, Anm. 17.
[38] Max Baldner. Siehe Dok. 21, Anm. 18.
[39] Pablo Casals (1876–1973), spanisch-katalanischer Cellist. Max Baldner hatte sich nach Paris begeben, da er „von der unvergleichlichen Kunst" Casals „profitieren" wollte. „Dieser Aufenthalt in Paris hat unendlich viel zu meiner Entwicklung beigetragen." Lebenslauf Max Baldner, in: LAB, C Rep. 120 (Magistrat von Berlin, Abteilung Volksbildung), Nr. 88, Bl. 21f., hier Bl. 21.
[40] Klingler-Quartett. Siehe Dok. 21, Anm. 19.
[41] Charlotte Baldner, geb. Lindemann. Siehe Dok. 21, Anm. 21.
[42] Siehe Dok. 21, Anm. 22.
[43] Siehe Dok. 21, Anm. 24.
[44] Es handelte sich nicht um ein Familienmitglied, sondern, so die Auskunft von Thomas Baldner (siehe Dok. 21, Anm. 24) in einem Telefongespräch mit Werner Breunig am 29. April 2009, um ein Mädchen aus dem Bekanntenkreis.
[45] Podbielskiallee 57. Siehe Dok. 21, Anm. 25.
[46] Hauptstadt des US-Bundesstaats Nebraska, wo Johnson mit seiner Familie wohnte und an der Universität lehrte.
[47] Johnsons Sohn John. Siehe Dok. 2, Anm. 15.
[48] Siehe Dok. 17 und Dok. 18.

Dok. 26
Schreiben an die Ehefrau
Berlin, Ihnestraße 14[1], 23. März 1946

Dearest Sweetheart –

I am very lonely and depressed tonight. The basic cause of it is the absence of news from you. It is some six weeks now since I have had any account of what is going on at home, and God knows what may have happened in this interval. This situation may end some time but it is not sure when it will end. Oh I resent this cutting off from my beloved ones. To be suddenly transported from the immediate delight of being loved and taken somewhat seriously by you and John (even Thomas was becoming aware of my existence) into a kind of darkness where the former immediacy becomes a memory and one cannot grasp the essential reality of his existence, is more than I can take at the moment. I can exert this memory. I can attempt to recapture all the details which go to make up you, and you and me, and all the combinations that result from our having John and Thomas. But this exertion is no substitute for the detail which comes from letters. The most important things in my life, in our lives, may have happened but I do not know them yet, nor will I ever know them from immediate experience. Darling, we must not prolong this precarious and impossible mode of existence. As I have written it is impossible to bring you over as long as I am unwilling to say that I shall stay here for as long as a year. The Switzerland business which I have spoken of[2] is almost out for at least the time being since for as far as I can see I am going to be in Berlin for most of my stay here, and not in Stuttgart[3] where I should be reasonably close to Switzerland. And I am not so sure that American families are going to be very happy over here.

I am going to interrupt this to ask you to be very careful about repeating things I tell you about 1) happenings in General Clay's[4] weekly staff meetings[5], which I attend and 2) happenings in any quadripartite meeting which I may have attended. In so far as I know these letters are not censored. Nor have I received any instructions here about the present security rules. But from what I know of my experience with OSS[6] I should say that anything I say which reflects *in detail* about our conduct here, or anything which reflects discredit or unusual difficulty with our Allies, should be treated by you with extreme caution. In case of doubt wait to be confirmed by stories in the press. Or confine your comments to general remarks which do not reflect detail. In any case don't risk anything that might get into the press. You know I have gone on the practice on telling you everything and it has worked perfectly. I want to go on with this practice with the same feeling of security. In many instances I am convinced that what I say should be well known and understood by Americans in order

---

[1] Siehe Dok. 15, Anm. 1.
[2] Siehe Dok. 23.
[3] Hauptstadt des Landes Württemberg-Baden in der amerikanischen Besatzungszone Deutschlands.
[4] Siehe Dok. 2, Anm. 6.
[5] Siehe Dok. 16, Anm. 10.
[6] Office of Strategic Services. Siehe Dok. 1, Anm. 9.

that they may understand the difficulties and tragedy of what is going over here. But I do not wish to embarrass my superiors or make anything more difficult for them. I must be absolutely loyal. If I am not they will simply send me home, and I have no desire to be sent home for this kind of cause. For Upper Austria, Yes. For a security violation No. So, if you pass on what I have to say, pass on the import and not the details, and pass on the import as though you gather this from your reading of the press.

This interruption I have written because in regard to the happiness of families over here, an incident reported in General Clay's staff meeting[7] this morning is revealing. In Stuttgart, the local M[ilitary] G[overnment] authorities were preparing to receive the April assignment of American wives and their children. Their idea is to put them into a compound. So they roped off an area designated for this American compound, and ordered all the people with the ropes to move out instantly.[8] It is a good example of our unwillingness to act wisely in this matter. We have never tried to distinguish between Nazis and non-Nazis in the requisition of dwelling space, a hot issue in this country where rooms are at premium.

In this instance if we wanted people in a given area to move out we should arrange to have some nice Nazi homes for them to move into. But we don't take this little precaution and simply asked them to get out. Accordingly there was in Stuttgart this morning a public demonstration of some 500 people protesting this move.[9] The demonstrators elected a Committee to deal with the lo-

---

[7] Siehe Protokoll der OMGUS-Stabskonferenz am 23. März 1946, in: Archiv des IfZ, OMGUS – Staff Conferences (Protokollkopien), Fg 12/3.
[8] Johnson spricht hier die angekündigte (Teil-)Räumung der Wohnsiedlung Sonnenberg im Süden von Stuttgart an. Im Protokoll der Stabskonferenz, S. 11 f., heißt es: "Just before the meeting, General McClure [siehe Dok. 17, Anm. 38] received a phone call from Stuttgart to the effect that M[ilitary] G[overnment] authorities had roped off a large area, advising Germans that M[ilitary] G[overnment] would take possession to make room for incoming American personnel. As a result, a demonstration was staged in front of the Buergermeister's office with about 500 people attending. A committee has been apppointed to talk with the Military Government authorities." Über die im Frühjahr und Sommer 1946 durchgeführte Räumung schreibt der „Sonnenberg-Verein": „Kaum hatten die Sonnenbergbewohner die Not des Krieges einigermaßen überstanden, als sie von einem schweren Schlag getroffen wurden: Im Frühjahr und Sommer 1946 musste fast der ganze Sonnenberg für die amerikanische Besatzungsmacht geräumt werden. [...] Insgesamt mussten 220 Häuser geräumt werden, und 2503 Sonnenberger mussten ihre Wohnungen verlassen. Der Sonnenberg wurde zu einer amerikanisch geprägten Siedlung. [...] Nach langem Kampf und zähen Verhandlungen wurde schließlich erreicht, dass Ersatzbauten für die Amerikaner erstellt wurden. Aber es dauerte volle neun Jahre, bis die Sonnenberger in ihre Häuser zurückkehren konnten. 1955 wurden ungefähr 100 Häuser freigegeben, und 1957 konnte man endlich die Freigabe des letzten Hauses feiern." http://www.sonnenberg-verein.de/ (letzter Zugriff am 30. Januar 2013).
[9] Hierzu die „Stuttgarter Zeitung": „Schätzungsweise 200 bis 300 Frauen des Stadtteils Sonnenberg, zum Teil mit ihren Kindern, versammelten sich am Samstagvormittag demonstrativ vor der Amtsstelle des Oberbürgermeisters in der Schönleinstraße. Eine Delegation von sechs Frauen trug dem Oberbürgermeister die Sorgen und Bedenken vor, die von der Bevölkerung des betroffenen Stadtteils empfunden werden. Dr. Klett versicherte bei der Gelegenheit noch einmal, daß von seiten der Stadt alles

cal M[ilitary] G[overnment] authorities who voted without consultation with higher-ups. The results of the negotiations were reported in the meeting as unsatisfactory. You can imagine how the American wives and their kids will be greeted by this town. And this I imagine is only the first of incidents of this kind. (I have just decided to write a small memorandum to General Clay on this subject). I just can't imagine that American families are going to feel very comfortable over here. American wives and their kids are going to be sporting around in swell clothes, well fed, and driving the own automobiles around. They are being encouraged to bring their own automobiles and some efforts are being made to have special favors tendered them with respect to the sale of a new American cars to them over here. This only emphasizes the differences between conquerors and conquered. And the mere fact that American families are coming over here is enough to indicate to the Germans that the conquerors are here for some time to come.

I am depressed also by a little incident I witnessed in coming home from the office this afternoon. The MP's (Military Police) inspect closely any packages brought out of Omgus[10] headquarters by Germans in our employ. Today I saw an unnecessarily gruff MP inspect the knapsack of a nice old German who was terrified. He found a piece of card-board which the old man was undoubtedly bringing home to burn (the sight of Berliners dragging home wood on Sundays is pathetic enough). The MP tore the card-board out of his knapsack and threw it on a pile. I found this hard to take. I would be a soft MP and an essentially soft (in some respects) conqueror.

I am also depressed by the food situation here. (Why can't you people at home disgorge a little bit). There are already reports of food riots in the British zone (shots being fired), people collapsing at their work, or serving notice that they can go on for only a little time longer. The coal production in the Ruhr[11] is already declining because of the starvation character of the British ration[12]. You can't teach democracy to people who are starving or threatened with starvation, and you don't help the situation by bringing in more troops.

I'll write an account of the Kommandatura[13] meeting tomorrow.[14] Goodnight my sweet. You can be thankful at least that you are not faced with what the German wives and Mothers and kids are faced with. My sweetest love to Emily and John and Thomas. Edgar

versucht werde, um allzu große Härten bei der Räumung zu vermeiden und die betroffenen Familien anderweitig unterzubringen." Vorläufig zwei Häuser beschlagnahmt, in: Stuttgarter Zeitung vom 27. März 1946, S. 3.

[10] Siehe Dok. 17, Anm. 45.
[11] Ruhrgebiet, bedeutende Industrieregion in der britischen Besatzungszone Deutschlands.
[12] Siehe Dok. 23, Anm. 15.
[13] Siehe Dok. 20, Anm. 11.
[14] Siehe Dok. 27.

Dok. 27
Schreiben an die Ehefrau
Berlin, Ihnestraße 14[1], 24. März 1946

Dearest Sweetheart –

I had a difficult moment at lunch today. I met this guy Thompson[2] from Colorado[3] whom you have heard me speak of[4] and he had with him at the table his wife and his little boy[5] whom he had just gathered in London. I don't know how long I shall be able to stand seeing these wives and children about. He is doing work for the Embassy in Warsaw[6] and is returning there Tuesday[7]. I suggested my coming there to study the Russians in Poland as a background for my work here. He said he would arrange it in Warsaw if I could arrange it here. I guess I'll try. It would be for only a week. He said that the present government in Poland[8] represents some 15-20 % of the people: that if a free election were to be held Mikolacyk(sp?)[9] the peasant party leader, would win by a 70 % majority, that the Russians have moved in new divisions to control the elections, that Russian officers control the Polish Secret Police and that Russians in Polish Uniforms are way down into the ranks of the Polish army. This is all very ugly.

I wonder if you could spare enough money to get me a wrist watch and send it over to me. The present system does not work. The crystal is always coming out. It is out now and I can't spend the time necessary to go and have it repaired constantly. About all I have had my secretary do recently is to keep me informed of the time so that I wouldn't miss my next appointment. At some

---

[1] Siehe Dok. 15, Anm. 1.
[2] Gemeint sein könnte Llewellyn E. Thompson Jr. (1904–1972), Diplomat, 1928 BA in Economics, University of Colorado, ab 1929 Department of State, 1944/1945 2nd Secretary and Consul, London, 1945/1946 1st Secretary and Consul, London, 1945 Political Adviser, Berlin Conference, 1946/1947 Chief, Division of Eastern European Affairs, 1952–1955 High Commissioner, Österreich, 1955–1957 Ambassador, Österreich, 1957–1962 und 1967–1969 Ambassador, Sowjetunion.
[3] Llewellyn E. Thompson Jr. wurde in Las Animas im US-Bundesstaat Colorado geboren.
[4] In den ab 12. Februar 1946 verfassten Briefen war Thompson noch nicht erwähnt worden. Johnson hatte ihn möglicherweise 1944/1945 in London kennengelernt.
[5] Llewellyn E. Thompson Jr. war zu diesem Zeitpunkt noch nicht verheiratet und hatte keine Kinder. Möglicherweise handelte es sich hier um eine Freundin und deren Sohn.
[6] Hauptstadt Polens.
[7] 26. März 1946.
[8] Stalin (siehe Dok. 39, Anm. 31) hatte einer Koalitionsregierung im befreiten Polen zugestimmt. Premierminister war der Sozialist Edward Osóbka-Morawski (1909–1997), der Kommunist Władysław Gomułka (1905–1982) war sein Stellvertreter, als zweiter Stellvertreter und Minister für Landwirtschaft kam Stanisław Mikołajczyk (siehe Anm. 9) hinzu, dessen Polnische Bauernpartei sich der Politik der kommunistisch dominierten Regierung widersetzte.
[9] Stanisław Mikołajczyk (1901–1966), polnischer Politiker, 1943/1944 Premierminister der polnischen Exilregierung, 1945 Wiederbelebung der Polnischen Bauernpartei, 1945–1947 Vizepremier der kommunistisch dominierten Regierung Polens, trat in Opposition zu den Kommunisten, 1947 Flucht nach England, anschließend in die USA.

moment in the future I am going to be embarrassed. If you ever find time or opportunity to send me anything you'd better send me cigarettes. They are worth their weight in gold here and are indeed to the Germans the preferred currency.[10] It is not right that I use PX[11] cigarettes for purposes of gratuities but I don't see why I shouldn't use cigarettes from home as long as I don't use them for black market[12] activities. Of course food parcels are a boon to these hungry people. The PX rations are very generous here. I counted them yesterday. 12 packages of cigarettes, 16 pieces of candy (including Smith's Cough drops), 5 cans of salted almonds, 1 can of fruit juice. I gave some things to the lady here who does my laundry. She smiled with delight; said it was very touching, and said "heissen Dank" which you don't hear very often. I have it in mind to suggest to General Clay[13] that an opportunity be given to Americans here to share their PX rations with Berlin orphans, Berlin old people, and Berliners in the hospitals by putting a box in the PX store into which they could drop their surplus. Many of them must feel a little guilty over the great abundance they are supplied. The snack-bars have everything from good pastry, sandwiches, and ice cream sundaes to peach melbas and chocolate milk shakes. The regular meals are, I am glad, not served in over-abundant portions but they are good and adequate. Breakfast is always served with two eggs and bacon or ham. There are oranges and apples about, and plenty of liquor at the bars. At dinner in the Harnack house[14] there is a wonderful orchestra, the first violinist of which I am told is a former symphony orchestra player. I am sending some request slips in case you or your friends want to be kind to hungry Germans. I shall try to get them to the right people.

At breakfast this morning I overheard this. A worker for the United Jewish Relief[15] was speaking. A little German kid (there are plenty of them about begging cigarettes for their papas and candy for their little sisters, 4 years old) approached and asked her if she were a Jew. She said yes and he was impressed because he said he had heard that the Jews were bringing bacon to the Germans and he would be glad to get in on it. Of course Jewish Relief is serving the Jews here. But what a magnificent gesture it would be if the Jews brought food to the Germans. Sometimes I think that is what is needed here – a magnificent display of generosity to the right people. We are so hesitant about tempering our punitive rigor with kindness. American latent generosity must be released at least to the innocent or least guilty of our enemies.

10 Da nach dem Krieg das Geld in Deutschland durch Inflation beständig an Wert einbüßte, wurde der direkte Warentausch bei den Menschen immer beliebter. Auch die Wertvergleichsfunktion des Geldes wurde von Waren übernommen, hauptsächlich von Zigaretten, die sich als allgemeiner Wertmaßstab einführten, sodass man schließlich von der Zigarettenwährung sprach.
11 Post Exchange, Verkaufsläden der amerikanischen Streitkräfte.
12 Siehe Dok. 21, Anm. 11.
13 Siehe Dok. 2, Anm. 6.
14 Siehe Dok. 15, Anm. 16.
15 Gemeint sein könnte der "United Jewish Appeal", durch dessen Spendensammlungen die Arbeit der amerikanisch-jüdischen Wohltätigkeitsorganisation "American Jewish Joint Distribution Committee" finanziert wurde. Siehe Angelika Königseder, Flucht nach Berlin. Jüdische Displaced Persons 1945-1948 (= Reihe Dokumente –

I worry sometimes that you are in financial straits. Perhaps by now you have gotten the check from OSS[16] (if not write them again). If not you have had to cash in the bonds or established some kind of credit with the banks or your friends. If I were you I'd write to the civil service commission also and try to speed up the permanent leave check. You can never be sure when you will be getting regular checks from here. These details are of course in your letters if ever I get them here.

Let me now try to give you some account of the Kommandatura[17] meeting which I attended last Friday[18].[19] The meeting was held in Kommandatura Headquarters[20] in a room much larger than that in which the Committee meeting was held about which I wrote earlier[21]. The participants were seated around a huge rectangular table. The 4 Generals sat facing each other at the center. Barker[22] sat next to Smirnov[23], the Russian who was chairman and across from them sat the French General Lanson[24] (his first meeting)[25] and the English General Nairs[26]. They were flanked by their Deputies and secretaries. Behind the Generals sat their interpreters. When the Russian spoke, his interpreters translated into English and French. When the Frenchmen spoke, his interpreters into Russian and English, etc. The interpreters were excellent and the meeting went much more smoothly than the other one I attended. But our interpreters came from Brooklyn[27] or New York and it was amusing to hear all the th's translated into d's – de generals and de words.[28]

The first question on the agenda was the question of reforming the Berlin police set up so that the respective Generals could control the orders given to the police in their sectors by the police president of Berlin[29]. The present Berlin government is the one set up by the Russians when they came in; it is dominat-

---

Texte – Materialien. Veröffentlicht vom Zentrum für Antisemitismusforschung der Technischen Universität Berlin, Bd. 27), Berlin 1998, S. 88.

[16] Office of Strategic Services. Siehe Dok. 1, Anm. 9.
[17] Siehe Dok. 20, Anm. 11.
[18] 22. März 1946.
[19] Siehe Protokoll der 8. Sitzung der Stadtkommandanten am 22. März 1946, BKC/M (46) 8, englischsprachige Fassung, in: LAB, B Rep. 036-01 (Office of Military Government, Berlin Sector [OMGBS]), 11/148-1/10.
[20] Kaiserswerther Straße 16/18, Berlin-Dahlem. Siehe Dok. 20, Anm. 11.
[21] Gemeint ist die Sitzung des Civil Administration Committee, Directorate of Internal Affairs and Communications, Allied Control Authority, vom 12. März 1946. Siehe Dok. 19.
[22] Siehe Dok. 20, Anm. 10.
[23] Siehe Dok. 25, Anm. 23.
[24] Charles J. M. Lançon (1890–1956), Général de Brigade, März–Oktober 1946 französischer Stadtkommandant, Alliierte Kommandantur Berlin. Foto mit Lançon im Bildanhang, Abb. 26.
[25] Lançon hatte das Amt des Stadtkommandanten erst seit dem 12. März 1946 inne.
[26] Eric Paytherus Nares (1892–1947), Major General, 1945–1947 britischer Stadtkommandant, Alliierte Kommandantur Berlin. Foto mit Nares im Bildanhang, Abb. 26.
[27] Stadtbezirk von New York City.
[28] Gemeint ist, dass in Brooklyn-Englisch „th" wie „de" ausgesprochen wird.
[29] Polizeipräsident war Paul Markgraf (1910–1993), ehemaliger Regimentskommandeur der Wehrmacht, in sowjetischer Kriegsgefangenschaft Mitglied des Nationalkomitees „Freies Deutschland".

ed by the Communists who are used by the Russians to effect their general program.[30] Hence the proposed reform was an attempt to control the influence of Berlin Communists in the respective sectors and thus indirectly to control Russian plans in these sectors. Smirnov began by saying that he could see no reason for the reform, that the new reform would be only an adaptation of the Hitler system, would mean additional expense for new police officials, and that the present system was functioning satisfactorily. Lanson countered by challenging Smirnov's comparison of the proposed reform with the Hitler system. It was actually the reverse. The reform aimed to decentralize the police whereas the Hitler system was completely centralized. (This is correct of course). Nairs joined in by saying that the Fr[ench] Eng[lish] and Americans regarded the present police system as unsatisfactory. The fact that Police H[ead]q[uarter]s were in the Russian Sector[31] meant that the Soviets could easily supervise the police. The other Allies couldn't do this. British want the reform but of course the Russians need not establish new offices in their sector unless they want to. Barker joined in with the Fr[ench] and English. He wanted a better system of police administration. Hitler[32] had nothing to do with it. In fact the present system more closely resembled the Hitlerian system than the proposed reform, if one wanted to go into that. The increase in expense was negligible. Americans too were interested in the welfare of Berliners (Smirnov had remarked something about the welfare of the people). He wanted additional police to act as an agency of his M[ilitary] G[overnment] in his sector. He agreed with Nairs that if the reform adopted the Soviets could do what they pleased in their own zone. It was now Smirnov's turn again. He had stated his own point of view. He objected to a solution by sectors. If the Allies wanted to come into Police Headquarters they were welcome. He had no intention of controlling the Police President. In fact he governed only 8 sectors of the city.[33] He advised that present plan be retained and the reform abandoned, and the question be stricken from the agenda. Barker said No. We can't just strike the question from the agenda. We must improve the present system. "There is nothing sacred about the present organization." We have to continue to study and work out a better arrangement. Nairs came to Barker's support. British wanted more control in their own

[30] Der Magistrat mit dem parteilosen Architekten Arthur Werner (1877–1967) als Oberbürgermeister war von den Sowjets im Mai 1945 eingesetzt worden. Als sich nach dem Eintreffen der Westmächte in Berlin die Alliierte Kommandantur im Juli 1945 als oberstes politisches Organ der Stadt konstituierte, beschlossen die drei Stadtkommandanten in ihrer ersten Sitzung, alle Anordnungen, die die Sowjets in der Zeit ihrer Alleinherrschaft erlassen hatten, in Kraft zu lassen, also auch den Magistrat im Amt zu belassen. Zur Zusammensetzung siehe Die Sitzungsprotokolle des Magistrats der Stadt Berlin 1945/46. Teil I: 1945, bearb. und eingel. von Dieter Hanauske (= Schriftenreihe des Landesarchivs Berlin, Bd. 2/I), Berlin 1995, S. 48–56; Dieter Hanauske, „… als leuchtendes Signal für ganz Deutschland". Der Berliner Magistrat von 1945/46 als „antifaschistisch-demokratisches" Musterbeispiel?, in: Berlin in Geschichte und Gegenwart. Jahrbuch des Landesarchivs Berlin 1999, S. 145–183, hier S. 151–154.
[31] Das Polizeipräsidium befand sich in der Linienstraße 83–85 im Berliner Verwaltungsbezirk Mitte.
[32] Siehe Dok. 22, Anm. 19.
[33] Der sowjetische Sektor Berlins bestand aus acht Verwaltungsbezirken: Friedrichshain, Köpenick, Lichtenberg, Mitte, Pankow, Prenzlauer Berg, Treptow und Weißensee.

sector. Barker returned to his demand for 2 or 3 officials in his sector with whom he could deal. Then Smirnov said: "I don't think I can change my point of view. I suggest we refer the question indefinitely to the future." Barker: "I suggest we postpone it to the next meeting." Smirnov: "Ok, but remember what I have said." And so it was postponed to the next meeting.

Here is the international situation in a nutshell. I don't think I have to press the analogy. I'll go on with the meeting in another letter. Please do not use these details in conversation until I have learned whether it is proper to do so. They are for your own orientation. The intelligent American public needs to be informed about how these things go or they will never understand the realities of the present situation.

I love you my sweet. (All these experiences increase my stature a little bit, I think). I kiss you and my sweet boys and long so much for you. When will there be word. Bye-bye Sweetheart. Edgar

Dok. 28
Schreiben an die Ehefrau
Berlin, Ihnestraße 14[1], 26. März 1946

Dearest Sweetheart –

I didn't write last night because I was quite tired and went to bed without even bothering to get fully undressed. And today has been a terribly busy day and my head is in a whirl. Let me give you a brief resumé of it.

I got down to what was supposedly going to be my new office in the Military Government Headquarters of Berlin[2] at 9 o'clock supposedly to see General Barker[3]. But he had not arrived as yet so I went to Col. Glaser's[4] office and worked on a T. O. for this new branch which I am going to set up for Barker.[5] Do you know what a T. O. is. I have heard about it a great deal, end-

---

[1] Siehe Dok. 15, Anm. 1.
[2] Siehe Dok. 25, Anm. 13.
[3] Siehe Dok. 20, Anm. 10.
[4] Louis Glaser (1890–1952), Lieutenant Colonel, amerikanischer Werbefachmann, 1908–1911 Studium am Georgetown University Law Center, gründete 1922 in Boston, Massachusetts, die Glaser Advertising Agency, Inc., ab 1942 US Army, 1945 Mil. Gov. Intelligence, OMGBD, Januar 1946-1948 Chief, Civil Administration Branch/ Civil Administration and Political Affairs Branch, OMGBD/OMGBS, 1948 Rückkehr in die USA, dann Tätigkeit für die CIA, ab 1951 Office of Defense Mobilization. Louis Glasers Sohn Anthony J. Glaser (siehe Dok. 59, Anm. 6) schreibt in einer E-Mail an Werner Breunig vom 22. August 2009: "[...] my father – in addition to being in military government – was involved with secret intelligence for the US within the Soviet Zone of Germany." Und in einer E-Mail vom 27. September 2009 heißt es: "The US Army awarded the Bronze Star medal to my father for his work in Military Government in Berlin – particularly, I believe, for the work on the constitution and the first free election (since 1933) in Berlin." Siehe Bildanhang, Abb. 35, Abb. 53, Abb. 68 und Abb. 77.
[5] Gemeint ist die Civil Administration Branch, OMGBD. "On the 25th of January a Civil Administration Branch was organized and started operations. On the 4th of

lessly in fact, but I have never really been concerned much with one. It is Table of Organization. It involves drawing a chart of your organization, deciding upon how many people you are going to need, giving them ratings, etc. and then going out to get them.

At ten o'clock I had to go to a Deputy Meeting of the Kommandatura[6] – that is a meeting of the Deputy Commanders of the Berlin District.[7] Col. Howley[8] for us, Col. Dalada[9] for the Russians, Col. (?) Cherdell[10] for the French, and Brigadier Hinde[11] for the British. The hot question on the agenda was elections for Berlin – the Russians stalling on quick elections, the French rather supporting the Russians, the British interested in elections but not wanting to go too fast with them, and we insisting upon speedy elections.[12] Nothing decided. You can't decide things as quickly as all that. The meeting lasted until about 2 o'clock with Col. Howley representing to be sure the American point of view but talking far too much. The Russian was efficient but none too sympathetic, the Frenchman melancholy and intelligent (I respond instinctively to the individual Frenchman as I respond to Paris even though I don't always respond to their policy). The British, clear and incisive, careful and a little bit petulant. These international meetings are fun.

Col. Howley, an advertising man,[13] invited me to lunch at his magnificent residence[14]. His Deputy was there, a Colonel Svoboda[15], who had something to do

April it was officially activated with terms of reference approved by the Commanding General". Civil Administration. Six Months Report 4 January-3 July 1946, in: Office of Military Government U. S. Berlin District (Hrsg.), Six Months Report 4 January-3 July 1946, Berlin 1946, S. 40-43, hier S. 41. Siehe Harold Hurwitz, Die Eintracht der Siegermächte und die Orientierungsnot der Deutschen 1945-1946 (= Demokratie und Antikommunismus in Berlin nach 1945, Bd. III), Köln 1984, S. 43; Jürgen Wetzel, Office of Military Government for Berlin Sector, in: OMGUS-Handbuch. Die amerikanische Militärregierung in Deutschland 1945-1949, hrsg. von Christoph Weisz (= Quellen und Darstellungen zur Zeitgeschichte, Bd. 35), München 1994, S. 671-738, hier S. 704. Organigramm der Civil Administration Branch im Bildanhang, Abb. 33.

[6] Siehe Dok. 20, Anm. 11.
[7] Siehe Protokoll der 15. Sitzung der stellvertretenden Stadtkommandanten am 26. März 1946, BKD/M (46) 15, englischsprachige Fassung, in: LAB, B Rep. 036-01 (Office of Military Government, Berlin Sector [OMGBS]), 11/148-1/12.
[8] Siehe Dok. 20, Anm. 18.
[9] Daniil Sergejewitsch Dalada (1900-1975), sowjetischer Oberst, 1933 Absolvent der Frunse-Militärakademie, 1945/1946 stellvertretender sowjetischer Stadtkommandant, Alliierte Kommandantur Berlin.
[10] René Cherdel (1900-1968), Capitaine de Vaisseau, ab 1945 stellvertretender französischer Stadtkommandant, Alliierte Kommandantur Berlin.
[11] William Robert Norris Hinde (1900-1981), Brigadier, 1945-1948 stellvertretender britischer Stadtkommandant, Alliierte Kommandantur Berlin.
[12] Siehe Stenographic Statement made by DOMG [Colonel Frank L. Howley] on the Deputy Commandants meeting held on 26 March 1946, in: LAB, B Rep. 036-01 (Office of Military Government, Berlin Sector [OMGBS]), 4/135-1/2. Zu den Auseinandersetzungen auf alliierter Seite um den Termin erster Wahlen siehe Werner Breunig, Verfassunggebung in Berlin 1945-1950 (= Beiträge zur Politischen Wissenschaft, Bd. 58), Berlin 1990, S. 174-183.
[13] Howley hatte in Philadelphia, Pennsylvania, eine Werbeagentur unterhalten.
[14] Gelfertstraße 32/34, Berlin-Dahlem. Foto des Hauses im Bildanhang, Abb. 55.

with the military gov[ernmen]t of Aachen[16] about which Saul Padover[17] and Paul Sweet[18] once wrote very unfavorably.[19] A Col. Bond[20] who is liaison with the Berlin municipal government, General or Colonel I don't know which Cherdell (who wants to go home. He has two children[21], a boy of two over which he almost went into ecstasy. He said many of the French want to go home because they are permitted to send only ½ of their salaries home to their families)[22]. There was champagne before lunch, and I had a chance to speak quite a bit of French. It was fun. I could build up my French.

I went back to my headquarters where some kind of an office had been fixed for me (it was severely plain, but is going to be more splendiferous). There was a German secretary[23] and the German driver[24] of my car.

I was soon drawn into discussion by Col. Glaser on the hot political question here at the moment – the union of the Communists with the Social Democrats

[15] Leo A. Swoboda (1898-1979), Lieutenant Colonel, amerikanischer Jurist, LLB, Kansas City School of Law, 1946 Deputy Director, OMGBD, 1946-1948 Chief, Military Government Courts Sub-Section, Legal Branch, OMGBD/OMGBS.
[16] Stadt in der britischen Besatzungszone Deutschlands, die zunächst von amerikanischen Truppen besetzt worden war.
[17] Siehe Dok. 20, Anm. 49.
[18] Siehe Dok. 2, Anm. 28.
[19] Johnson spricht hier einen Bericht aus dem besetzten Aachen an, den die Field Intelligence Officers Padover, Sweet und Lewis F. Gittler (1914-1974) der Psychological Warfare Division, SHAEF, vorgelegt und mit dem sie Aufsehen erregt hatten. Siehe S. K. Padover/L. F. Gittler/P. R. Sweet, The Political Situation in Aachen, in: Propaganda in War and Crisis. Materials for American Policy, edited with an introduction by Daniel Lerner, New York 1951 (Reprint 1972), S. 434-456. Siehe auch Klaus-Dietmar Henke, Die amerikanische Besetzung Deutschlands (= Quellen und Darstellungen zur Zeitgeschichte, Bd. 27), München 1995, S. 252-297, insbesondere S. 284-297.
[20] Charles C. Bond, Colonel, 1945/1946 Liaison Officer Berlin-Schöneberg, 1946-1949 Chief, Police Section, Public Safety Branch, OMGBD/OMGBS.
[21] René Cherdel hatte drei Kinder, zwei Töchter und einen Sohn: Françoise Cherdel, später verh. Haour (geb. 1936), Marie Cherdel, später verh. de Goy (geb. 1938) und Jean-Yves Cherdel (geb. 1944). Jean-Yves Cherdel in einer E-Mail an Werner Breunig vom 2. Dezember 2013: "I was already born in 1946, which makes us 3 children". René Cherdel ließ seine Familie später nachkommen.
[22] Die französischen Besatzungsangehörigen in Berlin durften ihre Familienangehörigen zunächst nicht nachkommen lassen. "French families will not be represented with Russian, English, and American dependents in the four-power occupation of Berlin. Wives and children of Russian officers, the only occupation families here now, will be joined by the Americans after April 1 and by English about June. 'We have no wish to bring our dependents into Berlin because of the acute food and housing shortage,' commented Lieutenant Jean Francais of the French Public Relations Office in reply to questions asked by THE GROOPER. Despite the French 'no family' policy here, their dependents are occupying other cities in the French Zone." Lynn Davis, French Won't Bring Families To Berlin, Russians Here Now, in: The Grooper vom 16. Februar 1946, S. 3. Im Frühjahr 1946 durften auch die Franzosen in Berlin ihre Familienangehörigen nachkommen lassen. Siehe Dorothea Führe, Die französische Besatzungspolitik in Berlin von 1945 bis 1949. Déprussianisation und Décentralisation, Berlin 2001, S. 48, Anm. 33, und 277.
[23] Möglicherweise Frau Donneck. Siehe Dok. 80.
[24] Möglicherweise Artur Sanow. Siehe Dok. 40, Anm. 13.

trying to consider steps as to how to keep the Communist + pro union SPD (Social Democratic Party) from using undemocratic methods to achieve their ends. Then I was summoned to a meeting in Mr. Steere's[25] office to discuss the same question. Then after dinner I went out to see General Barker to discuss the same question. (He lives in a magnificient and modern house overlooking the Wannsee[26]).[27] My early impressions of him are confirmed. He is a man definitely worth working for, takes a line somewhat different from Clay[28], is interested in a positive program here, and I shall get along. Then back to B[erlin] D[istrict] H[ead]q[uarter]s[29] to see Col. Glaser on the matter and then back here.

Tomorrow looks like the same with another quadripartite meeting[30] in the afternoon.

I am sorry to omit details because if I don't write them to you they will escape me forever (stories at lunch for example). But I must get some rest. If I don't get to write every day you will know I am pressed.

Good-night my dearest, sweetest beloved – hug my boys for me, and I wish I could be with you tonight. I love you dearest, and I think there is a chance for a job here. Edgar

---

[25] Siehe Dok. 20, Anm. 23.
[26] Gemeint ist der Große Wannsee, eine Ausbuchtung der Havel (siehe Dok. 74, Anm. 24) im Südwesten Berlins.
[27] Barker wohnte Am Sandwerder 27 im Berliner Verwaltungsbezirk Zehlendorf, Ortsteil Wannsee, am Ostufer des Großen Wannsees. Das von dem Architekten Fritz August Breuhaus de Groot (1883–1960) im Stil einer traditionell ausgeprägten Moderne entworfene Haus war 1934/1935 für den Kaufmann Carl H. Bauer (1881–1941), der den Generalvertrieb des „Zipp-Blitzverschlusses" hatte, erbaut worden. Bauer wohnte hier mit seiner Ehefrau Else Bauer, geb. Gutzeit (1882–1945) und den beiden Töchtern. „Für die damalige Zeit war es ein modernes Haus mit einem kupfernen Dach", so Bauers Enkeltochter Hedda Dutilh-von Schmidt Seidlitz in einem Schreiben an Werner Breunig vom 19. Oktober 2010. Die Enkeltochter berichtet von einer riesigen Fensterscheibe, die versenkt werden konnte, „so dass man einen herrlichen offnen Blick auf die Terrasse und weiter auf den Wannsee hatte". Ebd. 1961/1962 wohnte in dem Haus, das die Amerikaner als Gästehaus nutzten, Lucius D. Clay (siehe Dok. 2, Anm. 6), damals Berliner Sonderbeauftragter des US-Präsidenten. Siehe Helmut Engel, Villen und Landhäuser, fotografiert von Wolfgang Reuss (= Meisterwerke Berliner Baukunst, Bd. I), Berlin 2001, S. 81 und 83; Gartendenkmale in Berlin: Privatgärten, bearb. von Katrin Lesser, mit einer Einführung von Klaus-Henning von Krosigk und Beiträgen von Josef Batzhuber et al. (= Beiträge zur Denkmalpflege in Berlin, 21), Petersberg 2005, S. 208. Siehe Fotos im Bildanhang, Abb. 52, Abb. 53 und Abb. 54.
[28] Siehe Dok. 2, Anm. 6.
[29] Siehe Dok. 25, Anm. 13.
[30] Gemeint ist eine Sitzung des Local Government Committee, Allied Kommandatura Berlin. Siehe Dok. 29.

Dok. 29
Schreiben an die Ehefrau
Berlin, Ihnestraße 14[1], 27. März 1946

Dearest and my beloved:

The best thing that has happened to me since I left you happened today – a series of letters forwarded from the 25th Base Post Office[2] at Wurzburg[3].[4] There were seven of them dating from 20 February to 12 March.[5] I won't try to describe to you the manner in which I rushed from B[erlin] D[istrict] to Omgus[6] to get them, or the excited manner in which I tore through them. I have been through them now a second time, and I am comforted and a bit relaxed. Your last refers to the fact that you got my boat letters[7] on the Monday[8] before. We are therefore about two weeks apart in time, which is almost what we were when I was in Austria. It will be reduced soon to about 10 days which is about the best that we can hope for.

What you have been through – John's[9] illness, and Timmy's[10] almost departing from our midst and then his second little illness. I was in tears waiting to get through that letter telling me of his going to the hospital but I knew the ending was not his death – I had received no cable. I can imagine what you went through with John sick at home and Timmy's in the hands of fate under a steam tent, and not knowing whether you would have him in the morning. Oh I am grateful to you and to Hancock[11] and to the hospital that we still have him. Thank God you know how to call a doctor on time, and that he knows how to act quickly and properly. Tim's reaction to the hospital and to you when you came to see him; his final breaking down when he saw the train in the nursery all moved me very much. I shall be through the letters many times to catch the details and the nuances of the details which they contain. I feel I know Timmy a little bit after the stay at home, but only you and John know him well. At least now I am to have the opportunity of getting to know him better.

It is the same for John even though his care was not so desperate. Please tell him how much his father loves him and treasures every little detail of his life – the report card (the first report card) – and the first of many excellent report cards that are to come for many many years now: the practice and the regular

---

[1] Siehe Dok. 15, Anm. 1.
[2] Siehe Dok. 4.
[3] Würzburg, Stadt im Land Bayern in der amerikanischen Besatzungszone Deutschlands.
[4] Siehe Dok. 18.
[5] Briefe vom 20./21., 24., 27. und 27./28. Februar sowie vom 5., 10. und 12. März 1946, in: Unterlagen aus dem Nachlass Edgar N. Johnson, Privatbesitz Candice E. und Thomas R. Johnson, Denver, Colorado, USA.
[6] Siehe Dok. 17, Anm. 45.
[7] Gemeint sind die Briefe, die Johnson an seine Frau an Bord von USAT George W. Goethals geschrieben hatte. Siehe Dok. 9–12.
[8] 11. März 1946.
[9] Johnsons Sohn John. Siehe Dok. 2, Anm. 15.
[10] Johnsons Sohn Thomas. Siehe Dok. 2, Anm. 16.
[11] Siehe Dok. 4, Anm. 22.

series of five lessons, Herbert's[12] devotion and excitement, the continuation of the refreshments in accordance with a better system than I used to employ, the PTA[13] meeting with the dance program, the new stories, the teachers – all these fill in a horrible vacuum of these last few weeks.

And my sweet and adorable Emily. You say little about what all this has cost you. If I am devoted to you because of what you are I am no less devoted to you because of the beautiful and delicate understanding which you have of the boys – something which I shall never be able to achieve. I love you my dearest, and I trust that some day I shall be able to merit a little improvement on my "some understanding" of your "various foibles". You haven't any foibles, Sweetheart, anyway I love my dearest and I wish only to be everything to her.

I am depressed by the quadripartite meeting I attended today, the lowest level meeting I have attended – a sub-Committee on Local Government of the Kommandatura[14], discussing the question of an organization which has become Communist ridden, the Victims of Fascism[15].[16] The Russians blocked a compromise offered by the French, and so we and British stuck out against the French for our own point of view. The issues are becoming critical because political. The Russians want the German Communists to get a head start here, and we won't tolerate any strong arm methods. What is needed is little and great statesmen who at all levels are willing to sacrifice a point for the sake of international solidarity. You must urge the people at home to be patient and to insist that we do not push these things too fast. Otherwise things may come to a head sooner than anyone would wish.

But your letters came today and they are lovely and helpful. I'll write more about them tomorrow. Until then, my dearest and my boys a sweet kiss and all my love. Edgar

[12] Herbert Schmidt (1895-1987), amerikanischer Pianist und Professor für Klavier, BMus, absolvierte 1915 The University School of Music, Lincoln, Nebraska, und 1916 Institute of Musical Art, New York, ab 1917 Instructor in Pianoforte bzw. Professor of Piano, The University School of Music, Lincoln, Nebraska.

[13] Parent Teacher Association, Gesellschaft zur Förderung der engen Zusammenarbeit zwischen Eltern und Lehrern.

[14] Das Local Government Committee, Allied Kommandatura Berlin (siehe Dok. 20, Anm. 11), war ein personell nach dem Viererprinzip aufgebauter Fachausschuss; er beschäftigte sich mit "all governmental affairs and enterprises (such as the constitution of Berlin and the census of Berlin), all political matters, and the broad list which would be included under the term 'local government'". Civil Administration. Six Months Report 4 January-3 July 1946, in: Office of Military Government U. S. Berlin District (Hrsg.), Six Months Report 4 January-3 July 1946, Berlin 1946, S. 40-43, hier S. 41. Foto einer Sitzung des Local Government Committee im Bildanhang, Abb. 68.

[15] Am 3. Juni 1945 hatte Stadtrat Ottomar Geschke (1882-1957) die Bildung eines Hauptausschusses „Opfer des Faschismus" bei der von ihm geleiteten Magistratsabteilung für Sozialwesen bekannt gegeben. Das Sekretariat des Hauptausschusses leitete als Abteilung beim Hauptsozialamt mit Unterstützung von 20 Bezirksausschüssen die soziale und kulturelle Betreuung der politisch Verfolgten des NS-Regimes in Berlin.

[16] Siehe Protokoll der 11. Sitzung des Local Government Committee, Allied Kommandatura Berlin, am 27. März 1946, LG/M (46) 11, englischsprachige Fassung, in: The National Archives (TNA), Kew, Richmond, Surrey, Großbritannien, Allied Kommandatura: Directives, Minutes and Papers, FO 1112/378.

Dok. 30
Schreiben an die Ehefrau
Berlin, Ihnestraße 14[1], 30. März 1946

Dearest:

I must write you a little account (I wish I had sufficient time to be dictating to a secretary all of the details of what is going on here) of my first little victory here. There appeared in the German licensed press here, (and I imagine there is appearing in the American press, and periodicals as well – I wish you would take note of anything you see) this morning a release of General Barker[2] stating that in the coming referendum of the Social Democratic Party on the question of merger with the Communist Party (referendum to be held tomorrow) General Barker is anxious that a free and complete expression of opinion be had, and that, in the American Sector of Berlin, he intends to guarantee that sufficient protection and supervision be at hand so that people may vote as they please.[3] I made the suggestion to General Barker, and with slight

---

[1] Siehe Dok. 15, Anm. 1.
[2] Siehe Dok. 20, Anm. 10.
[3] Die Erklärung hatte folgenden Wortlaut: „Die *amerikanische Haltung* zum Plan der Verschmelzung von SPD und KPD ist in der Presse *eindeutig und klar* zum Ausdruck gebracht worden, nämlich, daß keine Verschmelzung anerkannt werden kann, die nicht freiwillig von der Mehrheit der Partei*mitglieder*, sondern nur von einer Gruppe von Partei*führern* verlangt wird. Es ist weiterhin klargelegt, daß jede Abstimmung in Berlin über diese Frage in Uebereinstimmung mit den allgemein gültigen demokratischen Regeln vor sich gehen muß. Es ist mir sehr daran gelegen, daß dies in der kommenden Urabstimmung am Sonntag der Fall ist, da sie nach meiner Ueberzeugung den ehrlichen Versuch der Parteimitglieder darstellt, ihren Standpunkt zum Ausdruck zu bringen. Die Ereignisse der vergangenen Woche deuten darauf hin, daß Versuche gemacht werden, eine freie und vollständige Meinungsäußerung der Mitglieder der SPD in dieser Urabstimmung zu verhindern. Im amerikanischen Sektor von Berlin werden Maßnahmen getroffen werden, damit jeder Wahlberechtigte, der beabsichtigt, seine Stimme abzugeben, sich unter entsprechendem Schutz und entsprechender Aufsicht ungehindert für oder gegen eine Verschmelzung aussprechen kann." Der Tagesspiegel vom 30. März 1946, S. 1. Siehe Stiftung Archiv der Parteien und Massenorganisationen der DDR im Bundesarchiv (SAPMO-BArch), Berlin, Nachlass Otto Grotewohl, NY 4090/278, Bl. 110; Berlin. Kampf um Freiheit und Selbstverwaltung 1945-1946, hrsg. im Auftrage des Senats von Berlin (= Schriftenreihe zur Berliner Zeitgeschichte, Bd. 1), 2., erg. und erw. Auflage, Berlin 1961, S. 401, Nr. 97. Der englische Wortlaut: "The American view regarding the SPD-KPD merger has been made clearly known in the press, namely that no merger can be recognized that is not demanded freely by a majority of the voters but only by a group of party leaders. It is further made clear that any voting conducted in Berlin on this question must be in accordance with the customary democratic principles. It is very important to me that this should be the case with the coming Sunday referendum as it is my conviction that this represents an honest attempt of the party membership to express its standpoint. Events in the past week have shown that efforts have been made to prevent a complete expression of opinion of the members of the SPD. In the American Sector of Berlin measures have been taken so that everyone entitled to vote will be afforded the necessary protection so that he may cast his vote unhindered for or against a merger." Special Report of the Military Governor, US Zone, vom

revisions, wrote the release. The story is as follows: The Communists here, backed by the Russians are favoring a merger with the Social Democratic party into a new Socialist Unitary Party (SEP). The Central Committee of the SPD (Social Democrats of Germany)[4] is using strong armed and high pressure methods to produce this merger in a hurry, before any elections can be held in Berlin, of any kind. The kind of methods they have been using has produced a revolt among the rank and file members who have demanded, and have been supported in their demand by the City Executive Committee of the Party[5] (not to be confused with the Central Committee), that a referendum on the question be held tomorrow. The Central Committee is not happy about this referendum and has tried to sabotage it by coming out with a statement in the Social Democratic Paper[6] urgently recommending all Social Democratic members of the Party to sabotage the referendum tomorrow by not going to the polls.[7] This made me mad and I went to Barker with the suggestion that he write a letter to the Central Committee reminding them that he wanted a free expression of opinion on the matter to be held and that he also release a statement to the press expressing his point of view. He agreed (he is a man of principle) and let me write the letter and the release. The letter was delivered to the Chairman of the Central Committee (Grotewohl)[8] as he was about to deliver an address (together with Pieck[9], the Communist leader) to a meeting of

---

15. Mai 1946: KPD-SPD Merger in Berlin and the Soviet Zone, S. 8, in: Bundesarchiv (BArch), Koblenz, Z 45 F, 11/147-2/21-47. Auch die amerikanische Presse berichtete über Barkers Statement. Siehe Berlin Poll in Question. Voting Today on Socialist-Red Union Off in Some Soviet Areas, in: The New York Times vom 31. März 1946, S. 20; J. Emlyn Williams, Berlin Vote Bars Communist Front, in: The Christian Science Monitor vom 2. April 1946, S. 7. Siehe auch Harold Hurwitz unter Mitarbeit von Andreas Büning/Johannes-Berthold Hohmann/Klaus Sühl/Ingolore Mensch-Khan, Die Anfänge des Widerstands, Teil 2: Zwischen Selbsttäuschung und Zivilcourage: Der Fusionskampf (= Demokratie und Antikommunismus in Berlin nach 1945, Bd. IV), Köln 1990, S. 1189.

[4] Der Zentralausschuss der SPD war das de facto nur für die sowjetische Besatzungszone und Berlin zuständige Leitungsgremium der SPD.
[5] Bezirksvorstand der SPD.
[6] Gemeint ist Das Volk. Tageszeitung der Sozialdemokratishen Partei Deutschlands.
[7] Erklärung des Zentralausschusses vom 27. März 1946 zur Urabstimmung in Berlin, in: Das Volk vom 28. März 1946, [S. 1].
[8] Otto Grotewohl (1894–1964), deutscher Politiker (SPD/SED), gelernter Buchdrucker, 1912 SPD, 1918 USPD, 1920 bis 1926 MdL Braunschweig, 1921/1922 Minister für Inneres und Volksbildung und 1923/1924 Minister für Inneres und Justiz des Freistaats Braunschweig, 1922 erneut SPD, 1925–1933 MdR, 1945/1946 Vorsitzender des Zentralausschusses der SPD, 1946 SED, 1946–1954 einer der zwei Vorsitzenden der SED, 1949–1964 Ministerpräsident bzw. Vorsitzender des Ministerrats der DDR. Foto mit Grotewohl im Bildanhang, Abb. 82.
[9] Wilhelm Pieck (1876–1960), deutscher Politiker (KPD/SED), gelernter Tischler, 1895 SPD, 1916 Spartakusbund, 1918 KPD, 1921–1928 und 1932/1933 Mitglied des Preußischen Landtags, 1928–1933 MdR, 1933–1945 Exil in der Tschechoslowakei, in Frankreich und in der Sowjetunion, ab 1934 in der Sowjetunion, 1945/1946 Vorsitzender der KPD, 1946 SED, 1946–1954 einer der zwei Vorsitzenden der SED, 1949–1960 Präsident der DDR. Foto mit Pieck im Bildanhang, Abb. 82.

railroad workers[10].[11] The letter made him more conciliatory on the question of referendum than he has hitherto been. The release this morning encourages all those here who believe we have a positive rather than a negative mission, and I believe will receive a warm welcome by the American press and people.

It was brought up at Clay's[12] staff meeting[13] this morning, and I was humiliated to have Clay, supported by Murphy[14], without knowing any of the facts concerning the matter, say that the Central Committee was within its rights in urging a sabotage of the referendum. It is the old question of leaning so far backwards in the support of democracy that you support those who are willing to destroy it. Later I learned that Clay would have been ready to forbid the referendum which would have raised an uproar at home. If Clay is supposed to be kept politically wise by Murphy then Murphy has failed in his job so far. I

---

[10] Am 29. März 1946 hatten Grotewohl und Pieck auf einer Kundgebung im Straßenbahnbetriebsbahnhof Charlottenburg gesprochen, die „von den Vereinigten Betriebsgruppen der SPD und KPD der BVG-Straßenbahn, der Wasserwerke, des Postamts I, des Telegrafen- und Bauamtes, der Technischen Hochschule und der Osramwerke einberufen worden war". Karl Honer, Machtvolle Vereinigungs-Kundgebung in Charlottenburg, in: Tägliche Rundschau vom 30. März 1946, S. 2.

[11] In dem an Max Fechner (siehe Dok. 39, Anm. 29) und Otto Grotewohl gerichteten Schreiben vom 29. März 1946 (in: SAPMO-BArch, Nachlass Otto Grotewohl, NY 4090/278, Bl. 109) heißt es in der deutschen Übersetzung: „In meiner Eigenschaft als kommandierender General der amerikanischen Streitkräfte und als Militär-Gouverneur des amerikanischen Sektors bitte ich Sie und Ihre Kollegen, von folgendem Kenntnis zu nehmen: 1) Am Sonnabend der vergangenen Woche erliess General Clay eine Verlautbarung an die Presse, in der er auf die amerikanische Haltung aufmerksam machte im Hinblick auf die beabsichtigte Verschmelzung der sozialdemokratischen und kommunistischen Parteien. In dieser Verlautbarung brachte er klar zum Ausdruck, dass er zwar nicht wünscht, die freie Wahl der an dieser Frage interessierten Deutschen zu beeinflussen, er aber keine Verschmelzung anerkennen würde, die nicht dem freien Willen der Mehrheit der betr. Parteimitglieder entspricht, sondern einer Aktion von seiten einer Gruppe von Partei-Führern. Er stellte ferner fest, dass er darauf bestehen würde, dass eine Wahl in dieser Frage in ganz Berlin und in der amerikanischen Zone durchzuführen ist gemäss dem anerkannten demokratischen Verfahren. Ich brauche nicht besonders zu betonen, dass das auch meine Stellungnahme ist. 2) Ich las im ‚Volk' vom 28.3.1946 den Aufruf Ihres Zentralausschusses, der allen Mitgliedern der sozialdemokratischen Partei dringend empfahl, an der kommenden Wahl am Sonntag nicht teilzunehmen. Ich finde, dass das im Widerspruch zu der Billigung der Wahl steht, die nach meinen Informationen in einer Sitzung des Zentralausschusses am 26.3.1946 beschlossen worden ist, an der auch die Leitungen der Verwaltungsbezirke teilgenommen haben. 3) Ich kann nur annehmen, dass die Mitglieder des Zentralausschusses sich wohl der Verwicklungen bewusst sind, die sich aus ihren Verlautbarungen im ‚Volk' ergeben. Nach meiner Ansicht sind die Pläne für die kommende Wahl ein ehrenhafter Versuch der Parteimitglieder, ihre Meinung zu einer lebenswichtigen Frage der Organisation der SPD und der politischen Zukunft Deutschlands zum Ausdruck zu bringen. Ich bin nur darauf bedacht, dass sie die Gelegenheit haben sollen, ihre Wünsche frei zu erkennen zu geben."

[12] Siehe Dok. 2, Anm. 6.

[13] Siehe Protokoll der OMGUS-Stabskonferenz am 30. März 1946, in: Archiv des IfZ, OMGUS – Staff Conferences (Protokollkopien), Fg 12/3.

[14] Siehe Dok. 8, Anm. 13.

intend, pardon the presumption, to take upon myself, with a little help, the job of making Clay politically informed.

I am a little happy over the event. I didn't expect to see my words translated so soon into headlines in the German press (the British did something similar). The issue between Soviet-Communist "democracy" and American "democracy" is becoming concrete here, and I know which side I am on.

I send all my love and many kisses to my sweet wife and my sweet boys. If it were not for them I could not be even a bit determined. I love them very very much. Edgar

Dok. 31
Schreiben an die Ehefrau
Berlin, Wannsee Hotel[1], Am Sandwerder 17/19, 31. März 1946

Dear Sweetheart –

I have moved out of my single room in Ihnestrasse[2] and into the quarters which General Barker[3] arranged for me in the Wannsee Hotel, the former house of the Nazi Minister of Economics Funk[4], now a prisoner at Nurnberg[5],[6]. I move into my own semi-permanent little apartment tomorrow when the present incumbent, a colonel, moves into his new quarters. There will be a bathroom, a bed-room, a sitting room, and a private dining room where I can entertain when necessary – mostly Germans, I hope. The apartment looks out on the Wannsee[7], a huge lake in Berlin's suburbs. Ultimately, I guess, I am to move into a large house, next door which they are taking over, – not the whole house of course, but an apartment which I can choose.[8] I don't know how wise this is going to be since it gets me away from the center of things. I suppose I could share quarters in a house closer to the center. Yet I should just as soon live alone. I am very very close to the subway station[9]. And here there is every facility for eating (the captain in charge says it is the best mess in Berlin) without having to bother about help and commissary purchases and the like. In any case I shall try it out. The idea of being near the lake is attractive, especially if it is going to be possible to swim and boat, and with spring coming on here now[10] it

---

[1] Siehe Dok. 25, Anm. 9.
[2] Siehe Dok. 15, Anm. 1.
[3] Siehe Dok. 20, Anm. 10.
[4] Siehe Dok. 25, Anm. 10.
[5] Nürnberg, Stadt im Land Bayern in der amerikanischen Besatzungszone Deutschlands.
[6] Siehe Dok. 25.
[7] Gemeint ist der Große Wannsee, eine Ausbuchtung der Havel (siehe Dok. 74, Anm. 24) im Südwesten Berlins.
[8] Gemeint ist das Haus Am Sandwerder 21/23. Siehe Dok. 25, Anm. 12.
[9] Gemeint ist der Bahnhof Wannsee.
[10] Am Vortag hatte Donald H. McLean Jr. (siehe Dok. 20, Anm. 42) in sein Tagebuch eingetragen: "What a beautiful spring day this is. For the first morning since fall, we wore no overcoats. I have the window open for the first time in weeks." E-Mail von Jack McLean, der das Tagebuch seines Vaters besitzt, an Werner Breunig vom 16. Juli 2008.

might to be quite nice. It gets you away too from the very American center of Omgus[11] headquarters and there may be a good chance here to sit quietly once in awhile, and reflect about the meaning of what is going on here.

I mentioned in my letter of yesterday, the vote which is being taken by Social Democrats today on the question of merger with the Communists into a new party.[12] I went out with Brewster Morris[13] (a State Department boy) to visit some of the election booths today. It was a good lesson in practical democracy. In the booths in the American and British sectors which we visited everything seemed to be going smoothly and people were turning out to vote. In the Russian sector no vote was being taken. In some districts this was because the local Social Democratic leaders had decided no vote would be taken and in somewhat controlled elections had secured this result. In others where the leaders wanted the voting the Russians had not yet given permission to vote. At one of the former districts a lone voter was asking for the vote and was told by a gruff party leader that there was no vote being taken. In one of the districts of the latter category, two Russians stood away from the booth, there was a group of ten voters about, but the Russian Commandant of the district had not yet given permission for the voting to take place. We brought the lone voter from the first place to the second place where he decided to wait to see if permission would be given or no. In a sense this is all symbolic – a good example in miniature of two different points of view. Careless Americans are often want to say that political democracy doesn't mean very much. In some cases it means very much, everything, especially in the case of a lone voter who is being denied the vote right in front of you.

We are going out tonight to see if there are any results.

I love you my sweet and my dear boys. I haven't had a chance to get at your letters again, but I am going to try when I get home tonight. Goodnight my lovely and dearest Emily. A kiss from me for you and the boys. Edgar

Dok. 32
Schreiben an die Ehefrau
Berlin, Wannsee Hotel[1], Am Sandwerder 17/19, 2. April 1946

My sweet Emily + my boys:

Just a note to say that I love you very much, and wish you were here in this new apartment. It is a little large for one person. Any room would be too large for one person for me.

---

[11] Siehe Dok. 17, Anm. 45.
[12] Siehe Dok. 30.
[13] Brewster H. Morris (1909–1990), amerikanischer Diplomat, ab 1936 Department of State, 1938/1939 Vice Consul, Wien, 1939/1940 Vice Consul, Dresden, 1940/1941 Vice Consul and 3rd Secretary, Berlin, 1944–1948 Office of US Political Adviser on German Affairs, 1961–1963 Consul General, Bonn, 1963–1967 Ambassador, Tschad.

[1] Siehe Dok. 25, Anm. 9.

I have worked hard all day and all evening writing a report on Sunday's[2] referendum[3] for General Barker[4]. The whole Berlin situation is a little chaotic and steps have to be taken quickly because political events are happening so fast. And when they have to be taken on a quadripartite basis they have to be so carefully taken. The British, e. g.[5] think Clay[6] is obsessed with the notion of not wanting to play their game and are not waiting for us to take the lead. I am of course willing to take it. It is clear too that some of the people in the State Department crowd wish to use me to prod General Barker, and Murphy[7] and Clay. Besides all this I am supposed to attend quadripartite meetings, start a new civil administration section[8] and consult about all its problems, and keep in touch with what is going on in Omgus[9]. It is too much. At least it is too much at the moment. Clay is a little exercised over these elections, and needs instructions. There are lots of things I should like to write. I need lots of time to think. Now I have a good place to do it. The sunset was nice over the Wannsee[10] tonight.

Goodnight – my beloved ones – sweet kisses and embraces for you. I love my sweet wife, and my John, and my Thomas. Edgar

Dok. 33
Schreiben an die Ehefrau
Berlin, Wannsee Hotel[1], Am Sandwerder 17/19, 6. April 1946

My dearest and sweetest beloved Emily –

Last night I read all over again your first and second batch of letters – a grand experience. The letters are coming direct now without going to 25th Base Post Office[2]. I think I'd better change to the B[erlin] D[istrict] APO[3] as soon as this seems to be a more or less permanent job. It seems a good while since I have had a chance to write a decent letter.

I am moved into my new quarters in the Wannsee Hotel which is soon to be transformed into the Wannsee Officers' Country Club for use, also, of wives and children when they arrive.[4] I have a large living room with two windows

---

[2] 31. März 1946.
[3] Urabstimmung über die Vereinigung von KPD und SPD durch die Mitglieder der SPD in den Westsektoren. Siehe Dok. 31.
[4] Siehe Dok. 20, Anm. 10.
[5] Exempli gratia, zum Beispiel.
[6] Siehe Dok. 2, Anm. 6.
[7] Siehe Dok. 8, Anm. 13.
[8] Gemeint ist die Civil Administration Branch, OMGBD. Siehe Dok. 28, Anm. 5.
[9] Siehe Dok. 17, Anm. 45.
[10] Gemeint ist der Große Wannsee, eine Ausbuchtung der Havel (siehe Dok. 74, Anm. 24) im Südwesten Berlins.

[1] Siehe Dok. 25, Anm. 9.
[2] Siehe Dok. 4.
[3] Army Post Office 755, Berlin-Lichterfelde, McNair Barracks.
[4] Die ersten Ehefrauen und Kinder von amerikanischen Besatzungsangehörigen sollten am 30. April 1946 in Berlin eintreffen. Siehe Dok. 42, Anm. 13.

looking out on the lake[5]. The room is nicely furnished with a couch, easy chairs, miscellaneous tables and a writing desk – glass container combination piece. There are three large oil paintings on the walls (nothing any good) and nice rugs on the floor. There is a telephone. I have also a bed-room with a handsome rug on the floor and built in closet space and a window looking out over the lake. Adjoining this is a large bathroom, with shower and tub (and the usual douche facilities for the ladies). It is done in black marble! which is so highly polished as to serve as a kind of mirror. I think I said this was Funk's[6] house.[7] I shall have the use of a private dining room, adjoining my living room whenever I need it. The food is very elegant and served in grand manner – the best mess in Berlin I am told. From the house there is a park – like lawn running down to the lake with a swimming pool and a boat house. Last night before supper a gasoline-engine yacht left the pier with officers on board for a ride. This place is now used for transient guests of General Barker[8]. Oh! The high officers live well in Europe, and I don't see why those of them who have been through battle shouldn't. Walter Dorn[9] is in Berlin now, and tried to get me to move into a huge house on the small Wannsee[10] which adjoins this lake. But I decided not to. General Barker went to a great deal of trouble to get me into this place, and he is, indeed, suspicious of Walter's red leanings: He told me the other day that he was glad he had me instead of Walter because I was not so left of center! I was also told by a Major Dollard[11] that the General had spoken affectionately of me. After being moved into these nice quarters I didn't see how I could immediately move into others with Walter. Besides Walter is leaving at long stretches. I can have peace and quiet here. I can think and work in the evenings without interference. This arrangement is not over-pretentious as the other one is, and it is lighter and brighter and altogether satisfactory. In fact I should like to remain independent of Walter. This place, also, is only a few steps from General Barker and he has asked me to drop down in the evenings whenever I please.[12] Walter is a kind of meddler and I don't want him meddling with me.

I am afraid Barker won't be here long and this I shall regret very very much. He is not well as I have explained, I think. He told me that for months now he has not been able to sleep without sleeping powders. He got up out of the hos-

---

[5] Großer Wannsee, eine Ausbuchtung der Havel (siehe Dok. 74, Anm. 24) im Südwesten Berlins.
[6] Siehe Dok. 25, Anm. 10.
[7] Siehe Dok. 25 und Dok. 31.
[8] Siehe Dok. 20, Anm. 10.
[9] Siehe Dok. 2, Anm. 10.
[10] Der Kleine Wannsee stellt die Verbindung zwischen dem Großen Wannsee (siehe Anm. 5) und dem Pohlesee dar. Am Ufer befinden sich repräsentative Anwesen.
[11] William A. S. Dollard (1901-2000), Major, 1926 MA, Columbia University, ab 1939 Instructor, Hunter College, English Department, 1942-1950 US Army Service, März/April 1946 Chief, Education and Cultural Relations Branch, OMGBD, dann Chief, Religious Affairs Section, Civil Affairs Division, Department of War, bis 1971 Professor, Lehman College (urspr. Bronx Campus des Hunter Colleges).
[12] Barker wohnte Am Sandwerder 27. Siehe Dok. 28, Anm. 27.

pital in Washington and left for this job on the next day.[13] There is also the fact that he and Clay[14] do not see eye to eye on all matters. He is suspected of being anti-red and pro-British and likes to run his job independently. I should not like to see him go. You never know what you will get in his place. But I think I'll try to stick in this place.

This is army day[15] here, a holiday, and it has been properly celebrated with appropriate ceremonies. I suppose I should have gone to those at Omgus[16] but I did not.[17] General Barker invited me to come to those at B[erlin] D[istrict].[18] I was given a card for my car which said "Official Guest", and a seat on the reviewing stand. On the front row were Murphy[19], Clay, Barker and Admiral Glassford[20]. Behind them were the Russian, French, and British Commandants and their Deputies. Behind these various colonels, and Mr. Steere[21], Don Heath[22] (State Department). I was in the back row. Barker made a speech and the parade passed by the review stand. About four companies of infantry, all recruits I was told, cavalry, Wacs[23], MP's[24], tanks, and planes flew overhead. But it rained. The poor Wacs must have been furious – makeup running down their faces and wet hair streaming behind. They looked tough. Afterwards there was a reception. Drinks and the most elaborate set-up of food you can imagine. Colonel Thayer[25] couldn't do better in Vienna. I talked a little with Colonel Nye[26]

---

[13] Barker hatte sein Amt in Berlin am 10. Oktober 1945 angetreten. Siehe Maj. Gen. Barker Assumes Command, in: The Berlin Sentinel vom 13. Oktober 1945, S. 1.

[14] Siehe Dok. 2, Anm. 6.

[15] "'To give special honor to our courageous soldiers,' April 6th was proclaimed 'Army Day,' a national holiday, on March 16, 1937, commemorating the day upon which the United States joined the Allies in World War I in 1917. The 'best dressed, best fed, best paid army in the world' receives today tribute from its country. Americans throughout the world are observing the first peacetime Army Day since the close of hostilities of World War II." Army Day at OMGUS, in: The Grooper vom 6. April 1946, S. 1 und 6, hier S. 1. Army Day wurde am 6. April 1949 zum letzten Mal landesweit begangen. Seit 1950 gibt es in den USA am dritten Samstag im Mai den Armed Forces Day.

[16] Siehe Dok. 17, Anm. 45.

[17] Siehe Army Day at OMGUS, in: The Grooper vom 6. April 1946, S. 1 und 6.

[18] Anlässlich des Army Day wurde am 6. April 1946 vor dem Telefunkenhaus in Berlin-Lichterfelde, dem US Headquarters Berlin District, eine Parade von ausgewählten Einheiten der verschiedenen in Berlin stationierten Truppenteile abgehalten. Siehe Der Tagesspiegel vom 2. April 1946, S. 6; Der Tagesspiegel vom 7. April 1946, S. 6; Der Tagesspiegel vom 10. April 1946, S. 3. Foto im Bildanhang, Abb. 26.

[19] Siehe Dok. 8, Anm. 13.

[20] William A. Glassford (1886–1958), Admiral, 1944 Deputy Commander US Naval Forces in Europe, 1945/1946 Commander US Naval Forces, Germany.

[21] Siehe Dok. 20, Anm. 23.

[22] Donald R. Heath. Siehe Dok. 8, Anm. 15.

[23] Members of the Women's Army Corps. Siehe Dok. 13, Anm. 14.

[24] Military Police officers.

[25] Charles W. Thayer (1910–1969), Lieutenant Colonel, amerikanischer Diplomat, 1933 Absolvent der United States Military Academy, ab 1934 Department of State, 1937/1938 Vice Consul, Berlin, 1939/1940 Vice Consul, Hamburg, 1943/1944 Secretary, European Advisory Commission, London, 1944–1946 US Army, 1944/1945 Chief, US Military Mission in Yugoslavia, 1945/1946 Chief, OSS Mission in Austria, 1950/1951 Political Liaison Officer, Bonn, 1952–1954 Consul General, München.

who is one of Barker's favorites. He agreed that such a display, most of it remaining uneaten should not be made in the midst of a hungry city. The British don't do it. They have cut their rations at the same time that they have cut the Germans' rations.[27] We are very spoiled and luxurious in these matters. I also talked with a Colonel Morgan[28], who is in charge of H[ead]q[uarter]s Command and he referred to the fact that the negro troops in Berlin District were not represented. Supposedly this is because they are raw recruits and would not make a good impression. But he thought it a mistake, nevertheless. It was my first experience on a reviewing stand. The display of local well-equipped power was somewhat impressive but under these conditions with the war over, the emotional fervor is not there.

I don't know how the week has gone but it certainly has gone. It has been chiefly concerned with the aftermath of the vote which the S[ocial] Democrats took last Sunday[29] on whether to join with the Communists.[30] There was no vote in the Russian sector. In the other sectors the vote went overwhelmingly against a merger.[31] The S[ocial] D[emocrat]'s have now decided to hold a meeting tomorrow to elect a new city Committee and cut loose from the present Central Committee[32], a pro-merger and somewhat tyrannical group. This meeting is to be hold in our sector and I shall be going.[33] When we heard of the meeting I thought we ought to let the other Allies know, since we are going to try to get them to agree to treat Berlin politics on a quadripartite basis. General Barker let me write an announcement that was read at the Kommandatura[34].[35]

---

[26] Wilbur S. Nye (1898–1970), Colonel, 1920 Absolvent der United States Military Academy, 1945/1946 G-3 Berlin District, 1950–1954 Chief Historian, US Army for Europe.

[27] Siehe Dok. 23, Anm. 15.

[28] Albert C. Morgan (1899–1964), Colonel, 1919 Absolvent der United States Military Academy, 1946 Headquarters Berlin District, US Army.

[29] 31. März 1946.

[30] Siehe Dok. 31.

[31] An der parteiinternen Urabstimmung über die Einheitsfrage beteiligten sich 71,8 Prozent der stimmberechtigten Parteimitglieder in den Westsektoren, von denen 82,6 Prozent gegen „den sofortigen Zusammenschluß beider Arbeiterparteien" votierten. Siehe Werner Breunig, Berlin 1945/46. Vom Kriegsende bis zum parlamentarischen Neubeginn, in: „Berlin kommt wieder". Die Nachkriegsjahre 1945/46 (= Ausstellungskataloge des Landesarchivs Berlin, 16), Berlin 2005, S. 7–43, hier S. 24.

[32] Zentralausschuss, das für die sowjetische Besatzungszone und Berlin zuständige Leitungsgremium der SPD.

[33] Der Parteitag der oppositionellen Sozialdemokraten sollte am 7. April 1946 in der Zinnowwaldschule im Berliner Verwaltungsbezirk Zehlendorf stattfinden.

[34] Siehe Dok. 20, Anm. 11.

[35] Die Erklärung, die in der 17. Sitzung der stellvertretenden Stadtkommandanten am 5. April 1946 von dem US-Vertreter verlesen wurde, hatte folgenden Wortlaut: "General Barker wishes to announce that he has approved for the near future a meeting requested by members of the Social Democratic Party in the American Sector, at which there may be present party members from all the Allied Sectors in Berlin. By informing the Kommandatura of this meeting he wishes to aid the promotion of a common Allied scrutiny and control over the political activities of Berlin." Protokoll der 17. Sitzung der stellvertretenden Stadtkommandanten am 5. April 1946, BKD/M (46) 17-220, englischsprachige Fassung, in: LAB, B Rep. 036-01 (Office of Military Government, Berlin Sector [OMGBS]), 11/148-1/12.

I also wrote a report on last Sunday's referendum for him.[36] There have been many informal conferences during the week. I had lunch one day with Murphy and Brewster Morris[37] (a cousin of Charlie Thayer[38]) and Murphy's secretary[39]. There were cocktails before lunch, wine during lunch, and brandy after lunch, and the lunch itself was elegant enough. The Ambassador lives well but not with the greatest of opulence. We talked mostly about the political situation in Berlin and its relation to the over-all picture. I found myself at odds on some matters. Murphy is very pleasant, and well intentioned. He has a good head but he is not what you would call a strong character. There are certain differences between him and the rest of the State Dep[artmen]t crowd.

There is a lack of coordination and measure here, and in this I may be of some use. Yesterday at the meeting of the Deputies[40] the Russians had to take it. There were complaints about the way they permitted one paper[41] to represent itself as an organ of the city government when it wasn't.[42] There were complaints about the arrest and detention for about 45 minutes last Sunday of two Americans (one Kathleen McLaughlin[43] – New York Times)[44] while they were trying to see what was going on in the Russian Sector with respect to the referendum.[45] There was a vigorous protest against the Russians for permitting their

[36] Siehe Dok. 32 und Dok. 32, Anm. 3.
[37] Siehe Dok. 31, Anm. 13.
[38] Charles W. Thayer. Siehe Anm. 25.
[39] Möglicherweise Henry C. S. Bush. Siehe Dok. 20, Anm. 4.
[40] Siehe Protokoll der 17. Sitzung der stellvertretenden Stadtkommandanten am 5. April 1946, BKD/M (46) 17, englischsprachige Fassung, in: LAB, B Rep. 036-01 (Office of Military Government, Berlin Sector [OMGBS]), 11/148-1/12.
[41] Gemeint ist die Berliner Zeitung.
[42] Die Berliner Zeitung hatte ihren Status als amtliches Publikationsorgan des Magistrats der Stadt Berlin verloren, als alleiniges amtliches Verkündungsblatt des Magistrats fungierte das Verordnungsblatt der Stadt Berlin. Siehe Die Sitzungsprotokolle des Magistrats der Stadt Berlin 1945/46. Teil II: 1946, bearb. und eingel. von Dieter Hanauske (= Schriftenreihe des Landesarchivs Berlin, Bd. 2/II), Berlin 1999, S. 19f., Anm. 101.
[43] Kathleen McLaughlin (1898–1990), Korrespondentin der amerikanischen Tageszeitung "The New York Times".
[44] Festgenommen worden war auch Peter H. Wyden, urspr. Weidenreich (1923–1998), Leiter des Berliner Büros der von der amerikanischen Besatzungsmacht in München herausgegebenen Zeitung „Die Neue Zeitung".
[45] Kathleen McLaughlin schrieb zu dem Vorfall: "Various Russian observers and newspaper correspondents visited the American and other zones to watch the polling, which was relatively quiet. However, this correspondent and Peter Weidenreich of New York, chief of the Berlin office of the United States Military Government newspaper published in Munich, the Neue Zeitung, ran afoul of Soviet military police while touring that sector and, despite our credentials, were taken into custody by two who climbed on our jeep and directed the German civilian driver to proceed to the Allied Control Council headquarters about a mile distant. Excited comment there over a Rolleiflex camera, which this correspondent was carrying, led to our detention for an hour until three Russian officers arrived to interrogate us. After a long conversation with higher headquarters, during which the phrase 'photo apparat' recurred intermittently, we were abruptly dismissed with the warning not to re-enter the Russian sector without having obtained special credentials for travel and for photography there." Kathleen McLaughlin, Berlin Socialists Reject Merger; Russians Bar Vote in Their Zone, in: The New York Times vom 1. April 1946, S. 1 und 3, hier S. 3.

paper for the Berliners (Tägliche Rundschau[46]) to printed an unwarranted attack upon Col. Howley[47], who is Barker's Deputy for M[ilitary] G[overnment].[48] Howley himself presided at the meeting and made the protest in person. There was my and Barker's little job about the lack of common control over politics in Berlin. All this (except my statement – which was written out) in unmeasured language. This protest should be well and finally but carefully made. Then there has been the case of two Communists, this week, sentenced for five years for trying to meddle in the affairs of M[ilitary] G[overnment].[49] The sentence is certainly excessive and I am sure it will be cut down or dismissed altogether. So you see how difficult it is for the powers to live together in the city of Berlin. But it is good that they can sit across the table from each other and discuss it. And they are small matters.

I hope you will try to get some help if Mrs. Brown[50] is not able to come back soon. You can't very well go on this way working yourself to death until the early hours of the morning. At least you should implement your resolve to send the washing out. You ought to get that practice established while I am away. I wish too you would get another pair of glasses, so that when the next lens breaks you won't have to go blind and sick for a few days. I am amazed to think that you have taken up gardening with such vehemence and enthusiasm. This relaxation of a firmer resolve I should never have expected. You will be having dogs and cats next. I wish I were there to see it all, and I can only express my admiration. Dad[51] can take over when he comes. Spring is about to break out here but I must say I am much less interested in it here than I am in Nebraska[52].

---

[46] Die Tägliche Rundschau wurde vom Kommando der Roten Armee als erste deutschsprachige Tageszeitung nach der Kapitulation seit dem 15. Mai 1945 herausgegeben.
[47] Siehe Dok. 20, Anm. 18.
[48] Gemeint ist eine Meldung der Prawda vom 31. März 1946, die in der Täglichen Rundschau vom 3. April 1946, S. 2 (Der Weltspiegel/Eine internationale Uebersicht), abgedruckt wurde. Darin heißt es unter anderem: „Der Stellvertreter des Chefs der Amerikanischen Militärkommandantur von Berlin, Oberst Howley, erklärte kürzlich dem Berliner Korrespondenten der Associated Press, daß *die Vereinigten Staaten in Deutschland eine aggressivere politische Führung für den Kampf gegen den Kommunismus sichern müssen.*"
[49] Der Leiter der KPD im Bezirk Schöneberg, Gerhard Jurr (siehe Dok. 41, Anm. 13), und der Vorsitzende der KPD-Betriebsgruppe im Bezirksamt Schöneberg, Wilhelm Kammermeier (siehe Dok. 41, Anm. 14), waren von einem amerikanischen Militärgericht zu je fünf Jahren Gefängnis verurteilt worden. Die beiden hatten versucht, Anordnungen der Militärregierung zu umgehen und die Bezirksverwaltung unter die Kontrolle ihrer Partei zu bringen. Siehe Berlin. Kampf um Freiheit und Selbstverwaltung 1945–1946, hrsg. im Auftrage des Senats von Berlin (= Schriftenreihe zur Berliner Zeitgeschichte, Bd. 1), 2., erg. und erw. Auflage, Berlin 1961, S. 408, Nr. 11; Protokoll der Verhandlung gegen Gerhard Jurr und Wilhelm Kammermeier vor dem Mittleren Amerikanischen Militärgericht für den amerikanischen Sektor Berlins in Lichterfelde-West am 2. und 3. April 1946, in: LAB, C Rep. 900-01 (Kommunistische Partei Deutschlands [KPD] – Bezirksorganisation Groß-Berlin), Nr. 56.
[50] Emily L. Johnsons Haushaltshilfe.
[51] Frank E. Johnson. Siehe Dok. 3, Anm. 12.
[52] US-Bundesstaat.

I should especially like to see the apple trees in bloom. You will tell me about the other things as they come along.

I am almost inclined to say that you should go ahead with the Steinway[53] in order that John[54] is not deprived of it longer than necessary. If you do not I must choose it when I return. I was sorry that you didn't subscribe to "Retort"[55]. You know how I feel about "Politics"[56] but you must not be without something to take its place.[57] What happened to the pictures I took at home.[58] You know I have no pictures except of those Washington ones of Timmy[59], and I don't like this.

I think I'll include some food package requests in case you think the consciences of your friends ought to be pricked. Mrs. Moore[60] of M + P[61] might want one. I haven't been able to deliver her package as yet because I haven't been to Kassel[62].[63] Maybe I'll mail it. I'll give this food to Germans, of course. Yesterday evening I noticed that the waiter in the hotel instead of taking uneaten rolls into the kitchen, stuck them in his pocket. Col. Morgan told me that the German keepers at the messes divide the garbage of uneaten food left on the plates among themselves.

Bye-bye, my sweet-heart. I love you and love you, and await the next letters from you. We are not so far apart temporally now. I send you a sweet kiss and many endearments. And remind the boys about me. Bye-bye my sweet-heart, my dearest. Edgar

---

[53] Siehe Dok. 4, Anm. 25.
[54] Johnsons Sohn John. Siehe Dok. 2, Anm. 15.
[55] Eine amerikanische Zeitschrift, 1942–1951 in Bearsville, New York, erschienen.
[56] Eine amerikanische Zeitschrift, 1944–1949 in New York City erschienen.
[57] Emily L. Johnson in ihrem Schreiben vom 10. März 1946: "My subscription to *Politics* ran out this month + I *shan't* renew it! However, I got a folder from *Retort*, 'an anarchist quarterly of social philosophy and the arts ... is the only political-cultural magazine that maintained an entirely uncompromising opposition to the war'. I'm tempted, dear one, but I guess I'll keep the dollar!" Brief in: Unterlagen aus dem Nachlass Edgar N. Johnson, Privatbesitz Candice E. und Thomas R. Johnson, Denver, Colorado, USA.
[58] Möglicherweise gehören Abb. 2 und Abb. 3 im Bildanhang zu den Fotos, die Johnson hier anspricht.
[59] Johnsons Sohn Thomas (siehe Dok. 2, Anm. 16), der in Washington, D. C., zur Welt kam.
[60] Hanna E. Moore, geb. Eberle (1887–1966), deutsch-amerikanische Kunst- und Antiquitätenberaterin, geboren in Vachingen, Deutschland, Kunststudium in Europa, wanderte 1909 in die USA aus, Witwe von Burton E. Moore (1866–1925), Professor of Physics, University of Nebraska, mit dem sie seit 1911 verheiratet war.
[61] Miller & Paine Department Store, Lincoln, Nebraska. Hanna E. Moore war Department Manager bei Miller & Paine, zuständig für Kunst und Antiquitäten.
[62] Stadt im Land Groß-Hessen in der amerikanischen Besatzungszone Deutschlands.
[63] In Kassel lebte Hanna E. Moores Schwester, Rosalie Eberle (geb. 1879). Siehe Dok. 76.

Dok. 34
Schreiben an die Ehefrau
Berlin, Wannsee Hotel[1], Am Sandwerder 17/19, 8. April 1946

Sweet dearest:

Before I forget it can you send me a can-opener? Some of the stuff I get in the PX[2] comes in cans (juice – nuts) and I haven't the slightest way of opening them. I am also enclosing the request slips I mentioned in a previous letter.[3] It is not necessary that you concern yourself about these. Cigarettes are handy but not necessary. Food I could distribute to hungry Germans. Last Saturday[4] I went to a Musikabend at which the cellist[5] I mentioned in a previous letter[6] was playing a Dvorak[7] Quintet I had never heard with four other colleagues. I remembered that they had 5 children[8] and were living next door in a bombed out house[9]. I thought some candy and nuts for the kids over which they were quite touched. Mrs. Balder[10] exclaimed that I was ein süsses Mensch and insisted that I come over there tomorrow. I brought along to this occasion a Colonel and a General whom I found here at the Hotel at dinner and who was going out night-clubbing for the evening. I told them what I was going to do and asked them to come along. They decided to come along for a while at least, but stayed all evening having a marvelous time talking with Germans. The General had never been in such a gathering before and he promised to get Balder's[11] cello from Salzburg[12] by plane if necessary. The Colonel found that he and Balder both had 14 year old twins (boy and girl).[13] I was somewhat impressed with the Colonel at dinner because he was saying that we ought to be doing something positive for these people, ought to be standing for something as an example. He told me that he takes a walk every morning before going to work and speaks to every German he meets. And he said if any one has a right to speak this way about doing things for the Germans, I have. They have come very close to killing me many times. During the conversation mention was made of at least helping German kids who have no guilt for this war. The Colonel said his rations go to them, and the General said he would see that a box was put up in his PX where surplus stuff could be dropped. Evidently this conversation was over-

---

[1] Siehe Dok. 25, Anm. 9.
[2] Post Exchange, Verkaufsläden der amerikanischen Streitkräfte.
[3] Siehe Dok. 27 und Dok. 33.
[4] 6. April 1946.
[5] Max Baldner. Siehe Dok. 21, Anm. 18.
[6] Siehe Dok. 21 und Dok. 25.
[7] Antonín Leopold Dvořák (1841–1904), böhmischer Komponist.
[8] Max Baldner und Charlotte Baldner, geb. Lindemann (siehe Dok. 21, Anm. 21) hatten vier Kinder. Siehe Dok. 21, Anm. 24. Bei dem fünften Kind handelte es sich nicht um ein Familienmitglied. Siehe Dok. 25, Anm. 44.
[9] Podbielskiallee 57. Siehe Dok. 21, Anm. 25.
[10] Charlotte Baldner, geb. Lindemann. Siehe Dok. 21, Anm. 21.
[11] Max Baldner. Siehe Dok. 21, Anm. 18.
[12] Stadt in der amerikanischen Besatzungszone Österreichs.
[13] Die Zwillinge Angelika und Lutz Baldner wurden 1931 geboren. Siehe Dok. 21, Anm. 24.

heard by General Myers[14] (you remember him from E. A. C.[15] days. His name was the only thing ever censored from my letters). He saw me in the PX today and came up to say that when it came to feeding kids he was for feeding American and English kids first. Of course I agree to this but you can't feed American and British kids from here, and there is enough to go around if only the Americans would insist upon tightening their belts a bit. I can't understand why it is not being done. My driver[16] is suffering from boils. The doctor told him it was a question of food and that many Germans are suffering from them. There are of course insufficient medicaments and a little shortage of doctors, since we won't permit Nazi doctors to practice in our Sector.[17] His doctor gave him a little bit of alcohol to use to cleanse the boil.

A letter from you today written the 29th.[18] I am writing Norman[19] tonight telling him to hurry up Dad[20] to Lincoln[21] if they want him to be of any help to you while it is most needed. Good God what a time you are having. It isn't fair that you should be alone, without help, with everything coming on at once, and with this veritable succession of critical illnesses. You are an admirable creature, my dear, in the way you are managing all this and I love you for all this but I wish you could be spared some of the constant day and night labor and fatigue, after almost losing Tim[22] you now have a serious case of measles, and Timmy's buttocks[23], and Timmy's finger[24], after all these incidental fevers and colds. And there is no help, and the garden needs attention, and there is no Dad in sight,

---

[14] Gemeint ist Vincent Meyer (1889-1974), Brigadier General, 1944/1945 Military Adviser, US Delegation, European Advisory Commission, 1945 Allied Control Council, Berlin, 1946/1947 Deputy Chief Operations, UNRRA, Germany.

[15] European Advisory Commission. Die 1944/1945 in London tagende EAC war von den USA, Großbritannien und der Sowjetunion eingerichtet worden, um alle im Zusammenhang mit Beendigung der Feindseligkeiten in Europa auftauchenden Probleme zu untersuchen und den Regierungen gemeinsam ausgearbeitete Empfehlungen zu unterbreiten. Siehe Hermann Weiß, European Advisory Commission (EAC), in: Deutschland unter alliierter Besatzung 1945-1949/55, hrsg. von Wolfgang Benz, Berlin 1999, S. 256-259.

[16] Möglicherweise Artur Sanow. Siehe Dok. 40, Anm. 13.

[17] Zur medizinischen Betreuung der Berliner Bevölkerung nach Kriegsende siehe Public Health. Six Months Report 4 January-3 July 1946, in: Office of Military Government U. S. Berlin District (Hrsg.), Six Months Report 4 January-3 July 1946, Berlin 1946, S. 89-100; Andreas Dinter, Berlin in Trümmern. Ernährungslage und medizinische Versorgung der Bevölkerung Berlins nach dem II. Weltkrieg (= Geschichte[n] der Medizin, Bd. 1), Berlin 1999, insbesondere S. 138-159 und 194-217.

[18] Brief in den Unterlagen aus dem Nachlass Edgar N. Johnson, Privatbesitz Candice E. und Thomas R. Johnson, Denver, Colorado, USA.

[19] Norman D. Johnson. Siehe Dok. 3, Anm. 13.

[20] Frank E. Johnson. Siehe Dok. 3, Anm. 12.

[21] Hauptstadt des US-Bundesstaats Nebraska, wo Johnson mit seiner Familie wohnte und an der Universität lehrte.

[22] Johnsons Sohn Thomas. Siehe Dok. 2, Anm. 16.

[23] Emily L. Johnson hatte am 29. März 1946 geschrieben: "Timmy had a good big shot of immunized human blood [...]. He couldn't sit down, poor kid. (They gave it to him in the buttock.)"

[24] Emily L. Johnson: "[...] we had to make a flying visit to the hospital with Timmy, because he hurt his finger in a drawer – flour drawer – and it was a mess."

and the weather is as rotten as Spring weather in Nebraska can be. I don't see how you have time for it all, and of course you don't. You are just killing yourself. On top of this constant day and night care of the kids you are going in for gardening with more vengeance than ever I did it seems. I hope it will turn out that we shall have fun doing it together, if once you have the chance you do not relax into the things you would prefer to do. I'd love to see the daffodils. We will get more King Alfredo[25]. But here you are raising your own plants, carrying on extensive spraying, transplanting hedge from rear to front, and even clipping the front hedge. My dear Sweetheart this is too much. Get your old gardener back again until Dad shows up. And please, if you haven't sent the laundry out as yet, send it out. You ask me to be careful. I beg it of you.

You complain about my not being shown sufficient attention here. I have an important job which somebody has to do. I have established myself as a person of some importance with General Barker[26] in a job which somebody with a little sense has to do. Political questions are coming to the fore which have to be decided in a clear cut fashion. They cannot be decided without information. The people who participate in the international machinery have to be briefed. American policy, such as it is, has to be enforced. I am in a position to be of help here. I have easy access to all the people that matter in the determination of these questions, and my position will become stronger as time goes on. Berlin is a center of importance, what is done here has significance for all of Germany and certainly it is an indication of what we stand for to all the world. I am not so sure that it is not perhaps as important as Stuttgart[27] (pardon). But I am not being tempted to stay on here. Except for the fact that they didn't tell me I would be doing this and that accordingly I might still be there with you, I think this is important enough. I only hope I don't lose General Barker.

I'd like to taste the asparagus.

Goodnight to my lovely tired devoted Emily. I love you with all of me. Kiss the sweet kids for me. Goodnight Sweetheart – Edgar

Dok. 35
Schreiben an die Ehefrau
Berlin, Wannsee Hotel[1], Am Sandwerder 17/19, 12. April 1946

Dearest –

A sweet and comforting letter from you today (3 April) telling me among other things of your wonderful gardening triumphs.[2] I wish I were there (I really

---

[25] Name einer Narzissensorte.
[26] Siehe Dok. 20, Anm. 10.
[27] Hauptstadt des Landes Württemberg-Baden in der amerikanischen Besatzungszone Deutschlands.

[1] Siehe Dok. 25, Anm. 9.
[2] Brief in den Unterlagen aus dem Nachlass Edgar N. Johnson, Privatbesitz Candice E. und Thomas R. Johnson, Denver, Colorado, USA.

mean this) to see "the unbearably beautiful" apple blossoms and the lovely daffodils and the other things that are coming along. You mention my being back in the fall to help. I have begun to think about this lately too – about the necessity for returning there.

I need comfort today and that is why your letter came as a blessing. From 10 o'clock this morning until 4 o'clock this afternoon, without lunch, I sat at a meeting of the Kommandatura[3] (the Commandants), the largest meeting on record, at which very important and touching political problems were being discussed.[4] It was really unpleasant and it was unpleasant because the Russians (there is a new Soviet Commandant – Kotikoff[5]) were so unreasonable, aggressive and at one point impudent. They have been impudent before. It is amazing to see how the western mind works. Most of the basic texts which Barker[6] used to-day were those I had written (that is why I haven't been able to write for the last few days). I have determined not to discuss these texts in advance of a meeting with one Ally, without, at the same time discussing them with all of the Allies, and for this I shall never have time. But it was striking to notice that the lines along which I was thinking were the lines along which the British also were thinking, and that in some instances they were ready to make the same special suggestions as me. And under all circumstances when you make a fair and decent democratic suggestion to the French and British, they accept without much discussion. But the Soviets don't seem to care much about what is fair or decent or democratic. They are only interested in their political aims here in Germany, and in this they won't compromise. Since we have really no basic political aims in Germany we are in a position to compromise. When I stop to think of it, it is amazing what we take from the Russians – we are inclined to forget that the Soviets are a Communist state, and that a Communist state supports Communism. We are inclined to forget that a Communist Party State is a one Party State not interested particularly in other parties or at least try to direct and control them. The Soviets support the Communist Party, we support no Party and in so doing give the impression of supporting all but the Communist Party and being anti-Communist. I'll write you at greater length about this over the weekend. It requires men of great patience, moderation, firmness and moral convictions and courage to survive this game.

How nice it is to be isolationist and to say to hell with it all.

I hope our little Timmy will be spared measles for a while – so soon after the incipient pneumonia. I am worried about you – with so much to do and so ex-

---

[3] Siehe Dok. 20, Anm. 11.
[4] Siehe Protokoll der 11. Sitzung der Stadtkommandanten am 12. April 1946, BKC/M (46) 11, englischsprachige Fassung, in: LAB, B Rep. 036-01 (Office of Military Government, Berlin Sector [OMGBS]), 11/148-1/10.
[5] Alexandr Georgijewitsch Kotikow (1902–1981), sowjetischer Generalmajor, 1933 Absolvent der Militärpolitischen Akademie, Leningrad, 1943 Absolvent der Frunse-Militärakademie, 1945–März 1946 Chef der Verwaltung der Militäradministration der Provinz Sachsen(-Anhalt) in Halle, April 1946-1950 Chef der Garnison des sowjetischen Sektors von Berlin und sowjetischer Stadtkommandant, Alliierte Kommandantur Berlin. Foto mit Kotikow im Bildanhang, Abb. 26.
[6] Siehe Dok. 20, Anm. 10.

hausted most of the time. I wish I were with you – all 108 pounds of you – my sweet and lovable wife. Oh! honey you are so much to me. I love you. Kiss my fine boys and all I can offer you is my endearment from a distance. Edgar

Dok. 36
Schreiben an die Ehefrau
Berlin, Wannsee Hotel[1], Am Sandwerder 17/19, 14. April 1946

Dear sweet Emily and my boys:

I have some idea of how lovely it would be to be at home this morning. It is something like a Spring morning here. The Wannsee[2] is smooth and there are sail boats in it. The trees are beginning to show their first green and red along the shores of the lake, and above them on the top of the ridge is the heavy dark green of the pines. The sun is out and the birds are making merry on the lawn. Two blue ones of a kind we do not have in the states were gaily active a few minutes ago beneath my window. At home there would be Spring in our hearts as there is not here. I can scarcely imagine certainly that there is any Spring in anyone's heart who has any real notion of what is going on here. There cannot be any Spring in any intelligent German's heart, for his future is, at all odds an uncertain one, and the best Spring one can provide is a little more adequate meal from time to time. It is certainly praiseworthy how, under these circumstances, there is as much cultivation of the arts as there happens to be. Of course the artist can get along with little, a musical instrument, some paint, some marble or wood and he can create. At home there would be Spring in our hearts – being together as an altogether happy little crowd, and on this kind of a morning we should be out in the yard. By now I take it the crab apple trees and the daffodils are beyond their best but there must be a few hyacinths about, and perhaps crocuses, and at least signs of much that is to come. But that Spring in the heart is what I should like to feel.

Instead I am going off this morning to a press conference which General Barker[3] is holding for a group of journalists who are making the rounds here.[4]

---

[1] Siehe Dok. 25, Anm. 10.
[2] Gemeint ist der Große Wannsee, eine Ausbuchtung der Havel (siehe Dok. 74, Anm. 24) im Südwesten Berlins.
[3] Siehe Dok. 20, Anm. 10.
[4] Die Gruppe bestand aus 14 amerikanischen "newspaper and magazine executives", die sich auf Einladung des War Department auf einer dreiwöchigen, vor allem in die amerikanischen Besatzungszonen in Deutschland und Österreich führenden Europareise befanden, "to see the operations of the American Military Government". News Executives Fly to Paris Today. 14 in Group Will Visit Austria and Germany to View the Operations of AMG, in: The New York Times vom 9. April 1946, S. 9; U. S. News Executives in Paris, in: The New York Times vom 12. April 1946, S. 16. Vom 12. bis 14. April 1946 hielt sich die Gruppe in Berlin auf. Siehe News Execs Arrive Today, in: OMGUS Observer vom 12. April 1946, S. 1; Editors Urge U. S. Aid. See Danger of Communist Rise Unless Germans Get Food, in: The New York Times vom 14. April 1946, S. 25. Nach Beendigung der Reise fand am 2. Mai 1946 im War Department in

They were introduced at General Clay's[5] staff meeting yesterday.[6] Mr. Adler[7] of the New York Times[8], Mr. Luce[9] of Time[10] and Fortune[11], Mr. Frank Gannet[12] of the Gannet newspapers[13] and others from various parts of the country including Des Moines[14], Kansas City[15] and Los Angeles[16]. Would you know what the SPD was if I mentioned it as such. Yesterday at Clay's conference, General Barker was talking about the split of the SPD in the city[17] and the editor of the New York Mirror[18] leaned over and asked me what the SPD was. He seemed relieved to think it was only the Social Democratic Party. This afternoon I am going to my first music in Berlin. Bach's[19] St. Matthew Passion[20] is being sung in a local church[21]. I haven't found anyone to go with me as yet (I have two tickets) but in a pinch I'll take the driver[22] in. This evening Brewster Morris[23], I think I have mentioned him,[24] is having a group of the anti-merger Social Democrats over to his house for supper and talk and he has invited me to come. That is Sunday in Berlin now. It will be like this on Sundays in Berlin for as long as I stay here. I find it is the same here with trying to get into a healthy frame of mind as it was in Vienna. It is just impossible. In the presence of ruin,

Washington, D. C., eine abschließende Pressekonferenz statt. Siehe Food, Russia Seen as Main Problems. Editors and Publishers Tell of Observations on 3-Week Journey in Europe, in: The New York Times vom 3. Mai 1946, S. 9.

[5] Siehe Dok. 2, Anm. 6.
[6] Siehe Protokoll der OMGUS-Stabskonferenz am 13. April 1946, S. 14, in: Archiv des IfZ, OMGUS – Staff Conferences (Protokollkopien), Fg 12/4.
[7] Julius O. Adler (1892-1955), amerikanischer Verleger, Brigadier General, Vice President and General Manager of The New York Times.
[8] Amerikanische Tageszeitung.
[9] Henry R. Luce (1898-1967), amerikanischer Verleger.
[10] Amerikanisches Nachrichtenmagazin.
[11] Amerikanisches Wirtschaftsmagazin.
[12] Frank E. Gannett (1876-1957), amerikanischer Verleger, President of Gannett Newspapers.
[13] Die Holding bestand aus mehreren Regionalzeitungen.
[14] Hauptstadt des US-Bundesstaates Iowa.
[15] Stadt im US-Bundesstaat Missouri.
[16] Stadt im US-Bundesstaat Kalifornien.
[17] Gemeint ist die Spaltung der Berliner SPD in Vereinigungswillige, die den Zusammenschluss mit der KPD unterstützten und in die SED gingen, und Vereinigungsgegner, die nach der Urabstimmung über die Einheitsfrage eine eigene sozialdemokratische Parteiorganisation in Berlin aufbauten.
[18] Executive Editor Glenn T. Neville (1907-1965) war der Vertreter des New York Daily Mirror in der Gruppe.
[19] Siehe Dok. 13, Anm. 20.
[20] Matthäus-Passion, BWV 244. Es ist umstritten, ob die Matthäus-Passion aus dem Jahre 1727 oder 1729 stammt.
[21] Die Matthäus-Passion wurde am 14. April 1946, 16.30 Uhr, von der Singgemeinschaft Rudolf Lamy und dem Orchester des Drahtfunks im amerikanischen Sektor Berlin in der Marienkirche am Neuen Markt (heute an der Karl-Liebknecht-Straße), Berlin-Mitte, aufgeführt. Siehe Der Tagesspiegel vom 13. April 1946, S. 6 (Berlin muss wissen).
[22] Möglicherweise Artur Sanow. Siehe Dok. 40, Anm. 13.
[23] Siehe Dok. 31, Anm. 13.
[24] Siehe Dok. 31 und Dok. 33.

in the presence of essential hopelessness, and more than anything else with the present unnatural life that one has to lead – away from those few who give real meaning and stability to one's existence how is it possible to enjoy anything – to wait joyfully for the arrival of Spring or to thrill at the rapture of a bird.
Later:
The conference has been held. General Barker stood up in front of the crowd and answered questions. He intended to give us all a chance to say a word but there was not time. These people are subjected to a high pressure program, which takes them here one moment and there the next according to a rigid schedule. They leave by plane this afternoon for the zone. As General Barker said it would have been better to divide them up into small groups and take them around to see how things are going on from the German point of view. Nothing very exciting happened at the press conference. Barker made a little speech and they then asked questions – not terribly interesting as it seemed to me very significant. I said to one of them as we were going out that I hoped they would be going back home to tell the people what their obligations are over here, and he replied that he thought there would be many missionaries returning home. There was a comparatively modest lunch afterwards, and at it the General sat me down next to Mr. Luce of Time and Fortune, husband of Claire Booth[25] etc. He is intelligent and we got to talking about the lack of a definite over-all policy here. I said I thought it might be best for not only Germany but for our relations with the Russians if we come out for a policy of straight democratic socialism, supporting the Social Democrats. He agreed about the need for a straightforward long range policy, agreed that for Europe it might be best for it to be democratic socialism but contested that it would smooth over our relations with Russia. He has a good point here, and we did not get far with our argument but he asked me to pursue it in writing for his benefit and send it on. I don't know whether I shall have time to do this. But in any case this issue may be discussed in the American press, and if you come across any references to it I wish you would note it. I imagine that Luce may try to get an article in Fortune about it.

I found a State Department guy to take over to the Marienkirche[26] to hear the Bach, and it is about time to go.

I send to my dearest Emily and my sweet boys all the love that a lonesome guy like me can send. It is, I suppose, too early for me to say that it has not been worthwhile for me to return here, but despite the interest and temporary excitement, it is going to have to be a lot more worthwhile than it has been up to date before I shall be relieved of my present discontent. I love you all, my dearest Em[ily], and my John and Timmy, very very much: Edgar

---

[25] Clare Boothe Luce, geb. Boothe (1903–1987), amerikanische Dramatikerin, Politikerin und Journalistin, von 1942 bis 1946 Mitglied des US-Kongresses, 1953–1957 Botschafterin in Italien, seit 1935 verheiratet mit Henry R. Luce.

[26] Am Neuen Markt (heute an der Karl-Liebknecht-Straße), Berlin-Mitte, eine der ältesten Kirchen Berlins, vermutlich in der zweiten Hälfte des 13. Jahrhunderts erbaut, 1292 erstmals urkundlich erwähnt. Im Zweiten Weltkrieg beschädigt, begann ihre Instandsetzung unmittelbar nach Kriegsende.

Dok. 37
Schreiben an die Ehefrau
Berlin, Wannsee Hotel[1], Am Sandwerder 17/19, 15. April 1946

Dear Sweetheart, my lovely Em[ily] –

The sun has just descended beneath the ridge on the other side of the Wannsee[2]. It has been a lovely Spring day. This is an especially beautiful and quiet place to return to after a day at the office, and it is going to be possible, by the first of May, to have one of the Faltboots to go out on the lake after the day's work. The swimming pool has already been filled. But I can't get excited about it all. The sun goes down in the west, and westward from here, it is so happens, is no other place than Nebraska, and what is going on in a certain house in Nebraska I know rather well, only I am not there to check up on the details. I think, my dearest, that this coming over, after my Austrian experiences, will put an end to all speculation, as to what I ought to do from next Fall on. This is not after all what I set out to do. Indeed I thought the other night that like Dad[3] I set out to do the wrong thing. I should have gone in for music no matter on how trivial a level. If it turns out that this is what John[4] ought to do, then by goodness, the mistake is not going to be made in the third generation. The world's affairs are in other hands, and into this circle I am too late to make any kind of intrusion. I had best content myself with trying to make young men and women aware of the world and to urge them to go out and take it over. Since you can't be here, and the boys can't be here (I doubt even that you would like it here) I am lost and will continue to be lost until I am back in your arms again. This is the one big fact. I feel responsible to the world in these moments, and there is undoubtedly a need here for responsible people. But there is a need at home, also, for responsible people, and one cannot properly carry out his responsibilities when he is separated from all that gives real substance to his life. I find myself counting the days that have past, and counting the days that are to come before I leave here. I am not one who is going to decide on what is to be done with Germany, or how we are going to solve our future relationship with the Soviet Union. And my obligations are not really here. I don't think it would have been any different had I gone to Stuttgart[5]. Under the present circumstances it is impossible to do anything very positive here. The basic conditions are all against it. We are engaged in making an essentially positive, and I do not say, unnecessarily positive settlement. The country is prostrate, essentially hopeless (I mean this only literally) and there is nothing that we are going to do for years to come to temper our punishment with generosity to the right people. There is a big job of education to be done here, but at the present moment General Barker[6] can't get

---

[1] Siehe Dok. 25, Anm. 9.
[2] Gemeint ist der Große Wannsee, eine Ausbuchtung der Havel (siehe Dok. 74, Anm. 24) im Südwesten Berlins.
[3] Frank E. Johnson. Siehe Dok. 3, Anm. 12.
[4] Johnsons Sohn John. Siehe Dok. 2, Anm. 15.
[5] Hauptstadt des Landes Württemberg-Baden in der amerikanischen Besatzungszone Deutschlands.
[6] Siehe Dok. 20, Anm. 10.

anybody to spend any money for the few American books and periodicals that these people would devour if they had them. There is work in religion to be done but at the moment, we haven't yet succeeded in getting the horribly Nazi Protestant Church in Germany, to get rid of the Nazi pastors.[7] It is hard to say that there is much fundamental progress of any kind, and I don't see how there can be much for many years to come. To be sure it is only a year now since the end of the war (a year ago I was in Caserta[8]), but how long is a year, short or long.

I attended a meeting of the Kommandatura[9] today which was a very discouraging affair. It was a meeting of the Education Committee.[10] I was asked to go by a Major Dollard[11] who teaches English at Hunter College[12], and who has done important work in Italy and Austria. At least he has been awarded the bronze star[13]. The man is overworked, and distraught. He is a bit fussy, possibly because he has taught so long in a women's college. Yet he is a devoted servant to the cause. He has practically no staff to work with to help run the educational system of Berlin. Three of the people – the best people have gone home. He has on his Committee a very stubborn Russian[14], and an utterly frivolous, supposedly brilliant Englishman (Creighton[15]) who looks down on his superiors because they do not come from a good enough family (meaning as good as his family[16]). At a recent luncheon this Creighton drank so much vodka that he

---

[7] Gemeint sind hier offenbar die den Nationalsozialisten nahestehenden Deutschen Christen.
[8] Stadt in der italienischen Region Kampanien, wo Johnson sich im Frühjahr 1945 aufgehalten hatte: "In April I moved to Caserta, Italy where various task forces for Austria were located." Edgar N. Johnson, Curriculum Vitae, undatiert [ca. 1963], S. 2, in: UChicago Library, Special Collections Research Center, Edgar N. Johnson Papers.
[9] Siehe Dok. 20, Anm. 11.
[10] Siehe Protokoll der Sitzung des Education Committee, Allied Kommandatura Berlin, am 15. April 1946, englischsprachige Fassung, in: LAB, B Rep. 036-01 (Office of Military Government, Berlin Sector [OMGBS]), 4/16-1/9.
[11] Siehe Dok. 33, Anm. 11. Dollard führte in der Sitzung den Vorsitz.
[12] College in New York City, 1870 gegründet, urspr. ein Frauencollege. Männer wurden erst in den 1950er-Jahren zum Studium aufgenommen.
[13] Eine Auszeichnung der US-Streitkräfte für herausragende Leistungen im Kampfeinsatz oder besondere Pflichterfüllung. Die Medaille wurde 1944 erstmals vergeben.
[14] Gemeint ist A. N. Sudakow, sowjetischer Oberstleutnant, 1945–1949 Chef der Abteilung Volksbildung in der Verwaltung des Kommandanten des sowjetischen Sektors von Berlin. Allerdings nahm Sudakow an der Sitzung des Education Committee am 15. April 1946 nicht teil; er wurde von Leutnant Lewin vertreten.
[15] Thomas Richmond Mandell Creighton (1915–1987), britischer Sprachwissenschaftler, 1941 MA, Trinity College, Cambridge, Großbritannien, arbeitete während des Zweiten Weltkriegs in Bletchley Park, war dann Leiter der Education Branch, Military Government British Troops Berlin (MGBTB), lehrte später am Makerere College, Uganda, an den Universities of Reading, Leeds und Edinburgh, Großbritannien, und war Professor of English, Fourah Bay College, Sierra Leone. Allerdings nahm Creighton an der Sitzung des Education Committee am 15. April 1946 nicht teil; er wurde von Dr. Middleton vertreten.
[16] Creightons Großvater war der Historiker Mandell Creighton (1843–1901), 1885–1891 Professor, University of Cambridge, 1897–1901 Bischof von London; seine Großmutter war die Autorin Louise Creighton, geb. von Glehn (1850–1936); sein Vater, Rev.

started to crawl underneath the table at the subsequent Committee meeting. He is a wild driver and killed the German manager of the opera[17] in an accident last Fall. The English interpreter is one of his buddies, a person named Tolstoi[18] (I don't know if there is any connection[19]). This young white Russian (most of the English interpreters are white Russians whom the Soviets suspect)[20] has been well educated in French and English and is an excellent linguist. But he treats his job as one that is beneath him, treats the secretaries with flippant scorn, and does his best to make the meeting utterly frivolous. If I had anything to do about it I'd throw him out on his ear. How can you hope to get anything done under these circumstances. If I were Dollard I should try to get home in a hurry, and indeed back to Hunter and my girls.

Brewster Morris[21] had some of the dissident Social Democrats over to his house last night and invited Don Heath[22] over. He treated them very generously: cocktails, wonderful food, brandy, and thereafter a night-cap. Two of the newly elected members of the anti-merger Berlin Committee[23] were there, one Germer[24] with his wife[25], and one Franz Neumann[26] who spent most of his life

---

Cuthbert Creighton (1876–1963), war 1919–1936 Headmaster und 1940–1942 Hon. Headmaster of King's School, Worcester. Thomas Richmond Mandell Creighton war ein entfernter Verwandter des deutschen Historikers Leopold von Ranke (1795–1886), der 1843 Helena Clarissa Graves (1808–1871) aus einer alten englischen Familie geheiratet hatte. Siehe Karl-Heinz Füssl, Die Umerziehung der Deutschen. Jugend und Schule unter den Siegermächten des Zweiten Weltkriegs 1945–1955 (Sammlung Schöningh zur Geschichte und Gegenwart), 2. Auflage, Paderborn, München, Wien und Zürich 1995, S. 325.

[17] Unklar ist, ob die Deutsche Staatsoper oder die Städtische Oper gemeint ist.
[18] Möglicherweise handelte es sich um Lew Tolstoi, der beim Nürnberger Hauptkriegsverbrecherprozess als Dolmetscher in der französischen Delegation arbeitete und ein Großneffe des russischen Schriftstellers Lew Nikolajewitsch Tolstoi (1828–1910) war. Siehe Arkadi Poltorak, Nürnberger Epilog, 5. Auflage, Berlin 1988, S. 32. Auch bei Francesca Gaiba, The Origins of Simultaneous Interpretation. The Nuremberg Trial (Perspectives on Translation), Ottawa 1998, S. 152, findet dieser Dolmetscher – "*Lieutenant Tolstoy*, Russian into French" – Erwähnung.
[19] Gemeint ist eine verwandtschaftliche Beziehung zu dem Schriftsteller Lew Nikolajewitsch Tolstoi.
[20] Weißrussen, die gegen die Bolschewiken gekämpft hatten und nach ihrer Niederlage nach Westeuropa oder in die USA emigriert waren.
[21] Siehe Dok. 31, Anm. 13.
[22] Donald R. Heath. Siehe Dok. 8, Anm. 15.
[23] Gemeint ist der Vorstand der neu organisierten Berliner SPD, der auf dem Parteitag der oppositionellen Sozialdemokraten am 7. April 1946 in der Zinnowwaldschule im Verwaltungsbezirk Zehlendorf gewählt worden war.
[24] Karl J. Germer Jr. (1913–1999), deutscher Politiker (SPD), 1931 SPD, Studium der Volkswirtschaft, Ausbildung im Verlagswesen, nach 1933 Widerstand gegen das NS-Regime, kaufmännischer Angestellter, 1945/1946 Mitglied des Zentralausschusses der SPD und Vorstandssekretär des FDGB, entschiedener Gegner der Fusion von SPD und KPD zur SED, April 1946 Wahl zu einem der drei gleichberechtigten Vorsitzenden der neu organisierten Berliner SPD, erklärte im Juli 1946 seinen Rücktritt, 1947–1951 selbstständiger Verleger, 1951/1952 politischer Berater bei HICOG, Berlin Element, Public Affairs Division, 1952–1955 Leiter des politischen Referats des Bundesministeriums für gesamtdeutsche Fragen, Abteilung II, Berlin, ab 1956 Referent des Regierenden Bürgermeisters von Berlin, ab 1957 Referent des Abgeordneten-

under the Nazis in prison and concentration camp. He knows, by the way, our Franz Neumann[27]. It was moving to hear them talk, they are for the most part young idealists and honest too. Good Democrats who are tired of the kind of tyranny the Russians have to offer. It was amusing to hear these simple workers, tell Don Heath, who is a strong supporter of American capitalism at its best, that capitalism was but an intermediary stage, and that it would have to superseded by the kind of socialism that puts the individual first of all. It was more pathetic to watch them eat. They take an occasion like this to fortify themselves for days to come. And it was also typically German to have one of the SPD's play music for everybody, a Brahms[28] intermezzo that I used to play and a Beethoven[29] Sonata. I had the feeling that this was his forte and not Social Democratic politics in a time like this. One has to admire the fortitude of these people – and after a little while what they are talking about seems very very far away from America, and certainly from you. One wonders how long he can stand the diet.

Did I ask you to send me a can-opener-cork-screw combination?[30]

Goodnight my sweet one. It's dark outside now. I'll go on with my evening alone, and try to make some sense out of it. I love you, love you, with all of me. Kiss the sweet boys for me. Edgar

Dok. 38
Schreiben an die Ehefrau
Berlin, Wannsee Hotel[1], Am Sandwerder 17/19, 18. April 1946

Dearest –

I slipped off to hear the Schubert[2] Quintett tonight played at an exhibition called Religion and Art.[3] Do you remember when we heard the Budapest

> hauses von Berlin, ab 1958 Referent beim Senator für Arbeit und soziale Angelegenheiten, 1990 Austritt aus der SPD.
> 25 Edith Germer, geb. Berndt (geb. 1921).
> 26 Franz Neumann (1904–1974), deutscher Politiker (SPD), gelernter Schlosser, 1920 SPD, 1925–1931 Deutsche Hochschule für Politik, Berlin, bis 1933 Jugendfürsorger, 1934 wegen angeblicher Vorbereitung zum Hochverrat zu eineinhalb Jahren Gefängnis verurteilt, danach unter Polizeiaufsicht gestellt, führender Gegner der Fusion von SPD und KPD zur SED, April 1946–1958 Vorsitzender der Berliner SPD, 1946–1960 Mitglied der Stadtverordnetenversammlung von Groß-Berlin bzw. des Abgeordnetenhauses von Berlin (1946/1947 und 1949–1958 Vorsitzender der SPD-Fraktion), 1949–1969 MdB (Berliner Vertreter), 1971 Ernennung zum Ehrenbürger von Berlin. Foto von Neumann im Bildanhang, Abb. 81.
> 27 Siehe Dok. 1, Anm. 8.
> 28 Johannes Brahms (1833–1897), deutscher Komponist der Romantik.
> 29 Ludwig van Beethoven (1770–1827), deutscher Komponist der Wiener Klassik.
> 30 Siehe Dok. 34.
> 1 Siehe Dok. 25, Anm. 9.
> 2 Franz Schubert (1797–1828), deutscher Komponist.
> 3 Das Streichquintett C-Dur von Franz Schubert wurde am 18. April 1946 von dem Zernick-Quartett, gegründet von dem Violinisten Helmut Zernick (1913–1970), im

Quartett[4] do it? It was played in a room filled with paintings by Berlin artists portraying very agonized types supposedly in tune with the Leiden period[5]. There was a large Crucifixion with the hands of Christ ripped loose from the nails and raised heavenward.[6] It was made by a man named Vetter[7] whom I met the other night at Rheinstein's[8].[9] Other water colors were of concentration

<blockquote>

Rahmen einer Veranstaltungsreihe zur Ausstellung „Das Religiöse in der Kunst" gespielt. Die Ausstellung des Minerva-Verlages in dessen Räumen in der Kurfürstenstraße 57, Berlin-Tiergarten, mit Werken moderner Malerei, Grafik und Plastik war am 7. April 1946 eröffnet worden und bis zum 24. April 1946 zu sehen. Siehe Friedrich Schwerdfeger, Das Religiöse in der Kunst. Eine Ausstellung und eine Vortragsreihe, in: Berliner Zeitung vom 11. April 1946, [S. 3]; LAB, B Rep. 036-01 (Office of Military Government, Berlin Sector [OMGBS]), 4/135-2/9.

[4] Das Budapest Quartet war ein international erfolgreiches, 1917 in Budapest gegründetes Streichquartett, das bis 1967 existierte, 1938 wegen der angespannten Lage in Europa Übersiedlung in die USA. Die Interpretationen des Budapest Quartets reichten von der Klassik bis zur zeitgenössichen Musik wie Zoltán Kodály (1882–1967) und Béla Bartók (1881–1945).

[5] Gemeint ist die Schaffensphase des niederländischen Malers Rembrandt van Rijn (1606–1669) in Leiden 1625–1631, in der er sich vor allem der Historienmalerei und physiognomischen Studien widmete.

[6] Es handelte sich um das Gemälde „Verklärung am Kreuz". Abb. in: The Grooper vom 30. März 1946, S. 3 (http://www.theberlinobserver.com/archive/1946V2/V2_N13_Mar_30.pdf [letzter Zugriff am 30. Januar 2013]).

[7] Ewald Vetter (1894–1981), deutscher Maler, der „zur Nachhut des deutschen Expressionismus" gehörte und „der Gestaltung des religiösen Themas und der Interpretation menschlicher Probleme in höchstem Maße verpflichtet" war. Rudolf Pfefferkorn in: Ausstellung Ewald Vetter, Walther-Rathenau-Saal, Rathaus-Wedding (Altbau), Berlin 65, Müllerstraße 146/147, 7.10.–11.11.75, Katalog zur Ausstellung des Kunstamts Wedding, Berlin 1975, [S. 3]. In einem Ende März 1946 in "The Grooper" erschienenen Artikel über Ewald Vetter heißt es: "Ewald Vetter was the unique and notable exception of a German artist who for many dark and gloomy years continued to produce works of art which will forever reflect all that was rotten, false and artificial in Hitler's Germany." Harold Kempner, Ewald Vetter. Anti-Nazi Painter, in: The Grooper vom 30. März 1946, S. 3 (http://www.theberlinobserver.com/archive/1946V2/V2_N13_Mar_30.pdf [letzter Zugriff am 30. Januar 2013]). Bilder von Ewald Vetter sollten in den USA ausgestellt werden: "About 25 of his paintings will be premiered in Rockefeller Center in New York next month under the sponsorship of Life magazine. They will later be on exhibition in all the prominent art galleries in the United States." Ebd.

[8] Siehe Dok. 11, Anm. 22.

[9] Von Vetter waren in der Ausstellung „zwei mächtige Tafeln" zu sehen, „eine ‚Verklärung am Kreuz' und eine ‚Entkleidung', sowie ein eindrucksvolles Blatt ‚In memoriam Ernst Barlach' und die aus geistiger Schau und Verinnerlichung entstandenen Bildnisse der Dichter Hölderlin und Novalis". Friedrich Schwerdfeger, Das Religiöse in der Kunst. Eine Ausstellung und eine Vortragsreihe, in: Berliner Zeitung vom 11. April 1946, [S. 3]. Im „Telegraf" heißt es: „Ewald Vetters grosse Ausdruckskunst, umwittert von der schmerzlichen Wahrheit ewiger Seelengeheimnisse, erschütterte aufs neue." M. J., Religion und Kunst, in: Telegraf vom 14. April 1946, S. 5. Bereits am 6. Januar 1946 war im Haus am Waldsee in Berlin-Zehlendorf eine Ausstellung mit Werken von Ewald Vetter und Käthe Kollwitz (1867–1945) eröffnet worden. Siehe Edwin Redslob, Zwölf Jahre im Spiegel der Kunst. Zur Eröffnung der Ausstellung im Kulturhaus Zehlendorf, in: Der Tagesspiegel vom 6. Januar 1946, S. 5.

</blockquote>

camp figures and experiences. Baldner[10] was the cellist in the Quartett. His wife[11] and children[12] were there, and when I told him you had purchased the hairs for his bow and had sent them on he beamed, and said we were angels.[13] He showed me his present bow. It is in bad shape. The Quintett I found very moving and of the grand character of the later Beethoven[14] Quartetts. It does have an especially religious character. It turned me inside out in a way that I have not been excited for a very long time. I was sitting close enough to Baldner to be able to read his music. He played his Stradivarius cello[15]. If there had been an especially good preacher about I might have been converted to something. It is so obvious here that there is great need of being converted to something. The Germans were also deeply moved, and applauded long and loudly – I should have gone to the Beethoven 130[16] the other night.

I came back to eat at the Officers' Mess on Kaiserstrasse[17]. For officers of Berlin District. It was rather loud, and some had too many drinks before dinner. It was certainly a far cry from Religion and Art. The conversation settled down to the ominous talk of the war with Russia after it was generally agreed that America at the present moment is hopeless. One officer from Dakota[18], a Colonel with a long time in the officers' reserve, said he wouldn't think of bringing his family to Berlin. He thought too much of them, and Berlin was too far from our security troops in the zone. Another remarked that he didn't see what was to stop the Russians from moving into all of Europe. This seems to me to be very wild talk. The officer from Dakota felt that people at home were greatly excited over the possibility of war with Russia. Is this so? Sometimes I think that one should hold any expression of views that are anti-Russian or that assume the possibility of war with Russia strictly to oneself. At other times I think that only a fair facing of the issues can ever resolve them.

I find myself taking on an ever stronger anti-Russian stand here. This is not the way actually to put it. I find myself when face to face with Russian methods strongly inclined to assert our own. And this is the way of course to shape up the fundamental issues. But what is one to do. There are fundamental issues, and as it works here in Berlin at the moment if you don't stand up for your own you will get run over. And the Russians don't care much whether they run over you or not in so far as I can see here in Berlin.

[10] Siehe Dok. 21, Anm. 18.
[11] Charlotte Baldner, geb. Lindemann. Siehe Dok. 21, Anm. 21.
[12] Siehe Dok. 21, Anm. 24.
[13] Siehe Dok. 25. Emily L. Johnson hatte in einem Schreiben an Ehemann Edgar vom 2. April 1946 mitgeteilt: "Miguel [A. Basoco; siehe Dok. 72, Anm. 5] got your cellists bow hairs today and I'll try to get them off for you. They are expensive: $ 2.40 for two sets, in case you are interested." Brief in: Unterlagen aus dem Nachlass Edgar N. Johnson, Privatbesitz Candice E. und Thomas R. Johnson, Denver, Colorado, USA.
[14] Siehe Dok. 37, Anm. 29.
[15] Streichinstrument, das von dem italienischen Geigenbaumeister Antonio Stradivari (latinisiert: Antonius Stradivarius) (um 1644 oder 1648–1737) gebaut wurde.
[16] Gemeint ist das Streichquartett B-Dur op. 130 von Ludwig van Beethoven (siehe Dok. 37, Anm. 29).
[17] Gemeint sein könnte die Kaiserstraße, heute Martin-Buber-Straße, im Berliner Verwaltungsbezirk Zehlendorf.
[18] US-Bundesstaat.

I have written about the split in the SPD between those who wish to join up with the Communists in a new Socialist Unity Party and those who wish to maintain the independence of their own party. As it is working itself out here this is a question between our methods and Russian methods. To date, although this a city supposedly governed by a Quadripartite machinery the Russians have paid no attention to our methods and have set out to get what they want in accordance with their own methods, and running over everyone else. You can take so much of this in the hope that eventually you will get a compromise. But when you don't get a compromise then you come to the point when you simply can't take any more without seeming to abandon your principles, everything you and your country stand for, and exhibiting weakness and indecision in the face of strong-armed methods. Weakness and indecision are in themselves demoralizing and only prove the way for the victory of strong-armed methods. Things are at this point here now. We are perfectly willing to recognize a democratic SEP throughout Berlin if at the same time the Russians are willing to recognize an independent SPD throughout Berlin. This as yet they show no intentions of doing. In fact they have blocked every attempt of ours to consider the question and to put the political situation here on a quadripartite basis. We are therefore obliged to show them that we mean what we say. We shall refuse to recognize the SEP in our sector until it has been officially recognized by the Kommandatura[19]. The British and French will probably do likewise. We shall indeed all along the line take similar steps refusing to compromise until we get the fair deal we think we ought to get. But as long as the Russians are unwilling to compromise this doesn't help matters. It simply divides the city into an eastern sector under the Soviets and a western sector under the rest of us. You have heard about the world being divided into two armed camps.

You have probably read in the press of the arrest in our sector of some Communists for interfering with the local government in our sector, and of the sentence of two of them to five years.[20] I think I have been instrumental, if only in a small way, in getting the first officer who is reviewing this case, to recommend suspending the sentences. Now it goes up to General Barker[21] and than to General Clay[22]. General Barker has thrown the whole thing in my lap for an opinion. It is interesting how things like this come ultimately your way when you are on the spot. I have read the trial record and I come to rather devastating conclusions. I think the original arrest was a political mistake. I think that the Court, in spite of desperate efforts to be fair was not quite aware of what they were trying to punish. I don't think for example that they quite understood the nature of the document which constitutes the main evidence upon which the Communists were convicted, not did they really understand the circumstances under which the document was published and circulated. That is I don't think that the Court should have found these men guilty of the offences

---

[19] Siehe Dok. 20, Anm. 11.
[20] Siehe Dok. 20 und Dok. 33.
[21] Siehe Dok. 20, Anm. 10.
[22] Siehe Dok. 2, Anm. 6.

they were found guilty of. I put these conclusions down in a document which I intend to submit to General Barker, and submit it first to my colleague Colonel Glaser[23] for criticism. Glaser takes exception to my criticizing the conclusions of the Court although he too thinks that the original arrest was a political mistake. The Court has come to a decision. Its decision must be defended to uphold its honor, and while the sentence ought to be suspended, they ought to be suspended out of clemency. One of the convicted has been in a concentration camp for a long time. General Barker will probably agree with Colonel Glaser. In any case my condemnation of the Court is now only a matter of academic interest since the important thing is to get the sentence suspended, no matter for what reason. I therefore revised the document accordingly with what was not a complete whitewash of the Court but only a pretense not to be able to comprehend completely all the legal niceties in the case. I shall however give my private opinion to General Barker and explain to him all the circumstances.

What he wanted from me (since he is inclined to believe that the sentences ought to be suspended) was a statement illustrating the fundamental issues in the case, why it wouldn't be taken lightly even though the sentences were suspended – a kind of justification to General Clay of the original harshness of the sentence. The basic issue is clear. These men were guilty of taking advantage of an unnatural political situation here (the Berlin Government is still the Government the Russians put in when they came in)[24] in order to place the interests of the Communist Party above the interests of the local administration of our sector and accordingly, indirectly, above what might be considered our own interests. It is a straight democratic issue and clear. But by getting at it and publishing it in the press you do not necessarily ease our relations with our Soviet Ally who takes offense at all action against Communists. One has to resort to the hope that by bringing the issues to a head rather than by covering them up, one enables them to be more easily discussed. But this is essentially a democratic and relativistic hope and there is no guarantee that it is justified. The Russians certainly don't work that way.

Your letter of the 8th came today.[25] I am heartsick about John's[26] eyes. I certainly never suspected they were that weak and I hope Hancock[27] is wrong. I feel guilty that we may have hurt them by putting him to reading regular sheet music without ever implementing our good intentions of getting some device made by which he would not have to strain his eyes to read the music. So he will have glasses when I see him again, poor kid. I resent not being there when the reading suddenly comes. Please tell me more about it. But thank God you are on hand to guide him into this wonderful new world. I hope he will always find it as exciting as he now finds it. Tell him I will write him again soon about

---

[23] Siehe Dok. 28, Anm. 4.
[24] Siehe Dok. 27, Anm. 30.
[25] Brief in den Unterlagen aus dem Nachlass Edgar N. Johnson, Privatbesitz Candice E. und Thomas R. Johnson, Denver, Colorado, USA.
[26] Johnsons Sohn John. Siehe Dok. 2, Anm. 15.
[27] Siehe Dok. 4, Anm. 22.

his excellent second report from school. Sweet old Timmy[28] – certainly now he has been able to go bye-bye again.[29] How about the sand box?

And my sweet darling Em[ily] – when is she going to get to go bye-bye. It will soon be three months since I left. Three months after that will bring me close to the time when I shall be returning. Our Minister-President in Bavaria[30] told the newspaper men I spoke of recently[31] that we ought to stay here for ten or 15 years if we really wanted to do a good job. Would you like to come over here and stay for 10 or fifteen years.

I got my per diem check the other day and am therefore in no need of money. I wonder if you have gotten a salary check at yet. Please let me know when you do, or if you are running short.

Goodnight my Sweetheart. I love you more than anything else in the world. Kiss the sweet boys for me and many fond endearments for my lovely one. Edgar

Dok. 39
Schreiben an die Ehefrau
Berlin, Wannsee Hotel[1], Am Sandwerder 17/19, 21. April 1946

Dearest wife and Sweetheart and my boys –

I was so lonesome yesterday I could have wept, and I am almost in the same state today – a lovely Easter Sunday. Lonesome of course for my sweet wife and for my boys. This being apart is no good, it is no good for any noble cause, since all noble causes are besmeared with the slimy activities of men who want to push people around. I wonder how you have celebrated Easter today. I wonder if that Easter Rabbit came again, whether John[2] wanted it to come, and whether it worked as successfully as it did the last year I was there, or as successfully as last year – I wonder if at least you have had this day free from worries over the outcome of diseases or the possibility of more. I do not have to say that I want nothing more at this present moment than to be home where I belong and not here, a relatively impotent observer of a tragedy involving some millions of people, not only in Germany but in all Europe. The war has brought more misery that it was possible to foresee. It won't be possible for me to stay over here I think even should you be able to come over with the kids. This is no place for them to be, nor do I think it is any place for you to be. It is too hard on the heart. I shall not be perfectly happy in University work again, at least to begin with, but at least that is where our security for the moment lies. May be

---

[28] Johnsons Sohn Thomas. Siehe Dok. 2, Anm. 16.
[29] Emily L. Johnson hatte am 8. April 1946 geschrieben: "Timmy is fine, still coughing, but no fever now for a few days. He does so want to go bye-bye, bless him."
[30] Wilhelm Hoegner. Siehe Dok. 11, Anm. 27.
[31] Siehe Dok. 36.

[1] Siehe Dok. 25, Anm. 9.
[2] Johnsons Sohn John. Siehe Dok. 2, Anm. 15.

you can arrange for some time in the mountains for the later part of the summer, and I can join you there when I come home. You have got to have some relief from this awful pace you have been going. After the frightful heat of the summer may be you will be ready for some escape. May be you will want to go for the whole summer. May be you could rent a car to go out. John too will need the refreshment that the mountains will bring after his pretty terrible siege of illnesses this year, not to mention our sweet Timmy[3] who can then be bye-bye most of the time. I worry a great deal about John's eyes. I keep blaming myself for having pushed the music without being careful enough to check whether it was right to ask him to read small notes at such great distances. We should have consulted an eye-doctor about it. May be it is not quite as bad as Doctor Hancock[4] guessed. Half vision is not very good vision. I love my sweet Em[ily], and my John and my Timmy very much. I want more than anything else to withdraw into the protective isolation of their company and love. I have had enough of the world's problems, or at least of this part of the world's problems for awhile, and I certainly need to escape from it for awhile, to hear nothing about it, to see nothing about it, absolutely to escape. May be we can do that best in the mountains. If you'll arrange for the last month before school opens. I'll do my best to be there for all or most of the time. I don't believe it's going to be good for me here from now on. The beauty of the outside world hurts too much as a cloak for the real picture and of what is Germany today and the beauty of the outside world is no satisfaction when the heart demands the beauty – the internal beauty – which only you and the kids give to my world.

I am low, I guess, because for one thing General Barker[5] is going and in his place comes a new General, a General Keating[6], who has no experience in this kind of work and who, I understand, has no other desire but to go home himself.[7] General Barker has principles, experience, and is himself a fighter. It will be a worthy task to do what I can to help the new General. But somehow or another I have become personally devoted to Barker in the little time that I have been permitted to work for him, and I don't like to see him go. He is one of the few in high places here who does have any principles. The enclosed pho-

---

[3] Johnsons Sohn Thomas. Siehe Dok. 2, Anm. 16.
[4] Siehe Dok. 4, Anm. 22.
[5] Siehe Dok. 20, Anm. 10.
[6] Frank A. Keating (1895-1973), Major General, Mai–Oktober 1946 Commanding General, US Headquarters Berlin District, US Commandant, Allied Kommandatura Berlin, Oktober 1946–1947 Assistant Deputy Military Governor for Operations and Deputy Commanding General, OMGUS, US Commandant, Allied Kommandatura Berlin, 1947 Deputy Military Governor, Germany (US), Commanding General, OMGUS, 1950 Chief US Military Adviser to Korea. Siehe Bildanhang, Abb. 27 und Abb. 28.
[7] Harold Hurwitz schreibt: „Barker wurde Anfang Mai von General Frank Keating abgelöst, einem politisch desinteressierten Organisationsmenschen, der unter Clay Karriere machte." Harold Hurwitz unter Mitarbeit von Andreas Büning/Johannes-Berthold Hohmann/Klaus Sühl/Ingolore Mensch-Khan, Die Anfänge des Widerstands, Teil 2: Zwischen Selbsttäuschung und Zivilcourage: Der Fusionskampf (= Demokratie und Antikommunismus in Berlin nach 1945, Bd. IV), Köln 1990, S. 1257.

tograph is taken at the entrance of his house[8].[9] You can see through to the big plate glass window in his living room and through it to the Wannsee[10]. I have under my arm the documents on the trial of the Communists.[11] The Colonel is Glaser[12], the head of the Civil Administration Section in B[erlin] D[istrict][13]. I have the same view of the lake from my window.[14]

I am low too, I guess, because of two political meetings I have attended yesterday and today. Yesterday it was a meeting of the anti-merger Social Democrats who gathered, to the number of some two thousand to listen to a Dr. Schumacher[15], the leader of the Social Democrats in the western and southern parts of Germany.[16] A gang of 20 to 30 pro-merger Social Democrats tried to break up the meeting in good Nazi fashion but the ring leaders were thrown out of the meeting and it then went on peacefully.[17] These are the people we ought to be supporting because they stand for the kind of democratic decency which we stand for. But we are doing nothing to support them. We won't even let them have a newspaper yet.[18]

---

[8] Barker wohnte Am Sandwerder 27. Siehe Dok. 28, Anm. 27.
[9] Foto im Bildanhang, Abb. 53.
[10] Gemeint ist der Große Wannsee, eine Ausbuchtung der Havel (siehe Dok. 74, Anm. 24) im Südwesten Berlins.
[11] Siehe Dok. 38.
[12] Siehe Dok. 28, Anm. 4.
[13] Civil Administration Branch, OMGBD. Siehe Dok. 28, Anm. 5.
[14] Blick von der Terrasse des damaligen Wannsee Hotels auf den Großen Wannsee im Bildanhang, Abb. 47.
[15] Kurt Schumacher (1895–1952), deutscher Politiker (SPD), 1926 Dr. rer. pol., Universität Münster, 1930–1933 MdR, 1933–1944 KZ-Haft, 1945 Einrichtung des sogenannten Büros Dr. Schumacher, Hannover, das im Februar 1946 zum „Büro der Westzonen" wurde, 1945–Mai 1946 Bevollmächtigter der Sozialdemokratischen Partei für die Westzonen, Mai 1946–1952 Vorsitzender der SPD, 1949–1952 MdB, Vorsitzender der SPD-Fraktion.
[16] Zu der Veranstaltung mit Schumacher im Mercedes-Palast im Berliner Verwaltungsbezirk Wedding siehe Wortprotokoll der Funktionärskonferenz der SPD-Opposition am 20. April 1946, in: LAB, C Rep. 900-02 (Sozialdemokratische Partei Deutschlands [SPD] – Bezirksorganisation Berlin [1945/46]), Nr. 12; Sozialismus und Demokratie untrennbar. Dr. Schumacher auf der Funktionärversammlung der SPD, in: Der Tagesspiegel vom 21. April 1946, S. 2; SPD will sozialistischen Neubau Deutschlands. Programmatische Erklärungen Dr. Schumachers, in: Telegraf vom 21. April 1946, S. 1 f.; Organisierte Versammlungs-Störung, in: Telegraf vom 28. April 1946, S. 3.
[17] Schumacher reagierte auf die Störungen während seines Referats unter anderem mit den Worten: „Ich habe mit Vergnügen festgestellt, dass ein Trupp von Lehrlingen der Demokratie im Saal ist." Wortprotokoll der Funktionärskonferenz der SPD-Opposition am 20. April 1946, in: LAB, C Rep. 900-02 (Sozialdemokratische Partei Deutschlands [SPD] – Bezirksorganisation Berlin [1945/46]), Nr. 12. Wie der „Telegraf" später berichtet, fand „der Störtrupp mit nachgedruckten, also *gefälschten Eintrittskarten* Einlass in die Versammlung". Organisierte Versammlungs-Störung, in: Telegraf vom 28. April 1946, S. 3.
[18] Die Zeitung „Der Sozialdemokrat. Organ der Sozialdemokratie Groß-Berlin" erschien erst ab dem 3. Juni 1946, unter britischer Lizenz. Die Lizenzierung des SPD-Organs „gehörte zu einem pressepolitischen Paket der CCG (BE), die sozialdemokratischen Kräfte in Berlin zu unterstützen". Susanne Grebner, Der Telegraf. Entstehung einer SPD-nahen Lizenzzeitung in Berlin 1946 bis 1950 (= Kommunikationsgeschichte,

This morning I went to a meeting where the union between the Social Democrats and the Communists of the Russian Zone and of Berlin was noted – that is the formation of the SEP which we, the Allies in Berlin, have not yet recognized![19] It was well prepared for – ran off as smoothly as a Nazi meeting, though I had the impression that the audience were a little sick of the enforced enthusiasm. In the royal box sat General Kotikoff[20] and all the speakers addressed him first. He is the Russian Commandant who at the last Kommandatura[21] meeting[22], had the effrontery to state, that he could not talk about Berlin politics because he was so newly arrived on the scene. Alongside of him sat the Communist major of Berlin, Dr. Werner[23]. On the platform sat the leader of the Communist Party here, Ullbrecht[24], who with his goatee looks nothing so much as like Lenin[25].[26] Other Communist leaders were there, including Pieck[27]. Ullbrecht and Pieck are Moscow trained. And alongside of them the Social Demo-

   Bd. 13), Münster, Hamburg und London 2002, S. 180. Bereits seit dem 9. April 1946 erschien mit sowjetischer Lizenz der zunächst vom Organisationsausschuss Groß-Berlin der SPD und KPD zur Vereinigung der beiden Parteien und dann vom Berliner Bezirksvorstand der SED herausgegebene „Vorwärts. Berliner Volksblatt".
[19] Am 21./22. April 1946 fand in der damaligen Spielstätte der Deutschen Staatsoper, im Admiralspalast im Berliner Verwaltungsbezirk Mitte, Friedrichstraße 101/102, der Vereinigungsparteitag von KPD und SPD statt. Siehe Protokoll des Vereinigungsparteitages der Sozialdemokratischen Partei Deutschlands (SPD) und der Kommunistischen Partei Deutschlands (KPD) am 21. und 22. April 1946 in der Staatsoper „Admiralspalast" in Berlin, Berlin 1946. Foto vom Vereinigungsparteitag im Bildanhang, Abb. 82.
[20] Siehe Dok. 35, Anm. 5.
[21] Siehe Dok. 20, Anm. 11.
[22] Siehe Protokoll der 11. Sitzung der Stadtkommandanten am 12. April 1946, BKC/M (46) 11, englischsprachige Fassung, in: LAB, B Rep. 036-01 (Office of Military Government, Berlin Sector [OMGBS]), 11/148-1/10.
[23] Oberbürgermeister Dr. Arthur Werner (siehe Dok. 27, Anm. 30) gehörte keiner politischen Partei an. Er sah sich in der Rolle eines parteipolitisch neutralen und allseitig loyalen „Stadtpräsidenten von Berlin" und beschränkte sich im Wesentlichen auf die Funktionen einer bürgerlichen Repräsentationsfigur des Magistrats. Die tatsächliche Leitung der Stadtregierung lag dagegen in kommunistischer Hand, was von Werner zu keinem Zeitpunkt in Frage gestellt wurde. Siehe Dieter Hanauske, „Ein ehrlicher Mann, aber etwas naiv". Arthur Werner – Berliner Oberbürgermeister von 1945/46, in: Der Bär von Berlin. Jahrbuch 2002 des Vereins für die Geschichte Berlins, S. 131–160.
[24] Walter Ulbricht (1893–1973), deutscher Politiker (KPD/SED), 1912 SPD, 1917 USPD, 1919 KPD, 1928–1933 MdR, 1929–1946 Mitglied des Politbüros des Zentralkomitees der KPD, 1933–1945 Emigration, kehrte 1945 als Chef der aus deutschen Kommunisten bestehenden „Gruppe Ulbricht" aus dem sowjetischen Exil nach Berlin zurück, organisierte den Wiederaufbau der KPD, 1946 SED, 1946–1971 stellvertretender Vorsitzender, Generalsekretär bzw. Erster Sekretär des Zentralkomitees der SED, 1949–1960 stellvertretender Ministerpräsident der DDR, 1960–1973 Vorsitzender des Staatsrats der DDR. Foto mit Ulbricht im Bildanhang, Abb. 82.
[25] Wladimir Iljitsch Lenin, eigentl. Uljanow (1870–1924), russischer Revolutionär, führender Kopf der Oktoberrevolution 1917 in Russland, wurde als Vorsitzender des Rates der Volkskommissare Gründer der Sowjetunion und deren erster Regierungschef.
[26] Mit seiner Barttracht wollte Ulbricht offenbar Lenin kopieren.
[27] Siehe Dok. 30, Anm. 9.

cratic leaders (Grotewohl[28], Fechner[29], etc.) who have been whipped and forced into the union, in large part, I think, by Russian methods and aid, and have tried thus to sell away their party. It was clear to see that henceforth they would be at the mercy of the Communists, whom I am coming to hate here, not because of their program, but because of their dirty, tricky, methods. I couldn't stand it, and left after a couple hours. As I went out, I noticed a book stall of the press of the Red Army[30] in Germany, at which was for sale a marvelous collection of books and pamphlets about Russia, Stalin[31] and Communism.

And where do we stand in this fight? Neutral! What does the liberal tradition of American democracy mean to these people? Nothing. They get up on the platform and damn the western powers (particularly the British today) as they please. What are we doing to present the American picture in a positive light? Nothing. Don't we care whether the real democrats have a chance here or not? Why did we fight this war? As I remember it was for the American way of life or at least it had something to do about democracy? If we don't care about democracy in Europe then we'd better get the hell out of here and turn the place over to the Communists and the Soviets, and if we do we had better organize ourselves in some positive way and make a display, and a protest. As it is we are permitting Russia to run away with the game here. There will be a reaction I'm sure but at the moment it is not encouraging. And if the leaders here don't want to fight there is not much the rest of us can do? What do the American people want to do.

I'm sick of it. May a democracy that is so spineless deserves to die.

I went sailing on the lake[32] yesterday afternoon to cure myself but it only helped for a while. I love you very much, you and my boys. Edgar

---

[28] Siehe Dok. 30, Anm. 8.
[29] Max Fechner (1892-1973), deutscher Politiker (SPD/SED), gelernter Werkzeugmacher, 1911 SPD, 1917 USPD, 1922 erneut SPD, 1925 bis 1928 Stadtverordneter in Berlin, 1928 bis 1933 Mitglied des Preußischen Landtags, 1933/34 KZ Oranienburg, 1934 bis 1945 selbstständiger Lebensmittelhändler in Berlin-Neukölln, 1944 KZ Sachsenhausen, 1945 Mitunterzeichner des Gründungsaufrufs der SPD, 1945–April 1946 Mitvorsitzender des Zentralausschusses der SPD für die sowjetische Besatzungszone, Befürworter des Zusammenschlusses von KPD und SPD zur SED, 1946 SED, April 1946–1953 Mitglied des zentralen SED-Parteivorstands bzw. des Zentralkomitees der SED, Oktober 1946–1948 Mitglied der Stadtverordnetenversammlung von Groß-Berlin, 1949–1953 Justizminister der DDR, nach dem Aufstand vom 17. Juni 1953 Amtsenthebung, Verhaftung, Ausschluss aus der SED, Untersuchungshaft in Berlin-Hohenschönhausen, Verurteilung durch das Oberste Gericht der DDR zu acht Jahren Zuchthaus, 1956 vorzeitig aus der Haft entlassen, 1958 Wiederaufnahme in die SED. Foto mit Fechner im Bildanhang, Abb. 82.
[30] Bis 1946 die offizielle Bezeichnung für die 1918 gegründeten Streitkräfte der Sowjetunion, anschließend Umbenennung in „Sowjetarmee".
[31] Iossif Wissarianowitsch Stalin, eigentl. Dschugaschwili (1879-1953), sowjetischer Politiker, 1922-1953 Generalsekretär des Zentralkomitees der Kommunistischen Partei der Sowjetunion, ab 1941 Vorsitzender des Rates der Volkskommissare und ab 1946 des Ministerrats der Sowjetunion, 1943 Marschall und 1945 Generalissimus der Sowjetunion.
[32] Gemeint ist der Große Wannsee, eine Ausbuchtung der Havel (siehe Dok. 74, Anm. 24) im Südwesten Berlins.

Dok. 40
Schreiben an die Ehefrau
Berlin, Wannsee Hotel[1], Am Sandwerder 17/19, 27. April 1946

Dear Sweetheart –
I have 3 wonderful letters before me which I have read many times but have not answered.[2] In fact I have not written, I believe, since last Sunday[3]. Not because I have not wanted to write. I want to write every night, but, for some reason it has been an especially hectic week. 3 of the five evenings were taken upon with engagements, one with work, and last night I was so discouraged and tired by a long all day session at the Kommandatura[4] that I couldn't do much else but go to bed after looking at a few German papers. I shall do better henceforth. By not giving you an account of each day, I not only keep you uninformed but I do not keep up the record for whatever use that might be. I ought to be writing some kind of a journal of goings on here because they all have some slight significance, and the details when not put down are lost. Since I don't write a journal letters to you fulfill somewhat that function, and I fancy that you do not mind having a journal written to you as long as it has some interest.

Monday[5] I went to call on Franz's[6] friends the Suhr's[7] who, in fact, asked me to call.[8] There were 2 others there[9], an editor of a Berlin paper, British licensed,

---

[1] Siehe Dok. 25, Anm. 9.
[2] Emily L. Johnsons Schreiben vom 10., 14. und 17. April 1946, in: Unterlagen aus dem Nachlass Edgar N. Johnson, Privatbesitz Candice E. und Thomas R. Johnson, Denver, Colorado, USA.
[3] 21. April 1946. Siehe Dok. 39.
[4] Siehe Dok. 20, Anm. 11; Protokoll der 12. Sitzung der Stadtkommandanten am 26. April 1946, BKC/M (46) 12, englischsprachige Fassung, in: LAB, B Rep. 036-01 (Office of Military Government, Berlin Sector [OMGBS]), 11/148-1/10.
[5] 22. April 1946.
[6] Franz L. Neumann. Siehe Dok. 1, Anm. 8.
[7] Das Ehepaar Otto und Susanne Suhr; Otto Suhr (1894–1957), deutscher Politiker (SPD), 1914–1920 Studium der Geschichte, Volkswirtschaft und Zeitungswissenschaft an der Universität Leipzig (unterbrochen durch Kriegsdienstjahre), 1919 SPD, 1923 Dr. phil., Universität Leipzig, 1925–1933 Leiter der wirtschaftspolitischen Abteilung des Allgemeinen Freien Angestelltenbunds, Berlin, 1926–1933 Dozent an der Deutschen Hochschule für Politik, 1933–1935 erwerbslos, danach als freier Schriftsteller und als Sachverständiger für Verpackungsfragen beim Reichskuratorium für Wirtschaftlichkeit tätig, 1945 Leiter des Referats Druck und Papier beim Magistrat der Stadt Berlin, Abteilung für Wirtschaft, 1945–März 1946 Hauptabteilungsleiter in der Deutschen Zentralverwaltung der Industrie in der sowjetischen Besatzungszone, August 1946–1947 Generalsekretär (davor geschäftsführender Generalsekretär) der neu organisierten Berliner SPD, November 1946–1955 Vorsteher der Stadtverordnetenversammlung von Groß-Berlin bzw. Präsident des Abgeordnetenhauses von Berlin, 1948/1949 Vertreter Berlins im Parlamentarischen Rat in Bonn, 1948–1955 Direktor der Deutschen Hochschule für Politik, 1949–1952 MdB (Berliner Vertreter), ab 1952 Honorarprofessor für Theorie der Politik an der Freien Universität Berlin, 1955–1957 Regierender Bürgermeister von Berlin; Susanne Suhr, geb. Pawel (1893–1989), deutsche Bibliothekarin, Journalistin, 1917–1921 Studium der Geschichte und Germanistik an den Universitäten München und Leipzig, 1922 SPD, 1946–1950 „Telegraf"-Redakteurin, 1948–1954 Mitglied der Bezirksverordnetenversammlung Berlin-Wilmers-

The Telegraph[10] and his rather wild-eyed wife[11]. Somehow or another the evening left a bad taste in my mouth. I had in my brief case a bottle of Canadian Club Whiskey which I had purchased as a part of my ration at Harnack House[12]. It occurred to me that it might be nice to offer these people a drink. So I did but evidently they thought I was offering them the whole bottle for they didn't offer to give it to me as I left. Then of course I had to offer to take the editor and his wife home, and this was somewhat out of the way. Meanwhile my driver, a good-natured, some-what absent-minded Berliner by the name of Sanow[13], had had little to eat and when I arrived here at the hotel I had to get him some chocolate. So I was furnishing to Germans food, drink, and transportation. This I would not have minded if I had had the feeling that it was somehow given to people who understood the American point of view, or were trying to understand it, and were willing to make some sacrifice to avail themselves of its privileges. But I came home with the feeling that I had simply been exploited, that feeling while so many Americans have with respect to what we do over here, that I had been soft when I should have told these people off in some way or another.

Suhr is a left-wing Social Democrat who has recently given up a job with the Russians because he couldn't withstand the pressure and wanted to go along

dorf, 1958–1963 Mitglied des Abgeordnetenhauses von Berlin. Foto von Otto Suhr im Bildanhang, Abb. 80.

8   Franz L. Neumann hatte bereits in den 1920er-Jahren zum Freundeskreis von Otto und Susanne Suhr gehört. Siehe Susanne Suhr, Biographische Einleitung, in: Otto Suhr. Eine Auswahl aus Reden und Schriften, mit einer biographischen Einleitung von Susanne Suhr, Geleitwort von Ernst Fraenkel, Tübingen 1967, S. 3–50, hier S. 15; Henrike Hülsbergen, Otto Suhr, in: Stadtoberhäupter. Biographien Berliner Bürgermeister im 19. und 20. Jahrhundert, hrsg. von Wolfgang Ribbe (= Berlinische Lebensbilder, Bd. 7), Berlin 1992, S. 465–483, hier S. 471; Gunter Lange, Otto Suhr. Im Schatten von Ernst Reuter und Willy Brandt. Eine Biographie (Reihe Praktische Demokratie), Bonn 1994, S. 71 f.

9   Wahrscheinlich fand die Zusammenkunft in der Wohnung von Otto und Susanne Suhr in der Sodener Straße 36 im Berliner Verwaltungsbezirk Wilmersdorf (siehe Anmeldung bei der polizeilichen Meldebehörde, 26. Oktober 1945, in: LAB, E Rep. 200-17 [Nachlass Otto Suhr], Nr. 528; Meldekarte Otto Suhr, in: LAB, B Rep. 021 [Einwohnermeldeamt Berlin]) statt.

10 Der „Telegraf", eine SPD-nahe Zeitung, die von dem Journalisten Arno Scholz (1904–1971) herausgegeben wurde. Am 15. März 1946 hatte Scholz die britische Lizenz erhalten. Siehe Britische Lizenz für neue Zeitung. Berlin erhält einen „Telegraf", in: Der Berliner vom 16. März 1946, S. 2. Otto Suhr sollte für den „Telegraf" Artikel über aktuelle Wirtschaftsfragen schreiben. Siehe Schreiben von Arno Scholz an Otto Suhr vom 9. April 1946, in: LAB, E Rep. 200-17 (Nachlass Otto Suhr), Nr. 662; Gunter Lange, Otto Suhr. Im Schatten von Ernst Reuter und Willy Brandt. Eine Biographie (Reihe Praktische Demokratie), Bonn 1994, S. 125. Susanne Suhr wurde „Telegraf"-Redakteurin. Siehe Susanne Grebner, Der Telegraf. Entstehung einer SPD-nahen Lizenzzeitung in Berlin 1946 bis 1950 (= Kommunikationsgeschichte, Bd. 13), Münster, Hamburg und London 2002, S. 143.

11 Wahrscheinlich Arno Scholz' damalige Lebensgefährtin Meta Strauß (1904–1959), mit der er ab 1952 verheiratet war.

12 Siehe Dok. 15, Anm. 16.

13 Artur Sanow (1910–1984), Chauffeur. Siehe Bildanhang, Abb. 44, Abb. 45 und Abb. 49.

with the anti-merger Social Democrats.[14] He, and I get the impression, many like-minded Germans, want all that we have to give them by way of freedom – and therefore they don't like Communist-Russian methods, but at the same time they want all that is to be had from the Russians by way of a radical social policy. Suhr was quite critical of our policy in general, and I go along with him to some extent. We are not offering to German workers a radical land reform program, a speedy program of nationalization and socialization, and a thoroughgoing program of workers' participation in the management of industry. But I told him that we were doing pretty well considering the fact that we had no Socialists in America. There is some kind of a compromise between these two but it is not to be had here under present circumstances, nor has the compromise been yet worked out anywhere, not even in England as yet. What disturbed me was that these Germans, I felt, would in the last analysis prefer what the Russians had to offer rather than what we had to offer – that is, they would prefer to give up their freedom again. After 12 years of the Nazis I should expect them to want to learn in the other direction if a choice is to be made.

The fact is, I guess, and I have often said it to you, that we can't expect to make much of our impression upon the German worker as long as we are in the state of economic development that we happen to be in at home. There is no longer any room in Europe for the kind of monopoly capitalism which we still have. So, and it is often said in the German press, they equate our freedom, which is genuine and real here under the circumstances, with freedom for reactionaries, (this is the Communist-Russian slogan), and our democracy, with the opportunity for the boys who ran Germany into the ground in 1914 and 1933 and 1939 to come to the front again and run it into the ground again. That is why we need here a positive policy which will go as far as is possible to the left but still proclaims and implements the few things we are able to stand for. We need books about America, and people who can speak to Germans in German about America. We need to introduce into the educational system a breath of the fresh air present in our schools and universities, into the German press some of the virtues of our press (and there are some) and into German political life some of the tolerance, the give and take which we do have. This it seems to me is what the Germans need now. They don't need Communism at the moment, certainly, if they need it at all.

On Tuesday[15] I went to a dinner given by Col. Glaser[16] at Col. Howley's[17] house[18] for the Local Government Committee of B[erlin] D[istrict][19]. It was accordingly to be an international meeting. But the Russians, although invited, and having accepted, did not show up. (They often do this) So it was only tripartite. I sat next to an English girl interpreter at dinner, whose Mother was

---

[14] Suhr war Hauptabteilungsleiter in der Deutschen Zentralverwaltung der Industrie in der sowjetischen Besatzungszone gewesen.
[15] 23. April 1946.
[16] Siehe Dok. 28, Anm. 4.
[17] Siehe Dok. 20, Anm. 18.
[18] Siehe Dok. 28, Anm. 14.
[19] Gemeint ist das Local Government Committee, Allied Kommandatura Berlin. Siehe Dok. 29, Anm. 14.

Swiss, and who does the French interpreting, and she was quiet, modest and intelligent. Cocktails were served before dinner, champagne at dinner and Benedictine[20] afterwards. On the table at dinner were lovely cherry blossoms or a kind of flowering almond, I do not know which. I spent the evening talking to Americans, unfortunately, about recent developments here and did not see much of the British or the French, who were not, under any circumstances, particularly distinguished representatives. This may be only self defense. In any case I don't like the tone Glaser sets at his parties. He is an advertising man,[21] as I may have told you, and rather proud of it. Yet it seems he doesn't want to go back to advertising and will stay here on a kind of vacationing lark. Besides he has said some not very nice things about his wife[22] who is, however, coming over here. He is the head of the Civil Administration Branch in B[erlin] D[istrict][23].

Thursday[24] I had what I thought was going to be my prospective German teacher out here to dinner in return for a similar favor. She is a middle aged woman who has been doing Russian interpretation for the English, and is in fact an English citizen. But she is Russian born (white Russian) and has studied a lot in Germany. But now I learn that she has been given work with my opposite number, if one may so speak, in the British Office of Political Affairs, a certain Major Spencer[25] who is the political advisor to the British Commanding General of B[erlin] D[istrict] – General Nares[26]. This I think is a little embarrassing since the British may think I am trying to get information. This Mrs. Delahaye[27], moreover, (I think her husband is dead) is a little bit boring, although quite nice, and her idea of German lessons is to spend an evening together. I only want an hour or so, once or twice a week, and not an evening. I tried it out first and she invited me to a British Club. The second time we met she had guests and it was at the same British Club. Not much German spoken and certainly none learned. I then had to return the favor. I now think I'll tell her that work has so piled up that I must discontinue German for the time being. Then I'll get a hold of a German who will come here for an evening or so for some methodical work in German. German and society don't really mix, or at least they haven't so far.

The week led up to what I thought was a disastrous climax on yesterday, the meeting of the Kommandatura. I think I reported on the last meeting[28] when I

[20] Ein Likör.
[21] Glaser hatte in Boston, Massachusetts, für die George Zain advertising firm gearbeitet und 1922 die Glaser Advertising Agency, Inc., gegründet.
[22] Marguerite K. Glaser, geb. Kaufman (1891–1985).
[23] Civil Administration Branch, OMGBD. Siehe Dok. 28, Anm. 5.
[24] 25. April 1946.
[25] Kenneth Angus Spencer (1916–2002), Major, 1937 BA (Deutsch, Französisch), University College, London, ab 1939 British Army, 1945–1947 British Military Government, Berlin, Political Adviser to the British Deputy Director, William Robert Norris Hinde (siehe Dok. 28, Anm. 11).
[26] Siehe Dok. 27, Anm. 26.
[27] Ina Delahaye (1906–1972), russisch-britische Schauspielerin und Sängerin, war verheiratet mit Colonel J. V. Delahaye (gest. 1955).
[28] Siehe Protokoll der 11. Sitzung der Stadtkommandanten am 12. April 1946, BKC/M (46) 11, englischsprachige Fassung, in: LAB, B Rep. 036-01 (Office of Military Government, Berlin Sector [OMGBS]), 11/148-1/10.

had carefully prepared statements for General Barker[29] to present at the previous meeting on such important subjects as elections in Berlin, the recognition of the anti-merger Social Democrats, and the supervision of political activities in the city of Berlin.[30] I thought we were getting somewhere at the last meeting. Everybody agreed, according to our proposal, that they would come to this meeting with the earliest possible date on which elections could be held, the Russians promised to telephone on the question of recognition of the anti-merger SPD's, and it was agreed that the Local Government Committee[31] would be permitted to discuss methods of bringing political activities in Berlin, under Allied Control. That seemed to be getting ahead, and I was congratulated by State Department people on the progress which had been made. But yesterday was a come-down. You have heard remarks from me to the effect that Kommandatura machinery may break down. That prediction may have been a little premature but nothing that has happened since has vitiated that sad prediction. A previous meeting was a further step in the way. An important question on the reorganization of the police had to be sent upwards to the Control Council[32] because it couldn't be decided in the Kommandatura, and it couldn't be decided in the Kommandatura because the Russians took a very stubborn stand. They just wouldn't tolerate the reorganization and they objected to its being handled on a sectoral basis.

Yesterday's meeting lasted from ten in the morning until after seven at night with a short break for lunch. The largest meeting of the Kommandatura yet. Only the last meeting was somewhat shorter. The initial question to be discussed was how soon elections could be held in Berlin. Remember the Russians had agreed at the last meeting to come to this meeting prepared to announce the earliest possible date at which they would be willing to hold elections. But they simply refused to carry out this promise and to name a date. The British and the French named their dates as they had promised, around the 1st of August. But the Russians – the new Russian Commandant is Kotikov[33], launched into terrific arguments to show that no date could be specified. Instead they proposed a long series of investigations which would have to be made before a date could be agreed upon, and took by and large an unpleasantly stubborn attitude. It is clear, that after the elections which have been held in Europe (Austria![34] and the local elections in the American zone[35]) the Russians are going to

[29] Siehe Dok. 20, Anm. 10.
[30] Siehe Dok. 35.
[31] Siehe Dok. 29, Anm. 14.
[32] Siehe Dok. 14, Anm. 5.
[33] Siehe Dok. 35, Anm. 5.
[34] In Österreich hatten am 25. November 1945 Wahlen zum Nationalrat stattgefunden, bei denen die Kommunistische Partei Österreichs lediglich 5,42 Prozent der gültigen Stimmen erzielte. Siehe Keesing's Archiv der Gegenwart, XV. Jg., 1945, S. 539 E. Von einem „Knalleffekt", mit dem die Wahlen endeten, „da sich die Kommunisten mit einem denkbar schlechten Ergebnis abzufinden hatten", spricht Richard Hufschmied, Sonderfall Wien? Die Alliierten und Österreich 1943–1955, in: Die Vier Mächte in Berlin. Beiträge zur Politik der Alliierten in der besetzten Stadt, hrsg. von Michael Bienert/Uwe Schaper/Andrea Theissen unter Mitarbeit von Werner Breunig (= Schriftenreihe des Landesarchivs Berlin, Bd. 9), Berlin 2007, S. 109–129, hier S. 114.

take no further chances. They will not consent to our election in so important a place as Berlin, until they are sure that it will go, if not entirely their way, at least in a way that is not altogether unfavorable. That is what this party maneuvering here is all about. Their arguments were absolutely stinking from any point of view except theirs. They know what Berlin means to Germany, and they want a victory of the new Communist dominated SED when elections are held in Berlin.

After about four hours of wrangling on this subject, it was passed on to the higher authorities, the Control Council. Everyone was tired and annoyed by this time. The next subject was the recognition of the anti-merger SPD's and the new SED – the Socialist Unity Party. I had written out a statement of our policy for the last meeting which was circulated among all the Commandants. It proposed simply that both parties be recognized. The Russians had, evidently, carefully studied this statement, and were impressed by its essential fairness. In fact they kept discussing and quoting it throughout their argument, which of course flattered me. But they were at the same time shrewd. Having blocked at the previous meeting the recognition of the anti-merger SPD's, they were now willing to come around on this point, if only, we would recognize without delay the SEP which they have been promoting. In all justice these were not entitled to this. They wanted it because there is to be a 1 May celebration here, and they wanted to have their party recognized for this celebration, and to show how quickly they could manage to gain this recognition. I was for going along with the Russians on this proposition. It meant sacrificing a bit but not very much, and we should have acquired a reputation on this issue at least, of meaning what we said. At it was General Barker, at the moment when it came to making a decision was physically exhausted. I believe I have told you what a heroic stand he takes in simply going through a day's work.[36] Moreover the British took an unexpected stand, one that contradicted their previous decision. They wanted recognition for the SPD, but as for the SED, they wanted this decision passed upwards. The French too took a strangely contradictory stand. Usually they are clear, precise and logical. This was an unexpected reverse. They would recognize the SPD but as for the SED, they would have to go upwards. At the moment of decision I was not called upon by General Barker for advice. I had briefed him the day before and we had agreed that under no considerations was the question to go upwards. This was a matter for the Kommandatura to decide. We were striving in fact to have the K[ommandatura] establish methods of controlling Berlin politics. But instead of going along with the Russians as he should have, and making clear that we meant what we said when we proposed that both SPD + SED should be recognized under similar conditions, he faltered, and essentially broke his word, and went along with the British and

---

[35] Bei den Kommunalwahlen, die im Januar 1946 in den kleineren Gemeinden der amerikanischen Besatzungszone Deutschlands stattgefunden hatten, erzielte die KPD enttäuschende Ergebnisse. Siehe Keesing's Archiv der Gegenwart, XVI. Jg., 1946, S. 628 D; Conrad F. Latour/Thilo Vogelsang, Okkupation und Wiederaufbau. Die Tätigkeit der Militärregierung in der amerikanischen Besatzungszone Deutschlands 1944–1947 (Studien zur Zeitgeschichte), Stuttgart 1973, S. 110f.

[36] Siehe Dok. 33.

French, with whom his sympathies naturally lie, and supported, contrary to our agreement of the evening before, sending up the matter to the Control Council. I do not know what the Russians thought but I know what I should have thought. Simply that the Americans make a proposition and do not keep their word. He missed a great chance in not going with the Soviets against the British and the French. It now goes up to General Clay[37], for whom I am going to prepare a memorandum on the subject. I was desolate about the outcome. My suggestions had been good. They had struck a responsive chord with the Russians and then we renigged. How can General Kotikov trust us henceforth. Two major questions which the Kommandatura could really have decided among themselves now go to higher authority. The reputation of the competency of the Kommandatura is now discredited. What we wanted, namely the right to manage our own affairs, is now discredited by the thought that maybe we are not capable of managing our own affairs. And the international machinery of Berlin is thus made to appear unworkable. I am laboring under the impression of immediate effects. These iron themselves out in the long run. But they iron themselves out better when there are not so many stubborn wrinkles and creases to flatten out. It is all very fascinating in a way. The important decisions depend upon so many factors that the historian cannot ever hope to get at from the documents. The fundamental explanation of all this is poor General Barker's spine[38]. That hole in his spine which will make him a cripple if he doesn't go home soon. He is a hero in spite of this disaster. In the long run he will be borne out.

I must stop now. I'll write again tomorrow and get to the precious details of these letters which really interest me more than all this. I love you, much more than all Berlin, than all Germany, than all Europe, than all the world. A sweet good-night to my beloved Em[ily]. Edgar

Dok. 41
Schreiben an die Ehefrau
Berlin, 30. April 1946

Dearest Emily –

I came home to the Club[1] tonight to find a photograph of General Barker[2] with a rewarding and cordial inscription, and a gracious note.[3] He has aban-

---

[37] Siehe Dok. 2, Anm. 6.
[38] Barker hatte ein Rückenleiden. Hierzu Frank L. Howley (siehe Dok. 20, Anm. 18): "Because of a bad back, he sat at meetings in a padded chair, with a big green pillow behind him, but always started to squirm in acute discomfort after the first half hour." Frank Howley, Berlin Command, New York 1950, S. 109.

[1] Gemeint ist das Wannsee Hotel bzw. der Wannsee Officers' Club, Am Sandwerder 17/19. Siehe Dok. 25, Anm. 9.
[2] Siehe Dok. 20, Anm. 10.
[3] Das Foto ist weder in den Edgar N. Johnson Papers (UChicago Library, Special Collections Research Center) vorhanden noch in den Unterlagen aus dem Nachlass Edgar N. Johnson, die sich im Privatbesitz von Candice E. und Thomas R. Johnson, Denver, Colorado, USA, befinden.

doned his job to General Keating[4] and will take off on Thursday[5].[6] He has been a fine person to come to know, and I regret very much his going. The new general is quite unpolitical, though not, I take it, without intelligence. I am told he is something of a hot headed Irishman.

I was going to say something about the details of the weekend. You will say I am being spoiled and demoralized, – a continuation of the corruption that OSS[7] started when they gave Paul[8] and me the blue Buick[9]. On Saturday[10] afternoon, for example, I took a little time out to go sailing with Captain Americus Mitchell[11], in the red sailboat we used the week before. It is a nice one, and, as the afternoon was somewhat breezy, we sped back and forth across the lake, with no helping to manage the craft at some intervals. I thought of our being at a lake somewhere, where we could have a sailboat, and go off with our boys for an afternoon. This is honest-to-God, conspicuous consumption.

When I came back I found an invitation from Ambassador Murphy[12] for dinner. Well I figured out that this was to be a colloquy on the paper I had written on the Jurr[13] and Kammermeier[14] case – (the two Communists whom we recently arrested and sentenced to five years)[15].[16] But it was nothing of the sort. I was by no means flattered to have it turn out to be a dinner given for a meandering Congressman (McGeehie[17] of Mississippi[18]) and his party, which included

---

[4] Siehe Dok. 39, Anm. 6.
[5] 2. Mai 1946.
[6] "Maj. Gen. R. W. Barker, Commanding General of Berlin District was transferred yesterday to Washington, D. C. He was replaced by Maj. Gen. Frank A. Keating who has had nine months occupation duty in Bavaria. Gen. Keating came overseas in 1944 with the 102nd Infantry Division." Barker Leaves, in: OMGUS Observer vom 3. Mai 1946, S. 3.
[7] Office of Strategic Services. Siehe Dok. 1, Anm. 9.
[8] Wahrscheinlich ist Paul R. Sweet gemeint. Siehe Dok. 2, Anm. 28.
[9] Amerikanische Automobilmarke.
[10] 27. April 1946.
[11] Möglicherweise Americus Mitchell Jr. (1916–2003), Captain, 1944 BA, College at Vanderbilt University, Patentanwalt.
[12] Siehe Dok. 8, Anm. 13.
[13] Gerhard Jurr (1905–1971), deutscher Parteisekretär (KPD), gelernter Installateur, 1929 KPD, 1934/1935 Besuch der Internationalen Leninschule der Komintern, Moskau, 1936 verhaftet und vom Volksgerichtshof zu 15 Jahren Zuchthaus verurteilt, bis 1945 im Zuchthaus Brandenburg, dann Bezirksverwaltung Berlin-Schöneberg, Sekretär der KPD Berlin-Schöneberg.
[14] Wilhelm Kammermeier (1889–1954), deutscher Verwaltungsangestellter, Leiter des Zentralbüros für die Unterbezirksverwaltungen in Berlin-Schöneberg und Vorsitzender der KPD-Betriebsgruppe im Bezirksamt Berlin-Schöneberg.
[15] Siehe Dok. 33.
[16] Murphy leitete eine Kommission, die am 8. April 1946 gebildet worden war, um die Urteile gegen Jurr und Kammermeier zu überprüfen. Siehe Harold Hurwitz, Die Eintracht der Siegermächte und die Orientierungsnot der Deutschen 1945–1946 (= Demokratie und Antikommunismus in Berlin nach 1945, Bd. III), Köln 1984, S. 216.
[17] Daniel (Dan) R. McGehee (1883–1962), amerikanischer Jurist und Politiker (Demokratische Partei), 1924–1928 und 1932–1934 Member of Mississippi State Senate, 1928–1932 Mississippi State House of Representatives, 1935–1947 Member of Congress.
[18] US-Bundesstaat.

the consul of Zurich[19], one Sam Brown[20]. There were some Frenchmen there (a Professor Siegfried[21] who teaches geography) and others. The Congressman I found a little bit colorful, but on the whole utterly obnoxious. He was a violent anti-New-Dealer,[22] and a representative of all the fine chivalry and potent prejudices of the deep South – about as sad a man to represent America to Europeans as I can imagine. And from the political point of view, certainly an utterly incomprehensible person. The quite personal and petty details which he described as governing Washington politics reveal how far removed any academic treatment of this subject is. There is hardly a principle involved that is not false and showy. Truman[23], he assured us all, was at heart a conservative. He knew him well from prolonged poker games. The Congressman was pot-bellied and drank a little too much. He and his party are off on a 12 day jaunt (arranged by Judge Rosenman[24]) between sessions of Congress. I questioned Brown (a staunch admirer of Wallace[25] – who is a professional gardener) about bringing families to Switzerland. He said that Geneva[26] was the best place, but that Zurich was also possible and offered his services. Do you want to come to Switzerland?

On Sunday[27] there was a reception for General Barker and General Keating, the departing and arriving generals of Berlin District. All people of importance were invited, and appeared for awhile. Murphy, General Millburn[28], Clay[29]. (I enclose a snap of Keating and myself taken by Americus.[30] I don't know who the other officer is. Also one of the grounds in front of the Club[31]). Drinks, food, and music by an orchestra led by a female violinist called Ingeborg[32], who

[19] Stadt in der Schweiz.
[20] Gemeint ist Sam E. Woods (1892–1953), amerikanischer Diplomat, BS, Mississippi State Teachers College, ab 1929 Foreign Service, 1937–1941 Commercial Attaché, Berlin, 1942–1947 Consul General, Zürich und Vaduz, 1947–1952 Consul General, München.
[21] André Siegfried (1875–1959), französischer Wirtschaftsgeograf, ab 1933 Professor, Collège de France, ab 1944 Membre de l'Académie Française.
[22] McGehee war "a New Deal critic in congress and an opponent of the fair employment practice act and anti-poll tax measures". War Hero Wins Congress Seat in Mississippi, in: Chicago Daily Tribune vom 28. August 1946, S. 6.
[23] Siehe Dok. 5, Anm. 19.
[24] Samuel I. Rosenman (1896–1973), amerikanischer Jurist, 1919 LLB, University of Columbia, 1932–1943 Justice New York Supreme Court, 1943–1945 Special Counsel to President Roosevelt, 1945/1946 to President Truman.
[25] Henry A. Wallace (1888–1965), amerikanischer Politiker (Republikanische Partei, dann Demokratische Partei und schließlich Progressive Partei), 1933–1940 US Secretary of Agriculture, 1941–1945 Vice President of the US, 1945/1946 US Secretary of Commerce.
[26] Stadt in der Schweiz.
[27] 28. April 1946.
[28] Bryan L. Milburn. Siehe Dok. 15, Anm. 20.
[29] Siehe Dok. 2, Anm. 6.
[30] Gemeint ist wahrscheinlich das Foto, das im Bildanhang als Abb. 28 abgedruckt ist.
[31] Gemeint ist wahrscheinlich das Foto, das im Bildanhang als Abb. 44 abgedruckt ist. Es wurde am Eingang des Wannsee Hotel/Wannsee Officers' Club (siehe Dok. 25, Anm. 9) aufgenommen.
[32] Ingeborg von Streletzky (1916–2011), Violinistin und Orchesterleiterin. „Auch die Amerikaner waren begeistert. Ingeborg eroberte die amerikanischen Clubs, sie spielte vor General Clay und General [Maxwell D.] Taylor, ‚erhielt glänzende Angebote

seems to be a favorite in Berlin. General Barker invited me to have a ride with him and his staff in his launch after the reception. And I went.[33]

The interesting thing about the reception to me was that Keating gave me the first indication that he wanted me to continue for him in the same capacity in which I have been acting for Barker. As I was sitting talking with him and Clay he mentioned to Clay that he would like to have me perform the rôle of an ambassador to him, such as Clay had in Murphy. He subsequently mentioned to me moving over from the present quarters in Berlin District[34] to his headquarters in the Telefunken Building[35]. Clay answered with the reminder that I was only loaned to B[erlin] D[istrict] on a temporary basis, and that I was subsequently to take on the job of Regional Military Governor[36] (this is the Stuttgart[37] job after Pollock[38] goes). I have scarcely been in my office across from Murphy in the Directors' Building at Omgus[39], although I have been told that there are piles of stuff coming through that office for me. To move over from B[erlin] D[istrict] to Keating would mean that I had three offices, which is rather impossible.

The point of all this is that Clay has evidently forgotten that he promised that I could return in the Fall, and is counting on me to take over Pollock's job when he returns to the states in August. I want to know what you really think. What I have said to you on this subject so far I have really meant, namely that I am not too much interested. I am perfectly ready to return to Nebraska in the Fall. At the same time there are considerations which I suppose we are obliged to think about. The two issues in my mind are 1. being with you and the boys; 2. security for you and the boys. There is also in the back of my mind – Dad[40]. If I am to stay on here, you should come nearer as soon as possible. How interested are you in some European experience? I don't know how long this occupation is to last. Certainly for several years. By staying here, I could have a 10,000 dollar job for this period. As a result of this experience I don't suppose I really have to worry about a job in the future. If I stayed another year, this would involve tearing up roots in Nebraska, unless Henry[41] were willing to say, one year more – Yes – but no further consideration. If we kept the house in Lincoln[42] we

nach drüben"', schreibt Gregor Eisenhauer in seinem Nachruf: Ingeborg von Streletzky. Geb. 1916. Es war keine gütige Fee, es war harte Arbeit und unbarmherzige Dressur, in: Der Tagesspiegel vom 25. November 2011, S. 12. „Aber sie blieb in Berlin. Was sie hielt? ‚Die Zuneigung so vieler Menschen hier, die mir wunderschöne Briefe schreiben, und meine dankbarsten und liebsten Zuhörer, die Kriegsblinden.'" Ebd.

[33] Fotos von der Bootsfahrt auf dem Wannsee im Bildanhang, Abb. 29, Abb. 30 und Abb. 31.
[34] Gemeint ist Johnsons Quartier beim OMGBD. Siehe Dok. 25, Anm. 13.
[35] Im Telefunkengebäude an der Goerzallee, Berlin-Lichterfelde, befand sich das US Headquarters Berlin District.
[36] Gemeint ist die Leitung des RGCO. Siehe Dok. 2, Anm. 11.
[37] Hauptstadt des Landes Württemberg-Baden in der amerikanischen Besatzungszone Deutschlands.
[38] Siehe Dok. 15, Anm. 12.
[39] Siehe Dok. 17, Anm. 45.
[40] Frank E. Johnson. Siehe Dok. 3, Anm. 12.
[41] Charles Henry Oldfather. Siehe Dok. 2, Anm. 19.
[42] Hauptstadt des US-Bundesstaats Nebraska, wo Johnson mit seiner Familie wohnte und an der Universität lehrte.

should always have some place to return to. Out of a salary of 10,000 for a few years we should be able to save enough to keep us going until we found a suitable job. How does this affect the boys? How does it affect Dad? Do we want to be adventurous enough to tear up roots at Nebraska and trust to our luck? If we saved enough we could live on our savings for awhile and I could do some writing which in itself might guarantee any security for the future, without too much of worry about teaching or any other kind of job. The question of serving your country is now – at this stage of the game – out. You would be serving your country but the pressure on this score, I now feel is over. I came back here honestly with this in mind and what I came back for is not now available. We have to think about ourselves, now, for a bit.

Have you any desires? any ideas? I'll go on with this again but we should be sketching out the future.

I love you my Sweetheart, and I don't want to miss the chance of our having in the years to come the best that can be arranged. Please tell the boys about me, and I send you my fondest and most tender caresses. I only want the finest for us all. Edgar

Dok. 42
Schreiben an die Ehefrau
Berlin, 1. Mai 1946

Dearest and Sweetest –

When I came in my office this morning there was a bouquet of tulips on my desk. I discovered they had been brought by my German driver[1], who told me his wife had gotten them for me. I have been sending some of my PX[2] rations home with him. And on the commode which contains coats and hats was a bouquet of apple blossoms brought by my German secretary[3] for whom I have done nothing. She is a Frau but about her family life I haven't inquired. This I think is the simple way to get along with the Germans – be so nice to them that they really want to bring you flowers.

I also went to the May day celebration today in the so-called Lustgarten[4].[5] I wanted any generals to go but at the last moment they turned me down – mistakenly I think. It was a celebration the organization of which I resent. We had tried to insist that it should be an unpolitical affair open to all workers' groups who wished to participate. General Barker[6] even went to see General

---

[1] Artur Sanow. Siehe Dok. 40, Anm. 13.
[2] Post Exchange, Verkaufsläden der amerikanischen Streitkräfte.
[3] Möglicherweise Frau Donneck. Siehe Dok. 80.
[4] Der urspr. zum Berliner Stadtschloss gehörende Lustgarten liegt auf dem nördlichen Teil der Spreeinsel im Verwaltungsbezirk Mitte.
[5] Am Maifeiertag fand im Lustgarten eine FDGB-Kundgebung statt, die im Zeichen der Vereinigung von KPD und SPD zur SED stand. Siehe B. K., Die Kundgebung der 500 000 im Lustgarten. Berlins Bekenntnis zur Einheit der Arbeiterklasse und zur Demokratie, in: Berliner Zeitung vom 3. Mai 1946, [S. 2]; Lustgarten im Zeichen der „Einheit", in: Der Tagesspiegel vom 3. Mai 1946, S. 4.
[6] Siehe Dok. 20, Anm. 10.

Kotikov[7] on this point and he gave his assurances. It wasn't a blatant celebration of the new SED but it was clearly under their auspices. Efforts to get other speakers from other parties failed and only speakers representing the right point of view were permitted to hold the platform.[8] They were more moderate than they have been but I don't like these methods. There were some 200,000 to 300,000 Germans on the square – workers who had marched from the suburbs into the center of the city. They were an awfully depressing sight to see. These Germans are thoroughly knocked out. They looked physically exhausted and they were dressed in all manner of old clothes. These were workers, metropolitan workers, who have no means to take care of themselves on the black market[9] or out in the country – and in Berlin it is hard to get out into the country, which is Russian country. They were so tired by the time they had marched into the city's center that they were not much interested in the speeches. The speakers, fresh and vigorous because they have better ration cards and receive extra supplements from the Russians were unable to awaken any enthusiasm. There were loud speakers about, but most of the people I could see were clapping because other people were clapping. They began to go home before the speeches were over. Maybe my driver is right. They have begun this political movement too early in Germany. People have to have more time to make up their minds. It seemed impossible to imagine that these were, not long ago, a part of the Herrenvolk. They came out in such numbers, I think, primarily because there had been nothing like this for such a long time. There is, after all, so little excitement for them in Germany.

Two letters from you today (April 22, April 26th!)[10] make me horribly lonesome. I am easily precipitated into this state. The one contained John's[11] very touching letter to the Easter Rabbit (how can this faith be translated into something real without in the meantime undergoing disillusion?) and the other your confession of your own loneliness. The passing remarks in this letter really contain the answer to all the questions I put in a letter of yesterday if only we could resolve ourselves not to discuss alternate answers. "These months are gone forever." "And sometimes I do wonder if it is all worth it." "To be released, oh when?" "I hope September, my darling." As you know I am ready to state September in Lincoln[12], rather than September here. It is September in either case. And it is September wherever you decide it to be. Or if you do not wish to decide, then it is September in Lincoln. Or to put it otherwise if you don't wish to come here then it is September in Lincoln. I don't really believe that when this episode is over it will have been worth it. To be with you for one day and

---

[7] Siehe Dok. 35, Anm. 5.
[8] Ansprachen hielten die beiden Vorsitzenden der SED, Otto Grotewohl (siehe Dok. 30, Anm. 8) und Wilhelm Pieck (siehe Dok. 30, Anm. 9), der 1. Vorsitzende des FDGB-Bundesvorstands, Hans Jendretzky (siehe Dok. 83, Anm. 113), SED, und die Leiterin des Berliner Frauenausschusses, Katharina Kern (1900–1985), SED.
[9] Siehe Dok. 21, Anm. 11.
[10] Briefe in: Unterlagen aus dem Nachlass Edgar N. Johnson, Privatbesitz Candice E. und Thomas R. Johnson, Denver, Colorado, USA.
[11] Johnsons Sohn John. Siehe Dok. 2, Anm. 15.
[12] Hauptstadt des US-Bundesstaats Nebraska, wo Johnson mit seiner Familie wohnte und an der Universität lehrte.

night is worth more than all this. To have been there over Easter is worth more than this. The money is all very tempting but we can't be led astray by this, and the kind of life which one leads over here is not the kind of life we are used to – I mean the quiet, scholarly kind. Here one does no reading, outside of the professional reading he is obliged to do. The patriotic motive diminishes when it is no longer a question of saving human lives of our own people at the moment. And I can work to stave off the coming war as well at home as here. Perhaps better there. In any case, I think, I shall retreat into our home, and nestle into your bosom, and not come out much again. Life is after all to be lived mostly for the moment, and not too much for the future, I shall not be completely satisfied teaching in Nebraska but neither, I think, should we be completely satisfied here. (The first batch of wives has arrived here.[13] I met a colonel's wife tonight. They occupy a beautiful mansion overlooking Wannsee[14]. This is hard for me to take.)

I want to be with you, my dearest, that is all, and that is enough. I don't want you overburdened in the way that you now are. I want to come back to a home where you are. I want to see your lovely face and your lovely body. I want to run my hands through your hair and kiss your eyes and lips and cheeks. I want to hold you close to me for a very long time. I want our naked bodies lovingly to be in touch. I want my hands and lips to be where you want them to be. I want to be able to come to you over and over again, and to be the boy you call me. We are blessed with a love that knows only how to grow. I want to give myself up to you, to share in the bliss which we can have. Oh my dear I want to come into you, and to stay there forever. I love you my darling Emily, and there is no comfort except that the days do pass and that there will be a release. Edgar

Dok. 43
Schreiben an die Ehefrau
Berlin, 5. Mai 1946[1]

Dearest Emily –

I have thought of a compromise solution to the question of our future which I would like to put to you, and also to Henry[2] when I next write. I just received a nice letter from him.

---

[13] Am 30. April 1946 waren die ersten Ehefrauen und Kinder von amerikanischen Besatzungsangehörigen in Berlin eingetroffen; ein Zug aus Bremerhaven hatte sie nach zehntägiger Schiffsreise in die Stadt gebracht. Siehe Kathleen McLaughlin, First U. S. Families Arrive in Berlin. Wives and Children Hailed in Poignant Reunions – Amazed at Beauty of Country, in: The New York Times vom 1. Mai 1946, S. 4; Lyn Davis, "Operation Dependency ...". Families' Arrival Has Rousing Climax, in: OMGUS Observer vom 3. Mai 1946, S. 1 und 4f.

[14] Gemeint ist wahrscheinlich der Große Wannsee, eine Ausbuchtung der Havel (siehe Dok. 74, Anm. 24) im Südwesten Berlins.

[1] Im Briefkopf heißt es: "Sunday, 6 May 1946". Nicht der 6., sondern der 5. Mai 1946 war ein Sonntag.

[2] Charles Henry Oldfather. Siehe Dok. 2, Anm. 19.

It is this: I decide to return to the University of Nebraska[3] in the Fall of 1947. This is irrevocable. Meanwhile I make arrangements to bring you and the boys over here as soon as possible. I tell Clay[4] that I will take the Stuttgart[5] job[6] when Pollock[7] goes in August and you and the boys will join me there. We shall stay there together until next June. The following summer we shall spend in Europe, or in England, or both, vacationing, seeing things. We shall return home to Lincoln[8] together in the Fall.

This plan leaves Dad[9] unprovided for, and depends upon a satisfactory solution of this question for adoption.

Its advantages are:

1. That it brings us together in this European experience and offers the opportunity for a little European travel, which, indeed, might never come again.

2. It gives us the advantage of this 10,000 salary for another year. Henry said in his letter that he has recommended me this Spring for 4200, the minimum salary of a full professor. This, of course, is more than twice that. By careful living here we should be able to save a great deal of it, even more perhaps than would be necessary to spend the next summer travelling. I really think of England in this connection, which you would love, and so would I. Something of the continent could be seen in between.

3. This would fill out my experience here. As it is my experience will be limited to Berlin. The Stuttgart job takes care of our whole zone, and puts me in touch with the leading people there, as well as with those in Omgus[10]. Although I am not any longer much moved by the patriotic motive, there is no doubt that staying here another year would be helpful to the USA. I would come to have a pretty good grip of the German problem as it appears to be a couple years after military defeat of Germany.

4. While I should be obliged to return to Nebraska for a few years, this prolonged experience might lead to something which would better suit our hearts' desire than permanently staying there.

The real point of this is whether you would like some European experience with the difficulties that are involved of having it with young children. I long to share the days' experience with you. That, together with being a part of you, is what I miss most. The Wannsee[11] is only a lake with boats on it to look at. This plan does not abandon our security at Nebraska, it does not abandon our lovely home there, it has the advantage of compromising with the advantages of my

---

[3] 1869 gegründete Universität in Lincoln, Nebraska.
[4] Siehe Dok. 2, Anm. 6.
[5] Hauptstadt des Landes Württemberg-Baden in der amerikanischen Besatzungszone Deutschlands.
[6] Die Leitung des RGCO in Stuttgart. Siehe Dok. 2, Anm. 11.
[7] Siehe Dok. 15, Anm. 12.
[8] Hauptstadt des US-Bundesstaats Nebraska, wo Johnson mit seiner Familie wohnte und an der Universität lehrte.
[9] Frank E. Johnson. Siehe Dok. 3, Anm. 12.
[10] Siehe Dok. 17, Anm. 45.
[11] Gemeint ist der Große Wannsee, eine Ausbuchtung der Havel (siehe Dok. 74, Anm. 24) im Südwesten Berlins.

position here and the advantages of being there. It depends, of course, upon Henry's decision. If he says that they can't wait for another year, then my decision I think is clear. I come home. We are not of the adventurous sort. At least, I am not.

What do you think? Would you like to see something of Europe now, under these unfortunate circumstances? Would you like to guide me in my work from day to day. Or would you prefer to have me come back to Lincoln to you rather than to come to Stuttgart to me?

I am writing a report on the SED for the Branch[12],[13] If you were here it would be much better.

I love you, oh my dearest, and my boys. Edgar

Dok. 44
Schreiben an die Ehefrau
Berlin, 6. Mai 1946

Sweet and dear Emily –

The best thing about the day was the gift from you – the watch came in perfect condition.[1] I put it on immediately, and it has run perfectly ever since, and I do not expect there will be any trouble with it. I am sorry you had to pay so much for it for I don't suppose we have any right really to afford so expensive a watch for me. But it is neat and handsome, just the right size so as not to make it conspicuous, and the black leather strap fits perfectly without an extra hole. I think I told you that I had a chance to buy a watch from a German – through my driver[2] – soldier who got it in the army. He wants two cartons of cigarettes for it. I thought it would be nice to get for John[3] who would be delighted to have a real watch. I can't pay for it with the cigarettes I get from the PX[4] for this is illegal but if you could send me a few cartons from Dalton's[5] I could get it for John. Certainly it is worth from our point of view 2 cartons of cigarettes. These cigarettes however cost on the German black market[6] 1400 marks a carton which is no less than $ 140 dollars a carton (140 marks – $ 14, a package).[7] But you can hardly figure this way. My new watch, with a second hand even, and if I read correctly 17 jewels! I shall treasure too as a memento of you always in sight. I have a ring from you on the same hand.

---

12 Civil Administration Branch, OMGBD. Siehe Dok. 28, Anm. 5.
13 Gemeint ist wahrscheinlich der Bericht über die SED in dem Special Report of Civil Administration Branch, OMGBD, vom 6. Mai 1946: Berlin Summary. May Day, Political Parties, Elections, SED review, in: BArch, Koblenz, Z 45 F, 17/258-3/2.

1 Siehe Dok. 27.
2 Artur Sanow. Siehe Dok. 40, Anm. 13.
3 Johnsons Sohn John. Siehe Dok. 2, Anm. 15.
4 Post Exchange, Verkaufsläden der amerikanischen Streitkräfte.
5 Kaufhaus in Lincoln, Nebraska.
6 Siehe Dok. 21, Anm. 11.
7 Siehe Dok. 27, Anm. 10.

On the way home tonight my driver took out of his pocket a purple velvet case with silver earings containing large brilliants. Some German had asked him to try to sell them for him. They belong to his aunt. He wanted ten cartons of cigarettes or in marks equivalent $ 1400 dollars (= 15 dollars in cigarettes). I was not interested. This is what is happening here, people getting rid of things in order to buy food that they need on the black market. Sanow[8] said that ten cartons of cigarettes would buy about 35 pounds of butter which is of course what people need most.

On the way down to work this morning Sanow told me his wife had cancer. She is 36 and he spoke of her in loving terms. She has had radium treatments, which burnt her somewhat badly, and these have helped keep it down I guess. But radium treatments are not available here now since the Russians are supposed to have taken it all and sent it back to Russia. He is now going to try to get her radium bath treatments, which I can't imagine will do much good. It is beginning to pain her. The doctor says she needs radium treatment. She told him that she wouldn't live long. Not a very nice way to begin the day. There is of course a general shortage of medicines here.[9] Even alcohol is hard to get and one does not know how much suffering is caused by this alone. I'd like to get Sanow's wife a radium treatment but I don't know whether we have any radium here or whether it is available to Germans if we have. There must be many cases like this.

Two Social Democrats came into my office today. They live in the Russian Sector and have refused to follow the Russian and Communist line and go in for the new party. One of them has been advised by his friends to get out of the Russian sector for fear that something might happen to him. These friends have been summoned to the headquarters of the local Russian Commandant and asked many questions about the man. What are his political opinions? What meetings has he recently attended? How does he conduct himself. The man has in his possession papers which he feels will incriminate others if they are taken. He now sleeps different places from night to night for fear of being found. The other man has a family. He is an independent Social Democrat. He has been summoned before the local Russian Commandant and told that his political views and activity are anti-Russian. He tried to explain that his political views and activity had nothing to do with being anti-Russian. They were just his political views. But the Russians professed not to understand. They both want to move into our Sector, and I shall try to do what I can. They live in terror, and under a terror which is not very different from the Nazi system. This makes you sick. Why do the Russians have to deal in terror methods. That they come to us is a great tribute. That is, in a sense, what America stands for. But we can't take in all the Germans who want to move from the Russian into the American Sector. Nor does this make for good American-Russian relations. The Russians will now say, if we take those men over, that they are being used by us as agents to

---

[8] Siehe Dok. 40, Anm. 13.
[9] Siehe Die Sitzungsprotokolle des Magistrats der Stadt Berlin 1945/46. Teil II: 1946, bearb. und eingel. von Dieter Hanauske (= Schriftenreihe des Landesarchivs Berlin, Bd. 2/II), Berlin 1999, Dok. 96, Anm. 59.

spy on the Russians. God knows how many Russian agents are in our Sector, or even in our offices. What would you do, take them in or not?

It is the same with the Liberal Democratic Party[10] here in Berlin – one of the two conservative parties[11]. They are being hamstrung by the Russians in their zone, and in the city. They want to move over into our sector for the freedom that it brings.[12] This is again what we stand for. We shall probably let them come over. But the Russians will use this to paint us as the supporters of reaction. They have already done this enough in the course of the merger struggle, and if the independent Social Democrats are the representatives of reaction you can imagine what the Liberal Democratic Party can be painted to be. It is likely that what the Russians are aiming at is something like a one party system. They hope, through the instrumentality of the new unity party to liquidate the Social Democrats. Having done that the other two conservative parties will be easy to liquidate.

Is all this worth fighting a war about if it should come to this? I must say I am not very hopeful tonight. When I read the press reports of the Council of Foreign Ministers in Paris[13] I am even less hopeful. They have returned the South Tyrol to Italy.[14] This is a decision which may not of course cause trouble enough to help bring on a war. But it is based on a kind of justice that I do not understand. Of course Austria is a defeated nation and Italy managed to scramble out of the war. The area in dispute is of course indisputably Austrian. It is given to Italy to help with her economic recovery. But the Italians, under Mussolini[15], used dastardly methods to Italianize the area to which they really have no right.

---

[10] Die Liberal-Demokratische Partei Deutschlands (LDP) war am 5. Juli 1945 mit einem Gründungsaufruf an die Öffentlichkeit getreten. Siehe Berlin. Quellen und Dokumente 1945-1951, hrsg. im Auftrage des Senats von Berlin, bearb. durch Hans J. Reichhardt/Hanns U. Treutler/Albrecht Lampe (= Schriftenreihe zur Berliner Zeitgeschichte, Bd. 4/1. Halbbd.), Berlin 1964, Nr. 472.

[11] Neben der bürgerlich-liberalen LDP war die CDU zugelassen, die sich als interkonfessionell-christlicher, bürgerlicher Zusammenschluss verstand. Siehe Dok. 21, Anm. 29.

[12] Die Geschäftsstelle des Landesverbands Berlin befand sich in der Taubenstraße 48/49 im Verwaltungsbezirk Mitte (sowjetischer Sektor).

[13] Die Pariser Konferenz des Rates der Außenminister, erste Sitzungsperiode, fand vom 25. April bis 15. Mai 1946 statt, die zweite Sitzungsperiode vom 15. Juni bis 12. Juli 1946. Siehe Oliver Jäkel, Außenministerkonferenz Paris (25. 4.-15. 5. und 15. 6.-12. 7. 1946), in: Deutschland unter alliierter Besatzung 1945-1949/55, hrsg. von Wolfgang Benz, Berlin 1999, S. 219.

[14] Im Friedensvertrag von Saint-Germain-en-Laye vom 10. September 1919 hatte Österreich das deutschsprachige Südtirol an Italien abtreten müssen. 1943 wurde das Land von deutschen Truppen besetzt. Nach dem Zweiten Weltkrieg bemühte sich Österreich um die Rückgabe von Südtirol. Am 1. Mai 1946 wiesen die vier Siegermächte die Forderung Österreichs nach einer Volksabstimmung in Südtirol endgültig ab. Siehe Rolf Steininger, Südtirol im 20. Jahrhundert. Vom Leben und Überleben einer Minderheit, Innsbruck und Wien 1997; Hans Heiss/Gustav Pfeifer (Hrsg.), Südtirol – Stunde Null? Kriegsende 1945-1946 (= Veröffentlichungen des Südtiroler Landesarchivs, Bd. 10), Innsbruck, Wien und München 2000; Rudolf Lill, Südtirol in der Zeit des Nationalismus, Konstanz 2002.

[15] Benito Mussolini (1883-1945), italienischer Politiker, 1922-1943 faschistischer Diktator Italiens, 1943-1945 Staatschef der Italienischen Sozialrepublik.

The talk about Trieste[16] and Venetia Giulia[17] also frightens me. There I am on the other side. Trieste is an Italian city. This even Molotov[18] admits but he thinks it should go to Jugo-Slavia, which, it's going to Jugo-Slavia puts Russia at the head of the Adriatic. I don't see how this Conference is to come to any common conclusions, or if it does that they are going to be any good. But I certainly should not like to be in Byrnes'[19] place. If Berlin is a tough job, Paris is a God-awful job.

I don't know why I wrote you my yesterday's proposal.[20] It was, I suppose, in part the aftermath of a meeting with Social Democrats during the previous week, and I thought that such people ought to be helped. But I don't know that I am very convinced of what I said. If I go down to Stuttgart[21] there won't be many Social Democrats to support although I suppose there are other decent people to support. There are of course some points in my proposal worth considering on their own, I suppose. At the moment I think perhaps I ought to come home right away. I am not actually necessary to the Berlin operation. I am sort of kept there by Clay[22] because he thinks I may go to Stuttgart later. If I don't this is of course a waste of the tax payer's money, though of course, having brought me over here they are obligated to keep me employed for the time I promised to come over. After all they kept me unemployed for some time at the beginning of this year. But the situation is really – the German situation I mean – so hopeless. Nothing much can be done under present circumstances. And you get tired working up your anti-Russian feelings which point to no good end. There is really not much hope for Europe and I wonder if we want to fight to keep it out of the Russian orbit! This is the kind of spirit Russian toughness creates! It is what the Nazis thrived on! I think it used to be called appeasement.

I think you were right about that second-hand piano at S + M[23].[24] I am terrified at the rise in price of the piano we wanted to buy. We, of course, don't have

16 Österreich hatte die seit 1382 zu seinem Staatsgebiet gehörende Stadt Triest im Frieden von Saint-Germain-en-Laye 1919 an Italien abtreten müssen. 1943 erfolgte die Besetzung durch deutsche Truppen, 1945 die Besetzung der Stadt sowie des nördlichen und westlichen Umlands (Zone A) durch angloamerikanische, des südlichen Umlands (Zone B) durch jugoslawische Truppen. Im Friedensvertrag von Paris vom 10. Februar 1946 wurde Triest Freistaat unter Aufsicht der UN. Aufgrund des Londoner Abkommens vom 5. Oktober 1954 erfolgte die Rückgabe der Stadt und der Zone A an Italien, die erweiterte Zone B blieb bei Jugoslawien.
17 Istrien musste Italien im Pariser Friedensvertrag an Jugoslawien abtreten.
18 Wjatscheslaw Michailowitsch Molotow (1890–1986), sowjetischer Politiker, 1926–1956 Mitglied des Politbüros der KPdSU, 1930–1941 Vorsitzender des Rates der Volkskommissare, 1939–1949 und 1953–1956 Außenminister der Sowjetunion.
19 Siehe Dok. 5, Anm. 17.
20 Siehe Dok. 43.
21 Hauptstadt des Landes Württemberg-Baden in der amerikanischen Besatzungszone Deutschlands.
22 Siehe Dok. 2, Anm. 6.
23 Schmoller & Mueller Music Store.
24 Emily L. Johnson hatte am 27. April 1946 geschrieben: "Schmoller + Mueller had a Style B second hand Steinway advertised and I was in yesterday to see it. Old and somewhat shabby looking." Brief in: Unterlagen aus dem Nachlass Edgar N. Johnson, Privatbesitz Candice E. und Thomas R. Johnson, Denver, Colorado, USA.

to buy a Steinway[25]. There are other good pianos: the Mason and Hamlin[26] and the Baldwin[27]. But their prices will also be up. I hope we can get a piano out of this sacrifice but we may have to decide on a smaller one. If you have time you might inquire elsewhere. I don't have any desire to trade with American Nazis.

O. K., let's paint the house ourselves. I ought to come home in time enough to do it.

I don't understand the notice you got about the allotment.[28] My salary began with February 8th. By May 8th you should have 1800 dollars coming to you, and I should have the residue of this three months' pay.[29] May be it will be this way. I have had no salary check here as yet. Please let me know.[30]

Tomorrow is the 7th of May. I have been away from you three months and here two months. Three months more will be August 8th. And a month after that I should be pretty close to you if I am not already with you. That is really my only comfort. Goodnight my sweet beloved. I take all those caresses which my imagination conjures up, and I send you all of me. I love you, dearest, and I wonder why I am away from you. Kiss the boys for me. Edgar

Dok. 45
Schreiben an die Ehefrau
Berlin, 8. Mai 1946

To my dearest and sweetest one:

Today is a holiday here – the first anniversary of V-E day[1]. As a day it is a brilliant one. Bright warm sun – fresh breeze. The lake[2] is rough and the sail boats are having a wonderful time. I ought to be out sailing with my Captain Americus Mitchell[3] in his red boat. A year ago – on the first V-E day I was in Caserta[4]. I still of course remember the great relief of that day. It was finally over. I remember the delicious quality of the Italian spring day. OSS[5] gave a

---

[25] Siehe Dok. 4, Anm. 25.
[26] Die Firma Mason and Hamlin wurde 1854 von Henry Mason (1831–1890) und Emmons Hamlin (1821–1885) in Boston, Massachusetts, gegründet.
[27] Firmengründer war Dwight H. Baldwin (1821–1899).
[28] Siehe Mitteilung über die monatliche Zuweisung von 600 Dollar an Emily L. Johnson im Bildanhang, Abb. 19.
[29] Siehe Dok. 15.
[30] Emily L. Johnson in ihrem Schreiben vom 10./13. Mai 1946: "The only money I've received from your new job was 600 on May 10th or thereabouts. It was marked 'for April'. You'd better enquire about Febr. 8–April 1." Brief in: Unterlagen aus dem Nachlass Edgar N. Johnson, Privatbesitz Candice E. und Thomas R. Johnson, Denver, Colorado, USA.

[1] V-E day steht für "Victory-in-Europe day" und bezeichnet den 8. Mai 1945, an dem der Zweite Weltkrieg in Europa zu Ende ging.
[2] Großer Wannsee, eine Ausbuchtung der Havel (siehe Dok. 74, Anm. 24) im Südwesten Berlins.
[3] Siehe Dok. 41, Anm. 11.
[4] Stadt in der italienischen Region Kampanien. Siehe Dok. 37, Anm. 8.
[5] Office of Strategic Services. Siehe Dok. 1, Anm. 9.

party in the garden of the hunting lodge belonging to the present crown prince of Italy[6]. I shall always remember this garden for the lovely wisteria which hung from the iron railing. It was at this party that a student of mine turned up. This boy who helped to plaster our house and who had been bombing Vienna and other Austrian cities. I remember also that General McNarney[7] was at the party – the general who is now running Germany. It did not seem to me then that this was the way to celebrate V-E day. To-day, in so far as I know, there is no official celebration except that people are taking the day off – going sailing, playing golf. The Allies are not even celebrating the day together – the British are to be sure taking the day off. But the Russians are celebrating tomorrow with some kind of a parade.[8] We, I guess, are making some kind of a taken contribution to their celebration.

It is natural to ask what has been accomplished in this year, and to answer it fairly one would have to balance what was possible with what has really been done. Of course you know my general point of view. On the international level – in Austria and Germany – I take it that as much has been done as could be done. The machinery is still standing and it functions in the solution of minor problems. Some major problems of a negative sort (level of industry for a future Germany) have also been settled. This is something even though there is no possibility yet of making peace with Austria let alone Germany. And peace is even far off yet in re Italy, the Balkans and Finland. In our own sphere of action, that is in our zones, I think much more could have been done if we had begun to collaborate immediately with those Germans and Austrians whom we could trust. It took us a long time to get around to this. In Berlin we have not really done it yet in our sector. At lunch today (with Mr. Muccio[9] State Department, Don Heath[10], ditto, and a Mr. Chase[11], ditto) there was still talk of the de-Nazification problem. This cannot be settled in a short time, and certainly we have made much progress, but we could have made much more by acting in this manner from the beginning, by taking, that is, the proper people in our confidence. To be sure other important things have been done – the German armed forces have in large part been demobilized and sent home. The displaced persons,[12] have for the most part been taken care of. The people have been kept alive and sufficiently well treated to avoid any disorder. But it would not be

---

[6] Umberto (1904–1983), Mai/Juni 1946 als Umberto II. König von Italien.
[7] Siehe Dok. 17, Anm. 41.
[8] Am 9. Mai 1946 fand auf der Charlottenburger Chaussee im Verwaltungsbezirk Tiergarten vor dem sowjetischen Ehrenmal eine Parade statt, an der sowjetische, amerikanische, britische und französische Truppen teilnahmen. Siehe Berliner Zeitung vom 10. Mai 1946, [S. 1].
[9] Siehe Dok. 20, Anm. 21.
[10] Donald R. Heath. Siehe Dok. 8, Anm. 15.
[11] Warren M. Chase (1905–1994), amerikanischer Diplomat, 1925 BA, Amherst College, ab 1929 Department of State, 1937–1939 Hamburg, 1945–1948 Foreign Service Officer, Staff of US Political Adviser on German Affairs.
[12] Zivilpersonen nichtdeutscher Staatsangehörigkeit, die während des Zweiten Weltkriegs von den deutschen Besatzungsbehörden in das Gebiet des Deutschen Reiches aus ihrer Heimat verschleppt wurden. Siehe Juliane Wetzel, Displaced Persons (DPs), in: Deutschland unter alliierter Besatzung 1945–1949/55, hrsg. von Wolfgang Benz, Berlin 1999, S. 338–342.

correct to say that much of a positive nature has been done. I suppose it is too much to expect that one can act negatively and positively at the same time, though that is what has to be done here. I suppose that what we have done positively compares none too well with what the Russians have done positively in their zone. But we could not have done what they did – our economic stage at home forbids it. And what we have done has been done with methods which are infinitely preferable – and one can hope that they will ultimately get the kind of results which we want for Germany.

I will give you an example, however, of the difficulties under which we labor. There is being held in Hannover[13], tomorrow and Friday[14], a meeting of Social Democrats of the western zones, S[ocial] D[emocrat]s who are maintainig a position of independence over and against the KPD[15].[16] The leaders of the group of S[ocial] D[emocrat]s here who have fought the unity party wanted to attend this convention. The British managed to transport about 12 of them today in the personal plane, I believe, of Sir William Strang[17], Ambassador Murphy's[18] counterpart. The question arose of whether we could get a plane for the rest of them to go. It was the State Department people who took up this possibility and showed sympathy but at the last moment this morning, Ambassador Murphy took the view that the getting of a plane was an operational matter with which he had nothing to do. So Don Heath threw the matter into my lap at noon. The leaders have been kept waiting all day today in the hope that a plane might be made available. I have been in touch with two generals – my General Keating[19], and General Harper[20], the head of the armed forces division here. I have still to receive an answer from Harper but it seems that it is too late. The general was afraid that if it became known in the states that we were transporting German Civilian Social Democrats to a convention by plane, when we were saying at the same time that we did not have enough planes to fly our own soldiers, that there would be trouble. He is going to call Don Heath and let me know. I think I shall try an admiral before giving up, since I understand there is an admiral here with a plane of his own. But it is sickening. The situation is of course that the State Department doesn't want to take the responsibility. They want to pass the [responsibility] back to me. I don't believe there is much point

---

[13] Stadt in der britischen Besatzungszone Deutschlands, ab 1. November 1946 Hauptstadt des Landes Niedersachsen.
[14] 10. Mai 1946.
[15] Siehe Dok. 20, Anm. 12.
[16] Vom 9. bis 11. Mai 1946 fand in Hannover der Parteitag der SPD der drei Westzonen statt, auf dem die offizielle Neugründung der Partei vollzogen und Kurt Schumacher (siehe Dok. 39, Anm. 15) zum Parteivorsitzenden gewählt wurde.
[17] Sir William Strang (1893–1978), britischer Diplomat, ab 1919 Foreign Office, 1943–1945 Vertreter Großbritanniens in der European Advisory Commission, 1945–1947 Politischer Berater des Oberbefehlshabers der britischen Besatzungstruppen in Deutschland, 1947–1949 Unterstaatssekretär, Foreign Office, Leiter der Deutschlandabteilung.
[18] Siehe Dok. 8, Anm. 13.
[19] Siehe Dok. 39, Anm. 6.
[20] Robert W. Harper (1900–1982), Major General, 1945–1947 Director, Armed Forces Division, OMGUS.

to this political neutrality. How in the hell can you be neutral unless you don't give a damn. And what is the point of trying to go ahead and formally giving the appearance of supporting the S[ocial] D[emocrat]s when in a pinch you can't really support them. May be I'll go on see Murphy and ask him. If the S[ocial] D[emocrat]s don't receive some support from us their best men will go where they can get support – our Russian friends. And that support will be at the price of joining the unity party.

I love you my Sweetheart – there is no neutrality about that Col. Glaser[21] has left for a two weeks motor trip in England. When he mentioned it I could only think of our doing a motor trip in England next summer – and I guess that is, in substance – my chief reason for being willing to consider, staying over here for another year. Kiss my dear boys – and my dear beloved one let me take you very closely to me – Edgar

P. S. I just had a call from the General who could have arranged the air trip. He talked to Don Heath and when put to it Don Heath backed down in face of certain reasonable objections of the General – particularly the lateness of the request. So Don Heath is another Murphy when it comes to the test. This is the sort of thing which makes me want to come home. How can you defend political neutrality. It is clear that under the present circumstances to defend our political democracy is to defend the Social Democrats, but we really aren't ready to do it. It would be so easy to become cynical. E[dgar]

Dok. 46
Schreiben an die Ehefrau
Berlin, 9. Mai 1946

Dearest –

A lovely letter today written on the first.[1] It makes me rather lonesome for the good things I am missing. The things that after all are everything to me. It is your sweet self that writes the letter and tells me these things. You who are tending this garden and taking care of these wonderful children. There is a garden here tended by a professor. There are still tulips, wonderful blues, especially a deep purple stock, and thousands of pansies, and vigorous delphinium on the malls. But I can't react to them. I am becoming quite insensitive to the natural world about me. There is a nightingale about here, and a cuckoo and I do hear them. But it is a world I cannot absorb. It is you and your garden, – it is really yours now – that I should like to see, and this I think could open me up. Our "big and fat and dimpled Hi Timmy[2]" I have really never come to know and what you say of him does not make it easy to go on not knowing him. Our

---

[21] Siehe Dok. 28, Anm. 4.

[1] Emily L. Johnsons Brief vom 1. Mai 1946, in: Unterlagen aus dem Nachlass Edgar N. Johnson, Privatbesitz Candice E. und Thomas R. Johnson, Denver, Colorado, USA.

[2] Johnsons Sohn Thomas. Siehe Dok. 2, Anm. 16. Emily L. Johnson hatte geschrieben: "When he sees you, he says 'Hi, Timmy'."

sweet John going out with his May baskets, playing his Sonatina before the judges as you say we have come to expect he would play it and then going out to the recital on Sunday[3], this boy's growing life I am not experiencing. And what I am doing here has really no great importance, and will not have. I sometimes feel myself caught in the web of very ambitious people like Col. Glaser[4] even, and Col. Howley[5], who are out to make this show a pleasure and an adventure for themselves.

You say you have written Mrs. Zumwinkel[6]. It is just possible that she may have something for us, let us say for the month before school starts again. I hope so. I am ready to stop talking about staying over here, unless your reaction to my recent proposal is stronger than I think it is going to be. We might as well stop being tempted by a 10,000 dollar salary which we really don't believe in anyway, and to which we should never be proud of succumbing. The presence of so many wives over here does not help my present mood but I doubt if you would strike up much intimacy with them, and I sometimes doubt very much the quality of people who are staying over here. I suppose it is really no place for John and Hi-Timmy, and there would not be for you as there is not for me any pleasure in living in the midst of these poor people. The papers are already beginning to speak of a winter next year harder than the one which these people have gone through. So why should we continue to speculate and threaten to be adventurous. Why don't I say that I'll be home on or about September first. Tell me why.

I had a rather hurried and cool letter from Norman[7] today saying that Dad[8] had gotten a job repairing pianos in a music store and couldn't possibly be gotten away from Milwaukee[9] at the moment. He seems to be happy in his work and would not even take off a day to go with them to La Porte[10]. La Porte I guess is too painful for him now. He did go to Chicago recently to visit Auntie[11] and Mildred[12], but especially to go out to the cemetery[13] – the poor sweet man. How utterly lonesome he must be.

I love you my sweet and need you very very much – need you to share the days and nights, and to keep my zeal burning. I love you, my heart very tenderly. Edgar

---

[3] 5. Mai 1946.
[4] Siehe Dok. 28, Anm. 4.
[5] Siehe Dok. 20, Anm. 18.
[6] Essie Zumwinkel (1892–1981), Vermieterin von Ferienhäusern in den Rocky Mountains im US-Bundesstaat Colorado.
[7] Norman D. Johnson. Siehe Dok. 3, Anm. 13.
[8] Frank E. Johnson. Siehe Dok. 3, Anm. 12.
[9] Stadt im US-Bundesstaat Wisconsin.
[10] Stadt im US-Bundesstaat Indiana, wo Edgar N. Johnson die High School besucht hatte und seine Eltern einen Großteil ihres Lebens verbrachten.
[11] Hannah Walstrom. Siehe Dok. 4, Anm. 14.
[12] Mildred H. Williams. Siehe Dok. 4, Anm. 12.
[13] Zum Grab seiner Frau, Mabel A. Johnson, geb. Walstrom (1876–1944), Edgar N. Johnsons Mutter, geboren in Chicago, Illinois, Tochter von 1868 aus Schweden eingewanderten Eltern, heiratete 1895, starb am 29. Dezember 1944 in Chicago, wo sie auch beerdigt wurde.

Dok. 47
Schreiben an die Ehefrau
Berlin, Wannsee Hotel¹, Am Sandwerder 17/19, 11. Mai 1946

Dear Sweetheart –

I am very lonely and really am not able to take this very well. It is not only the wives, but now there are children. I believe a second boat-load has arrived.[2] Tonight at dinner, a little American lady, a little older than Hi-Timmy[3] did not appreciate the splendor of the Wannsee Hotel in Berlin. She protested so violently that her Mother had to carry her out – to the embarrassment of papa who was left alone at the table with his coffee. I leave you to imagine what was going through my mind during all this. I have perhaps made a fatal mistake in not insisting that I should stay over long enough this time to bring you along. Without that decision I can't bring you here, although I understand that it is possible to make application for your coming over just in case it should be possible later on. This, I think, I had better do.

I went down to sit on the pier a bit after my solitary meal in order to get rid of my melancholy. On the way back to the house I chatted a bit with the gardener[4] of this place. He has been here for 25 years. He first worked for an Englishman who was a member of the Reparations Commission after the last war.[5],[6] The next inhabitant was a Jewish banker (Anholt[7]) for whom he worked for

---

[1] Siehe Dok. 25, Anm. 9.
[2] Die ersten Ehefrauen und Kinder von amerikanischen Besatzungsangehörigen waren am 30. April 1946 in Berlin eingetroffen. Siehe Dok. 42, Anm. 13. Am 10. Mai 1946 kamen weitere Angehörige. Siehe More U. S. Families Come to OMGUS, in: OMGUS Observer vom 17. Mai 1946, S. 4.
[3] Johnsons Sohn Thomas, der damals 22 Monate alt war. Siehe Dok. 2, Anm. 16, und Dok. 46, Anm. 2.
[4] Albert Redmann (1891–1978).
[5] Die alliierte Reparationskommission setzte nach dem Ersten Weltkrieg die deutschen Reparationsverpflichtungen fest.
[6] Bei dem Mitglied der alliierten Reparationskommission in Berlin handelte es sich um den belgisch-britischen Botaniker und Geografen Dr. Marcel Hardy (1876-ca. 1944/1945), "who was selected to organize the Agricultural Section of the Commission". News and Notes, in: The American Journal of Sociology, Vol. 26, No. 4 (Januar 1921), S. 519–523, hier S. 520. Seine Tochter Miette (1899–1996) erinnert sich: "[...] Father was nominated as one of the five representatives of the Reparations Commission started in early 1920. Father went first and looked for a house for the family, as well as being briefed in what he was supposed to do in the Commission. And that was how we came to Berlin, Germany, in time to spend our first Christmas there, in a large well-appointed house in Wansee whose garden led right up the lake, where we were able to learn to skate in the winter and sail in the summer." Seven Chapters of Miette Dernbach's (née Hardy) Family Biography, S. 37, in: University of Strathclyde Archives, Glasgow, Großbritannien, T-MIN/31. Wie Miette mitteilt, war ihr Vater bis 1923 für die Reparationskommission tätig. Siehe ebd., S. 38f. Miette lernte in Berlin den Architekten Eckart Muthesius (1904–1989) kennen und heiratete ihn später. Siehe ebd., S. 37f. und 42. In zweiter Ehe war sie mit dem Bildhauer, Maler und Kunsthandwerker Joseph Dernbach-Mayen (1908–1990) verheiratet.
[7] Hans Arnhold (1888–1966), deutsch-amerikanischer Bankier, ab 1911 Repräsentant und ab 1918 Filialleiter des Bankhauses Gebr. Arnhold, Dresden, in Berlin, 1921 Umwandlung in Gebr. Arnhold, Dresden-Berlin, ab 1931 Interessengemeinschaft mit

sixteen years until 1938,[8] when the Nazis caught up with the Jewish banker and he had to flee to Holland.[9] It was at that moment that Herr Funk[10], the innocent Herr Funk of Nürnberg[11] took over the place.[12] Viewing the garden, however, did not help my mood much. I did not realize that the spinach we have been eating came from his garden. He has everything coming. There is much to learn from him. He has for example berry bushes – gooseberries and currants in the form of little trees, which could be easily strewn throughout our garden without interfering with the sun on the vegetables. And cherry trees which grow alongside of a wall – a modification of the ones we saw at Mount Vernon[13]. His gardening has brought him through the crises all right – Englishman – Jew – Nazi – Americans, and he goes on growing his flowers and his vegetables.

I learned today that a new job may be offered me. I went up to my office in the Director's Building[14] today to look over the stuff which, I had been told was coming into my office there. I had consented recently to its being occupied by a certain Col. Oppenheimer[15], who is a personal assistant to Clay[16] on matters of De-Nazification. When I saw him I recognized him as a man with whom I had had something to do in London. He was then working with a Special Legal Unit which was dealing with Austrian affairs.[17] He recognized me also and we had some talk, and then had lunch together in the Snack Bar next to the Director's Building. He is going home around May 20th and is looking for someone to

---

    dem Berliner Bankhaus S. Bleichröder, Emigration in die USA, Seniorpartner des Bankhauses Arnhold & S. Bleichroeder, Inc.

[8] Im Berliner Adreßbuch ist Hans Arnhold 1938 letztmals aufgeführt. Siehe Berliner Adreßbuch, 1938: Arnhold, Hans.

[9] Arnhold emigrierte in die USA, möglicherweise über Holland. "Forced to emigrate in 1938 because they were Jewish, the Arnhold family sold their property for a token price to the German Ministry of Finance. They moved first to Paris and then to New York City, where Hans Arnhold re-founded his banking partnership, Arnhold & S. Bleichroeder, which exists to this day." http://www.americanacademy.de/home/about-us/hans-arnhold-center/ (letzter Zugriff am 30. Januar 2013).

[10] Siehe Dok. 25, Anm. 10.

[11] Stadt im Land Bayern in der amerikanischen Besatzungszone Deutschlands.

[12] Im Berliner Adreßbuch werden ab 1940 das Reichswirtschaftsministerium als Eigentümer und Funk als Bewohner genannt. Siehe Berliner Adreßbuch, 1940–1943: Nikolassee, Am Sandwerder 17.19.

[13] Der ehemalige Landsitz des ersten Präsidenten der USA, George Washington (1732–1799), im US-Bundesstaat Virginia.

[14] Auf dem Gelände der OMGUS-Zentrale. Siehe Dok. 17, Anm. 45.

[15] Fritz E. Oppenheimer (1898–1968), deutsch-amerikanischer Jurist, Lieutenant Colonel, geboren in Berlin, Deutschland, 1922 Dr. jur., Universität Breslau, ab 1925 Anwalt für internationales Recht, Berlin, 1936 Emigration nach Großbritannien, 1940 USA, 1943–1946 US Army, 1945/1946 Special Assistant, OMGUS, verantwortlich für die Entnazifizierung, die deutsche Gesetz- und Gerichtsreform, Mitarbeit an der Ausarbeitung der von OMGUS und der Alliierten Kontrollbehörde erlassenen Gesetze, 1946–1948 Special Assistant for German-Austrian Affairs, Department of State.

[16] Siehe Dok. 2, Anm. 6.

[17] Beim gemeinsamen Hauptquartier der amerikanischen und britischen Expeditionsstreitkräfte (Supreme Headquarters, Allied Expeditionary Forces [SHAEF]) war Oppenheimer Mitarbeiter der Special Legal Unit – Germany/Austria (SLUGA) der Stabsabteilung für zivile Angelegenheiten (Civil Affairs Section [G-5]) gewesen.

take his place. In fact he told me that he had recommended to Clay that either Dorn[18] or I should take his place.[19]

He is the author of the plan to turn over the whole question of De-Nazification to the Germans in our zone. As you perhaps know from the press after long and rather extreme measures of our own to solve the De-Nazification problem – the matter was turned over to the Germans. This man is the author of the law which was finally worked out with the Germans, and accepted in our zone as the law for the final solution of the Nazi problem.[20] It is now in the process of being executed. All the Nazis in the zone have been registered, and they are to be tried in special tribunals and prosecuted by special prosecutors. In Bavaria[21] many of these tribunals have been set up, the prosecuting offices have been set up and things are ready to go. In Baden-Wurttemburg[22], and in Hesse[23] things are going a little bit more slowly. It would be my job, as a special assistant of Clay to see that the Germans push through this program successfully, to be responsible for any improvements in the system, to report on the progress made, and to be responsible for reporting on the political implications of the process. Oppenheimer thinks that if the machinery gets properly set up and is able to function, the De-Nazification of our zone ought to be carried through in about 9 months. It is of course a challenge of a kind. There have been many who have insisted that this task should never have been turned over to the Germans, and that they are bound to fail. It involves keeping in close touch with the De-Nazification machinery in the zone, with the Military Government officials with the German officials responsible, and coordinating the whole matter with the proper people here in Omgus[24]. It involves also attending the meetings of the De-Nazification Committee of the Länderrat[25] in Stuttgart[26]. I saw Oppenheimer's memorandum to Clay outlining the organization he would like to leave behind him and proposing my name, along with Dorn's,

---

[18] Siehe Dok. 2, Anm. 10.
[19] Dorn wurde dann im Juni 1946 zu Clays Personal Adviser on Denazification unter Beibehaltung seiner bisherigen Pflichten ernannt. Siehe Josef Henke/Klaus Oldenhage, Office of Military Government for Germany (U. S.), in: OMGUS-Handbuch. Die amerikanische Militärregierung in Deutschland 1945–1949, hrsg. von Christoph Weisz (= Quellen und Darstellungen zur Zeitgeschichte, Bd. 35), München 1994, S. 1-142, hier S. 45f.
[20] Gemeint ist das Gesetz zur Befreiung von Nationalsozialismus und Militarismus vom 5. März 1946, abgedruckt in: Sammlung der Länderratsgesetze (LRGS), o. O. und J., S. 95-112. Das Gesetz übertrug die praktische Durchführung der Entnazifizierung an deutsche Behörden. Zur Entnazifizierung siehe Angelika Königseder, Entnazifizierung, in: Deutschland unter alliierter Besatzung 1945–1949/55, hrsg. von Wolfgang Benz, Berlin 1999, S. 114-117.
[21] Land in der amerikanischen Besatzungszone Deutschlands.
[22] Gemeint ist das Land Württemberg-Baden in der amerikanischen Besatzungszone Deutschlands.
[23] Gemeint ist das Land Groß-Hessen in der amerikanischen Besatzungszone Deutschlands.
[24] Siehe Dok. 17, Anm. 45.
[25] Siehe Dok. 15, Anm. 10.
[26] Hauptstadt des Landes Württemberg-Baden in der amerikanischen Besatzungszone Deutschlands.

as his successor. How he came across my name, I don't know. He didn't identify me until today.

I don't know, of course, what decision Clay and Adcock[27] will make. But if the job comes to me I am inclined to take it. I have always been interested in the problem. I have always thought that it should be done with the help of the Germans. It is a job that has to be accomplished before much that is positive can go ahead. It involves the whole question of the Church and of Youth. In the case of the Church the un-de-Nazified condition of the clergy is simply scandalous. The job with Berlin District has lost a bit of its spice – now that General Barker[28] has gone. I think that Col. Glaser[29] would be only too glad to get rid of me, since my position as political advisor to the Commanding General sort of cramps his style. He is moreover a jealous and ambitious person, an advertising man, who takes, I think a certain amount of pleasure in shoving people about. This job involves acting on one's own. It gets me out of this island in the Soviet Zone Berlin, and in close touch with our own work in the zone. And what we do in our own zone in this respect may have something to do with the way in which the problem is handled in the rest of Germany. It might be nice to be able to say that you saw the De-Nazification policy through in Germany.

But it brings up again the question of our future together and this I shall not be able to let go unsolved for very much longer. The Berlin District job does not make it desirable that I should stay here any longer than next Fall. My staying here, from the standpoint of a job, depends upon either the Stuttgart or this de-Nazification job.[30] If the plan for a central administration for Germany goes through in the near future, the bottom is knocked out of the Stuttgart job, since, with a central administration for Germany, the Länderrat is no longer necessary. Besides, the Länderrat job is, as I have come to conceive of it, primarily a high-powered administrative job and as you will know I am not the best administrator in the world. Staying on here for the Stuttgart job is primarily to stay on for the 10,000 dollars and the possibility that we might do some traveling together next summer.

The de-Nazification job, however, aside from the 10,000 dollars and the same prospect of doing some traveling together next summer does bring a little more to the fore the motive of helping your government complete a job which it has more or less bungled heretofore and upon which it has now got a secure footing. I would promise, if Henry[31] agreed to let me go for another year, and you would agree to come over here with the boys, to see this thing through – since it could been seen through by the summer of next year.

---

[27] Siehe Dok. 14, Anm. 9.
[28] Siehe Dok. 20, Anm. 10.
[29] Siehe Dok. 28, Anm. 4.
[30] "The Stuttgart job appears from here the most important", schrieb Franz L. Neumann (siehe Dok. 1, Anm. 8) ein paar Tage später aus Washington, D. C., an Johnson. "That does not mean that the De-Nazification job is not important. It merely means that there ought to be more Edgar Johnsons in Germany." Schreiben vom 17. Mai 1946, in: UChicago Library, Special Collections Research Center, Edgar N. Johnson Papers.
[31] Charles Henry Oldfather. Siehe Dok. 2, Anm. 19.

I wonder if you could help me make this decision, or to get ready to make it. You must decide whether you would prefer to have me home by next Fall, or whether you would be willing to go to the trouble of bringing yourself and the boys over here by next Fall. There is still the advantage of a 10,000 salary for another year, and the opportunity of doing some travel, I think it ought to be in England, next summer.

If you decided that you wanted to come here, I should do my best to arrange for excellent quarters for you and the boys to live in. For our headquarters would be in Berlin. Moreover, you would be free, here, of responsibility for everything except management. It is easy and cheap enough to provide for cooks, maids, and even nurses for the children. I believe that most of this would be at government expense. If we made such a decision it would be, as I suggested in my previous letter, only for another year. We should then return to Nebraska. Sometimes I think we should take this chance. Suppose, for example, we never got back to Europe. I should do a much better job with you and the boys at my side, because then life would be full each day.

I've got to have you by my side either here or in Lincoln[32]. I am not trying to pass the buck to you, but in a sense it is really your decision. Do you want me there or do you want to come here? If you think of coming here you might sound out Henry on the possibility of another year without any tergiversation at the end of this period. There is something to be said for this war experience culminating in an experience which we really share on the spot. Here we could have some of the experience of a metropolitan existence – there is much opera and music here which I have no desire to go in for alone. There would also be a good music teacher for John[33] here. Personally I have no great desire for more European experience as such unless it be with you. I can't stand being alone. It is not good for me. These wives and children here make life unbearable and this hotel is obviously a place where they congregate.

I love you my darling and I want you close to me all the time. If you don't want to come here, I shall be in Lincoln in the Fall. I love you, my Emily. Edgar

Dok. 48
Schreiben an die Ehefrau
Berlin, 14. Mai 1946

Dear Sweet Ones:

I shan't have a decent chance to write a good letter until Thursday[1] but I must write a little note tonight, after the departure of guests, to say how much contentment recent letters[2] have brought, and the things which they contained.

---

[32] Hauptstadt des US-Bundesstaats Nebraska, wo Johnson mit seiner Familie wohnte und an der Universität lehrte.

[33] Johnsons Sohn John. Siehe Dok. 2, Anm. 15.

[1] 16. Mai 1946.

[2] Briefe in: Unterlagen aus dem Nachlass Edgar N. Johnson, Privatbesitz Candice E. und Thomas R. Johnson, Denver, Colorado, USA.

I was mad to come back here without my lovely pictures.³ The snaps have done my heart wonderfully good. The ones of you my dearest are the best thing I have seen since I left you. I love you, my sweet heart. The ones of the boys are simply grand. These precious and fine human beings. Then another letter contained John's⁴ recital program⁵ and another a description of his magisterial commencement of the program.⁶ I resent not being there to see him bring them to order, and to hear him play, and I'm glad for John's and Herbert's⁷ sake that it was an auspicious beginning (Eugene List⁸ has been hanging around here the last few days and I have longed to talk with him about John but there has been no chance)⁹. You also mention the first columbine, an experience of such intense delight that we seem to have shared similarly.¹⁰ And then you tell me that you are reading some papers for Ray Franz¹¹,¹². You are quite wonderful. You of course have nothing to do – but this temptation is too great. When I get back

---

3   Siehe Dok. 33 und Dok. 33, Anm. 58.
4   Johnsons Sohn John. Siehe Dok. 2, Anm. 15.
5   Als jüngster Teilnehmer hatte John sich am 5. Mai 1946 mit einem Klaviervortrag – Rondo in F des italienischen Komponisten Muzio Clementi (1752–1832) – an einer Veranstaltung der Lincoln Music Teachers' Association mit jungen Schülerinnen und Schülern beteiligt. Programmheft in: Unterlagen aus dem Nachlass Edgar N. Johnson, Privatbesitz Candice E. und Thomas R. Johnson, Denver, Colorado, USA. Siehe Bildanhang, Abb. 18.
6   Emily L. Johnson in ihrem Schreiben vom 6. Mai 1946: "[...] your little boy played at his recital. Herbert [Schmidt; siehe Dok. 29, Anm. 12] termed it an 'auspicious beginning'. Poor dear, he was the only 6 year old, and he had to play first. It was a very noisy audience, and John just sat and calmly looked at them waiting for silence, which he finally got! He played very well indeed."
7   Herbert Schmidt. Siehe Dok. 29, Anm. 12.
8   Eugene List (1918–1985), amerikanischer Pianist.
9   Eugene List und seine Ehefrau, die Violinistin Carroll Glenn List, geb. Glenn (1918–1983), hatten am 11. Mai 1946 ein gemeinsames Konzert im Titania-Palast in der Schloßstraße im Berliner Verwaltungsbezirk Steglitz gegeben, "for an audience of U. S. and Allied Troops. [...] After their Berlin engagement List and his wife will go to Prague, Czechoslovakia, where they will represent the U. S. in the forthcoming Prague International Music Festival. Before their return to the U. S., this couple will give concerts in Paris, Budapest, Vienna and Rome." Lists to Give Joint Recital At Titania, in: OMGUS Observer vom 10. Mai 1946, S. 2. Siehe Barbara E. Scott Fisher, Carroll and Eugene List Carry Musical Language of Good Will Overseas. Young Artists Share Careers In Work, Play, in: The Christian Science Monitor vom 8. Mai 1946, S. 13; List, Pianist, Returns From Tour Of Europe, in: The New York Times vom 19. Juni 1946, S. 17.
10 Emily L. Johnson in ihrem Schreiben vom 6. Mai 1946: "Do you remember our *first* sight of a columbine, on the path up among the rocks behind the Gasses [siehe Dok. 63, Anm. 29] cabin at Evergreen [siehe Dok. 63, Anm. 31]? I'll never forget it. You just can't believe such a flower is possible."
11 Ray W. Frantz. Siehe Dok. 11, Anm. 15.
12 Emily L. Johnson in ihrem Schreiben vom 6. Mai 1946: "Ray Frantz called me tonight and asked if I'd read his exam papers and a few English 21 papers he now has on hand. His reader has gone to the hospital all of a sudden + he's left in a pinch – I shouldn't do it, but I'm terribly flattered that anyone should think after 10 years that I've brains enough to read English papers." Im Juni 1935 hatte sie den Bachelor of Arts in Englisch und Geschichte an der University of Nebraska erworben.

to you that is one thing I shall never neglect again – sharing a rich intellectual life with you. You must let me. I can't say either that I was not pleased to be put on the Council of the Mediaeval Academy[13].[14] These things, combined with your comments on coming over here, lead to one conclusion which I think you know. I love my sweet ones very much, and I feel rather close to them tonight. I wish I really were. Such treasures, Edgar

Dok. 49
Schreiben an die Ehefrau
Berlin, Wannsee Officers' Club[1], Am Sandwerder 17/19, 19. Mai 1946

My beloved Emily –

I am a bit lonesome this morning after what has been a rather strenuous week. I feel a great need of talking to you. I have read your recent letters[2] over again and they have comforted me, and of course, now, I have always the new snaps[3] in front of me. These are fine likenesses of my dear ones in that batch.

On Monday[4] evening I had dinner with the Colonel in Military Government, Berlin District,[5] who has charge of labor. It is Colonel Abe Kramer[6] who has had a tremendous amount of experience with the National Labor Relations Board[7]. He had just come back from the Leipzig[8] Fair[9]. The Russians put them-

[13] The Mediaeval Academy of America, 1925 gegründet. Siehe http://www.medievalacademy.org/ (letzter Zugriff am 30. Januar 2013).
[14] Johnson war auf dem am 27. April 1946 in Cambridge, Massachusetts, abgehaltenen 21. Annual Meeting of the Corporation of the Mediaeval Academy of America zum Mitglied des Council (Councillor) gewählt worden. Siehe Historical News, in: The American Historical Review, Vol. 51, No. 4 (Juli 1946), S. 788–804, hier S. 794f.; The Mediaeval Academy of America. Proceedings of the Twenty-first Annual Meeting of the Corporation 1946, in: Speculum, Vol. 21, No. 3 (Juli 1946), S. 362–375, hier S. 362. Bis 1949 blieb Johnson Mitglied des Council.

[1] Siehe Dok. 25, Anm. 9.
[2] Briefe in: Unterlagen aus dem Nachlass Edgar N. Johnson, Privatbesitz Candice E. und Thomas R. Johnson, Denver, Colorado, USA.
[3] Gemeint sind Fotos von der Ehefrau und den Söhnen. Siehe Dok. 48.
[4] 13. Mai 1946.
[5] Siehe Dok. 25, Anm. 13.
[6] Abe Kramer (1908–1968), Major, 1941/1942 Field Examiner, National Labor Relations Board, 1942–1947 US Army, 1946/1947 Chief, Manpower Branch, OMGBD/OMGBS, 1947–1949 Deputy Manpower Adviser, OMGBY.
[7] Die 1935 gegründete Bundesbehörde für Arbeitsbeziehungen, organisiert Wahlen zur Zulassung von Gewerkschaften als Repräsentanten in Betrieben und ermittelt wegen unfairer Arbeitsbedingungen.
[8] Stadt im Land Sachsen in der sowjetischen Besatzungszone Deutschlands.
[9] Älteste und bedeutendste Warenmesse Deutschlands. Vom 8. bis 12. Mai 1946 hatte die erste Leipziger Nachkriegsmesse stattgefunden. Vertreten waren Aussteller aus allen vier Besatzungszonen und der Sowjetunion. "In the 2,750 exhibits were household items, stoves, refrigerators, dresses and furs, jewelry, textile goods, and all the other sundry articles formerly turned out by the nation's industry." Leipzig Fair, in: OMGUS Observer vom 17. Mai 1946, S. 5.

selves out to arrange a good show in Leipzig (I should have gone perhaps). There was much on display but absolutely nothing to sell, and of course no raw materials to make anything with. All the Americans who went had the experience of being stopped many times by Germans and asked when the Russians were leaving, and when we were coming back (we had Leipzig to begin with you remember[10]). But the Germans are only doing what the Austrians were doing when we came in there. I am sick of this kind of talk, and incidentally, sick of the Germans as well. But I suppose there is no helping the fact that after 12 years of anti-Russian talk, of the war, and of experience with the Russians they should feel this way. And they know very well of course that quadripartite relations do not run very smoothly. But their attitude, in that it contributes to hostility is no good. If it leads, or helps to lead to war they are the chief sufferers. And I don't like to have them deliberately try to stimulate the differences. An assistant Burger-meister of Kreuzberg[11] told my driver[12] the other day that he was sure that the U. S. and Britain would soon present an ultimatum to the Russians telling them to get out of Germany. Kramer is a leftist and labor union man, and he went through the history of this fight to get them into some kind of line. The unions are organized into one large federation here and it is largely under the control of the Communists, many of them trained in Russia.[13] It is supposed to be unpolitical, but as a matter of fact it has gone over strongly to the new SED party. In its organizational steps it has thumbed its nose pretty consistently at the Allies and gone its own way, and it threatens to do so again with new elections which it is planning to hold in the various industrial branches of the union. The Russians permit no employers' associations (we do) and consequently in their zone the unions have a pretty strong hand, and they are making strong demands to share in the complete management of the plants. But there is going to be more and more unemployment here since stocks of raw materials are dwindling. Kramer was a comfort. There are few men so capable and so energetic here, and I am glad he is planning to stay on. But he has only one or two people help him control the labor activities of a huge city, and of the American sector of it.

---

[10] Im April 1945 war Leipzig von amerikanischen Truppen besetzt worden. Nach dem Rückzug in die ihnen im Londoner Protokoll (siehe Dok. 83, Anm. 88) zugewiesene Besatzungszone kam die Stadt unter sowjetische Kontrolle.

[11] 1. stellvertretender Bürgermeister des Berliner Verwaltungsbezirks Kreuzberg war Georg Henschel (1912–1981), SPD, 2. stellvertretender Bürgermeister war Karl Krüger, parteilos.

[12] Artur Sanow. Siehe Dok. 40, Anm. 13.

[13] Zum Freien Deutschen Gewerkschaftsbund (FDGB), der im Februar 1946 für die gesamte Sowjetzone in Berlin gegründet worden war, siehe Werner Müller, Freier Deutscher Gewerkschaftsbund (FDGB), in: SBZ-Handbuch. Staatliche Verwaltungen, Parteien, gesellschaftliche Organisationen und ihre Führungskräfte in der Sowjetischen Besatzungszone Deutschlands 1945–1949, im Auftrag des Arbeitsbereiches Geschichte und Politik der DDR an der Universität Mannheim und des Instituts für Zeitgeschichte München hrsg. von Martin Broszat/Hermann Weber, München 1990, S. 626–664; Michael Fichter, Gewerkschaften, in: Deutschland unter alliierter Besatzung 1945–1949/55, hrsg. von Wolfgang Benz, Berlin 1999, S. 129–134.

On Tuesday[14] I had dinner with Rodnick[15] and his wife[16]. Do you remember my talking about Rodnick, a cultural anthropologist who uses the word culture and pattern so many times in every five minutes as to make you sick. They did an interesting thing while working for the Information Control Services branch here.[17] They went to a little town in Hesse, Eschwege[18], close to the Russian and the French borders[19] and sat down there for a period of about six months to find out what was going on. They got to know most of the people of the town and had occasion to watch the detailed activity of military government there. It was a sad picture they paint both of the Germans and of military government, so sad that I was utterly in despair when they left and wondered whether there was actually any hope in the Germans, or indeed in us, and whether, if this was the general situation prevailing in our zone, we should not simply get out of here and not bother with a job for which we are not fitted either by experience or interest. This was worse than Upper Austria[20], and Rodnick evidently had some of the spirit in him that we had when in Austria. Walter Dorn[21] says his report was not fair. Dorn had to go down and fire the Military Government officer. Well – it was not so much that there was anything happening in Eschwege that we have not heard about but that it was all lumped together in one little place, having an altogether disastrous effect on the Germans. Much drunkenness, for example. Officers starting to drink around noon, then going out and

---

[14] 14. Mai 1946.
[15] David Rodnick (1908–1980), amerikanischer Soziologe und Anthropologe, 1936 PhD, University of Pennsylvania, arbeitete während des Zweiten Weltkriegs für das OSS, 1947–1951 Berater, Columbia University, Project in Contemporary Cultures, 1955–1959 Assistent Director, Institute for International Social Research, Princeton, New Jersey, 1959–1961 Professor, Interamerican University, Puerto Rico, 1961–1963 Professor of Sociology and Anthropology, Iowa Wesleyan College, 1963–1965 Senior Sociologist, Operations Research, Inc., Washington, D. C., 1965–1975 Professor of Sociology and Anthropology, Texas Technological University, 1975–1977 Gastprofessor, Universität Hamburg. "Following World War II, he began cultural analysis of European countries and cultures including posts at the Office of Military Government in occupied Germany, the Paris office of Air University, the University of Oslo, Columbia University, and Princeton University. In the 1950s he became a professor at Inter-American University, San German, Puerto Rico, before moving to Iowa Wesleyan College and then Texas Technological University (1965-1975)." http://www.lib.utexas.edu/taro/utcah/02351/cah-02351.html (letzter Zugriff am 30. Januar 2013).
[16] Elizabeth A. Rodnick, geb. Amis (1911–1999), arbeitete während des Zweiten Weltkriegs für das OSS.
[17] David Rodnick schreibt später in der Einleitung zu seinem Buch "Postwar Germans. An Anthropologist's Account": "The book is based on five months of intensive anthropological field work in central and northeastern Hesse, carried on with the assistance of my wife, Elizabeth Amis Rodnick, between December, 1945, and June, 1946, as part of our duties with the Information Control Division of the Office of Military Government." David Rodnick, Postwar Germans. An Anthropologist's Account, New Haven, Connecticut, 1948, S. IX.
[18] Kleinstadt im Nordosten des Landes Groß-Hessen in der amerikanischen Besatzungszone Deutschlands.
[19] Eschwege lag in der Nähe der sowjetischen, aber nicht der französischen Besatzungszone Deutschlands.
[20] Oberösterreich grenzte an die damalige Tschechoslowakei und Deutschland.
[21] Siehe Dok. 2, Anm. 10.

trying to play ball with German kids, unable to do so and falling down and having to be picked up. Mistresses – the Rodnicks claim they were put up in a house where four M[ilitary] G[overnment] officers were openly living with Fräuleins – indeed one of the bedrooms was always open and the blue silk night dress of one of the ladies always draped over the bed in proud display. Black Market[22]. The PX[23] supplies coming into town for a small contingent of M[ilitary] G[overnment] officers were originally sent for a whole company which had as a matter of fact gone but the supplies continued to come in the same amount. The Rodnicks were offered 48 chocolate bars each for one week. This in addition to all the rest including cameras and radios. You know where most of this went. They told me the story of 2 GI's[24] who took 2 cartons of cigarettes from the bed of a captain and arranged between them that one was to sell it to a black market dealer and the other was to hi-jack the dealer on the way home. The cigarettes were accordingly returned to the bed of the captain who was annoyed, not because of their dishonesty but because they had not informed him they were taking the cigarettes away. The situation in the local government is bad if not worse than what we found in Upper Austria. The Nazis in and the anti-Nazis out or in very unimportant positions, and this because the M[ilitary] Governor thought that the Nazis were the right people to turn over things to. They were the kind of people he would deal with at home, whereas the anti-Nazis were riff-raff-no-account. All this was accompanied by a perfectly cold-blooded attitude to the whole situation. The Rodnicks were told by officers that they knew of course that at home they would have to occupy a very small and unimportant position in life. But here they were cock of the walks – they ran the government and the people as they never could do at home, and by God they were going to stay here just as long as they could. In fact one of them said he was going to stay at least until he had made 20,000 dollars. I only hope Eschwege is not typical. Walter Dorn says that it is not but he has concern about the growing resentment of the Germans in the zone to us. Here people say we are Bolshevists with creased trousers. What the Rodnicks had to say about the Germans themselves was not encouraging. They visited schools and youth groups, political meetings and they like and had nothing to report of initiative, vitality, or ideas. This of course can't be expected. But you have got to have some groups upon which you can depend. May be these people are really hopeless.

Wednesday[25] night I had dinner with a British Major Hayes[26] who is Chairman of the Local Government Committee in the Kommandatura[27], and who is leaving. His place is being taken by a Major Ashton[28], a merchant from Liver-

---

22 Siehe Dok. 21, Anm. 11.
23 Post Exchange, Verkaufsläden der amerikanischen Streitkräfte.
24 Government Issues, ugs. für amerikanische Soldaten.
25 15. Mai 1946.
26 Harold Hays (1896–1980), Major, Administration and Local Government Section, Military Government British Troops Berlin (MGBTB), britischer Vertreter im Local Government Committee, Allied Kommandatura Berlin. Fotos mit Hays im Bildanhang, Abb. 68 und Abb. 77.
27 Siehe Dok. 29, Anm. 14.
28 John Pennington Ashton (1891–1978), Major, 1953/1954 Mayor of Wallasey (bei Liverpool in England).

pool[29] who has dealt with cotton in Texas[30].[31] The dinner was in a British Mess and it was put on in considerable style. The French and Russians were invited but the Russians as usual did not show up. The Frenchman had been in the banking business. At the conclusion of the dinner there was a toast to the king. I almost made the mistake of smoking before it but I was warned by Ashton that it was not done. Nobody smokes before the toast. The table is cleared of everything except one glass of wine per person. The person presiding stands. All stand. Then he says, "Mr. *Vice* – (this is the person at the other end of the table) I give you the King." And Mr. Vice says "To the King." And they all drink, and that is that. The Major Ashton is proud to belong to a regiment whose history stretches back to the Revolution[32], and he was afraid that the Labor Government might break up these old regiments and these fine traditions. I don't see that they do any harm. I heard from Major Hayes much criticism of English Military Government. I don't suppose they really make much more of an impression than we. But they are much more willing to impose their way upon the Germans than we are. It was the same in Austria. They have had a much larger time to get used to doing things in a certain way, and it seems therefore natural to them but that others should do it in the same way. They annoy the Russians, I am afraid, very very much. Yet they are comparatively easy to get along with, and you don't have to be afraid of trickery at least where they are concerned.

Thursday[33] I should have written you but I was completely worn out and went to bed. On Friday[34] Robert Eisenberg[35] (OSS[36] Washington) invited me over to dinner with three Germans, one Herr Mommsen[37], grandson of the

[29] Stadt an der Nordwestküste Englands.
[30] US-Bundesstaat.
[31] Ashton vertrat Hays als Vertreter Großbritanniens im Local Government Committee und als Chairman in den Sitzungen am 17., 23. und 31. Mai 1946. Siehe Protokoll der 18. Sitzung des Local Government Committee, Allied Kommandatura Berlin, am 17. Mai 1946, LG/M (46) 18, englischsprachige Fassung, in: TNA, Allied Kommandatura: Directives, Minutes and Papers, FO 1112/378; Protokoll der 19. Sitzung des Local Government Committee, Allied Kommandatura Berlin, am 23. Mai 1946, LG/M (46) 19, englischsprachige Fassung, in: ebd.; Protokoll der 20. Sitzung des Local Government Committee, Allied Kommandatura Berlin, am 31. Mai 1946, LG/M (46) 20, englischsprachige Fassung, in: ebd.; Protokoll der 21. Sitzung des Local Government Committee, Allied Kommandatura Berlin, am 31. Mai 1946, LG/M (46) 21, englischsprachige Fassung, in: ebd.
[32] Gemeint ist die Glorious Revolution von 1688, durch die der Stuartkönig James II. (1633–1701) vertrieben wurde und seine Tochter als Königin Maria II. (1662–1694) mit ihrem Gemahl Wilhelm III. von Oranien (1650–1702) den englischen Thron bestieg.
[33] 16. Mai 1946.
[34] 17. Mai 1946.
[35] Robert Eisenberg (1908–1987), amerikanischer Jurist, geboren in Waidhofen, Niederösterreich, 1931 Dr. jur., Deutsche Universität Prag, 1939 Emigration nach Italien und Frankreich, 1941 USA, 1943 US-Staatsbürgerschaft, 1943–1945 US Army (OSS), 1945–1968 Department of State.
[36] Office of Strategic Services. Siehe Dok. 1, Anm. 9. Gemeint ist hier eine Nachfolgebehörde des OSS.
[37] Konrad Mommsen (1896–1973), deutscher Kaufmann, in der NS-Zeit wegen Unterstützung versteckt lebender Juden zu einer Gefängnisstrafe von sechs Monaten verurteilt, nach 1945 Berater der amerikanischen Militärregierung.

famous classical historian[38] and a friend of Felix Gilbert's[39], a Herr Haas[40] who is the treasurer of the city of Berlin, and a Willi Brandt[41], a Marxist professor at the Russian controlled University of Berlin[42]. It was an interesting evening, a good deal of it being spent on the Nurnberg[43] trials[44] in condemnation of

[38] Theodor Mommsen (1817–1903), deutscher Altertumswissenschaftler, 1902 für sein monumentales Werk „Römische Geschichte" mit dem Nobelpreis für Literatur geehrt.

[39] Felix Gilbert (siehe Dok. 1, Anm. 11) war ebenso wie Konrad Mommens Bruder Theodor Ernst Mommsen (1905–1958) ein aus Deutschland stammender Historiker, beide waren Schüler von Friedrich Meinecke (siehe Dok. 1, Anm. 11) gewesen, und beide waren in den 1930er-Jahren in die USA emigriert.

[40] Friedrich Haas (1896–1988), deutscher Jurist und Politiker (CDU), Studium der Naturwissenschaften, Volkswirtschaft und Rechtswissenschaft, Universitäten Freiburg im Breisgau und München, 1922 Promotion zum Dr. oec. publ., 1925–1928 Hilfsrichter für Besatzungsschäden beim Reichswirtschaftsgericht, Berlin, 1929–1931 Tätigkeit als Magistratsrat in der Bezirksverwaltung Charlottenburg, ab 1931 in der Hauptverwaltung der Stadt Berlin (ab 1937 als Obermagistratsrat, ab 1938 als Stadtdirektor), bis 1933 Deutsche Zentrumspartei, 1945 CDU, Oktober–Dezember 1945 stellvertretender Leiter des Rechtsamts, ab Dezember 1945 stellvertretender Leiter der Finanzabteilung des Magistrats, in dieser Position März–Dezember 1946 kommissarischer Leiter der Finanzabteilung (Abteilung A), Dezember 1946–1951 Leiter der Magistratsabteilung für Finanzen (Stadtkämmerer), 1951–1958 Senator für Finanzen, gleichzeitig 1953–1955 Senator für Bundesangelegenheiten, 1958–1961 Präsident des Oberverwaltungsgerichts Berlin. Foto von Haas im Bildanhang, Abb. 83.

[41] Gemeint ist der deutsche Jurist Dr. Günter Brandt (1894–1968), „einer der heute völlig vergessenen unabhängig-linken Köpfe der Berliner Intellektuellenszene der Jahre 1945–48". Wolfgang Schivelbusch, Vor dem Vorhang. Das geistige Berlin 1945–1948, München und Wien 1995, S. 273. Gemeinsam mit Konrad Mommsen und Arno Scholz (siehe Dok. 40, Anm. 10) hatte Günter Brandt bei der britischen Militärregierung die Lizenzierung der Zeitung „Telegraf" (siehe Dok. 40, Anm. 10) beantragt, als Lizenzträger trat dann aber nur Scholz auf, Mommsen war abgesprungen, „weil Scholz sich geweigert hatte, mit Brandt, einem Kommunisten, zusammenzuarbeiten". Peter Köpf, Die Mommsens. Von 1848 bis heute – die Geschichte einer Familie ist die Geschichte der Deutschen, Hamburg, Leipzig und Wien 2004, S. 85. Brandt wurde Chefredakteur der vom Kulturbund zur demokratischen Erneuerung Deutschlands herausgegebenen Wochenzeitung „Sonntag", die erstmals im Juli 1946 erschien. Außerdem schrieb er regelmäßig für „Die Weltbühne". Brandt war Professor mit Lehrauftrag für bürgerliches Recht an der Universität Berlin, ab 1950 lehrte er an der Freien Universität Berlin.

[42] 1810 gegründete, am 29. Januar 1946 feierlich wiedereröffnete Universität. Zur Sicherstellung des sowjetkommunistischen Einflusses auf die Universität heißt es bei Reimer Hansen, Neuer Name in historischer Tradition. Von der Friedrich-Wilhelms- zur Humboldt-Universität 1945–1949, in: Berlin in Geschichte und Gegenwart. Jahrbuch des Landesarchivs Berlin 2009, S. 349–375, hier S. 373: „Nach der auf den Kriegskonferenzen in Jalta und Potsdam vereinbarten Deutschlandpolitik der ‚Großen Drei' sollte Berlin keiner der Besatzungszonen angehören und von der Alliierten Kommandantur und dem Berliner Magistrat verwaltet werden. Die Deutsche Zentralverwaltung für Volksbildung riss jedoch mit konspirativer Billigung der Sowjetischen Militäradministration die Zuständigkeit für die Universität an sich. Hiermit war die Universität widerrechtlich der kommunistischen sowjetischen Militär- und deutschen Zivilverwaltung der sowjetischen Besatzungszone unterstellt worden."

[43] Nürnberg, Stadt im Land Bayern in der amerikanischen Besatzungszone Deutschlands.

[44] Nürnberger Prozess gegen 22 Hauptkriegsverbrecher und sechs als verbrecherisch angeklagte Organisationen. Die Verhandlung fand vor einem eigens eingerichteten

Schacht[45] and in ridicule of Raeder[46]. But I was discouraged about the way these Germans talk about each other. They were quite insistent, and this was a sound note, that the Germans should pursue an internationalist line rather than their present nationalist one. But they called the Germans simply political idiots who could not now be trusted with the management of their own affairs. Brandt told the story of being at a movie where shots were displayed of the Nurnberg and Dachau[47] trials[48], at the latter of which the Mauthausen[49] boys[50] were being tried, that ugly bunch which I saw in their cells when I was there. When Jackson[51] appeared on the screen, the lady next to him leaned over to him and said that he looked like a war criminal, and when the criminals themselves were shown she commented on what fine looking Germans they were. Brandt said nothing. When the Mauthausen murderers were shown she broke out again with the remark that they were such fine looking men. He then had to silence her with the remark, "Were you ever in Mauthausen." She just took it for granted that any German in the audience would share her point of view. I am afraid this has to be a very long occupation, and that we have to make very long range plans. These people have literally to be re-educated over a long

Ad-hoc-Tribunal, dem Internationalen Militärgerichtshof, statt und dauerte vom 20. November 1945 bis zum 1. Oktober 1946. Siehe Heinz Boberach, Strafrechtliche Verfolgung von NS-Verbrechen, in: Deutschland unter alliierter Besatzung 1945–1949/55, hrsg. von Wolfgang Benz, Berlin 1999, S. 181–186; Manfred Görtemaker, Rache der Sieger oder Suche nach Gerechtigkeit? Der Nürnberger Hauptkriegsverbrecherprozess 1945/46, in: Die Vier Mächte in Berlin. Beiträge zur Politik der Alliierten in der besetzten Stadt, hrsg. von Michael Bienert/Uwe Schaper/Andrea Theissen unter Mitarbeit von Werner Breunig (= Schriftenreihe des Landesarchivs Berlin, Bd. 9), Berlin 2007, S. 133–145.

[45] Hjalmar Schacht (1877–1970), deutscher Bankier und Politiker, 1923–1930 Reichswährungskommissar und Reichsbankpräsident, 1933–1939 erneut Reichsbankpräsident und 1934–1937 zugleich Reichswirtschaftsminister, 1935–1937 Reichsbevollmächtigter für Wehrwirtschaft, 1937 bis 1943 Reichsminister ohne Geschäftsbereich, 1944/1945 KZ, wurde vom Internationalen Militärgerichtshof in Nürnberg gegen die Hauptkriegsverbrecher angeklagt und freigesprochen.

[46] Erich Raeder (1876–1960), deutscher Marineoffizier, 1928 Beförderung zum Admiral, 1928–1935 Chef der Marineleitung, 1935–1943 Oberbefehlshaber der Kriegsmarine, 1939 Beförderung zum Großadmiral, vom Internationalen Militärgerichtshof in Nürnberg zu lebenslanger Haft verurteilt, 1955 aus gesundheitlichen Gründen entlassen.

[47] Stadt nordwestlich von München im Land Bayern in der amerikanischen Besatzungszone Deutschlands.

[48] Die Dachauer Prozesse waren Militärgerichtsprozesse der US-Armee gegen Angeklagte, denen Kriegsverbrechen und Verbrechen gegen die Menschlichkeit vorgeworfen wurden. Sie fanden von 1945 bis 1948 im Internierungslager Dachau statt, wo sich bis Ende April 1945 das Konzentrationslager Dachau befunden hatte.

[49] Gemeint ist das Konzentrationslager Mauthausen in Oberösterreich, in dem zwischen 1938 und 1945 mehr als 200 000 Personen inhaftiert waren, von denen etwa die Hälfte ermordet wurde.

[50] Gemeint ist das Lagerpersonal des Konzentrationslagers Mauthausen, gegen das vom 29. März bis zum 13. Mai 1946 im Mauthausen-Hauptprozess, dem zweiten Dachauer Prozess, verhandelt wurde.

[51] Robert H. Jackson (1892–1954), amerikanischer Jurist, 1940/1941 US Attorney General, 1941–1954 Associate Justice, US Supreme Court, 1945/1946 US Chief Prosecutor, International Military Tribunal, Nürnberg.

period by themselves but under our direction. I think now we should go very slowly in letting them resume responsibility for themselves over anything like a centralized state.

Last night I had dinner or rather an after dinner talk with this Mrs. Delahaye[52], whom I have mentioned.[53] I waited for 45 minutes for my driver to come and get me but he didn't show up. On the way home from here in the afternoon, he had been picked up by the MP's[54] for speeding – they are terribly strict here because of the numerous accidents – and kept waiting until about 11:30 last night in the MP police station. He called me about mid-night and was rather furious, I gathered. I had to rescue him once before from the MP's for leaving his car open while he was in his house. He was doubtful last night if they would continue him in his job, but said he could get other work. He insisted they would not let him call me. I shall intervene for him if I can but I was certainly at a loss last night. When I got to Harnack house[55] this Russian lady has already begun to eat. Afterwards our conversation was a bit trivial and she left early. I had a difficult time in getting back to the hotel. Our car got lost and never arrived, but I finally got another from the Berlin District Motor Pool. There was drinking and dancing at Harnack house. I noticed they are now selling wine with meals and most people had bottles. When I went home there was a very unpleasant drunken scene in front of the house. A belligerent officer whom they couldn't get into a cab. I am afraid there is far too much drinking here, by the wrong kind of people. I don't like the looks of many I see about me. We just aren't a colonial people, and for many this is just another racket.

There have been many meetings during the week. I took Col. Glaser's[56] place at a meeting of the Local Government Committee[57],[58] We were supposed to talk about future elections in Berlin but the Russians don't want to talk about elections in Berlin. They stalled unmercifully at the last meeting and at this meeting the Russian Major Feldman[59], a rather nice chap, wasted one hour and

---

52 Johnsons Deutschlehrerin. Siehe Dok. 40, Anm. 27.
53 Siehe Dok. 40.
54 Military Police officers.
55 Siehe Dok. 15, Anm. 16.
56 Siehe Dok. 28, Anm. 4. Glaser befand sich auf einer Englandreise. Siehe Dok. 45.
57 Siehe Dok. 29, Anm. 14.
58 Siehe Protokoll der 18. Sitzung des Local Government Committee, Allied Kommandatura Berlin, am 17. Mai 1946, LG/M (46) 18, englischsprachige Fassung, in: TNA, Allied Kommandatura: Directives, Minutes and Papers, FO 1112/378.
59 Iossif Moissejewitsch Feldman (geb. 1905), sowjetischer Major, 1928 WKP(B), 1927–1937 und wieder ab 1939 Rote Armee, 1930 Absolvent der Militärtechnischen Luftfahrtschule, 1941 Absolvent des Leningrader Instituts für Sprachen, 1945 stellvertretender Chefredakteur der „Berliner Zeitung", SMAD-Zensor, 1946–1949 stellvertretender Chefredakteur der „Täglichen Rundschau", Chefredakteur des „Nacht-Expreß", 1949 als Mitarbeiter der Informationsverwaltung der SMAD unter Spionageverdacht verhaftet und in die Sowjetunion verbracht. Wolfgang Schivelbusch schreibt: „Feldmann war, wie die SMAD-Mitarbeiterin Eugenia Kazewa sich erinnert, einer der in der Informationsabteilung so zahlreich vertretenen jüdischen Leningrader Intellektuellen, ein ‚kleiner runder beweglicher und sehr schlauer Mann'." Wolfgang Schivelbusch, Vor dem Vorhang. Das geistige Berlin 1945–1948, München und Wien 1995, S. 262. Der britische Vertreter im Local Government Committee, Harold Hays (siehe

a half quarrelling over the minutes. He resents the English particularly, resented something Major Hayes had inserted into the minutes, and because his own translation was inaccurate there was a long fuss. In fact the whole afternoon was wasted. There was also a Kommandatura[60] meeting in the morning at which nothing important happened.[61] But things will soon begin to happen there again. The pro-merger SPD people have written what I think is an intolerably fresh letter to the Kommandatura.[62] Yesterday[63] I went to a meeting of the Political Directorate[64] (Don Heath[65] + opposites) at which the question of the recognition of SPD + SED came up, and went through this for. Don called me to his side in the course of the discussion. The tone of this meeting was very different. Quick, rapid-fire negotiation unlike anything I have ever seen. The Russian, Ivanov[66], about the smoothest Russian I have seen here. He made slighting remarks about Commandants. It was so quick it was difficult for me to follow. For this kind of exchange you have to be very skilled and very experienced. There was no translation of French because everybody knew it.

The Military Government people in Berlin District come to me more and more with their problems. There is too much to do.

Kathleen McLaughlin[67] called on me the other day. She seems a very quiet, modest and capable person. She said she might be in again.

    Anm. 26), erinnert sich später an Feldman: "[...] Feldman was trained in law and had been educated at the university at Kiev. He was a Ukrainian Jew"; und: "Feldman was not only uncompromising and unhelpful, but at times plainly insolent." Erinnerungen von Harold Hays, Chapter 10: Berlin Constitution 1946, S. 147, in: Imperial War Museum (IWM) Duxford, Cambridgeshire, Großbritannien, Lieutenant Colonel Harold Hays MBE Collection. Foto mit Feldman im Bildanhang, Abb. 68.

[60] Siehe Dok. 20, Anm. 11.
[61] Gemeint ist die 14. Sitzung der Stadtkommandanten am 17. Mai 1946. Siehe Protokoll dieser Sitzung, BKC/M (46) 14, englischsprachige Fassung, in: LAB, B Rep. 036-01 (Office of Military Government, Berlin Sector [OMGBS]), 11/148-1/10.
[62] Im Protokoll der 14. Sitzung der Stadtkommandanten, BKC/M (46) 14-142, heißt es: "The Meeting had before it a letter from the Pro-Fusion Committee of the SPD asking for clarification upon its status vis à vis the Allies." Möglicherweise handelte es sich um das Schreiben des ehemaligen Zentralausschusses der SPD vom 9. Mai 1946, in dem um eine Entscheidung über die Verteilung des Eigentums und der Guthaben der ehemaligen SPD gebeten wurde. Siehe BK/O (46) 261 vom 13. Juni 1946, in: LAB, F Rep. 280 (Quellensammlung zur Berliner Zeitgeschichte [LAZ-Sammlung]), Nr. 12601.
[63] 18. Mai 1946.
[64] Siehe Protokoll der 36. Sitzung des Politischen Direktorats, Alliierte Kontrollbehörde, am 18. und 20. Mai 1946, DPOL/M (46) 19, französischsprachige Fassung, in: Archives de l'Occupation Française (AOF) en Allemagne et en Autriche, Ministère des Affaires Etrangères, Colmar, Frankreich, Services Français à Berlin, Groupe Français du Conseil de Contrôle (GFCC), Bureau des Archives, caisse 1140, paquet 51.
[65] Donald R. Heath (siehe Dok. 8, Anm. 15) war der amerikanische Vertreter im Politischen Direktorat, Alliierte Kontrollbehörde.
[66] Nikolai Wassiljewitsch Iwanow (1905–1996), sowjetischer Diplomat, 1938/1939 Erster Sekretär der sowjetischen Botschaft in Berlin, 1944/1945 Berater der sowjetischen Delegation bei der Europäischen Beratenden Kommission, London, 1945–1947 Chef der Politischen Abteilung in der Verwaltung des Politischen Beraters, SMAD, und Stellvertreter des Politischen Beraters für allgemeine Fragen.
[67] Siehe Dok. 33, Anm. 43.

Your letters make it quite clear that you don't want to bring the boys over here. I certainly am not the one to say that this is not wise. They make clear also that you do not feel able to make a decision for yourself on over there or over here. I take it my recent letter on this subject will bring the same response. This I think leads in only one direction, the direction you speak of when you say that you guess I might decide to return to Nebraska. I have never thought that if I returned to Nebraska I should not be happy there. You underestimate your importance to me when you say "I don't think that you can necessarily be happy wherever I am." I expect that there will be some necessary readjustment to my work, but I think that will not take a long time. Once having made the decision to come back, I shan't be out looking for trouble. From what I gather from your letters, and what I read and what I learn from others who are returning from home no serious person can be completely happy with the present situation at home. Nor at Nebraska will things be any better. But there is much to do at home to try to get the country into some shape for assuming its responsibilities in the world and to try to clean house at home (the one-party system in the South struck me as a phrase the other day). I have also still to educate myself. I don't think, therefore, I'll bring up the subject again unless something unusual happens. When shall I plan to be there. I should say somewhere in the neighborhood of Sept. 1st. May be you will have secured some kind of an answer from Mrs. Zumwinkel[68]. I need you all so very very much. I am no good alone. The prospect and the definite decision will help. Keep the phlox blooming until I get there, my own sweet beloved Emily.

In this connection Henry[69] has written saying that they lost Paul Sweet[70] but got a young instructor[71].[72] They certainly did not offer Paul very much.[73] Henry says also that he plans to give up the chairmanship and plans to support a system of election of a chairman within the department and appointment by the chancellor. I suppose Glenn[74] ought to have it.[75] Well he also told me that he recommended to Boucher[76] that I be raised from my present level 3980 to 4200

---

[68] Siehe Dok. 46, Anm. 6.
[69] Charles Henry Oldfather. Siehe Dok. 2, Anm. 19.
[70] Siehe Dok. 2, Anm. 28.
[71] Es handelte sich um David L. Dowd (1918–1968), amerikanischer Historiker, 1946 PhD, University of California, 1946–1949 Instructor, University of Nebraska, lehrte dann an der University of Florida und schließlich an der University of Kentucky.
[72] Siehe Dok. 2 und Dok. 11.
[73] Hierzu Emily L. Johnson in ihrem Schreiben vom 10./13. Mai 1946: "In answer to my query about Paul S[weet], Jim Sellers [siehe Anm. 77] yesterday said he'd taken a job at Chicago at 4500. Henry had offered him 3600." Brief in: Unterlagen aus dem Nachlass Edgar N. Johnson, Privatbesitz Candice E. und Thomas R. Johnson, Denver, Colorado, USA.
[74] Glenn W. Gray (1900–1979), amerikanischer Historiker, 1928 PhD, Cornell University, lehrte 1924–1926 an der Cornell University, ab 1926 an der University of Nebraska, Professor.
[75] Johnson wurde im Herbst 1946, nach seiner Rückkehr an die University of Nebraska, temporary Chairman des Department of History.
[76] Chauncey S. Boucher (1886–1955), amerikanischer Historiker, 1914 PhD, University of Michigan, lehrte an der University of Michigan, Washington University, Ohio State

the minimum salary of a full professor. He did the same for Jim[77] and others. Boucher sliced all these recommendations but in the case of Jim and me he sliced them 200 dollars apiece, giving us a raise of twenty dollars apiece. This is nothing less than a deliberate affront. I am going to write him and tell him so and refuse to accept the twenty dollars, the effrontery.[78] If he were going to be the chancellor next year certainly I should hesitate to come back.[79]

You will have to send the lawn-mower downtown to get it sharpened. They do it at the sporting goods store I think.

Did you ever get any money from the government? Did you ever receive a package I sent from Washington containing papers? Have you ever received similar packages from Washington, sent by Coburn Kidd[80].

Bye-bye Sweetheart. I'll try not to wait so long next time. I love you and the boys with all my heart. Kiss and hold them closely for me. It would be so wonderful if I could be with you for only a little while. Bye-bye Sweet, my lovely Emily. Edgar

Dok. 50
Schreiben an die Ehefrau
Berlin, Wannsee Officers' Club[1], Am Sandwerder 17/19, 20. Mai 1946

Dear Sweetheart –

Let me try to summarize a busy day in order to prove to you that there are things to do over here.

I must say I overslept a bit this morning after being up a bit late at Walter Dorn's[2] last night. Walter Lichtenstein[3] was there and a Professor Gewehr[4],

---

University, University of Texas und University of Wisconsin, ab 1923 University of Chicago, 1926–1935 Dean, College of Arts, Literature, and Science, University of Chicago, 1935–1938 President, West Virginia University, 1938–1946 Chancellor, University of Nebraska, lehrte 1947–1952 am Knox College.

[77] James L. Sellers (1891–1966), amerikanischer Historiker, 1922 PhD, University of Wisconsin, 1922–1930 Instructor, University of Wisconsin, 1930–1959 Professor, University of Nebraska.

[78] Alison G. Murie (siehe Dok. 68, Anm. 5) schreibt in einer E-Mail an Werner Breunig vom 10. Januar 2010: "[...] there was a story that Chancellor Boucher wrote to him offering him a derisory salary raise if he would come back, and Edgar refused it with contempt. This was naturally applauded among his friends."

[79] "Boucher was replaced the following year, to general relief among my parents' friends", schreibt Alison G. Murie (siehe Dok. 68, Anm. 5) in einer E-Mail an Werner Breunig vom 15. Januar 2010. Boucher blieb bis 31. August 1946 im Amt, sein Nachfolger wurde der Biochemiker Reuben G. Gustavson (1892–1974), der das Amt dann bis 1953 innehatte.

[80] Coburn B. Kidd (1909–1981), 1935 PhD, University of St. Andrews, Schottland, 1937–1940 Assistant Archivist, National Archives, 1939 LLB, Georgetown University, 1943–1945 US Army, ab 1946 Department of State (1946/1947 Research Analyst).

[1] Siehe Dok. 25, Anm. 9.
[2] Siehe Dok. 2, Anm. 10.
[3] Siehe Dok. 20, Anm. 39.

who was responsible for getting Gene Anderson[5] away from us when we first tried to get him for Nebraska.[6] Walter D[orn] has been down to Bavaria[7] for a couple of weeks and he is filled with somewhat the same ideas as those I referred to in my yesterday's letter[8]. He is concerned with the growing resentment against us in our zone. He is concerned, not so much with the prevalence of a Nazi type of mind, but with the persistence of the imperialist-nationalist old German type of mind, which regards the war and Hitlerism as a passing incident, and takes for granted that Germany will be permitted to revert to its old practices but Europe can't get along without Germany's coal and steel and Germany's industry and skill. Walter seems to be convinced at the moment also that our most important effort should be an educational one and that it should be planned over a long period. He speaks of having to stay here for at least ten years. All these things I tend to share also.

Not long after I got to the office Col. Abe Kramer[9] came in to give me the latest dope on the trade unions. They have decided, in a kind of way, to ask for permission to hold elections in their industrial branches – this is a bit of a victory for him. But I learned later in the day that his efforts to get additional personnel for his section[10] have been turned down, and I imagine that, as the result of this, he will simply pack up and go home – a great loss to Military Government here.

My driver[11] was furious this morning at the way he was treated yesterday.[12] The motor pool operator let him sit for 8 hours in the M. P. station without trying to get him out. "He is no friend of the Germans," Artur remarked, and then added by way of trying to understand: "Perhaps he lost a friend of relative in the war." But he couldn't forgive this treatment. I reminded him that he had been driving a little bit too fast, and that in Vienna, we arrested Chancellors of the Republic as well as drivers. He referred to the fact that the Oberburgermeister of Berlin, Werner[13], was also arrested recently and kept sitting in the MP station for hours. He admired this lack of distinction made in arrests. But still he wore sore. I can never forget that he has a young wife who will soon die with cancer, the poor devil. He says she has a great craving for lemonade. Could you get ahold of some lemon powder, and possibly orange powder also with

---

[4] Wesley M. Gewehr (1888–1961), amerikanischer Historiker, 1922 PhD, University of Chicago, lehrte 1919–1922 am Morningside College, 1922–1929 an der Denison University, 1924/1925 Austauschprofessor, Tsing Hua College, Peking, 1929–1940 American University, 1940–1958 University of Maryland, 1945/1946 Head of History, Army University, Shrivenham, Great Britain, Professor in US Army University, Biarritz, France, attached to Army Lecture Bureau, Germany.
[5] Eugene N. Anderson. Siehe Dok. 1, Anm. 1.
[6] Anderson war 1936 als Professor an die American University in Washington, D. C., berufen worden, wo Gewehr seit 1929 lehrte, und kam nicht an die University of Nebraska.
[7] Land in der amerikanischen Besatzungszone Deutschlands.
[8] Siehe Dok. 49.
[9] Siehe Dok. 49, Anm. 6.
[10] Manpower Branch, OMGBD.
[11] Artur Sanow. Siehe Dok. 40, Anm. 13.
[12] Siehe Dok. 49.
[13] Siehe Dok. 27, Anm. 30, und Dok. 39, Anm. 23.

which they might make some beverages? I keep giving him stuff for her. I think I told you there is no radium here for her to be treated with. She speaks now constantly of death.

At 10:30 I went to another meeting of the Political Directorate[14] in the Allied Control Authority Building[15] which was to discuss the question of a date for elections in Berlin.[16] Ivannov[17], the Russian delegate was quite compromising. The British began by quoting the Potsdam agreement[18] on the necessity for holding early elections,[19] and Ivanov[20] countered by asking when the British were going to hold elections in their zone.[21] Since the British have had no elections they were not in a very good position to argue for early elections in Berlin, although they tried to argue that Berlin was not the British zone. The Russians excepted us in their attack because they admitted that we had held elections comparable to those in Berlin and were in a position to advocate early elections. They then proposed that elections be held in Berlin comparable to those held in the zones outside of the American and indeed proposed the month of October. This was indeed a couple months earlier than had been proposed in

---

[14] Siehe Protokoll der 36. Sitzung des Politischen Direktorats, Alliierte Kontrollbehörde, am 18. und 20. Mai 1946, DPOL/M (46) 19, französischsprachige Fassung, in: AOF, Services Français à Berlin, GFCC, Bureau des Archives, caisse 1140, paquet 51.

[15] Gebäude des Kammergerichts. Siehe Dok. 19, Anm. 9.

[16] Siehe Dok. 49.

[17] Nikolai Wassiljewitsch Iwanow. Siehe Dok. 49, Anm. 66.

[18] Als „Potsdamer Abkommen" wird das Ergebnis der Potsdamer Konferenz vom 17. Juli–2. August 1945 auf Schloss Cecilienhof in Potsdam bezeichnet. Es regelt die Behandlung Deutschlands nach der bedingungslosen Kapitulation. Teilnehmer dieser Konferenz waren die Staats- und Regierungschefs der drei Siegermächte USA, Großbritannien und Sowjetunion und deren Außenminister. Siehe Manfred Görtemaker, Potsdamer Konferenz (17. 7.–2. 8. 1945), in: Deutschland unter alliierter Besatzung 1945–1949/55, hrsg. von Wolfgang Benz, Berlin 1999, S. 214–218.

[19] Im „Potsdamer Abkommen" vom 2. August 1945 heißt es unter III. Deutschland, A. Politische Grundsätze: „9. Die Verwaltung Deutschlands muß in Richtung auf eine Dezentralisation der politischen Struktur und der Entwicklung einer örtlichen Selbstverantwortung durchgeführt werden. Zu diesem Zwecke: (I) wird die lokale Selbstverwaltung in ganz Deutschland nach demokratischen Grundsätzen, und zwar durch Wahlausschüsse (Räte), so schnell wie es mit der Wahrung der militärischen Sicherheit und den Zielen der militärischen Besatzung vereinbar ist, wiederhergestellt; (II) sind in ganz Deutschland alle demokratischen politischen Parteien zu erlauben und zu fördern mit der Einräumung des Rechtes, Versammlungen einzuberufen und öffentliche Diskussionen durchzuführen; (III) soll der Grundsatz der Wahlvertretung in die Gemeinde-, Kreis-, Provinzial- und Landesverwaltungen, so schnell wie es durch die erfolgreiche Anwendung dieser Grundsätze in der örtlichen Selbstverwaltung gerechtfertigt werden kann, eingeführt werden; [...]." Berlin. Quellen und Dokumente 1945–1951, hrsg. im Auftrage des Senats von Berlin, bearb. durch Hans J. Reichhardt/Hanns U. Treutler/Albrecht Lampe (= Schriftenreihe zur Berliner Zeitgeschichte, Bd. 4/1. Halbbd.), Berlin 1964, Nr. 54, S. 86.

[20] Siehe Dok. 49, Anm. 66.

[21] Erst am 15. September 1946 fanden in den Ländern der britischen Besatzungszone Deutschlands Gemeindewahlen statt. Siehe Keesing's Archiv der Gegenwart, XVI. Jg., 1946, S. 868 A. Es folgten am 13. Oktober 1946 Landkreis- und Stadtkreiswahlen, Bürgerschaftswahlen in Bremen und Hamburg. Siehe ebd., S. 895 G und 896 A.

the Kommandatura[22]. The British, French and ourselves proposed August. October is a kind of compromise between August and December. But the Russians proposed also holding elections in only what corresponds to the wards in Berlin, and not for the city as a whole. Since this seemed to be an unnecessary waste we wanted to think this over for a week, and as it was decided. It is nice to see the questions which we initiated in the Kommandatura get some kind of push in higher quarters. Indeed the Russians seem, on the whole, to be in a more conciliatory mood.

I had lunch with Roger Wells[23] who also attended the Directorate meeting.

After lunch I had to undertake a fight with the Control and Personnel offices of Omgus[24] over the classification of a couple positions in our newly established branch[25]. They had cut the classifications down from what we had expected. This was fighting for large salaries for Col. Glaser[26] and Capt. Biel[27]. I think the salaries given them are really large enough. But they, apparently, don't and rather than see them refuse the jobs and the section go to smash I am willing to take up the battle. I urged people to reconsider the classification and they promised to, but what will come out of it finally I don't know. But I'm not going to fight their battles any more.

Then I had conferences with Roger Wells again and Don Heath[28] over the proposal to be made to the Russians next Friday[29] on the question of Berlin elections. These went on until about 5:30 and I got back to Berlin District about six.

Tomorrow is lunch with Walter Dorn. Tomorrow is dinner out. And Wednesday[30] is dinner out with Herr Grotewohl[31] the leader of the new SED party here. This ought to be interesting but it looks like another strenuous week.

At dinner I talked with Col. Babcock[32] about making a protest in the Kommandatura about political and religious impartiality in appointments to public office. Those Communists! And so it goes.

I long for a bit of peace. No time to think about anything. I long for you too and for the boys. Maybe I will get a letter tomorrow. I love you my sweetheart, my dearest one. Goodnight. Edgar

---

[22] Siehe Dok. 20, Anm. 11.
[23] Siehe Dok. 19, Anm. 16.
[24] Siehe Dok. 17, Anm. 45.
[25] Gemeint ist die Civil Administration Branch, OMGBD. Siehe Dok. 28, Anm. 5.
[26] Siehe Dok. 28, Anm. 4.
[27] Siehe Dok. 20, Anm. 31.
[28] Donald R. Heath. Siehe Dok. 8, Anm. 15.
[29] 24. Mai 1946.
[30] 22. Mai 1946.
[31] Siehe Dok. 30, Anm. 8.
[32] William T. Babcock (1898–1950), Lieutenant Colonel, 1946 Chief, Public Safety Branch, OMGBD, 1946-1949 Deputy Director, OMGBD/OMGBS, 1947-1949 US Deputy Commandant, Allied Kommandatura Berlin, 1949 Director, OMGBS, 1949/1950 Deputy Commissioner, Berlin Element, HICOG.

**Dok. 51
Schreiben an die Ehefrau
Berlin, 23. Mai 1946**

Dearest –

I'm dreadfully tired tonight and am going straight to bed. Last night Brewster Morris[1] had Grotewohl[2] (the head of the pro-merger Social Democrats and member of the Executive Committee of SED) to dinner, and I was there. It lasted too late. I am no good after this kind of a late evening the next day. This was after a night out the night before. And I sat from two until seven today on a meeting of the Local Government Committee of the Kommandatura[3], discussing a new constitution for Berlin and electoral procedure.[4] Since I am going to a meeting of the Political Directorate[5] tomorrow I've got to be fresh since they work like a whirl-wind. I'll tell you about Grotewohl later.[6]

Just now I want to say a sweet hello and to confirm, after another letter from you on the subject, what I said in a recent letter about coming home. Let us consider the matter closed. I am coming home. Nothing could keep me from you and the boys any longer than next fall. And although you are willing to come over here if I want to stay for the Stuttgart job[7], I haven't the slightest intention of asking you to do so. First of all I am not sufficiently interested in it. And secondly, it is quite clear that you don't care much about coming here simply for the sake of coming here or going any place else in Europe. And I think your reactions are healthy and sound. This is not a good place for introverts and people with sensibilities to be. I believe the atmosphere is becoming more corrupt – corrupt in the sense of creating a privileged conqueror-class which is interested in nothing much more than what they can get out of it. That is most of them. Walter Dorn[8] admitted to me the other day that he found himself thinking things which under normal circumstances he never would consider – his sensibilities being corrupted. The decision gives me comfort. I now have this to look forward to. But I shall be desperately lonely until I can see you. If you can get something in the mountains for a little while I should like it very much. At the same time I agree on painting the house ourselves – I should say myself. If I start to paint a house it will take a very very long time.

I checked on my pay recently. I haven't been getting any money because nobody has ever turned in a time sheet. It is taken care of now and I shall be paid

---

[1] Siehe Dok. 31, Anm. 13.
[2] Siehe Dok. 30, Anm. 8.
[3] Siehe Dok. 29, Anm. 14.
[4] Siehe Protokoll der 19. Sitzung des Local Government Committee, Allied Kommandatura Berlin, am 23. Mai 1946, LG/M (46) 19, englischsprachige Fassung, in: TNA, Allied Kommandatura: Directives, Minutes and Papers, FO 1112/378; Bildanhang, Abb. 66 und Abb. 67.
[5] Politisches Direktorat, Alliierte Kontrollbehörde.
[6] Siehe Dok. 52.
[7] Gemeint ist die Leitung des RGCO. Siehe Dok. 2, Anm. 11.
[8] Siehe Dok. 2, Anm. 10.

full salary until April when your first allotment was paid.[9] I'll send this to you and suggest seriously that you use it to buy a new car, if you can get one. You need this in your present desperate plight.

I send you all my love – my dearest Emily. Edgar

Dok. 52
Schreiben an die Ehefrau
Berlin, Wannsee[1], 25. Mai 1946[2]

Dear Sweetheart –

Another week gone – I must say they go quickly enough and I don't seem to accomplish much in the course of them. But the passing is now beginning to have real significance for me since I know that the date for leaving here is thus approaching. I know I shall never regret not staying on, and once having made the decision will quickly find my way back into American life – such as it happens to. From here everything seems to be chaotic there. Of course I see no American papers except the awful Stars and Stripes[3] and the almost as awful Paris edition of the Herald Tribune[4],[5] I try to keep up mostly with the German newspapers, and except for those under American and British and French license they keep me in pretty constant turmoil. Censorship is an ugly thing and under Russian auspices very unpleasant. Everything possible is done to put us in a bad light and to make the Russians seem the guiding angels of the world. There is always, however, something to put us in a bad light. Even our strikes are held against us. You would think that there would be at least enough fairness to recognize that here are workmen trying and succeeding in improving their standard of living. Instead it is always to illustrate the chaotic nature of our economy and incidentally to intimidate workers here. In Russia there are no such things as strikes. I prefer to have strikes. There are strikes taking place here now – "sit-down strikes" to force upon employers the acceptance of the right of co-management on the part of the workers –

---

[9] Siehe Dok. 44.

[1] Gemeint ist entweder der Große Wannsee, eine Ausbuchtung der Havel (siehe Dok. 74, Anm. 24) im Südwesten Berlins, oder Berlin-Wannsee, Ortsteil im Verwaltungsbezirk Zehlendorf.
[2] Das Schreiben ist vom 25. März 1946 datiert; wie aber aus dem Inhalt hervorgeht, wurde es am 25. Mai 1946 verfasst.
[3] Amerikanische Soldatenzeitung.
[4] New York Herald Tribune, amerikanische Tageszeitung, republikanisch orientiert.
[5] "'Stars and Stripes' – the unofficial paper of the US Armed Forces in the European theater. Printed in Germany with international coverage. Distributed by subscription. 'New York Herald Tribune' – Printed in Paris and distributed by subscription. Will be sold also at Post Exchange news stands." US Sector of Berlin. Information for New Arrivals, published by Headquarters, Berlin District, 25 April 1946/15 July 1946, S. 19, http://www.berlinbrats.org/pdfs/46Guide.pdf (letzter Zugriff am 30. Januar 2013).

the sort of thing which the CIO[6] attempted with General Motors[7] when I was home.

I attended Clay's[8] staff meeting[9] this morning, the first I have been able to attend for a couple of weeks. It is not encouraging to attend one because so little that is actually important is happening to put Germany on its feet. It is not sure that the new denazification law[10] which the Germans put into effect is really going to work out well. There is much dissatisfaction with it, especially on the part of the church, which doesn't want to get rid of its Nazi clergy, and has protested to Clay who rejected their complaints. Incidently I am not to have the de-Nazification job I referred to.[11] Walter Dorn[12] is going to take it over. I suppose they haven't quite enough for him to do, and in any case he is better qualified for it from some points of view. De-Nazification is already a joke among the Germans when it is not a tragedy. Grotewohl[13] told the story the other night[14] of the man working at cleaning away debris in the streets. He was approached ruefully by a passerby who said he wished he had a job like that. He used to have he said. "And why did you lose it?" "Oh, I was a Nazi and was fired." "Well", replied the other, "I am a Nazi too and that's why they put me on this job." There is also going around the statement that "In the Russian zone you see three smoke-stacks on every factory going, in the British zone two, but in the American zone the only activity you see is wasps chasing Nazis." It came out in Clay's meeting this morning that the camps for civilian internees (these are mostly Nazis put away for safe keeping) are much better fed than the ordinary German civilian. So if you don't mind your loss of freedom you can be better fed. The Germans are of course irritable over the loss of houses to American families. Some 362 houses are now occupied by American families in Berlin, and 51 more have to be taken over to accommodate those on the spot. Of course there is such a shortage of proper houses in our sector that practically anything that is available has to be taken over, irrespective of who has it. This is just a situation which has to be faced. If there are not enough Nazi houses available others have to be taken. And of course the Germans believe that we are going out of our way to keep the Nazis in their houses and drive the others out. It is true that concentration camp people have had to get out to make room for the conquerors.

I had a good little example yesterday of the danger inherent in not having a little understanding of the situation one is dealing with. There suddenly ap-

---

[6] Congress of Industrial Organizations, 1935–1955 Gewerkschaftsbund, der überwiegend ungelernte Industriearbeiter in den USA und Kanada organisierte.
[7] 1908 gegründetes amerikanisches Automobilunternehmen, Firmenzentrale in Detroit im US-Bundesstaat Michigan.
[8] Siehe Dok. 2, Anm. 6.
[9] Siehe Protokoll der OMGUS-Stabskonferenz am 25. Mai 1946, in: Archiv des IfZ, OMGUS – Staff Conferences (Protokollkopien), Fg 12/4.
[10] Siehe Dok. 47, Anm. 20.
[11] Siehe Dok. 47.
[12] Siehe Dok. 2, Anm. 10.
[13] Siehe Dok. 30, Anm. 8.
[14] Siehe Dok. 51.

peared in my office three officers with my driver[15]. They said they had seen him give the Nazi salute in the courtyard and that the other drivers had received it with laughter. They wanted to arrest him and have him tried. I just couldn't believe that Sanow had seriously given the Nazi salute[16] or that it had been received in a mocking spirit. He was not a member of the party[17], is a good anti-Merger Social Democrat[18] and a typical Berliner who likes a joke, and is generally speaking, when not thinking of his poor wife[19], in good humor. He said he had done it as a joke and that it had been received as a joke by the drivers. This seemed to me, from what I knew of him to be the truth. I think that I might even give the Hitler salute in a jovial mood. But I had a hard time convincing these officers that this was so. They were about to go home to the USA, and wanted to arrest him before going. They had fought the war to keep things like this from happening. I finally told them I would have Sanow call together the drivers and given them a serious talk on the possibility of such action being misunderstood when done on US property + observed by those who did not know what was going on. They were then persuaded to let him go. Sanow called together the drivers. The atmosphere between Germans and many Americans is not pleasant. The barriers of misunderstanding are very high and wide.

Sunday morning [26. Mai 1946].

I thought this morning that it was now four months since I have seen you and that if I stay on through August there will be only three more to go – more than half the time, at least is gone. In a sense I have promised to stay on here until the fall. I have thought that a convenient terminus date would be Sept. 8. That would be seven months. And I take it my services are terminated where they began – in Omaha[20]. When does school begin in September? If however you manage to get a place in the mountains for August and September (you speak of putting the Sellers[21] on the look out)[22] I should be tempted to leave earlier, even though I suppose we should have this extra month of salary for the months that are ahead. Moving out to the mountains after Labor Day[23] seems a little strenuous if we are to be there for only a week or so. If I paint the house (where are we going to get the equipment) that will take plenty of time, and there are undoubtedly plenty of other things to do. What, by the way, did you ever do

---

[15] Artur Sanow. Siehe Dok. 40, Anm. 13.
[16] Gemeint ist der nach 1945 verbotene Hitlergruß, im nationalsozialistischen Sprachgebrauch auch als „Deutscher Gruß" bezeichnet, bei dem der rechte Arm mit flacher Hand auf Augenhöhe schräg nach oben gestreckt wurde. Siehe Tilman Allert, Der deutsche Gruß. Geschichte einer unheilvollen Geste, Frankfurt am Main 2005.
[17] Gemeint ist die NSDAP.
[18] Ein Sozialdemokrat, der gegen die Fusion von SPD und KPD eintrat.
[19] Seine Frau war krebskrank. Siehe Dok. 44 und Dok. 50.
[20] Stadt im US-Bundesstaat Nebraska, nordöstlich von Johnsons Wohnort Lincoln.
[21] James L. Sellers (siehe Dok. 49, Anm. 77) und seine Ehefrau Nell K. Sellers, geb. Kennedy (gest. 1946).
[22] Siehe Emily L. Johnsons Schreiben vom 10./13. Mai 1946, in: Unterlagen aus dem Nachlass Edgar N. Johnson, Privatbesitz Candice E. und Thomas R. Johnson, Denver, Colorado, USA.
[23] US-Nationalfeiertag seit 1894, wird immer am ersten Montag im September begangen.

about those chairs that I left on your hands? Are they still where I left them. I should be content to stay at home with you and the kids and getting robes and things together in preparation for the beginning of school. In any case it is downhill again for the next two or three months with some little steep up-hill grades on the way.

The bow-hairs, by the way, did come and I delivered them.[24] Mr. Baldner[25] said I was an angel. Thanks for getting them. I have not seen him since. I am a little beware of Germans for whom I have done favors, because they have always more for you to do, and after a while you get fed up.

It was here a less strenuous week than last but not much less. I had to go out on Tuesday[26] to an evening prepared by a member of the staff in the office. Then on Wednesday[27] came Mr. Grotewohl's evening at Brewster Morris's[28].[29] It was an interesting one because we were in the presence of a shrewd politician who had for the moment compromised his best principles in order to roll with what he thinks is the wave of the future – the unity party here. It was clear, however, that if the wave recedes, he will try to get back into the fold which he left. I hope they reject him if he does. He has moved into the Russian Sector and is, of course, provided with all the things he needs. I didn't like the look in his eye nor react to his proposition that now that the dirt was over we should forget it, establish peace, and work together for the future. Things are not quite so simple. He has a vigorous mind, speaks by way of reference to Communist orators, of "epileptic politicians who foam at the mouth", and makes easy comparisons between "the Germany of Goethe[30] and the Germany of Göring[31]". We put him through a rather hard evening, and he took it well. But he was hardly a man in whom you could really put your trust.[32]

Friday[33] I went with Walter Dorn to the theatre – my first here. It was Sternheim's[34] "The Snob"[35] in Max Reinhardt's[36] "Deutsches Theatre"[37].[38] But I

---

[24] Gemeint sind die Bogenhaare, die Johnson in den USA für den Cellisten Max Baldner (siehe Dok. 21, Anm. 18) besorgen ließ. Siehe Dok. 25 und Dok. 38.
[25] Siehe Dok. 21, Anm. 18.
[26] 21. Mai 1946.
[27] 22. Mai 1946.
[28] Siehe Dok. 31, Anm. 13.
[29] Siehe Dok. 51.
[30] Johann Wolfgang von Goethe (1749–1832), deutscher Dichter.
[31] Siehe Dok. 22, Anm. 24.
[32] Brewster H. Morris brachte nach dem Abend mit Grotewohl in einem Bericht die Meinung zum Ausdruck, dass der SED-Vorsitzende "is still at heart a democrat and is therefore well worth keeping contact with". Zitiert nach Anjana Buckow, Zwischen Propaganda und Realpolitik. Die USA und der sowjetisch besetzte Teil Deutschlands 1945-1955 (= USA-Studien, Bd. 13), Stuttgart 2003, S. 77.
[33] 24. Mai 1946.
[34] Carl Sternheim (1878–1942), deutscher Schriftsteller.
[35] Komödie in drei Aufzügen, Uraufführung 1914 in den Kammerspielen des Deutschen Theaters in Berlin, gehört zu Sternheims Komödienzyklus „Aus dem bürgerlichen Heldenleben".
[36] Max Reinhardt (1873–1943), österreichischer Schauspieler, Regisseur und Intendant, leitete 1905-1930 das Deutsche Theater in Berlin, gründete 1906 die Kammerspiele im Nebengebäude.

couldn't take very well the way in which the play was worked out – since the snob won out, and pushed everyone aside. The leading man Grundjens[39] was a Nazi. We OK'd him before we knew too much about him, and then tried to un-O. K. him. But the Russians objected to this. The Theatre is in their Sector, and so he goes on. He certainly looked like a good Nazi. I went to Walter's big house on the Kleiner Wannsee[40] afterwards, and we talked mostly about what is going on here. Walter is not fundamentally more hopeful than I. I think he is going home at the end of the summer but he is much more flattered by his position here than I should be under similar circumstances. He is after all a German trained to be respectful of his superiors. Nevertheless men like him are needed here.

I went to two meetings of the Political Directorate during the week.[41] The question of the recognition of the parties[42] is stalled on account of the French who do not know whether they can recognize the new Socialist Unity Party and have sent home for instructions. It is of course a vital matter with them. A strong Socialist-Communist Party here would be a strong impetus to a similar one in France which could then take over the government. The last elections[43]

[37] Deutsches Theater, Schumannstraße 13a, Berlin-Mitte. Das 1850 eröffnete Friedrich-Wilhelmstädtische Theater hatte 1883 den Namen „Deutsches Theater" erhalten.
[38] Die Vorstellung begann um 18 Uhr. Siehe Berliner Zeitung vom 24. Mai 1946, [S. 4]. Die Erstaufführung hatte am 3. Mai 1946 stattgefunden. Siehe Walther Karsch, Sternheims und Gründgens' Wiederkehr. „Der Snob" in Max Reinhardts Deutschem Theater, in: Der Tagesspiegel vom 5. Mai 1946, S. 3 (Beilage); Paul Rilla, Carl Sternheim: „Der Snob". Gustaf Gründgens im Deutschen Theater, in: Berliner Zeitung vom 5. Mai 1946, [S. 3]; Georg Zivier, Ein Grosser kehrt wieder. Carl Sternheim: „Der Snob" im Deutschen Theater, in: Telegraf vom 5. Mai 1946, S. 5. Siehe auch Ein Gespräch mit Gustaf Gründgens. „Was ich schon immer spielen wollte ..." – Wie es zur Aufführung des „Snob" kam, in: Telegraf vom 1. Mai 1946, S. 6.
[39] Die Rolle des Christian Maske spielte Gustaf Gründgens (1899–1963), deutscher Schauspieler, Regisseur und Intendant, war in der NS-Zeit Generalintendant des Preußischen Staatstheaters, trat 1946 nach der Rückkehr aus einem sowjetischen Internierungslager wieder als Schauspieler auf.
[40] Siehe Dok. 33, Anm. 10.
[41] Gemeint sind die Sitzungen des Politischen Direktorats, Alliierte Kontrollbehörde, vom 20. und 24. Mai 1946. Siehe Protokoll der 36. Sitzung des Politischen Direktorats, Alliierte Kontrollbehörde, am 18. und 20. Mai 1946, DPOL/M (46) 19, französischsprachige Fassung, in: AOF, Services Français à Berlin, GFCC, Bureau des Archives, caisse 1140, paquet 51; Protokoll der 37. Sitzung des Politischen Direktorats, Alliierte Kontrollbehörde, am 24. Mai 1946, DPOL/M (46) 20, französischsprachige Fassung, in: ebd.
[42] Gemeint ist die Anerkennung der SED und der neu organisierten SPD in Berlin.
[43] Gemeint ist die Volksabstimmung vom 5. Mai 1946, durch die der Verfassungsentwurf, der mit den Stimmen der kommunistisch-sozialistischen Mehrheit von der Verfassunggebenden Nationalversammlung verabschiedet worden war, abgelehnt wurde. Siehe Keesing's Archiv der Gegenwart, XVI. Jg., 1946, S. 741 D. In einem Leitartikel der französisch lizenzierten Zeitung „Der Kurier" heißt es, das Ergebnis des Referendums „beweist eindeutig, daß die Mehrheit in der Nationalversammlung nicht mehr der Mehrheit im Lande entspricht. [...] Die Sozialisten und Kommunisten hatten bei den letzten Wahlen am 21. Oktober zehn Millionen Stimmen erhalten gegen neun Millionen sämtlicher übrigen Parteien. Die Volksabstimmung zeigt, daß sich dieses Verhältnis umgekehrt hat. Diesmal hat die äußerste Linke nur neun Millionen

however moved from the left to the right, and it's a question whether the French Gov[ernmen]t[44] wants, before the next elections[45], to encourage in even the slightest way, the French forces of the left. They might wait therefore until after the elections before making up their minds. At the second meeting the handsome, clever and reasonably conciliatory Russian representative, Mr. Ivanov[46], annoyed and disappointed over this postponement, said, that although he was willing privately to have elections held in Berlin in October, he could not discuss the question officially until the matter of recognition had been settled, which was a perfectly fair proposition. And so the stalemate will go on for some time. It seems to be the case with all important questions. It is difficult to arrive at a common basis in a hurry. Take the fundamental question of the Potsdam agreement[47] providing for central agencies in certain fields.[48] It has been held up by the French for months, and there is no prospect that it will be settled for many months to come.[49] As long as Germany is not treated as an economic unit things will stagnate. It is clear that the Russians do not wish to share their zone with the rest. The only club we have here is to refuse reparations to them from the west for so long as they refuse to carry out the Potsdam agreement as a whole. This I think we are ready to do but it will take a long time to implement.

It is rather fun representing your government in even the smallest negotiations. I sat on the Local Gov[ernmen]t Committee[50] for a couple of sessions in

Stimmen erreicht, während die Gegner der Verfassung zehneinhalb Millionen zusammengebracht haben, das macht 53,9 gegen 46,1 Prozent." Liberale gegen autoritäre Demokratie, in: Der Kurier vom 6. Mai 1946, S. 1f., hier S. 1.

[44] Provisorische Regierung der Französischen Republik, Koalitionsregierung aus Kommunisten (Parti Communiste Français [PCF]), Christdemokraten (Mouvement Républicain Populaire [MRP]) und Sozialisten (Section Française de l'Internationale Ouvrière [SFIO]). Präsident der Provisorischen Regierung war (Januar–Juni 1946) der Sozialist Félix Gouin (1884–1977).

[45] Am 2. Juni 1946 wurde eine neue Verfassunggebende Nationalversammlung gewählt. Siehe Keesing's Archiv der Gegenwart, XVI. Jg., 1946, S. 771 D; Schwergewicht verlagert, in: Der Kurier vom 3. Juni 1946, S. 1.

[46] Siehe Dok. 49, Anm. 66.

[47] Siehe Dok. 50, Anm. 18.

[48] Das „Potsdamer Abkommen" sah die Errichtung „einiger wichtiger zentraler deutscher Verwaltungsabteilungen" vor, „an deren Spitze Staatssekretäre stehen, und zwar auf den Gebieten des Finanzwesens, des Transportwesens, des Verkehrswesens, des Außenhandels und der Industrie. Diese Abteilungen werden unter der Leitung des Kontrollrates tätig sein." Berlin. Quellen und Dokumente 1945–1951, hrsg. im Auftrage des Senats von Berlin, bearb. durch Hans J. Reichhardt/Hanns U. Treutler/Albrecht Lampe (= Schriftenreihe zur Berliner Zeitgeschichte, Bd. 4/1. Halbbd.), Berlin 1964, Nr. 54, S. 86.

[49] Frankreich hatti massive Vorbehalte gegenüber der Einrichtung zentraler deutscher Verwaltungsstellen und wollte duch dezentrale politische und wirtschaftliche Strukturen ein Wiedererstarken Deutschlands verhindern. Siehe Elisabeth Kraus, Ministerien für das ganze Deutschland? Der Alliierte Kontrollrat und die Frage gesamtdeutscher Zentralverwaltungen (= Studien zur Zeitgeschichte, Bd. 37), München 1990; Gunther Mai, Der Alliierte Kontrollrat in Deutschland 1945–1948. Alliierte Einheit – deutsche Teilung? (= Quellen und Darstellungen zur Zeitgeschichte, Bd. 37), München 1995, S. 83–92.

[50] Siehe Dok. 29, Anm. 14.

discussions on the future constitution of Berlin, and some progress was made.[51] Whether I shall continue I do not know. Col. Glaser[52] is back and may want to take over.[53] Since he knows no German he is hardly the person to take over these negotiations.

It is interesting to see how many little things are thrown on to you. A small group of students from the U[niversity] of Berlin[54] were sent to me by the education people[55] to help arrange a program of lecture discussions on America. I shall be able to help a little and will probably talk a little myself on one occasion. A publisher[56] who is going to put out an edition of Franklin's[57] Autobiography[58] and Bowers'[59] Jefferson and Hamilton[60] wants Forewords by Americans and he has been sent to me.[61] I may try the one on Franklin whose Autobiography I am just now reading it so happens. The people in Military Government of

---

[51] Siehe Protokoll der 17. Sitzung des Local Government Committee, Allied Kommandatura Berlin, am 10. Mai 1946, LG/M (46) 17, englischsprachige Fassung, in: TNA, Allied Kommandatura: Directives, Minutes and Papers, FO 1112/378; Protokoll der 18. Sitzung des Local Government Committee, Allied Kommandatura Berlin, am 17. Mai 1946, LG/M (46) 18, englischsprachige Fassung, in: ebd.; Protokoll der 19. Sitzung des Local Government Committee, Allied Kommandatura Berlin, am 23. Mai 1946, LG/M (46) 19, englischsprachige Fassung, in: ebd.

[52] Siehe Dok. 28, Anm. 4.

[53] Glaser, der an den Sitzungen des Local Government Committee am 10., 17. und 23. Mai 1946 nicht teilnahm, war von seiner Englandreise zurückgekehrt. Siehe Dok. 45.

[54] Siehe Dok. 20, Anm. 44.

[55] Gemeint sind die mit Erziehungsfragen betrauten Vertreter der amerikanischen Militärregierung.

[56] Gemeint ist der Berliner Verleger Karl Heinz Henssel (1917–2014). Sein Verlag, der Karl H. Henssel Verlag (Sitz: Rheinstraße 46, Berlin-Friedenau), ein Verlag für Belletristik und geisteswissenschaftliche Literatur, war im Dezember 1945 von der amerikanischen Militärregierung lizensiert worden. Siehe Publishers licensed by the U. S. authorities, Mitteilung der Information Services Control Section, U. S. Headquarters Berlin District, Publications Sub-Section, vom 13. Dezember 1945, in: LAB, B Rep. 036-01 (Office of Military Government, Berlin Sector [OMGBS]), 4/17-1/33. Eine Visitenkarte, die Johnson von Henssel überreicht bekam, befindet sich in: Unterlagen aus dem Nachlass Edgar N. Johnson, Privatbesitz Candice E. und Thomas R. Johnson, Denver, Colorado, USA.

[57] Benjamin Franklin (1706–1790), amerikanischer Politiker, Naturwissenschaftler und Schriftsteller, einer der Gründerväter der Vereinigten Staaten von Amerika.

[58] Franklins unvollendete, nach seinem Tod veröffentlichte Autobiografie. „Gegen das Ende seines Lebens unternahm er es, zu Nutz und Frommen seines Sohnes eine Autobiographie zu schreiben, die er jedoch im Drange seiner vielfältigen Geschäfte nicht beenden konnte." Benjamin Franklin. Auszug aus der Autobiographie, in: Die Neue Zeitung vom 26. April 1946, Feuilleton- und Kunst-Beilage.

[59] Claude G. Bowers (1878–1958), amerikanischer Schriftsteller und Diplomat.

[60] Das Buch "Jefferson and Hamilton. The Struggle for Democracy in America" erschien erstmals 1925.

[61] Noch 1946 erschien im Karl H. Henssel Verlag, Berlin, „Benjamin Franklin. Sein Leben von ihm selbst erzählt" mit einem Vorwort von Edgar N. Johnson; die Übersetzung von Berthold Auerbach aus dem Jahre 1875 war hier überarbeitet wiedergegeben. Siehe Cover des Buches im Bildanhang, Abb. 65. 1948 folgte „Jefferson und Hamilton" von Claude G. Bowers (deutsche Übertragung von Grete Rambach, geb. Lorch).

Berlin come to me. The director of public safety[62] wants to know whether it is wise to forbid police to join political parties (this is directed against the Communists who are trying desperately to control the police). I said No. This is more than we ask at home. The Director of Welfare[63] wants to do somewhat the same with Welfare Workers (the Communists control them too). Local personnel officers in our Sector refuse jobs to qualified applicants because they do not belong to the party or are too religious. "We don't want pious people around who pray all day." The Food people come to me wanting to know what to do about the Main Food Office[64] which is still full of Nazis as well as Communists and there is much food being lost, and stolen and wasted, etc., etc.

There are not enough qualified people here to do the job.

I love you my dearest Emily, my sweet wife and I long for you. I hope those damn English papers are through.[65] Kiss my sweet boys for me and I send you every tender caress. The time when we shall really be close to each other again is at least in sight. I love her very very dearly. Edgar

Dok. 53
Schreiben an die Ehefrau
Berlin, Wannsee Officers' Club[1], Am Sandwerder 17/19, 27. Mai 1946

My own sweet Emily –

One of the nicest things you ever said about me was in a recent letter[2] when you were commenting on Mary Lancaster's[3] imminent marriage. You said simply that you wished that we had met long before we did meet and had been married thereupon.[4] I do not like to think of what we actually have missed by that's not having occurred. But it is so much the more reason for my hastening back to you.

As you know by now the decision about my coming home is made, not to be reconsidered or to be discussed except in terms of anticipation. I have written

---

[62] William T. Babcock. Siehe Dok. 50, Anm. 32.
[63] Albert W. Paddock, Major, Januar–Juni 1946 Chief, Public Welfare Branch, OMGBD.
[64] Gemeint ist die Magistratsabteilung für Ernährung.
[65] Emily L. Johnson las Klausurarbeiten für Ray W. Frantz (siehe Dok. 11, Anm. 15). Siehe Dok. 48, Anm. 12.

[1] Siehe Dok. 25, Anm. 9.
[2] Emily L. Johnsons Schreiben vom 15. Mai 1946, in: Unterlagen aus dem Nachlass Edgar N. Johnson, Privatbesitz Candice E. und Thomas R. Johnson, Denver, Colorado, USA.
[3] Mary Lancaster, später verh. Hopkins, Tochter von Mary B. Lancaster, geb. Brown (ca. 1892–1948) und Lane W. Lancaster (1892–1962), amerikanischer Politikwissenschaftler, 1923 PhD, University of Pennsylvania, 1930–1960 Professor, University of Nebraska. Mary Lancaster heiratete am 28. Mai 1946 Robert E. Hopkins. Siehe Emily L. Johnsons Schreiben vom 28. Mai 1946, in: Unterlagen aus dem Nachlass Edgar N. Johnson, Privatbesitz Candice E. und Thomas R. Johnson, Denver, Colorado, USA.
[4] Emily L. Johnson hatte geschrieben: "I wish we had met and been married long before we did."

Jim[5] to that effect and yesterday I wrote a long letter to Henry[6] to that effect, telling him incidently some of the things I expected from the University upon my return in order that the full hope and promise of academic life might be in some measure realized at Nebraska. I hope he will understand the letter. Because I went out of my way to say some nice things to him and I do not want it considered as flattery. For, after all, if Henry were not there, in some position of authority, it would not be so easy to come back to the Univ[ersity] of Nebraska. Whatever may be his odd decisions at the moment, he is an honest and decent human, and there are few like him.

My present mood is indeed to return immediately and abandon the petty men about me and the corrupting atmosphere, and to return to the strength and comfort of your bosom and the delicacy of your spirit. It is perhaps better that I should not abandon the scene quite so easily. General Keating[7] is quite innocent of politics. He has some trust in me, and I'd rather have him in my hands in what is to come in the next few months, than in the hands of a comparatively ignorant, grasping, envious and ambitious advertising man such as Colonel Glaser[8], even though I have to suffer a little at Glaser's hands. It is quite clear in my mind that Glaser would like nothing better than for me to abandon the field to him. And since he doesn't know a word of German this is not quite what I propose to do. Four months have now passed and there are at the most only three left. I'd better leave what imprint I can before I leave, and if it is nothing else, it must be that of one who can put the interests of his country a little bit above those of himself. This sounds awfully bombastic and stuff-shirted but it really is not. I do not say that my motives are of the purest but I do say that the guiding ones are not concerned with the guarantee of my present position or the jealous exclusion of any one who threatens it. Anyone can have my position who can crowd me out of it. But he will have to be worth it. And I refuse to be bothered with the petty annoyances set in my way by men who have influence to bear in petty affairs but who are incapable of rising to any greater consideration than their own little empire in the months or days that are to come.

I don't think they will put pressure on me to stay. Oh! Clay[9] may say some nice things about the need for my taking Pollock's[10] place[11] but he is quite sufficient to his task, and there are always others. I shall ask, before I go, for the privilege of taking a round of our zone, so that I may come home pretty well informed about what Americans are doing here. This I think will be granted me. I'll write a final report for Clay, and then come home to you and John[12] and Timmy[13]. I have the feeling that I shall remain secluded from all but your and mine and our boys' and my student world for a long time to come. The values

---

[5] James L. Sellers. Siehe Dok. 49, Anm. 77.
[6] Charles Henry Oldfather. Siehe Dok. 2, Anm. 19.
[7] Siehe Dok. 39, Anm. 6.
[8] Siehe Dok. 28, Anm. 4.
[9] Siehe Dok. 2, Anm. 10.
[10] Siehe Dok. 15, Anm. 12.
[11] Gemeint ist die Leitung des RGCO. Siehe Dok. 2, Anm. 11.
[12] Johnsons Sohn John. Siehe Dok. 2, Anm. 15.
[13] Johnsons Sohn Thomas. Siehe Dok. 2, Anm. 16.

of this world are so clear and indisputable, they can be so easily destroyed again (I mean only the possibility of enjoying them) that it would be folly to do much else than to cultivate them to the last refinement.

So from the world of affairs, such as I have been able to touch it, I shall return to your most precious self, with no greater desire than to cultivate you in so far as in me lies, and to realize those potentialities of our love and life together that we are aware of but have not really probed. Aside from being the companion and husband that you most desire, I shall be there to order to be a proper associate for our fine boys. I am very conscious of this responsibility. And after this will come my students. And after this the world. You are always, and so correctly insistent upon this "Time which does not tarry". Let us resolve, my own sweet darling, when once we are together again in each other's arms, that all our moments together shall be calculated to achieve the dream of an almost perfect happiness that we are capable of. Only its realization, in the few years that are ahead of us, will justify this wanton abandonment of you, especially this last one, that I have been guilty of. I love you my sweet and lovely Emily, with you, and in your constant presence I can hope to be what I am capable of being. That will not be bad for you or John or Timmy. And that can only be where we are all together. Goodnight, my dearest, my beloved. Edgar

Dok. 54
Schreiben an die Ehefrau
Berlin, Wannsee Officers' Club[1], Am Sandwerder 17/19, 28. Mai 1946

Dear Sweetheart –

I went to my first meeting of the Coordinating Committee[2] today.[3] This is the Committee just below the Control Council[4] itself. Clay[5] represents us, General Robertson[6] the British, General Koeltz[7] the French and General Dratvin[8] the Russians. I got to go because they were discussing the recognition of the SPD and the SED. This was being held up because the French had to consult their

---

[1] Siehe Dok. 25, Anm. 9.
[2] Siehe Dok. 15, Anm. 21.
[3] Siehe Protokoll der 57. Sitzung des Koordinierungskomitees, Alliierte Kontrollbehörde, am 28. Mai 1946, CORC/M (46) 28, französischsprachige Fassung, in: AOF, Services Français à Berlin, GFCC, Bureau des Archives, caisse 1133, paquet 7.
[4] Siehe Dok. 16, Anm. 11.
[5] Siehe Dok. 2, Anm. 6.
[6] Sir Brian Hubert Robertson (1896-1974), Lieutenant General, 1945-1947 Deputy Military Governor, Germany (UK), 1947-1949 Military Governor, Germany (UK), and Commander-in-Chief of British Forces of Occupation in Germany, 1949/1950 High Commissioner (UK), Allied High Commission, Germany.
[7] Louis Marie Koeltz (1884-1970), Général de Corps d'Armée, 1945-Juni 1946 Leiter der Groupe Français du Conseil de Contrôle.
[8] Michail Iwanowitsch Dratwin (1897-1953), sowjetischer Generalleutnant, 1945-1947 Stabschef der SMAD, 1947-1949 Erster Stellvertreter des Obersten Chefs der SMAD.

government. It passed easily enough this afternoon after the French had received word that they could recognize the two parties. This gives a chance for the Political Directorate tomorrow to discuss the question of elections.[9] I am going to that also with the consent of Don Heath[10]. Since I am here I want to follow up these questions through the hierarchy. With the setting of a date for elections and the recognition of the two parties the stage is set for an election campaign here during the summer. The election will probably be in October, after I have left. It will be the same here as it was in Austria. All the excitement without waiting for the event. But I can think of something much more exciting than an election in Berlin, and I don't have to tell you what it is.

General Robertson presided in a rather austere manner, as the British are inclined to do, showing evident displeasure at some of the attitudes struck by the Russians. Across from him sat Dratvin, even more formidable and unpleasant. To Robertson's right was Koeltz, agreeable and civilized, and on his left our capable General Clay.

It started out unpleasantly with the consideration of a quadripartite Commission to investigate in all the four zones the disarmament of Germany. The Russians had rejected the proposal on the previous meeting on the ground that in so far as the western zones were concerned there was no disarmament that had taken place in the economic field and therefore nothing to investigate. What is clear of course is that the Russians don't want a Commission monkeying around in their zone investigating what has happened to the industry in their zone. The Russians did not change their tune at this meeting. Then Robertson wanted an agreement on a text of a Communique to the press stating that the Soviets opposed a disarmament commission. The Russians would not agree to consider such a Communique and wanted it postponed until the next meeting. Clay and Robertson said they felt free to communicate themselves to their respective presses. The Russians objected to this. It was agreed to the disgust of everyone except the Russians to put the Communique off until the next meeting.

There was not much else that happened. Clay made a plan for national trade unions in connection with a paper on trade unions. And Koeltz ended the meeting with a plea that more coal from the Saar[11] be delivered to France and less to the Germans. I don't believe there will be much left of Germany when everybody gets through taking what he wants, and of course there is much justice in this. After fighting together they all went into a neighboring room for what Robertson called tea, which was indeed a very high tea. I went in for a moment to see what it was like. The principals all sat around one big table and the lesser lights sat around in the corners.

---

[9] Siehe Protokoll der 38. Sitzung des Politischen Direktorats, Alliierte Kontrollbehörde, am 29. Mai 1946, DPOL/M (46) 21-192, französischsprachige Fassung, in: AOF, Services Français à Berlin, GFCC, Bureau des Archives, caisse 1140, paquet 51.

[10] Donald R. Heath (siehe Dok. 8, Anm. 15) war der amerikanische Vertreter im Politischen Direktorat, Alliierte Kontrollbehörde.

[11] Gemeint ist das Gebiet des heutigen Saarlandes, das zunächst zur französischen Besatzungszone Deutschlands gehörte, dann der Zuständigkeit der Alliierten Kontrollbehörde entzogen und zu einem französischen Protektorat wurde.

I want to go to one meeting of the Control Council itself in order to get a complete picture of the international machinery.

I have just finished Franklin's[12] Autobiography[13],[14] It is by far too episodic but it makes you long for the comparative simplicity of 18th century America.

I love you my sweet heart and my boys and give you a tender good-night. I am very tired and shall go straight to bed. I hope those papers are over.[15] Goodnight my sweet ones – Edgar

Dok. 55
Schreiben an die Ehefrau
Berlin, Wannsee Officers' Club[1], Am Sandwerder 17/19, 31. Mai 1946

Dear Sweetheart –

If today is any example of how the world is run or can be run under quadripartite leadership, then I fear for the world. I have sat at quadripartite meetings from 10 this morning until six this evening with almost nothing accomplished. For most of the day it was the local government committee[2] trying to come to some agreements about electoral procedure for the forthcoming elections in Berlin (October) and about a provisional constitution for the city of Berlin.[3] We had decided to hold a special meeting this morning in order to make up for lost time. To begin with the French representative, a clear headed French lawyer by the name of Ziegelmaier[4] (all Frenchmen of importance here seem to have German names – the commanding General is Koeltz[5]) made a suggestion which I made three weeks ago but was then put aside, that we ask the Germans to frame the text of an electoral procedure and then base our discussions upon this text. This was now accepted by everyone, and the Committee sat down to draft a letter. This took until 1 o'clock. We then went along to have lunch at the English Blue and White Club. After lunch we got into a discussion of how this

---

[12] Siehe Dok. 52, Anm. 57.
[13] Siehe Dok. 52, Anm. 58.
[14] Siehe Dok. 52.
[15] Emily L. Johnson las Klausurarbeiten für Ray W. Frantz (siehe Dok. 11, Anm. 15). Siehe Dok. 48, Anm. 12.

[1] Siehe Dok. 25, Anm. 9.
[2] Siehe Dok. 29, Anm. 14.
[3] Siehe Protokoll der 20. Sitzung des Local Government Committee, Allied Kommandatura Berlin, am 31. Mai 1946, LG/M (46) 20, englischsprachige Fassung, in: TNA, Allied Kommandatura: Directives, Minutes and Papers, FO 1112/378; Protokoll der 21. Sitzung des Local Government Committee, Allied Kommandatura Berlin, am 31. Mai 1946, LG/M (46) 21, englischsprachige Fassung, in: ebd.
[4] Jean Victor Ziegelmeyer (1911–1987), Capitaine, französischer Jurist, Section Juridique du Gouvernement Militaire Français du Grand-Berlin, dann französischer Verbindungsoffizier beim Berliner Magistrat, gründete und leitete später in Frankreich eine Société d'électronique. Fotos mit Ziegelmeyer im Bildanhang, Abb. 68 und Abb. 77.
[5] Siehe Dok. 54, Anm. 7.

letter was to get to the proper Berlin authorities. A terrific argument developed, led by the Soviet representative (a Major Feldman[6] – a young boy who has been able to make no sense out this business of electoral procedure and constitutions and who does not therefore want to reveal his insecurity by going in for a discussion of them). In order to settle our difficulties we had to drag down the English and Soviet representatives of the Allied Secretariat of the Kommandatura[7], and they only muddled the waters. It was finally agreed at about 4:30 that the text of the letter we had drawn up should be turned over to the Secretariat and gotten to the proper Berlin authorities in some way or another. The British chairman was really insufferable also. I may have mentioned him,[8] a Major Ashton[9] who is a former cotton importer from Liverpool[10] (whom the English Labor government is now liquidating because they intend to take over the cotton importing business) and who is leading member of the Conservative Party in the City Council at Liverpool[11]. He was simply terrible, so terrible in fact, that I deliberately refused to go out tonight to any English mess where I should have had to spend the evening with him and another of his kind a Major Hayes[12]. They are fine people, all right. You can't help liking them in their way. But these two certainly don't know how to get along with other people. They just antagonize everybody by their insistence that there is only one way to do a thing and that is the English way. Well after the letter was finally gotten off we started off on our regular meeting which was supposed to discuss the Berlin Constitution. Before a meeting can go ahead the minutes of the last meeting have to be approved. The Russians usually stall a great deal on the actual text of the minutes, and this time was nothing new. Then Major Feldman was at it again. Captain Ziegelmaier also had some objections to make and by the time we got through approving three sets of minutes, it was time to go home. And so as the result of a day's discussion we got a letter and some minutes approved but no headway made on the Berlin elections or the Berlin constitution. It reminded me of Fling's[13] course on the Paris Peace Conference[14],[15]

---

[6] Siehe Dok. 49, Anm. 59.
[7] Siehe Dok. 20, Anm. 11.
[8] Siehe Dok. 49.
[9] Siehe Dok. 49, Anm. 28.
[10] Stadt an der Nordwestküste Englands.
[11] Ashton betätigte sich kommunalpolitisch in Wallasey bei Liverpool und war seit 1935 Mitglied des Wallasey Council.
[12] Harold Hays. Siehe Dok. 49, Anm. 26.
[13] Fred M. Fling (1860–1934), amerikanischer Historiker, 1883 BA, Bowdoin College, 1890 Dr. phil., Universität Leipzig, lehrte ab 1891 an der University of Nebraska, Professor of European History.
[14] Gemeint ist die Pariser Friedenskonferenz 1919/1920, auf der insgesamt 32 Staaten über die Friedensbedingungen beraten hatten, die dem Deutschen Reich und seinen Kriegsverbündeten gestellt werden sollten.
[15] Fling hatte in Paris, während der Friedenskonferenz, als Beauftragter der Historical Branch of the General Staff Material für eine Geschichte der Konferenz gesammelt. "[...] Fling has sailed to France with the group who accompanied President Wilson, to represent at Paris, during the period of the peace conference, the interests of the Historical Branch of the General Staff and to accumulate materials for that portion

In the course of the meeting, I was called into the Commandants' meeting[16], where upon my initiative, final recognition was made of the SPD and SED throughout Berlin.[17] May be that's enough for a day. But there was an unpleasant fight about a Youth Celebration which the Youth Committee of the Magistrat[18] wants to hold in Berlin on 5 June. We opposed it and held to our guns because the Russians had been holding up discussions on the problem of youth organizations in the Education Committee[19]. This seems to be the only way you can get along with them.[20]

Yesterday was Memorial Day[21] and I worked all day. At eleven I saw a young German publisher[22] who wants me to write a little foreword for a translation of Franklin's[23] autobiography[24] which he is putting out.[25] This I think I'll do since I have just read it. In the late afternoon, after working all day on Berlin elections and constitution which came to nothing today I took Col. Glaser[26] over to General Keating's[27] to discuss the recognition of the parties at today's Commandants' meeting. I was made melancholy by General Keating's informing us that he had broken three strikes during the war (a coal strike in West Virginia, a street car strike in Philadelphia, and an air-plant strike in California). He also thinks that because of the labor difficulties we are now having in America, we

of its history of which he has charge, the portion relating to the diplomatic history of the war and the peace." Historical News, in: The American Historical Review, Vol. 24, No. 2 (Januar 1919), S. 308–348, hier S. 311. "[...] his proposed account of the 1919 Versailles Peace Conference, which he attended as a research historian, never appeared." Robert E. Knoll, Prairie University. A History of the University of Nebraska, Lincoln, Nebraska, 1995, S. 65. Fling war bekannt für seinen Hang "to precision, completeness, and detail". Ebd.

16 Siehe Protokoll der 15. Sitzung der Stadtkommandanten am 31. Mai 1946, BKC/M (46) 15, englischsprachige Fassung, in: LAB, B Rep. 036-01 (Office of Military Government, Berlin Sector [OMGBS]), 11/148-1/10.
17 Siehe BK/O (46) 247 vom 31. Mai 1946, in: LAB, C Rep. 901 (Landesleitung Berlin der SED), Nr. 517; BK/O (46) 248 vom 31. Mai 1946, in: LAB, F Rep. 280 (Quellensammlung zur Berliner Zeitgeschichte [LAZ-Sammlung]), Nr. 4865.
18 Jugendausschuss, der bei der Magistratsabteilung für Volksbildung bestand. Siehe Hermann Weber, Freie Deutsche Jugend (FDJ), in: SBZ-Handbuch. Staatliche Verwaltungen, Parteien, gesellschaftliche Organisationen und ihre Führungskräfte in der Sowjetischen Besatzungszone Deutschlands 1945-1949, im Auftrag des Arbeitsbereiches Geschichte und Politik der DDR an der Universität Mannheim und des Instituts für Zeitgeschichte München hrsg. von Martin Broszat/Hermann Weber, München 1990, S. 665-690, hier S. 667.
19 Komitee der Alliierten Kommandantur Berlin.
20 Die Veranstaltung wurde schließlich bewilligt und fand am 18. Juni 1946 statt. Siehe Berlin. Kampf um Freiheit und Selbstverwaltung 1945-1946, hrsg. im Auftrage des Senats von Berlin (= Schriftenreihe zur Berliner Zeitgeschichte, Bd. 1), 2., erg. und erw. Auflage, Berlin 1961, S. 461, Nr. 38.
21 Amerikanischer Feiertag zu Ehren der Kriegsgefallenen. Siehe Memorial Day – 1946, in: OMGUS Observer vom 31. Mai 1946, S. 1.
22 Gemeint ist der Berliner Verleger Karl Heinz Henssel. Siehe Dok. 52, Anm. 56.
23 Siehe Dok. 52, Anm. 57.
24 Siehe Dok. 52, Anm. 58.
25 Siehe Dok. 52 und Dok. 54.
26 Siehe Dok. 28, Anm. 4.
27 Siehe Dok. 39, Anm. 6.

are about to go Socialist or Communist in the USA. A person like this you have to stick with in order to get things properly done. Afterwards I went to one of the nicest evenings I have had in Berlin. You remember my cellist friend Baldner[28]. Well two of his younger children[29] were confirmed yesterday[30]. A table in the living room was covered with confirmation presents, two of which were drawings, handsome drawings which Baldner himself had made as gifts for his kids. One was a view of a small town in Silesia[31] whither they had gone during the war to escape bombing,[32] and the other of a head of the crucified Christ which he had seen once in a church in Perpignan[33]. He is an extraordinary person. His quartet[34] played a lovely Mozart[35] quartet, the only one I was told that Mozart wrote in a minor key, and a Terzett of Dvorak[36] which I had never heard before. They also played the theme and variations movement from the Death and the Maiden Quartet[37]. We sat out on a terrace of a bombed-out house[38] while the music came from an inside room. The children sat in the inside room and were in audible rapture during most of the music. There were a lot of people there – both Americans and Germans including my old friend of steamer days, Dr. Max Rheinstein[39].

The evening before was taken up also. I had to go to a cocktail party of General Keating's at which I talked to Chinese, Brazilians and Danes and also considerably with General Clay[40] about the KPD and the future of America in Germany. He has a terribly good head. Thereupon I had to go to a party at the Lakeside Club[41], which is now housed in what was formerly General Eisen-

[28] Siehe Dok. 21, Anm. 18.
[29] Gemeint sind die Zwillinge Angelika und Lutz Baldner. Siehe Dok. 21, Anm. 24.
[30] Christi Himmelfahrt, 30. Mai 1946.
[31] Gebiet im Südosten des Staates Preußen, nach dem Zweiten Weltkrieg unter polnischer Verwaltung.
[32] Um dem Bombenkrieg zu entgehen, hatte sich die Familie Baldner 1943 auf die niederschlesische Besitzung des Widerstandskämpfers Paul Graf Yorck von Wartenburg (1902-2002) zurückgezogen und kam in der Försterei bei dem Ort Niehmen unter. Nach dem 20. Juli 1944 erfolgte die Rückkehr nach Berlin. Auskunft von Thomas Baldner (siehe Dok. 21, Anm. 24) in einem Telefongespräch mit Werner Breunig am 29. April 2009.
[33] Stadt in Südfrankreich.
[34] Gemeint ist das Zernick-Quartett (siehe Dok. 38, Anm. 3), mit dem Max Baldner 1945/1946, bis zu seinem Tod, spielte.
[35] Wolfgang Amadeus Mozart (1756-1791), österreichischer Komponist.
[36] Siehe Dok. 34, Anm. 7.
[37] Streichquartett Nr. 14 „Der Tod und das Mädchen" von Franz Schubert (siehe Dok. 38, Anm. 2).
[38] Podbielskiallee 57. Siehe Dok. 21, Anm. 25. In dem Haus „fanden", so Thomas Baldner in einer E-Mail an Werner Breunig vom 20. September 2010, „Zusammenkünfte der großen Geister Berlins mit den amerikanischen Freunden statt, was wohl auf der überragenden Persönlichkeit meines Vaters fußte. Es versteht sich fast von selbst, dass da [...] viel Musik gemacht wurde, an der ich als blutjunger Student als Begleiter meines Vaters und anderer Musiker auch immer wieder teilnahm."
[39] Siehe Dok. 11, Anm. 22.
[40] Siehe Dok. 2, Anm. 6.
[41] Siehe Dok. 17 und Dok. 18. Der Lakeside Club war zuerst Am Großen Wannsee 2/4 untergebracht. Siehe Dok. 18, Anm. 20.

hower's[42] house on an island[43] in the Wannsee[44]. This was given by Col. Taylor[45] and his wife[46]. I ran into a certain Olsen[47] there who was active in Nebraska doing rehabilitation work with farmers. He complained of how little help he could get from the University. It was a large party with people walking about on the terraces looking down on the lake. The Heaths[48] were there, and at Keating's party. I had had lunch with them before going to the Political Directorate[49] to hear the discussion about Berlin elections. At the Directorate the Russian delegate (Ivanov[50]) called upon me to help with the discussion. Feldman in today's Committee meetings referred to this. The Soviets have their eyes open as to persons. Sometimes I think I could negotiate with them.

Doesn't this sound perfectly rotten – all this party talk. I am sick of it. It's got to the point now where there has to be one huge party after the other to pay debts. I can't stand this pace. It's one reason why I don't want to stay here, and I don't think you would like it either.

I thought the Civil Service money might amount to a little more. If you are sure there is going to be more and considerable inflation in the USA it is better to convert this money into something other than the equivalent of money, unless we hold the bond until the dollar gets stabilized again. A thousand dollars

---

[42] Siehe Dok. 18, Anm. 25.
[43] Inselstraße 16 auf der Insel Schwanenwerder (siehe Dok. 17, Anm. 13 und 14). Hier hatte General Eisenhower im August 1945 Quartier genommen. Eigentümer war ab 1938 der Chemieindustrielle Maximilian Baginski (1891–1964) gewesen. Siehe Rüdiger Reitmeier, Sonnenwenden – Geschichte, Glanz und Parties, in: Burkhardt Sonnenstuhl (Hrsg.), Prominente in Berlin-Wannsee und ihre Geschichten, Berlin 2006, S. 17–67, hier S. 44; Harry Balkow-Gölitzer, Dwight D. Eisenhower, in: ebd., S. 130–132, hier S. 132; Georg Schertz, Schwanenwerder. Eine Insel im Spiegelbild der Geschichte, in: Berlin in Geschichte und Gegenwart. Jahrbuch des Landesarchivs Berlin 2005, S. 209–223, hier S. 218–220; Lothar Uebel, Neue Hoffnung nach Verfall und Stagnation?, in: Janin Reif/Horst Schumacher/Lothar Uebel, Schwanenwerder. Ein Inselparadies in Berlin, Berlin 2000, S. 129–138, hier S. 129; Meldekarten Max Baginski, in: LAB, B Rep. 021 (Einwohnermeldeamt Berlin). Foto des Hauses im Bildanhang, Abb. 60.
[44] Gemeint ist der Große Wannsee, eine Ausbuchtung der Havel (siehe Dok. 74, Anm. 24) im Südwesten Berlins.
[45] Siehe Dok. 17, Anm. 26.
[46] Katherine W. Taylor, geb. Wright.
[47] C. Arild Olsen (1898–1990), 1920 Candidate Theology, Grand View College Seminary, 1927 MA, University of Chicago, lehrte 1925–1930 History and Social Sciences, Grand View College, 1932–1938 President, Grand View College, 1939–1945 Farm Security Administration, Lincoln, Nebraska, bzw. Washington, D. C., ab 1945 OMGUS, 1947 Chief, Office of Religious Affairs, Education and Religious Affairs Branch, Internal Affairs and Communications Division, OMGUS, 1948/1949 Chief, Religious Affairs Branch, Education and Cultural Relations Division, OMGUS, dann Office High Commissioner Germany, ab 1951 National Council of the Churches of Christ in the USA, 1952 Honorary Doctorate, Augustana College.
[48] Donald R. Heath (siehe Dok. 8, Anm. 15) und Louise B. Heath, geb. Bell (1895–1981).
[49] Siehe Protokoll der 38. Sitzung des Politischen Direktorats, Alliierte Kontrollbehörde, am 29. Mai 1946, DPOL/M (46) 21, französischsprachige Fassung, in: AOF, Services Français à Berlin, GFCC, Bureau des Archives, caisse 1140, paquet 51.
[50] Siehe Dok. 49, Anm. 66.

bond, if we had to cash it, might only buy 500 dollars worth of stuff when we had to cash it. If we just forgot it however – that's something else. To spend it on reducing the balance on the house, on a car, on a piano would hardly be a mistake. Perhaps we should save it to spend on the boys in the right manner.

I hope John[51] gets to learn how to swim. May be there would be a camp available for him somewhere near Lincoln[52]. I am terribly anxious to hear him read. Give him a big tight hug from me. And Timmy[53] too. What you say about him is alarming (milk and glass) and ingratiating.[54] I hope those terrible papers are through, honey.[55] Don't take any more in this summer. If you are willing they will always come to you for there is no better. Good night, my lovely Emily. I love you with all my heart, and send you the tenderest caresses I know. Edgar

Dok. 56
Schreiben an die Ehefrau
Berlin, Wannsee Officers' Club[1], Am Sandwerder 17/19, 2. Juni 1946

Dearest Emily –

You have been in my mind almost all the day. I cannot tell you in how many ways. In very very intimate and tender ways. In one's imagination, many many thousands of miles away from the object of his love, one contemplates how he would act were he to have his love beside him, in a fashion somewhat different from what he actually would do were he really to have his love beside him. That is, I suppose, because he cannot quite imagine what his love would do. She has left him on one occasion to accept the most delicate caresses of which his imagination was capable. Sometimes these are infinite. They have been infinite today. When I should have had my mind on other things I have been able only to consider, how would it be to be with my love, today and tonight, for many days and many nights. Could we find new ways to tell each other how much we loved each other? I think so.

As it is I must go on with the account of my social engagements. You will be interested at least to know that in General Clay's[2] staff meeting[3] of yesterday, General Keating[4] complained of the number of parties that were being held at

---

[51] Johnsons Sohn John. Siehe Dok. 2, Anm. 15.
[52] Hauptstadt des US-Bundesstaats Nebraska, wo Johnson mit seiner Familie wohnte und an der Universität lehrte.
[53] Johnsons Sohn Thomas. Siehe Dok. 2, Anm. 16.
[54] Siehe Emily L. Johnsons Schreiben an Ehemann Edgar vom 23. Mai 1946, in: Unterlagen aus dem Nachlass Edgar N. Johnson, Privatbesitz Candice E. und Thomas R. Johnson, Denver, Colorado, USA.
[55] Emily L. Johnson las Klausurarbeiten für Ray W. Frantz (siehe Dok. 11, Anm. 15). Siehe Dok. 48, Anm. 12.

[1] Siehe Dok. 25, Anm. 9.
[2] Siehe Dok. 2, Anm. 6.
[3] Siehe Protokoll der OMGUS-Stabskonferenz am 1. Juni 1946, in: Archiv des IfZ, OMGUS – Staff Conferences (Protokollkopien), Fg 12/4.
[4] Siehe Dok. 39, Anm. 6.

the expense of the Berlin commissary. You will be interested to know also that General Clay himself joined in with Keating's complaint, and suggested that some steps ought to be taken to diminish the lavish display of food that is made at some buffet parties. He said that it was a bit anomalous that the Americans over here should be eating better than the Americans at home. General Clay is usually on the right side, but I have learned enough to know that it takes a long while before orders from the top get down to where they are really effective. Clay went out of his way to recommend that at least, on the mess tables, here we could do as much as was being done at home, we could take off the bread, and we could put signs about urging people to be careful with food. I don't know what the Germans think when they see such lavishness. It hardly fits the picture. There are still to be seen in our PX's[5] what I hoped, soon after my arrival here would be the case, huge boxes in which could be deposited, the surplus supplies which no one would ever use. It is a little embarrassing, when in the PX, to have a GI[6] ahead of you determined to buy everything that is possible to buy. For you know very well that he isn't going to use all this stuff. He just buys it in order to make money on the Black Market[7]. We are much too generous with all these things. It is simply the pressure of people back home to have things sold over here. After all, as Lt. Fromson[8] remarked to me in Austria, you can't expect American business men to let a market as big as this one get away from them. The Germans have to use the Black Market. My new driver (Sanow[9] has been suspended a week for exceeding the speed limit) frankly declares that it is necessary for him to patronize the B[lack] M[arket] if he is to get enough of the proper food to support his wife, a 4 ½ y[ea]r old daughter, and his Mother. Where his Father is he does not know. The Poles took his Father away last summer, and he has not been heard of since.

At Clay's staff meeting it was also announced that an American officer who was motoring through the countryside with his wife and child was shot at.[10] This is the only example of this kind of action that I have heard of.

The number of automobile accidents here continues to be shocking. At least one death a day. And the number of attacks upon American soldiers, and the

---

[5] Post Exchanges, Verkaufsläden der amerikanischen Streitkräfte.
[6] Government Issue, ugs. für amerikanischer Soldat.
[7] Siehe Dok. 21, Anm. 11.
[8] Howard A. Fromson (geb. 1921), amerikanischer Wirtschaftsexperte, 1943 BA, Harvard University, 1943–1945 OSS-Mitarbeiter, Economic Intelligence Officer in Nordafrika, Italien und Österreich, 1958 Gründung der Anocoil Corporation, Rockville, Connecticut.
[9] Siehe Dok. 40, Anm. 13.
[10] Im Protokoll der OMGUS-Stabskonferenz am 1. Juni 1946, S. 11f., in: Archiv des IfZ, OMGUS – Staff Conferences (Protokollkopien), Fg 12/4, heißt es hierzu: "During the period twenty-one incidents involving attacks on US personnel were reported. This past week saw fifteen such incidents and six were shown the previous week. In the majority of cases, US soldiers were beaten up by groups of young Germans, altho in six cases the attacks were made with firearms. In Ebersbach a captain driving with his newly arrived wife and child was fired at and the bullet passed thru the windshield and rear window of the car without, however, injuring any of the occupants. The Mannheim area showed the greatest concentration of such incidents and this particular city for months has been the scene of incidents of all categories."

number of attacks of American soldiers upon Germans, does not abate. The % of colored soldiers participating in these attacks is high. In many cases it is simply the result of their attempting to get their prostitute friends out of jail where they have been put awaiting physical examinations. It is a long way from the lofty decisions of General Clay, and the activities of political parties in Berlin, the colored GI's spending the nights with German prostitutes. I don't suppose that any historian, or other person can quite comprehend it all.

Keating admitted to me at the staff meeting that the number of incidents involving Germans + GI's is still alarming. At the same time it must not be forgotten that daily there are being held court martials involving such cases, and that every day American officers are sending GI's to jail for years on end because they have been guilty of assaulting Germans. But the court martials do not get into the press. Indeed they hardly get around to anybody except those who participate in the court martials. My friend, Captain Americus Mitchel[11], is now sitting on a court martial, and he participates daily in trials which result in penning up American soldiers for unwarranted assaults upon Germans. So we try to do right.

Yesterday I went sailing with Americus in our red boat. It was a good day. And I was glad for the release since after the difficulties on Friday[12,13] I could not quite combat the lull on Saturday[14], and wondered whether it was not my duty to save the American tax payers the large salary they are paying me and come home. In the course of our sail we had thrust upon us a German Fraulein who was being carried about in a launch of the Major who supervises the sailing upon the Wannsee[15]. She wanted a ride in a sail-boat. She was a pretty piece but an apparent phony because when once cast in our midst she tried to impress us with how, in Hamburg[16], she used to spend the summers in her brother's yacht sailing around Copenhagen[17]. Actually I don't think she had ever been in a sail-boat before. And I could not help but think of the many American girls who are working here who would have enjoyed being in our sail-boat, rather than this pretty and shapely little German bitch.

Today I actually did a bit of studying. I worked on my foreword to the German translation of Franklin's[18] autobiography[19,20]. I am re-reading it, taking notes as I go. But I must confess this Franklin is just a little bit too American for me. He had his eyes a little too securely fixed upon the dollar work or upon its colonial equivalent, and if anything, I shall have to soft-pedal this in my foreword. I wonder what a Soviet historian would do with this piece of Benjamin's. Do you remember the lady he came across in London who was living the life of

[11] Americus Mitchell Jr. Siehe Dok. 41, Anm. 11.
[12] 31. Mai 1946.
[13] Siehe Dok. 55.
[14] 1. Juni 1946.
[15] Gemeint ist der Große Wannsee, eine Ausbuchtung der Havel (siehe Dok. 74, Anm. 24) im Südwesten Berlins.
[16] Stadt in der britischen Besatzungszone Deutschlands.
[17] Hauptstadt Dänemarks.
[18] Siehe Dok. 52, Anm. 57.
[19] Siehe Dok. 52, Anm. 58.
[20] Siehe Dok. 52, Dok. 54 und Dok. 55.

a nun, because she could find no nunnery to enter in England. What impressed Franklin was not the general austerity of her life and the sacrificial quality of it. He learned that she lived on cold oatmeal water and nothing else. Therefore he felt inclined to warn his son that it was possible to live on only a penny or so a day – as much as it would take to supply enough oat-meal water to keep one alive.

I saw Otto Suhr[21] this afternoon and brought him a package that Franz[22] sent. He is a very able fellow, and I only wish he were the actual leader of the Social Democrats rather than the temporary General Secretary.[23] After this I went to a cocktail party given by General Millbourne[24] who treated me very warmly (General Clay's Chief of Staff). I spent most of the time talking to Joe Keenan[25], Clay's labor adviser, a hard boiled, close to the earth, Irish Catholic, Federation of Labor, Trade Union man who wants to send some Jesuit priests and American nuns over here to teach the Germans democracy. How confused we are getting.

I love you my sweet and must return to my imaginings as I go to sleep. It is now June, and the weeks go by. Ultimately I shall be in your arms. Good-night my beloved, my dearest Em[ily]. Edgar

Dok. 57
Schreiben an die Ehefrau
Berlin, 3. Juni 1946

Dear lovely one –

You are a difficult person. When once I think I have a question decided, and write all around that I have it decided, behold a letter[1] comes from you throwing the whole question open again. I had the impression that you didn't want to come to Europe, that you didn't want to bring the boys[2] to Europe. Now you say,

---

[21] Siehe Dok. 40, Anm. 7.
[22] Franz L. Neumann. Siehe Dok. 1, Anm. 8.
[23] Suhr war zunächst geschäftsführender Generalsekretär der neu organisierten Berliner SPD. Siehe Dok. 40, Anm. 7. Franz Neumann (siehe Dok. 37, Anm. 26), einer der drei SPD-Vorsitzenden, hatte ihn überzeugt, „daß er mit seinem Organisationstalent der richtige für den Posten des geschäftsführenden Parteisekretärs sei". Gunter Lange, Otto Suhr. Im Schatten von Ernst Reuter und Willy Brandt. Eine Biographie (Reihe Praktische Demokratie), Bonn 1994, S. 125. Auf dem Parteitag der Berliner SPD am 17./18. August 1946 wurde Suhr dann zum Generalsekretär gewählt. Siehe Telegraf vom 20. August 1946, S. 4.
[24] Bryan L. Milburn. Siehe Dok. 15, Anm. 20.
[25] Joseph D. Keenan (1896–1984), amerikanischer Gewerkschaftsfunktionär, ab 1937 Secretary, Chicago Federation of Labor, 1943–1945 Vice Chairman for Labor, War Production Board, 1945–1947 Labor Adviser to Lucius D. Clay (siehe Dok. 2, Anm. 6), 1954–1976 International Secretary, International Brotherhood of Electrical Workers. Clay und Keenan hatten bereits beim War Production Board zusammengearbeitet. Siehe John H. Backer, Die deutschen Jahre des Generals Clay. Der Weg zur Bundesrepublik 1945–1949, München 1983, S. 294.

[1] Gemeint ist Emily L. Johnsons Brief vom 28. Mai 1946, in: Unterlagen aus dem Nachlass Edgar N. Johnson, Privatbesitz Candice E. und Thomas R. Johnson, Denver, Colorado, USA.
[2] Gemeint sind die Söhne John und Thomas. Siehe Dok. 2, Anm. 15 und 16.

after an evening with Ola and Orin[3] during which they tried to persuade you to come over here for a year "for the things it would give us together" that "I am not unaware of this aspect of it and if *you* want to stay on another year, I'd *most happily* join you." You never said this before, that is the *most happily* part of it and I have gone on the theory that you really didn't want to come over, and to suffer the responsibility of bringing the kids over. Well I'm not switching over immediately to the other point of view but it does put a little different light on it. I think that what I'd better do is to go and see Clay[4] and make sure that the job is mine if I want it. Then I'd better make sure that there will be such a job for the time that we might want to stay here. We are getting a little tough on the Russians and are refusing to dismantle any more plants in our zone until Russia consents to treat Germany as an economic unit. Treating Germany as an economic unit involves setting up some central administrative agencies. Central administrative agencies spell the doom of our set-up at Stuttgart[5,6]. I don't want to be without a job again. But if he says definitely I can have the job, and it seems likely that the job will last until next summer then I shall reconsider this matter. The thing to do then is to decide it in a hurry so as to get you over here as soon as possible if case we stay, or to get me back in Lincoln[7]. I just won't live without you at my side any longer than I have to, and the end of when I have to is in sight. Of course I love you very much for all the indecision. I love you very much for consenting to read those papers[8] at my expense. But I hope you won't do it again. Tomorrow I'll answer your wonderful letter of today more in detail. Goodnight my adorable one. I send you all of me. Edgar

Dok. 58
Schreiben an die Ehefrau
Berlin, 5. Juni 1946

Dear Sweetheart:

They called another holiday today – D day.[1] If only we had a few more Allies here we shouldn't have to work there would be so many holidays. I have spent

---

[3] Olga F. Stepanek (1906-1998), geb. Folda, 1930 MA (English), University of Chicago, und ihr Ehemann Orin Stepanek (1888-1955), amerikanischer Neuphilologe, 1914 MA, Harvard University, lehrte ab 1920 an der University of Nebraska, ab 1930 als Associate Professor of English and Slavonic Languages.

[4] Siehe Dok. 2, Anm. 6.

[5] Hauptstadt des Landes Württemberg-Baden in der amerikanischen Besatzungszone Deutschlands.

[6] Gemeint ist, dass zentrale deutsche Verwaltungsstellen den Länderrat der amerikanischen Besatzungszone Deutschlands und das RGCO in Stuttgart überflüssig machen würden. Siehe Dok. 2, Anm. 11.

[7] Hauptstadt des US-Bundesstaats Nebraska, wo Johnson mit seiner Familie wohnte und an der Universität lehrte.

[8] Gemeint sind die Klausurarbeiten, die Emily L. Johnson für Ray W. Frantz (siehe Dok. 11, Anm. 15) korrigierte. Siehe Dok. 48, Anm. 12.

[1] Es handelte sich um den zweiten Jahrestag des D-Day, des Beginns der Landung alliierter Truppen in der Normandie am 6. Juni 1944. "The second anniversary of

the day so far rereading Franklin's[2] Autobiography[3] by way of getting ready to open this Foreword over the week-end.[4] Tonight I have to go to Brewster Morris's[5] to meet Pieck[6] the former Communist leader, and now one of the Chairmen of the Executive Committee of the SED. The SED is showing itself a little more conciliatory. They have evidently received orders to cooperate. The other night Ullbricht[7], another of their Russian trained Communists came to our office[8] and talked a long time.[9] They are like the Nazis now and want to forget the past. But it is to be feared that this calm is only the preliminary to another offensive and where it will land no one knows. You remember when I came here I said that our relations with the Soviets were gradually getting worse. They have continued to go in that direction so that now it is a matter of official comment and are all urged to keep up good personal relations while the official relations are not good. I think I mentioned the last meeting of the Coordinating Committee[10] I attended, the one which continued to fight over a Disarmament Commission to view the extent to which disarmament had gone in the four zones.[11] The Russians do not want investigation into economic disarmament. I hope they are not making munitions. In any case with their usual wearing down tactics they succeeded in getting the question held up for another meeting. There was unusually frank talk to them by Robertson[12] and Clay[13] both of whom complained of the utter futility to which the Russians were reducing the Committee. Robertson told them plainly that what was in the document upon which they were trying to agree was the plain truth but that the Soviet Delegation was not interested in having the plain truth go into the record. But Robertson, at the same time, is very lofty and a bit supercilious in his approach. Somebody said to me the other day that they wished the war would come so we could get it over in a hurry while we have the atom bomb[14]. This is vile talk and

D-Day, when United States and British troops breached the continental defense of Germany, will be observed as a holiday throughout the E[uropean] T[heater]", hatte General Joseph T. McNarney (siehe Dok. 17, Anm. 41) bekannt gegeben. 2nd Anniversary of D-Day Is ET Holiday Tomorrow, in: The Stars and Stripes, European Edition, vom 5. Juni 1946, S. 1. Siehe D-Day Anniversary, in: OMGUS Observer vom 7. Juni 1946, S. 3.

[2] Siehe Dok. 52, Anm. 57.
[3] Siehe Dok. 52, Anm. 58.
[4] Siehe Dok. 52, Dok. 54, Dok. 55 und Dok. 56.
[5] Siehe Dok. 31, Anm. 13.
[6] Siehe Dok. 30, Anm. 9.
[7] Walter Ulbricht. Siehe Dok. 39, Anm. 24.
[8] Office of the Civil Administration Branch, OMGBD.
[9] Siehe Special Report of Civil Administration Branch, OMGBD, vom 10. Juni 1946: Berlin Elections. Political Opinion and Summary, S. 2-6, in: BArch, Koblenz, Z 45 F, 17/258-3/2.
[10] Siehe Dok. 15, Anm. 21.
[11] Siehe Dok. 54.
[12] Siehe Dok. 54, Anm. 6.
[13] Siehe Dok. 2, Anm. 6.
[14] Als Gegengewicht zum vermuteten deutschen war das amerikanische Atomprojekt begonnen worden. Am 6. und 9. August 1945 wurden die ersten Luftangriffe mit Atombomben im Krieg gegen Japan gegen die Städte Hiroshima und Nagasaki geflo-

I don't believe it will necessarily come to this but it is hard to see what the compromise is going to be. Perhaps we are lucky in having the UNO[15] in existence in case these normal methods of reaching decisions do not work. It would all be a little better if we could give everybody a chance to express himself. But as long as all of eastern Europe, with the exception of Czecho-Slovakia[16] and possibly Austria[17] is kept under minority governments who use terroristic methods there is nothing they cannot do. The Russian controlled press here,[18] and radio[19] are horrible to me. Our press is bad enough but it's wonderful compared to this. Elections for city governments were carried out in our zone a week ago Sunday[20].[21] They were not mentioned in the Berlin radio. Instead the municipal elections in Turkey were being talked about.[22] They were not mentioned in the overt Russian newspaper here. And the way they distort all the news to point the guilty finger at the USA is maddening. I wonder what the people at home would really think if they knew just how they were being treated by the Russian licensed newspapers here. I hope the ice will be broken at Paris.[23] If not there can only be a further deterioration in relationships. It is not easy to see the outcome.

Two years ago I was on the high seas abandoning you, it has seemed, forever.[24] I shall of course never forget the early morning of this day aboard the New Amsterdam[25] when we were ordered through the first boat drill and then told

gen. Die Amerikaner verfügten zunächst über ein Kernwaffenmonopol, das erst 1949 durch eine erfolgreiche Explosion einer sowjetischen Atombombe gebrochen wurde.

[15] United Nations Organization, 1945 gegründete Staatenverbindung, wichtigste Aufgaben: Sicherung des Weltfriedens, Einhaltung des Völkerrechts, Schutz der Menschenrechte und Förderung der internationalen Zusammenarbeit.

[16] Die Tschechoslowakische Republik wurde 1948 kommunistisch, als die Kommunisten durch einen Staatsstreich die Macht vollständig an sich rissen.

[17] Österreich war getrennt und unabhängig von Deutschland wiederhergestellt worden und wie Deutschland in Besatzungszonen aufgeteilt.

[18] Hierzu zählten Tageszeitungen wie die Berliner Zeitung und die Tägliche Rundschau.

[19] Gemeint ist der Berliner Rundfunk, der von der sowjetischen Besatzungsmacht kontrolliert wurde. Bei Kriegsende hatten die Sowjets das Haus des Rundfunks an der Masurenallee im Bezirk Charlottenburg übernommen, und auch nach Ankunft der Westmächte und Übernahme des Bezirks durch die Briten behielten die Sowjets die Kontrolle bei.

[20] 26. Mai 1946.

[21] Kommunalwahlen für die Stadtkreise in Bayern, Groß-Hessen und Württemberg-Baden. Siehe Keesing's Archiv der Gegenwart, XVI. Jg., 1946, S. 763 A; Das Ergebnis der Städtewahlen. Hohe Wahlbeteiligung – CSU und SPD als stärkste Parteien, in: Die Neue Zeitung vom 31. Mai 1946, S. 3; Conrad F. Latour/Thilo Vogelsang, Okkupation und Wiederaufbau. Die Tätigkeit der Militärregierung in der amerikanischen Besatzungszone Deutschlands 1944–1947 (Studien zur Zeitgeschichte), Stuttgart 1973, S. 111.

[22] Am 26. Mai 1946 waren in der Türkei Gemeindewahlen durchgeführt worden. Siehe Der Tagesspiegel vom 30. Mai 1946, [S. 1] (Spiegel des Erdballs).

[23] Gemeint ist die Pariser Außenministerkonferenz. Siehe Dok. 44, Anm. 13.

[24] Im Juni 1944 hatte Johnson sich als Mitarbeiter der Research and Analysis Branch, OSS, auf dem Weg nach London befunden.

[25] Der Transatlantik-Liner „Nieuw Amsterdam" war 1938 als das Flaggschiff der Holland-Amerika Lijn und das bis dahin größte Schiff unter niederländischer Flagge

that the invasion of France had been launched.[26] Nor of course the first day of arrival in London when we were greeted by the first V-1[27]. That was not an easy summer and fall for any of us. The world is at least freed for the moment of such terrors, though the terrors it has are serious enough.

When I think over these two years and try to relate it to the prospect of staying on here it seems now that I have had enough. I have not been to Clay as I suggested in my last note to you, and I don't know when I shall go.[28] I thought today that perhaps I should ask to go to Stuttgart[29] and look over the job[30] in some detail but I don't know as I shall. If we should go there we would be contented enough, I suppose, as contented as it is possible to be under these circumstances. Somebody mentioned the other day that Pollock[31] does an awful lot of entertaining of various people there, and I don't look forward to a lot of entertaining. I have had enough of these parties and can't really keep up the pace. It is for the professional diplomats. We should see some parts of Europe while we were here but it would be difficult to see them properly with the boys as young as they are, and there is a great deal to be said for waiting until Europe revives a bit and the boys are a bit older before going on sight-seeing tours. I sometimes feel moreover that if I stay over here another year I shall be quite spoiled for the scholarly life. Maybe I am already. Jim[32] said in a recent letter that "you can hardly imagine what an attractive home and family you are denying yourself". Without more enthusiasm from you I don't imagine I shall be able to work up enough enthusiasm to stay on. I suppose this is very unadventurous.

I had the finance office here send you a check for 1600 dollars which brings up my salary to June 1st.[33] I kept out $ 148.51 to keep me going here for awhile since I was running rather low, having had no check since my arrival.[34] I don't know how you want to use this. I have suggested a car for your needs there which goodness knows are heavy enough.[35] There is the piano for John[36] than which there is nothing more important. We also have to keep some reserve for

---

    vom Stapel gelaufen und wurde im Zweiten Weltkrieg für den Truppentransport eingesetzt, "completing 44 war time voyages carrying nearly 400,000 passengers (mostly troops)". http://www.hollandamerica.com/news/NewsRelease.action?newsReleaseId= 593 (letzter Zugriff am 30. Januar 2013). Siehe http://www.gallagher.com/ww2/chapter11.html (letzter Zugriff am 30. Januar 2013).

[26] Am 6. Juni 1944 hatte die Landung alliierter Truppen in der Normandie begonnen. Siehe Anm. 1.
[27] Fieseler Fi 103, auch V 1 (Vergeltungswaffe 1) genannt, eine raketenbetriebene Flugwaffe, von der deutschen Luftwaffe ab Juni 1944 gegen englische Städte, insbesondere London, eingesetzt.
[28] Siehe Dok. 57.
[29] Hauptstadt des Landes Württemberg-Baden in der amerikanischen Besatzungszone Deutschlands.
[30] Gemeint ist die Leitung des RGCO. Siehe Dok. 2, Anm. 11.
[31] Siehe Dok. 15, Anm. 12.
[32] James L. Sellers. Siehe Dok. 49, Anm. 77.
[33] Siehe Dok. 44 und Dok. 51.
[34] Siehe Dok. 51.
[35] Siehe Dok. 51 und Dok. 55.
[36] Johnsons Sohn John. Siehe Dok. 2, Anm. 15.

taxes. If I stay until Sept. 1 you will get 1800 dollars more in allotments. What I get here will be a little more than I need for expenses, and we can count on about 275 from retirement at some later date. Nor do I think that I shall take any leave since that will give us another half months salary. May be we can squeeze both the car and the piano out of this.

I'm so happy that Mrs. Brown[37] has returned.[38] Congratulate my dear John on his going to the lesson alone.[39]

I should like to have seen you in your black dress with the beads, daisies in your hair, white gloves.[40] Also your new hat. Your mention of our wedding day with what went on before and what has gone on since stirs up more than usual, and I think about you pretty constantly wonderful memories and emotions. I wonder if this is the place to continue the honeymoon. I must have some gray hairs also to match yours. I can't believe they are very important – You will always be very lovely to me. If there are lovely ladies here I have not noticed them to the extent that I have been tempted to seek them out. I love you very much, my darling, and I long for you and wish only for the swift passing of the months. Edgar

Dok. 59
Schreiben an die Ehefrau
Berlin, 9. Juni 1946

Dear Sweetheart –

The Germans and English are celebrating a Whitsuntide holiday today and tomorrow but the Americans go on irreligiously with their affairs. It happens to be a rather rainy day and the boats on the lake[1] are turning in with their wet sails. There was a handsome vase with lovely delphinium in it in the window at breakfast this morning. I have noticed that the flowers here bloom at about the same time as at home, possibly a bit later.

At breakfast there was a colonel who is stationed at Frankfurt[2] and is up here on some kind of a furlough. He is from Mississippi[3] though he now lives in Texas[4]. His plans for bringing his family over are, I imagine, typical of those

---

[37] Siehe Dok. 33, Anm. 50.
[38] Siehe Emily L. Johnsons Brief vom 28. Mai 1946, in: Unterlagen aus dem Nachlass Edgar N. Johnson, Privatbesitz Candice E. und Thomas R. Johnson, Denver, Colorado, USA.
[39] Siehe ebd.
[40] Emily L. Johnson hatte über die Hochzeit von Mary Lancaster berichtet, und ihr Ehemann nimmt darauf Bezug. Siehe Dok. 53, Anm. 3.

[1] Gemeint ist der Große Wannsee, eine Ausbuchtung der Havel (siehe Dok. 74, Anm. 24) im Südwesten Berlins.
[2] Frankfurt am Main, Stadt im Land Groß-Hessen in der amerikanischen Besatzungszone Deutschlands.
[3] US-Bundesstaat.
[4] US-Bundesstaat.

who are making similar plans. He has two daughters, one 11 and one 17. They are coming too. For the 17 year old he is going to try to find a University in Switzerland or France if she can come home once a month. Otherwise he is going to keep her home. She is studying painting (the best southern tradition) and he will get a private tutor in painting for her, and a language tutor. The eleven year old will also have a language tutor (German and French) and will study the piano. He hopes that while they are here they can do a lot of traveling in western Europe, and indeed in Germany which he admits is very very beautiful. Col. Glaser[5] is going to bring over an 18 year old son[6] if he is released from the Marines, and is seeking a University for him in Europe which will not require a knowledge of German.[7] I met a wife at a party last night. Mrs. Clay[8] was at the opera with Don Heath[9]. I saw Col. Rosengren[10] going through the halls with his six year old son[11] in the Internal Affairs and Administration building[12].

From your note of May 31 I gather that your earlier reactions to my staying here and your coming over with the boys correspond to your real wishes, and that the "most happily" has to do chiefly with your conforming to a decision I would make.[13] At least in this present note you seem to have no regrets about my coming home around the first of September rather than staying here. I have found it difficult to reopen in my mind the question of staying here since we seem to have been agreed that it was, on the whole, best that I should come home. I shall have to give Clay[14] my decision soon since he may wish to arrange for giving someone else the Pollock[15] job[16], and also be of the opinion that if I

[5] Siehe Dok. 28, Anm. 4.
[6] Anthony J. Glaser (geb. 1927), studierte 1944/1945 am Tufts College (seit 1954: Tufts University) Engineering, 1945/1946 Marine Corps, 1946-1948 Aufenthalt in Berlin, Besuch der American University of Berlin, 1951 Absolvent des College of Engineering, Syracuse University, 1951-1953 Air Force, 1953-1993 Industrial Engineer.
[7] In einer E-Mail an Werner Breunig vom 22. August 2009 schreibt Anthony J. Glaser: "My mother, Marguerite [siehe Dok. 40, Anm. 22], joined my father in late summer, 1946 and I followed shortly thereafter – probably in October – after being discharged from the US Marine Corps where I had served since March, 1945 when I became 18. I was 19 and a half when I arrived in Berlin and 21 and a half when I left two years later (9/48) during the Soviet blockade of Berlin." Ferner: "I had completed one year of engineering before joining the Marines. I considered continuing my education at a university, but instead I attended a few courses at the American University of Berlin (a United States Armed Forces Institute – USAFI school)."
[8] Marjorie McK. Clay, geb. McKeown (1898-1992), Ehefrau von Lucius D. Clay (siehe Dok. 2, Anm. 6).
[9] Donald R. Heath. Siehe Dok. 8, Anm. 15.
[10] Siehe Dok. 19, Anm. 17.
[11] Erik L. Rosengren (geb. ca. 1940).
[12] Rosengren war seinerzeit für die Civil Service Branch der Civil Administration Division tätig.
[13] Johnson nimmt hier Bezug auf Emily L. Johnsons Briefe vom 28. und 31. Mai 1946, in: Unterlagen aus dem Nachlass Edgar N. Johnson, Privatbesitz Candice E. und Thomas R. Johnson, Denver, Colorado, USA. Siehe Dok. 57.
[14] Siehe Dok. 2, Anm. 6.
[15] Siehe Dok. 15, Anm. 12.
[16] Pollock hatte die Absicht, sein Amt als Director, RGCO, OMGUS, aufzugeben und in die USA zurückzukehren.

am not going to Stuttgart[17] it is a waste of government money for me to stay here.

I had a fine long letter from Harold Vedeler[18], the first one, really, I have had, since I saw him in Washington.[19] He has come to the conclusion, and I gather that this is the conclusion of those he works with in the state department that it is useless to continue to maintain the present pretense of international solidarity since it is only too clear that the Soviets are interested in achieving their particular aims (an international Communist world) at the expense of all cooperation if necessary. He thinks we must organize the so-called western world in accordance with new international institutions and that when once that is accomplished it will be so strong that the Russians will have to deal with it on a full reciprocal basis. Only after the western world has been organized as a unit strong enough to bargain collectively with the Soviets (not weakly separated into national fragments) will the Russians see that they cannot take advantage (as the Nazis did) of a divided western world, and will be obliged to modify their aims. Only after this can there be some accommodation of East and West into a one world, and that can only come after a long development. I think he is right. It is a dangerous policy but it is less dangerous than making constant concessions to the Russians, and failing to organize ourselves.

I went to Mozart's[20] "Abduction from the Seraglio" which was put on for the first time at the Staatsoper yesterday afternoon.[21] I had seen it only once before at Munich[22] and had forgotten what a wonderfully rich opera it was. Afterwards Col. Glaser gave a party for some of the leading members of the cast and other guests – the tenor Peter Anders[23] (whom I had met previously), the leading soprano, Erna Berger[24], a quiet, modest person and an excellent musician, her understudy, an Elizabeth Streik[25] (21 years) old, with a slight but beautifully trained coloratura voice. There were others there, a grand baritone named Greindl[26], a

[17] Hauptstadt des Landes Württemberg-Baden in der amerikanischen Besatzungszone Deutschlands.
[18] Siehe Dok. 2, Anm. 12. Vedelers Brief vom 30. Mai 1946 ist vorhanden in: UChicago Library, Special Collections Research Center, Edgar N. Johnson Papers.
[19] Siehe Dok. 2 und Dok. 4.
[20] Siehe Dok. 55, Anm. 35.
[21] Die Premiere der Oper „Die Entführung aus dem Serail" von Wolfgang Amadeus Mozart fand am 8. Juni 1946, 17 Uhr, in der Deutschen Staatsoper im Admiralspalast im Bezirk Mitte, Friedrichstraße 101/102, statt. Die musikalische Leitung hatte Karl Schmidt (1895-1950), Regie führte Karl August Neumann (1897-1947). Siehe Kurt Westphal, „Die Entführung aus dem Serail". Neuinszenierung in der Staatsoper, in: Berliner Zeitung vom 12. Juni 1946, [S. 3]; Lina Jung, Die Entführung aus dem Serail. Mozart in der Staatsoper, in: Der Tagesspiegel vom 13. Juni 1946, Beiblatt. Die Staatsoper hatte nach der Zerstörung ihres Hauses Unter den Linden ihren Spielbetrieb am 23. August 1945 im Admiralspalast wieder aufgenommen.
[22] Hauptstadt des Landes Bayern in der amerikanischen Besatzungszone Deutschlands.
[23] Peter Anders (1908-1954), Tenor (Belmonte in „Die Entführung aus dem Serail").
[24] Erna Berger (1900-1990), deutsche Sopranistin (Konstanze in „Die Entführung aus dem Serail").
[25] Gemeint ist Rita Streich (1920-1987), deutsche Koloratursopranistin (Blonde in „Die Entführung aus dem Serail").
[26] Josef Greindl (1912-1993), deutscher Bassbariton.

powerful mezzo-soprano, Frau Bose[27], and the director of the opera, one Legal[28]. Unfortunately Legal and Greindl have a more or less Nazi past. Col. Glaser had some of them sing at his party. Greindl sang some Wagner[29], (Wotan's farewell[30]), Anders some Schubert[31] and Schuman[32] songs, and Bose, an aria from Samson and Delilah[33]). This was all very wonderful singing. But somehow the affair left me cold because it was so patently arranged. Col. Glaser, as I have told you, is a publicity man and he naturally sees things from the point of view of public relations. So all the right people were there, right from the point of view of his position, and there were some Germans there who would be nice to have in order that the right people could talk to them. He invited a Social Democrat who might be the future mayor of Berlin[34] because somebody else wanted to talk about politics and he wanted to be in contact with anyone who might be a future mayor of Berlin. I suppose this is only proper. But instead of being a group of people who came to hear and talk about music and associate with German artists it was rather a miscellaneous assortment of Americans for whom the Germans were performing. Social Democrats, Communists, Nazis. The Col. said he had no objection using a Nazi singer for his party.

I am glad the papers[35] are finished for I expect to profit a little from it and I know that you are relieved. I hope you will use the money for a new dress or at

---

[27] Gemeint ist Petronella Boser, geb. Hofmann (1910–1994), deutsche Mezzosopranistin.
[28] Ernst Legal (1881–1955), deutscher Schauspieler, Regisseur und Intendant, Buchhändlerlehre, danach Großherzogliche Musik- und Theaterschule Weimar, 1933–1936 Direktor des Theaters in der Saarlandstraße, Berlin, dann Oberspielleiter am Berliner Schiller-Theater, 1945–1952 Leiter der ehemaligen Preußischen Staatstheater und Intendant der Deutschen Staatsoper, Berlin.
[29] Richard Wagner (1813–1883), deutscher Komponist.
[30] Wotans Arie „Leb' wohl, du kühnes, herrliches Kind!" (Wotans Abschied von Brünnhilde) aus dem dritten Akt, dritte Szene der Oper „Die Walküre" von Richard Wagner.
[31] Siehe Dok. 38, Anm. 2.
[32] Robert Schumann (1810–1856), deutscher Komponist.
[33] Oper des französischen Komponisten Camille Saint-Saëns (1835–1921).
[34] Unklar ist, um welchen Sozialdemokraten es sich handelte. Nach den Stadtverordnetenwahlen vom 20. Oktober 1946 standen der Berliner SPD zwei Kandidaten zur Nominierung für die Oberbürgermeisterwahl zur Verfügung: der frühere preußische Finanzminister Hermann Lüdemann (1880–1959), 1947–1949 Ministerpräsident von Schleswig-Holstein, und der Bezirksbürgermeister von Berlin-Wilmersdorf, Otto Ostrowski (1883–1963). Nominiert wurde am 29. Oktober 1946 Ostrowski, der dann am 5. Dezember 1946 von der Stadtverordnetenversammlung von Groß-Berlin zum Oberbürgermeister gewählt wurde. Siehe Wolfgang Ribbe, Otto Ostrowski, in: Stadtoberhäupter. Biographien Berliner Bürgermeister im 19. und 20. Jahrhundert, hrsg. von Wolfgang Ribbe (= Berlinische Lebensbilder, Bd. 7), Berlin 1992, S. 357–371, hier S. 357 und 365. Der SPD-Politiker Ernst Reuter (1889–1953) kehrte Mitte Dezember 1946 zu spät aus dem türkischen Exil nach Berlin zurück, um als möglicher Oberbürgermeister berücksichtigt werden zu können. Nach dem Rücktritt von Ostrowski wurde er im Juni 1947 zum Oberbürgermeister gewählt, aber von der Alliierten Kommandantur infolge sowjetischen Einspruchs nicht bestätigt. Siehe Daniel Koerfer, Ernst Reuter, in: ebd., S. 419–442, hier S. 429–431.
[35] Gemeint sind die Klausurarbeiten, die Emily L. Johnson für Ray W. Frantz (siehe Dok. 11, Anm. 15) korrigierte. Siehe Dok. 48, Anm. 12.

least something to adorn your person. Ray[36] ought to be very grateful. I hope that the late hours you complain of have not contributed to the arthritis you complain of. This has me worried. You know I have always in the back of my mind the prepossession that someday you are going to pay with your health for the manner in which you do not take care of yourself. When you speak of arthritis I can conjure up dreadful pictures of people (the wife of our former graduate dean) who have suffered painfully and chronically from this ailment. So please go to the doctor, and take it easy for awhile. I love my sweet Emily very much. I know how sensitive she is to any pain and the prospect of her suffering from anything like chronic arthritis is unbearable. Please take care of yourself, honey. I have a hunch I'll get a letter from you tomorrow and that will start the week off well. I love you my sweet one. Hug the boys for me and take my fondest embraces. Edgar

Dok. 60
Schreiben an die Söhne[1]
Berlin, 9. Juni 1946

Dear Sweet Kid:

These are still Vienna cards.[2]

Mother wrote me about how you went to your music lesson all alone, and I wanted to tell you how proud that makes me. But I'm kind of sorry too because now I can't take you to your music lessons any more, and we had good times doing that. I love my Bre'r Rabbit[3]. Father Bear

Dok. 61
Schreiben an die Ehefrau
Berlin, 13. Juni 1946

Dearest –

I have felt somewhat better today. Because, for one, I did go to bed early last night, and escaped, as you would say, from this baffled immediate world. I therefore felt somewhat refreshed this morning. But, for two, I have succeeded in

---

[36] Ray W. Frantz. Siehe Dok. 11, Anm. 15.

[1] John und Thomas. Siehe Dok. 2, Anm. 15 und 16. Die Karte ist zwar an beide Söhne adressiert, Johnson spricht aber im Text nur John an.
[2] Johnson schrieb eine Postkarte, die er noch aus Wien hatte.
[3] "Brother Rabbit", die zentrale Figur in den Uncle Remus-Fortsetzungsgeschichten von Joel Chandler Harris (1848–1908), die erstmals 1879 in der Zeitung "The Atlanta Constitution" erschienen und aufgrund ihres optimistischen Bildes der amerikanischen Rassenbeziehungen nach dem offiziellen Ende der Rassentrennung schnell populär wurden. „Bruder Hase" setzt sich stets mittels List gegen stärkere Gegner durch.

justifying my existence a bit by participating in getting something done. Tomorrow at the meeting of the Commandants,[1] General Keating[2] under the item of the Agenda called unfinished business, will say to the Soviet Commandant, General Kotikov[3], "General, it has come to my attention, through several of my officers, that the judges in my (American Sector) sector have been interrogated by the president of the Kammergericht[4] (a Russian appointee of the highest court in Berlin) as to their political affiliations. Such an interrogation is contrary to the best principles of American administration. We do not believe that judges have any political interests to serve. They have only justice to serve. This interrogation, according to our information was upon orders of the Russian Kommandatura. I have ordered my officers to conduct an investigation through the instrumentality of the Legal Committee, but meanwhile I wonder if you know anything about the order, and if you do, whether you could tell us something about it, or arrange to tell us something about it at our next meeting."[5] This I helped to arrange through a personal conference with Keating this afternoon, attended also by Colonel Glaser[6], and a Colonel McNeil[7]. The German judges in our sector are particularly sensitive to political intimidation. They are sensitive to it not only because under the Nazis judges had to be political, and interpret the will of the people but because it so happens that since our arrival here, four of our judges (i. e. in the American sector) have simply disappeared, and have never been heard of since. Everyone knows that the Russians have carried them off but how and where and why nobody seems to be able to find out, even after prolonged quadripartite negotiations. Accordingly when judges in our sector are asked by their superiors to indicate their present political affiliations (the recent political history of Berlin is behind this) they fear that this is the prelude to their being carried off in some mysterious manner and disappearing behind what is beginning to be called the Soviet iron curtain[8].

[1] Siehe Protokoll der 16. Sitzung der Stadtkommandanten am 14. Juni 1946, BKC/M (46) 16, englischsprachige Fassung, in: LAB, B Rep. 036-01 (Office of Military Government, Berlin Sector [OMGBS]), 11/148-1/10.
[2] Siehe Dok. 39, Anm. 6.
[3] Siehe Dok. 35, Anm. 5.
[4] Präsident des Kammergerichts war Georg Strucksberg (1884–1965), deutscher Jurist, Dr. jur., 1945–Januar 1946 Vizepräsident und Februar 1946–1951 Präsident des Kammergerichts in Berlin (ab 1949 West-Berlin). Das Kammergericht war von der Alliierten Kommandantur als oberste Gerichtsinstanz in Berlin anstelle des unmittelbar nach dem Zusammenbruch geschaffenen Stadtgerichts wiedererrichtet worden und hatte ein Gebäude im sowjetischen Sektor, in der Neuen Friedrichstraße (heute: Littenstraße), erhalten.
[5] Siehe hierzu das Memorandum (Subject: Representations to be made at Allied Kommandatura Meeting in Connection with Intimidation of Judges) von Louis Glaser an Frank A. Keating vom 13. Juni 1946, in: LAB, B Rep. 036-01 (Office of Military Government, Berlin Sector [OMGBS]), 4/136-1/9.
[6] Siehe Dok. 28, Anm. 4.
[7] John P. MacNeill, Lieutenant Colonel, Chief, German Courts Section, Legal Branch, OMGBD.
[8] Der britische Politiker Winston Churchill (1874–1965), 1940–1945 und 1951–1955 Premierminister, hatte am 12. Mai 1945 in einem Telegramm an US-Präsident Harry S. Truman (siehe Dok. 5, Anm. 19) erstmals von einem „Eisernen Vorhang" gespro-

This came to my attention this afternoon after Col. Glaser consulted me as to what to do about the matter. Judges who had thus been intimidated came to our officers in some fright. Consider how impudent this is, the Russian Kommandatura orders an interrogation of the political affiliation of the judges in the American sector of Berlin! The matter was first brought to the attention of one Col. Pape[9] who was disinclined to do anything about it, disclined because orders have come out to the effect that our relations with the Russians are so bad that everything must be done to avoid any unpleasantness. This, of course, because of the conference of the ambassadors and foreign ministers which is to open in Paris on Saturday[10].[11] But the information came to us independently, and we learned, moreover, from one of the judges who is a legal consultant of ours, that among the highest judges of the Kammergericht, the same interrogation was being made upon the behest of the Soviet authorities. What Col. Pape was unwilling to do we were willing to do. Col. Glaser wanted to draft a memorandum suggesting to Keating that he take up the matter. I dislike this paper way of getting things done and suggested that we go to see Keating immediately about the matter. The general, for all his political innocence, has never yet refused to do the correct thing, and when once he sensed the situation agreed that a protest should be made in the Kommandatura[12]. Accordingly, it will be made. The Soviet authorities will at least be informed that we know what they are up to, and do not like it.

While we were with Keating he proceeded to tell us some of the difficulties he is having with the Russians during what it supposed to be a quiescent period. There are almost a million people in our sector.[13] There is constant difficulty because Soviet soldiers come over and rape, steal and plunder. Keating has had to protest 27 such cases in recent weeks. It so happens that this is something our soldiers do not do. If they want to rape and plunder and loot they do it in our sector and do not go over to the Russian sector. But we are very stringent when it comes to traffic regulations, because there have been so many accidents with untoward fatalities in our sector. And when it comes to traffic regulations a Russian soldier or officer is treated no differently than anyone else. All our drivers are terrified at the sight of an M. P. The Russians are reckless drivers, and rather than come under military arrest they drive hell bent for election through all traffic lights into all parts of the city. Our M. P.'s are armed and

chen, dann in seiner Rede am 5. März 1946 in Fulton, Missouri: „Von Stettin an der Ostsee bis hinunter nach Triest an der Adria ist ein ‚Eiserner Vorhang' über den Kontinent gezogen." Keesing's Archiv der Gegenwart, XVI. Jg., 1946, S. 669 B.

[9] Wesley F. Pape (1893–1967), Colonel, amerikanischer Jurist, 1918 und 1940–1946 US Army, 1922 LLB, Southeastern University, 1924 MPL, National University, 1945–Juni 1946 Deputy Chief, Legal Branch, OMGBD, Juli 1946–1949 Chief, Legal Branch, OMGBD/OMGBS, dann Chief, Legal Affairs Division, HICOG-BE.

[10] 15. Juni 1946.

[11] Vom 15. Juni bis 12. Juli 1946 fand die zweite Sitzungsperiode der Pariser Außenministerkonferenz statt. Siehe Dok. 44, Anm. 13.

[12] Siehe Dok. 20, Anm. 11.

[13] Der amerikanische Sektor wies am 29. Oktober 1946 eine Wohnbevölkerung von 979 846 Einwohnern auf. Siehe Berlin in Zahlen 1947. Taschenbuch, Hrsg.: Hauptamt für Statistik, Berlin 1949, S. 76.

some of them are a little nervous at the trigger. Consequently there have been not only wild chases of M. P.'s after Russian soldiers and officers but shooting matches in which Russians have been wounded and killed. It is all very nasty and unpleasant business. But I guess it is inevitable when thousands of soldiers of different nationalities are placed beside each other within rather narrow confines.

I had lunch with Walter Dorn[14] today and he is quite pessimistic over what can be done to speed up the German handling of the de-Nazification question.[15] You remember that he now has this responsibility.[16] A main part of the difficulty is that the Germans who can handle the problem are so poorly fed that they haven't the energy to carry on with the problem. German officials faint in their offices continuously for lack of strength. Nor is there much by way of salary to encourage them. You remember what I said earlier about the moral courage to fight the battle, our battle. When that is present there has to be food to nourish it. Pieck[17], the Communist leader here, is a pot-bellied leader of the workers. The Russians keep him, and all of their supporters well fed.

I visited the quarters I may have to move into today. They are quite nice. The ground floor of a house close to the Schlachtensee[18] which is surrounded by a pinewood. There is a piano and there is a housekeeper who says she loves to cook. I think I am permitted to buy a certain amount of supplies from the commissary.

I waited for a letter today but I know you have much to do. Anyway I feel a little better and I love you and our fine boys and I kiss and hug you all very closely. Edgar

Dok. 62
Schreiben an die Ehefrau
Berlin, 15. Juni 1946

Dearest Emily –

I have felt a little abandoned by you this week. For some reason or other I have longed intensely for a word from you, more intensely than usual, and nothing has come since Monday[1].[2] Don't think I am blaming you. I have some understanding of what you have on your hands, and after the experiences you have been through since I left I can well imagine that some other untoward thing has turned up to drive you frantic. And I guess I put too much hope on

---

[14] Siehe Dok. 2, Anm. 10.
[15] Siehe Dok. 47 und Dok. 52.
[16] Siehe Dok. 52.
[17] Siehe Dok. 30, Anm. 9.
[18] See in dem zum amerikanischen Sektor gehörenden Bezirk Zehlendorf.

[1] 10. Juni 1946.
[2] Gemeint ist wahrscheinlich Emily L. Johnsons Brief vom 4. Juni 1946, in: Unterlagen aus dem Nachlass Edgar N. Johnson, Privatbesitz Candice E. und Thomas R. Johnson, Denver, Colorado, USA.

your completion of those papers[3] for Ray[4], and believed that it would be possible to have the benefit of your gracious and facile pen in somewhat greater abundance after they were through. I shall be rewarded in any case next week, perhaps even on Monday[5]. Soon this kind of dependence upon the mail will be over. Today is the 15th of June and within two months or close to thereabouts I should be starting back to you. That seems, all in all a short time if we consider how long I really have been away. For I have been able to work out in my own mind no good reasons for prolonging my stay here let alone whipping up enthusiasm to take the place of reasons. I do not look forward to returning to America. Though I am anxious to return to certain people there.

My desire to return is not fortified by the news in today's press. I refer to the defeat of Griswold[6] by Butler[7].[8] This happens to come at a moment when it makes a great impression upon my mind. Yesterday I sat for hours again in the local government committee of the Commandatura[9].[10] We had finally got to the point of deciding which draft of the constitution of Berlin we would discuss, the constitution of 1920[11], or the draft recently prepared by the present municipal government[12]. Since the present municipal government is largely Soviet appointed[13] Major Feldmann[14], the Soviet delegate will consider no other draft as the basis for discussion. Major Hayes[15], however, the British delegate, after consulting German constitutional experts and what appears to be veritable legions of English constitutional lawyers has come to the conclusion that the Magistrat's

[3] Gemeint sind die Klausurarbeiten, die Emily L. Johnson korrigierte. Siehe Dok. 48, Anm. 12.
[4] Ray W. Frantz. Siehe Dok. 11, Anm. 15.
[5] 17. Juni 1946.
[6] Dwight P. Griswold (1893–1954), amerikanischer Politiker (Republikanische Partei), 1941–1947 Gouverneur des US-Bundesstaats Nebraska, 1946 erfolglos bei der Nominierung als Kandidat der Republikaner für den US-Senat, 1947 Director, Internal Affairs and Communications Division, OMGUS, 1947/1948 Chief, American Mission for Aid to Greece, 1953/1954 Senator des US-Bundesstaats Nebraska.
[7] Hugh A. Butler (1878–1954), amerikanischer Politiker (Republikanische Partei), 1941–1954 Senator des US-Bundesstaats Nebraska.
[8] Als Kandidat für den US-Senat war am 11. Juni 1946 bei den Vorwahlen der Republikanischen Partei in Nebraska der Isolationist Butler nomiert worden, der sich gegen den Internationalisten Griswold durchsetzte. Siehe Warren Moscow, Griswold Beaten in Nebraska Vote. Candidate Backed by Stassen Loses in Primary Linked to 1948 White House Race, in: The New York Times vom 12. Juni 1946, S. 1.
[9] Siehe Dok. 29, Anm. 14.
[10] Siehe Protokoll der 23. Sitzung des Local Government Committee, Allied Kommandatura Berlin, am 14. Juni 1946, LG/M (46) 23, französischsprachige Fassung, in: TNA, Allied Kommandatura: Directives, Minutes and Papers, FO 1112/378; englischsprachige Fassung in: TNA, Control Commission for Germany (British Element), CCG (BE), FO 1012/246.
[11] Gesetz über die Bildung einer neuen Stadtgemeinde Berlin vom 27. April 1920, in: Preußische Gesetzsammlung, 1920, S. 123–150.
[12] Magistratsentwurf vom 29. April 1946, in: Vorläufige Verfassung von Groß-Berlin, erl. von Dr. Haas, Kämmerer von Groß-Berlin, 4., neubearb. Auflage, Berlin 1947, S. 115–126.
[13] Siehe Dok. 27, Anm. 30.
[14] Iossif Moissejewitsch Feldman. Siehe Dok. 49, Anm. 59.
[15] Harold Hays. Siehe Dok. 49, Anm. 26.

(the present city administration's) draft is an impossible one and that it would be a waste of time to discuss it. We who have consulted no German experts, and have no constitutional lawyers available, have stood with the Soviets, since it was agreed earlier that this was the draft that would be discussed, and since we feel that it doesn't make much difference which draft we discuss if we get down to discussing some draft. The constitution is due 15 July[16] and we have it all to discuss at the moment. The Soviet delegate became perfectly enraged at the lecturing of Major Hayes, a little superior and a little patronizing. At one moment, in utter disgust he took out a Russian newspaper and began to read it while the Britisher was talking. Since the French chairman[17] was not adamant on the point, though as a lawyer he was inclined to be sympathetic to the English proposal, we soon had Major Hayes out on a limb, and when confronted with a proposal to report to the Commandants that the Committee could not agree and that a new one should be appointed, he capitulated, after insisting that a statement of his point of view be incorporated into the minutes[18] – when once we got down to discussing actual terms of the constitution we got along better. But I shall always remember that at a moment when Allied relations are at their worst since the conclusion of the war, and at a moment when we are told that at the present meeting of the foreign ministers[19] the split is likely to come between east and west the relations between the Soviets and ourselves in the local government committee were friendly. Maybe Major Feldman will remember that too as we get ready to fight the next war (which I really don't believe).

I am glad too that at this crucial point I was able to go to the Russian political adviser of General Kotikov[20], a certain Mr. Panim[21] and pay my respects. I had been made known to him by Colonel Kramer[22], our labor officer, who gets along with him. I suggested that it might be possible to have dinner sometime and he responded that that would be very agreeable. May be I'll have a chance to talk heart to heart with a Russian yet, before leaving this theatre. It would be a great event for me.

I think I made reference to the incident of the Russians calling for the political affiliations of the judges in our sector.[23] Well General Keating[24] made the

---

[16] Die Zeit drängte angesichts des Wahltermins. Aus Sorge um die Durchführung der Oktoberwahlen hatten die Stadtkommandanten das Local Government Committee angewiesen, "to hasten its work and to submit a draft of the constitution by the 15th July". Protokoll der 16. Sitzung der Stadtkommandanten am 14. Juni 1946, BKC/M (46) 16-157, englischsprachige Fassung, in: LAB, B Rep. 036-01 (Office of Military Government, Berlin Sector [OMGBS]), 11/148-1/10.
[17] Jean Victor Ziegelmeyer. Siehe Dok. 55, Anm. 4.
[18] Siehe Statement by the British Member vom 17. Juni 1946, in: TNA, Allied Kommandatura: Directives, Minutes and Papers, FO 1112/378.
[19] Zur Pariser Außenministerkonferenz siehe Dok. 44, Anm. 13.
[20] Siehe Dok. 35, Anm. 5.
[21] Alexei Wassiljewitsch Panin (geb. 1911), sowjetischer Major, ab 1945 Vertreter des Politischen Beraters, Verwaltung des Militärkommandanten des sowjetischen Besatzungssektors der Stadt Berlin.
[22] Siehe Dok. 49, Anm. 6.
[23] Siehe Dok. 61.
[24] Siehe Dok. 39, Anm. 6.

protest at the Kommandatura[25] meeting on Friday[26].[27] It was a desultory meeting. General Kotikov seemed weary of trying to combat the French-Anglo-American agreement on most questions. In fact the Russians in the Kommandatura have been trying to reduce the number of meetings that are held. They want to reduce the number of committee meetings, the number of meetings of the deputy commandants, and the number of meetings of the commandants themselves. In Omgus[28] too they are trying to reduce the number of occasions when it is necessary to talk things over across the table. This may be the prelude to the break which is to come at Paris[29], a preliminary announcement that the Russians are withdrawing to their own sphere and to hell with the consequences. General Keating got a strong reaction to his protest. Kotikov said he knew nothing about it and had given no such orders, that this was just an attempt of the Germans to sow discord among the Allies and that he would conduct a thoroughgoing investigation. We also investigated and found out that whether or not Kotikov had knowledge of it, the fact was that some Russian had ordered it, and the order was conveyed to the president of the supreme court by a vice-president[30] who was a member of the SED. When we tried to contact the president of the Kammergericht (a Dr. Strucksberg[31]) he had already been summoned to Russian headquarters, and told to cancel the order inasmuch as it had been misunderstood. What the Russians wanted was not the present political affiliation of judges but their political affiliation as of 1 January and 1 May 1945 which indeed makes absolutely no sense whatever. In any case our protest, based on the correct premises, resulted in a Russian cancellation of their order, and this is a little victory. At the same time that we can be friendly with the Russians, we can also make protests, and all this we can do by adhering to a simple American creed which has no anti- or pro-Soviet bias but only is attempting to carry out what we as a nation represent.

At this moment comes the news from Nebraska[32]. Walter Lippmann[33] has an article on the result in the New York Herald Tribune[34] (Paris edition) in which he opines that it is a confirmation of the American trend towards isolation-

---

[25] Siehe Dok. 20, Anm. 11.
[26] 14. Juni 1946.
[27] Siehe Protokoll der 16. Sitzung der Stadtkommandanten am 14. Juni 1946, BKC/M (46) 16-158, englischsprachige Fassung, in: LAB, B Rep. 036-01 (Office of Military Government, Berlin Sector [OMGBS]), 11/148-1/10.
[28] Siehe Dok. 17, Anm. 45.
[29] Zur Pariser Außenministerkonferenz siehe Dok. 44, Anm. 13.
[30] Gemeint ist Richard Hartmann (1902–1965), deutscher Jurist, 1923 Dr. jur., 1945–Februar 1946 Amtsgerichtsrat, Amtsgericht Berlin-Treptow bzw. Amtsgericht Berlin-Köpenick, März 1946–1949 Vizepräsident des Kammergerichts in Berlin, anschließend Rechtsanwalt und Notar, Berlin (Ost). Hartmann war SED-Mitglied und kam aus der KPD, der er ab 1. Juli 1945 angehört hatte.
[31] Siehe Dok. 61, Anm. 4.
[32] US-Bundesstaat.
[33] Walter Lippmann (1889–1974), amerikanischer Journalist, politischer Kommentator und Schriftsteller, 1909 BA, Harvard University, ab 1931 erschien seine Zeitungskolumne "Today and Tomorrow" in der "New York Herald Tribune".
[34] Amerikanische Tageszeitung, republikanisch orientiert.

ism.[35] The other papers are full of it. It is given especial significances because of Stassen's[36] support of Griswold. I wonder if the Nebraskans realize the extent to which this is world news, and how much the Europeans will seek in it a confirmation of their notion that we are certain to abandon them again. There is no point in going over the details. But I resolved upon reading the news today what when I got home I should try to arrange for a speaking tour throughout Nebraska, may be you could go with me, in the course of which I should try to chide them in correct fashion for this one thing only their abandonment of their responsibility and this return to their hay-like gorging on their own corn. I think I could prepare an effective speech and at least raise some questions. May be the University could arrange this tour, or perhaps I should do it on behalf of the democratic candidate who is opposing Mr. Butler. I should rather like, I think, campaigning against Mr. Butler. That's carrying on the battle at home, if one can't carry it on in Berlin.

Good night my blessed one, and my dear boys. I shall end on the note I began with. Today is the 15 June and in eight weeks or so I shall be setting forth from here on the way back to you. This time it is for good. No more prolonged interruptions of our life together, a life which I shall try to live to the very full, devoted to the most intimate cultivation of one another. Good-night my beloved. I love you as no other person or thing, and I long for you. Edgar

Dok. 63
Schreiben an die Ehefrau
Berlin, 17. Juni 1946

Dearest –

I was rewarded today with two fine letters from you.[1] Another from Paul Sweet[2,3] and another from Henry[4,5] Henry's letter refers to his bringing over Dowd[6] to meet you and to see the house. "Nobody was there. But we walked

---

[35] Lippmann hatte den Artikel "Portent From Nebraska" für seine Kolumne "Today and Tomorrow" verfasst. Siehe New York Herald Tribune, European Edition, vom 13. Juni 1946, S. 4.

[36] Harold E. Stassen (1907–2001), amerikanischer Jurist und Politiker (Republikanische Partei), 1939–1943 Gouverneur des US-Bundesstaats Minnesota, 1948–1953 President, University of Pennsylvania, zwischen 1948 und 1992 neunmal unterlegen bei der Nominierung des Präsidentschaftskandidaten der Republikanischen Partei.

[1] Emily L. Johnsons Schreiben vom 10. und 11./12. Juni 1946, in: Unterlagen aus dem Nachlass Edgar N. Johnson, Privatbesitz Candice E. und Thomas R. Johnson, Denver, Colorado, USA.

[2] Siehe Dok. 2, Anm. 28.

[3] Sweets Brief vom 10. Juni 1946 ist vorhanden in: UChicago Library, Special Collections Research Center, Edgar N. Johnson Papers.

[4] Charles Henry Oldfather. Siehe Dok. 2, Anm. 19.

[5] Oldfathers Brief vom 13. Juni 1946 ist vorhanden in: Unterlagen aus dem Nachlass Edgar N. Johnson, Privatbesitz Candice E. und Thomas R. Johnson, Denver, Colorado, USA.

[6] Siehe Dok. 49, Anm. 71.

around the yard and certainly every prospect was one to please. I could wish that the Oldfathers[7] had such an attractive home. And you are blest in your family. No doubting that." Undoubtedly a good deal of tragedy back of Henry's remarks in so far as it concerns the Oldfathers. And much tribute to you. I can imagine how well everything looks.

You are aware by this time that aside from the first reaction of mine to your "most happily" joining me, I have understood it pretty well, and come to a pretty final conclusion about my fate here. I have not been to General Clay[8] about staying on, nor do I think that I shall go to him. In fact I have begun to compose in my own mind the letter which I shall soon have to submit to him, telling him that I have decided to return to the University, and asking for the privilege of doing a little bit of travel in the zone[9] before returning. There is every patriotic reason to stay on here. There is every patriotic motive to return home. They both are of a piece. Paul wrote that had he to do it over again he would stay with the government until he got the academic job of his choosing. He has, in fact, accepted the Chicago job.[10] If under present circumstances I have decided not to stay here, I do not see what could, in the way of a job, persuade me to change my mind. But I come back in the expectation of rejoining you and the boys and not of being especially happy with the University, Nebraska[11], or the USA.

The Knabe[12] sounds like a real compromise if it is at all in any kind of shape. It is a well made piano though not in the Steinway[13] or Mason and Hamlin[14] class. May be we just can't afford the latter right now. Would it be possible to get Mr. Heller[15] to investigate the mechanism of the thing, and to get Herbert[16] to try it out? I like the size of it. The Stein[17], I think, is a kind of neither here nor there piano. The Knabe could be turned in for something later if we could afford a new piano, or if Gretchen[18] decided some day that she wanted to sell her Steinway. I don't think the age necessarily means anything. I am in favor of getting some kind of a decent piano for John[19], out of

---

[7] Die Familie von Charles Henry Oldfather und seiner Ehefrau Margaret K. Oldfather, geb. McLelland (1887–1956).
[8] Siehe Dok. 2, Anm. 6.
[9] Gemeint ist die amerikanische Besatzungszone Deutschlands.
[10] Siehe Dok. 49, Anm. 73. Sweet lehrte 1946/1947 an der University of Chicago. Siehe Dok. 2, Anm. 28.
[11] US-Bundesstaat.
[12] Gemeint ist ein Klavier der Knabe Piano Company, die 1837 in Baltimore, Maryland, gegründet wurde.
[13] Siehe Dok. 4, Anm. 25.
[14] Siehe Dok. 44, Anm. 26.
[15] Wahrscheinlich William F. Heller, Klavierstimmer und -reparateur.
[16] Herbert Schmidt. Siehe Dok. 29, Anm. 12.
[17] Klavier der Charles Frederick Stein Piano Company.
[18] Gemeint sein könnte Margarete (Gretchen) H. Rogers, geb. Hochdoerfer, ab 1960 verh. Carstensen (1886–1969), amerikanische Sprachwissenschaftlerin, 1909 MA, University of Illinois, 1929 PhD, University of Chicago, studierte auch in Deutschland (an den Universitäten Marburg und Berlin), lehrte bis zu ihrer Verehelichung mit George H. Rogers im Jahre 1937 an der University of Nebraska als Professor of Germanic Languages.
[19] Johnsons Sohn John. Siehe Dok. 2, Anm. 15.

all this. Otherwise we shall find our little accumulation slipping away from us as the inflation gets worse. Buy the Knabe if it will last until the day when John really has to have a first class instrument. It must be better than that up-right Steinway of the Sellers[20]. I even think dear John's ear is to be trusted in this matter.

You are so evidently in need of a rest and a complete one. Can't something be arranged for a few weeks in September in the mountains? What we should have is a hotel arrangement so that you would be quite free from cooking, etc. How about the Meeker Lodge[21]? That, as I remember it was a pleasant and comparatively inexpensive place. Or may be just something on a Minnesota[22] or an Iowa[23] lake. I could take care of the kids[24] most of the time. It would be a great treat after all this separation. If we take a cottage or cabin someplace, it will be very hard work for you. If we stay at home, I shall be tempted to get into notes and be thinking about lectures. Away from Lincoln[25] there would be no such opportunity. Or may be the Ozarks[26]. Or may be something in the Black Hills[27]. Your descriptions of these unbearable Nebraska days with the bad withering winds is discouraging. Early September can be bad too. The Hamiltons[28] know Minnesota places. If you can escape to someplace by September first, I could join you in that place. How about that wonderful Lodge we ran into the day after we arrived in the Gass'[29] cottage in Bear Creek Canyon[30].[31] What lake was it on?

There is an unpleasant intensity about Berlin, these days, as the immediate future of the world is being decided at Paris.[32] Most ugly rumors are going

[20] James L. Sellers (siehe Dok. 49, Anm. 77) und seine Ehefrau Nell K. Sellers, geb. Kennedy (siehe Dok. 52, Anm. 21).
[21] Ferienhaus im Meeker Park, in der Nähe von Allenspark, Colorado.
[22] US-Bundesstaat, nordöstlich von Nebraska gelegen.
[23] US-Bundesstaat, östlich von Nebraska gelegen.
[24] Gemeint sind die Söhne John und Thomas. Siehe Dok. 2, Anm. 15 und 16.
[25] Hauptstadt des US-Bundesstaats Nebraska, wo Johnson mit seiner Familie wohnte und an der Universität lehrte.
[26] Das Ozark-Plateau ist eine Hügellandschaft, die den größten Teil des Südens des US-Bundesstaats Missouri einnimmt.
[27] Eine Bergkette im westlichen Gebiet des US-Bundesstaats South Dakota, die bis ins nordöstliche Wyoming hineinreicht.
[28] Gemeint ist wahrscheinlich die Familie von Cliff S. Hamilton (1889–1975), 1922 PhD, Northwestern University, 1923–1927 und 1929–1957 Professor of Chemistry (1939–1956 Chairman of Department of Chemistry and Chemical Engineering), University of Nebraska.
[29] Gemeint ist die Familie von Sherlock B. Gass (1878–1945), 1904 PhB, University of Chicago, ab 1905 University of Nebraska, Professor of English.
[30] Im US-Bundesstaat Colorado, westlich von Denver.
[31] Geoffrey A. Gass, Sohn von Sherlock B. Gass, in einer E-Mail an Werner Breunig vom 30. Dezember 2009: "The cottage was located just outside the little town of Evergreen, about 20 miles WSW of Denver. I'm not sure of the name of the little creek across the road from the cabin. We spent summers there until 1936 when my father's first heart attack precluded his going to any high-altitude locations. The cabin there was built by my father and his brothers probably back in the 1920's. It was sold [...] around 1940."
[32] Zur Pariser Außenministerkonferenz siehe Dok. 44, Anm. 13.

about with respect to Russian intentions. I talked with somebody yesterday who ought to know, if anybody, what is going on and he speaks of five Russian armies being concentrated in the Russian zone from the Czech border to Stettin[33], so powerful that, if anything were to happen they could sweep the rest of the western powers out of Germany and not be stopped until they reacted the Atlantic and the Spanish border. It is quite possible that it is Franco's[34] armies which are preserving him in Western eyes. General Keating[35] let me attend his staff meeting this morning and he is taking the normal precautions of a military leader who must protect the most important installations under his command, the Tempelhof airfield[36], for example. And the troops are being provided with extra ammunition. You must be very very cautious in your mention of these things. They can be exaggerated way beyond their real significance. I am not an alarmist. But it is interesting to see what happens when a political situation gets tense. I wonder if this place, at least, is a good one for you and the boys to be.

Your baby and boy (there are appellations which I am only too willing to take from you) was dumped into the lake[37] yesterday. Walter Dorn[38] and I were out getting a little exercise paddling and withdrew into a boathouse to escape a bad rain. In getting out of the house, our sensitive craft quite unexpectedly turned over and we were thrown into the water and the boat got nicely filled. So it was a mess bailing the water out and getting back home. My watch is indeed waterproof.[39]

I went to the General[40] today about staying in my nice quarters[41], and he said I was to stay here.[42] This is really more convenient even if I don't have a piano.

I love you, my sweet Emily. 4½ months are gone. There are 2½ left. Then we shall be together for a very long time. Goodnight, my blessed one, my dearest. Edgar

---

[33] Bis 1945 Hauptstadt der preußischen Provinz Pommern, danach unter polnischer Verwaltung.
[34] Francisco Franco (1892-1975), spanischer General und Diktator, 1939-1975 Staatschef von Spanien.
[35] Siehe Dok. 39, Anm. 6.
[36] Flughafen Berlin-Tempelhof, der 1923 den Linienverkehr aufgenommen hatte.
[37] Gemeint ist wahrscheinlich der Große oder der Kleine Wannsee.
[38] Siehe Dok. 2, Anm. 10.
[39] Siehe Dok. 44.
[40] Wahrscheinlich Frank A. Keating. Siehe Dok. 39, Anm. 6.
[41] Am Sandwerder 17/19. Siehe Dok. 25, Anm. 9.
[42] Johnson hatte in seinem Schreiben vom 13. Juni 1946 (Dok. 61) von einem möglichen Umzug in eine Unterkunft nahe am Schlachtensee gesprochen.

Dok. 64
Schreiben an die Ehefrau
Berlin, 18. Juni 1946

My darling –

I am sending you, under separate cover, a carbon copy of the Foreword I prepared for this German translation of Franklin's[1] Autobiography[2].[3] If you will pardon, I shall say that I don't think it's bad. Indeed I think that it is perhaps the best thing I have ever written. Properly understood there is much of myself in it, the meaning of the war for me, the experience in Austria, and especially the experience here, which I think, the intelligent German can catch, all these things rising up through Franklin's text and catching hold of certain phrases and sentences which seem to have particular meaning for this sad Berlin of June 1946. I shall be anxious to hear what you think. If you think it good enough I wish you would give it to Orin[4] to read, and if he thinks it's good enough, ask him to give it to Wimberly[5] for publication in the Prairie Schooner[6]. If it is possible I should like to have some off-prints of it there. One says continuously that the Germans need talking to. After Butler's[7] victory[8] I am sure the Nebraskans[9] need talking to. I am not sure they are in a position to understand Franklin, but if you agree, I shouldn't mind giving this Foreword a little publicity.[10]

I have got a momentary political bug. It is the one I mentioned to you in a recent letter.[11] The nomination of Butler et al. is an enormous disgrace and cannot represent the real convictions of simple Nebraskans who have been properly instructed as to what is going on over here. I propose to offer my services to the Democratic Party of Nebraska to campaign against Butler for as much as

---

[1] Siehe Dok. 52, Anm. 57.
[2] Siehe Dok. 52, Anm. 58.
[3] Siehe Dok. 52, Dok. 54, Dok. 55, Dok. 56 und Dok. 58.
[4] Orin Stepanek. Siehe Dok. 57, Anm. 3.
[5] Lowry C. Wimberly (1890–1959), amerikanischer Neuphilologe, 1925 PhD, University of Nebraska, bis 1956 Professor of English, University of Nebraska.
[6] Literarische Zeitschrift, die Wimberly 1926 an der University of Nebraska begründet hatte und deren erster Herausgeber er bis 1956 war.
[7] Siehe Dok. 62, Anm. 7.
[8] Siehe Dok. 62, Anm. 8.
[9] Die Bewohner des US-Bundesstaats Nebraska.
[10] Ursula Seyffarth geht in ihrer Besprechung des noch 1946 erschienenen Buches (siehe Dok. 52, Anm. 61) auch auf Johnsons Vorwort ein: „Das Vorwort von Edgar N. Johnson stellt die Verbindung zwischen diesem Dokument eines vergangenen Jahrhunderts und unserer heutigen Welt her, indem es, menschenwürdig erhaben über jegliche Parteilichkeit oder pharisäisches Erziehenwollen, eine deutsche Aufgabe zwischen Ost und West als immanent annimmt und das Franklin'sche Ethos als Anliegen der ganzen heutigen Menschheit sieht." Welt und Wort. Literarische Monatsschrift, November 1946, S. 188. In Auszügen wurde das Vorwort in „Horizont. Halbmonatsschrift für junge Menschen" veröffentlicht. Siehe Benjamin Franklin und die deutsche Jugend, in: Horizont, 20. Heft, 1. Jg., 1. September 1946, S. 19.
[11] Siehe Dok. 62.

they want to use me. I can't believe that the new Chancellor[12] would object, and if he did I should do it anyway. If I felt that I was having any kind of influence upon Nebraska audiences, and sometimes I think I could let go my academic reserve and get down to basic sentiments which might have a popular emotional appeal. The Democrats might think I were worth trying for a candidacy for Congress[13]. In any case I wish you would give me Paul Good's[14] address. He is one of the leading Democrats in the state, and I should like to write him about it. He would know whether or not it is a foolhardy idea. My general outlook, and recent experience are such as should, if properly expressed evoke some kind of response. In any case I should like to give it a try. There would then be some kind of life to balance the sedentary academic existence, and I could raise, in our backward state some pertinent and awkward questions.

By the way, Paul Sweet[15] mentioned in a recent letter that some part of my medieval text was quoted on the editorial page of a recent issue of the Christian Science Monitor[16].[17] Have you heard anything about it?

The tale of John's[18] urinating on the floor of the porch off the dining room was indeed a strange one.[19] The way in which you handled it was, I think, quite extraordinary. If he really could not explain why he did it then there is, I believe, little point in punishing him – punishing him, that is, for something he himself could not understand. Such punishment would seem to him quite unforgivable.

I have been working on the new Constitution for Berlin all day. A draft is due for the Commandants on 15 July 1946.[20] After that there will be the matter of electoral procedure to decide upon and that will have to be ready about 1 August.[21] After that I think my job will be about done here. I can't wait until the

---

[12] Gemeint ist der künftige Chancellor der University of Nebraska. Das Amt sollte ab September 1946 der Biochemiker Reuben G. Gustavson (siehe Dok. 49, Anm. 79) innehaben.

[13] Der Kongress, die Legislative der USA, setzt sich aus dem Senat und dem Repräsentantenhaus zusammen.

[14] Paul F. Good (1893–1971), amerikanischer Jurist und Politiker (Demokratische Partei), 1921 MA, Oxford University, England, 1933–1935 Nebraska State Attorney General, 1936–1956 Chancellor, Diocese of Nebraska, Protestant Episcopal Church.

[15] Siehe Dok. 2, Anm. 28.

[16] Publikationsorgan der amerikanischen Christian Science Publishing Society.

[17] Siehe Dok. 63, Anm. 3. Unter der Überschrift "The Weavers of the Thirteenth Century" waren in The Christian Science Monitor vom 7. Juni 1946, S. 14, Textpassagen aus James Westfall Thompson/Edgar Nathaniel Johnson, An Introduction to Medieval Europe 300–1500, New York 1937, Kapitel 19 ("The Revival of Trade and Industry"), S. 566–568, abgedruckt.

[18] Johnsons Sohn John. Siehe Dok. 2, Anm. 15.

[19] Johnson bezieht sich hier auf ein Schreiben von Emily L. Johnson vom 11./12. Juni 1946, in: Unterlagen aus dem Nachlass Edgar N. Johnson, Privatbesitz Candice E. und Thomas R. Johnson, Denver, Colorado, USA.

[20] Siehe Dok. 62, Anm. 16.

[21] Das Local Government Committee, Allied Kommandatura Berlin, erhielt dann am 4. Juli 1946 vom Magistrat den Entwurf einer Wahlordnung. "[…] the Committee will give this document immediate consideration." LOC GOV/R (46) 30 vom 5. Juli 1946, Appendix A, englischsprachige Fassung, in: TNA, Allied Kommandatura: Directives, Minutes and Papers, FO 1112/377.

elections are held,[22] and the electoral campaign itself won't be worth prolonging my stay here. If Clay[23] lets me do a little trip through the zone I should be ready to start for home, perhaps, sometime shortly after the middle of August, and perhaps get there around the first of September rather than around the 8th. We shall need the extra week together. I found two good experts at Omgus[24] today who will help with some of the technical side of the Constitution, with proportional representation, for example, about which I hardly understand anything. I must say though, I find it a little amusing to be working on the Constitution of Berlin, though it is no less amusing than some of the other things I have been into in recent years. Colonel Glaser[25] is quite helpless with this since he knows no word of German, and the draft of the Constitution as submitted by the City Government[26] is of course not in English. There is an English translation but it is pretty frightful and no one could make much sense of it. This is a good example of what could happen if there were no-one around who could handle the German in some fashion.

So I shall be busy until this is done and that is some comfort. Then I shall have the great excitement of preparing to go home. I have the impression that many of the best people are not staying on another year. The stalemate reached on the quadripartite level has a bad effect on morale. Americans like to get some place.

I love you my darling. Kiss the sweet boys for me, and let's plan on a little get-away before school takes up. My own sweet girl, good-night. Edgar

Dok. 65
Schreiben an die Ehefrau
Berlin, 19. Juni 1946

Dearest –

A letter from you today telling me of the farewell dinner with the Marshalls[1].[2] I don't understand how they have been mistreated. He was hired for a year and the department has not re-hired him. It is quite accurate to say that we don't

---

[22] Am 3. Juni 1946 hatte das Koordinierungskomitee der Alliierten Kontrollbehörde (siehe Dok. 15, Anm. 21) entschieden, im Oktober 1946 Wahlen in Berlin abhalten zu lassen. Siehe Werner Breunig, Verfassunggebung in Berlin 1945–1950 (= Beiträge zur Politischen Wissenschaft, Bd. 58), Berlin 1990, S. 183.
[23] Siehe Dok. 2, Anm. 6.
[24] Siehe Dok. 17, Anm. 45.
[25] Siehe Dok. 28, Anm. 4.
[26] Magistratsentwurf vom 29. April 1946. Siehe Dok. 62, Anm. 12.

[1] Familie von Leon S. Marshall (1904–1989), amerikanischer Historiker, 1928 MA, University of Colorado, lehrte ab 1930 am Westminster College, New Wilmington, Pennsylvania, 1937 PhD, University of Pittsburgh, 1945/1946 Visiting Professor of European History, University of Nebraska, September 1946–1970 Kent State University (ab 1948 Full Professor).
[2] Emily L. Johnsons Brief vom 13. Juni 1946, in: Unterlagen aus dem Nachlass Edgar N. Johnson, Privatbesitz Candice E. und Thomas R. Johnson, Denver, Colorado, USA.

want another man in English history.[3] If we are to emphasize anything it is hardly English history. None of us would want that – certainly not Glenn[4] who may be somewhat terrified at the thought of two volumes on Manchester[5],[6] I'm a little terrified myself – Manchester – the cultural patterns of Manchester. I don't see that his age has anything to do with it. It is understandable that you don't like to tell a man to his face that you don't think his teaching was good enough to warrant what would then have been a permanent appointment at the University. Marshall must have had some idea of why he wasn't being re engaged, and why he couldn't be told the whole truth. I don't think it is necessary to accuse Glenn of some kind of conspiracy. Of course it is very hard not to have made good, but in this case I don't see that the department is to blame for this.

As for Glenn's being chairman I don't know as I am in favor of that either.[7] Henry[8] suggested in a recent letter that we ought to elect a chairman among ourselves and then have the chancellor make the appointment.[9] I don't know as I favor that either in so small a department voting against each other might cause unforgivable resentments. Henry would never vote for Jim[10], and Alden[11] I should suspect would feel obliged to vote for him. Since Glenn has never published anything except the two chapters in my book[12] which nobody has liked I don't think he is entitled to the distinction, no matter how excellent an administrator he might be or how much he knows. Nor with Jim's awkwardness does he make a likely chairman. I think the chancellor better make the appointment or that we should have it together – one a year. Jim has never published very much either. I don't think Glenn wants me to have it. He said something about my not being burdened with it when I was home. I am not anxious for it since it

---

[3] Mit englischer Geschichte beschäftigte sich am Department of History der University of Nebraska bereits Glenn W. Gray (siehe Dok. 49, Anm. 74).

[4] Glenn W. Gray. Siehe Dok. 49, Anm. 74.

[5] Stadt in England.

[6] Emily L. Johnson in ihrem Schreiben vom 13. Juni 1946: "The great point is, I am convinced, that he [Leon S. Marshall] has one book on *Manchester* now on the press + another nearly finished, and Glenn just can't take it." 1946 erschien in Syracuse, New York, Leon S. Marshalls Buch "The Development of Public Opinion in Manchester 1780–1820". So auch der Titel seiner Dissertation aus dem Jahre 1937.

[7] Emily L. Johnson: "*I am against Glenn as chairman of the department. He is lazy, selfish, and willing to cut off an other's head if it's in his interest. Very sweet, to be sure, but not sweet to those who get in his way.*"

[8] Charles Henry Oldfather. Siehe Dok. 2, Anm. 19.

[9] Siehe Dok. 49.

[10] James L. Sellers. Siehe Dok. 49, Anm. 77.

[11] John R. Alden (1908–1991), amerikanischer Historiker, 1939 PhD, University of Michigan, lehrte am Michigan State Normal College, an der Bowling Green State University, ab 1945 an der University of Nebraska (1946 als Assistant Professor), 1955–1976 an der Duke University.

[12] James Westfall Thompson/Edgar Nathaniel Johnson, An Introduction to Medieval Europe 300–1500, New York 1937. Glenn W. Gray hatte Kapitel 15 ("The Development of the English State [1066–1272]"), S. 432–462, und Kapitel 25 ("The Development of the English State [1272–1485]"), S. 833–862, verfasst. Johnson nahm diese beiden Kapitel über England auf, um alle Felder abzudecken.

would be only extra administrative and personal problems pain, having to do with raises and promotions. Should Glenn get a full professorship without ever having to publish anything, etc. But should I refuse it, if it comes my way?[13] Ben Franklin[14] said he would never ask for, never refuse, and never resign from an office.[15]

In some ways I hate to enter this small world again, and I think perhaps I shouldn't. You will be interested to know that I wrote the first draft of my letter to Clay[16] today – saying that I wanted to be home on or about the first of September.[17] I think when I get there I shall want, despite all my talk about trying to get into politics[18] to do nothing much more than stay at home and tend to my classes. Staying at home will mean cultivating you, cultivating the boys, and I suppose the garden. We have lost over two years, and you are always rightly reminding me of how really little time there is left. It is rather futile to think that I shall ever be able to do anything much outside of the rôle of teacher, and there is much still that I have to make up for. May be the time is coming with the boys getting a little older when you will get a better break, and when we can share more fully than we have ever shared, and cultivate more than we have ever cultivated a larger intellectual life. I have always in mind too being adequate for the boys. All this is enough without worrying about others promotions and salaries.

Tomorrow will be a full day at the Kommandatura[19],[20] talking about the Constitution of Berlin – whether the councilmen of Berlin shall have free rides on the trolleys or not.[21] But that is an easy one. I say no.

---

[13] Johnson wurde im Herbst 1946 temporary Chairman. Siehe Dok. 49, Anm. 75.
[14] Benjamin Franklin. Siehe Dok. 52, Anm. 57.
[15] "[…] I had read or heard of some Public Man, who made it a Rule never to ask for an Office, and never to refuse one when offer'd to him. I approve, says I, of his Rule, and will practise it with a small Addition; I shall never *ask*, never *refuse*, nor ever *resign* an Office." Benjamin Franklin, The Autobiography, with an introduction by Daniel Aaron, New York 1990, S. 109. In der deutschen Übertragung von Berthold Auerbach, revidiert von Heinz Förster, heißt es: „[…] ich habe von einem Manne in öffentlicher Stellung gehört oder gelesen, der es sich zur Regel gemacht hatte, sich niemals um ein Amt zu bewerben, aber auch niemals eines auszuschlagen, wenn es ihm angeboten wurde. ‚Ich pflichte dieser Regel bei und werde sie, nur mit einem kleinen Zusatz, befolgen', sagte ich; ‚ich werde mich nie um ein Amt *bewerben*, nie eins *ablehnen*, aber auch nie eins *aufgeben*. […]'" Benjamin Franklin, Autobiographie, mit einem Nachwort von Klaus Harpprecht (= Beck'sche Reihe, 1510), 2. Auflage, München 2010, S. 155.
[16] Siehe Dok. 2, Anm. 6.
[17] Siehe Dok. 63.
[18] Siehe Dok. 62 und Dok. 64.
[19] Siehe Dok. 20, Anm. 11.
[20] Johnson spricht hier die für den 20. Juni 1946 anberaumte Sitzung des Local Government Committee, Allied Kommandatura Berlin, an.
[21] Art. 11 des Magistratsentwurfs vom 29. April 1946 lautet: „Die Mitglieder der Abgeordnetenversammlung erhalten das Recht zur freien Fahrt innerhalb von Berlin auf den öffentlichen Verkehrsmitteln, Sitzungsgeld und Erstattung des durch die Sitzungen entstandenen Lohnausfalls." Vorläufige Verfassung von Groß-Berlin, erl. von Dr. Haas, Kämmerer von Groß-Berlin, 4., neubearb. Auflage, Berlin 1947, S. 119. Art. 8 der von den Alliierten erlassenen Vorläufigen Verfassung von Groß-Berlin vom

Goodnight my sweet one. In ten more days June will have gone. I love you very much. I think may be you have some idea how much. This is really an impossible existence here. Goodnight, sweetheart. Edgar

Dok. 66
Schreiben an die Ehefrau
Berlin, 23. Juni 1946

Dearest –

I have not written for a couple days. The evenings have been taken up for the last three days. Wednesday[1] the French threw an orchestra concert at which some French woman with a very complicated name[2] played the Tschaikowsky[3] second piano concerto[4], I think it was, and the Berlin Philharmonic Orchestra[5], conducted by a Roumanian (Cellibidache)[6] played the Beethoven 5th[7].[8] I went with Colonel Glaser[9] after a very unsatisfactory meeting of the Local Government Committee[10],[11] It was the first time I had heard the Philharmonic. It is not a bad orchestra at present and the conducter is above average. The orchestra was obliged to play, to begin with, the four national anthems of the Allies. This must be a little painful to do. This puts them in their places right away. They are a kind of slave labor. But they must feel a little rewarded when their efforts at

---

13. August 1946 lautet: „Die Mitglieder der Stadtverordnetenversammlung erhalten das Recht zur freien Fahrt innerhalb von Groß-Berlin auf den öffentlichen Verkehrsmitteln nebst Sitzungsgeld und Erstattung des durch die Sitzung entstandenen Lohnausfalles." Ebd., S. 9.

[1] Richtig: Thursday. Gemeint ist der 20. Juni 1946.
[2] Monique de la Bruchollerie (1915-1972), französische Pianistin.
[3] Peter Iljitsch Tschaikowsky (1840-1893), russischer Komponist.
[4] Es handelte sich um das 1874 entstandene 1. Klavierkonzert op. 23 in b-Moll.
[5] Das Berliner Philharmonische Orchester war 1882 gegründet worden. Nach dem Zweiten Weltkrieg konzertierte es erstmals am 26. Mai 1945 im Titania-Palast in der Schloßstraße im Berliner Verwaltungsbezirk Steglitz. Die alte Philharmonie, in der Bernburger Straße im Verwaltungsbezirk Tiergarten gelegen, war zerstört, und der Titania-Palast wurde ständiger Spielort des Orchesters.
[6] Sergiu Celibidache (1912-1996), deutscher Dirigent rumänischer Abstammung, leitete 1945-1952 ad interim die Berliner Philharmoniker.
[7] 5. Sinfonie op. 67 in c-Moll von Ludwig van Beethoven (siehe Dok. 37, Anm. 29).
[8] Das Konzert fand am 20. Juni 1946, 21 Uhr, in der Deutschen Staatsoper im Admiralspalast im Bezirk Mitte, Friedrichstraße 101/102, statt. Siehe Der Tagesspiegel vom 20. Juni 1946, Beiblatt; roi, Französische Pianistin in Berlin, in: Telegraf vom 21. Juni 1946, S. 5; Erwin Kroll, Philharmonisches Konzert. Solistin: Monique de la Bruchollerie, in: Der Tagesspiegel vom 22. Juni 1946, Beiblatt; Fritz Brust, Schwer erkämpftes Musikerlebnis. Am Flügel Monique de la Bruchollerie, in: Telegraf vom 22. Juni 1946, S. 5.
[9] Siehe Dok. 28, Anm. 4.
[10] Siehe Dok. 29, Anm. 14.
[11] Siehe Protokoll der 24. Sitzung des Local Government Committee, Allied Kommandatura Berlin, am 20. Juni 1946, LG/M (46) 24, französischsprachige Fassung, in: TNA, Allied Kommandatura: Directives, Minutes and Papers, FO 1112/378.

playing German music (the 5th) are heavily applauded by the Allies, and this in a manner to indicate that they are not being applauded simply as slaves who have done good work. In a sense therefore the Germans had the victory, and I wonder whether in the longer sense they might not get it again by having us leave here sooner than we should. Sometimes I feel very insecure about this – feel indeed that they may be running us. I had the feeling tonight, for example, when I discovered, at the mess in Harnack house[12], that the two girls seated at our table were not Americans but Germans. Now German girls are not permitted in this mess. These tried to put on a good show by talking broken English but when we began to question them, they got up and left hastily. Evidently two German girls, who, of course, may be in our employ, but who evidently had crashed this mess. If they can do this, there are other things they can do.

Last night Don Heath[13] gave a musicale, and afterwards supper. He had a German trio (viola, clarinet, piano), an unusually beautiful combination which I had not heard before, play a lovely Schumann[14] and a Mozart[15] trio. Then he had Erna Bergner[16], whom I believe I have mentioned to you in another connection,[17] sing a Mozart aria, and a wonderful Schubert[18] song with clarinet and piano accompaniment. It was all very nice and intimate, a small group and the proper music. I talked with the clarinetist some. He knew all about Benny Goodman[19], and would like to come to America. A great majority of Germans, I think, would now like to emigrate, if only they had some place to go. Having ruined their own country they would now like to escape the consequences of that ruin.

I spent this morning talking with a German professor (Drum[20]) about the Constitution of Berlin.[21] He is now a consultant for Omgus[22].[23] His wife's[24] un-

---

[12] Siehe Dok. 15, Anm. 16.
[13] Donald R. Heath. Siehe Dok. 8, Anm. 15.
[14] Siehe Dok. 59, Anm. 32.
[15] Siehe Dok. 55, Anm. 35.
[16] Erna Berger. Siehe Dok. 59, Anm. 24.
[17] Siehe Dok. 59.
[18] Siehe Dok. 38, Anm. 2.
[19] Benny Goodman (1909–1986), amerikanischer Jazzmusiker (Klarinettist) und Bandleader.
[20] Gemeint ist Friedrich Glum (1891–1974), deutscher Jurist, 1920 Dr. jur., Universität Tübingen, 1920–1937 Generalsekretär bzw. -direktor der Kaiser-Wilhelm-Gesellschaft zur Förderung der Wissenschaften, 1923 Habilitation, Universität Berlin, 1923–1937 Privatdozent bzw. außerordentlicher Professor für Staats- und Verwaltungsrecht, Universität Berlin, ab 1939 Grundstücks- und Finanzmakler, 1945–Juli 1946 Berater der amerikanischen Militärregierung in Berlin in Verfassungs- und Verwaltungsfragen, ab August 1946 Ministerialdirigent in der Bayerischen Staatskanzlei, 1948 CSU, ab 1949 Lehrbeauftragter, Universität München.
[21] Glum war Ende 1945 von der amerikanischen Militärregierung engagiert worden, um zunächst an der Schaffung einer vorläufigen Verfassung für Berlin mitzuwirken. Hierzu Friedrich Glum, Zwischen Wissenschaft, Wirtschaft und Politik. Erlebtes und Erdachtes in vier Reichen, Bonn 1964, S. 561: „Richmond, der der politische Offizier der Amerikaner für Berlin war, wollte meine Hilfe hauptsächlich haben, um einen Entwurf für eine neue Stadtverfassung von Berlin von mir ausgearbeitet zu erhalten. [...] Ich sollte also Richmond die künftige Verfassung für Groß-Berlin entwerfen. Wir

cle was a famous Bavarian sculptor, Hildebrand[25], who did a lot of Munich's public fountains[26]. His house[27] was full of his stuff some of which he would like to sell. Do you want me to bring home a Hildebrand's St. Cecilia[28].[29] It is rather

sammelten dafür Material, und ich machte einen Entwurf, von dem Richmond hochbefriedigt war. Es fiel mir dies ja auch nicht schwer, hatte ich doch schon an dem Gesetz für Groß-Berlin 1919 und 1920 mitgearbeitet." Richmond war der Legal Officer Clarence Richmond (1896–1989), Lieutenant Colonel, amerikanischer Jurist, 1917 Absolvent der Boston University Law School, Teilnahme am Ersten Weltkrieg, in den 1920er- und 1930-Jahren City Solicitor, Welfare Commissioner, Alderman, Library Trustee and School Committee Member, Chelsea, 1941–1946 US Army's Judge Advocate Corps, 1945/1946 Chief, Local Government and Administration Sub-Section, Political Affairs Sub-Section, Legal Section, A1A1 Military Government Detachment, G-5 Section, US Headquarters Berlin District/OMGBD, bis 1982 als Anwalt tätig.

[22] Siehe Dok. 17, Anm. 45.
[23] Glum war vom 1. Dezember 1945 bis 31. Juli 1946 Berater der amerikanischen Militärregierung in Berlin. Siehe BArch, Koblenz, Nachlass Friedrich Glum, N 1457/2.
[24] Elisabeth Glum, geb. Hildebrand (1896–1984); Vater: Otto Hildebrand (1858–1927), ab 1904 ordentlicher Professor der Chirurgie an der Universität Berlin und Direktor der chirurgischen Universitätsklinik der Charité, Geheimer Medizinalrat; Mutter: Frieda Hildebrand, geb. Freiin von Seebach (1868–1940).
[25] Adolf von Hildebrand (1847–1921), deutscher Bildhauer, in seiner Zeit auf dem Gebiet der Brunnen- und Denkmalkunst deutschlandweit führend.
[26] In München stehen drei große Stadtbrunnen Adolf von Hildebrands: der Wittelsbacher Brunnen, der Hubertusbrunnen und der Reinhardbrunnen. Siehe Sigrid Esche-Braunfels, Adolf von Hildebrand (1847–1921), Berlin 1993, insbesondere S. 210–225, 228–243 und 261–285; Sigrid Braunfels, Skulptur und Architektur des Wasserspiels. Die Brunnen Adolf von Hildebrands, München und Berlin 2005, insbesondere S. 9–79.
[27] Glum wohnte im Kirchweg 28, Berlin-Nikolassee. Siehe Jörg Riedel, Friedrich Glum, in: Harry Balkow-Gölitzer/Rüdiger Reitmeier/Bettina Biedermann/Jörg Riedel, Prominente in Berlin-Wannsee und ihre Geschichten, hrsg. von Burkhardt Sonnenstuhl, Berlin 2006, S. 143–146, hier S. 144 (Abb.: „Kirchweg 28 heute").
[28] Cäcilia, soll im 3. Jahrhundert n. Chr. in Rom gelebt haben, Märtyrerin, Heilige, Patronin der Kirchenmusik.
[29] Wahrscheinlich sah Johnson ein Terracottarelief, das sich heute im Besitz des Museums für Kunst und Kulturgeschichte der Philipps-Universität Marburg befindet. Es handelt sich um die Zweitfassung eines Reliefs, das Adolf von Hildebrand nach dem Tod der mit dem Komponisten Heinrich von Herzogenberg (1843–1900) verheirateten Pianistin und Musikförderin Elisabeth von Herzogenberg, geb. von Stockhausen (1847–1892) für ein Grabmal aus weißer Majolika gefertigt hatte und das die als heilige Cäcilia dargestellte, Orgel spielende Verstorbene abbildet. Das Grabmal befindet sich auf dem alten Friedhof des italienischen Kurorts San Remo. Siehe Sigrid Esche-Braunfels, Adolf von Hildebrand (1847–1921), Berlin 1993, S. 181–183 und 370–372. Wie das Marburger Universitätsmuseum in einer E-Mail an Werner Breunig vom 29. Mai 2009 mitteilt, war die Zweitfassung des Reliefs tatsächlich zeitweise Eigentum der Glums. Auf der Inventarkarte des Museums wird das Relief, das eine Höhe von 79 cm (oben abgerundet) und eine Breite von 44 cm hat, wie folgt beschrieben: „Unter einem Kreuzgratgewölbe sitzt, nach links gewendet, eine Frau (Kniestück), deren beide Hände auf der Tastatur einer vom linken Bildrand überschnittenen Orgel liegen. Über dem Kopf mit teils im Nacken zusammengefaßten, teils frei herabfallendem Haar schwebt ein Heiligenschein." Außerdem findet sich auf der Inventarkarte die Information, dass Adolf von Hildebrand das Terracottarelief 1897 für Heinrich von Herzogenberg angefertigt hatte und dass es nach dessen Tod (1900) wieder in die Hildebrand-Familie zurückkam. Das Museum erwarb es 1979 von der Galerie Arnoldi-Livie, München.

nice but I don't know where we would put it. One of his sons is a painter[30] and the house was full of modern paintings. He has four other children[31] and they all play musical instruments. His wife is a pianist,[32] and he a very elegant professor with a neat moustache and a sleek grey beard. I don't understand it. All this city elegance and the Nazis. Of course he is horrified with the Russians.

The rest of the day I spent with Harold Trevors[33], a colleague of Harold Vedeler's[34] in the state department who is doing the rounds after a mission to London. I think he was amazed at the luxury of this place. We took a ride through the ruins of Berlin – a horribly depressing ride. My driver[35] says the Berliners could rebuild the city in five years.

Good-night my sweetheart. I love you. June is soon over. I think I'll hear from you tomorrow. Edgar

Dok. 67
Schreiben an die Ehefrau
Berlin, Wannsee Officers' Club[1], Am Sandwerder 17/19, 26. Juni 1946

Dearest, my own dearest:

It is amazing what company one falls into. Tonight I had dinner with a group of officers who are in charge of court martial and military police work here. The man in charge is a Colonel Karl Frank[2] who invited me after hearing me talk before the officers of Berlin District. He used to teach Military Science at the University of Kansas[3] and there is from his point of view a mid-western bond. At the table were a colonel, a couple of majors, a couple of captains, and a civil-

---

[30] Peter Glum (geb. 1920), „eine durch und durch künstlerische Natur", so Friedrich Glum, Zwischen Wissenschaft, Wirtschaft und Politik. Erlebtes und Erdachtes in vier Reichen, Bonn 1964, S. 528. Peter Glum lebt heute in Japan.

[31] Hildebrand (1922–2010), Ursula (geb. 1923), Michael (1925–2012) und Christine (geb. 1928).

[32] Friedrich Glum, Zwischen Wissenschaft, Wirtschaft und Politik. Erlebtes und Erdachtes in vier Reichen, Bonn 1964, S. 164: „Alle drei Töchter meines Schwiegervaters waren musikalisch und hatten eine sehr gute Ausbildung erhalten, [...] die älteste, meine Braut, als Pianistin bei Edwin Fischer." Edwin Fischer (1886–1960) war ein Schweizer Pianist, Dirigent und Musikpädagoge, der lange Zeit in Berlin wirkte.

[33] Gemeint ist Howard Trivers (1909–1987), amerikanischer Diplomat, 1932 MA, Harvard University, 1932/1933 Universität Heidelberg, 1934/1935 Teaching Assistant, Harvard University, 1935–1938 Universität Freiburg im Breisgau, 1941 PhD, Harvard University, 1941–1969 Department of State, zuletzt als Generalkonsul in Zürich.

[34] Harold C. Vedeler (siehe Dok. 2, Anm. 12) war wie Howard Trivers seit April 1946 Foreign Affairs Specialist, Division of Central European Affairs, Department of State.

[35] Artur Sanow. Siehe Dok. 40, Anm. 13.

[1] Siehe Dok. 25, Anm. 9.

[2] Karl C. Frank (1899–1993), Lieutenant Colonel, 1935–1940 Assistant Professor of Military Science and Tactics, Kansas State College of Agriculture and Applied Science (seit 1959: Kansas State University), lehrte 1952–1954 Military Science and Tactics am Utah State Agricultural College (seit 1957: Utah State University).

[3] 1865 gegründete Universität in Lawrence, Kansas.

ian. The colonel looks forward to nothing but bringing his wife and children here, and installing them in a beautiful house at Heidelberg[4], overlooking the Neckar-valley[5]. One of the majors was (and is) a stalwart and intelligent organizer of military police. The other major and the two captains are hard-boiled first sergeants (formerly) who have acquired commissions. One, an Irishman, who loves to tell stories about Catholic priests, conducts the local rifle range. The two others, one a Mainer[6] + the other from the south, run the stockade in which over two hundred and fifty criminal GI's[7] are kept. The civilian[8] grew up in gangster politics in New Jersey[9] (Mayor Hague[10]).[11] (The Colonel from Kansas told me this). He is an Italian who has just had imported from the States some records of Caruso[12], Scipa[13] and Gigli[14]. He speaks the hard-boiled language of the American tough and he is head of CID here, i. e., Criminal Investigation Department. He directs all investigations against GI's and officers who violate military regulations, and against Germans who do the same. Many cases were being discussed at the table including that of a chaplain who was such a notorious thief that he was ordered by General Barker[15] to get out of the theater. I go to General Clay's[16] Staff Meetings[17] every week and I hear about the incidents committed by American GI's against German civilians. These are the boys who investigate these incidents, that for instance of the GI who entered an apartment of a German and raped his twelve-year old daughter. My imagination is not quite rich enough to take this all in. Your's would be. I ought to have a private secretary on hand to whom I would dictate every evening. Or I ought to have the imagination and capacity of a novelist who has the ability to put this rich detail in dramatic setting. As it is I am keeping no journal, no diary. Only my letters to you contain a chronicle of what is happening to me. These omit so much rich detail that a large part of this experience will have been lost, except as it cuts certain grooves in the cranial convolutions.

[4] Universitätsstadt im Land Württemberg-Baden in der amerikanischen Besatzungszone Deutschlands, hatte den Zweiten Weltkrieg nahezu unversehrt überstanden.
[5] Romantisches Flusstal.
[6] Aus dem US-Bundesstaat Maine kommend.
[7] Government Issues, ugs. für amerikanische Soldaten.
[8] Gemeint ist Orazio R. Carlucci (1910–1985), 1st Lieutenant, 1946–1949 Director, Criminal Investigation Division, US Army, Berlin.
[9] US-Bundesstaat.
[10] Frank Hague (1876–1956), amerikanischer Politiker (Demokratische Partei), 1917–1947 Bürgermeister von Jersey City, New Jersey, 1924–1949 Vice-Chairman, Democratic National Committee. "His name is synonymous with that early 20th century urban American blend of political favoritism and social welfare known as bossism." http://www.cityofjerseycity.org/hague/index.shtml (letzter Zugriff am 30. Januar 2013).
[11] Informationen zu Carluccis Vorleben in: LAB, B Rep. 036-01 (Office of Military Government, Berlin Sector [OMGBS]), 4/137-3/7.
[12] Enrico Caruso (1873–1921), italienischer Tenor.
[13] Tito Schipa (1888–1965), italienischer Tenor.
[14] Beniamino Gigli (1890–1957), italienischer Tenor.
[15] Siehe Dok. 20, Anm. 10.
[16] Siehe Dok. 2, Anm. 6.
[17] Siehe Dok. 16, Anm. 10.

Monday[18], Tuesday[19], and today have been hard. 5 hours of Monday was spent arguing the constitution of Berlin with the Russians,[20] and little Major Feldmann[21] succeeded in keeping anything at all from being done, after we thought that at last the stage was set for smooth running. We were so depressed and even outraged at the outcome that we decided that General Keating[22] ought to make a strong protest to the Commandants at the Kommandatura[23] on Tuesday. My advertising colonel[24] and I worked until midnight on Monday (I writing and he, for the most part typing) preparing statements for Keating to make to the Commandants on Tuesday. We saw him early yesterday morning, and thought that we had him well briefed. But in spite of our (my) well prepared statements, the General muffed the ball at the meeting of the Commandants[25] and supported an utterly illogical and impossible position. We missed out again taking a stand which would make the Russians feel good, feel that they were supporting us and we them. Today I have sat in Committee[26] Meeting for 8 hours.[27] Major Feldmann, having, together with the English, blocked all progress to date had over him today a Colonel[28] who did all the talking, and things went better. At least we got through a few articles of the new constitution. The fact that the obstructionist, Major Hayes[29], was supplanted by an Englishman who knows Russian,[30] and who moreover is conciliatory, helped a great

---

[18] 24. Juni 1946.
[19] 25. Juni 1946.
[20] Siehe Protokoll der 25. Sitzung des Local Government Committee, Allied Kommandatura Berlin, am 24. Juni 1946, LG/M (46) 25, französischsprachige Fassung, in: TNA, Allied Kommandatura: Directives, Minutes and Papers, FO 1112/378.
[21] Iossif Moissejewitsch Feldman. Siehe Dok. 49, Anm. 59.
[22] Siehe Dok. 39, Anm. 6.
[23] Siehe Dok. 20, Anm. 11.
[24] Gemeint ist Louis Glaser. Siehe Dok. 28, Anm. 4.
[25] Siehe Protokoll der 17. Sitzung der Stadtkommandanten am 25. Juni 1946, BKC/M (46) 17-162, englischsprachige Fassung, in: LAB, B Rep. 036-01 (Office of Military Government, Berlin Sector [OMGBS]), 11/148-1/10.
[26] Local Government Committee, Allied Kommandatura Berlin. Siehe Dok. 29, Anm. 14.
[27] Siehe Protokoll der 26. Sitzung des Local Government Committee, Allied Kommandatura Berlin, am 26. Juni 1946, LG/M (46) 26, französischsprachige Fassung, in: TNA, Allied Kommandatura: Directives, Minutes and Papers, FO 1112/378.
[28] Gemeint ist Alexandr Michailowitsch Sosulja (geb. 1910), sowjetischer Oberstleutnant, ab 1945 Referent für Innenpolitik in der Verwaltung des Politischen Beraters, SMAD, dann politischer Berater des sowjetischen Stadtkommandanten, Oktober 1946–1947 sowjetischer Chef des Stabes der Alliierten Kommandantur Berlin. Louis Glaser über Sosulja: "a Soviet political officer evidently with considerable discretionary power and a skillful debater". Bericht Glasers vom 26. August 1946 über die Entstehung der Vorläufigen Verfassung von Groß-Berlin, in: Archiv des IfZ, OMGUS-Akten (Mikrofiche-Reproduktion), 1945-46/10/5. Jean Victor Ziegelmeyer (siehe Dok. 55, Anm. 4) über Sosulja: « un jeune et sémillant officier de l'Armée Rouge », « ancien professeur d'histoire à l'Université d'Odessa ». Jacques Robichon/J. V. Ziegelmeyer: L'affaire de Berlin 1945–1959 (L'air du temps), 9. Auflage, Paris 1959, S. 88.
[29] Harold Hays. Siehe Dok. 49, Anm. 26.
[30] Wahrscheinlich handelte es sich um Kenneth Angus Spencer (siehe Dok. 40, Anm. 25), den politischen Berater des stellvertretenden britischen Stadtkommandanten (siehe Dok. 28, Anm. 11), der über Russischkenntnisse verfügte und an Sitzungen des Local

deal. But an 8 hour session is a long session in three languages and I was worn out at the end of it. I was slightly amused also (no more than that) to have the Colonel (my advertising colonel) leave the meeting for a few hours (I being therefore responsible while he was gone) in order to go to a press conference at which there were to be such important people as representatives of the NAM[31], officers of the National City Bank of New York City, etc., etc.[32] When he came back he announced that he had made an impromptu speech before them. Well OK. It is good for Glaser's[33] business when he gets back home. It would not contribute to my business, though I leave you to deduce who should have made the speech. I also noticed with similar amusement that the stationery which the Colonel, my advertising colonel, chose for typing the statements which the General was to make to the Commandants on Tuesday, was stationery which

Government Committee teilnahm. In seinen Erinnerungen schreibt Spencer: "Though without any formal training, my fluent German and French, and useful knowledge of Russian, and in particular my background interest in politics for the previous 20 years and understanding of political processes, enabled me to carry out my duties with reasonable efficiency." K. A. Spencer, Flycatcher. Memoirs of an amateur entomologist, The Hague 1992, S. 20. "During my time in Berlin, my knowledge of Russian, limited as it was, proved invaluable. It also greatly improved through contacts with Red Army officers and particularly by attendance at the four-power meetings of the Allied Kommandatura. Everything said in English was translated into French and Russian, everything said in French into English and Russian, and everything said in Russian into English and French. Each meeting thus provided a three-hour Russian lesson." Ebd., S. 24. "In Berlin from 1945 to 1947 my knowledge of Russian, although imperfect, was nevertheless invaluable and greatly helped establish friendly relations with the numerous Red Army officers with whom I had frequent official contact." Ebd., S. 26. Spencer nahm an Sitzungen des Local Government Committee, Allied Kommandatura Berlin, teil, als die vorläufige Berliner Verfassung beraten wurde. Siehe Bericht Louis Glasers vom 26. August 1946 über die Entstehung der Vorläufigen Verfassung von Groß-Berlin, in: Archiv des IfZ, OMGUS-Akten (Mikrofiche-Reproduktion), 1945-46/10/5.

[31] National Association of Manufacturers, amerikanischer Herstellerverband.
[32] Sechs amerikanische "business executives" hielten sich als Gäste der amerikanischen Militärregierung in Berlin auf, um sich über die deutsche Wirtschaftslage zu informieren. "The men who flew here from Paris where they had attended sessions of the council of the International Chamber of Commerce, were Philip D. Reed, chairman of the General Electric Company and chairman of the United States section of the International Chamber of Commerce; Robert R. Wason, president of the National Association of Manufacturers; Robert Gaylord, chairman of the Executive Committee of the National Association of Manufacturers; John Abbink, chairman of the National Foreign Trade Council; Randolph Burgess, vice chairman of the National City Bank of New York and chairman of the International Chamber of Commerce's committee on monetary relations, and Benjamin H. Beckhart, economist of the Chase National Bank of New York." U. S. Executives in Berlin. Six Business Leaders Plan Study of Economic Conditions, in: The New York Times vom 23. Juni 1946, S. 21. Siehe Positive Aktionen notwendig, in: Der Tagesspiegel vom 26. Juni 1946, [S. 3]; Want Curbs Eased on German Market. Six American Business Chiefs on Visit There Call for Move to Develop Foreign Trade. Task Thus Far Negative. Burgess, Reed Hold Time Ripe for Positive Action to Spur Two-Way Commerce, in: The New York Times vom 26. Juni 1946, S. 33; Deutschlands Exportaussichten. USA-Industrielle über die deutsche Wirtschafts- und Finanzlage, in: Die Neue Zeitung vom 28. Juni 1946, S. 4.
[33] Siehe Dok. 28, Anm. 4.

contained the information that there was such a thing as the Civil Administration Branch[34], and that Col. Glaser was its chief. General Barker told me when I came to him that it was just as well that I should get along with the colonel, and that perhaps I ought to retain him in the section. I only say these things to illustrate.

Your letters of the last couple days (two of them) are both depressing and exciting.[35] For one who is encouraging me to come back to Nebraska[36] this fall, you do not do a very good job of telling me that except for my family, there is much to return to, except the most despicable of climates, and a pretty sorry lot of human beings. You go so far as to say that those persons with whom I shall be most intimately associated, are indeed people whom you now loathe, and I take it this means only Glenn[37], Jimmy[38] Henry[39] and Alden[40]. Harold Trevors[41] told me yesterday (I mentioned him in a previous letter[42]) that he thought it very strange and absurd that I should be abandoning my position here, which was of considerable importance, to return to the academic life of Nebraska. Here I would be associated with the making of history rather than the teaching of it. He insisted that if I stayed on here for a few more years, I could accumulate enough money to carry us over an interim period until I could get an academic position which would be worthy of my experience in the past few years. Sometimes I think, particularly after the receipt of Henry's last letter[43], that the boys whom you now loathe, are resentful of what I have been engaged in for the last couple of years and that they take particular pleasure in bringing me back, in reducing the 10,000 to 4,000, and in subjecting me to petty academic routine and to petty university politics and to provincial isolationism of our backward mid-west. You yourself indicate that you want to get out. I say to you, my sweetest, let us pick the place we want to be, whether the Pacific NW or New England[44], whether the glorious SW or a choice spot in the south. If I abandon this life (and I do not desire to preserve it) it is only because I want with you and the boys, to engage upon a manner of living which will do justice to our capacities to live well. We shall seek out our place no matter where it is. We could get it.

---

[34] Civil Administration Branch, OMGBD. Siehe Dok. 28, Anm. 5.
[35] Briefe in: Unterlagen aus dem Nachlass Edgar N. Johnson, Privatbesitz Candice E. und Thomas R. Johnson, Denver, Colorado, USA.
[36] US-Bundesstaat.
[37] Glenn W. Gray. Siehe Dok. 49, Anm. 74.
[38] James L. Sellers. Siehe Dok. 49, Anm. 77.
[39] Henry Charles Oldfather. Siehe Dok. 2, Anm. 19.
[40] Siehe Dok. 65, Anm. 11.
[41] Howard Trivers. Siehe Dok. 66, Anm. 33.
[42] Siehe Dok. 66.
[43] Gemeint ist wahrscheinlich Charles Henry Oldfathers Schreiben vom 13. Juni 1946, in: Unterlagen aus dem Nachlass Edgar N. Johnson, Privatbesitz Candice E. und Thomas R. Johnson, Denver, Colorado, USA.
[44] Neuengland ist eine Region im Nordosten der USA und ist, neben Virginia, der Ursprung der englischen Besiedlung Nordamerikas. Das Gebiet Neuenglands umfasst die Staaten Connecticut, Maine, Massachusetts, New Hampshire, Rhode Island und Vermont.

The news about the possibility, no the certainty, of getting back our old cottage is too good to be true.[45] I have not submitted my letter to General Clay,[46] but when I do I think I shall change the date upon which I said I should like to be in Lincoln[47] (i. e. Sept. 1) to August 21. I am so glad you seized upon the opportunity of taking the place at the moment it was presented. Papa will join you as soon as he can. He will try to arrange to be there before you set off for Colorado[48] (in this instance, I think, money is no consideration) but he may not be able to make it. You go ahead and make your own plans. If I am there in time, O. K., if not then I shall join you at the cottage. And we shall ask Henry and the boys to announce that I shall be back for classes after the preliminary monkey business is over. I am not sure you are wise about the car (how are we to get to the High Drive[49] for example?) but I am willing to submit to your decision in this regard.[50] (Did you get my 1600 dollars?).[51] It will be no inconvenience for me to be in Lincoln without a car. I only ask that on one of these days in Colorado you will arrange that the boys will be taken care of, and that you and I will start off in the early morning on a hike which will take us to the highest peak in Colorado[52] (we have been there before), and that this shall be the inauguration, if not before, (I should say continuation), of the sweetest and most intimate life that two people have ever lived together. Then no matter what our life, as associated with the University, will turn out to be, together with our sweet kids, it will be such as no untoward exterior circumstances can disturb. If we miss this wonderful chance, we shall have only ourselves to blame. I love you my darling. I have only one chance to make my life somewhat complete, and that is through you. I take you into my arms and hold you very close. I love you. We must try to realize this. Kiss sweet John and Timmy. Your "darling boy", Edgar

---

[45] Emily L. Johnson in ihrem Schreiben vom 17. Juni 1946: "I am also happy – vaguely – because I had a note from Mrs. Zumwinkel [siehe Dok. 46, Anm. 6] saying we could have a cabin – our old one – on Aug. 22, for as long as we want it." Brief in: Unterlagen aus dem Nachlass Edgar N. Johnson, Privatbesitz Candice E. und Thomas R. Johnson, Denver, Colorado, USA.

[46] Siehe Dok. 63 und Dok. 65.

[47] Hauptstadt des US-Bundesstaats Nebraska, wo Johnson mit seiner Familie wohnte und an der Universität lehrte.

[48] US-Bundesstaat.

[49] Ein Scenic Drive in den Rocky Mountains, Colorado.

[50] Emily L. Johnson in ihrem Schreiben vom 17. Juni 1946: "About a car: I am against getting one now, even if I could. The inconveniences of not having one are many, but we do get along, and 'think of the money we save'." Brief in: Unterlagen aus dem Nachlass Edgar N. Johnson, Privatbesitz Candice E. und Thomas R. Johnson, Denver, Colorado, USA. Siehe Dok. 51.

[51] Siehe Dok. 58.

[52] Wahrscheinlich ist der höchste Berg im Rocky Mountain National Park gemeint, der bei Bergsteigern beliebte, über 4300 m bzw. fast 14 300 Fuß hohe Longs Peak.

Dok. 68
Schreiben an die Ehefrau
Berlin, Wannsee Officers' Club[1], Am Sandwerder 17/19, 29. Juni 1946

My sweet one:

It is a lovely day, and the Americans, I take it, are making the most of it. I shall not conceal that I am very lonesome for you and the boys. But the end of this comes suddenly into view. It seems silly not to try to get home by the 21st of August in order to go out with you and the boys to Colorado[2]. I, of course, may not make it by that date in which case I shall have to join you in Meeker Park[3]. In any case I think you should try to take someone along. Not only to help you until I get there in case I don't make it in Lincoln[4], but it might be nice to have someone stay with the children in case we wanted to go out for a hike alone on some of these days. You would appear to be lucky if you could get Alison[5] to go along.

I have not done anything more with my letter to Clay[6].[7] He announced this morning at the staff conference[8] that he was going to Paris[9] on Tuesday[10], where, I suppose, the German problem will be taken up. I imagine, however, that he will be back at the end of the week, and I shall try to get a letter to him by that time. In it I shall ask for the privilege of going to the zone for a couple of weeks. I do not know whether it will be possible for me to fly home. I rather doubt it inasmuch as it has been announced that flying facilities have been much curtailed, and I do not intend to spend money on paying for my own transportation home by air.

If it is to be by boat then I suppose I should be leaving here around the first of August. That might get me to New York around the 15th. I don't know whether I have to go to Washington or not. In case I don't have to, I don't think I

---

[1] Siehe Dok. 25, Anm. 9.
[2] US-Bundesstaat.
[3] Feriengebiet in der Nähe von Allenspark, Colorado.
[4] Hauptstadt des US-Bundesstaats Nebraska, wo Johnson mit seiner Familie wohnte und an der Universität lehrte.
[5] Alison E. Gass, später verh. Murie (1931-2013), Tochter von Sherlock B. Gass (siehe Dok. 63, Anm. 29), Babysitterin für die Kinder von Emily L. und Edgar N. Johnson. In einer E-Mail an Werner Breunig vom 10. Januar 2010 schreibt sie: "[...] I remember the Johnsons very well. They were dear friends of my parents. Given the times & manners of the day, my relationship with them was somewhat more formal. I knew Emily better, since the kids were largely her province. They had a nice record player and an interesting collection of records. I discovered a taste for Schubert's [siehe Dok. 38, Anm. 2] string quintets there (after putting the kids to bed). [...] My mother and I left Lincoln permanently in 1947, and I don't believe I ever saw the Johnsons after that, though my mother would have kept in touch with them by mail."
[6] Siehe Dok. 2, Anm. 6.
[7] Siehe Dok. 63, Dok. 65 und Dok. 67.
[8] Siehe Protokoll der OMGUS-Stabskonferenz am 29. Juni 1946, in: Archiv des IfZ, OMGUS – Staff Conferences (Protokollkopien), Fg 12/4.
[9] Zur Außenministerkonferenz siehe Dok. 44, Anm. 13.
[10] 25. Juni 1946.

shall even though it would be nice to see Polly[11] and Gene[12], and Marguerite[13] and Harold[14], and perhaps wise to call on some people in the State Department. I could then go on straight to Chicago where I must see Aunt Hannah[15], and Mildred[16] and David[17], and go up to Milwaukee[18] to see Dad[19] (whom I have very shamefully neglected) and inevitably Norman[20] and Lucille[21]. Then to Omaha[22], where I take it, a final cutting off of relations with the War Department could be made, and then to you in Lincoln, or if not in Lincoln then in Colorado. If this is the way it is to be and I am to have the privilege of going to the zone for a couple of weeks. I should not be in Berlin longer than about two weeks more which seems incredible. As a matter of fact I suppose I should really leave here for good and go to Le Havre[23], from which port I suppose one sails, via Frankfurt[24]. I left there for you in November of last year, and got back very quickly by air.

But by the 15 July at least my main task in Berlin will have been done,[25] I think. We are supposed to have the constitution of Berlin, together with an electoral procedure ready for the Commandants by their next meeting which is the 9th of July.[26] I don't know whether we shall quite be able to make this, but at the present moment it looks as if we might, and in that event, as long as I am not going to stay here, there is not much point in my staying much longer. When they sent me down here there were two big problems to be solved, the problem of the merger[27] (you remember letters on that subject) and the problem of elections in Berlin. By the time the constitution and electoral procedure are completed these two problems will have been settled. The plan of the electoral campaign will have been begun, and there is not much point in my getting started on that.

[11] Pauline R. Anderson. Siehe Dok. 2, Anm. 2.
[12] Eugene N. Anderson. Siehe Dok. 1, Anm. 1.
[13] Marguerite D. Vedeler. Siehe Dok. 2, Anm. 13.
[14] Harold C. Vedeler. Siehe Dok. 2, Anm. 12.
[15] Hannah Walstrom. Siehe Dok. 4, Anm. 14.
[16] Mildred H. Williams. Siehe Dok. 4, Anm. 12.
[17] David G. Williams. Siehe Dok. 4, Anm. 17.
[18] Stadt im US-Bundesstaat Wisconsin.
[19] Frank E. Johnson. Siehe Dok. 3, Anm. 12.
[20] Norman D. Johnson. Siehe Dok. 3, Anm. 13.
[21] Lucille Johnson. Siehe Dok. 3, Anm. 17.
[22] Stadt im US-Bundesstaat Nebraska, nordöstlich von Johnsons Wohnort Lincoln.
[23] Französische Hafenstadt an der Atlantikküste.
[24] Frankfurt am Main, Stadt im Land Groß-Hessen in der amerikanischen Besatzungszone Deutschlands.
[25] Siehe Dok. 62 und Dok. 62, Anm. 16; Dok. 64.
[26] Die Stadtkommandanten hatten in ihrer Sitzung am 25. Juni 1946 beschlossen, "to instruct the Local Government Committee to continue its work on the draft constitution and electoral procedure without delay and to submit to the Meeting of the Commandants on 9th July (i) A draft of the constitution (ii) a recommendation on electoral procedure taking into account, in particular, the four points submitted by the British representative (para 350 of BKD/M (46) 28)". Protokoll der 17. Sitzung der Stadtkommandanten am 25. Juni 1946, BKC/M (46) 17-162, englischsprachige Fassung, in: LAB, B Rep. 036-01 (Office of Military Government, Berlin Sector [OMGBS]), 11/148-1/10.
[27] Gemeint ist der Zusammenschluss von KPD und SPD zur SED.

This morning at nine o'clock I saw Mrs. Heath[28], the wife of Don Heath[29] who is Murphy's[30] second here and head of the division of political affairs. She is the vice-president or something of the sort of the wives' organization[31] here (there are now about 170 of them[32]) and she has to organize a program for the club which these wives are forming. She wanted me to talk over the possible program for such a club, and it turned out also that she wanted me to open up the program by a speech to the ladies. I did not consent to do it immediately but I am to give her an answer by tomorrow, and although it involves a lot of extra work, I think I'll do it. My notion would be that the ladies should undertake something positive in Berlin, that they should not sit back and enjoy their luxurious houses, and their retinues of servants, and organize the social life of a military post, a university campus, or a missionary compound but that they should get busy and associate themselves with the elements in Berlin life which are working towards the same goals as we are. Insofar as I can gather they are much dominated by military hierarchy, and want to get back to bridge and possibly lectures on German porcelain, which they hope to acquire while here. I will suggest associating themselves with forward-looking elements in German life, and acting as a liaison with American women at home who have to be led into the notion of seeing this thing through. I have too good a notion of what happens at dinner-tables not to know that such a talk would not have repercussions in, let us say, the best circles. I know something about the power of women. And I know how I shall begin my little speech. I hope it will be psychologically correct. I shall say, "There is only one person whom I should like to be added to the members of this organization (I mean only present in the audience) but I am not sure, that if she were here, she would bother to come out and listen to her husband talk." This interview kept me from attending General Keating's[33] staff meeting and he did not like it. At least there was a summons for me at 35 Grunewaldstrasse[34] to attend. But since Mrs. Heath kept me I did not wish to interrupt the meeting and the General took it all right. As a matter of fact I had lost interest because after last week's meeting at which certain problems were discussed, Colonel Howley[35] demanded (he is director of MGBD[36]) that General Keating should be presented not with the failures of M[ilitary] G[overnment], but with their accomplishments. In other words we

---

[28] Siehe Dok. 55, Anm. 48.
[29] Donald R. Heath. Siehe Dok. 8, Anm. 15.
[30] Siehe Dok. 8, Anm. 13.
[31] Gemeint ist der American Women's Club of Berlin, der am 25. Juni 1946 im Harnack House (siehe Dok. 15, Anm. 16) zu seiner ersten offiziellen Sitzung zusammentrat. Für die ersten drei Monate waren Marjorie McK. Clay (siehe Dok. 59, Anm. 8) als President, Louise B. Heath als Vice President und General Program Chairman eingesetzt. Siehe U. S. Wives Form Club, in: OMGUS Observer vom 31. Mai 1946, S. 2; Women's Club Members Adopt Constitution, in: OMGUS Observer vom 28. Juni 1946, S. 2.
[32] Gemeint sind die seit Kurzem in Berlin lebenden Frauen von amerikanischen Besatzungsangehörigen.
[33] Siehe Dok. 39, Anm. 6.
[34] Grunewaldstraße 35 im Bezirk Steglitz, Sitz von OMGBD. Siehe Dok. 25, Anm. 13.
[35] Siehe Dok. 20, Anm. 18.
[36] Military Government, Berlin District. Siehe Dok. 25, Anm. 13.

are doing an impeccable job. And I was disappointed to hear from General Keating that the meeting went much better this morning. Then I went to Clay's staff meeting[37]. It was announced there that on next Tuesday[38], American officials would proclaim an amnesty (from all de-Nazification laws) for anybody born after July 1, 1919.[39] This means all these kids who were 14 at the time when Hitler[40] came to power would be exempted from any de-Nazification process if they were not in the worst categories of Nazis[41]. This would include people who are now 27 years of age. Clay admitted this was dangerous, and for the first time, I heard from him a statement to the effect that its success would depend upon a successful positive program for the youth of this age – such as we have not had yet and such as – I wonder – we are not likely to get from the people who are here responsible. It is meant to suggest however our great trust in the German youth, our faith that they are not a lost generation and can therefore be brought around. But at this same meeting it was announced that the attacks by bands of German youth upon American personnel (including women) were increasing noticeably and that stringest measures are now necessary in those communities where these attacks are most numerous. These attacks, however, bear a certain relationship to the attacks of American soldiers upon German civilians. These things should not be overemphasized, but they do take place.

The work on the Constitution has been going along more smoothly. These were two full day meetings this week, Wednesday[42] and Friday[43].[44] The Russians have made a complete turn-about (vide Molotov[45] at Paris[46]) and the English have been not quite so sticky. The little Russian major[47] has been virtu-

---

[37] Siehe Anm. 8.
[38] 2. Juli 1946.
[39] Am 2. Juli 1946 verlas der Direktor des RGCO, James K. Pollock (siehe Dok. 15, Anm. 12), auf der 10. Tagung des Länderrats (siehe Dok. 15, Anm. 10) eine Botschaft des stellvertretenden amerikanischen Militärgouverneurs Lucius D. Clay, in der dieser die Bereitschaft der amerikanischen Militärregierung zum Ausdruck brachte, einem Antrag des Länderrats auf eine allgemeine Amnestie für die deutsche Jugend stattzugeben. Siehe 10. Tagung des Länderrates des amerikanischen Besatzungsgebietes in Stuttgart, 2. Juli 1946, in: Akten zur Vorgeschichte der Bundesrepublik Deutschland 1945-1949, Bd. 1: September 1945-Dezember 1946, bearb. von Walter Vogel/Christoph Weisz, München und Wien 1976, Nr. 24, S. 572f.; Amnestie für die Jugend. Milderung im Schicksal der Evakuierten? – Botschaft General Clays, in: Die Neue Zeitung vom 5. Juli 1946, S. 3; Keesing's Archiv der Gegenwart, XVI. Jg., 1946, S. 799 E.
[40] Siehe Dok. 22, Anm. 19.
[41] Gruppen I und II (Kriegsverbrecher und Aktivisten) des Gesetzes zur Befreiung von Nationalsozialismus und Militarismus vom 5. März 1946 (siehe Dok. 47, Anm. 20).
[42] 26. Juni 1946.
[43] 28. Juni 1946.
[44] Siehe Protokoll der 26. Sitzung des Local Government Committee, Allied Kommandatura Berlin, am 26. Juni 1946, LG/M (46) 26, französischsprachige Fassung, in: TNA, Allied Kommandatura: Directives, Minutes and Papers, FO 1112/378; Protokoll der 27. Sitzung des Local Government Committee, Allied Kommandatura Berlin, am 28. Juni 1946, LG/M (46) 27, französischsprachige Fassung, in: ebd.
[45] Siehe Dok. 44, Anm. 18.
[46] Zur Pariser Außenministerkonferenz siehe Dok. 44, Anm. 13.
[47] Gemeint ist Major Iossif Moissejewitsch Feldman. Siehe Dok. 49, Anm. 59.

ally supplanted by a Russian colonel[48], who has evidently been instructed to get work done, and the understanding we achieved in fighting the British on a previous occasion has now developed into a kind of friendship. Since the Russians know that I attend meetings of the Commandatura[49], Political Directorate[50] and Coordinating Committee[51] they listen to me, and since I am reasonable are quite willing to get along. I was amazed yesterday to have a proposition (and an important one) accepted by them, almost without debate. I am enclosing a menu of the luncheon held in the Kommandatura after our Wednesday meeting.[52] This month is French chairmanship and the menu is typically French – that is mediatory.[53] To a great extent these negotiations depend upon persons – persons who are not stubborn and in re the Soviets not positively anti-Russian. Liberal Americans have a great rôle to play in diplomatic negotiations but there are not many of them here.

Thursday[54] evening I spent with a group of University of Berlin[55] students who are interested in the USA. I brought them a handsome American lady who spoke on Social Welfare in the USA (Miss Beklin[56] who has worked in

[48] Es handelte sich um Oberstleutnant Alexandr Michailowitsch Sosulja. Siehe Dok. 67, Anm. 28.
[49] Siehe Dok. 20, Anm. 11.
[50] Politisches Direktorat, Alliierte Kontrollbehörde.
[51] Siehe Dok. 15, Anm. 21.
[52] Siehe Bildanhang, Abb. 38.
[53] Das Menü, das unter anderem aus „Potage Windsor", „Salade Russe" und „Pommes Anglaises" bestand, spiegelte die ausgleichende, vermittelnde Rolle wider, um die sich die Franzosen im Kreis der Alliierten bemühten. Siehe Wolfgang Benz, Vorwort, in: Dorothea Führe, Die französische Besatzungspolitik in Berlin von 1945 bis 1949. Déprussianisation und Décentralisation, Berlin 2001, S. VII–IX, hier S. VIII. Die Besatzungsmacht, die den Vorsitz führte, war auch für die Verpflegung zuständig. Hierzu der Brite Kenneth Angus Spencer (siehe Dok. 40, Anm. 25): "Chairmanship of the meetings at all levels rotated monthly, with the duty country being responsible not only for arranging the agenda of the meetings but also for providing the lunches, which played an important part in the day's work. Without being jingoistic I can fairly claim that the British month produced the best work, with more problems being solved under British chairmanship than was achieved by any of the other Allies. However, by general consensus the meals provided by the British were by far the most inferior. During the Russian month the reverse applied. Few effective decisions were reached but the Russian food was magnificent, with ample vodka, wines and champagne from the Crimea. After such lunches little was achieved. One aspect of the American months was interesting. They daily flew in from Copenhagen supplies of fresh dairy produce for the large American colony in Berlin. At their lunches, no alcohol was provided but merely fresh cold milk. It was amusing to watch the vodka-swilling Russians having to be content with milk. At least everyone kept awake after these lunches!" K. A. Spencer, Flycatcher. Memoirs of an amateur entomologist, The Hague 1992, S. 21 f.
[54] 27. Juni 1946.
[55] 1810 gegründete, am 29. Januar 1946 feierlich wiedereröffnete Universität.
[56] Mildred L. C. Biklen, später Mildred B. Smith (1903–1993), amerikanische Sozialfürsorgerin, 1928 BA, University of Iowa, graduate work, University of Chicago and University of Nebraska, 1934/1935 Case Work Supervisor and Director of Lancaster County Relief Bureau, 1935/1936 Supervisor of Employment District 3 Works Progress Administration, Associate Director of Works Progress Administration for Ne-

Nebraska). There was president of Columbia Teacher's College[57] guy (Alexander[58]) who is a prohibitionist and a North Carolinian[59].[60] We need some very alive people in this field of Education and Religion.

I love you, my sweetheart, and it won't be long now. Edgar

Dok. 69
Schreiben an den Vater[1]
Berlin, Wannsee Officers' Club[2], Am Sandwerder 17/19, 29. Juni 1946

Dear Dad –

I am ashamed for not having written you long before this. When I left you in February I thought you would be going out to Lincoln[3] soon but Norman[4] has written me to the effect that you have gotten a job with a music store in Milwaukee[5] repairing pianos, and that you did not feel that you could go.[6] I can understand this very well. A chance to go back to the kind of work you used to do, you couldn't very well afford to pass up, and I know how important keeping busy is to you as it is to every one.

---

braska, ab 1936 Supervisor of Assistance, Nebraska State Assistance and Child Welfare Department, Januar–Juni 1946 Deputy Chief, Public Welfare Branch, OMGBD, Juni 1946/1947 Chief, Public Welfare Branch, OMGBD/OMGBS, 1947/1948 Chief, Public Welfare Branch, Internal Affairs and Communications Division, OMGUS, 1948/1949 Chief, Public Welfare Branch, Civil Administration Division, OMGUS.

[57] Teachers College, Columbia University, New York City, 1887 gegründet.
[58] Richard T. Alexander (1887–1971), amerikanischer Erziehungswissenschaftler, unterrichtete 1910/1911 am Robert College, Türkei, 1911/1912 erster Aufenthalt in Deutschland, lehrte 1914–1924 am George Peabody College for Teachers, 1918 PhD, Columbia University, 1924–1951 Teachers College, Columbia University, Professor of Education, 1946/1947 Education and Religious Affairs Branch, Internal Affairs and Communications Division, OMGUS, 1947/1948 Chief, Education and Religious Affairs Branch, Internal Affairs and Communications Division, OMGUS, 1948 Chief, Education Branch, Education and Cultural Relations Division, OMGUS. John W. Taylor (siehe Dok. 17, Anm. 26), sein früherer Schüler, hatte ihn gebeten, als Mitarbeiter der Militärregierung nach Deutschland zu kommen. "[…] John had contacted or had revised and made arrangements for the state department to talk to my dad", erinnert sich später Richard T. Alexanders Sohn, Richard T. Alexander Jr. (geb. 1917). http://web.utk.edu/~csws/interviews/alexander2.pdf (letzter Zugriff am 30. Januar 2013).
[59] Bewohner des US-Bundesstaats North Carolina.
[60] Richard T. Alexander war mit dem Leiter (1927–1949 Dean, 1949–1954 President) des Teachers College, William F. Russell (1890–1956), eng befreundet. Siehe https://my.tennessee.edu/pls/portal/docs/PAGE/WAR/WAR_SOCIETY/ORAL/INTERVIEW_LISTING/INT_ALEXANDERR.PDF (letzter Zugriff am 30. Januar 2013).

[1] Frank E. Johnson. Siehe Dok. 3, Anm. 12.
[2] Siehe Dok. 25, Anm. 9.
[3] Hauptstadt des US-Bundesstaats Nebraska, wo Johnson mit seiner Familie wohnte und an der Universität lehrte.
[4] Norman D. Johnson. Siehe Dok. 3, Anm. 13.
[5] Stadt im US-Bundesstaat Wisconsin.
[6] Siehe Dok. 46.

I have been a little disappointed in coming back here. As Norman may have told you, the job I thought I was going to get wasn't ready for me when I came because of the long time it took for me to get back here. Consequently I was sent down to Berlin to become the political adviser of the Commanding General of the troops in the Berlin area. This work has been interesting and important enough, and I have not felt that my time was wasted. During the first part of it there was a nasty political fight going on here between the Communists and the Socialists. The Communists, with the support of Russia, wanted the Socialists to join with them in a united workers' party, and the Socialists wanted to retain their independence. The Socialists lost out in the Russian zone, but in Berlin, with the help of the British, French, and ourselves they managed to preserve their independence. I had something to do with this and for this I am glad. Since that time we have been busy trying to get ready for elections in Berlin in October. This has meant preparing a constitution for the city and preparing for the machinery of elections. In another week or so this work should be done.

Then I think I am coming home. It is something of a temptation to stay on here but Emily does not want to come over with the children, and I am not sure that I want to abandon the university for work of this kind inasmuch as there is really no guarantee of how long it will last. I shall have to take a huge salary cut, which, with the inflation imminent in America will make things a bit difficult but I have made up my mind. I couldn't stay over here another year in any case without my family. On my way out to Lincoln from New York or Washington I shall stop off in Chicago and come up to Milwaukee to see you. According to my present plans this should be somewhere between the 15th and 21st of August. Emily is going out to Colorado[7] with the boys around the 21st of August, and I shall try to join her either in Lincoln or in Colorado.

So it won't be too long before I shall be seeing you and we can then have another chance at talking things over. I am glad you have been well, and that you have got something like your old work back again. I have some idea of how hard things are for you. I love you very much, my fine Father, and I shall be very happy to see you again. Your son, Edgar

Dok. 70
Schreiben an die Ehefrau
Berlin, 2. Juli 1946[1]

Dearest –

Just a note. I shall have to neglect you a bit until the Constitution for Berlin is finished and until my speech for the ladies[2] is through. But I just wanted to

---

[7] US-Bundesstaat.

[1] Siehe das Schreiben und den dazugehörigen Briefumschlag im Bildanhang, Abb. 13 und Abb. 14.

[2] Gemeint ist der geplante Vortrag vor dem American Women's Club of Berlin. Siehe Dok. 68 und Dok. 68, Anm. 31.

say tonight that I have completed letters to Generals Clay[3] and Keating[4] saying that I wished to be returned to the USA in time for arrival in Lincoln[5] Nebraska, on or before 21 August 1946.[6] I also asked General Clay for the privilege of spending a couple of weeks in the zone[7] previous to my departure. This I think he will grant me. If so I shall be in Berlin for only a couple of weeks more.

Yesterday's meeting at the Kommandatura[8] was rather successful.[9] As a result of a Russian lunch (they are chairmen this month), which included much vodka and wine, it all got rather friendly. Major Feldman[10] remarked to me that the Soviets had found a way of speaking with the Americans that they couldn't find with the British. And I took occasion to ask a Russian what they meant by accusing us of atomic diplomacy. I didn't get a good answer but I did get a promise to come and talk it over some time. This I hope I can arrange before I leave. I was with the Berlin students[11] against last night. Bob Schmidt[12] sang with guitar accompaniment some folk songs for them.

Two years ago you were about to give birth to our sweet Timmy.[13] Not long after we shall have been married 10 years.[14] I love you my blessed darling.
Edgar

Dok. 71
Schreiben an die Ehefrau
Berlin, Wannsee Officers' Club[1], Am Sandwerder 17/19, 7. Juli 1946

My beloved:

I walked down to the lake[2] after dinner, and while there I suddenly smiled. I thought that today was the 7 July. In six weeks then we should be on our way to Colorado[3] together. I haven't received an answer from my letter to Clay[4].[5] He

---

[3] Siehe Dok. 2, Anm. 6.
[4] Siehe Dok. 39, Anm. 6.
[5] Hauptstadt des US-Bundesstaats Nebraska, wo Johnson mit seiner Familie wohnte und an der Universität lehrte.
[6] Siehe Dok. 63, Dok. 65, Dok. 67 und Dok. 68.
[7] Gemeint ist die amerikanische Besatzungszone Deutschlands.
[8] Siehe Dok. 20, Anm. 11.
[9] Siehe Protokoll der 28. Sitzung des Local Government Committee, Allied Kommandatura Berlin, am 1. Juli 1946, LG/M (46) 28, russischsprachige Fassung, in: TNA, Allied Kommandatura: Directives, Minutes and Papers, FO 1112/378.
[10] Siehe Dok. 49, Anm. 59.
[11] Siehe Dok. 68.
[12] Möglicherweise einer der Studenten.
[13] Sohn Thomas (siehe Dok. 2, Anm. 16) wurde am 8. Juli 1944 geboren.
[14] Edgar N. und Emily L. Johnson waren seit dem 14. Juli 1936 verheiratet.

[1] Siehe Dok. 25, Anm. 9.
[2] Gemeint ist der Große Wannsee, eine Ausbuchtung der Havel (siehe Dok. 74, Anm. 24) im Südwesten Berlins.
[3] US-Bundesstaat.
[4] Siehe Dok. 2, Anm. 6.
[5] Siehe Dok. 63, Dok. 65, Dok. 67, Dok. 68 und Dok. 70.

has been in Paris.[6] He returned yesterday afternoon to Berlin, and is leaving again tonight for Paris. As yet the matter of Germany has not come up before the Foreign Ministers of Paris and Clay is supposed to be in a bad frame of mind. Supposedly it will come up before the Ministers during the early part of the next week, and he is supposed to be back in a few days. I doubt if my letter has been put in his hands during the brief interval of his return from Paris. It will have to wait accordingly until the end of the week. I understand that Pollock[7] is going back to Michigan[8] even though Clay does not wish him to go. Clay will be losing, accordingly his three chief professional assistants, Pollock, Dorn[9], and myself and that is, I believe, a thing which he cannot take very lightly. I understood also that the return is now made to the U. S. from Bremen[10] instead of Le Havre[11] on the many ships which bring supplies here. A boat is supposed to leave almost every day. Therefore I imagine that I shall be leaving from there somewhere in the neighborhood of the first of August. Henry[12] wrote recently that they had not been able to get a man of professorial rank for Harold's[13] place, and that instead they would try to get another instructor.[14] And from what you continue to report of the academic atmosphere in Nebraska, I wonder, indeed, to what I am returning in the University. Am I returning to Glenn[15], Jim[16], Alden[17] and a couple of young instructors. This I must confess is not returning to very very much. But I am not really returning to the University. I am returning to you and to the boys, and to our establishment. It will not be easy to give up a sense of being a small part of what is really going on in the world and I shall be tempted to continue a little along this line. I don't imagine, however, that it will last long. I imagine that except for the classroom I shall soon abandon all these plans for participating in public life and return only too willingly to you, the boys and what houses us there, to books, to writing and to the perfection of our little way of life. I might even return a little to the piano.[18]

---

[6] Clay nahm an der Pariser Außenministerkonferenz teil. Siehe Dok. 44, Anm. 13.

[7] Siehe Dok. 15, Anm. 12.

[8] US-Bundesstaat. Pollock lehrte an der University of Michigan als Professor für Politikwissenschaft.

[9] Siehe Dok. 2, Anm. 10.

[10] Bremen mit Bremerhaven war amerikanische Exklave im Küstengebiet der britischen Besatzungszone. Siehe Andreas Röpcke, Office of Military Government for Bremen, in: OMGUS-Handbuch. Die amerikanische Militärregierung in Deutschland 1945–1949, hrsg. von Christoph Weisz (= Quellen und Darstellungen zur Zeitgeschichte, Bd. 35), München 1994, S. 597–670, hier S. 599–637.

[11] Französische Hafenstadt an der Atlantikküste.

[12] Charles Henry Oldfather. Siehe Dok. 2, Anm. 19.

[13] Harold C. Vedeler. Siehe Dok. 2, Anm. 12.

[14] Als Instructor in History wurde, neben David L. Dowd (siehe Dok. 49, Anm. 71), eingestellt: Albin T. Anderson (1911–1996), 1933 MA und 1947 PhD, University of California, Berkeley, bis 1979 Professor, University of Nebraska, 1984/1985 President, Institute for Continued Learning, University of California, San Diego.

[15] Glenn W. Gray. Siehe Dok. 49, Anm. 74.

[16] James L. Sellers. Siehe Dok. 49, Anm. 77.

[17] Siehe Dok. 65, Anm. 11.

[18] Johnson war ein versierter Klavierspieler. Siehe Dok. 21, Anm. 6.

You seem to have been very sensible about this piano business. I'm glad, after what you have said about it, that you turned down this Knabe instrument which, from all you say would have been just another piano.[19] There is no point in having just another piano. It must be something different, fine, brilliant, mellow and definitely exciting to play. And if you are in any doubt about these things don't buy. We should be eternally dissatisfied with it and John[20] would never feel the thrill of having a wonderful instrument to go to. I know what I am talking about. I used to go from our good upright at home to practice on Mr. Sooter's[21] piano and it was always an exciting experience. The reason why I want a larger piano is just because of this experience – the little ones don't have the difference. If I could buy that big one of our friend in Washington (we certainly, as you say, missed out on that deal)[22] for somewhere near 1,000 dollars, I'd go to Washington to buy. Your experience shows however, that there are plenty of pianos about, people trying to take advantage of the scarcity. I wouldn't therefore rush it if you aren't sure. I rather go in debt some and get a proper new one than to buy a doubtful old one. In fact the only one you can really be sure about is a new one.

It has been an interesting day. I got up early to go to a meeting of SPD functionaries and trade union leaders.[23] They were meeting to protest the kind of elections which have been held earlier in the industrial branches by the present unitary (SED controlled) Federation of Free German Trade Unions[24]. It was encouraging to me because I hear and see so few Germans who are really democratic. In this meeting, however, a simple young woman got up, who works in a factory in the Russian sector which makes telephones. She has never been active in trade union activities or politics before but she has had enough of dictation and espionage and has revolted in a most courageous manner and speaks out her mind. It so happens that the women in this factory outnumber the men about 70 to 30, and she has got the women under her leadership, and is in a position to control the factory. She was bitter against the Russians, in a most undiplomatic fashion. I don't know whether there were any Russian officers present or not. I didn't see any. She condemned the way she is being spied upon by the SED (Communist) people in the factory who watch her every movement and listen to her every telephone call. The Russians recently sent a delegation of their Trade Union people here and they visited this factory. But the Commu-

---

[19] Siehe Dok. 63.
[20] Johnsons Sohn John. Siehe Dok. 2, Anm. 15.
[21] Offensichtlich ein Bekannter in den USA, mit dem er die Leidenschaft zum Klavierspiel teilte.
[22] Siehe hierzu Emily L. Johnsons Schreiben vom 26./28. Juni 1946, in: Unterlagen aus dem Nachlass Edgar N. Johnson, Privatbesitz Candice E. und Thomas R. Johnson, Denver, Colorado, USA.
[23] Die Funktionärsversammlung zum Thema „Gewerkschaften und Betriebsratswahlen" fand am 7. Juli 1946 in Kliems Festsälen in der Hasenheide 10 im Berliner Verwaltungsbezirk Kreuzberg statt. Siehe Die Unsicherheit in Berlin. Die verschwundenen SPD-Funktionäre – Kampf um Betriebsdemokratie, in: Der Sozialdemokrat vom 8. Juli 1946, S. 2; „Keine zweite Arbeitsfront". Konferenz sozialdemokratischer Betriebsfunktionäre, in: Telegraf vom 9. Juli 1946, S. 3; Kritische Aeusserungen, in: Der Kurier vom 8. Juli 1946, S. 2; pr., SPD und Betriebsratswahlen, in: Der Tagesspiegel vom 9. Juli 1946, [S. 2].
[24] Zum Freien Deutschen Gewerkschaftsbund (FDGB) siehe Dok. 49, Anm. 13.

nists didn't permit her to speak. It is very clear to these SPD people that the Communists are no different from the Nazis. She also speaks out boldly to the Russian officers with whom she comes into contact. I had a chance to say "gut" to her after her speech. She may disappear any day. A couple of SPD leaders have recently disappeared.[25] She doesn't care. She is in this business to speak out her mind and to act accordingly. This is the kind of person we ought to seek out and support. There are so few of them. We have haven't got sense enough, however, to make this selection. I ran into a man who came to me for protection from the Russians lately and whom, I thought, might have disappeared.[26] But he has moved into the American sector.

After the meeting I went to a concert of the Philharmonic.[27] They played the Prokofieff Classical Symphony[28], which I think as delightful as ever. Erna Berger[29], whom I mentioned before,[30] and whom I met going into the hall sang a Concerto for Soprano and Orchestra written by Glière[31]. The first movement was one of the most beautiful things of its kind I have ever heard. The program ended with Shostakovich's 5th Symphony.[32] It is in some instances heavy handed as the Russians are often apt to be, and in other passage there is long dull Communist argument. But there is also much that is stunning, and some that is beautiful. I'd like to know it better. It seemed to me a far different work from the 7th[33], a long winded speech that bored me very much in Vienna.

[25] Verschwunden waren Hermann Löwenthal (1900–1947), Leiter der SPD-Betriebsgruppe beim Berliner Magistrat, und Julius Scherff (1886–1947), Mitglied des Vorstands der Berliner SPD. Sie waren Ende Juni 1946 von der sowjetischen Besatzungsmacht verhaftet worden und starben 1947 in der Haft. Siehe Harold Hurwitz unter Mitarbeit von Ursula Böhme/Andreas Malycha, Die Stalinisierung der SED. Zum Verlust von Freiräumen und sozialdemokratischer Identität in den Vorständen 1946–1949 (= Schriften des Zentralinstituts für sozialwissenschaftliche Forschung der Freien Universität Berlin, Bd. 79), Opladen 1997, S. 54 und 157f.; Günter Fippel, Demokratische Gegner und Willküropfer von Besatzungsmacht und SED in Sachsenhausen (1946 bis 1950). Das sowjetische Speziallager Sachsenhausen – Teil des Stalinschen Lagerimperiums, unter Mitarbeit von Paul Radicke, mit einem einführenden Essay von Klaus-Dieter Müller, Herausgabe und Redaktion: Klaus-Dieter Müller/Mike Schmeitzner, Leipzig 2008, S. 122.

[26] Möglicherweise handelte es sich um einen der beiden Sozialdemokraten, die ihn am 6. Mai 1946 aufgesucht hatten, da sie sich als Fusionsgegner im sowjetischen Sektor bedroht fühlten und in den amerikanischen Sektor ziehen wollten. Siehe Dok. 44.

[27] Sinfoniekonzert des Berliner Philharmonischen Orchesters unter der Leitung von Sergiu Celibidache (siehe Dok. 66, Anm. 6) um 11 Uhr in der Deutschen Staatsoper im Admiralspalast im Bezirk Mitte, Friedrichstraße 101/102. Gespielt wurden Werke namhafter russischer Komponisten der damaligen Zeit. Siehe bog., Die fünfte Symphonie von Schostakowitsch. Symphonie-Konzert der Berliner Philharmoniker, in: Berliner Zeitung vom 9. Juli 1946, [S. 3]; Erwin Kroll, Russische Symphonik, in: Der Tagesspiegel vom 9. Juli 1946, [S. 6].

[28] Sinfonie Nr. 1 (Symphonie classique) von Sergei Sergejewitsch Prokofjew (1891–1953), russischer Komponist.

[29] Siehe Dok. 59, Anm. 24.

[30] Siehe Dok. 59 und Dok. 66.

[31] Konzert für Koloratursopran und Orchester von Reinhold Glière (1875–1956), russischer Komponist belgischer Abstammung.

[32] Sinfonie Nr. 5 des russischen Komponisten Dmitri Dmitrijewitsch Schostakowitsch (1906–1975). Es handelte sich um die deutsche Erstaufführung.

I then went to Don Heath's[34] for lunch after which I read to Mrs. Heath[35] the speech I have written for the women on Tuesday[36].[37] She liked this very much, thank God, so I don't have to think about recasting it. But after my experience with the little trade union leader today I shall have to add some things. Their son[38] is arriving here tomorrow, and they are especially excited. He is an 18 year old who has just graduated from the Salisbury school[39] at Salisbury Connecticut[40], and going to Hamilton College[41] (Erhardt's[42] College) this fall. Someday we shall have a couple of 18 year olds going off to college.

Then I went to Col. Glaser's[43] to talk about briefing General Keating[44] for the session on the Constitution of Berlin for the Commandants on Tuesday[45].[46] He begged me before I left to urge General Keating not to get another political adviser when I left but to content himself with Col. Lou[is] Glaser as political adviser. He is afraid of being pushed out of the picture. All very human enough. Nobody likes being pushed out of the picture.

There is much that I have omitted during the last few days but I'll keep it until we see each other which won't be very long. Good-night, my sweet and dearly beloved. Tell John to have the Bach[47] Invention[48] ready for me[49] and tell Timmy about Father. I love you, my sweetheart. Edgar

[33] Sinfonie Nr. 7, genannt Leningrader Sinfonie.
[34] Donald R. Heath. Siehe Dok. 8, Anm. 15.
[35] Siehe Dok. 55, Anm. 48.
[36] 9. Juli 1946.
[37] Siehe Dok. 68 und Dok. 70. Unter der Überschrift "Women's Club Meets Tuesday" schreibt der OMGUS Observer vom 5. Juli 1946, S. 2, unter anderem: "The second meeting of the Women's Club of Berlin will take place at Harnack House [siehe Dok. 15, Anm. 16] this Tuesday, July 9, at 3 p.m. A short business meeting will be held, followed by a talk given by Dr. E. N. Johnson, Special Assistant to the Commanding General, Headquarters Berlin District. His topic is to be 'The Relationship of Dependents to Occupation.' A special invitation is extended to all women who have just arrived in Berlin as well as to those who have not attended the previous meeting."
[38] Donald R. Heath Jr. (geb. 1928).
[39] College-preparatory school, gegründet 1901.
[40] Stadt im US-Bundesstaat Connecticut.
[41] College in Clinton, New York, gegründet 1793 als Hamilton-Oneida Academy, 1812 als Hamilton College.
[42] Siehe Dok. 20, Anm. 30.
[43] Siehe Dok. 28, Anm. 4.
[44] Siehe Dok. 39, Anm. 6.
[45] 9. Juli 1946.
[46] Siehe Dok. 68. Das Local Government Committee, Allied Kommandatura Berlin, hatte seine Beratungen am 5. Juli 1946 abgeschlossen. Siehe LOC GOV/R (46) 30 vom 5. Juli 1946, englisch- und russischsprachige Fassung, in: TNA, Allied Kommandatura: Directives, Minutes and Papers, FO 1112/377; Bildanhang, Abb. 70. Foto von Johnson in einer Arbeitspause des Local Government Committee am 5. Juli 1946 im Bildanhang, Abb. 69.
[47] Siehe Dok. 13, Anm. 20.
[48] Bachs Inventionen sind als Spiel- und Kompositionsübungen gedacht.
[49] Emily L. Johnson in ihrem Schreiben vom 29. Juni 1946: "John has a Bach invention for his lesson – hard, but beautiful." Brief in: Unterlagen aus dem Nachlass Edgar N. Johnson, Privatbesitz Candice E. und Thomas R. Johnson, Denver, Colorado, USA.

Dok. 72
Schreiben an die Ehefrau
Berlin, Wannsee Officers' Club[1], Am Sandwerder 17/19, 9. Juli 1946

My beloved –

It was very exciting to come back after my talk to the American wives[2] and find two letters from my lady – those of July 3 + 4th[3]. The one contains the account of the acquisition of the Steinway[4], and the other the account of the 4th of July with the Basoco's[5]. I am very very excited!!!! too over the acquisition of the piano, but I am sorry you had to get sick over it. It seems to me you have been very wise, very careful and have got what sounds like an excellent instrument. It is everything that we wanted. It is beyond the ordinary baby grand size. It is a Steinway of some vintage. You have paid less for it than we were willing to pay for a new one. It seems to be in very excellent condition

---

[1] Siehe Dok. 25, Anm. 9.

[2] Gemeint ist der Vortrag, den Johnson in der zweiten Sitzung des American Women's Club of Berlin am 9. Juli 1946 im Harnack House (siehe Dok. 15, Anm. 16) hielt. Siehe Dok. 68, Dok. 70, Dok. 71 und Dok. 71, Anm. 37. Unter der Überschrift "'Shun Nazis', Wives Told At Women's Club Meeting" schreibt der OMGUS Observer vom 12. Juli 1946, S. 2: "American families should have no toleration for Nazi-Germans, no matter how cultured or charming they seem to be, stated Dr. E. N. Johnson, Special Assistant to the Commanding General, Headquarters, B[erlin] D[istrict] at the second meeting of the American Women's Club of Berlin, Tuesday, when he discussed the responsibilities of American women in occupation. 'But Germans who conspicuously fought and resisted the influence of distorted Nazi minds should be fought and resisted the influence of [sic!] build their country along democratic lines,' he pointed out. 'The American women should reach out to German women like Helen Weber who are now trying to organize healthy political parties in a wholesome German government, or to persons like Gunther Weisenborn, who after imprisonment in concentration camps for underground activities against the Nazis, is still trying to direct the people away from the hypnotic influence of Nazism.' As Berlin is the nerve center of the world, Dr. Johnson said that what happened here would have lasting influence on the world of tomorrow. Therefore it is up to American women, who other women of the world are closely watching, to study international situations and keep abreast of world problems, particularly those to which they are so close. As the American families are apt to lose their sense of value and timing because of their comfortable communities, he advised them not to isolate themselves from the German people and their problems. 'The coming of American wives and families to Europe,' Dr. Johnson said, 'is but a further extension of America into Europe, a further representation of the best that America stands for in a Germany which has sore need for it. Your coming, in fact, amounts to the introduction into Germany of another American institution, the American home.'" Siehe Bildanhang, Abb. 64.

[3] Briefe in: Unterlagen aus dem Nachlass Edgar N. Johnson, Privatbesitz Candice E. und Thomas R. Johnson, Denver, Colorado, USA.

[4] Siehe Dok. 4, Anm. 25.

[5] Doris Basoco (1910–2000) und Miguel A. Basoco (1900–1981), amerikanischer Mathematiker, 1929 PhD, California Institute of Technology, lehrte ab 1930 an der University of Nebraska, 1944/1945 amtierender Direktor und 1947–1954 Direktor des Mathematischen Instituts.

and to have been little played on. If Byler[6] was willing to buy it, and Herbert[7] was willing to buy it, being as you say enthusiastic over it, and John[8] loved it, I don't see what better checking you could have. And you did check on the sounding board, and hammers, and keys. It is all too good to be true. I'm so glad you didn't pick up the indifferent Knabe.[9] If I have done nothing else in the war, I have made it possible for you to get a piano for our lovely John. It is one of the best things we have done, and we shall never regret it. Your suggestion that I take a lesson a week strikes a warm note in my heart, and I think I'll take it up. I suppose it would be a certain stimulus for John, and it would be good for me. Maybe I can get learn how to play nicely some things. It would be a bond with our dear boy too. Can you stand so much practicing around the house. John will thank us some day for this. I'll remember to keep the secret. You are superb.

The day with the Basoco's was one I would not covet. I am reminded again of how well you have done again with the boys. As I remember it there is nothing John does not like except peanuts, and there is something organic about that. And Timmy likewise. I am so anxious to see you and them.

And it won't be long now. General Clay[10] did see my letter while he was here.[11] I had a call from Colonel (formerly General) Millburn[12], saying that he had approved of my trip to the zone, and that I should come to his office at any time and make arrangements. General Keating[13] also wrote me a very nice letter, saying he hoped I would get the trip to the zone, and that he did not know how he would have gotten along without me here.[14] That is saying too much but I am glad he feels that I have not been utterly useless. I was trying to figure out a time schedule last night which would make it possible for me to get to Lincoln[15] by 21 August, and I think I should leave here on or about the first of August. If I take two full weeks in the zone, which I should do that means actually leaving here in a few days. But this, I think, I cannot do. The constitution and electoral procedure will not actually be finished until the 19th of August,

---

[6] Gemeint sein könnte Arthur W. Byler, amerikanischer Pianist und Professor, 1919–1925 Studium am Bethany College, Lindsborg, Kansas, lehrte ab 1927 am Doane College, Professor of Piano and Theory, Chairman, Department of Music.
[7] Herbert Schmidt. Siehe Dok. 29, Anm. 12.
[8] Johnsons Sohn John. Siehe Dok. 2, Anm. 15.
[9] Siehe Dok. 63 und Dok. 71.
[10] Siehe Dok. 2, Anm. 6.
[11] Siehe Dok. 63, Dok. 65, Dok. 67, Dok. 68, Dok. 70 und Dok. 71.
[12] Bryan L. Milburn. Siehe Dok. 15, Anm. 20.
[13] Siehe Dok. 39, Anm. 6.
[14] In dem Schreiben vom 5. Juli 1946, vorhanden in: Unterlagen aus dem Nachlass Edgar N. Johnson, Privatbesitz Candice E. und Thomas R. Johnson, Denver, Colorado, USA, heißt es unter anderem: "It is hoped that your request for release, as well as a tour of the zone for two weeks, will be approved. You deserve anything that may be granted. It has been a genuine pleasure to work with you, and in leaving, you will take back the heartfelt gratitude of my office for the magnificent assistance you rendered in your present capacity. I do not know what I would have done without your help." Siehe Bildanhang, Abb. 75.
[15] Hauptstadt des US-Bundesstaats Nebraska, wo Johnson mit seiner Familie wohnte und an der Universität lehrte.

when they come before the Commandants for final approval.[16] I could leave for Frankfurt[17] on the evening of that day, have twelve days in the zone, and plan to get back here by 1 August and off to Bremen[18] that night. That would be about 12 days. I suppose I ought to try to go to Vienna again, and catch up with the situation there. Maybe I could get some material for writing. But that would take time off from the zone. In any case my days here are numbered – 10 more at the most. It seems almost incredible. These departures come suddenly. Then I shall be off to you and the boys, and we shall be off to the mountains. There was an article in the Stars and Stripes[19] about the polio epidemic in Colorado[20].[21] May be we have no business to take this chance. Most of the cases seem to be concentrated in Denver[22] which we should try to avoid. Isn't there someplace else we can get off by taking a slower train perhaps, and make our way to Meeker lodge[23]. Or else can arrangements be made in advance to meet us at the train and away we go. Couldn't Mrs. Zumwinckel[24] make arrangements with a local driver at Meeker to come to Denver and meet the train, so that there would be no delay whatsoever in getting out of the city. You'd better get good accommodations. At the worst you could sleep with Timmy in a lower berth and John and I could sleep in an upper. He would think that this is fun.

The Constitution was presented to the Commandants this morning.[25] Keating used statements I had drawn up to present the American case. The generals were quite amazed that we presented an agreed upon report[26], and Kotikov[27]

---

[16] Gemeint ist der 19. Juli 1946. Die Stadtkommandanten genehmigten in ihrer Sitzung am 9. Juli 1946 den Verfassungsentwurf des Local Government Committee grundsätzlich, gaben ihn aber zur Klärung einzelner Fragen dem Committee zurück. Die Endfassung sollte den Stadtkommandanten am 19. Juli 1946 vorliegen. Siehe Protokoll der 18. Sitzung der Stadtkommandanten am 9. Juli 1946, BKC/M (46) 18-170, englischsprachige Fassung, in: LAB, B Rep. 036-01 (Office of Military Government, Berlin Sector [OMGBS]), 4/132-3/11.

[17] Frankfurt am Main, Stadt im Land Groß-Hessen in der amerikanischen Besatzungszone Deutschlands.

[18] Siehe Dok. 71, Anm. 10.

[19] Amerikanische Soldatenzeitung.

[20] US-Bundesstaat.

[21] Unter der Überschrift "Polio Cases Spread In Colorado Area" berichtet The Stars and Stripes, European Edition, vom 9. Juli 1946, S. 5: "Infantile paralysis was nearing epidemic proportions in Colorado today as the state was given emergency status by the National Foundation for Infantile Paralysis. Dr. Roy Cleere, executive secretary for the state board of health, announced that 99 cases of poliomielitis had been reported recently in Colorado, with 56 of them in the metropolitan Denver area. Eight victims have died. All public pools and beaches have been closed in Denver in an effort to halt the disease."

[22] Hauptstadt des US-Bundesstaats Colorado, am östlichen Fuß der Rocky Mountains gelegen.

[23] Siehe Dok. 63, Anm. 21.

[24] Essie Zumwinkel. Siehe Dok. 46, Anm. 6.

[25] Siehe Protokoll der 18. Sitzung der Stadtkommandanten am 9. Juli 1946, BKC/M (46) 18-170, englischsprachige Fassung, in: LAB, B Rep. 036-01 (Office of Military Government, Berlin Sector [OMGBS]), 4/132-3/11.

[26] Siehe LOC GOV/R (46) 30 vom 5. Juli 1946, russisch- und englischsprachige Fassung, in: TNA, Allied Kommandatura: Directives, Minutes and Papers, FO 1112/377; Bildanhang, Abb. 70.

had prepared a special statement of commendation which was to go into the minutes. I understand also that Keating is going to make some kind of a citation for Glaser[28] and me for our work on the Committee[29].[30] It will all seem rather petty some weeks hence but it has been fun doing. These last meetings have been strenuous under Russian chairmanship what with their terrible luncheons. But the Russians are going all out to be friendly these days. At the end of the meeting yesterday,[31] they gave a tea with all their drinks accompanying. You know you have to drink bottoms up with the Russians. At the end of the Commandants meeting today Kotikov invited the crowd to lunch as a kind of celebration. I had another engagement but in any case I couldn't have taken it. Col. Zozulya[32], with whom I have got rather friendly was very disappointed. The Russians are sensitive on this score.

The ladies seemed to like the speech and asked for copies.[33] I referred to you at the beginning and at the end. Soon I shall be leaving here for you. I love you my blessed one, oh so much. There are wonderful days ahead of us. Kiss the sweet boys. I love you. Edgar

Dok. 73
Schreiben an die Ehefrau
Berlin, Wannsee Officers' Club[1], Am Sandwerder 17/19, 12. Juli 1946

Dearest:

I am aware that on Sunday[2] we shall have been married for ten years.[3] I have thought I would call you by long distance telephone on that date but in view of the excessive cost (4 dollars a minute), and of the fact that we really wouldn't

---

[27] Siehe Dok. 35, Anm. 5.
[28] Siehe Dok. 28, Anm. 4.
[29] Local Government Committee, Allied Kommandatura Berlin.
[30] Glaser wurde ein "Certificate of Commendation" zuerkannt: "For meritorious service during the period 1 January 1946 to 1 July 1946 while serving as Chief of Civil Administration Branch for Military Government distinguished himself by outstanding performance of duty. The capability and resourcefulness displayed in addition to his untiring energy and loyal devotion to duty reflect great credit upon himself and the military service. Lieutenant Colonel GLASER is hereby authorized to wear the Army Commendation Ribbon by direction of the Secretary of War." Certificate of Commendation vom 30. Juli 1946, in: Unterlagen aus dem Nachlass Louis Glaser, Privatbesitz Anthony J. Glaser, Bethesda, Maryland, USA. Siehe Bildanhang, Abb. 34.
[31] Siehe Protokoll der 32. Sitzung des Local Government Committee, Allied Kommandatura Berlin, am 8. Juli 1946, LG/M (46) 32, russischsprachige Fassung, in: TNA, Allied Kommandatura: Directives, Minutes and Papers, FO 1112/378.
[32] Siehe Dok. 67, Anm. 28.
[33] Siehe oben.

[1] Siehe Dok. 25, Anm. 9.
[2] 14. Juli 1946.
[3] Edgar N. und Emily L. Johnson waren seit dem 14. Juli 1936 verheiratet.

get anything said to each other, I have decided to save the money. I think may be you will approve. I have talked with some who have done it and they find it quite unsatisfactory. Since we can't be together on that date we shall have to postpone our festivity until we see each other. The details of that day are precious and fresh in my mind and I have to go over them. I think I have gone over them in many letters to you since we have been apart I am going over them now. I love you very much sweetheart. The days of that summer which followed, and indeed most of the days, I meant almost every one of them, and almost every hour of every one of them that has since gone have only served to make clear how great a misfortune it is that we were not married at least ten years earlier. They have been the only years of my life which really count. What we have lost it is impossible to retrieve, but it can heighten an awareness of the necessity to live out our remaining years to the full. We shall have to remind each other in the morning, or in the evening that the day which is to come or which has just gone will be one less or is one less among the few which are still allotted to us. Until the great separation we shall have none such as we have had for the past two years and more. I shall try to be worthy of your presence in the days that are to come. I love you, my darling and my sweetheart.

I actually took some steps to get back to you today by the 21st[4]. I went to General Clay's[5] administrative officer, a Mr. Baird and told him I was leaving between 1 August and 5 August, and that he should be getting orders ready. He says it will be quite necessary to leave by that time if I hope to make it. I guess it is possible to terminate one's services with the War Department in New York. Accordingly it will not be necessary to go to Washington, and since I am really not looking for a job, I don't think I'll go unless there is an abundance of time. I care to see there only Gene[6] and Polly[7] and Harold[8] and Marguerite[9]. It is more important that I spend a little time with Dad[10], and Mildred[11] and Aunt Hannah[12]. I think I should like to go to the cemetery also,[13] then come out straight to you. I also made some preliminary arrangements for trips to the zone. I'll leave here for that trip after the Commandants meeting on next Friday[14], or on Saturday[15] next. I asked for the privilege of going to Vienna but I don't know whether it will be granted, or if I really have time to go. I'd like to catch up on the situation there because it is, for the moment, so very tense. But I have put Stuttgart[16] on the list. I at least ought to get a glimpse of the job I was to have, and I have

---

[4] 21. August 1946.
[5] Siehe Dok. 2, Anm. 6.
[6] Eugene N. Anderson. Siehe Dok. 1, Anm. 1.
[7] Pauline R. Anderson. Siehe Dok. 2, Anm. 2.
[8] Harold C. Vedeler. Siehe Dok. 2, Anm. 12.
[9] Marguerite D. Vedeler. Siehe Dok. 2, Anm. 13.
[10] Frank E. Johnson. Siehe Dok. 3, Anm. 12.
[11] Mildred H. Williams. Siehe Dok. 4, Anm. 12.
[12] Hannah Walstrom. Siehe Dok. 4, Anm. 14.
[13] Zum Grab der Mutter in Chicago, Illinois. Siehe Dok. 46, Anm. 13.
[14] 19. Juli 1946.
[15] 20. Juli 1946.
[16] Hauptstadt des Landes Württemberg-Baden in der amerikanischen Besatzungszone Deutschlands.

put Heidelberg[17] on the list too. I'll try to get as much done as I can, but evidently I am going to be rushed. I'll come back here for only a day or so, and then off to Bremen[18] where, I understand, I shall be delayed for a couple of days.

I shall leave here with regret because there is much to do but I have never thought that my decision to leave is unwise. We do not have the resources to go adventuring here. Many of the important people here who are staying on, have, I imagine, independent means. Anyway I am coming back to you, my sweetheart, for a very very long time and first of all for a wonderful re-experiencing of our last Colorado[19] experience. I love you, my Emily, and boys. It is hardly more than five weeks now. I kiss you all. Edgar

Dok. 74
Schreiben an die Ehefrau
Berlin, Wannsee Officers' Club[1], Am Sandwerder 17/19, 14. Juli 1946

My sweet Emily –

This is the day 10 years ago.[2] 10 full and precious years. And 5 weeks from today I should be there. And five weeks from tonight we should be starting off together on a holiday in the mountains in our old cabin. This all turns out very beautifully. I imagine you have arranged to take Alison[3] or Tascha[4] along so that we may have some hiking together.[5] You were after all a very determined climber and I can't imagine that you will be very contented to remain confined to the environment of the cabin for any great length of time. I can't wait to share John's[6] excitement about it all.

This then is, I suppose, my last Sunday in Berlin. It is a lovely Sunday. The sporting Americans have just made their appearance on the lake[7] in what amounts almost to a fleet of sail-boats. I can hear the shouts of the children over at the Wannsee beach[8] which is not so far from here. It is a pleasant sound –

---

[17] Universitätsstadt im Land Württemberg-Baden in der amerikanischen Besatzungszone Deutschlands.
[18] Siehe Dok. 71, Anm. 10.
[19] US-Bundesstaat.

[1] Siehe Dok. 25, Anm. 9.
[2] Gemeint ist der zehnte Hochzeitstag, Edgar N. und Emily L. Johnson waren seit dem 14. Juli 1936 verheiratet. Siehe Dok. 73.
[3] Alison E. Gass. Siehe Dok. 68, Anm. 5.
[4] Natasha (Tasha) Stepanek (geb. 1933), Tochter von Olga F. und Orin Stepanek (siehe Dok. 57, Anm. 3).
[5] Emily L. Johnson in ihrem Schreiben vom 3. Juli 1946: "I am still toying with the idea of taking Alison Gass or Tasha Stepanek along as a babysitter so we can be free to go on a few points together." Brief in: Unterlagen aus dem Nachlass Edgar N. Johnson, Privatbesitz Candice E. und Thomas R. Johnson, Denver, Colorado, USA.
[6] Johnsons Sohn John. Siehe Dok. 2, Anm. 15.
[7] Gemeint ist der Große Wannsee, eine Ausbuchtung der Havel (siehe Dok. 74, Anm. 24) im Südwesten Berlins.
[8] Gemeint ist das 1929/1930 errichtete Strandbad Wannsee am Ostufer des Großen Wannsees.

the kind of sound that you don't often hear in Berlin – shouts of delight over the release from the dingy houses and rubble of the city and over the chance to frolic in the sunshine. Artur[9] is coming at about one o'clock and I am going out for an hour or so and take some pictures of this forlorn city so that you can see something of what has happened to it.[10] I shall work here in the afternoon. Tonight I have been invited to go to Suhr's[11] to meet some of the Social Democrats. I have to go because he postponed a gathering from last-night to tonight in order that I might come. I suppose it is the last time I shall see the Social Democrats – those people who put up such a good fight when I first came here, but who have since lost a good deal of this drive, and are now quibbling about very small things.

Yesterday I suppose was the last staff meeting of General Keating[12] and Colonel Howley[13] that I shall attend. They had a sign at my chair this time. "Political Advisor". Then I went to Clay's[14] Staff meeting[15]. He had not returned as yet from Paris[16], and I imagine he will return a rather disappointed man since the German matter has really been postponed until November,[17] and not much further progress can be expected here until fundamental decisions have been taken. These meetings have in fact been rather dull for several weeks. Except for keeping the machinery going not much is happening. I discovered that a sign had been put at my chair for these meetings also. "Adviser to the Deputy Military Governor". Walter Dorn[18] told me yesterday that Clay feels that he has been at this job long enough, and that a civilian should take over. I wonder who that civilian is going to be if and when. There seems to be a general feeling about here that we are not going to stay here very long – a very horrible mistake, I think. The Germans think this also. I had lunch with Walter Dorn and he

[9] Artur Sanow. Siehe Dok. 40, Anm. 13.
[10] Fotos, die von Johnson möglicherweise an diesem Tag gemacht wurden, im Bildanhang, Abb. 50 und Abb. 51.
[11] Otto Suhr. Siehe Dok. 40, Anm. 7.
[12] Siehe Dok. 39, Anm. 6.
[13] Siehe Dok. 20, Anm. 18.
[14] Siehe Dok. 2, Anm. 6.
[15] Siehe Protokoll der OMGUS-Stabskonferenz am 13. Juli 1946, in: Archiv des IfZ, OMGUS – Staff Conferences (Protokollkopien), Fg 12/5.
[16] Clay hatte an der bis zum 12. Juli 1946 stattgefundenen Pariser Außenministerkonferenz teilgenommen. Siehe Dok. 44, Anm. 13.
[17] Wie die Presse nach Beendigung der Pariser Konferenz mitteilte, sollte im Herbst 1946 eine Sonderkonferenz der Außenminister über Deutschland abgehalten werden. „Die Außenminister kamen überein, *im Herbst* – nach der Vertagung der im September beginnenden Vollversammlung der Vereinten Nationen – *eine Sonderkonferenz über die deutsche Frage* abzuhalten. Der genaue Zeitpunkt dieser Konferenz wurde noch nicht festgelegt. Nach Mitteilung der französischen Nachrichtenagentur ‚AFP' sollen sich die Außenminister auf den *November* geeinigt haben." Deutschland-Konferenz im November. Die Grundsätze der amerikanischen Politik in Deutschland, in: Der Tagesspiegel vom 13. Juli 1946, Beiblatt. „[...] die deutsche Frage wird bis in den November hinein in der Schwebe bleiben, bis zu dem Tage, da nach der Pariser Absprache die Minister zusammentreffen wollen, um sich endgültig über das zukünftige Gesicht Deutschlands klar zu werden." Die Ergebnisse von Paris, in: Der Tagesspiegel vom 14. Juli 1946, [S. 1].
[18] Siehe Dok. 2, Anm. 10.

was wrapped up in his de-Nazification problems, which are, indeed, serious enough. The church, for example, that church which I once thought was going to be such a great help in bringing back Germany to its feet, while it has, to be sure, dismissed some of its Nazi adherents, is now taking the stand that preachers who are punished by the De-Nazification law[19] in our zone we can't force it to keep from the pulpit because only the church can say who may preach the word of God, and for us to say that preachers may not preach, is an unwarranted interference by us (the state) in the affairs of the church. They may have to take this interference.

After lunch I went back to the office for awhile and then took off to a French fête given in honor of a certain famous speech which De Gaulle[20] made at London on 18 June 1940 when he said that France may have lost a battle, but it had not lost the war,[21] and in honor too of today – Bastille Day[22]; yet De Gaulle overshadows the Bastille. It was in the nature of an aquatic and athletic display at one of Berlin's outing places, Tegelort[23] on the Havel[24].[25] I could only stay a few minutes because I had an appointment with Dr. Haas[26] and his wife[27] to go to the opera.

Dr. Haas is a member of the Magistrat[28] who wrote the first draft of the constitution of Berlin upon which we have been working.[29] He is trying desperately to correct some of the mistakes which we have had to make but I don't know

---

[19] Gesetz zur Befreiung von Nationalsozialismus und Militarismus vom 5. März 1946. Siehe Dok. 47, Anm. 20.
[20] Charles de Gaulle (1890-1970), französischer General und Politiker, 1943/1944 Präsident des Comité Français de la Liberation Nationale, 1944/1945 Regierungschef der Provisorischen Regierung, 1945 Wahl zum Ministerpräsidenten und vorläufigen Staatspräsidenten durch die verfassunggebende Nationalversammlung, Januar 1946 Rücktritt, nachdem die Nationalversammlung seiner Forderung nach einem Präsidialsystem nicht entsprochen hatte, 1947-1953 Gründer und Vorsitzender des Rassemblement Populaire Français, 1958/1959 Ministerpräsident, 1959-1969 Staatspräsident.
[21] In seiner Rede am 18. Juni 1940 hatte de Gaulle vom Exil in London aus die Franzosen aufgefordert, an der Seite Großbritanniens von den Kolonien aus den Krieg gegen die Achsenmächte fortzusetzen. Danach wurde er der führende Kopf des französischen Widerstands gegen die deutsche Besatzungsmacht und das Vichy-Regime.
[22] Seit 1880 französischer Nationalfeiertag. Am 14. Juli 1789 erfolgte die Erstürmung der Bastille, am 14. Juli 1790 fand das Föderationsfest statt.
[23] Eine Ortslage im Ortsteil Konradshöhe im Berliner Verwaltungsbezirk Reinickendorf (französischer Sektor von Berlin).
[24] Fluss, der Berlin in einer Länge von rund 30 km durchfließt.
[25] Mit der Veranstaltung in Tegelort begannen am 13. Juli 1946 die Feierlichkeiten zum französischen Nationalfeiertag. "The three-day holiday celebration began Saturday afternoon with a combination regatta and fair at the French Nautique Sport Club of Tegelort. Sailing, rowing and swimming races were followed by dancing and a water carnival with decorated floats which ended in a burst of fireworks." Bastille Day Observed By French Here, in: OMGUS Observer vom 19. Juli 1946, S. 3.
[26] Siehe Dok. 49, Anm. 40.
[27] Charlotte Haas, geb. Wegener (1905-1963).
[28] Haas hatte im März 1946 kommissarisch die Kämmereigeschäfte übernommen.
[29] Haas hatte dem Magistrat am 9. April 1946 einen Verfassungsentwurf zur Beratung vorgelegt, der überarbeitet und dann der Alliierten Kommandantur vorgelegt wurde; es folgte die Beratung im Local Government Committee der Alliierten Kommandantur.

whether I shall be able to get them out or not. He is a practising Catholic, a southern German[30], who has been in the city government since 1939[31], a simple modest unambitious and principled man who tries first of all to do his duty. He may leave Berlin to become the mayor of Heidelberg[32],[33] though he feels that he would be missing the international show here if he went down there. Yesterday was his 50th birthday.[34] He married late,[35] a very simple woman, and they have no children. He showed me the flowers and inscription which the 8000 people who work for him in the Finance section presented him.[36] He showed me a bottle of champagne which the Communist Vice-Mayor (Maron[37] – trained in Russia) gave to him. I noticed it was the same as the Russians serve at the Kommandatura[38]. Germans to Russians to a Communist Vice-Mayor to a Catholic German city treasurer. The Ober-Burgermeister[39] wrote him a flowery letter. A subordinate in our sector gave him a bottle of schnaps. There were other flowers and the city porcelain factory[40] gave him one of its pieces. The little satisfactions go on underneath the tragic covering. The opera was Butter-

Siehe Vorläufige Verfassung von Groß-Berlin, erl. von Dr. Haas, Kämmerer von Groß-Berlin, 4., neubearb. Auflage, Berlin 1947, S. 26f. Einen allerersten Verfassungsentwurf hatte Haas am 8. November 1945 dem Magistrat vorgelegt. Siehe ebd., S. 25f.

[30] In Untereggingen/Kreis Waldshut in Baden geboren.

[31] Haas war ab 1929 Magistratsrat in der Bezirksverwaltung Charlottenburg gewesen.

[32] Universitätsstadt im Land Württemberg-Baden in der amerikanischen Besatzungszone Deutschlands.

[33] Am 27. Juli 1946 wählte der Heidelberger Stadtrat den Kandidaten der CDU, Dr. Hugo Swart (1885-1952), zum Oberbürgermeister. Siehe Oberbürgermeisterwahl in Heidelberg, in: Rhein-Neckar-Zeitung vom 30. Juli 1946, S. 1; Gerhard Hinz, Ernst Walz †, in: Ruperto-Carola. Zeitschrift der Vereinigung der Freunde der Studentenschaft der Universität Heidelberg e.V., Juni 1967, S. 46f., hier S. 46. Trotz der freundlichen Unterstützung durch das Stadtarchiv Heidelberg hat sich nicht nachweisen lassen, dass Haas der Heidelberger CDU als Kandidat für das Amt des Oberbürgermeisters zur Verfügung stand.

[34] Haas wurde am 13. Juli 1896 geboren.

[35] Haas war seit 1936 verheiratet.

[36] Die Hauptverwaltung des Magistrats hatte im Mai 1946 9000 Beschäftigte. Siehe Das erste Jahr. Berlin im Neuaufbau. Ein Rechenschaftsbericht des Magistrats der Stadt Berlin, hrsg. im Auftrage des Magistrats der Stadt Berlin, Berlin 1946, S. 26. Vermutlich waren in der Finanzabteilung etwa 800 (nicht 8000) Personen beschäftigt.

[37] Karl Maron (1903-1975), deutscher Politiker (KPD/SED), 1925 KPD, 1934 Emigration nach Dänemark und 1935 in die Sowjetunion, ab 1943 stellvertretender Chefredakteur von „Freies Deutschland" (Zeitung des Nationalkomitees „Freies Deutschland"), 1945 Rückkehr nach Berlin als Mitglied der „Gruppe Ulbricht", 1945-Dezember 1946 Erster Stellvertreter des Oberbürgermeisters der Stadt Berlin, 1946 SED, November 1946-1948 Mitglied der Stadtverordnetenversammlung von Groß-Berlin, 1954-1975 Mitglied des Zentralkomitees der SED, 1955-1963 Innenminister der DDR und Chef der Deutschen Volkspolizei.

[38] Siehe Dok. 20, Anm. 11.

[39] Arthur Werner. Siehe Dok. 27, Anm. 30, und Dok. 39, Anm. 23.

[40] Ehemalige Staatliche Porzellanmanufaktur, die als Berliner Porzellanmanufaktur weitergeführt und von der Finanzabteilung des Magistrats betreut wurde. Siehe Die Sitzungsprotokolle des Magistrats der Stadt Berlin 1945/46. Teil I: 1945, bearb. und eingel. von Dieter Hanauske (= Schriftenreihe des Landesarchivs Berlin, Bd. 2/I), Berlin 1995, Dok. 52, S. 699f.

fly[41] and it was not very well done – nothing like the performances in Vienna. I brought them out here for dinner and they stayed until after twelve – the first Germans, I imagine, who have been entertained in this expensive club[42]. It is an event which I suppose he will long remember and he is the kind of German upon whom Germany will have to rebuild. He is going to introduce me to Cardinal Preysing[43] before I go, and I shall try to get Preysing to introduce me to Faulhaber[44] whom I shall try to see in Munich[45]. Since I once was interested in the Church I ought to try to see a few of these people before I leave.[46]

Were we going to stay here for a very long time it would be fun to devote oneself's to the rebirth of Germany. But I believe that, at the moment, I have other things to devote myself to. You know what I mean. I love my sweet wife and my very sweet boys. A kiss for them. Edgar

Dok. 75
Schreiben an die Ehefrau
Berlin, Wannsee Officers' Club[1], Am Sandwerder 17/19, 15. Juli 1946

My sweet and only one:
After a rather long and difficult meeting of the local government committee[2] on yesterday I came back to find two lovely letters from you awaiting me. One was a letter that had gone somewhat astray, since it dated back to the 3 July.[3] The other was as recent as the 9th of July.[4] The first reminded me of how far I am from

---

[41] Madame Butterfly, Oper von Giacomo Puccini (1858–1924), Aufführung der Deutschen Staatsoper im Admiralspalast im Bezirk Mitte, Friedrichstraße 101/102, am 13. Juli 1946, 18 Uhr. Premiere: 26. Januar 1946. Siehe Kurt Westphal, Puccini und seine „Butterfly". Zur Neuinszenierung in der Staatsoper, in: Berliner Zeitung vom 29. Januar 1946, [S. 3].
[42] Gemeint ist das Wannsee Hotel bzw. der Wannsee Officers' Club. Siehe Dok. 25, Anm. 9.
[43] Konrad Kardinal Graf von Preysing-Lichtenegg-Moos (1880–1950), deutscher Bischof, 1932–1935 Bischof von Eichstätt, ab 1935 Bischof von Berlin, führend im kirchlich-katholischen Widerstand gegen die nationalsozialistische Kirchenpolitik, 1946 Ernennung zum Kardinal, gründete zahlreiche Hilfsorganisationen für den Wiederaufbau Berlins.
[44] Siehe Dok. 11, Anm. 26.
[45] München, Hauptstadt des Landes Bayern in der amerikanischen Besatzungszone Deutschlands.
[46] Siehe Dok. 21, Anm. 35.

[1] Siehe Dok. 25, Anm. 9.
[2] Siehe Dok. 29, Anm. 14; Protokoll der 34. Sitzung des Local Government Committee, Allied Kommandatura Berlin, am 15. Juli 1946, LG/M (46) 34, russischsprachige Fassung, in: TNA, Allied Kommandatura: Directives, Minutes and Papers, FO 1112/378.
[3] Siehe Schreiben vom 2. Juli 1946 (Poststempel vom 3. Juli 1946), in: Unterlagen aus dem Nachlass Edgar N. Johnson, Privatbesitz Candice E. und Thomas R. Johnson, Denver, Colorado, USA.
[4] Siehe Schreiben vom 8. Juli 1946 (Poststempel vom 9. Juli 1946), in: Unterlagen aus dem Nachlass Edgar N. Johnson, Privatbesitz Candice E. und Thomas R. Johnson, Denver, Colorado, USA.

the kids what with a young son who has to be reprimanded and punished for saying Yipe and Jeez too frequently, and another who learns phrases upon their mere mention to him. "That's all right." "You are two years old." The second was an account of Timmy's birthday party[5] (wherein the imaginative aptitude of my sweet Emily came into play. I am thinking of Pooh[6]!) and of the chairs which we now have of our new piano, and of Gretchen's[7] piano. Your characterization of the two pianos strikes home with me. I don't know our new one except from your descriptions of your experiences with pianos. But I do remember Gretchen's piano from having played on it and your description is as I experienced it. The difference consists of the contrast between your adjective "brilliant" from which I deduce a clear, volatile treble and a rather resounding bass, and your adjective "sweet" which implies no especial contrast but rather a satisfactory tone throughout treble and bass. You are right. The ordinary pianist prefers the brilliance which means the contrast rather than the sweetness, which is all right for Christmas carols but hardly for a Chopin[8] Étude. John[9] I am sure will come to prefer the brilliance to the sweetness for without brilliance there is no pianism. I think indeed that through your perspicacity we have been saved from a piano which is only sweet.

Things have begun to hum a bit today in preparation for my trip to the zone. It is very convenient to have generals on the tip of your tongue. It looks at present as if I shall take my driver, Sanow[10], and my car along with me. They are, at least, on my orders at present, and I am seeing Keating[11] tomorrow morning to get his consent. I saw the Education and Religion people[12] this morning and made arrangements to see some of the so-called church heroes about which I wrote while I was in R + A, OSS[13].[14] They do not happen to be at the moment, the heroes I thought they were going to be. I have an appointment for Thursday[15] morning to meet Cardinal Preysing[16], the prelate of Berlin, one of the Catholic heroes, and I am going to try to get him to give me a letter of introduction to Cardinal Faulhaber[17] of Munich[18], one of the heroes of southern Germany. I made arrangements this morning to see the important political people in the zone, and also to attend a meeting of the Nurnberg[19] trial[20] in case I

---

[5] Johnsons Sohn Thomas (siehe Dok. 2, Anm. 16) war am 8. Juli 1946 zwei Jahre alt geworden.
[6] Gemeint sein könnte Winnie-the-Pooh, eine Kinderbuchfigur von Alan A. Milne (1882–1956).
[7] Siehe Dok. 63, Anm. 18.
[8] Frédéric Chopin (1810–1849), polnischer Komponist und Pianist, 1831 Übersiedlung nach Frankreich, wo der Vater herstammte.
[9] Johnsons Sohn John. Siehe Dok. 2, Anm. 15.
[10] Siehe Dok. 40, Anm. 13.
[11] Siehe Dok. 39, Anm. 6.
[12] Gemeint sind Mitarbeiter der Education and Religious Affairs Branch, Internal Affairs and Communications Division, OMGUS.
[13] Research and Analysis Branch, Office of Strategic Services. Siehe Dok. 1, Anm. 9.
[14] Siehe Dok. 21, Anm. 35.
[15] 18. Juli 1946.
[16] Siehe Dok. 74, Anm. 43.
[17] Siehe Dok. 11, Anm. 26.
[18] München, Hauptstadt des Landes Bayern in der amerikanischen Besatzungszone Deutschlands.

should get to Nurnberg, which I think I should try to do. I'd like to get a look at Göring[21] and at Funk[22] whose bathroom I happen now to be using. Vienna is also on my orders, or at least I think it is going to be by tomorrow, and I shall therefore have the chance to talk with my friends there, and bring my Vienna experience up to date. I dropped in to see Don Heath[23] this morning, whom I have often mentioned. He expressed regret at my leaving and said quite sincerely that if I found the life of the University to be a little too much to take, I should write him here at Berlin with the idea of coming into the service of the State Department here. I think he meant it. And I am glad that I spoke for his wife[24] before the wives here.[25] Your suggestion that I should perhaps make it a point to go to Washington, just in case, I think I may follow. It will be good to see Gene[26] and Harold[27] again. Gene will perhaps be coming over here later on.[28] And I could speak to General Hilldring[29] also who is the big man on occupation matters now. You may be interested to know that the Education people would be glad to take me on for an important job if I wished to come back here.

It may be a little difficult, with all this, to get back to you by the 20th or the 21st[30]. This is however my aim. I shall get in touch with you upon my arrival in New York. I don't see why you could not wait for me in case I were a day or two late, although I am perfectly willing to admit that there is no reason why you should wait for me. A day or two extra in the mountains, is a day or two extra in the mountains. I think, however, that with the chance to do a good job

---

[19] Nürnberg, Stadt im Land Bayern in der amerikanischen Besatzungszone Deutschlands.
[20] Siehe Dok. 49, Anm. 44.
[21] Siehe Dok. 22, Anm. 24.
[22] Siehe Dok. 25, Anm. 10.
[23] Donald R. Heath. Siehe Dok. 8, Anm. 15.
[24] Louise B. Heath. Siehe Dok. 55, Anm. 48.
[25] Johnson spricht hier den Vortrag an, den er am 9. Juli 1946 vor dem American Women's Club of Berlin gehalten hatte. Siehe Dok. 72, Anm. 2.
[26] Eugene N. Anderson. Siehe Dok. 1, Anm. 1.
[27] Harold C. Vedeler. Siehe Dok. 2, Anm. 12.
[28] Anderson sollte als Vertreter des Department of State, Occupied Areas Division, mit einer amerikanischen Kommission von Erziehungssachverständigen, der United States Education Mission to Germany, nach Deutschland reisen. "Gene plans to come over in August + hopes to get permission from Clay [siehe Dok. 2, Anm. 6] to travel a bit – some educational group", hatte Emily bereits am 10. Juni 1946 ihrem Ehemann mitgeteilt. Brief in: Unterlagen aus dem Nachlass Edgar N. Johnson, Privatbesitz Candice E. und Thomas R. Johnson, Denver, Colorado, USA. Am 24. August 1946 traf die Delegation, die über den Zustand des Bildungswesens in der amerikanischen Besatzungszone berichten und ein Programm für notwendige Reformen ausarbeiten sollte, in Berlin ein. Dort wurden Gespräche mit Angehörigen der amerikanischen Militärregierung geführt, anschließend bereiste die Delegation die Länder der US-Zone. Nach knapp einmonatiger Tätigkeit schloss sie ihre Arbeit ab. Siehe Die Neue Zeitung vom 23. August 1946, S. 1, vom 30. August 1946, S. 1, vom 6. September 1946, S. 2, vom 23. September 1946, S. 2, und vom 18. Oktober 1946, S. 2; Educators Tour American Zone To See Schools, in: OMGUS Observer vom 30. August 1946, S. 4; James F. Tent, Mission on the Rhine. Reeducation and Denazification in American-Occupied Germany, Chicago und London 1982, S. 114f.
[29] Siehe Dok. 2, Anm. 4.
[30] August 1946.

in the zone, and with the chance to go to Vienna, I should do both. The itinerary I worked out today brings me to Bremen[31] about the 5th of August. I understand I lose a couple of days there, and that one must count on at least ten days on the Atlantic. This may leave me little enough time to get from New York to you, or I may have luck and have some extra days to spare. In any case I shall do my best.

Letters may be a little sporadic from now on, and I may not be able to write very regularly. Yet I shall be gathering up experience to relate to you when I see you. This is, I think, a good way to end it all. I shall wait to see General Clay[32] and other important ones until I return from the zone. I shall get in touch with you soon after my arrival in New York to learn from you what I should really do next.

Goodnight, my love, a sweet kiss for you and for the boys. Tell John there is much fun in store for us in the mountains and forever afterwards. Get the fishing rod ready if you can find it. I love you all very very much. My sweet ones to whom I am returning. Edgar

Dok. 76
Schreiben an die Ehefrau
Butzbach[1], Groß-Hessen, Officers' Club – vormals Deutsches Haus[2], 21. Juli 1946

Dearest –

According to our plans I was to be with you a month from today in Colorado[3]. Considering what has happened today and yesterday it is unlikely that I shall ever get there. For my trip to the zone[4] has had a very unsuspicious start. I started out with what I thought was a car in very good condition – neither the driver[5] nor the motor pool ever led me to believe otherwise. We started yesterday morning, after I had spent a whole day (except for a meeting of the Kommandatura[6] at which the constitution was finally adopted[7]) trying to get papers

---

[31] Siehe Dok. 71, Anm. 10.
[32] Siehe Dok. 2, Anm. 6.

[1] Stadt im Land Groß-Hessen in der amerikanischen Besatzungszone Deutschlands, am nordöstlichen Übergang des Taunus zur Wetterau.
[2] Das am Bahnhof gelegene Deutsche Haus, in der NS-Zeit neben dem Hessischen Hof das beste Hotel der Stadt, war nach dem Einmarsch der Amerikaner Offiziersklub geworden, „d. h. hier wohnten die amerikanischen Offiziere. Außerdem wurde der Offiziersclub auch von zahlreichen ‚Fräuleins' besucht, die hier ihre Freunde hatten (zeitüblich)." E-Mail von Dieter Wolf, Leiter des Museums und Stadtarchivs der Stadt Butzbach, an Werner Breunig vom 12. Juli 2007.
[3] US-Bundesstaat.
[4] Gemeint ist die amerikanische Besatzungszone Deutschlands.
[5] Artur Sanow. Siehe Dok. 40, Anm. 13.
[6] Siehe Dok. 20, Anm. 11.
[7] Am 19. Juli 1946 billigten die Stadtkommandanten die Verfassung. Siehe Protokoll der 19. Sitzung der Stadtkommandanten am 19. Juli 1946, BKC/M (46) 19-175, englischsprachige Fassung, in: LAB, B Rep. 036-01 (Office of Military Government, Berlin Sector [OMGBS]), 5/36-1/5.

for my driver to come along.[8] The papers worked very well – nobody made any trouble and we were on our way. Outside of Kassel[9] we got a flat tire but had an extra one with us so that was no trouble. In Kassel I delivered to Mrs. Moore's[10] sister[11] the things which I took with me from Lincoln[12].[13] I had a most unpleasant time there, not with Mrs. Moore's sister, who seems to be pleasant enough but with her husband, a retired bureaucrat who occupied a low civil service position who told me right away in the usual fashion the usual German story and what was wrong with the occupation. The chief complaint was of course that he had lost his house to the Americans, and was now forced to live in a couple of rooms. Kassel is one of the worst bombed out places in all Germany,[14] and he is lucky to have these rooms. Besides they have a garden. I reminded him that many places in London were wiped out by German bombing[15] and that there were serious housing shortages in all the places where Germans had been in any form. This made no impression upon him. He didn't think the bombing of London was serious. The officers who now live in his house have mistresses, and the mistresses take the fruit and the vegetables from the garden which he has there too. I heard about our favoring victims of the concentration camps in public office (he means Social Democrats and Communists) to the exclusion, I think he meant, of people like himself. He even said they were worse than the Nazis which made me very angry and I asked him please not to say that to me. He then complained violently about our de-Nazification program, and indicated that he was a witness for what he considered local and harmless Nazis in the tribunals which are now being set up by the Germans to try the Nazis. I replied that until the Germans had enough moral strength to deal with this problem vigorously they would not win the respect of the world. Everything he said annoyed me. He expects us to bring a paradise to the Germans, as their right, immediately, utterly unmindful of anything the Ger-

---

[8] Siehe Headquarters Berlin District, United States Army, Subject: Orders, 19. Juli 1946, in: Unterlagen aus dem Nachlass Edgar N. Johnson, Privatbesitz Candice E. und Thomas R. Johnson, Denver, Colorado, USA.
[9] Stadt im Land Groß-Hessen in der amerikanischen Besatzungszone Deutschlands.
[10] Siehe Dok. 33, Anm. 60.
[11] Rosalie Eberle. Siehe Dok. 33, Anm. 63.
[12] Hauptstadt des US-Bundesstaats Nebraska, wo Johnson mit seiner Familie wohnte und an der Universität lehrte.
[13] Siehe Dok. 33.
[14] Das schwerste Bombardement hatte Kassel am 22. Oktober 1943 erlebt, bei dem etwa 10 000 Menschen starben. Siehe Werner Dettmar, Die Zerstörung Kassels im Oktober 1943. Eine Dokumentation, Fuldabrück 1983.
[15] "From 7 September 1940 until 11 May 1941, an estimated 18,800 tons of explosive were dropped on London by German bombers. According to conservative estimates, over 15,000 people were killed and 3.5 million homes damaged during the attacks, which became known as the Blitz (from the German Blitzkrieg, meaning 'lightning war'). Some historians suggest that the number of deaths was closer to 30,000." Blitz, in: Kenneth J. Panton, Historical Dictionary of London (= Historical Dictionaries of Cities of the World, No. 11), Lanham, Maryland, und London 2001, S. 60f. Auf einer interaktiven Karte kann genau nachvollzogen werden, wo während des Zweiten Weltkriegs in London deutsche Bomben niederfielen: http://bombsight.org/#15/51.5050/-0.0900 (letzter Zugriff am 30. Januar 2013).

mans may have brought to the world in the last few years. I didn't stay any longer than I had to, and was not very nice I think. But I found myself asking myself afterwards, just why am I over here trying to help the Germans in the face of this attitude. It is well to let them stew in their own juice or to turn them over to the Russians. Of course I don't really believe this.

Incidently Mrs. Moore's sister remarked that when she was in Lincoln she met the Werkmeister's[16] and upon her arrival at the house, Werkmeister hauled out a recent picture of Hitler[17] which he expected her to admire. I guess there is no doubt he was a good Nazi supporter. We ought to de-nazify our own faculty.

But to get back to my own woes. On the way from Kassel to Frankfurt[18], the motor developed a bad clanky sound which made it impossible to proceed. I hitched a ride to the nearest service station on the autobahn, and made arrangements to have the car towed in. Then Sanow[19] and I were sent to this town of Butzbach to stay for the night, I in the Officers' Club and he in a PW[20] work camp[21]. On the way here (and it was about a 25 mile trip) the lights of the jeep went out and we had to travel most of the way over pretty terrible roads in a pretty black night. Previously we had done some pretty wild chasing over fields. It reminded me of our introduction to Bear Creek Canyon[22]. When I got here the local officers were having a dance with their fräuleins. It is the center of an Ordnance Depot[23] and an Engineering school[24]. I was exhausted and went to bed. Today the car was hauled from the Service Station to the workshop here.

[16] Lucyle T. Werkmeister, geb. Thomas (1908–1999) und ihr Ehemann William H. Werkmeister (1901–1993), amerikanischer Philosophieprofessor, geboren in Asendorf, Deutschland, studierte zunächst an den Universitäten Münster und Frankfurt am Main, wanderte in den 1920er-Jahren in die USA aus, wurde amerikanischer Staatsbürger, 1927 PhD, University of Nebraska, lehrte bis 1953 als Professor an der University of Nebraska, im Wintersemester 1936/1937 Austauschprofessor an der Universität Berlin, Amerika-Abteilung des Englischen Seminars, 1953–1966 University of Southern California, Direktor der dortigen School of Philosophy, schließlich Distinguished Professor an der Florida State University.
[17] Siehe Dok. 22, Anm. 19.
[18] Frankfurt am Main, Stadt im Land Groß-Hessen in der amerikanischen Besatzungszone Deutschlands.
[19] Siehe Dok. 40, Anm. 13.
[20] Prisoner of War.
[21] Dieter Wolf, Leiter des Museums und Stadtarchivs der Stadt Butzbach, hält es für denkbar, dass Johnsons Fahrer im Marstallgebäude der Schlosskaserne, die bis Ende März 1945 als Wehrmachtskaserne gedient hatte, eine Schlafgelegenheit zugewiesen bekam. Wolf hat „gelegentlich von deutschen Zeitzeugen erzählt bekommen, sie hätten zeitweise im Marstallgebäude der Schlosskaserne, wo ein Kriegsgefangenenlager zeitweise eingerichtet worden war, gearbeitet". E-Mail von Dieter Wolf an Werner Breunig vom 9. Dezember 2011.
[22] Siehe Dok. 63, Anm. 30.
[23] Das Butzbach Ordnance Depot „war der zentrale US-Ausbesserungsbetrieb für Militärfahrzeuge für ganz Süddeutschland", so Dieter Wolf, Leiter des Museums und Stadtarchivs der Stadt Butzbach, in einer E-Mail an Werner Breunig vom 12. Juli 2007.
[24] Im April 1946 war das US Army Engineer Training Center von Epernay in Frankreich nach Butzbach gezogen. Siehe http://www.usarmygermany.com/School_Comd/ USAREUR_SchoolCommand.htm (letzter Zugriff am 30. Januar 2013).

The engine has developed bad defects and new parts are needed which are practically impossible to get. We have called both Frankfurt and Stuttgart[25]. Accordingly I shall have to send the car and Sanow back to Berlin tomorrow, and go on my own way, depending upon local transportation. By the time I get out of here I shall have lost 2 ½ days of my trip which is just a little bit tough. I almost feel like returning to Berlin with Sanow and the car.

If my conversation here with the subordinate officers and civilians is any evidence, the situation here is pretty rotten. The top officers, a Major Stephens[26], and a Captain Rosendale[27] are OK. But the others, outside of duty cannot make a very good impression upon the local population. I think they do their own particular jobs here all right but the place is overridden with mistresses. I saw them at the party last night, and they were in the Club this morning waiting for their men. In fact Sgt. Herman told me that the men have been with their fräuleins so long that when they have a party it is like husbands and wives being together. His fraulein has a three year old daughter to whom he is devoted and gives all his rations. After the party they all go home with their frauleins and sleep with them for awhile. I don't suppose there is any point in getting exciting about this. These men would all have families at home. The sergeant at the Service Station said that he had been fornicating all night. And if you believe the local officers (there is no military government here) the town is still Nazi and is running by Nazis or Nazi sympathizers. The attitude of the major officers is defeatist. We should just get out of here. An occupation can do no good. It reminds me of Eschwege[28],[29] and I suppose it is like this everywhere.

Bye-bye my sweet one, whom I shall soon see. Edgar

---

[25] Hauptstadt des Landes Württemberg-Baden in der amerikanischen Besatzungszone Deutschlands.
[26] Thomas M. Stephens, Major, 1945–November 1946 Commanding Officer, Butzbach Ordnance Depot.
[27] David Rosendale (1906–2009), Captain, geboren in Dokkum, Niederlande, 1934 US-Staatsbürgerschaft, University of Denver, 1942–1948 US Army, Executive Officer, 47th Ordnance Battalion, 1948/1949 Deputy Chief, Liaison and Security Control Division, OMGHE, ab 1949 Foreign Service Staff Officer, Field Operations Division, Office of Land Commissioner for Hesse (OLCH).
[28] Kleinstadt im Nordosten des Landes Groß-Hessen in der amerikanischen Besatzungszone Deutschlands.
[29] Siehe Dok. 49.

Dok. 77
Schreiben an die Ehefrau
Stuttgart[1], 26. Juli 1946

Dearest –

A note to tell you of the progress of the journey. I left Wiesbaden[2] at about 9 this morning and came on here mostly via the Autobahn. The one interesting stop was at Darmstadt[3] where I visited an internment camp[4] where 17,000 Nazis considered dangerous enough to be put away are kept. In some ways it was an amazing institution. They have organized a university within the camp and there are all sorts of workshops, and artists' ateliers busy doing things, I am afraid, for American officers. There is a theatre and an orchestra. Indeed they played the Egmont Overture[5] for me. But I hardly know what to think. I learned that these people were being fed 1700 calories a day which is a good deal more than the average German gets. And one man at a machine who was doing especially hard work was getting a ration of 2500 calories which is more than the heavy workers ration in Germany. A German guard outside the camp, a PW[6], told Sanow[7] that he would gladly enter the camp, and the driver himself can't understand this treatment. I had only a casual glimpse of something more than an hour but they were a hard looking crew. I got a view of Darmstadt which has been almost destroyed by a 20 minute raid in November 1943[8] I think it was.[9]

---

[1] Hauptstadt des Landes Württemberg-Baden in der amerikanischen Besatzungszone Deutschlands.

[2] Hauptstadt des Landes Groß-Hessen in der amerikanischen Besatzungszone Deutschlands.

[3] Stadt im Land Groß-Hessen in der amerikanischen Besatzungszone Deutschlands.

[4] Gemeint ist das amerikanische Internierungslager "Civil Internment Enclosure 91" (CI Camp 91) in Darmstadt, an der Rheinstraße, in dem bis zu 25 000 Internierte festgehalten wurden. Siehe http://www.digam.net/einfuehrung.php?lput=632& (letzter Zugriff am 30. Januar 2013); Dieter Emig/Alfred G. Frei, Office of Military Government for Hesse, in: OMGUS-Handbuch. Die amerikanische Militärregierung in Deutschland 1945–1949, hrsg. von Christoph Weisz (= Quellen und Darstellungen zur Zeitgeschichte, Bd. 35), München 1994, S. 317–453, hier S. 428f.

[5] Egmont-Ouvertüre von Ludwig van Beethoven (siehe Dok. 37, Anm. 29).

[6] Prisoner of War.

[7] Siehe Dok. 40, Anm. 13.

[8] In der Nacht vom 11. zum 12. September 1944 war Darmstadt durch einen Großangriff der Royal Air Force mit anschließendem Feuersturm weitgehend zerstört worden. Siehe Klaus Schmidt, Die Brandnacht. Dokumente von der Zerstörung Darmstadts am 11. September 1944, 3. Auflage, Darmstadt 1964.

[9] Unerwähnt bleibt der Besuch, den Johnson am 26. Juli 1946 mit Major William R. Sheehan dem Darmstädter Regierungspräsidenten Ludwig Bergsträsser (1883–1960) abstattete. In Bergsträssers Tagebuch liest man: „Gegen Mittag kam Sheehan mit Professor Edgar N. Johnson, der bald in die Staaten zurückkehrt und dort gegen die Illusionisten und für die Entwicklung der deutschen Zustände auch in der Öffentlichkeit wirken will. Er besucht jetzt drei Wochen die amerikanische Zone, um sich im einzelnen zu informieren. Langes, sehr interessantes Gespräch. Er stellte vielerlei Fragen und war erstaunt, wie ich ihm sagte, es sei doch eine Dummheit, daß uns nicht von drüben Bücher geschickt werden dürften. Schließlich sähe ich den Grund nicht ein, warum wir nur Briefe privaten Inhalts hinüberschicken dürften. Wenn ich

This trip is going to be somewhat unsatisfactory because it is so rushed. I have been late in getting started, as you know, and it seems foolish, having made the effort, not to do it as well as I can. I think I'll cut out Vienna, however, since that will make me too late but I hate to cut out a visit to the Nuremberg[10] trials[11]. I will get back to Berlin, according to my present schedule, a little late, but I won't delay. I understand also that there is a jam on transportation home from Bremen[12]. It looks therefore as if I shall not be able to make it home by the 20th or 21st[13]. I won't know very definitely, of course, until I see when I get away from Bremen, and I can cable you, en voyage, or telephone you immediately upon arrival in New York.

I got to talk with some of the important Germans in Wiesbaden but not as many as I hoped because they are off on vacation. The trip to Marburg[14] was interesting to see how we work through the Universities, and to see how American life goes on in this kind of a town. I think you might enjoy life in a smaller German town in the zone. The trip is however in many respects anti-climactical. My work is really over and the uncertainty of our future in Germany makes it seems pointless to consider how much positive good we can do here. The Germans, I am sure, are itching for us to leave in order to get control themselves.

I love you my darling and it won't be many weeks now before I shall see you and the lovely boys. A sweet kiss and a tight squeeze. Goodnight, my darling. Edgar

z.B. über politische Dinge nach drüben schreiben wolle, müsse ich Sheehan bitten, diese weiterzugeben, und könne das nicht direkt tun. Er fragte auch nach den Möglichkeiten der demokratischen Weiterentwicklung und vielen anderen Dingen. Ich betonte die wirtschaftliche Notwendigkeit, auch das Hereinkommen von Rohstoffen für unseren Export, verwies auf die Offenbacher Industrie. Er hat in der Internationalen Kommandantur in Berlin gearbeitet und erzählte, wie umständlich es sei, schon der Sprache wegen. Sie hätten allein über die Frage des Eides und das Wort ‚unparteiisch‘, das die Russen krampfhaft als ‚unpolitisch‘ auffassen wollten, zwei Stunden diskutiert. Meiner Meinung, daß Austausch von Professoren und Studenten, auch Lehrern im großen Maßstab geschehen müsse, stimmte er sehr zu. Als ich im Gespräch sagte, ich wäre noch nie in den Staaten gewesen, sagte er, das müsse arrangiert werden, daß ich bald einmal hinüberkomme. Er betonte sehr stark die Bedeutung der Denazifizierung für die öffentliche Meinung in USA." Ludwig Bergstrasser, Befreiung, Besatzung, Neubeginn. Tagebuch des Darmstädter Regierungspräsidenten 1945-1948, hrsg. von Walter Mühlhausen (= Biographische Quellen zur deutschen Geschichte nach 1945, Bd. 5), München 1987, S. 149f. Eine Visitenkarte, die Johnson von Bergsträsser überreicht bekam, befindet sich in: Unterlagen aus dem Nachlass Edgar N. Johnson, Privatbesitz Candice E. und Thomas R. Johnson, Denver, Colorado, USA.

[10] Nürnberg, Stadt im Land Bayern in der amerikanischen Besatzungszone Deutschlands.
[11] Siehe Dok. 49, Anm. 44.
[12] Siehe Dok. 71, Anm. 10.
[13] August 1946.
[14] Universitätsstadt im Land Groß-Hessen in der amerikanischen Besatzungszone Deutschlands.

**Dok. 78
Schreiben an die Ehefrau
Stuttgart[1], 28. Juli 1946**

My dearest –

Col. Dawson[2], the director of the M[ilitary] G[overnment] set up in Baden-Wurttemberg[3] has let me stay in his villa here, as Col. Newman[4], the director of M[ilitary] G[overnment] in Greater Hesse let me stay with him in Wiesbaden[5]. They are both academic people. Newman was a superintendent of schools in Long Island[6] some place, and Dawson is a Professor of Law at Western Reserve[7] in Cleveland[8]. An executive officer of Dawson's (Col. Winning[9]) is on the faculty of the Business School of New York University[10]. At Wiesbaden, the head of the Civil Administration Branch was a friend of Glenn's[11] at Cornell[12] (Landin[13]), and here in Civil Administration there is a pupil of Shumate's[14] at

[1] Hauptstadt des Landes Württemberg-Baden, das zur amerikanischen Besatzungszone gehörte.
[2] William W. Dawson (1892–1947), Colonel, amerikanischer Jurist, lehrte ab 1927 an der School of Law, Western Reserve University, Professor, 1945/1946 Director, OMGWB, ab August 1946 Director, RGCO, OMGUS.
[3] Richtig: Württemberg-Baden, Land in der amerikanischen Besatzungszone Deutschlands.
[4] James R. Newman (1902–1964), Colonel, amerikanischer Erziehungswissenschaftler, 1930 MA und 1940 EdD, Teachers College, Columbia University, Schullehrer, Supervising Principal for the 16th District Schools of Long Island, ab 1941 US Army, 1945–1949 Director, OMGGH/OMGHE, 1949–1952 Land Commissioner for Hesse. Foto mit Newman im Bildanhang, Abb. 21.
[5] Hauptstadt des Landes Groß-Hessen in der amerikanischen Besatzungszone Deutschlands.
[6] Insel, die zum US-Bundesstaat New York gehört.
[7] Western Reserve University (seit 1967: Case Western Reserve University).
[8] Stadt im US-Bundesstaat Ohio.
[9] Charles D. Winning (1894–1988), Colonel, amerikanischer Literaturwissenschaftler, 1932 PhD, New York University, Professor of General Literature, School of Commerce, Accounts and Finance, New York University, 1945–März 1946 Deputy Director, OMGWB, Juni 1946–1947 Director, Government Group/Government Affairs Office, OMGWB, 1947/1948 Director, RGCO, OMGUS, 1948/1949 Director, Education and Cultural Relations Division, OMGBY, dann Chief, Public Affairs Division, Office of Land Commissioner for Bavaria (OLCB).
[10] School of Commerce, Accounts and Finance (heute Leonard N. Stern School of Business), New York University, New York City.
[11] Glenn W. Gray. Siehe Dok. 49, Anm. 74.
[12] Cornell University, Ithaca, New York. Glenn W. Gray war 1928 an der Cornell University promoviert worden.
[13] Harold W. Landin (1903–1991), Major, amerikanischer Historiker, 1928 PhD, Cornell University, lehrte bis 1942 am Smith College und an der Ohio State University, 1945–1947 Director, Civil Administration Division, OMGGH/OMGHE, ab 1947 Chief, Democratization Branch, Civil Administration Division, OMGUS.
[14] Roger V. Shumate (1900–1954), amerikanischer Politikwissenschaftler, 1933 PhD, University of Minnesota, lehrte 1929–1931 an der University of Cincinnati, 1931–1933 University of Minnesota, 1933–1937 University of Pittsburgh, ab 1937 University of Nebraska, Professor of Political Science, Director of Research, Legislative Council des US-Bundesstaats Nebraska.

Minnesota[15] (Scammon[16]). So there are plenty of academic people scattered about this show. Dawson and Winning were home recently and decided to come back for at least another year. They are bringing their wives[17]. Everyone feels some insecurity about the future of M[ilitary] G[overnment] here and there are bets being made on the chance that M[ilitary] G[overnment] will not be here a year from now. Aside from all other questions, it is, I think, just as well that I am coming home now. It is unlikely that the M[ilitary] G[overnment] character of the occupation will last so long that there is much of a chance, were there even the desire, to pursue a long range policy here. And there are those on the spot who feel that because of the conduct of our troops, and the impression this makes on the Germans, it is just as well that we withdraw our troops as soon as possible. There seems to be much greater trust of the Germans here in the zone where, of course, the relationship is first hand, and not removed, as it is in Berlin.

This is a lovely spot, and it would have been pleasant to be here. I think possibly, if it had worked out that way, that you would have been reasonably contented here, but not for the short space of a year. Somebody mentioned at breakfast that 5000 dependents are arriving in August and 4000 in September, and that already in Frankfurt[18], the shipment of dependents has had to be curtailed because of the shortage of housing. This will be a more serious than ever problem because the Germans are already considerably annoyed at the situation.[19] Maybe you and the boys couldn't have come over in any case, which, if I had stayed, would have made it intolerable for me. I visited Pollock[20] at the Länderrat[21] quarters yesterday morning (quarters of the former Gauleiter[22]).[23]

---

[15] University of Minnesota, Minneapolis and Saint Paul, Minnesota.

[16] Richard M. Scammon (1915–2001), First Lieutenant, amerikanischer Politikwissenschaftler, 1935 BA, University of Minnesota, 1938 MA, University of Michigan, 1939–1941 Research Secretary, Radio Office, University of Chicago, 1941–1946 US Army, 1945/1946 Administration and Local Government Officer, OMGWB, 1946–1948 Chief, Election Affairs Branch/Election and Political Parties Branch/Political Activities Branch, Civil Administration Division, OMGUS, 1948–1955 Department of State (Chief, Division of Research for Western Europe), 1961–1965 Director, Bureau of the Census, Department of Commerce.

[17] Marguerite Dawson; Freda G. Winning, geb. Gerwin (1901–1978), PhD, New York University, Professor of Education, Chairman, Home Economics Department, School of Education, New York University, 1975–1978 President, Cleveland Branch, American Association of University Women.

[18] Frankfurt am Main, Stadt im Land Groß-Hessen in der amerikanischen Besatzungszone Deutschlands.

[19] Am 23. März 1946 schrieb Johnson über die geplante Räumung der Wohnsiedlung Sonnenberg im Süden von Stuttgart. Siehe Dok. 26 sowie Dok. 26, Anm. 8 und 9.

[20] Siehe Dok. 15, Anm. 12.

[21] Siehe Dok. 15, Anm. 10.

[22] Wilhelm Murr (1888–1945), NS-Politiker, 1928–1945 Gauleiter der NSDAP in Württemberg-Hohenzollern, 1930–1932 und 1933–1945 MdR, 1932/1933 MdL Württemberg, 1933–1945 Reichsstatthalter in Württemberg und Hohenzollern.

[23] Der Länderrat und das RGCO hatten ihren Sitz in der Villa Reitzenstein, heute Dienstsitz des Ministerpräsidenten von Baden-Württemberg.

He has the most palatial and colonial office I have yet seen in Germany. I can see that he is a very difficult person – capable, to be sure, but a little of a stuffed shirt. At least he treated me rather coldly and off-hand, leaving me to be impressed with his importance. Yet at the same time he was polite, has invited me to dinner today, and I am to have a chance to see the Länderrat at work tomorrow and Tuesday[24] by attending a couple of Committee meetings.

I took a pleasure ride yesterday into the French zone and visited a wonderful Cistercian abbey (Bebenhausen)[25] which I saw during my first stay[26] here.

I am going to drive to Heidelberg[27] this afternoon to see some of the professors there.

According to my present schedule I shall arrive in Bremen[28], the evening of 8 August. When I get out of there is a question. I am very lonesome for you, feel very far away from you and the boys. But it will be less than a month now. I love you my darling, and shall never leave you again. Edgar

Dok. 79
Schreiben an die Ehefrau
München[1], 1. August 1946

Dearest –

I am very lonesome for you and am in a mood to cut this trip short + go back to Berlin. The chief cause of this is that I came here last night, on from Nurnberg[2], hoping to get started on a little talking here today, only to find that it is a holiday here: "Air Corps Day"[3] and that there is no one around. I shall try to do something this afternoon by way of seeing UNRRA[4] people in Pasing[5] and per-

---

[24] 30. Juli 1946.
[25] Kloster Bebenhausen, ein ehemaliges Zisterzienserkloster in Bebenhausen bei Tübingen, in dem ab 22. November 1946 die Beratende Landesversammlung und ab 3. Juni 1947 der Landtag des zur französischen Besatzungszone Deutschlands gehörenden Landes Württemberg-Hohenzollern tagten.
[26] Gemeint ist Johnsons Studienaufenthalt in Deutschland 1927/1928.
[27] Universitätsstadt im Land Württemberg-Baden in der amerikanischen Besatzungszone Deutschlands.
[28] Siehe Dok. 71, Anm. 10.

[1] Hauptstadt des Landes Bayern in der amerikanischen Besatzungszone Deutschlands.
[2] Nürnberg, Stadt im Land Bayern in der amerikanischen Besatzungszone Deutschlands.
[3] Tag der Luftstreitkräfte. Am 1. August 1907 war die Aeronautical Division, US Signal Corps, eingerichtet worden, der erste Vorläufer der heutigen amerikanischen Luftsteitkräfte.
[4] United Nations Relief and Rehabilitation Administration, Hilfsorganisation der Vereinten Nationen zur Unterstützung notleidender Personenkreise, besonders der Flüchtlinge und Displaced Persons in den von den Alliierten besetzten Gebieten. Siehe Gioia-Olivia Karnagel, United Nations Relief and Rehabilitation Administration (UNRRA), in: Deutschland unter alliierter Besatzung 1945–1949/55, hrsg. von Wolfgang Benz, Berlin 1999, S. 310f.

haps arranging to see some of their camps[6] this afternoon. The brass is also down from Berlin, General Clay[7] and General Adcock[8] to witness the opening of some kind of an industrial exhibition here.[9] I suppose actually there is no point in getting back to Berlin, inasmuch as I should arrive there over the weekend, and could accordingly get nothing done but get ahold of some letters from you that will be there.

I perhaps labor under the spell of the Nurnberg trial[10] yesterday, which I could have attended in the afternoon as well as the morning had I known there was a holiday here.[11] It is hardly what you would call a spectacle since the court room is none too large.[12] The 22 prisoners are crowded into 2 rows of benches. These were not all there yesterday. Hess[13] wasn't there. Nor Ribbenthrop[14] nor Raeder[15] but the rest were, and except for one or two, they are a horrible looking bunch. Göring[16] looks like a violent degenerate. Streicher[17] the Jew barker an Unter-Mensch if there ever was one. Von Papen[18] looks like a monkey, and

---

[5] Seit 1938 Stadtteil von München. In München-Pasing befand sich das Hauptquartier der UNRRA für die amerikanische Besatzungszone Deutschlands. Siehe UNRRA. The History of the United Nations Relief and Rehabilitation Administration, prepared by a special staff under the direction of George Woodbridge, Vol. I, New York 1950, S. 193 (Chart VII: Field organization chart, Displaced Persons operations, Germany).

[6] Von der UNRRA betreute Lager zur vorübergehenden Unterbringung von Displaced Persons.

[7] Siehe Dok. 2, Anm. 6.

[8] Siehe Dok. 14, Anm. 9.

[9] Am 3. August 1946 wurde im Haus der Kunst in München eine „Exportschau, Leistungsschau der Bayerischen Wirtschaft" eröffnet. Siehe Die Neue Zeitung vom 2. August 1946, S. 8, und vom 5. August 1946, S. 1f. und 8.

[10] Siehe Dok. 49, Anm. 44.

[11] Johnson war am 30. Juli 1946 und in der Vormittagssitzung am 31. Juli 1946 Prozessbeobachter.

[12] Der Prozess fand im Saal 600 des Nürnberger Justizpalastes statt.

[13] Rudolf Heß (1894–1987), NS-Politiker, ab 1933 Reichsminister ohne Geschäftsbereich, von Adolf Hitler (siehe Dok. 22, Anm. 19) zu seinem Stellvertreter in der NSDAP ernannt, flog 1941 nach Schottland, um mit Douglas Douglas-Hamilton, 14. Herzog von Hamilton (1903–1973) über Frieden zu verhandeln, geriet dabei in britische Kriegsgefangenschaft, vom Internationalen Militärgerichtshof als Hauptkriegsverbrecher zu lebenslanger Haft verurteilt, die er im Spandauer Kriegsverbrechergefängnis bis zu seinem Tode absaß.

[14] Joachim von Ribbentrop (1893–1946), NS-Politiker, 1936–1938 deutscher Botschafter in Großbritannien, 1938–1945 Reichsaußenminister, vom Internationalen Militärgerichtshof als Hauptkriegsverbrecher zum Tode verurteilt und hingerichtet.

[15] Siehe Dok. 49, Anm. 46.

[16] Siehe Dok. 22, Anm. 24.

[17] Julius Streicher (1885–1946), NS-Politiker, ab 1923 Herausgeber der antisemitischen Wochenschrift „Der Stürmer", 1924–1932 MdL Bayern, 1925–1939 Gauleiter der NSDAP in Mittelfranken/Franken, 1932–1945 MdR, vom Internationalen Militärgerichtshof als Hauptkriegsverbrecher zum Tode verurteilt und hingerichtet.

[18] Franz von Papen (1879–1969), deutscher Politiker (Deutsche Zentrumspartei), 1932 Reichskanzler, ebnete 1933 den Weg zur Machtübernahme von Adolf Hitler (siehe Dok. 22, Anm. 19), in dessen Regierung er als Vizekanzler eintrat, 1934 Rücktritt als Kabinettsmitglied und Berufung als Außerordentlicher Gesandter an die deutsche

so indeed does Frick[19], the Minister of the interior. Schacht[20] too is a very inferior looking person. Except for a few they seemed to be all in a fairly cheerful state of mind, and munched bread during the hearing. Their trial is over, and now the organizations of the Party[21] are being tried. Yesterday they had a Gauleiter (Hoffman[22] from Hamburg[23]), an Ortsgruppenleiter (also Bürgermeister)[24] and Blockleiter[25] on the stand trying to tell the court how harmless all this activity was.[26] The microphone system does not work any too well. It broke down during the proceedings and stalled things for awhile. It might have been a going of ordinary criminals instead of extraordinary criminals.

Last night I went out to see Frau Engelhorn[27] and her daughter[28]. She looks much less well than when I saw here in November[29]. And she has now had the

Botschaft in Österreich, 1936 Botschafter in Österreich, 1939 Botschafter in der Türkei, vom Internationalen Militärgerichtshof freigesprochen, jedoch im Spruchkammerverfahren zu acht Jahren Arbeitslager verurteilt, 1949 vorzeitig entlassen.

[19] Wilhelm Frick (1877-1946), NS-Politiker, 1930/1931 Innen- und Volksbildungsminister im Land Thüringen, 1933-1943 Reichsinnenminister, 1943-1945 Reichsprotektor von Böhmen und Mähren, vom Internationalen Militärgerichtshof als Hauptkriegsverbrecher zum Tode verurteilt und hingerichtet.

[20] Siehe Dok. 49, Anm. 45.

[21] Nationalsozialistische Deutsche Arbeiterpartei (NSDAP).

[22] Karl Kaufmann (1900-1969), NS-Politiker, 1928-1930 MdL Preußen, 1929-1945 Gauleiter der NSDAP in Hamburg, 1930-1945 MdR, 1933-1945 Reichsstatthalter in Hamburg.

[23] Stadt in der britischen Besatzungszone Deutschlands.

[24] Hans Wegscheider (geb. 1885), deutscher Schmiedemeister und Tierheilkundiger, 1933-1945 Ortsgruppenleiter der NSDAP und Bürgermeister in Hirschdorf bei St. Lorenz im Kreis Kempten-Land.

[25] Dr. Ernst Hirth (geb. 1896), deutscher Landgerichtsrat, 1942-1945 Blockleiter der NSDAP in Nürnberg.

[26] Am 30. Juli standen Kaufmann und Willi Meyer-Wendeborn (geb. 1891), 1934-1945 Kreisleiter der NSDAP in Cloppenburg (Oldenburg) im Gau Weser-Ems, davor Ortsgruppenleiter der NSDAP, im Zeugenstand, in der Vormittagssitzung am 31. Juli Meyer-Wendeborn, Wegscheider und Hirth. Siehe Internationaler Militärgerichtshof Nürnberg (Hrsg.), Der Prozeß gegen die Hauptkriegsverbrecher vor dem Internationalen Militärgerichtshof, Nürnberg 14. November 1945-1. Oktober 1946, Bd. XX: Verhandlungsniederschriften 30. Juli 1946-10. August 1946, Nürnberg 1948, S. 7-118.

[27] Anna Engelhorn, geb. Winnecke (1875-1957), geboren im damals deutschen Straßburg, Elsass, Tochter von August Winnecke (1835-1897), Professor für Astronomie an der Universität Straßburg und Direktor der dortigen Sternwarte, und einer Deutschrussin (Hedwig Winnecke, geb. Dell [1846-1919]), betätigte sich als Malerin und Lithografin, lebte nach 1919 in München, heiratete 1920 den verwitweten, früheren Bankdirektor Kommerzienrat Karl Engelhorn (1856-1927), ab 1931 Mitglied der Anthroposophischen Gesellschaft. Über die künstlerische Arbeit von Anna Winnecke informiert François Lotz avec la collaboration de Joseph Fuchs/Léon Kieffer/René Metz, Artistes-Peintres Alsaciens de jadis et de naguère (1880-1982), Kaysersberg 1987, S. 358. Einen Überblick über die künstlerische Arbeit geben auch A. Bauer/ J. Carpentier, Répertoire des Artistes d'Alsace des XIXe et XXe siècles. Peintres – Sculpteurs – Graveurs – Dessinateurs, V-Z, Straßburg 1991, S. 425. 1908 war Anna Winnecke auf der Großen Berliner Kunstausstellung mit einer Lithografie vertreten. Siehe Verzeichnis der ausgestellten Kunstwerke nach Sälen geordnet, in: Katalog der Grossen Berliner Kunst-Ausstellung 1908, Berlin, Stuttgart und Leipzig 1908, S. 1-176, hier S. 18. Edgar N. Johnson wohnte 1927/1928, während seines Studienaufenthalts in

misfortune of having her house³⁰ and furniture confiscated by the Americans as part of the so-called American Military Communities³¹ which are established here in the zone: blocks of barbed-wire surrounded houses. The Germans don't react well to this separation. They don't take well the insistence upon letting houses remain empty in the compound. In Frankfurt³² they call the American enclosure – the Ghetto of the Pharisees³³. Frau Engelhorn urged me to stay over here and bring the family. Evidently they don't run into too many congenial Americans. She is, however, still sprightly and full of good humor. They have to use the black market³⁴. They had 2 pancakes apiece for supper.

I'll leave here over the weekend for Berlin and get away from there as soon as possible. It is all over anyway, insofar as I can see, and I sometimes ask why, indeed, I ever came down here to the zone. I love you my sweetheart, and the month begins today during which we shall be together again. Kiss the sweet boys for me, and let me hold you very tight. Edgar

Dok. 80
Schreiben an die Ehefrau
Bremerhaven¹, 7. August 1946

My darling –
I am at last on the way to you, to be with you for a very very long time I hope. I am trying to write this in a huge lounge at this staging area². Five feet

---

    München, in der Gästepension, die von Anna Engelhorn in der Hohenstaufenstraße 10/II betrieben wurde. Siehe Personenstand der Ludwig-Maximilians-Universität München, Winter-Halbjahr 1927/28, München 1928, S. 116. Foto von Engelhorn im Bildanhang, Abb. 79.

²⁸ Gemeint ist die mit Anna Engelhorn zusammenlebende Stieftochter Hedwig Engelhorn (1893–1968), geboren in Straßburg, Elsass, Studium der Rechte und Staatswirtschaft, Promotion an der Universität Freiburg im Breisgau.

²⁹ Im November 1945, als Johnson nach Beendigung seiner Aufgaben in Österreich und vor seiner Rückkehr in die USA Deutschland bereiste.

³⁰ Harthauser Straße 90. Nach Auskunft des Stadtarchivs München vom 4. August 2009 bzw. 26. März 2010 hatte Anna Engelhorn seit 1937 in der Harthauser Straße 90 gewohnt, zum 8. Juli 1946 wurde ihr Umzug in die Dr.-Max-Straße 15 in Grünwald gemeldet.

³¹ Zu den Militärgemeinden siehe Thomas Leuerer, Die Stationierung amerikanischer Streitkräfte in Deutschland. Militärgemeinden der U. S. Army in Deutschland seit 1945 als ziviles Element der Stationierungspolitik der Vereinigten Staaten (= Politik und Gesellschaft. Würzburger Universitätsschriften, Bd. 6), Würzburg 1997.

³² Frankfurt am Main, Stadt im Land Groß-Hessen in der amerikanischen Besatzungszone Deutschlands.

³³ Pharisäer, hebräisch „perushim", die Abgesonderten, Angehöriger einer altjüdischen, die religiösen Gesetze streng einhaltenden Partei, übertragen für hochmütiger, selbstgerechter Heuchler.

³⁴ Siehe Dok. 21, Anm. 11.

¹ Siehe Dok. 71, Anm. 10.
² Bremerhaven Staging Area.

away someone is trying to play boogie woogie[3] on the bass of a tin-pan piano[4]. They are getting ready for some kind of a performance. Whether, under these circumstances I can manage to get anything written I don't know.

I don't believe I have written you since I went to Oberammergau[5]. I started something there which I didn't finish and where it is now I don't know – somewhere in the mess of papers I have piled along.[6] After the nice treatment I got in Wiesbaden[7] and Stuttgart[8] I was treated somewhat shabbily in Munich I thought: At least General Müller[9] paid no attention to me, nor any of his henchmen, and the people on his M[ilitary] G[overnment] staff whom I could find in their offices were a little condescending or else a little dead. The nicest thing about the trip was, I guess, the couple visits to Frau Engelhorn[10].[11] I think I mentioned that she had been thrown out of her house to make room for one of those so-called American Communities[12], a compound surrounded by barbedwire. She doesn't know quite where she is going to land for the winter. She doesn't look as well as when I saw her last November[13] but she still has sharp intelligence, good humor, and is certainly one of the best if not really the best German, I have ever met. I also talked with Högner[14], the S[ocial] D[emocrat] Minister President, Baumgartner[15], the CSU[16] Minister of Food and Agricul-

[3] Im ersten Jahrzehnt des 20. Jahrhunderts in den USA entstandener Solo-Klavierstil schwarzer Musiker.
[4] Ein billiges, verstimmtes Klavier.
[5] Gemeinde im Land Bayern in der amerikanischen Besatzungszone Deutschlands, bekannt vor allem durch die seit 1634 alle zehn Jahre stattfindenden Passionsspiele.
[6] Das nicht unterzeichnete und nie abgesandte Schreiben aus Oberammergau vom 1. August 1946 befindet sich in: Unterlagen aus dem Nachlass Edgar N. Johnson, Privatbesitz Candice E. und Thomas R. Johnson, Denver, Colorado, USA. Johnson berichtet in diesem Schreiben von seinem Abstecher nach Oberammergau, wo er im Gästehaus der European Theater Intelligence School unterkam.
[7] Hauptstadt des Landes Groß-Hessen in der amerikanischen Besatzungszone Deutschlands.
[8] Hauptstadt des Landes Württemberg-Baden in der amerikanischen Besatzungszone Deutschlands.
[9] Walter J. Muller (1895–1967), Brigadier General, 1918 Absolvent der United States Military Academy, 1945–1947 Director, OMGBY, 1953–1955 Mitglied bzw. Vorsitzender des deutsch-alliierten Begnadigungsausschusses in Bad Godesberg zur Überprüfung von Kriegsverbrecherurteilen, einem Amt im Geschäftsbereich des amerikanischen Hohen Kommissars für Deutschland. Foto mit Muller im Bildanhang, Abb. 21.
[10] Siehe Dok. 79, Anm. 27.
[11] Siehe Dok. 79.
[12] Siehe Dok. 79, Anm. 31.
[13] November 1945, als Johnson nach Beendigung seiner Aufgaben in Österreich und vor seiner Rückkehr in die USA Deutschland bereiste. Siehe Dok. 79.
[14] Wilhelm Hoegner. Siehe Dok. 11, Anm. 27.
[15] Joseph Baumgartner (1904–1964), deutscher Volkswirt und Politiker, 1929 Dr. oec. publ., Universität München, 1945 CSU, 1945–1948 bayerischer Landwirtschaftsminister, 1946 Mitglied der Verfassunggebenden Landesversammlung Bayerns, 1946–1962 MdL Bayern, 1948 Bayernpartei, 1948–1959 Landesvorsitzender der Bayernpartei, 1949–1951 MdB, 1954–1957 bayerischer Landwirtschaftsminister und stellvertretender Ministerpräsident.
[16] Christlich-Soziale Union, eine christlich-konservative Partei in Bayern. 8. Januar 1946 Gründungsversammlung auf Landesebene.

ture, Pfeiffer[17], the Minister of De-Nazification, and Dr. Seifrid[18], the SPD Minister of the Interior. I had a long talk with Dr. Josef Müller[19], the head of the CSU (Christian Social Union) in Bavaria, and with a certain Herr Herwarth[20], a so-called Ambassadorial Adviser, formerly in the foreign service of the Nazis, whom OSS[21] helped a great deal when we were in Salzburg[22], and who is very very grateful for this help. All the big shots from Berlin were down to witness the opening of an export-import expedition[23], a rather elegant but pathetic attempt of the Bavarians to show us how ready they are to go ahead. I had planned to see others – and go elsewhere in Bavaria but when Saturday[24] noon came, and things closed up, I could not make up my mind to stay any longer, nor to try a trip to Austria. Instead Sanow[25] and I decided to go back to Berlin. We had to stop at Stuttgart to get my coat which I had absent-mindedly left at Col. Dawson's[26], and at Oberursel[27] to pick up the Mercedes-Benz[28], which you remember went blouie[29] our first day out of Berlin.[30] We had very bad luck on this way back. Small goings – wrong with the motor on two occasions which Sanow fortunately was able to repair, and three flats mind you. We got into Oberursel about 1 a. m. and were met by a very cordial, considerate, and effi-

[17] Anton Pfeiffer (1888–1957), deutscher Politiker (CSU), 1913 Dr. phil., Universität München, Neuphilologe, Lehrer, 1918–1933 Generalsekretär der Bayerischen Volkspartei, 1928–1933 MdL Bayern, 1945–Juli 1946 und Dezember 1946-1950 Leiter der Bayerischen Staatskanzlei, Juli–Dezember 1946 bayerischer Staatsminister für Sonderaufgaben (Entnazifizierung), 1946–1950 MdL Bayern, 1948 Mitorganisator und Leiter des Verfassungskonvents auf Herrenchiemsee, 1948/1949 Mitglied des Parlamentarischen Rates, dort Vorsitzender der CDU/CSU-Fraktion, 1950/1951 Generalkonsul in Belgien, 1951–1954 Botschafter in Belgien.
[18] Josef Seifried (1892–1962), deutscher Politiker (SPD), 1928–1933 und 1946–1950 MdL Bayern, 1945–1947 bayerischer Staatsminister des Innern, 1946 Mitglied der Verfassunggebenden Landesversammlung Bayern, 1948 Mitglied des Parlamentarischen Rates.
[19] Josef Müller (1898–1979), deutscher Politiker (CSU), 1925 Dr. oec. publ., Universität München, ab 1927 Rechtsanwalt, 1943–1945 Verhaftung wegen Hochverrats und Haft in Berlin, Buchenwald, Flossenbürg sowie Dachau, 1946 Mitglied der Verfassunggebenden Landesversammlung Bayern, 1946–1949 Landesvorsitzender der CSU, 1946–1962 MdL Bayern, 1947–1952 bayerischer Justizminister, bis 1950 zugleich stellvertretender Ministerpräsident.
[20] Hans-Heinrich Herwarth von Bittenfeld (1904–1999), deutscher Diplomat, 1931–1939 Attaché und Legationssekretär, deutsche Botschaft in Moskau, 1945–1949 Bayerische Staatskanzlei (1946 Regierungsdirektor), 1955–1961 Botschafter in Großbritannien, 1961–1965 Statssekretär und Chef des Bundespräsidialamts, 1965–1969 Botschafter in Italien, 1969–1977 Präsident des Goethe-Instituts.
[21] Office of Strategic Services. Siehe Dok. 1, Anm. 9.
[22] Stadt in der amerikanischen Besatzungszone Österreichs.
[23] Siehe Dok. 79, Anm. 9.
[24] 3. August 1946.
[25] Siehe Dok. 40, Anm. 13.
[26] Siehe Dok. 78, Anm. 2.
[27] Stadt im Land Groß-Hessen in der amerikanischen Besatzungszone Deutschlands.
[28] Deutsche Automarke, 1926 mit dem Zusammenschluss der Daimler-Motoren-Gesellschaft und der Benz & Cie. entstanden.
[29] Gemeint ist "went blooey", Slang für "broke down".
[30] Siehe Dok. 76.

cient Mr. Henry Bose[31] in charge of the motor pool who turned over to us the repaired Mercedes-Benz, put us up for the night (Sanow too), gave us an elegant breakfast and sandwiches to take along. He is of German descent he said and prefers the Germans who work for him to many of the Americans who do.

There was no more difficulty on the way to Berlin on Sunday[32] and we got in about 7 o'clock. I went to see Col. Glaser[33] in the hope that he had your mail for me but he didn't. In fact his wife[34] was arriving that evening, and he was not particularly interested in me. But he did have a German phrase that he wanted translated. I then tried to find your letters at the office but without luck and went out to Wannsee[35] to go to bed. For on the last days of the trip I developed this stomach trouble which I had in Austria and was in none too vigorous a condition. It is still with me but I think it will be over by the time I get home. I think it is only a question of a good deal of fatigue and will clear up on the boat over.

The letters[36] were in my hand on Monday[37] morning and they bucked me up no end. I will leave the decision about Colorado[38] to you. From what I read here Minnesota[39] is as bad as Colorado.[40]

Monday I cleaned out my desk. Col. Glaser had me to dinner with his wife and with Col. Howley[41] and his wife[42], and the English representative[43] on the Local Gov[ernmen]t Committee[44] who wanted my signature on his specially prepared copy of the Berlin Constitution which he is going to present to the Museum of the 5th Royal Engineers[45] I think it was. It was not an espe-

[31] Möglicherweise Henry H. Bose (geb. 1913), Army Serial Number: 32214673 (civilian occupation: semiskilled mechanics and repairmen, motor vehicles).
[32] 4. August 1946.
[33] Siehe Dok. 28, Anm. 4.
[34] Marguerite K. Glaser. Siehe Dok. 40, Anm. 22.
[35] Zum Wannsee Officers' Club, Am Sandwerder 17/19. Siehe Dok. 25, Anm. 9.
[36] In: Unterlagen aus dem Nachlass Edgar N. Johnson, Privatbesitz Candice E. und Thomas R. Johnson, Denver, Colorado, USA.
[37] 5. August 1946.
[38] US-Bundesstaat.
[39] US-Bundesstaat.
[40] Johnson spricht hier die Ausbreitung der Polioepidemie an und meint, dass eine Reise mit der Familie nach Minnesota (siehe Dok. 63) genauso problematisch sei wie der geplante Coloradoaufenthalt. Siehe Dok. 72 und Dok. 72, Anm. 21; Minnesota Reports 86 New Polio Cases, in: The New York Times vom 6. August 1946, S. 21; Polio Cases Reach 706 In Minnesota. 46 Added in Day to Year's Total – Woodring Says Curare Cured His Daughter, in: The New York Times vom 7. August 1946, S. 28; 660 Polio Cases Listed In Minnesota Epidemic, in: New York Herald Tribune, European Edition, vom 7. August 1946, S. 4.
[41] Siehe Dok. 20, Anm. 18.
[42] Edith Howley, geb. Cadwallader (1910–1985), 1930 BS in Ed, University of Pennsylvania, 1930–1935 Lehrerin, Springfield Township High School, Montgomery County, Pennsylvania, 1962 MLS, Rutgers University, ab 1962 Bibliothekarin.
[43] Gemeint ist wahrscheinlich Harold Hays. Siehe Dok. 49, Anm. 26.
[44] Local Government Committee, Allied Kommandatura Berlin. Siehe Dok. 29, Anm. 14.
[45] Gemeint ist wahrscheinlich The Royal Engineers Museum in Gillingham, Kent, Großbritannien. Nach Auskunft des Royal Engineers Museum vom 24. Juni 2009

cially encouraging farewell dinner. Col. Glaser has admitted to me that his wife was difficult, and that I could see. Mrs. Howley, much like the Colonel, admitted that she was being utterly spoiled here with so much elegance, and so many servants. I wish we had better people to represent M[ilitary] G[overnment] in Berlin. By better I mean unadvertising and able to get closer to the Germans.

I tried to do good-byes yesterday but didn't have much luck. Frau Donneck, my German secretary had beautiful dahlias on my desk. I saw Mr. Muccio[46] and Brewster Morris[47]. Louis Wiesner[48] was out of town. Lloyd Steere[49] was very cordial and wanted me to stop in Washington and talk with people there. Mr. Murphy[50] was not in town. General Clay[51] was not in town. General Adcock[52] was not in town. Walter Dorn[53] was not in town. I had a very nice talk with General Keating[54] who is definitely on the ball. I also saw Col. Howley again. They were trying desperately to get up some kind of a citation for me, legion of merit, or ribbon of merit, or some such thing but there were some technical difficulties. Instead they are going to write a letter to the new Chancellor[55] about me.[56] I guess they are really grateful for what I tried to do. I said good-bye to Sanow who could not be with me the last two days because of more difficulties with the car.

About the middle of the afternoon I went out to the Club[57] to pack, distributed some cigarettes to those who had been kind to me there, left some PX[58] supplies for my driver, and made for the station at 6:00. The train left at 6:32 and we had to sit up all night. I have developed a very bad back (may be its

befindet sich das Verfassungsexemplar nicht in den Beständen des Museums. Auch ist das Exemplar nicht in der Lieutenant Colonel Harold Hays MBE Collection enthalten, die das IWM Duxford verwahrt. In einer E-Mail an Werner Breunig vom 30. Juni 2009 teilt das IWM Duxford, Department of Documents, mit, die Sammlung enthalte leider keine "copy of the Provisional Constitution – in his memoirs Hays writes that 'My colleagues and I [on the Committee] were quite frankly jubilant with the result. This was the greatest individual measure ever agreed by the Allied Kommandatura to date. We gleefully signed copies of the documents for each other as mementos ...' – there is, however, no further reference to these signed copies. I am unable to say what might have happened to the copy signed by Johnson", so der Archivar Stephen Walton.

46 Siehe Dok. 20, Anm. 21.
47 Siehe Dok. 31, Anm. 13.
48 Siehe Dok. 8, Anm. 11.
49 Loyd V. Steere. Siehe Dok. 20, Anm. 23.
50 Siehe Dok. 8, Anm. 13.
51 Siehe Dok. 2, Anm. 6.
52 Siehe Dok. 14, Anm. 9.
53 Siehe Dok. 2, Anm. 10.
54 Siehe Dok. 39, Anm. 6.
55 Reuben G. Gustavson. Siehe Dok. 49, Anm. 79.
56 Der Entwurf eines Schreibens des stellvertretenden US-Militärgouverneurs Lucius D. Clay an Gustavson vom 8. August 1946 befindet sich in: LAB, B Rep. 036-01 (Office of Military Government, Berlin Sector [OMGBS]), 4/135-2/14.
57 Gemeint ist der Wannsee Officers' Club, Am Sandwerder 17/19. Siehe Dok. 25, Anm. 9.
58 Post Exchange, Verkaufsläden der amerikanischen Streitkräfte.

sacro-iliac) which I think will also be over by the time I see you. Conditions are rather crude at this. Staying one-thousands waiting to go home. But not so bad as Camp Home-Run[59].

It is the 7th. It is almost certain that I shall be here three or four days. I think it is equally certain that the boat will take at least ten days to New York. I don't think you'd better wait for me in Lincoln[60]. Get away as soon as possible and I'll join you there[61]. I am longing to be with you, and it will certainly be before the end of the 3 weeks. I love my very sweet ones very much. Kisses to them.
Edgar

Dok. 81
Schreiben an die Ehefrau
Bremerhaven[1], 9. August 1946

Sweetheart –

Still here but things are moving. The processing is complete today with baggage inspection, currency control, and physical examination. We get orders and tickets this afternoon. But I don't suppose we shall actually get on the boat until tomorrow. That is the 10th. Someone remarked here that it takes the boat eight or nine days to get across. It is a so-called Victory Ship[2]. "Colby-Victory"[3]. If she really makes it that quickly there is some chance that I'll make it in time to leave with you on the 21st for Meeker Park[4]. I do not actually have to go to Washington. Lloyd Steere[5] asked me to go in order to talk with Riddleberger[6] and General Hilldring[7] especially. My friend from Austrian days is now in Wash-

---

[59] In Le Havre. Siehe Dok. 13 und Dok. 13, Anm. 8.
[60] Hauptstadt des US-Bundesstaats Nebraska, wo Johnson mit seiner Familie wohnte und an der Universität lehrte.
[61] Gemeint ist der Ferienort in den Rocky Mountains im US-Bundesstaat Colorado, wo Johnson nach seiner Rückkehr mit seiner Familie Urlaub machen wollte.

[1] Siehe Dok. 71, Anm. 10.
[2] Als „Victory"-Schiffe wurden Transportschiffe bezeichnet, die in den USA während des Zweiten Weltkriegs innerhalb kürzester Zeit nach standardisierten Plänen und in großer Stückzahl gebaut worden waren. Victory-Schiffe waren die Weiterentwicklung der „Liberty"-Schiffe (siehe Dok. 2) und übertrafen diese bezüglich Geschwindigkeit und Reichweite.
[3] Das nach Colby College in Waterville im US-Bundesstaat Maine benannte Schiff war am 5. August 1946 in Bremerhaven angekommen. Es stach am 11. August wieder in See. Siehe Bd. 2 der Hafenverkehrsbücher Bremerhaven, Überseehäfen und Columbuskaje – Seeschifffahrt, in: Staatsarchiv Bremen (StAB), 4,72/2-57. Das Schiff traf am 20. August 1946 in New York ein. Siehe Hospital Ship With 414 Patients To Arrive Today, in: The Washington Post vom 21. August 1946, S. 3; Marine and Aviation Reports, in: The New York Times vom 19. August 1946, S. 39.
[4] Siehe Dok. 68, Anm. 3.
[5] Loyd V. Steere. Siehe Dok. 20, Anm. 23.
[6] Siehe Dok. 8, Anm. 2.
[7] Siehe Dok. 2, Anm. 4.

ington – Joe Gray[8], taking over Erhardt's[9] former job as personnel manager for the State Department. He would be the man to see about a job. I learn that Francis Cunningham, Jr.[10], is taking over the Scandinavian desk in the department, and that my very good friend Charlie Thayer[11] is taking over the Southern European desk. But I don't want to see them. Nor do I think that this is especially the time to go looking about for a job. After all I am committed to go back to the University, and that means, at least, for about a year. If at the end of that time I don't seem to have settled down in the University, and we think I ought to look for something else, I can always go to Washington and inquire. Lloyd wanted me to talk about my impressions of Berlin and Germany but this I can put down in some form of writing. So if there is any chance of getting to you on time I shall just skip Washington. But I've got to stop over in Chicago – possibly to see Biddy[12], certainly to see Auntie[13], Dad[14], Mildred[15], and, if it can be managed, Paul Sweet[16]. I should hope this wouldn't take longer than a day. In case of severe difficulties I can try to fly some of the way, say from Chicago to Omaha[17] which would some considerable. In any case if it is so close, you might hold over for a day. If for no other reason I think I could be of some help with the kids. The papers here are now full of the Minnesota[18] polio epidemic, as if the Colorado[19] one were dying down.[20] I hope so. It would be more than we can stand to have anything happen to either of the boys because we decided to spend a little time in Colorado.

I am loafing here quite easily. I did read some articles in Life[21] by Dulles[22] concerning what our policy in re Russia should be, and while the first one was

[8] Cecil W. (Joe) Gray (1898–1983), amerikanischer Diplomat, 1920 BA, Roanoke College, ab 1923 Department of State, 1944–1946 Counselor of Mission, Office of US Political Adviser on Austrian Affairs, Commanding General, US Army Forces, Mediterranean Theater, ab April 1946 Chief, Division of Foreign Service Personnel im Department in Washington, D. C., ab 1948 Consul General, Paris.
[9] Siehe Dok. 20, Anm. 30.
[10] H. Francis Cunningham Jr. (1912–1999) aus Lincoln, Nebraska, amerikanischer Diplomat, 1933 BA, University of Nebraska, 1938–1969 Department of State, Juni 1946–1948 Division of Northern European Affairs, 1957–1959 Consul General, Bonn.
[11] Charles W. Thayer. Siehe Dok. 33, Anm. 25.
[12] Alice D. Bickford, geb. Dean (geb. 1864), die Mutter von John D. Bickford (siehe Dok. 14, Anm. 3).
[13] Hannah Walstrom. Siehe Dok. 4, Anm. 14.
[14] Frank E. Johnson. Siehe Dok. 3, Anm. 12.
[15] Mildred H. Williams. Siehe Dok. 4, Anm. 12.
[16] Siehe Dok. 2, Anm. 28, und Dok. 63, Anm. 10.
[17] Stadt im US-Bundesstaat Nebraska, nordöstlich von Johnsons Wohnort Lincoln.
[18] US-Bundesstaat.
[19] US-Bundesstaat.
[20] Siehe Dok. 80 und Dok. 80, Anm. 40; 660 Stricken by Polio In Minnesota Epidemic, in: The Stars and Stripes, European Edition, vom 8. August 1946, S. 4.
[21] Amerikanisches Reportagemagazin.
[22] John Foster Dulles (1888–1959), amerikanischer Jurist und Politiker (Republikanische Partei), 1911 LLB, The George Washington University Law School, 1911–1949 Mitglied der New Yorker Anwaltskanzlei Sullivan & Cromwell (ab 1926 Senior Partner), 1919 Mitglied der amerikanischen Friedensdelegation in Paris, 1945 US-Delegierter bei der Gründungskonferenz der Vereinten Nationen und bei folgenden Voll-

good as an analysis of the problem, the second on what we should do about it seemed none too helpful.[23] He suggests making it plain to the Russians that we believe that our democratic principles are of divine origin. I am not so sure this will impress them. If we can't do more than he says then we have already lost to Russia. I have also read here Carl Van Doren's[24] book on Liberal Education[25], a sort of modified Hutchins[26] – Buchanan[27] treatment of the problem.[28] It did put me in the frame of mind of considering students again. His big point is, I think, the one Sherlock[29] made when he read his paper before some club or meeting that we attended, (Rosenlof[30] presided you remember + spoke on obituaries) viz., that in American there is no large and common basis of ideas that the teacher or writer can take for granted is present in every cultivated mind. He therefore recommends the St. John's[31] curriculum[32] – the best books notion. I shall have to introduce a little of that in my culture course[33] this year. As a result of the loafing the stomach is better and also the back. I took a little walk yesterday.

My thoughts, however, are really centering upon one thing only – upon you first of all whom I have not seen now for seven months, and upon John, soon to

versammlungen, 1951 als Sonderbotschafter am Abschluss des Friedensvertrags mit Japan maßgeblich beteiligt, 1953–1959 Außenminister der USA.

[23] Siehe John Foster Dulles, Thoughts on Soviet Foreign Policy and What To Do About It, in: Life vom 3. Juni 1946, S. 112-126 (Part I), und vom 10. Juni 1946, S. 118-130 (Part II); ders., Gedanken über die Sowjet-Außenpolitik und was dazu zu tun ist, der Zeitschrift „Life" entnommen, Hamburg 1947.

[24] Gemeint ist nicht Carl Van Doren (1885–1950), sondern dessen Bruder Mark Van Doren (1894–1972), amerikanischer Schriftsteller, 1920 PhD, Columbia University, lehrte 1920-1959 an der Columbia University, ab 1942 als Full Professor of English.

[25] Liberal Education, New York 1943.

[26] Robert M. Hutchins (1899–1977), amerikanischer Jurist und Pädagoge, 1921 BA, Yale University, 1925 LLB, Yale Law School, 1927-1929 Professor of Law, Yale Law School, 1929 LLD, West Virginia University, 1929-1945 President, University of Chicago, 1945-1951 Chancellor, University of Chicago.

[27] Scott M. Buchanan (1895–1968), amerikanischer Philosophieprofessor und Pädagoge, Begründer des Great Books Program am St. John's College, Annapolis, Maryland (siehe Anm. 32), 1925 PhD, Harvard University, 1929-1936 Professor of Philosophy, University of Virginia, 1936/1937 University of Chicago (von Robert M. Hutchins berufen, um bei der Schaffung eines Committee on Liberal Arts zu helfen), 1937-1946 Dean, St. John's College.

[28] Siehe Mary Ann Dzuback, Robert M. Hutchins. Portrait of an Educator, Chicago und London 1991.

[29] Sherlock B. Gass. Siehe Dok. 63, Anm. 29.

[30] George W. Rosenlof (1891–1974), amerikanischer Erziehungswissenschaftler, 1929 PhD, Columbia University, Registrar, University Examiner, and Director of Admissions, Professor of Secondary Education (Secretary of the Faculties and of the University Senate), University of Nebraska.

[31] St. John's College in Annapolis, Maryland, seit 1964 zweiter Campus in Santa Fe, New Mexico, gegründet 1696 als preparatory school, King William's School, seit 1784 St. John's College.

[32] Seit 1937 folgt das St. John's College einem ausgefallenen Lehrplan, dem Great Books Program, das auf Werke der westlichen Philosophie und Literatur basiert.

[33] Gemeint ist eine Lehrveranstaltung an der University of Nebraska.

be 7,[34] and upon Thomas, now over 2[35] – and how quickly I can get to you. The world of larger affairs has faded from my mind for the time being – first, because in this kind of a set-up there is no point in it (going through the mill is dreadful on the ego), and second, because it is really behind me this time. At present I'm just anonymous. But I am making for you and the boys. I love you with all my heart and soon hope to be able to demonstrate this with something more than words. Edgar

Dok. 82
Schreiben an die Ehefrau
Bremerhaven[1], 9. August 1946

Dearest –

It's all very sad here at the present moment. Just as we completed our processing yesterday a notice was put on the bulletin board saying that the War Department had ordered that no civilians in its employ were to travel on Victory Ships[2]. We were scheduled to go off tomorrow on a Victory Ship, and now of course we are not going. Nobody seems to know the reason for this order. Whether, that is, it is because civilians who have gone home on these Victory Ships have complained so much, or whether, as was suggested by a Colonel this morning, it has to do with the cost of transportation home. It is a most extraordinarily arbitrary thing to do. Not only to make it applicable without further notice but to make it retroactive to include those who was already booked for passage. Just another horrible example of the danger of inconsiderate bureaucracy. Well I went to see the Commanding Officer of this Port, a nice Colonel Pirtle[3], who called in another Colonel. They tried to get an exemption made in Frankfurt[4] for those civilians who were scheduled to go tomorrow but to no avail. It now appears that there is a ship in port that is not a Victory Ship, the Marine Robin[5]. It appears also that civilians may sail on it. But when it is to sail nobody knows whether that is before or after many more victory ships have sailed. These ships can't sail empty, and there are not enough troops here at

---

[34] Sohn John (siehe Dok. 2, Anm. 15) wurde am 15. September 1939 geboren.
[35] Sohn Thomas (siehe Dok. 2, Anm. 16) wurde am 8. Juli 1944 geboren.

[1] Siehe Dok. 71, Anm. 10.
[2] Siehe Dok. 81, Anm. 2.
[3] James J. Pirtle (1896–1967), Colonel, 1925 BA, Wabash College, Commanding Officer, 3rd Replacement Depot, Bremerhaven Staging Area.
[4] Frankfurt am Main, Stadt im Land Groß-Hessen in der amerikanischen Besatzungszone Deutschlands.
[5] Das amerikanische Truppenschiff „Marine Robin" hatte am 4. August 1946, aus Schanghai kommend, in Bremerhaven angelegt. An Bord des Schiffes wurden 1100 Deutsche, die während des Krieges in China und Singapur interniert waren, in ihre Heimat zurückgeführt. Siehe Die Neue Zeitung vom 9. August 1946, S. 1 (Bilder vom Tage). Das Schiff stach am 15. August 1946 wieder in See. Siehe Bd. 2 der Hafenverkehrsbücher Bremerhaven, Überseehäfen und Columbuskaje – Seeschifffahrt, in: StAB, 4,72/2-57.

present to fill them rapidly. The Robin carries some 2000 troops. If Victory Ships go off before she does, they will have to wait before enough troops pile up to fill her before she can go. So I don't know when I am going to get away. The other possibility is to hire passage on a commercial freighter. There is one here that is leaving the 14th, and if the situation doesn't otherwise clear up I may try to get passage on it. It is supposed to make the trip in 10 days but if it is a tramp freighter one doesn't know when it will ever get to America.

If it seems worth it I shall call Clay[6] this afternoon, after consulting more people here.

So don't count on anything. Get off to the mountains on time with some help. I'll come when it is possible to come, and no one knows at the present moment when that will be. It is all very disgusting.

But I love you, my dearest, and my sweet boys. If there is no good chance to get away otherwise, I'll pay my way on this commercial ship. Though so far as the money is concerned, this will be making a present to the government. Edgar

Dok. 83
Bericht "Five Months in Berlin"
Schreibmaschinenmanuskript, nicht datiert

[I]

It had been rather discouraging in Austria the year before. The fine zeal of the Moscow Declaration of November 1943[1] could not undo the essential absurdity of imposing upon this little country a quadripartite occupation[2]. For as long as this lasted Austria would necessarily remain a sacrifice to the international rivalry which no clumsy occupational machinery could conceal. The starving and

---

[6] Siehe Dok. 2, Anm. 6.

[1] Moskauer Deklaration über Österreich, die am 1. November 1943 von den Außenministern der USA, der Sowjetunion und Großbritanniens unterzeichnet wurde. Darin wird Österreich als erstes freies Land bezeichnet, das der Angriffspolitik von Adolf Hitler (siehe Dok. 22, Anm. 19) zum Opfer gefallen sei. Der „Anschluss" Österreichs an das Deutsche Reich vom März 1938 wird für null und nichtig erklärt. Siehe Richard Hufschmied, Sonderfall Wien? Die Alliierten und Österreich 1943–1955, in: Die Vier Mächte in Berlin. Beiträge zur Politik der Alliierten in der besetzten Stadt, hrsg. von Michael Bienert/Uwe Schaper/Andrea Theissen unter Mitarbeit von Werner Breunig (= Schriftenreihe des Landesarchivs Berlin, Bd. 9), Berlin 2007, S. 109–129, hier S. 109f.

[2] Die Alliierten hatten sich entschieden, Österreich aufgrund des Fehlens einer Exilregierung vorerst zu besetzen und ein gemeinsames Kontrollsystem einzurichten. Das Abkommen über die Alliierte Kontrolle in Österreich (Erstes Kontrollabkommen) vom 4. Juli 1945, das von der European Advisory Commission in London beschlossen wurde, sah die Errichtung einer „Alliierten Kommission für Österreich" vor. Siehe ebd., S. 114f.

dead at Mauthausen³, however, had demonstrated that there was much to be done in the country, no matter what the obstacles. The sentences of the Moscow Declaration had been re-inforced by encouraging directives in handbooks of military government, and papers of the State Department. There were some people in positions of authority who took these directives seriously and were impatient to carry them out. In general, however, moral fervor in the support of the simple democratic principles we were supposed to represent, was, in the early days of the occupation, weak. The nasty question always remained, "Did we really, under the circumstances, have anything positive to offer this people?"

When the government of the United States so mutilated the Office of Strategic Services⁴ as to render it essentially innocuous, there was nothing to do but to return to the University. It did not seem quite right. There were still voices making themselves heard in American public circles who were talking about winning the peace. The peace was not actually being won in Austria. It might be won elsewhere; perhaps in Germany. At the moment a promising experiment was being inaugurated in the American zone: Bavaria, Baden-Wurttemberg and Greater-Hesse.⁵ This was the Länderrat⁶, the Council of States, located at Stuttgart⁷. Those in authority in Germany suggested a return to help with this Council. The gluttonous and somewhat gaudy America of the early winter of 1945–46 was a little difficult to absorb. The petty and long-suffering complacency of important elements in a mid-western college community was a little alien to the bleak ruins of Cologne⁸ and Kassel⁹. Yet if those in authority in Germany wished help, those in authority in the War Department at Washington did not know how, in time, to get it where it was needed. At the moment of the return to Germany it had long been necessary to send someone else to Stuttgart. The generals were, I am afraid, a little puzzled over what to do with me when I arrived.

It was to have been via plane. It was explained, however, at the last moment that demobilization had so crippled the ground forces that it was impossible to maintain sufficient planes in the air. Accordingly it must be via the George W. Goethals¹⁰. There had been talk of hunger and starvation in Europe. I knew indeed that I had detected starvation on the ashen faces of the Viennese. Except

---

3   Siehe Dok. 49, Anm. 49.
4   Siehe Dok. 1, Anm. 9.
5   In der amerikanischen Besatzungszone wurden mit der Proklamation Nr. 2 der Militärregierung vom 19. September 1945 die drei als Staaten bezeichneten Länder Bayern, Groß-Hessen und Württemberg-Baden gebildet. Siehe Keesing's Archiv der Gegenwart, XV. Jg., 1945, S. 440 A. Textabdruck: Der Länderrat des amerikanischen Besatzungsgebietes, hrsg. im Auftrag der Ministerpräsidenten von Bayern, Hessen, Württemberg-Baden und des Präsidenten des Senats der Freien Hansestadt Bremen vom Direktorium des Länderrats, zusammengestellt von Lia Härtel, ehemalige Archivarin beim Länderrat, Stuttgart und Köln 1951, S. 201 f.
6   Siehe Dok. 15, Anm. 10.
7   Hauptstadt des Landes Württemberg-Baden in der amerikanischen Besatzungszone Deutschlands.
8   Stadt in der britischen Besatzungszone Deutschlands.
9   Stadt im Land Groß-Hessen in der amerikanischen Besatzungszone Deutschlands.
10 USAT George W. Goethals. Siehe Dok. 7, Anm. 18.

for its small contingent of civilians, however, and for the supply of baby equipment which was to administer to the comfort and necessity of returning French brides, the boat was empty.

These civilians were the people who were going to Germany to assist in winning the peace.[11] There were those who were high-minded and earnest, aware of the difficulties of the problem and of the awful import of its outcome. A few of these were Germans who had taken refuge with us from the land they were now hoping to rescue.[12] Many of those in a similar category, whom one met or later heard of in Germany, did their rescue work in a fashion contrary to the principles and methods of the America of their adoption, embarrassing their country and making more difficult its occupational task. The professor of administrative law at the University of Chicago[13] was not one of these.[14] He was to be responsible on the American side for the elimination of Nazism from German law. The amount of additional good he did in eliminating from German minds unfortunate prejudices about Americans, it would be difficult to measure. There were American academics on board who had not yet had their opportunity of participating very actively in the cause of their country. The very roly-poly professor of economics[15] in a California women's college[16], for example, who was as suspicious as one of his good nature could be of the ultimate feasibility of the occupation of Germany. There were specialist civil servants summoned from Washington for their expert opinion on particular phases of the occupation. The New York road builder[17] who had to inspect the bridges and roads of our zone, and who, when he was through, foretold disaster for efficient military transportation if material for surfacing these roads were not imported from the United States in great abundance. The specialist in administration of whom all empire builders had to beware before they could staff their branches and divisions with the improper number of high civil service ratings. There were also the opportunists and adventurers, the gravy lappers, who were concerned with leaves, how long they would have to work, and how much they would get paid for overtime, husky-throated, hard-faced women among them. Some of these had been well instructed in the possibilities of the black market[18] abroad, and came well supplied with the articles they knew would sell for handsome prices. I saw one of these again in Paris.[19] He was flushed with his first successful deal on the black market. I saw him the day after he arrived in Berlin. He displayed to me the first fruits of his operations on the Berlin black market. It

---

[11] Gemeint sind zivile Mitarbeiter der amerikanischen Militärregierung in Deutschland.
[12] Es handelte sich um Deutsche, die in der NS-Zeit Zuflucht in den USA gefunden hatten und als Mitarbeiter und Berater der amerikanischen Militärregierung nach Deutschland zurückkehrten.
[13] 1890 gegründete Universität in Chicago, Illinois.
[14] Gemeint ist der Emigrant Max Rheinstein (siehe Dok. 11, Anm. 22), der sich an Bord befand.
[15] Glenn E. Hoover. Siehe Dok. 9, Anm. 10.
[16] Mills College in Oakland, California.
[17] William J. Anderson. Siehe Dok. 9, Anm. 8.
[18] Siehe Dok. 21, Anm. 11.
[19] Siehe Dok. 21.

was jewelry which some poor German had felt obliged to exchange for his cigarettes or his chocolate.[20] These Germans, ruined middle class families or old retired heads of families deprived of their pensions, assembled in such numbers about places where Americans congregated that special guards were established to drive them off. These were not exactly, in spite of the excellence of a few, the best Americans who could have been chosen to assist in winning the peace. The best Americans, it appeared, were not that interested in winning the peace.

If Mauthausen had been an incentive to work in Austria, the German scientist aboard the Goethals was a similar incentive to work in Germany. He was a young man whom, together with many of his kind, we had picked up after the close of hostilities and sent to work on rockets and remote control projectiles in Maryland[21]. He was not indeed the worst kind of a Nazi scientist. He said he had never joined the Party[22] despite all the pressure to which he had been subjected. He held indeed the reassuring opinion, which I had always held, that it was actually never necessary for anyone to join the Party. Yet he was that worst kind of a scientist who, with perfect amorality, was willing to prostitute his talents for any political cause. He had worked on V-1 and V-2[23]. He was a leader in the research at Peenemünde[24]. He could talk exultantly about the great "progress" made when V-2 supplanted V-1. His imagination leaped into the future. There was not reason why, in a few years, rockets should not be carrying passengers across the Atlantic in forty minutes. They would, in fact, soon be able to circle the earth in continuous rounds. He had had, however, to pay his price with personal tragedy. His wife was awaiting him for burial in the cold darkness of a mortuary. She had contracted pneumonia on a voyage from the British zone to Frankfurt[25] to learn why, after his removal to the States, she had never heard from him. In the Germany he had really helped to destroy he would have to begin anew, and find a place for his two children. There is no doubt that he will be able to do so. Scientists of his training are at a premium with the occupiers. Scientists, too, of his training would be used not only by the kind of Germany which would arise if the peace were won, but also by the kind of Germany which could arise if the peace were lost.

---

[20] Siehe Dok. 27, Anm. 10.
[21] US-Bundesstaat. In White Oak, Maryland, befand sich das Naval Ordnance Laboratory.
[22] Gemeint ist die Nationalsozialistische Deutsche Arbeiterpartei (NSDAP).
[23] Vergeltungswaffe 1 und Vergeltungswaffe 2, Waffensysteme, die während des Zweiten Weltkriegs im nationalsozialistischen Deutschland entwickelt wurden, zur „Vergeltung" der alliierten Luftangriffe auf deutsche Städte. Der Marschflugkörper V 1 wurde erstmals im Juni 1944 auf London abgefeuert, die Flüssigkeitsgroßrakete V 2 ab September 1944 eingesetzt. Siehe Walter Dornberger, Peenemünde. Die Geschichte der V-Waffen, mit einem Geleitwort von Eberhard Rees, Huntsville/Alabama, Eßlingen 1981.
[24] Gemeinde auf der Ostsee-Insel Usedom. 1936 war hier eine Heeresversuchsanstalt („Peenemünde-Ost") errichtet worden. Sie wurde 1938 durch die Erprobungsstelle der Luftwaffe „Peenemünde-West" ergänzt. Während in Peenemünde-Ost die Flüssigkeitsgroßrakete V 2 entwickelt wurde, testete parallel in Peenemünde-West die Luftwaffe den Marschflugkörper V 1. Siehe ebd.
[25] Frankfurt am Main, Stadt im Land Groß-Hessen in der amerikanischen Besatzungszone Deutschlands.

When the Goethals tumbled its civilians into the capacious lap of OMGUS (Office of Military Government U. S.)[26] in Berlin, this headquarters was about to gather into its bosom a child it had never learned quite how to control, the headquarters for the military government of the American zone[27] at Frankfurt. While the advantages of consolidation could be seen, it was not so easy to understand why the consolidation should not have been made at Frankfurt rather than Berlin. To be sure there was necessary quadripartite business to be done at Berlin, but to control the military government of the American zone more effectively, moving into, rather than away from the zone might seem more satisfactory. Those who were actually directing the military government of the zone from the local capitals might welcome this remote control, regard it even as an enhancement of the efficiency of military government itself. The distance from Berlin, however, made it easier for officials to remain isolated there, and to feel the necessity for an old Carolingian institution, the missi dominici[28].

Yet the amalgamation in Berlin enlarged the American family which gathered for work each morning the building clustering around Kronprinzenallee[29] and Saargemünderstrasse[30].[31] This community, situated pleasantly in the midst of its tulip beds was fast taking on the nature of a university campus, an army post, or a missionary compound. Removed from the actualities of the zone, this little region in Dahlem[32] was almost as far removed from the actualities of Berlin, the Tiergarten transformed into a vegetable garden,[33] the dead streets from which nobody had ever yet tried to extricate the dead, the millions of shabby and hungry Berliners, who, somehow, still managed to make the city their habitation. Nobody could say that these Americans were not being well taken care of. It cannot be assumed that, except for a few in very responsible positions, they were over-worked. American food was abundantly available in attractive messing centers. It was not necessary to eat without the accompaniment of a German orchestra, or without the stimulation of preparatory cocktails, served, as in the Harnack House[34], in the atmosphere of a sophisticated metropolitan cocktail lounge. For awhile all Americans seemed to be going around with bottles under their arms. There were few forms of entertainment in which one could not indulge. There was the Russian directed opera and orches-

---

[26] Siehe Dok. 17, Anm. 45.
[27] Gemeint ist das OMGUSZ in Frankfurt am Main, das die Aufgabe hatte, die von OMGUS beschlossene Politik in der amerikanischen Besatzungszone auszuführen. Als OMGUSZ aufgelöst wurde, gingen die Aufgaben, von geringfügigen Ausnahmen abgesehen, auf OMGUS über. Siehe Dok. 15, Anm. 32.
[28] Siehe Dok. 24, Anm. 17.
[29] In Berlin-Dahlem. Seit 1949 heißt die Straße Clayallee.
[30] Saargemünder Straße, Berlin-Dahlem.
[31] Gemeint ist das Gelände in Berlin-Dahlem, das OMGUS beherbergte. Siehe Dok. 17, Anm. 45.
[32] Ortsteil im Berliner Verwaltungsbezirk Zehlendorf.
[33] Der größte Berliner Park, im gleichnamigen Bezirk gelegen, wurde von der hungernden Bevölkerung zum Anbau von Gemüse genutzt.
[34] Siehe Dok. 15, Anm. 16.

tra,³⁵ the lively theatre, the art exhibits and the night clubs. There were horses to canter through the Grunewald³⁶. The Wannsee³⁷ on week-ends was gaily covered with a great variety of sailing and motor craft, confiscated from the Germans who were now confined to bathing on a portion of the Strandbad³⁸, and serviced by the various yacht clubs.

Nobody from the lowliest to the high could complain about quarters. We had simply taken over the best available, and could not be bothered much about the political histories of those we obliged to get out. The professor of administrative law³⁹ on the boat found himself sharing a house⁴⁰ which belonged to a distinguished German cellist⁴¹, who because of his Jewish wife⁴², had been harassed by the Nazis.⁴³ With his five children⁴⁴ he had moved into an adjoining bombed-out house⁴⁵ where he had been offered American supplies at black market prices by the very American officer who was responsible for his withdrawal. The professor invited him back, not to re-occupy his house but to participate in social gatherings at which Americans and Germans were present. And this distinguished cellist (Max Baldner of the Klinger Quartet⁴⁶) brought his Stradivarius⁴⁷ and played for his American expropriators in his own house, in order, as he hoped, to help bridge the chasm between Germans and Americans.

The very important people lived in the houses of the very important people of the preceding era in a atmosphere of what would have to be described as elegant luxury. The large electrically operated plate glass windows which opened the living rooms into the gardens were a sign of rank. The Wannsee region was among the most select. I was permitted to occupy quarters in the Wannsee Officers' Club⁴⁸, operated for the officers of Berlin District. It had formerly been the abode of the Nazi Minister of Economics, Mr. Funk⁴⁹, who now occupies

---

35 Gemeint sind die Deutsche Staatsoper und deren Orchester. Da das Gebäude der Staatsoper Unter den Linden zerstört war, wurde im August 1945 der Admiralspalast, Friedrichstraße 101/102 im Bezirk Mitte, ständige Spielstätte.
36 Ein rund 3000 ha großes, sich über weite Gebiete der Bezirke Wilmersdorf (britischer Sektor) und Zehlendorf (amerikanischer Sektor) sowie einen kleinen Teil von Charlottenburg (britischer Sektor) erstreckendes Waldgebiet östlich der unteren Havel (siehe Dok. 74, Anm. 24).
37 Gemeint ist der Große Wannsee, eine Ausbuchtung der Havel (siehe Dok. 74, Anm. 24) im Südwesten Berlins.
38 Das 1929/1930 errichtete Strandbad Wannsee am Ostufer des Großen Wannsees.
39 Max Rheinstein. Siehe Dok. 11, Anm. 22.
40 Podbielskiallee 65. Siehe Dok. 21, Anm. 17.
41 Max Baldner. Siehe Dok. 21, Anm. 18.
42 Charlotte Baldner, geb. Lindemann. Siehe Dok. 21, Anm. 21.
43 Siehe Dok. 21, Anm. 22.
44 Max Baldner hatte vier Kinder. Siehe Dok. 21, Anm. 24. Bei dem fünften Kind handelte es sich nicht um ein Familienmitglied. Siehe Dok. 25, Anm. 44.
45 Podbielskiallee 57. Siehe Dok. 21, Anm. 25.
46 Klingler-Quartett. Siehe Dok. 21, Anm. 19.
47 Siehe Dok. 38, Anm. 15.
48 Am Sandwerder 17/19 im Berliner Verwaltungsbezirk Zehlendorf, Ortsteil Wannsee. Siehe Dok. 25, Anm. 9.
49 Siehe Dok. 25, Anm. 10.

quarters of an entirely different character at Nürnberg[50]. Mr. Funk, the gardener[51] explained, and gardeners like bureaucrats have a nice ability to survive all regimes, had acquired it from a Jewish banker[52] now in Holland[53], who, in turn, after the last war[54], had acquired it from a British member[55] of the Reparations Commission[56]. If its architecture was insignificant, it did afford commodious and even opulent services. "This", asserted the officer in charge, a genial yachting enthusiast, "is the best mess in Berlin." I never had any reason to doubt it. Elegant food served by a corps of professional waiters from some of Berlin's best hotels. You could have German and French champagne with dinner, served in the proper ice-containers. The grounds were beautifully landscaped, and the flower gardens supplied gorgeous blooms, plucked and arranged by a special member of the staff. The exotic lavender rhododendrons were followed by tall spikes of blue delphinium, these in turn by the roses and the snapdragons. Over the air-raid shelter the gardener grew his lettuce, his spinach and his beans. In the garden, not far to the right of the swimming pool on the front lawn, he grew his fruit. The lawn itself, kept carefully groomed, sloped down to the lake. Of a late evening you could find fishing from the pier, to which came every afternoon a motor launch for the use of the guests of the club, the melancholy pastry cook who had once had his own shops in Sofia[57] and Constantinople[58]. On this pier one could sit, suffering the humiliation of being bitten by German mosquitoes, gazing into the western skies across the lake as a usually magnificent sun descended, thinking about winning the peace and the formation of a new group of American colonial governors.

Into this bountiful life the dependents were coming.[59] At the Officers' Club the shrieks of a young daughter, protesting so violently against the unaccustomed elegance of her surroundings that her embarrassed mother had to carry her from the room, broke upon the calm of the diners. It was, however, now no more difficult for them than it had been previously for their husbands. Indeed they were frank to admit that it was much less difficult than it had been at home. High ranking officers gave purpose to their lives in organizing the forces and equipment necessary to do over quarters for the family that was about to arrive. In some instances the stuffy furniture of an old mansion had to be replaced with its stream-lined equivalent even if the continent had to be scoured to do it. In others, the plan of a too militaristically conceived formal garden had

---

[50] Stadt im Land Bayern in der amerikanischen Besatzungszone Deutschlands. Funk und andere beim Kriegsverbrecherprozess Angeklagte waren in dem zum Nürnberger Justizpalast gehörenden Gefängnis untergebracht.
[51] Albert Redmann. Siehe Dok. 47, Anm. 4.
[52] Hans Arnhold. Siehe Dok. 47, Anm. 7.
[53] Siehe Dok. 47, Anm. 9.
[54] Gemeint ist der Erste Weltkrieg (1914–1918).
[55] Marcel Hardy. Siehe Dok. 47, Anm. 6.
[56] Die alliierte Reparationskommission hatte der Festsetzung und Überwachung der vom Deutschen Reich zu leistenden Reparationen gedient.
[57] Hauptstadt Bulgariens.
[58] Früherer Name für Istanbul, türkische Stadt am Bosporus.
[59] Am 30. April 1946 trafen die ersten Ehefrauen und Kinder von amerikanischen Besatzungsangehörigen in Berlin ein. Siehe Dok. 42, Anm. 13.

to be modified along more democratic lines. In spite of the efforts of some wives to create one, there was no servant problem. There were more cooks and maids, more chauffeurs and gardeners, and of course more governesses than had ever been made available to these people before. They admitted and liked it. It was something of a relief to come from a troubled environment where there were such things as strikes, to the serenity of Dahlem, Zehlendorf or Wannsee[60]. If it was to continue like this they would be prepared to stay a long time. Some women were worried about their figures under such an easy routine. Others felt the danger of being completely spoiled with such complete staffs. Yet the organization of the Berlin Women's Club[61], with departments calculated to fit any interest from bridge to porcelain, promised to relieve whatever boredom might be in store with so much leisure time, even if it did not bring the women into any closer contact with German Berlin. Indeed this closer contact was at the moment not encouraged. In the American zone the American Military Communities[62] were protected from the Germans by fences and forbidding rolls of barbed wire.[63] Some Germans were sensitive about this. Some, whose empty houses stood within, were bitter. In Frankfurt, the American compound behind its barbed-wire was even called, 'the Ghetto of the Pharisees'[64].

II

Beyond this pleasant American world was Berlin. There could be no doubt that this city was still the most important in Germany even if the French were considerably annoyed when a local newspaper, for reasons other than the fact, adopted as part of its masthead the phrase *Zeitung der Hauptstadt Deutschlands*.[65] From the point of view of what was going on here, it was even the most important city in Europe. From the point of view of the struggle between East and West it was one of the most fascinating, if discouraging, focal points in the world. It was still the capital of Germany in the minds not only of the Berliners, but of those outside of Berlin who suffered from the isolation imposed by the four zones. The political parties organized here[66] did not regard themselves as anything other than parts of the national parties. No political convention was limited to members from Berlin, or to members from Berlin and the enveloping Russian Zone. 'Guests' from all the zones were invited and came whenever it was possible. It was clear to an outsider who attended such conventions that the

---

[60] Ortsteile im Berliner Verwaltungsbezirk Zehlendorf.
[61] Gemeint ist der American Women's Club of Berlin. Siehe Dok. 68, Anm. 31.
[62] Siehe Dok. 79, Anm. 31.
[63] Siehe Dok. 79.
[64] Siehe Dok. 79, Anm. 33.
[65] Die vom Berliner Bezirksvorstand der SED herausgegebene Tageszeitung „Vorwärts. Berliner Volksblatt" hatte den zweiten Untertitel „Das Abendblatt der Hauptstadt Deutschlands".
[66] Zugelassen waren in Berlin zunächst die KPD, die SPD, die CDU und die LDP. Siehe Dok. 20, Anm. 12 und 13, Dok. 21, Anm. 29, und Dok. 44, Anm. 10. Nach dem Zusammenschluss von KPD und SPD zur SED wurden in Berlin sowohl die SED als auch die von den Vereinigungsgegnern neu konstituierte SPD anerkannt.

chief joy of the German participants was to feel reunited again in an assembly consisting of Germans from all over the Reich. If in such an assembly a capable orator spoke movingly of the sufferings and tragedy of the fatherland, he could easily reduce his audience to tears. If, in such a gathering, the guest from Bavaria, a roughly-hewn native son (Josef Müller[67], the leader of the Christian Social Union[68]) spoke of the desirability of Berlin and Bavaria's acting together, he called forth a dramatic response not necessarily to be expected from a Berlin audience for a Bavarian.[69] With Germany so obviously and variously atomized, the exhibition of any kind of a partial unity was the occasion for unwonted excitement.

If Berlin was still in the German mind the capital of the Reich, it was even more interesting to speculate whether Berlin was actually to become again the capital of the Russian zone. As it was Berlin was an international island in the Russian sea, or if you would believe some Germans, an international oasis in the Russian desert. Before the inauguration of the quadripartite government of the city, the Kommandatura[70], Berlin had actually been the capital of the Russian Zone.[71] In abandoning Berlin as a military objective to pursue the Wehrmacht[72] elsewhere,[73] we had permitted the Russians to execute the plans for the government of the city that they had long worked out with the Free Germany Committee[74]. The leading officials in this government, trained in

---

[67] Siehe Dok. 80, Anm. 19.
[68] Siehe Dok. 80, Anm. 16.
[69] Müller hatte als Gast an dem vom 15. bis 17. Juni 1946 in Berlin stattfindenden Parteitag der CDU der sowjetischen Besatzungszone und Berlins teilgenommen. Siehe Berlin. Kampf um Freiheit und Selbstverwaltung 1945–1946, hrsg. im Auftrage des Senats von Berlin (= Schriftenreihe zur Berliner Zeitgeschichte, Bd. 1), 2., erg. und erw. Auflage, Berlin 1961, S. 459, Nr. 31. Ob Johnson den Parteitag besucht hatte, geht aus seinen Briefen nicht hervor.
[70] Siehe Dok. 20, Anm. 11.
[71] Nach Kriegsende hatte Berlin zwei Monate lang, bis zur Ankunft der Westmächte, unter der ausschließlichen Kontrolle der sowjetischen Besatzungsmacht gestanden. Faktisch gehörte die Stadt in dieser Zeit zur sowjetischen Besatzungszone Deutschlands.
[72] Die deutschen Streitkräfte.
[73] Gegen Kriegsende hatten sich die Amerikaner dafür entschieden, die Eroberung Berlins den sowjetischen Streitkräften zu überlassen; die angloamerikanischen Streitkräfte sollten die verbliebenen deutschen Kräfte südlich von Berlin vernichten und sich nahe Dresden mit den Sowjets vereinigen. Siehe Jean E. Smith, Der Weg ins Dilemma. Preisgabe und Verteidigung der Stadt Berlin, Berlin 1965, S. 42–59.
[74] Das 1943 gegründete Nationalkomitee „Freies Deutschland" war eine von der sowjetischen Regierung gestützte Organisation deutscher Kriegsgefangener und kommunistischer Emigranten. Es hatte die Aufgabe, sowohl an der Front deutsche Soldaten für den Kampf gegen das NS-Regime zu gewinnen als auch gefangen genommene Soldaten und Offiziere in der Sowjetunion für Propagandazwecke einzusetzen. Nach 1945 erhielten zahlreiche Angehörige des Nationalkomitees Schlüsselstellungen in der sowjetischen Besatzungszone und in der späteren DDR. Siehe Bodo Scheurig, Verräter oder Patrioten. Das Nationalkomitee „Freies Deutschland" und der Bund Deutscher Offiziere in der Sowjetunion 1943–1945, Berlin und Frankfurt am Main 1993; Das Nationalkomitee „Freies Deutschland" und der Bund Deutscher Offiziere, hrsg. von Gerd R. Ueberschär (Die Zeit des Nationalsozialismus. Eine Buchreihe), Frankfurt am Main 1995.

Russia, were ready at hand when the conquest of the city was complete.[75] When, accordingly, the Magistrate was set up[76] it contained such men as Bürgermeister Maron[77], who was to do the actual governing of the city while Oberbürgermeister Werner[78], whom everybody know to be a kind of nincompoop, made the speeches and stopped to bow in deferential acknowledgement whenever he was applauded. The president of the police, Marquard[79], was also a Russian trained Communist. The head of the department of personnel[80] was the son of Wilhelm Pieck[81], the venerable if somewhat empty-headed Communist leader who had spent his last years of exile in Russia. Together with him came Walter Ulbricht[82], whose German long residence in the Soviet Union[83] had given a slightly Russian accent, trying desperately to look like Lenin[84],[85] an unscrupulous and clever demagogue. So, in a capital city which the Russians had captured, there

[75] Die drei wichtigsten Posten im Magistrat wurden von Kommunisten besetzt, die in der Sowjetunion geschult worden waren: Karl Maron (siehe Dok. 74, Anm. 37) wurde 1. Stellvertreter des Oberbürgermeisters, Arthur Pieck (1899-1970) Leiter der Abteilung für Personalfragen und Verwaltung, Otto Winzer (1902-1975) Leiter der Abteilung für Volksbildung. Maron und Winzer waren mit der „Gruppe Ulbricht" aus Moskau zurückgekehrt. Maron, KPD-Mitglied seit 1925, hatte seit 1935 in der Sowjetunion gelebt und sich als Mitarbeiter der Presseabteilung der Komintern, ab 1943 als stellvertretender Chefredakteur der Zeitung des Nationalkomitees „Freies Deutschland" betätigt. Pieck war seit 1919 KPD-Mitglied, hatte nach seiner Emigration in die Sowjetunion unter anderem für die Presseabteilung der Komintern gearbeitet, war 1938 sowjetischer Staatsbürger geworden und hatte sich nach dem deutschen Überfall auf die Sowjetunion als Offizier in der Politischen Hauptverwaltung der Roten Armee betätigt. Winzer, der 1919 dem Kommunistischen Jugendverband Deutschlands und 1925 der KPD beigetreten war, hatte bis 1935 als Redakteur und Verlagsleiter kommunistischer Zeitungen und Zeitschriften in Deutschland und anderen europäischen Ländern gearbeitet, ging dann in die Sowjetunion, wo er für die Komintern, den Verlag für fremdsprachige Literatur, am Deutschen Volkssender und als Lehrer an einer Antifa-Schule tätig war.

[76] Der von der „Gruppe Ulbricht" zusammengestellte und anschließend vom sowjetischen Stadtkommandanten, Generaloberst Nikolai Erastowitsch Bersarin (1904-1945), und vom Oberbefehlshaber der Gruppe der sowjetischen Besatzungsstreitkräfte in Deutschland, Marschall der Sowjetunion Georgi Konstantinowitsch Schukow (siehe Anm. 155), bestätigte erste Nachkriegsmagistrat Berlins wurde am 19. Mai 1945 öffentlich vorgestellt und offiziell in seine Tätigkeit eingeführt. Zur Etablierung des Magistrats siehe Die Sitzungsprotokolle des Magistrats der Stadt Berlin 1945/46. Teil I: 1945, bearb. und eingel. von Dieter Hanauske (= Schriftenreihe des Landesarchivs Berlin, Bd. 2/I), Berlin 1995, S. 31-48; Werner Breunig, Berlin 1945/46. Vom Kriegsende bis zum parlamentarischen Neubeginn, in: „Berlin kommt wieder". Die Nachkriegsjahre 1945/46 (= Ausstellungskataloge des Landesarchivs Berlin, 16), Berlin 2005, S. 7-43, hier S. 12-17.

[77] Siehe Dok. 74, Anm. 37.
[78] Siehe Dok. 27, Anm. 30, und Dok. 39, Anm. 23.
[79] Paul Markgraf. Siehe Dok. 27, Anm. 29.
[80] Arthur Pieck. Siehe Anm. 75.
[81] Siehe Dok. 30, Anm. 9.
[82] Siehe Dok. 39, Anm. 24.
[83] Seit 1938 hatte Ulbricht in der Sowjetunion gelebt.
[84] Siehe Dok. 39, Anm. 25.
[85] Siehe Dok. 39, Anm. 26.

was installed a central government dominated by men who can be considered as the agents of Russian policy. In the administration appointed to assist them in the central departments and in the districts of the city, it was inevitable that the Communists received a larger percentage of the jobs than their actual strength in the electorate warranted.

When the western Allies were finally admitted into Berlin,[86] and when in accordance with the terms worked out in the European Advisory Commission[87] in London, the Kommandatura was put to work,[88] the character of the Berlin *Magistrat* remained unchanged. The Red Army[89], understandable, would have considered it an unnecessary affront to have suggested that the government of the city would now have to be modified. In point of fact, except for its essentially undemocratic character, it was, as a temporary expedient, hardly as bad as that. In this spirit, and in the desire to get on with the new international control of the city, the western Allies went so far as to approve all that this Berlin government had previously done.[90] It may be questioned whether they knew quite

---

[86] Nachdem am 1. Juli 1945 der Rückzug der alliierten Truppen in die ihnen zugewiesenen Besatzungszonen begonnen hatte, konnte die Besetzung der westlichen Sektoren Berlins durch die Truppen der Westmächte erfolgen. Siehe Wolfgang Ribbe, Berlin 1945-2000. Grundzüge der Stadtgeschichte (= Kleine Schriftenreihe der Historischen Kommission zu Berlin, Heft 6), Berlin 2002, S. 28-30.

[87] Siehe Dok. 34, Anm. 15.

[88] Die Grundlage für die gemeinsame Verwaltung Berlins durch die Alliierten war mit dem sogenannten Londoner Protokoll, das die European Advisory Commission am 12. September 1944 vereinbart und am 14. November 1944 ergänzt hatte, und dem sogenannten Londoner Abkommen vom 14. November 1944 gelegt worden. Siehe Protokoll zwischen den Vereinigten Staaten, Großbritannien und der Sowjetunion vom 12. September 1944 über die Besatzungszonen in Deutschland und die Verwaltung von Groß-Berlin, in: Dokumente zur Berlin-Frage 1944-1966, mit einem Vorwort des Regierenden Bürgermeisters von Berlin, hrsg. vom Forschungsinstitut der Deutschen Gesellschaft für Auswärtige Politik e.V., Bonn, in Zusammenarbeit mit dem Senat von Berlin (= Schriften des Forschungsinstituts der Deutschen Gesellschaft für Auswärtige Politik e.V., Bonn, Reihe: Internationale Politik und Wirtschaft, Bd. 52/I), 4. Auflage, München 1987, Dok. 1; Abkommen zwischen den Vereinigten Staaten, Großbritannien und der Sowjetunion vom 14. November 1944 über Ergänzungen zu dem Protokoll vom 12. September 1944 über die Besatzungszonen von Deutschland und die Verwaltung von Groß-Berlin (Auszug), in: ebd., Dok. 2; Londoner Abkommen vom 14. November 1944 über die Kontrolleinrichtungen in Deutschland in der durch das Ergänzungsabkommen vom 1. Mai 1945 über den Beitritt der Französischen Republik abgeänderten Fassung (Auszug), in: ebd., Dok. 3. Bereits das Londoner Protokoll sah die Errichtung einer interalliierten Verwaltungsbehörde für Berlin (Kommandatura) vor. Im Londoner Abkommen war festgelegt, dass die Kommandatura unter der allgemeinen Leitung des Kontrollrats für Deutschland (siehe Dok. 14, Anm. 5) arbeiten und über das Koordinierungskomitee (siehe Dok. 15, Anm. 21) Befehle erhalten sollte.

[89] Bis 1946 die offizielle Bezeichnung für die Streitkräfte der Sowjetunion.

[90] Mit ihrem Befehl Nr. 1 vom 11. Juli 1945 ordnete die Alliierte Kommandantur an: „Alle früher vom Chef der Garnison und Militärkommandanten der Roten Armee der Stadt Berlin und von den unter alliierter Kontrolle stehenden deutschen Behörden ausgegebenen Befehle und Anordnungen, die die Ordnung und Haltung der Bevölkerung der Stadt Berlin regulieren, sowie die Verantwortung der Bevölkerung für die Verletzung der Befehle und Anordnungen und für gesetzwidrige Handlungen ge-

of what they were approving. When they came to understand it in part they were not satisfied with what they had approved. Yet it was difficult, if not impossible, to secure any very fundamental modifications by way of negotiation in the Kommandatura.[91] The only recourse left open to them was to keep close watch on the functioning of the central administration and, if necessary, to place obstacles in its way in their own national sectors of the city. At the moment that these avenues of action became open, the American reduction of the personnel engaged in military government in Berlin was so drastic that it was neither possible to keep close watch on the *Magistrat*, or to keep in close enough contact with what was going on in the American sector of Berlin, a sector whose population is approximately a million[92]. We had one liaison officer at the *Magistrat*[93], and four liaison officers in our six *Verwaltungsbezirke*[94]. What, moreover, had once been approved was somewhat sacred to the Soviet authorities. It was accordingly always a delicate matter to introduce local changes in the districts. It was, too, always a question of how far it was wise to go in breaking up the unity of a politically partial and none too efficient administration of the city. It was always embarrassing to have to admit that the international administration of a city meant it gradual separation into four parts. Yet this meant that the government remained the government which the Russians had set up, and that Berlin, instead of a fifth zone, was still a kind of capital of the Russian zone.

The city was always subject to the pressure of events in the Russian zone. All the central organizations for that zone were still located there.[95] It was no dis-

    gen die alliierten Okkupationstruppen betreffend, bleiben bis auf besondere Verfügung in Kraft." Berlin. Quellen und Dokumente 1945-1951, hrsg. im Auftrage des Senats von Berlin, bearb. durch Hans J. Reichhardt/Hanns U. Treutler/Albrecht Lampe (= Schriftenreihe zur Berliner Zeitgeschichte, Bd. 4/1. Halbbd.), Berlin 1964, Nr. 73. Die Westmächte erkannten somit die in der Phase der alleinigen sowjetischen Besatzung entstandenen Strukturen an.

[91] Beschlüsse konnten auf allen Ebenen der alliierten Verwaltung Berlins nur einstimmig gefasst werden.

[92] Siehe Dok. 61, Anm. 13.

[93] Verbindungsoffizier beim Magistrat war Joseph C. Joublanc (1894-1965), Lieutenant Colonel. Siehe Roster of Officers assigned to OMG BD, 25. Juni 1946, S. 1, in: LAB, B Rep. 036-01 (Office of Military Government, Berlin Sector [OMGBS]), 4/136-1/9.

[94] Es handelte sich um die Berliner Verwaltungsbezirke Steglitz (VBK 1), Zehlendorf (VBK 2), Kreuzberg (VBK 3), Tempelhof (VBK 4), Schöneberg (VBK 5) und Neukölln (VBK 6). Verbindungsoffiziere waren im Juni 1946 Lee H. Burnham, Major (Steglitz), Matthew J. Kasprzycki (1915-1984), Captain (Tempelhof und Neukölln), George F. Pawling, Major (Kreuzberg und Schöneberg) und John A. Sabo, Major (Zehlendorf). Siehe Roster of Officers assigned to OMG BD, 25. Juni 1946, S. 1 f., in: LAB, B Rep. 036-01 (Office of Military Government, Berlin Sector [OMGBS]), 4/136-1/9.

[95] Die aufgrund des Befehls Nr. 17 des Obersten Chefs der Sowjetischen Militärverwaltung in Deutschland vom 27. Juli 1945 errichteten Zentralverwaltungen in der sowjetischen Besatzungszone waren im sowjetischen Sektor Berlins untergebracht. Siehe Um ein antifaschistisch-demokratisches Deutschland. Dokumente aus den Jahren 1945-1949, Hrsg.: Ministerium für Auswärtige Angelegenheiten der DDR/Ministerium für Auswärtige Angelegenheiten der UdSSR, Berlin 1968, Dok. 32; Wolfgang Ribbe, Berlin 1945-2000. Grundzüge der Stadtgeschichte (= Kleine Schriftenreihe der Historischen Kommission zu Berlin, Heft 6), Berlin 2002, S. 31.

tance at all to the Russian headquarters at Karlshorst[96],[97] and it was no secret that Communist leaders, in and out of the *Magistrat*, went there for instructions. The political parties which had been organized for the Russian zone were identical with those of Berlin.[98] Indeed the leaders of these parties regarded themselves as national and not local leaders. Membership on national, zonal or purely Berlin executive boards was interchangeable. What was done in the Russian zone it was always felt had to be done in Berlin in order to complete or at least to restore the former unity. The zonal organization of the trade unions,[99] with a common governing board for Berlin, always took it for granted that what happened in the zone automatically happened in Berlin as it had before the introduction of quadripartite control. The zonal organization of youth,[100] wedged into the city in the Russian sector, took for granted its final assumption of the leadership of the Berlin youth. The whole press of the city, except finally for the Social Democratic press under English and French license,[101] and the American licensed *Tagesspiegel*[102] was under rigid Russian censorship. Nobody had been able to do anything effective about the Berlin radio[103]. It had always been a matter of astonishment to some observers that after the initiation of quadripartite government this radio remained what it was and where it was. It remained

---

[96] Ortsteil im Berliner Bezirk Lichtenberg.
[97] Im Befehl Nr. 1 des Obersten Chefs der Sowjetischen Militärverwaltung in Deutschland vom 9. Juni 1945 heißt es unter anderem: „Der Standort der Sowjetischen Militärverwaltung ist die Stadt Berlin." Befehle des Obersten Chefs der Sowjetischen Militärverwaltung in Deutschland. Aus dem Stab der Sowjetischen Militärverwaltung in Deutschland, Sammelheft 1: 1945, Berlin 1946, S. 9.
[98] Bereits am 10. Juni 1945 hatten die Sowjets in ihrem Besatzungsbereich – also in der sowjetischen Besatzungszone und Berlin – die Bildung und Tätigkeit „antifaschistischer" politischer Parteien erlaubt. Siehe Befehl Nr. 2 des Obersten Chefs der Sowjetischen Militärverwaltung in Deutschland vom 10. Juni 1945, in: ebd., S. 9f.
[99] Zum Freien Deutschen Gewerkschaftsbund (FDGB) siehe Dok. 49, Anm. 13.
[100] Zur Freien Deutschen Jugend (FDJ), die aus den antifaschistischen Jugendausschüssen hervorging, siehe Hermann Weber, Freie Deutsche Jugend (FDJ), in: SBZ-Handbuch. Staatliche Verwaltungen, Parteien, gesellschaftliche Organisationen und ihre Führungskräfte in der Sowjetischen Besatzungszone Deutschlands 1945-1949, im Auftrag des Arbeitsbereiches Geschichte und Politik der DDR an der Universität Mannheim und des Instituts für Zeitgeschichte München hrsg. von Martin Broszat/ Hermann Weber, München 1990, S. 665-690; Katharina Lange, Freie Deutsche Jugend (FDJ), in: Deutschland unter alliierter Besatzung 1945-1949/55, hrsg. von Wolfgang Benz, Berlin 1999, S. 264f.
[101] Mit der ersten britischen Zeitungslizenz in Berlin erschien seit dem 5. März 1946 das „Spandauer Volksblatt". Seit dem 22. März 1946 erschien die SPD-nahe, von der britischen Militärverwaltung lizensierte Zeitung „Telegraf". Ebenfalls mit Genehmigung der Briten gab die Berliner SPD seit dem 3. Juni 1946 die Tageszeitung „Der Sozialdemokrat" heraus. Französisch lizenziert war das seit dem 12. November 1945 erscheinende Abendblatt „Der Kurier". Siehe Berlin. Kampf um Freiheit und Selbstverwaltung 1945-1946, hrsg. im Auftrage des Senats von Berlin (= Schriftenreihe zur Berliner Zeitgeschichte, Bd. 1), 2., erg. und erw. Auflage, Berlin 1961, S. 259, Nr. 32; S. 378, Nr. 13; S. 393, Nr. 71, und S. 452, Nr. 7.
[102] „Der Tagesspiegel" erschien erstmals am 27. September 1945. Siehe ebd., S. 202, Nr. 85.
[103] Der von der sowjetischen Besatzungsmacht kontrollierte Berliner Rundfunk. Siehe Dok. 58, Anm. 19.

an essentially Russian station whose programs were subject to a kind of censorship which made German artists often furious when they were not more amused. This when Goethe[104] lyrics were interrupted and forbidden as fascist or militaristic. It remained in the *Rundfunkhaus*[105] in the British sector where it had always been, and why, without any change in status or character the British permitted it to remain there, nobody quite understood. It was always the Russian theory that this was a radio originally set up for the Russian zone, and that quadripartite control of the city made no difference.

Thus one had in Berlin the European situation in miniature. In the Russian zone about the city, into which no ordinary mortal thought of trespassing, the Soviet authorities were carrying out long prepared plans for introducing as much of the Soviet system as they could, or preparing by gradual stages for its introduction. There was no doubt about this. My Russian friend told me when I accused him of it that he was not one of those Russians who was so absurd as to think it could be done. The pattern, however, was unmistakable, and the methods, to Germans and western Allies alike, so repugnantly familiar. It was difficult to feel that our Soviet ally, in spite of all her protestations, was much concerned with what happened to Germans or to Germany. It had been the same in Austria where Americans were inclined to take the Moscow Declaration[106] seriously. It was easy from the past to understand this point of view, but to one who had hopes of cultivating a better future, this cynical, one is almost tempted to say unscrupulous realism, was disheartening. If, however, they were not seriously concerned with the German future, they would have the German people believe that they were the only power who was so concerned. Certainly any German future in which they would be interested would have to be within the Russian orbit, and as close to the Communist order as possible. The Germans must be convinced of the necessity, the superiority, and the inevitability of this outcome by the use of every kind of persuasion. The German peasant and working man, the future social foundations of whatever German state there might be, must be weaned from the attraction of American capitalism and English socialism, both associated with certain democratic liberties. In the Russian controlled papers in Berlin, Communist or otherwise, little was left undone to discredit these powers for what they were doing in Germany, at home, or elsewhere in the world. No American who read the Berlin daily press (and there were not enough of them) but who was regularly antagonized by the cynical distortion of the news, and by the abject following of the Russian lead by the German Communists and the Berlin radio.

At the same time that in the Russian zone society was being remodeled by the agrarian reform[107], by the dismantling of German industry[108], and by the

---

[104] Siehe Dok. 52, Anm. 30.
[105] Haus des Rundfunks. Siehe Dok. 58, Anm. 19.
[106] Siehe Anm. 1.
[107] Die im September 1945 unter der Losung „Junkerland in Bauernhand" improvisierte Bodenreform entmachtete durch die entschädigungslose Enteignung des privaten Grundbesitzes über 100 ha dauerhaft eine traditionelle soziale und politische Elite und veränderte grundlegend die ländliche Besitz- und Gesellschaftsstruktur. Siehe Günter J. Trittel, Bodenreform, in: Deutschland unter alliierter Besatzung 1945–1949/55, hrsg. von Wolfgang Benz, Berlin 1999, S. 105–108.

socialization of remaining industries, formerly belonging to Nazis or war profiteers or those whom local committees decided to expropriate,[109] the attack on the inert, weary, and hungry German mind and body began. The watchword was always unity – *Einheit*. The word that had done more than any one thing to ruin the German people[110] was now dinned into their ears again with such sickening frequency and such hollow mockery that it drove many to seek security in the far removed centuries of the worst feudal anarchy. These wondrously patriotic perorations, these touching appeals to human brotherhood were made to beaten, broken, bent, and bewildered Germans by stooges who were kept fat and sleek by the special gift packages and extra rations of their Soviet paymasters. The belly of Pieck lost none of its bulk, the goatee of Ulbricht none of its trim, the voice of Fechner[111] none of its bark, and the gleam of Grotewohl's[112] eyes nothing but its trustworthiness, as they beat the tom-tom for the Germans to go through their paces.

It was first the unity of unpolitical trade unions preached by a shrewd, exasperating and Communist Jendretsky[113], who preferred to thumb his nose at American military government rather than to work with it. There followed the political unity of the working classes.[114] The great love of the Communists for their Social Democratic comrades, so plain to the careful student of the

---

[108] Die Sowjetunion demontierte in ihrer Besatzungszone und Berlin rund 3470 Objekte, 5 114 000 t Material wurden abtransportiert. Siehe http://www.zzf-pdm.de/site/mid__2870/ModeID__0/EhPageID__303/369/default.aspx (letzter Zugriff am 30. Januar 2013). Siehe auch Werner Bührer, Reparationen, in: Deutschland unter alliierter Besatzung 1945–1949/55, hrsg. von Wolfgang Benz, Berlin 1999, S. 161–167.

[109] Siehe Elke Scherstjanoi, Sowjetische Besatzungspolitik, in: Deutschland unter alliierter Besatzung 1945–1949/55, hrsg. von Wolfgang Benz, Berlin 1999, S. 73–89, hier S. 86; Befehl Nr. 124 des Obersten Chefs der Sowjetischen Militärverwaltung in Deutschland vom 30. Oktober 1945, in: Befehle des Obersten Chefs der Sowjetischen Militärverwaltung in Deutschland. Aus dem Stab der Sowjetischen Militärverwaltung in Deutschland, Sammelheft 1: 1945, Berlin 1946, S. 20–22; Befehl Nr. 126 des Obersten Chefs der Sowjetischen Militärverwaltung in Deutschland vom 31. Oktober 1945, in: Um ein antifaschistisch-demokratisches Deutschland. Dokumente aus den Jahren 1945–1949, Hrsg.: Ministerium für Auswärtige Angelegenheiten der DDR/Ministerium für Auswärtige Angelegenheiten der UdSSR, Berlin 1968, Dok. 72; Befehl Nr. 97 des Obersten Chefs der Sowjetischen Militärverwaltung in Deutschland vom 29. März 1946, in: ebd., Dok. 96.

[110] Johnson denkt hier offenbar an das Gesetz zur Sicherung der Einheit von Partei und Staat vom 1. Dezember 1933 (in: Reichsgesetzblatt, Teil I, 1933, S. 1016), mit dem der nationalsozialistische Einparteienstaat rechtlich verankert wurde.

[111] Siehe Dok. 39, Anm. 29.

[112] Siehe Dok. 30, Anm. 8.

[113] Hans Jendretzky (1897–1992), deutscher Politiker (KPD/SED), 1919 USPD, 1920 KPD, 1928–1932 MdL Preußen, 1945/1946 Leiter der Magistratsabteilung für Arbeitseinsatz bzw. für Arbeit, Mitunterzeichner des Gründungsaufrufs des vorbereitenden Gewerkschaftsausschusses für Groß-Berlin vom 15. Juni 1945, bis Anfang Februar 1946 provisorischer 1. Vorsitzender des Berliner FDGB, Februar 1946–1948 1. Vorsitzender des FDGB-Bundesvorstands, 1946 SED, 1948–1953 1. Sekretär der Landesleitung bzw. Bezirksleitung Groß-Berlin der SED, 1950–1954 und 1958–1990 Mitglied der Volkskammer der DDR, 1990 PDS.

[114] Gemeint ist die Vereinigung von KPD und SPD zur SED.

history of the German working class, was now to find its fulfillment in the great effacement. The Communist party would simply disappear. The Social Democratic party would do likewise. Out of this mutual and magical disappearance would come a new mystic fusion, – the Socialist Unity Party of Germany (Sozialistische Einheitspartei Deutschlands – SED). The gates to a new paradise, the paradise being established in the Russian zone, would now be opened.

It was then the unity of unpolitical youth. The wasteful competition of rival political and religious youth movements was to yield to a cooperative movement, properly guided and disciplined by Communists from above. It was finally the unity of the German women.[115] One trade union, one political party, one youth movement, one women's organization, it all had a familiar ring. It would have been more exciting had it been more spontaneous. Still the awful and frightening thing was the pressure, real and threatened, yes, even the terror. These unities were what one of the occupying powers wanted, was determined to have, knew how to get. There were privileges for those who knew how to comply and penalties for those who refused. The NKVD[116] was active. People disappeared and things happened to them. One knew about specific cases. People were watched. They were questioned. They came pleading for protection. This was the system that was crowding in on quadripartite Berlin from the Russian zone and the Russian sector. Could it be stopped? Could it be modified? Could East and West really come together in the city?

III

My orientation along the highways and by-ways of OMGUS was interrupted when it was suggested that I go to help with the situation in Berlin by acting as a political adviser to the commanding general[117]. It was late March. The politi-

---

[115] Zunächst hatten sich Frauen in antifaschistischen Frauenausschüssen zusammengeschlossen. Die sowjetische Besatzungsmacht strebte die Gründung eines einzigen Frauenbundes an, und im März 1947 wurde in Berlin der Demokratische Frauenbund Deutschlands gegründet. Siehe Gerda Weber, Demokratischer Frauenbund Deutschlands (DFD), in: SBZ-Handbuch. Staatliche Verwaltungen, Parteien, gesellschaftliche Organisationen und ihre Führungskräfte in der Sowjetischen Besatzungszone Deutschlands 1945–1949, im Auftrag des Arbeitsbereiches Geschichte und Politik der DDR an der Universität Mannheim und des Instituts für Zeitgeschichte München hrsg. von Martin Broszat/Hermann Weber, München 1990, S. 691–713; Katrin Wehry, Demokratischer Frauenbund Deutschlands (DFD), in: Deutschland unter alliierter Besatzung 1945–1949/55, hrsg. von Wolfgang Benz, Berlin 1999, S. 244f.

[116] NKWD (Narodny Komissariat Wnutrennich Del, Volkskommissariat für Inneres), 1934 gebildetes sowjetisches Unionsministerium, dem als wichtigstes Ressort die GPU (Gossudarstwennoje Polititscheskoje Uprawlenije), die politische Geheimpolizei, eingegliedert war; zuständig vor allem für politische Überwachung, Nachrichtendienst, politische Strafjustiz, Verwaltung der Straf- und Verbannungslager, Grenzschutz; war das Instrument des stalinistischen Terrors zur Zeit der Großen Tschistka (1935–1939).

[117] Commanding General, US Headquarters Berlin District, war Ray W. Barker. Siehe Dok. 20, Anm. 10.

cal atmosphere of the city was tense. To be sure the Christian Democratic Union[118] and the Liberal Democratic Party[119] were safely hamstrung by the limitations put upon their activity by the Soviet authorities. In the political camp of the workers, however, revolt was in the air. The drive conducted by the Soviet authorities for the unification of the Communist and the Social Democratic parties into the new Socialist Unity Party was reaching its climax.[120] The Soviet authorities had evidently decided that the union must be completed by May first, and every step was being taken to meet this schedule. The pressure in the Russian zone was so great that the Social Democrats there had been completely intimidated. Under no circumstances had it been necessary to intimidate the Communists, whose prospects with the new party were so fair, whose power so enlarged, and whose rewards so great, that, except possibly for a very few, they needed no prodding from their Russian overlords. The international occupation of Berlin, however, made it possible for the Social Democrats there to resist the pressure of the Soviets upon their party leaders. They were quite willing to prove false the assumption that what could be done in the Russian zone could be done also in Berlin. A principle of party organization was at stake. Could a party executive irrespective of the wishes of its members, determine the future of the party? Could it alone decide that the party was no longer to exist? The independents said no. At a meeting of party functionaries on the first of March[121] they decided upon the simple democratic expedient of taking a vote of all members of the Social Democratic Party (they called it an *Urabstimmung*) on whether they desired an immediate amalgamation with the Communist Party. The vote was to be taken on the thirty-first of March.

The official policy of the United States Government in all internal German political struggles was neutrality. This was a policy which some Americans could not understand. It was rather obvious to them that there was no such thing as political neutrality. To the extent that this meant political indifference it was undesirable. If it means, as it meant to many military government officers when they were first called upon to establish German or Austrian governments, reliance upon officials who claimed to adhere to no political party, this was only to put into power political amorality which in practice usually meant political reaction. If a policy of political neutrality meant that the American government did not care which party came to control Germany, this view was short sighted. In the present situation, however, the doctrine of political neu-

---

[118] Zur CDU siehe Dok. 21, Anm. 29, und Dok. 44, Anm. 11.
[119] Zur LDP siehe Dok. 44, Anm. 10.
[120] Auf die SPD wurde massiver Vereinigungsdruck ausgeübt, repressive Maßnahmen der sowjetischen Besatzungsmacht gegen sozialdemokratische Gegner einer Fusion von SPD und KPD zur SED reichten bis hin zu Verhaftungen. Siehe Dok. 30.
[121] Funktionärskonferenz der Berliner SPD am 1. März 1946 im Admiralspalast im Bezirk Mitte, Friedrichstraße 101/102. Siehe Berlin. Kampf um Freiheit und Selbstverwaltung 1945-1946, hrsg. im Auftrage des Senats von Berlin (= Schriftenreihe zur Berliner Zeitgeschichte, Bd. 1), 2., erg. und erw. Auflage, Berlin 1961, S. 374f., Nr. 5; Harold Hurwitz unter Mitarbeit von Andreas Büning/Johannes-Berthold Hohmann/Klaus Sühl/Ingolore Mensch-Khan, Die Anfänge des Widerstands, Teil 2: Zwischen Selbsttäuschung und Zivilcourage: Der Fusionskampf (= Demokratie und Antikommunismus in Berlin nach 1945, Bd. IV), Köln 1990, S. 1022-1030.

trality conflicted with the democratic doctrine we were also called upon to uphold. It conflicted as well with the program of international cooperation. It was clear that in this Berlin struggle the Communists, and the pro-merger Social Democrats who had gone over to them, were using methods which under no circumstances could be called democratic. The idea of an *Urabstimmung* corresponded altogether too simply to our notions of democratic procedure to call forth any kind of a protest. Therefore in supporting the right of the Social Democrats to take this vote, we had to oppose the Communists and their Social Democratic hangers-on, who were denying it. In so doing we were opposing our Soviet ally, who wanted nothing more anxiously than to see this merger carried through speedily and without opposition. There had always been, of course, the academic question of the respective nature of democracy as used by the Soviets and ourselves. It was instructive, therefore, to observe that in supporting what we felt instinctively to be democratic we were running head on into the Russians. There was more, however, in the struggle than supporting what we felt to be democratic. We were supporting also what we felt to be a little heroic. Elsewhere the Social Democrats had lacked the courage to fight this superimposed unity. In Berlin, at considerable risk to themselves, this courage was not lacking. Men like Otto Suhr[122], the present General Secretary of the Berlin Social Democrats, gave up their jobs with the Russian zonal administration in order to take up the fight.[123] These were the kind of Germans we wanted to support, the kind in whose hands a future Germany ought to be. They seemed to have learned something from the abdication of the Social Democrats in 1933.[124]

Mr. Grotewohl, and the members of his purged Executive Committee[125], unwilling to trust the results of a referendum, tried to thwart it. They did not succeed. When it showed that they had been repudiated they tried to misinterpret it. This only showed to what lengths they were willing to go. The fact that the referendum was not held in the Russian sector of Berlin only made the fundamental issue clearer. In Berlin the Social Democratic Party continued to exist. In Berlin the Russian plans had for the moment been halted. They had been halted by a vote.

This snag in the program of a speedy amalgamation brought a change in the person of the Russian commander-in-chief for Berlin. General Smirnov[126]

---

[122] Siehe Dok. 40, Anm. 7.
[123] Otto Suhr war bis März 1946 Hauptabteilungsleiter bei der Deutschen Zentralverwaltung der Industrie in der sowjetischen Besatzungszone und wurde nach der Neukonstituierung der Berliner SPD deren Generalsekretär.
[124] Die SPD war am 22. Juni 1933 verboten worden. Zuvor hatte sie einen Anpassungskurs eingeschlagen, ohne das Parteiverbot verhindern zu können. Siehe Ossip K. Flechtheim, Die Anpassung der SPD: 1914, 1933 und 1959, in: Politologie und Soziologie. Otto Stammer zum 65. Geburtstag, hrsg. von Jürgen Fijalkowski, Köln und Opladen 1965, S. 182–202.
[125] Zentralausschuss der SPD, das für die sowjetische Besatzungszone und Berlin zuständige Leitungsgremium der SPD, von dem sich die Vereinigungsgegner getrennt hatten.
[126] Siehe Dok. 25, Anm. 23.

brought along with him in early April General Kotikov[127],[128] who, it was understood, had successfully managed the merger in Saxony[129].[130] The new general was tall and good-looking, if somewhat flabby. His white hair was streaked with yellow. His face was usually weary and troubled, and it seemed anxious for the occasion when it could break into a smile. Obviously he was a hard worker and a hard fighter. When the Social Democrats, reorganized after their democratic revolt, repudiated their old and elected new leaders, and proposed to the Kommandatura the recognition of their efforts,[131] the General, with a certain amount of scornful indifference, would not hear of it. These new leaders were, he said, unknown to him. Although he must have known that he could hardly be believed, he asserted that he was unfamiliar with the political situation in Berlin and that he was not able to discuss the question. He preferred evidently to await developments. Yet he must also have realized that if the new and as yet unrecognized Socialist Unity Party wished to organize throughout Berlin the same privilege would have to be accorded to the reorganized Social Democratic Party. One couldn't encourage a revolt and still permit it to be crushed.

Accordingly, until the SED was officially recognized, it was not permitted to organize in the western sectors of the city, while, at the same time, the new leadership of the Social Democrats was permitted to take over the old organization in these sectors. The Soviet authorities soon recognized the situation. In order to facilitate the organization of the SED in all Berlin they were soon anxious to accord recognition to the Social Democrats they had hoped to obliterate. The empty formalities of conventions completing the merger in both the Russian zone and Berlin were nevertheless carried out. At the final meeting[132] Mr. Pieck and Mr. Grotewohl staged the dramatic scene of standing with clasped hands while the audience rose.[133] General Kotikov was sitting in the royal box.

[127] Siehe Dok. 35, Anm. 5.
[128] Am 2. April 1946 stellte Generalleutnant Smirnow in der Sitzung der alliierten Stadtkommandanten Generalmajor Kotikow als seinen Nachfolger vor. Siehe Die 32. (10. im Jahre 1946) Sitzung der Alliierten Kommandantur der Stadt Berlin. Generalmajor A. G. Kotikow – neuer Kommandant des sowjetischen Sektors der Stadt Berlin. Kommuniqué, in: Tägliche Rundschau vom 3. April 1946, S. 1.
[129] Provinz Sachsen(-Anhalt).
[130] Kotikow war 1945–März 1946 Chef der Verwaltung der Sowjetischen Militäradministration der Provinz Sachsen(-Anhalt) in Halle gewesen.
[131] Die Vereinigungsgegner veranstalteten am 7. April 1946 einen Parteitag in der Zehlendorfer Zinnowwald-Schule, auf dem sie einen eigenen Bezirksvorstand wählten. Dieser beantragte am 8. April die Lizenzierung der neukonstituierten Berliner SPD bei der Alliierten Kommandantur. Siehe Die Sitzungsprotokolle des Magistrats der Stadt Berlin 1945/46. Teil II: 1946, bearb. und eingel. von Dieter Hanauske (= Schriftenreihe des Landesarchivs Berlin, Bd. 2/II), Berlin 1999, S. 6.
[132] Gemeint ist der Vereinigungsparteitag von KPD und SPD am 21./22. April 1946 in der damaligen Spielstätte der Deutschen Staatsoper, im Admiralspalast im Berliner Verwaltungsbezirk Mitte, Friedrichstraße 101/102. Siehe Dok. 39, Anm. 19.
[133] „Das Orchester spielte die Fidelio-Ouvertüre von Ludwig van Beethoven [siehe Dok. 37, Anm. 29]. Einige Minuten später kamen Wilhelm Pieck und Otto Grotewohl von verschiedenen Seiten auf die Bühne, trafen sich in der Mitte und reichten sich unter minutenlangem stürmischem Beifall die Hände." So die Schilderung von Wolfgang Leonhard, Die Revolution entläßt ihre Kinder, 8. Auflage, München 1985,

When recognition for both parties finally came,[134] it turned out to be but the beginning of another phase of the struggle. The Soviet authorities were not willing to permit the Social Democrats to organize in the Russian sector in quite the same way as the SED was being permitted to organize in other sectors of the city. If the Social Democrats could not be prohibited they could be controlled. Some Social Democrats disappeared.[135] The newly elected leaders of the Party in the various districts in the Russian sector were not recognized if they had displayed an attitude called 'anti-Soviet' or 'anti-Red Army'. The essential test of this attitude was whether the elected leaders had been for or against the merger. The Social Democrats were faced with a nice dilemma: how could a party which had been born out of opposition to the fusion choose leaders which had not opposed the fusion. At the same moment a larger issue was raised. The SED leaders, with the consent of the western Allies, were beginning their invasion of the western zones. I heard them shouting in the ruined market place of Nürnberg and wondered if the event were symbolic. Social Democrats there were amazed. The Soviets had destroyed the Social Democrats in their zone. There was no question of western Social Democrats going into the Russian zone to reorganize the fold. Even if invited they would have been afraid to go and run the risk of simply disappearing. It was suggested, therefore, that the Soviet authorities might again see the point if no SED activity were permitted in the West for as long as no Social Democratic activity were permitted in the East. Yet something had been done in Berlin to relieve the pressure from the East, and it had been done finally with the reluctant consent of the East. The iron grip of unity, uniformity and unanimity had been loosened, and this because there were four powers instead of one.

IV

In the course of the battle over the merger the question of elections for Berlin had arisen. It was clearly recognized by the American authorities uninterested in preserving for an unnecessarily long period the regime of the existing *Magistrat*, that the simplest way to undo this regime was to prepare for elections for a new municipal government. It was a program which the Americans could pur-

---

S. 386. Der Händedruck zwischen Pieck und Grotewohl besiegelte symbolisch die Vereinigung von KPD und SPD. Als Emblem wurden die ineinander verschlungenen Hände das Parteiabzeichen der SED.

[134] Da in der Alliierten Kommandantur keine Einigung über die Zulassungsanträge von SED und neukonstituierter SPD erzielt werden konnte, wurde die Angelegenheit dem Koordinierungskomitee der Alliierten Kontrollbehörde vorgelegt. Dort vereinbarten die Vertreter der vier Mächte am 28. Mai 1946, SED und SPD in ganz Berlin zuzulassen. Dementsprechend genehmigte die Alliierte Kommandantur die Zulassung und Tätigkeit beider Parteien in allen vier Sektoren. Siehe BK/O (46) 248 vom 31. Mai 1946, in: LAB, F Rep. 280 (Quellensammlung zur Berliner Zeitgeschichte [LAZ-Sammlung]), Nr. 4865.

[135] Es verschwanden beispielsweise Hermann Löwenthal und Julius Scherff. Siehe Dok. 71, Anm. 25.

sue with propriety inasmuch as they had already instituted the series of elections in their zone which aimed at creating popular governments.[136] Although the British and French were not to hold elections in their zones until the autumn,[137] they were willing to see earlier elections in Berlin. The Soviet authorities, however, for as long as the political situation remained unclarified, were unwilling to touch the question of elections, and prepared a most elaborate and irrelevant defence against them. When, it was settled that the SED was to be permitted to spread throughout Berlin, and the date for their own municipal elections in their zone had been decided upon,[138] they came quickly and easily to an agreement on an election date. It was later than the western Allies had wanted, but it was earlier than had first been suggested by Soviet officials.

If there were to be elections in October,[139] then the Local Government Committee of the Kommandatura[140] would have to rouse itself from its lethargy to produce a constitution for Berlin, and an electoral ordinance in accordance with which such elections might be held. This Committee had been standing still for months. It had been standing still because the Soviet authorities had not decided upon the main lines of their policy on these matters. It was the Russian representative's job to keep the Committee inert until these decisions were made. Everybody like the Russian Major[141]. He was short, stocky and black-haired.

---

[136] In der amerikanischen Besatzungszone Deutschlands hatten im Januar 1946 Kommunalwahlen in den kleineren Gemeinden stattgefunden (siehe Dok. 40, Anm. 35), es folgten Wahlen zu Kreistagen sowie in den größeren Gemeinden und für die Stadtkreise (siehe Dok. 58, Anm. 21). Siehe Conrad F. Latour/Thilo Vogelsang, Okkupation und Wiederaufbau. Die Tätigkeit der Militärregierung in der amerikanischen Besatzungszone Deutschlands 1944–1947 (Studien zur Zeitgeschichte), Stuttgart 1973, S. 109–111; Wolfram Werner, Wahlen, in: Deutschland unter alliierter Besatzung 1945–1949/55, hrsg. von Wolfgang Benz, Berlin 1999, S. 194–200.

[137] Am 15. September 1946 fanden Gemeindewahlen in den Ländern der britischen (siehe Dok. 50, Anm. 21) und der französischen Besatzungszone Deutschlands statt. Siehe Keesing's Archiv der Gegenwart, XVI. Jg., 1946, S. 868 A und C. Es folgten am 13. Oktober 1946 in der britischen Zone Landkreis- und Stadtkreiswahlen, Bürgerschaftswahlen in Bremen und Hamburg, in der französischen Zone Wahlen für die Kreisversammlungen. Siehe ebd., S. 895 G und H sowie 896 A. Am 17. November 1946 wählten in der französischen Zone die Mitglieder der Kreistage und die Vertreter der Gemeinderäte von Städten über 7000 Einwohnern in zwei Wahlkörpern die beratenden Landesversammlungen der drei Länder, die zugleich verfassunggebende Versammlungen waren. Siehe ebd., S. 927f. E.

[138] Die Gemeindewahlen in der sowjetischen Besatzungszone Deutschlands fanden am 1. September 1946 in Sachsen statt, am 8. September in Sachsen-Anhalt und Thüringen und am 15. September in Brandenburg und Mecklenburg. Siehe Keesing's Archiv der Gegenwart, XVI. Jg., 1946, S. 859 C, 863 G und 868 B.

[139] Am 29. Mai 1946 hatten sich die Mitglieder des Politischen Direktorats, Alliierte Kontrollbehörde, darauf geeinigt, im Oktober 1946 Wahlen durchführen zu lassen. Siehe Protokoll der 38. Sitzung des Politischen Direktorats, Alliierte Kontrollbehörde, am 29. Mai 1946, DPOL/M (46) 21-192, französischsprachige Fassung, in: AOF, Services Français à Berlin, GFCC, Bureau des Archives, caisse 1140, paquet 51; Werner Breunig, Verfassunggebung in Berlin 1945–1950 (= Beiträge zur Politischen Wissenschaft, Bd. 58), Berlin 1990, S. 182.

[140] Siehe Dok. 29, Anm. 14.

[141] Iossif Moissejewitsch Feldman. Siehe Dok. 49, Anm. 59.

His studies in the law had been interrupted by the war in which he had covered himself with glory. His chest bore an impressive array of Soviet decorations. His superiors, however, did not give him much latitude in the conduct of the negotiations in the Committee. It was clear too that the little, and at times somewhat belligerent Major was terrified of his superiors. It was rumored at least that his predecessor on the Committee[142] had been given other work to do because he was unnecessarily conciliatory. The combination of legal logic and Marxist logic served well to cover up what some members of the Committee felt were purely dilatory tactics. In any case the Major could waste more time in correcting the minutes of the previous meeting than probably any other person in Berlin. If, in the preparation of any document or report there was more than a word or a comma to insert, his efforts to get the decision postponed until the next meeting were often clumsy and obvious. Yet those of us who had no such superiors, who were left comparatively free to come to agreements, were sympathetic with the Major's plight, even though at times, the lack of agility of his mind seemed to explain the circumspection of his superiors. At any rate if a constitution were to be produced in a hurry he would have to have help. At the last moment this was supplied in the person of an academic colonel[143]. The new colonel was the principal of a little school in the Caucasus. His graduate studies had been interrupted at the moment when he was about to take his doctorate. His thesis on some phase of the history of the Caucasus region was waiting to be published. He was an atheist and a Communist, the son of a working man, and proud of what the Soviet state had done for him and for simple people like him. His superiors evidently trusted his ability for it was clear upon his first appearance that he had been given instructions to agree upon a constitution for Berlin. In the subsequent sessions the little Major was little more than a secretary. The Colonel carried on the argument, made the speeches and the concessions.

It was, nevertheless, somewhat anomalous that this Committee should presume to act as a constitutional assembly for the city of Berlin. Except for the French representative[144], none of the regular members of the Committee know very much German,[145] nor were they any too conversant with the constitutional history of the city. They had passed off the preliminary work to the *Magistrat* with an order that it was to prepare, on the basis of the constitutional laws be-

---

[142] Sein Vorgänger war Hauptmann Kasatkin. Siehe Die Entstehung der Verfassung von Berlin. Eine Dokumentation, Bd. I, im Auftrag des Präsidenten des Abgeordnetenhauses von Berlin hrsg. von Hans J. Reichhardt unter Mitarbeit von Werner Breunig/Josephine Gabler, Berlin und New York 1990, Dok. 37, S. 242, Dok. 44, S. 255, und Dok. 45, S. 256. Der britische Vertreter im Local Government Committee, Harold Hays (siehe Dok. 49, Anm. 26), erinnert sich später an Kasatkin: "[...] a geologist with little or no knowledge of constitutional matters. He was a very charming man, quiet, tactful, and helpful, but was obviously working strictly according to instructions". Erinnerungen von Harold Hays, Chapter 10: Berlin Constitution 1946, S. 145, in: IWM Duxford, Lieutenant Colonel Harold Hays MBE Collection.

[143] Es handelte sich um Alexandr Michailowitsch Sosulja. Siehe Dok. 67, Anm. 28.

[144] Jean Victor Ziegelmeyer. Siehe Dok. 55, Anm. 4.

[145] Der französische Vertreter im Komitee war ein Elsässer, der einer alten Colmarer Familie entstammte.

fore 1933, the draft of a temporary constitution for the city.[146] This meant that after some preliminary discussions as to what the constitution was to contain, the actual drafting was left to the only technically competent member of this body, the very busy acting treasurer of the city, Dr. Friedrich Haas[147], who, it can be easily understood, in spite of his preliminary work upon the question, was obliged to prepare this draft somewhat hurriedly.[148] To the Soviet representatives it was a draft prepared by their Magistrat. To the British representatives, when once they learned how quickly it had been drafted,[149] it was an impossible text. They proposed instead that the texts of the Municipal Ordinance of 1857[150], the Constitution of 1920[151], and the amendments of 1931[152], be used as the basis of discussion. This last proposal was clearly impossible if a constitution were to be produced at all. The British representative was finally beaten down by the other members of the Committee. He withdrew his proposal upon the threat that a report be made to the Commandants that the Committee could not agree on how to begin to discuss a constitution for Berlin.

The draft constitution of Berlin began to be discussed paragraph by paragraph. It was not easy. The interpreters were not so expert that they could always reproduce in another tongue the very precise meaning of the original language. One therefore often had the feeling that he was agreeing to what he thought he understood. It was, of course, not enough to understand and agree with each other in three different languages. It was necessary also to agree upon the wording of the German text and this involved the use of additional interpreters. This produced at moments almost inextricable crises. The Soviet delegates at one point discovered that they had agreed to a clause providing that

---

[146] Den ersten Magistratsentwurf einer vorläufigen Verfassung, der am 16. Januar 1946 der Alliierten Kommandantur zur Genehmigung übermittelt worden war, hatte das Local Government Committee am 8. Februar 1946 abgelehnt. Mit BK/O (46) 144 vom 28. März 1946 wurde der Magistrat angewiesen, bis zum 1. Mai 1946 einen neuen Verfassungsentwurf auszuarbeiten, der auf dem Gesetz über die Bildung einer neuen Stadtgemeinde Berlin vom 27. April 1920 (in: Preußische Gesetzsammlung, 1920, S. 123-150) und dem Gesetz über die vorläufige Regelung verschiedener Punkte des Gemeindeverfassungsrechts für die Hauptstadt Berlin vom 30. März 1931 (in: Preußische Gesetzsammlung, 1931, S. 39-44), soweit diese demokratischen Grundsätzen entsprach, basieren sollte. Siehe Werner Breunig, Verfassunggebung in Berlin 1945-1950 (= Beiträge zur Politischen Wissenschaft, Bd. 58), Berlin 1990, S. 154-169.

[147] Siehe Dok. 49, Anm. 40.

[148] Siehe Dok. 74, Anm. 29.

[149] Für die Ausarbeitung des neuen Verfassungsentwurfs hatte nur ein Monat zur Verfügung gestanden. Siehe Werner Breunig, Verfassunggebung in Berlin 1945-1950 (= Beiträge zur Politischen Wissenschaft, Bd. 58), Berlin 1990, S. 169.

[150] Gemeint ist die Städte-Ordnung für die sechs östlichen Provinzen der Preußischen Monarchie vom 30. Mai 1853, in: Gesetz-Sammlung für die Königlichen Preußischen Staaten, 1853, S. 261-290.

[151] Gemeint ist das Gesetz über die Bildung einer neuen Stadtgemeinde Berlin vom 27. April 1920. Siehe Anm. 146.

[152] Gemeint ist das Gesetz über die vorläufige Regelung verschiedener Punkte des Gemeindeverfassungsrechts für die Hauptstadt Berlin vom 30. März 1931. Siehe Anm. 146.

the members of the newly elected *Magistrat* were to take on oath to administer their offices impartially. The German word was *unparteiisch*. The Russian colonel understood this German word to mean unpolitically. He could not understand therefore how a member of the *Magistrat*, elected from a political party, could be expected to administer his office unpolitically. When, after prolonged discussion, he was convinced that *unparteiisch* meant impartial at the same time.[153] For those who fret over the seeming lack of speed in the conduct of international negotiations it is to reflect whether it is not remarkable that they can be conducted at all.

The necessity for meeting in long sessions at frequent intervals soon broke down whatever official character there was to these meetings. The members of the Committee became friends. As meeting after meeting passed and every difficulty was settled, it became clear that no difficulty was to be too great; the Committee would come out with an agreed report. It was not only necessary to work and argue and discuss together. It was also necessary to eat and drink together, now at one mess and now at another. During the last month[154] the Russians were in the chair, and their luncheons at the Kommandatura became notoriously strenuous. The Russians liked late luncheons. The tables were heavy with bottles. Vodka made from the best German potatoes, vermouth, and General Zhukov's[155] beer, reputed to be 12 %. This, when mixed with caviar, smoked salmon, borsch, and sour cream dressing, broke down the staid character of the conversation and relaxed the negotiations for what was left of the afternoon's work. "What did the Russian papers mean when they accused America of atomic diplomacy?"[156] If the Soviet representatives were hungry for all views on contemporary events why didn't they simply subscribe to the London[157] or the New York Times[158]? Would our Russian friends ever come to see us in America or we them in Russia? Was it possible then that there would be another war this time between East and West? If the Local Government Committee had the world in its hands there would be no such war. Back in the Committee room, the question of whether the Germans should be permitted to hold secret sessions of their councils became less serious when the French (represented in Germany only by Alsatians[159]) explained that in Colmar[160], his home town, the municipal council used to hold secret sessions. His father[161], however, was the

---

[153] Siehe hierzu Dok. 77, Anm. 9.
[154] Juli 1946.
[155] Georgi Konstantinowitsch Schukow (1896–1974), Marschall der Sowjetunion, 1919 WKP(B), nahm am 8. Mai 1945 als Oberbefehlshaber der 1. Belorussischen Front die Kapitulation der deutschen Wehrmacht entgegen, 1945–März 1946 Oberbefehlshaber der Gruppe der sowjetischen Besatzungsstreitkräfte in Deutschland und Oberster Chef der SMAD, 1955–1957 Minister für Verteidigung der Sowjetunion.
[156] Siehe Dok. 70.
[157] Gemeint ist "The Times", eine britische Tageszeitung, die manchmal als "The London Times" oder "The Times of London" bezeichnet wird.
[158] Amerikanische Tageszeitung.
[159] Elsässer wurden gerne wegen ihrer Deutschkenntnisse in Deutschland eingesetzt.
[160] Stadt im Elsass.
[161] Joseph Ziegelmeyer (1877–1947), 1935–1940 und 1945 1. Stellvertreter des Bürgermeisters, Colmar.

mayor of Colmar and after every secret session he reported its discussion and conclusions to his wife[162], and the secrecy was not long maintained. The British were inclined to grow more lyrical about the superiority of their own municipal and governmental institutions. Did we realize what a fine charter the city of Liverpool[163] possessed, and how good it would be for Berlin, it was intimated, if some features of this charter could be imported from England? Was it not just a little bit ordinary to permit the elected chairman of the new city assembly to be called a mere "Vorsitzende"? Now take the example of the Speaker of the House of Commons.[164] He did not speak but on ceremonial occasions he marched before the Prime Minister.

The Constitution for Berlin was in fact becoming less and less German and more and more international. The fact that the existing *Magistrat* was none too popular with some members of the Committee made it seem desirable to limit the independent position which Prussian municipal law granted to this organ. The British and the Soviets were, at the same time, anxious to introduce the parliamentary system into Berlin. Not only were the individual members of the *Magistrat* made subject to recall for cause, but the *Magistrat* as a collective body was made subject, under certain conditions, to dismissal by the city council. This principle was even carried so far as to make the local administrations in the wards, subject, under limitations, to the will of the councils of the wards. There were those in the Committee who felt that as a result of certain legislative powers left to the Magistrat, the unnatural conception of a constitution by four powers had produced an abnormal child. For the rest, however, the Magistrat's draft was repaired as the Allies thought necessary. The gravity of the decisions was tempered somewhat by the provision that this was to be only a temporary constitution, and that the new city assembly itself was to have the opportunity of correcting the mistakes of the Local Government Committee in a new constitution for Berlin. While it was felt that the German specialists need not be deprived of a smile at some of the things the constitution might contain, nobody wanted them to laugh.

The documents were ready for the Commandants at the required date.[165] There was general amazement. This was the first agreed-upon, i. e., unanimous report upon a major problem that the Kommandatura had witnessed for months. The question of the reorganization of the police, for example, had long been sent upward by the Commandants, and had been drifting for months in the higher reaches of the Control Council[166].[167] The question of the organiza-

---

162 Jeanne Ziegelmeyer, geb. Meyer (1872–1948).
163 Stadt an der Nordwestküste Englands.
164 Das House of Commons, das Unterhaus des britischen Parlaments, wählt zu Beginn jeder Legislaturperiode aus seiner Mitte einen Vorsitzenden, der als Parlamentspräsident fungiert und als Speaker (Sprecher) bezeichnet wird, obwohl er gar keine Reden hält und nicht an Debatten teilnimmt. Er tritt vor dem Monarchen als Sprecher der Abgeordneten auf, daher sein Name.
165 Das Local Government Committee schloss seine Beratungen am 5. Juli 1946 ab, und am 9. Juli lag der Verfassungsentwurf fristgemäß den Stadtkommandanten vor. Siehe Dok. 71, Anm. 46; Werner Breunig, Verfassunggebung in Berlin 1945–1950 (= Beiträge zur Politischen Wissenschaft, Bd. 58), Berlin 1990, S. 199.
166 Siehe Dok. 14, Anm. 5.

tion of the Berlin youth had reached nowhere in the Committee on Education[168].[169] Yet the Local Government Committee was saying to the Commandants that after its initial difficulties, there was no word, or phrase, or sentence in this new temporary constitution upon which they did not all agree. This session of the Commandants was necessarily made a little festive.[170] General Kotikov made a very complimentary speech congratulating the Committee on its exemplary accomplishment, and proposed that the other Commandants join him in expressing their commendation.[171] He thereupon invited everyone to another strenuous luncheon, a luncheon to celebrate the institution of a democratic government for post-war Berlin. Except for minor details and approvals the constitution was actually finished.[172] In October elections would be held in accordance with its provisions, an election which would overturn the system of government which the Russians had first set up in the city, and indicate to some degree the choice of the Berliners between East and West. After this election

---

[167] Am 4. Oktober 1946 stimmten die Stadtkommandanten mit BK/O (46) 391 einem vom Alliierten Kontrollrat beschlossenen Plan über die Neuorganisation der Berliner Polizei zu. Siehe Berlin. Kampf um Freiheit und Selbstverwaltung 1945–1946, hrsg. im Auftrage des Senats von Berlin (= Schriftenreihe zur Berliner Zeitgeschichte, Bd. 1), 2., erg. und erw. Auflage, Berlin 1961, S. 544, Nr. 13 a; LAB, F Rep. 280 (Quellensammlung zur Berliner Zeitgeschichte [LAZ-Sammlung]), Nr. 5504.

[168] Education Committee, Allied Kommandatura Berlin.

[169] "[...] the Russians had been holding up discussions on the problem of youth organizations in the Education Committee", so Johnson in seinem Schreiben an Ehefrau Emily vom 31. Mai 1946 (Dok. 55).

[170] Gemeint ist die 18. Sitzung der Stadtkommandanten am 9. Juli 1946. Siehe Protokoll der 18. Sitzung der Stadtkommandanten am 9. Juli 1946, BKC/M (46) 18, englischsprachige Fassung, in: LAB, B Rep. 036-01 (Office of Military Government, Berlin Sector [OMGBS]), 5/36-1/5.

[171] Kotikow sagte laut Wortprotokoll: "I think we ought to express in the minutes of the Commandants today the light of spirit prevalent here today. I would like to read to you the formula which I have prepared for our appreciation for the work of the Local Government Com. The committee of Local Affairs has done its work well and fulfilled its obligations in time, the work it has been ordered to do. In expressing our appreciation we have to keep in mind the fact the draft constitution which has been presented by the Local Government Com. to the Magistrat had to be studied very thoroughly and very deeply. Very many points in the draft submitted by the Magistrat had to be worked and re-studied and re-edited many times. I, therefore, propose for the the various attitudes and for the great amount of work the committee has done, I propose that we express our appreciation of the Local Government Com." Wortprotokoll der 18. Sitzung der Stadtkommandanten am 9. Juli 1946, englischsprachige Fassung, S. 7, in: LAB, B Rep. 036-01 (Office of Military Government, Berlin Sector [OMGBS]), 4/132-3/11.

[172] Zwar genehmigten die Stadtkommandanten in ihrer Sitzung am 9. Juli 1946 den Verfassungsentwurf grundsätzlich, gaben ihn aber zur Klärung einzelner Fragen dem Local Government Committee zurück. Dieses Komitee beschloss am 17. Juli den endgültigen Text, den die Stadtkommandanten am 19. Juli billigten und der dann der Alliierten Kontrollbehörde übermittelt wurde. Nach der Beratung im Koordinierungskomitee beschäftigten sich die Stadtkommandanten am 9. August abschließend mit dem Verfassungstext, der mit BK/O (46) 326 vom 13. August 1946 dem Oberbürgermeister übermittelt wurde. Siehe Werner Breunig, Verfassunggebung in Berlin 1945–1950 (= Beiträge zur Politischen Wissenschaft, Bd. 58), Berlin 1990, S. 199–225.

the Communists would certainly lose their predominant position in the municipal government which would then reflect the political opinions of the electorate. Once again the Soviet pressure had been limited. Once again it had been limited, this time with open cordiality, with the aid of the Soviet authorities themselves. Once again this had been done because they were four powers in the city instead of one.

V

Suddenly this world vanished overnight into the rather tawdry environment of the Third Replacement Depot[173] at Bremerhaven[174], where, in conversations punctured with four-letter words it was possible to learn what the occupation was really about. In the miserable quarters which the War Department furnished its soldiers, officers, and civilians returning home aboard the Marine Robin[175], where GI's[176] were asked to think of the steak dinner they would be given at the Separation Centers[177] in order to take their minds off their inadequate rations on board, it was possible to reflect, in the awkward postures which the total absence of chairs made necessary, about the meaning of these months in Berlin.

Certainly this occupation of Germany was one of the most, if not the most, important tasks which the United States had ever undertaken beyond its borders. The main reasons for our being in Germany were still good reasons for our staying there for some time to come. The German war potential was not yet destroyed, and the de-Nazification was, still incomplete in our zone, no matter how much more seriously we had taken this problem than the other powers. The inability to implement the clauses of the Potsdam Agreement[178] on treating Germany as an economic unit was responsible for the former situation, and when all is said and done, our own inadequacy was responsible for the latter. We had not known how, from the very beginning, to work closely enough with the proper Germans in solving speedily the Nazi problem. We had, consequently, been obliged to turn over this problem to the Germans themselves. Nobody could be really sure that, at this late date, they would really be able to see it through. Even granted that it would be carried through, it would necessarily be done with a mildness which our war and peace aims did not contemplate. Were it solved to everyone's general satisfaction, there still remained those ultra-conservative, nationalist groups in German society who were waiting once more to take over. Those who understood Bavaria, for example, were worried over how little would have been accomplished when once de-Nazification had been reasonably completed. We had been nicely successful with our program of elections, and with the coordination of the administration of the Länder in the Län-

---

[173] Durchgangs- und Sammelstation für amerikanische Soldaten.
[174] Siehe Dok. 71, Anm. 10.
[175] Siehe Dok. 82, Anm. 5.
[176] Government Issues, ugs. für amerikanische Soldaten.
[177] Entlassungsabteilung der US Army.
[178] Siehe Dok. 50, Anm. 18.

derrat at Stuttgart. Yet it was still a question here of whether we had not gone a little bit too fast. No German in a position of responsibility would admit this, inasmuch as the relative independence to be achieved from a government established upon popular support was something to be coveted. One could feel how eager in spite of all their deferential courtesy, the Germans were to get rid of us, provided, of course, that certain others left at the same time. Military Government would find it more difficult to direct democratic governments of the Länder. It too would have to respect the constitutions. It was inevitably a serious question whether in so rapidly depleting our personnel in military government, and entrusting more and more responsibility to the Germans, we were not risking letting the German situation get out of our hands again as it had after the last war[179],[180] Since the main objectives of our war had not yet been achieved, certainly this time we could afford to be a little more cautious in abandoning our controls to the Germans. If we had erred on the wrong side after the last war, we might err on the right side after this one.

Undoubtedly much excellent work was being done in promoting the positive side of a democratic program, but not enough. The careful directives prepared by military government were often enough ignored or violated by parallel occupational military authorities. It was no good to write out a procedure which would make the requisitioning of houses less painful to the Germans, if the Air Corps[181], for example, simply swooped down and evacuated blocks of houses over-night, and made away with all the furniture when they departed. It was confusing to spend millions of dollars to bring in food for the Germans, and then to inform them, by public notices over the door-ways of certain messes in officers' clubs that they would not be permitted to utilize the scraps which fell from our tables. These would have to go into the garbage cans.[182] More serious perhaps was the absence of any feeling that knew exactly what we were trying to do in Germany beyond the vague phrases of the Potsdam Agreement, or how long, for example, we were going to stay. How long would we stay within the confines of so-called political neutrality? Was it not possible to see now what was the democratic political hope of this forlorn country? How long were we going to postpone the implementation of a program of the widest and most generous scope in aid of the really forward-looking groups in German education and in the youth movement? How long were we going to postpone weeding out the undesirable elements, both military and civilian, in the forces of the

[179] Gemeint ist der Erste Weltkrieg (1914–1918).
[180] Nach dem Ersten Weltkrieg hatten sich die USA von Europa abgewandt und mit einer isolationistischen Politik begonnen.
[181] Die Luftstreitkräfte der US Army.
[182] Georg Schertz, Anwohner der Insel Schwanenwerder und von 1987 bis 1992 Polizeipräsident in Berlin, erinnert sich in einer E-Mail an Werner Breunig vom 26. Juni 2007 an den Lakeside Club, der in der unmittelbaren Nachkriegszeit auf Schwanenwerder untergebracht war (siehe Dok. 55): „Für uns bei Kriegsende hungernde Anwohner hatte der ‚Lakeside Club' eine – das kann man sich heute nicht mehr vorstellen – enttäuschende Praxis. Nicht verbrauchte Lebensmittel – darunter schönste und sogar verpackte Sachen – wurden vor den Augen der Bewohner mit Benzin übergossen und verbrannt. Die Wünsche der Anwohner, sich da zu bedienen, wurden schroff zurückgewiesen."

occupation, those callous, cynical, and adventurous youngsters with high civil-service ratings, those untrained officers looking for sinecures, those officers and troops who didn't know how to represent the best which a great democracy exemplifies? How could we keep in Germany, and how could we summon from America to work in Germany, the best forces that we have, if the opportunity were not given to pursue over a relatively vixed period, a constructive policy which would really guarantee the execution of our war aims and support those Germans whom, by now, we should have learned to trust. How long were we going to postpone a publicity and educational program at home which would attempt to persuade the American people that the peace, having not yet been won, was as vital to win as the war?

This inability to give adequate expression abroad to the best, positive, democratic forces in our nation was a constant embarrassment to Americans abroad, and an embarrassment to all those Germans who sought hope and guidance from us. It put us in a false light with respect to our other, and especially our Soviet Allies, who were only too anxious to find fault with us. Here again the instability of our future in Germany precluded our taking a well-worked out and positive stand. The experience in Berlin had shown that there was no reason on earth why we couldn't work well with the Soviet authorities. To be sure we could not hope to come to complete agreement on all matters. If, however, we knew what we wanted, and if we were willing also to pound the table to get it, we had a better chance to be understood and thus to be met half way. The distrust between East and West could be broken only by the utmost frankness, by our own frankness even when and if the Russians did not feel free to be frank. Suspicions could be removed only by dealings in the simplest human terms among people who had convictions which they were willing to defend, and who were likewise friendly, sympathetic and really anxious to understand the other's point of view and to go out of their way to learn it. The Russians do not and dare not underrate the power of democratic principles. They are not so secure and so venerated that they are able to combat beyond measure the popularity of and basic devotion to, these principles among the peoples of Europe. But for so long as we do not demonstrate our unwavering devotion to these principles both at home and abroad, and with something more than talk, and exhibit tangibly our determination to support them in the future at any cost, we cannot expect aid from the Soviets in making ourselves popular. Certain elements of their program appear to many Germans whose sincerity cannot be questioned, more fundamentally democratic than anything we have been able to conceive for Germany, in spite of the unpalatable methods used to carry them out.

Without underestimating our accomplishments to date, we can do a still better job in Germany. We are in a position therewith to make a splendid, positive contribution to the pacification of Europe and to the world. To do so, however, the American people through their government will have to display more real interest than hitherto, and put into this critical and peaceful effort their very best and most generous efforts: they must see to it that the great positive task that remains to be done is not cast aside through sheer national indifference and the neglect which accompanies it.

phang

Abb. 1 *Edgar N. Johnson,*
ca. Ende der 1930er-Jahre.
Candice E. und Thomas R. Johnson, Denver, Colorado, USA

Abb. 2 *Edgar N. Johnson*
vor seinem Haus in Lincoln, Nebraska, USA,
wahrscheinlich Ende 1945 oder Anfang 1946.
Candice E. und Thomas R. Johnson, Denver, Colorado, USA

Abb. 3 *Emily L. Johnson mit den Söhnen John (links) und Thomas, Lincoln, Nebraska, USA, Ende 1945 oder Anfang 1946.*
Candice E. und Thomas R. Johnson, Denver, Colorado, USA

Abb. 4 *Emily L. und Edgar N. Johnson mit Sohn John.*
Candice E. und Thomas R. Johnson, Denver, Colorado, USA

Abb. 5 *Emily L. und Edgar N. Johnson.*
Candice E. und Thomas R. Johnson, Denver, Colorado, USA

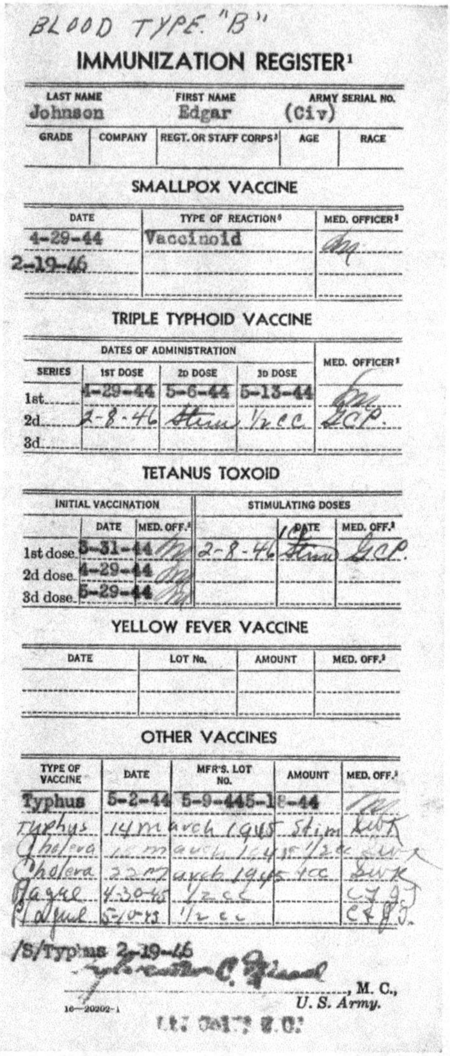

BLOOD TYPE "B"

IMMUNIZATION REGISTER[1]

LAST NAME	FIRST NAME	ARMY SERIAL NO.
Johnson	Edgar	(Civ)

GRADE	COMPANY	REGT. OR STAFF CORPS[2]	AGE	RACE

SMALLPOX VACCINE

DATE	TYPE OF REACTION[6]	MED. OFFICER[3]
4-29-44	Vaccinoid	
2-19-46		

TRIPLE TYPHOID VACCINE

SERIES	DATES OF ADMINISTRATION 1ST DOSE	2D DOSE	3D DOSE	MED. OFFICER[3]
1st	4-29-44	5-6-44	5-13-44	
2d	2-8-46	Stim	1/2 cc	GCP.
3d				

TETANUS TOXOID

	INITIAL VACCINATION DATE	MED. OFF.[3]	STIMULATING DOSES DATE		MED. OFF.[3]
1st dose	3-31-44		2-8-46	1cc Stim	GCP.
2d dose	4-29-44				
3d dose	5-29-44				

YELLOW FEVER VACCINE

DATE	LOT No.	AMOUNT	MED. OFF.[3]

OTHER VACCINES

TYPE OF VACCINE	DATE	MFR'S. LOT NO.	AMOUNT	MED. OFF.[3]
Typhus	5-2-44	5-9-445-1	8-44	
Typhus	14 March 1945		Stim	
Cholera	15 March 1945		1/2 cc	
Cholera	22 March 1945		1 cc	
Plague	4-30-45	1/2 cc		
Plague	5-10-45	1/2 cc		

/S/Typhus 2-19-46

, M. C.,
U. S. Army.

16—20202-1

Abb. 6 *Immunization Register, 1944–1946.*
Candice E. und Thomas R. Johnson, Denver, Colorado, USA

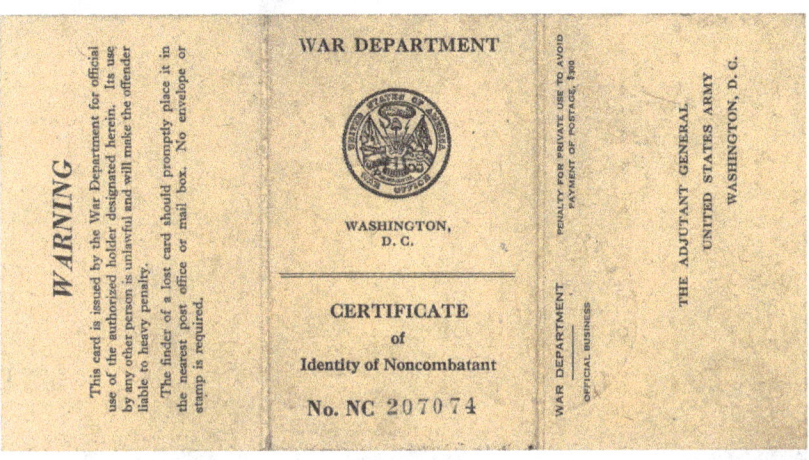

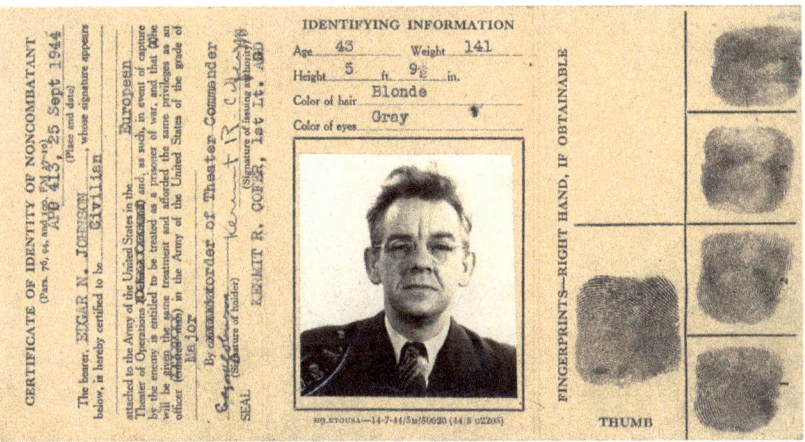

Abb. 7 und Abb. 8 *Certificate of Identity of Noncombatant, 1944.*
Candice E. und Thomas R. Johnson, Denver, Colorado, USA

Abb. 9 *Edgar N. Johnson (rechts)
und sein Executive Officer Elliott W. Schryver,
München, Juli 1945.*
The University of Chicago Library, Special Collections Research Center,
Chicago, Illinois, USA, Edgar N. Johnson Papers

Abb. 10 *Amerikanische Historiker in Deutschland (von links):
Edgar N. Johnson, Felix Gilbert, John L. Clive und Carl E. Schorske,
Wiesbaden, November 1945.*
Rechteinhaber nicht bekannt, freundlicherweise zur Verfügung gestellt von
Barry M. Katz, Palo Alto, California, USA

Abb. 11 *Erste Seite eines Schreibens von Edgar N. Johnson
aus New York City an seine Ehefrau,
20. Februar 1946.*
The University of Chicago Library, Special Collections Research Center,
Chicago, Illinois, USA, Edgar N. Johnson Papers

374 Bildanhang

Abb. 12 *USAT George W. Goethals, das Armeetransportschiff,
mit dem Edgar N. Johnson 1946 nach Europa kam,
Aufnahme aus dem Jahre 1945.*
National Archives and Records Administration, College Park, Maryland, USA,
photo no. 111-SC-223790

Abb. 13 *Umschlag eines Briefes von Edgar N. Johnson
aus Berlin an seine Ehefrau,
Poststempel vom 3. Juli 1946.*
The University of Chicago Library, Special Collections Research Center,
Chicago, Illinois, USA, Edgar N. Johnson Papers

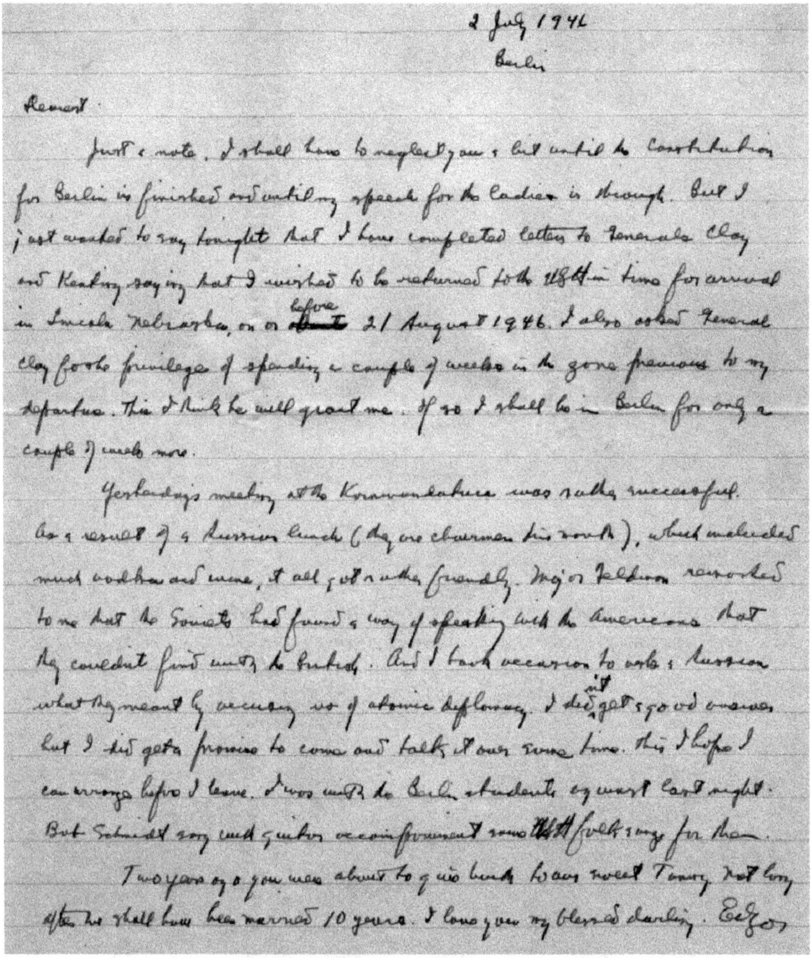

Abb. 14 *Schreiben von Edgar N. Johnson
aus Berlin an seine Ehefrau,
2. Juli 1946.*
The University of Chicago Library, Special Collections Research Center,
Chicago, Illinois, USA, Edgar N. Johnson Papers

Abb. 15 *Umschlag eines Briefes von Emily L. an Edgar N. Johnson, Internal Affairs and Communications Division, OMGUS, Poststempel vom 12. April 1946.*
Candice E. und Thomas R. Johnson, Denver, Colorado, USA

Abb. 16 *Umschlag eines Briefes von Emily L. an Edgar N. Johnson, Civil Administration Branch, OMGBD, Poststempel vom 12. Juni 1946.*
Candice E. und Thomas R. Johnson, Denver, Colorado, USA

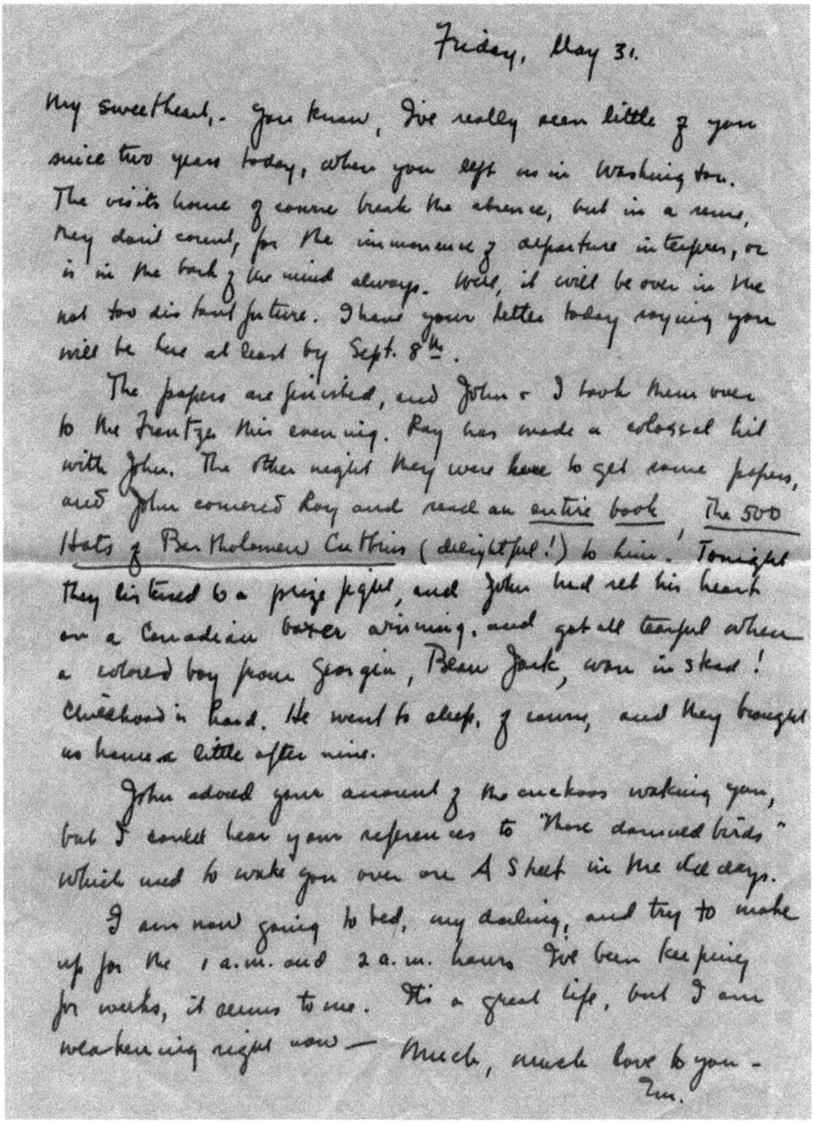

Friday, May 31.

My sweetheart, – You know, I've really seen little of you since two years today, when you left us in Washington. The visits home of course break the absence, but in a sense, they don't count, for the imminence of departure interferes, or is in the back of the mind always. Well, it will be over in the not too distant future. I have your letter today saying you will be here at least by Sept. 8th.

The papers are finished, and John & I took them over to the Frantzes this evening. Ray has made a colossal hit with John. The other night they were here to get some papers, and John cornered Ray and read an entire book, The 500 Hats of Bartholomew Cubbins (delightful!) to him. Tonight they listened to a prize fight, and John had set his heart on a Canadian boxer winning, and got all tearful when a colored boy from Georgia, Beau Jack, won instead! Childhood in hand. He went to sleep, of course, and they brought us home a little after nine.

John adored your account of the cuckoos waking you, but I could hear your references to "those damned birds" which used to wake you over on A Street in the old days.

I am now going to bed, my darling, and try to make up for the 1 a.m. and 2 a.m. hours I've been keeping for weeks, it seems to me. It's a great life, but I am weakening right now — Much, much love to you –

Em.

Abb. 17 *Schreiben von Emily L. an Edgar N. Johnson,
31. Mai 1946.*
Candice E. und Thomas R. Johnson, Denver, Colorado, USA

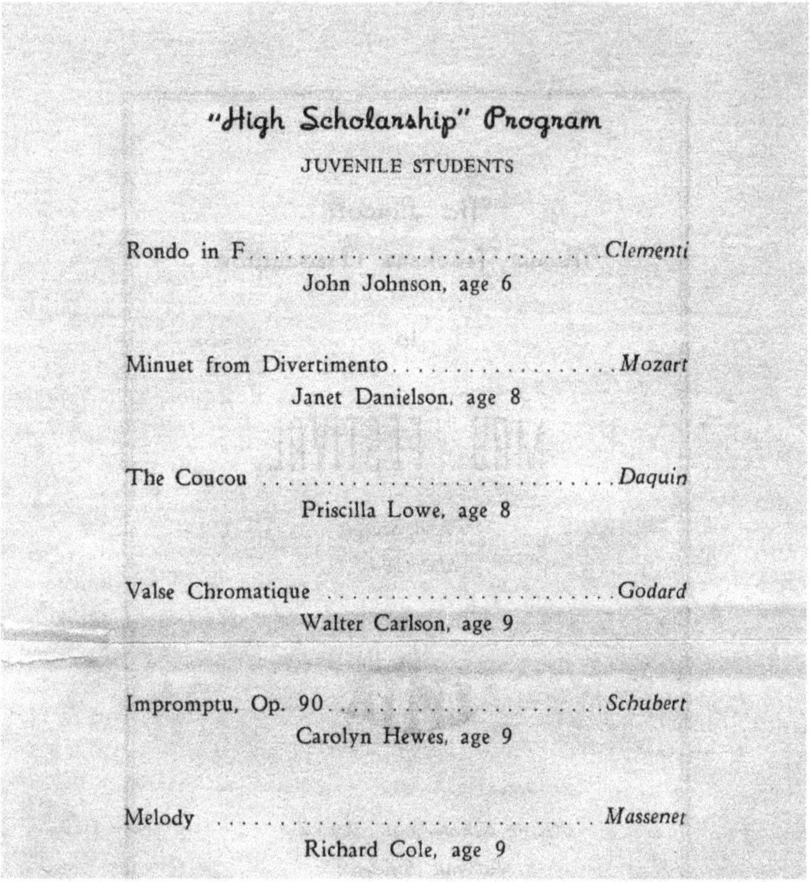

"High Scholarship" Program

JUVENILE STUDENTS

Rondo in F . . . . *Clementi*
John Johnson, age 6

Minuet from Divertimento . . . . *Mozart*
Janet Danielson, age 8

The Coucou . . . . *Daquin*
Priscilla Lowe, age 8

Valse Chromatique . . . . *Godard*
Walter Carlson, age 9

Impromptu, Op. 90 . . . . *Schubert*
Carolyn Hewes, age 9

Melody . . . . *Massenet*
Richard Cole, age 9

Abb. 18 *Programmzettel (Ausschnitt) der Lincoln Music Teachers' Association, Klaviervortrag von Sohn John, 5. Mai 1946.*
Candice E. und Thomas R. Johnson, Denver, Colorado, USA

ALLOTTER'S LAST NAME	FIRST	M. I.	ARMY SERIAL NUMBER
JOHNSON	EDGAR	N	Z-9952
GRADE OR RANK	MONTHLY AMOUNT		BEGINNING 1ST DAY OF
CIV	$ 600.00		4/46
CREDIT OF (IF ALLOTTEE IS BANK)			ACKNOWLEDGMENT DATE
			18 APR 46

IMPORTANT—THE FIRST PAYMENT ON THIS ALLOTMENT WILL BE MADE ON OR ABOUT:
15 MAY 46
SUBSEQUENT PAYMENTS WILL BE MADE AS THEY FALL DUE SHORTLY AFTER THE BEGINNING OF EACH SUCCEEDING MONTH.

ALLOTTEE:
MRS EMILY L JOHNSON
3268 SO 31ST ST
LINCOLN 2 NEBRASKA

ADDRESS OF ALLOTTER:

ASF ODB FORM NO. 29
REV. JAN 1946 271-471-E305 VDG Mail To This Address
PLEASE READ REVERSE SIDE
UARCO—CLEVELAND

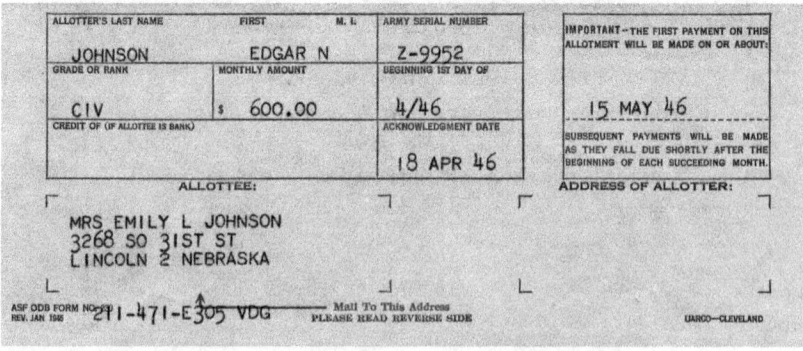

Abb. 19 *Monatliche Zuweisung von 600 Dollar an Emily L. Johnson.*
Candice E. und Thomas R. Johnson, Denver, Colorado, USA

Abb. 20 *James K. Pollock, 1945–August 1946 Leiter des Regional Government Coordinating Office, OMGUS, an seinem Schreibtisch in Stuttgart.*
University of Michigan, Bentley Historical Library, Ann Arbor, Michigan, USA, James K. Pollock Papers, Box 84, Folder OMGUS

Abb. 21 *Vertreter der amerikanischen Besatzungsmacht, Stuttgart, 17. Mai 1946, von links: James K. Pollock, General Lucius D. Clay, 1945–1947 Deputy Military Governor, Germany (US), General Walter J. Muller, 1945–1947 Director, Office of Military Government, Bavaria, und Colonel James R. Newman, 1945–1949 Director, Office of Military Government, Greater Hesse/Hesse.*
ullstein bild, Berlin/dpa

Abb. 22 *Robert D. Murphy, 1944–1949 Ambassador, Political Adviser for Germany, an seinem Schreibtisch in Berlin, Aufnahme aus dem Jahre 1946.*
Stanford University, Hoover Institution Archives, Stanford, California, USA, Robert D. Murphy Papers, Envelope X

Abb. 23 *Walter L. Dorn, 1946/1947 Special Adviser for German Civil Administration und Personal Adviser on Denazification von General Lucius D. Clay, Aufnahme aus dem Jahre 1940.*
Columbia University in the City of New York, USA, Rare Book & Manuscript Library, Walter L. Dorn Papers, Box 2

Abb. 24 *General Lucius D. Clay (links) und General Charles K. Gailey Jr., 1945–April 1946 Chief, Civil Administration Branch, Internal Affairs and Communications Division, OMGUS, Aufnahme ca. 1946, oben rechts persönliche Widmung von Clay für Gailey:*
"To Charlie Gailey
The honor was mine.
Lucius D. Clay".
US Army, freundlicherweise zur Verfügung gestellt von
Charles K. Gailey III, Springfield, Virginia, USA

Abb. 25 *General Ray W. Barker,*
1945–Mai 1946 US Commandant, Allied Kommandatura Berlin.
US Army, freundlicherweise zur Verfügung gestellt von der
Dwight D. Eisenhower Library, Abilene, Kansas, USA

Abb. 26 *General Ray W. Barker nimmt am Army Day die Parade ab, US Headquarters Berlin District, Berlin-Lichterfelde, 6. April 1946, hinter Barker in der ersten Reihe links: General Eric Paytherus Nares, britischer Stadtkommandant, in der ersten Reihe von rechts: General Alexandr Georgijewitsch Kotikow, sowjetischer Stadtkommandant, und General Charles J. M. Lançon, französischer Stadtkommandant.*
Rechteinhaber nicht bekannt, freundlicherweise zur Verfügung gestellt vom Archiv der sozialen Demokratie der Friedrich-Ebert-Stiftung, Bonn-Bad Godesberg

Abb. 27 *General Frank A. Keating,*
Mai 1946–1947 US Commandant, Allied Kommandatura Berlin,
Aufnahme aus dem Jahre 1947.
Archiv der sozialen Demokratie der Friedrich-Ebert-Stiftung, Bonn-Bad Godesberg

Abb. 28 *Empfang für den scheidenden amerikanischen Stadtkommandanten, General Ray W. Barker, und seinen Nachfolger, General Frank A. Keating (Zweiter von links), Zweiter von rechts: Edgar N. Johnson, Wannsee Hotel/Wannsee Officers' Club, Berlin-Wannsee, 28. April 1946.*
The University of Chicago Library, Special Collections Research Center, Chicago, Illinois, USA, Edgar N. Johnson Papers

Abb. 29 *Bootsfahrt auf dem Wannsee, 28. April 1946, hinten links: Edgar N. Johnson, hinten rechts: General Ray W. Barker, Mitte links: Major Robert A. Holzman, Mitte rechts: Colonel Elmer E. Barnes, am Steuer: Colonel John C. MacDonald.*
The University of Chicago Library, Special Collections Research Center, Chicago, Illinois, USA, Edgar N. Johnson Papers

Abb. 30 *Bootsfahrt auf dem Wannsee,*
28. April 1946.
The University of Chicago Library, Special Collections Research Center,
Chicago, Illinois, USA, Edgar N. Johnson Papers

Abb. 31 *Edgar N. Johnson (hinten links) im Gespräch mit*
General Ray W. Barker,
28. April 1946.
The University of Chicago Library, Special Collections Research Center,
Chicago, Illinois, USA, Edgar N. Johnson Papers

Abb. 32 *Colonel Frank L. Howley,
1945–1949 Director, OMGBD/OMGBS,
Aufnahme aus dem Jahre 1949.*
US Army, freundlicherweise zur Verfügung gestellt vom
Archiv der sozialen Demokratie der Friedrich-Ebert-Stiftung, Bonn-Bad Godesberg

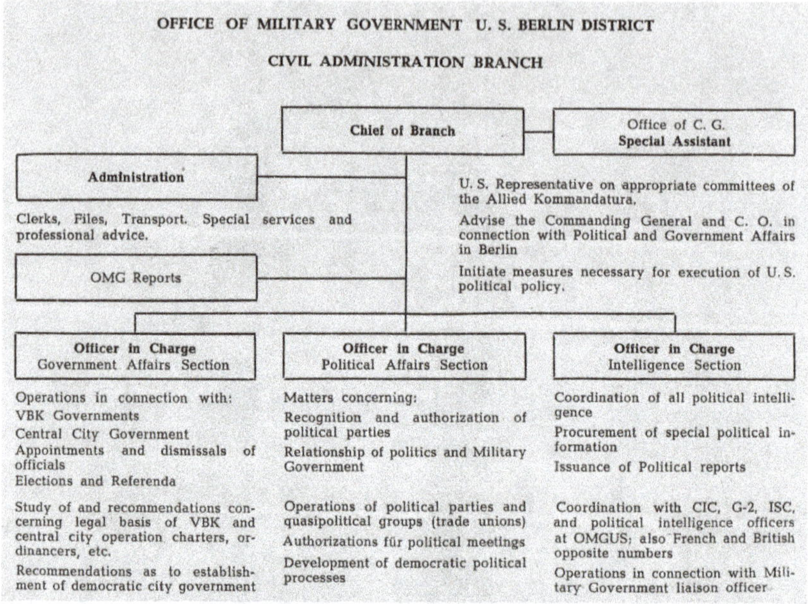

OFFICE OF MILITARY GOVERNMENT U. S. BERLIN DISTRICT
CIVIL ADMINISTRATION BRANCH
Chief of Branch
Office of C. G. Special Assistant
Administration
Clerks, Files, Transport. Special services and professional advice.
OMG Reports
U. S. Representative on appropriate committees of the Allied Kommandatura.
Advise the Commanding General and C. O. in connection with Political and Government Affairs in Berlin
Initiate measures necessary for execution of U. S. political policy.
Officer in Charge Government Affairs Section
Operations in connection with:
VBK Governments
Central City Government
Appointments and dismissals of officials
Elections and Referenda
Study of and recommendations concerning legal basis of VBK and central city operation charters, ordinancers, etc.
Recommendations as to establishment of democratic city government
Officer in Charge Political Affairs Section
Matters concerning:
Recognition and authorization of political parties
Relationship of politics and Military Government
Operations of political parties and quasipolitical groups (trade unions)
Authorizations für political meetings
Development of democratic political processes
Officer in Charge Intelligence Section
Coordination of all political intelligence
Procurement of special political information
Issuance of Political reports
Coordination with CIC, G-2, ISC, and political intelligence officers at OMGUS; also French and British opposite numbers
Operations in connection with Military Government liaison officer

Abb. 33 *Civil Administration Branch, OMGBD, Chief of Branch: Lieutenant Colonel Louis Glaser, Special Assistant: Edgar N. Johnson.*
Office of Military Government U. S. Berlin District (Hrsg.), Six Months Report 4 January–3 July 1946, Berlin 1946, S. 40

HQ BERLIN DISTRICT

UNITED STATES FORCES, EUROPEAN THEATER
UNITED STATES ARMY

This

Certificate of Commendation

is awarded to

LT COL LOUIS GLASER 0508575
OMG BD

For meritorious service during the period 1 January 1946 to 1 July 1946 while serving as Chief of Civil Administration Branch for Military Government distinguished himself by outstanding performance of duty. The capability and resourcefulness displayed in addition to his untiring energy and loyal devotion to duty reflect great credit upon himself and the military service.

Lieutenant Colonel GLASER is hereby authorized to wear the Army Commendation Ribbon by direction of the Secretary of War.

FRANK A. KEATING
MAJOR GENERAL USA
COMMANDING

30 July 1946

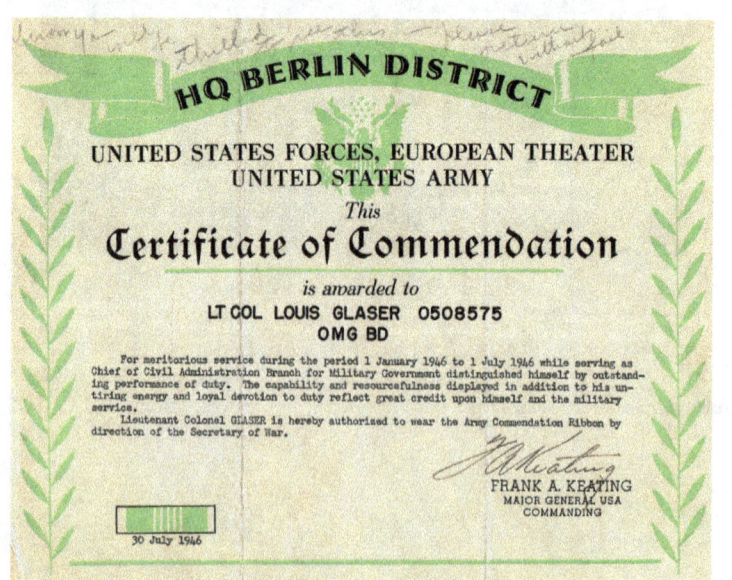

Abb. 34 *Certificate of Commendation für Lieutenant Colonel Louis Glaser, 30. Juli 1946.*
Anthony J. Glaser, Bethesda, Maryland, USA

Abb. 35 *Louis Glaser,*
Januar 1946–1948 Chief, Civil Administration Branch/
Civil Administration and Political Affairs Branch, OMGBD/OMGBS,
Aufnahme ca. 1947.
Rechteinhaber nicht bekannt, freundlicherweise zur Verfügung gestellt von der
Harry S. Truman Library, Independence, Missouri, USA

Abb. 36 *Alliierte Kontrollbehörde für Deutschland, am Kleistpark, Berlin-Schöneberg.*
Views and Facts of Berlin. As seen through the eyes of the American soldier and intended for the folks and friends at home, o. O. und J.

Abb. 37 *Alliierte Kommandantur Berlin, Kaiserswerther Straße 16/18, Berlin-Dahlem.*
Views and Facts of Berlin. As seen through the eyes of the American soldier and intended for the folks and friends at home, o. O. und J.

Abb. 38 *Menükarte, Alliierte Kommandantur Berlin, 26. Juni 1946.*
Candice E. und Thomas R. Johnson, Denver, Colorado, USA

Abb. 39 *OMGUS*,
Kronprinzenallee (heute Clayallee), Berlin-Dahlem.
Berlinische Galerie. Landesmuseum für Moderne Kunst, Fotografie und Architektur,
Berlin/Henry Ries

Abb. 40 *OMGBD,*
Grunewaldstraße 35, Berlin-Steglitz.
Office of Military Government U. S. Sector, Berlin (Hrsg.),
A Four Year Report July 1, 1945–September 1, 1949, Berlin 1949, S. 125

Abb. 41 *Harnack House,*
unter anderem Offizierskasino,
Ihnestraße 16, Berlin-Dahlem, Gartenansicht.
Archiv der Max-Planck-Gesellschaft, Berlin

Abb. 42 *Edgar N. Johnsons erste Unterkunft in Berlin: damals Ihnestraße 14, heute Brümmerstraße 74, Berlin-Dahlem, Aufnahme aus dem Jahre 2009.*
Landesarchiv Berlin/Barbara Esch-Marowski

Abb. 43 *Edgar N. Johnsons zweite Unterkunft in Berlin: Am Sandwerder 17/19, Berlin-Wannsee, damals Wannsee Hotel/Wannsee Officers' Club, heute The American Academy in Berlin, Hans Arnhold Center, Aufnahme aus dem Jahre 2009.*
Landesarchiv Berlin/Barbara Esch-Marowski

Abb. 44 *Edgar N. Johnson und sein Chauffeur Artur Sanow am Eingang des Wannsee Hotel/Wannsee Officers' Club, 1946.*
The University of Chicago Library, Special Collections Research Center, Chicago, Illinois, USA, Edgar N. Johnson Papers

Abb. 45 *Artur Sanow, Wannsee Hotel/Wannsee Officers' Club, 1946.*
The University of Chicago Library, Special Collections Research Center, Chicago, Illinois, USA, Edgar N. Johnson Papers

Abb. 46 *Am Sandwerder 17/19, Gartenansicht,*
Aufnahme aus dem Jahre 2009.
Landesarchiv Berlin/Barbara Esch-Marowski

Abb. 47 *Am Sandwerder 17/19, Blick von der Terrasse auf den Großen Wannsee,*
Aufnahme aus dem Jahre 2012.
Candice E. und Thomas R. Johnson, Denver, Colorado, USA

Abb. 48 *Sowjetisches Panzerdenkmal im amerikanischen Sektor Berlins, 1946.*
The University of Chicago Library, Special Collections Research Center,
Chicago, Illinois, USA, Edgar N. Johnson Papers

Abb. 49 *Artur Sanow, 1946.*
The University of Chicago Library, Special Collections Research Center,
Chicago, Illinois, USA, Edgar N. Johnson Papers

Abb. 50 *Blick auf die zerstörte Kaiser-Wilhelm-Gedächtniskirche, Berlin-Charlottenburg, 1946.*
The University of Chicago Library, Special Collections Research Center, Chicago, Illinois, USA, Edgar N. Johnson Papers

Abb. 51 *Ruinenlandschaft mit dreisprachigem Schild "YOU ARE LEAVING THE AMERICAN SECTOR", 1946.*
The University of Chicago Library, Special Collections Research Center, Chicago, Illinois, USA, Edgar N. Johnson Papers

Abb. 52 *Am Sandwerder 27, Berlin-Wannsee, 1945–Mai 1946 Residenz von General Ray W. Barker, Aufnahme vermutlich aus der zweiten Hälfte der 1930er-Jahre.*
Hedda Dutilh-von Schmidt Seidlitz, Aerdenhout, Niederlande

Abb. 53 *Edgar N. Johnson (links) und Lieutenant Colonel Louis Glaser am Eingang der Residenz, 21. April 1946.*
The University of Chicago Library, Special Collections Research Center, Chicago, Illinois, USA, Edgar N. Johnson Papers

Abb. 54 *Am Sandwerder 27, Gartenansicht, Aufnahme aus dem Jahre 2009.*
Landesarchiv Berlin/Barbara Esch-Marowski

Abb. 55 *Gelfertstraße 32/34, Berlin-Dahlem,*
ab 1945 Residenz von Colonel Frank L. Howley,
Aufnahme aus dem Jahre 2011.
Landesarchiv Berlin/Thomas Platow

Abb. 56 *Podbielskiallee 65, Berlin-Dahlem,*
ehemalige Villa des Cellisten Max Baldner,
1945 von der amerikanischen Besatzungsmacht requiriert,
Aufnahme aus dem Jahre 2009.
Landesarchiv Berlin/Barbara Esch-Marowski

Abb. 57 *Max Baldner, 1942.*
Thomas Baldner, Bloomington, Indiana, USA

Abb. 58 *Der Cellist Max Baldner, Ölgemälde von Ewald Vetter, 1946.*
Kunstpostkarte, freundlicherweise zur Verfügung gestellt von
Helmut Hoffmann, Berlin

Abb. 59 *Am Großen Wannsee 2/4, Berlin-Wannsee, ehemalige Villa der Filmschauspielerin Brigitte Helm, 1946 Lakeside Club für hohe amerikanische Offiziere, Aufnahme aus dem Jahre 2011.*
Landesarchiv Berlin/Thomas Platow

Abb. 60 *Inselstraße 16 auf der Insel Schwanenwerder, Berlin-Wannsee, ab 1946 Lakeside Club, Aufnahme aus dem Jahre 1953.*
Landesarchiv Berlin/Gert Schütz, F Rep. 290 (Allgemeine Fotosammlung), Nr. 29956

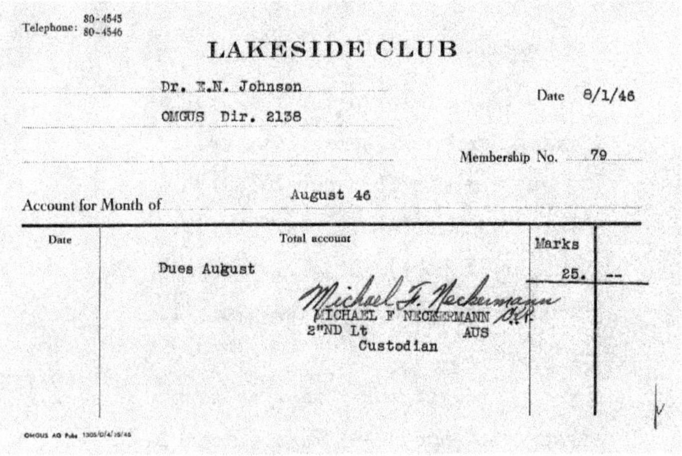

Telephone: 80-4545 80-4546

LAKESIDE CLUB

Dr. E.N. Johnson

OMGUS Dir. 2138

Date 8/1/46

Membership No. 79

Account for Month of August 46

Date	Total account	Marks	
	Dues August	25.	--
	Michael F. Neckermann MICHAEL F NECKERMANN 2"ND Lt AUS Custodian		

OMGUS AG Form 1305/0/4/15/46

Abb. 61 *Abrechnungsbeleg für Edgar N. Johnson, 1. August 1946.*
Candice E. und Thomas R. Johnson, Denver, Colorado, USA

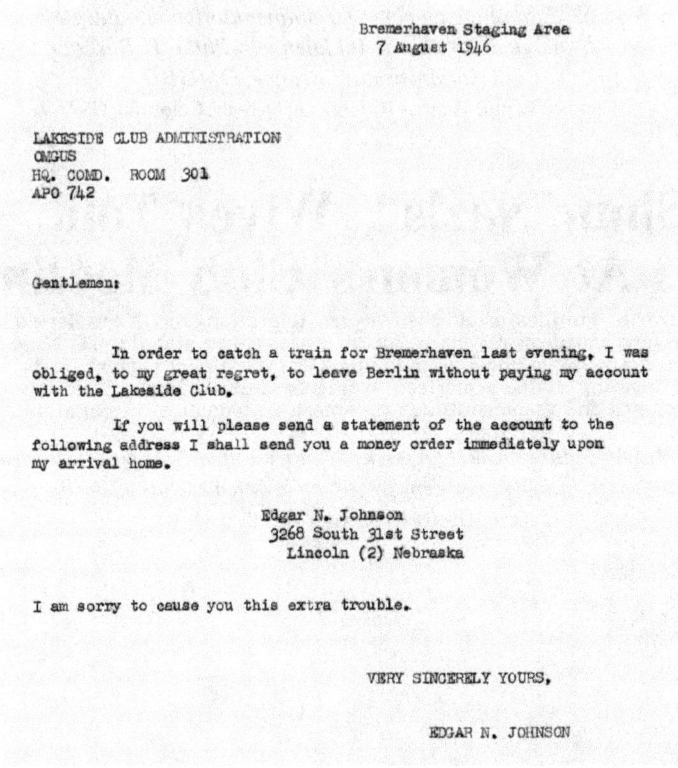

Bremerhaven Staging Area
7 August 1946

LAKESIDE CLUB ADMINISTRATION
OMGUS
HQ. COMD. ROOM 301
APO 742

Gentlemen:

In order to catch a train for Bremerhaven last evening, I was obliged, to my great regret, to leave Berlin without paying my account with the Lakeside Club.

If you will please send a statement of the account to the following address I shall send you a money order immediately upon my arrival home.

Edgar N. Johnson
3268 South 31st Street
Lincoln (2) Nebraska

I am sorry to cause you this extra trouble.

VERY SINCERELY YOURS,

EDGAR N. JOHNSON

Abb. 62 *Schreiben von Edgar N. Johnson aus Bremerhaven an die Lakeside Club Administration, 7. August 1946.*
Candice E. und Thomas R. Johnson, Denver, Colorado, USA

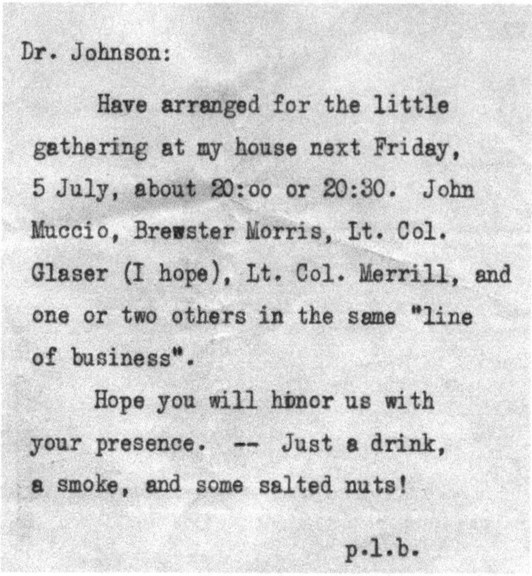

> Dr. Johnson:
>
> Have arranged for the little gathering at my house next Friday, 5 July, about 20:oo or 20:30. John Muccio, Brewster Morris, Lt. Col. Glaser (I hope), Lt. Col. Merrill, and one or two others in the same "line of business".
>
> Hope you will honor us with your presence. -- Just a drink, a smoke, and some salted nuts!
>
> p.l.b.

Abb. 63 *Einladung zu einer Zusammenkunft am 5. Juli 1946, p. l. b.: möglicherweise die Initialen von Philip L. Barbour, Civil Administration Branch, OMGBD.*
Candice E. und Thomas R. Johnson, Denver, Colorado, USA

"Shun Nazis", Wives Told At Women's Club Meeting

American families should have no toleration for Nazi-Germans, no matter how cultured or charming they seem to be, stated Dr. E. N. Johnson, Special Assistant to the Commanding General, Headquarters, B. D. at the second meeting of the American Women's Club of Berlin, Tuesday, when he discussed the responsibilities of American women in occupation.

Abb. 64 *Zeitungsartikel (Ausschnitt) über Edgar N. Johnsons Vortrag am 9. Juli 1946 vor dem American Women's Club of Berlin.*
OMGUS Observer vom 12. Juli 1946, S. 2

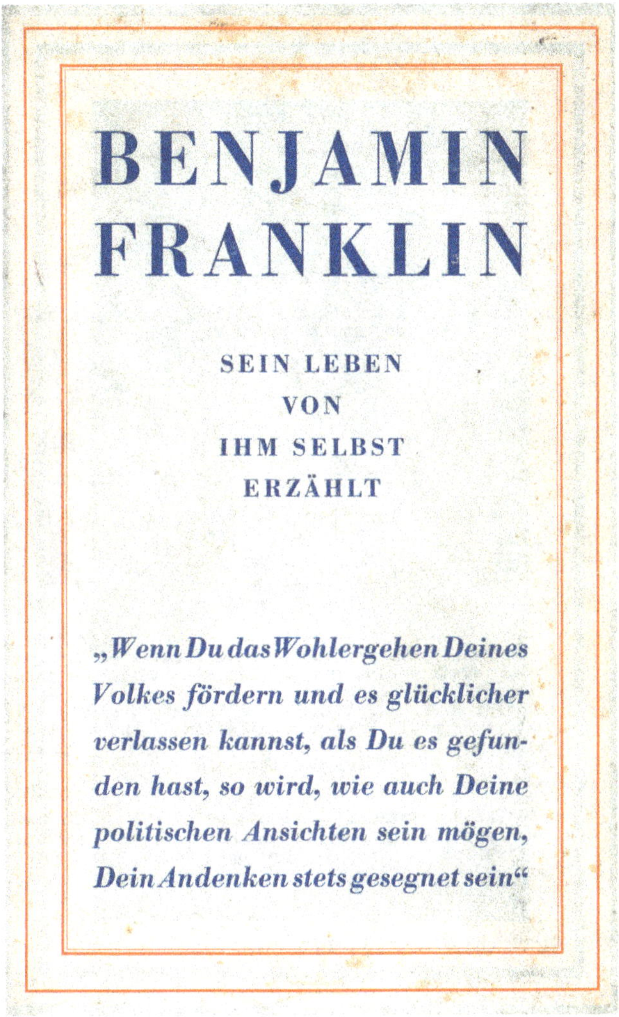

BENJAMIN FRANKLIN

SEIN LEBEN
VON
IHM SELBST
ERZÄHLT

„Wenn Du das Wohlergehen Deines Volkes fördern und es glücklicher verlassen kannst, als Du es gefunden hast, so wird, wie auch Deine politischen Ansichten sein mögen, Dein Andenken stets gesegnet sein"

Abb. 65 *Deutsche Ausgabe von Benjamin Franklins Autobiografie, 1946 im Karl H. Henssel Verlag, Berlin, mit einem Vorwort von Edgar N. Johnson erschienen.*
Freundlicherweise zur Verfügung gestellt von
Candice E. und Thomas R. Johnson, Denver, Colorado, USA

24 May 1946   R E S T R I C T E D   LG/M(46)19

ALLIED KOMMANDATURA BERLIN
Local Government Committee

MINUTES
of the
NINETEENTH MEETING

held in the Allied Kommandatura Building, Berlin-Dahlem,
at 1400 Hours, on 23 May 1946.

Present:

BR
Major J.P. ASHTON (Chairman)

FR
Capt. ZIEGELMAIER

USSR
Major FELDMAN
Capt. KASATKINE

USA
Dr. JOHNSON

----

1. The CHAIRMAN submitted the amended minutes of the seventeenth Meeting together with the minutes of the eighteenth Meeting for approval and signature.
 The SOVIET REPRESENTATIVE stated that before approval and signature he would like a translation of the minutes of both meetings and suggested they be submitted at the next meeting of the Local Government Committee for consideration.
 This was AGREED.

 The SOVIET REPRESENTATIVE submitted a paper on procedure in connection with Minutes and suggested that, after translation, consideration be given to the paper at the next meeting of the Committee.
 This was AGREED.

2. CITY OF BERLIN CONSTITUTION

 (1) The CHAIRMAN produced a copy of the German Draft of the City of Berlin Constitution as submitted by the Kommandatura and stated that in order to make progress he would request the Committee to consider the first point, mentioned in the paper on suggested procedure, accepted by the Committee at the last meeting.
 First point therefore would be "The Assembly".

 (2) The CHAIRMAN asked for suggestions as to the title the Committee should confer on the members of the Assembly.

- 2 -

Abb. 66 und Abb. 67 *Erste und letzte Seite des Protokolls der Sitzung des Local Government Committee, Allied Kommandatura Berlin, am 23. Mai 1946, unterzeichnet haben (von links): Major John Pennington Ashton (Großbritannien), Capitaine Jean Victor Ziegelmeyer (Frankreich), Major Iossif Moissejewitsch Feldman (Sowjetunion) und Edgar N. Johnson (USA).*
The National Archives, Kew, Richmond, Surrey, Großbritannien,
Allied Kommandatura: Directives, Minutes and Papers, FO 1112/378

RESTRICTED

- 5 -

The CHAIRMAN also stated that the Magistrat had undertaken to prepare the Electoral Machinery within three months after a decision is made upon the following points:-
   (1) What are we going to elect?
   (2) How are we going to elect them?
   (3) Who shall vote?

First point concerns the Constitution.

Questions arising on the second point were:-
   (1) On Basis of Proportional Representation
   (2) On a direct vote of each person
   (3) A combination of the two (alternative vote).

To initiate a discussion, the CHAIRMAN suggested that two thirds be elected by direct vote and one third from a modified form of Proportional Representation.

The US REPRESENTATIVE suggested that instead of going ahead with this question to-day, an extraordinary meeting be called of the Local Government Committee to discuss Electoral Procedure.

4. After some discussion, it was

   AGREED to hold an extraordinary meeting of the Local Government Committee on Friday 31 May 1946, at 1000 Hours for the purpose of discussing Electoral Procedure, and the Electoral Roll.

5. NEXT ORDINARY MEETING

It was

   AGREED that the next ordinary meeting of the Local Government Committee be held on Friday 31 May 1946, at 1400 Hours.

| GR BR | FR | USSR | USA |

Abb. 68 *Sitzung des Local Government Committee, Allied Kommandatura Berlin, Anfang Juni 1946, von links im Uhrzeigersinn: die britische Delegation (Sekretär, Dolmetscher [russisch], Beobachter der Control Commission, Major Harold Hays und Dolmetscher [französisch]), die französische Delegation (Sekretärin und Capitaine Jean Victor Ziegelmeyer [Vorsitz]), der amerikanische Vertreter (Lieutenant Colonel Louis Glaser) und die russische Delegation (Dolmetscherin [französisch], Oberstleutnant Alexandr Michailowitsch Sosulja und Major Iossif Moissejewitsch Feldman).*
Rechteinhaber nicht bekannt, freundlicherweise zur Verfügung gestellt von Anthony J. Glaser, Bethesda, Maryland, USA

Abb. 69 *Edgar N. Johnson in einer Arbeitspause des Local Government Committee, Allied Kommandatura Berlin, 5. Juli 1946.*
The University of Chicago Library, Special Collections Research Center, Chicago, Illinois, USA, Edgar N. Johnson Papers

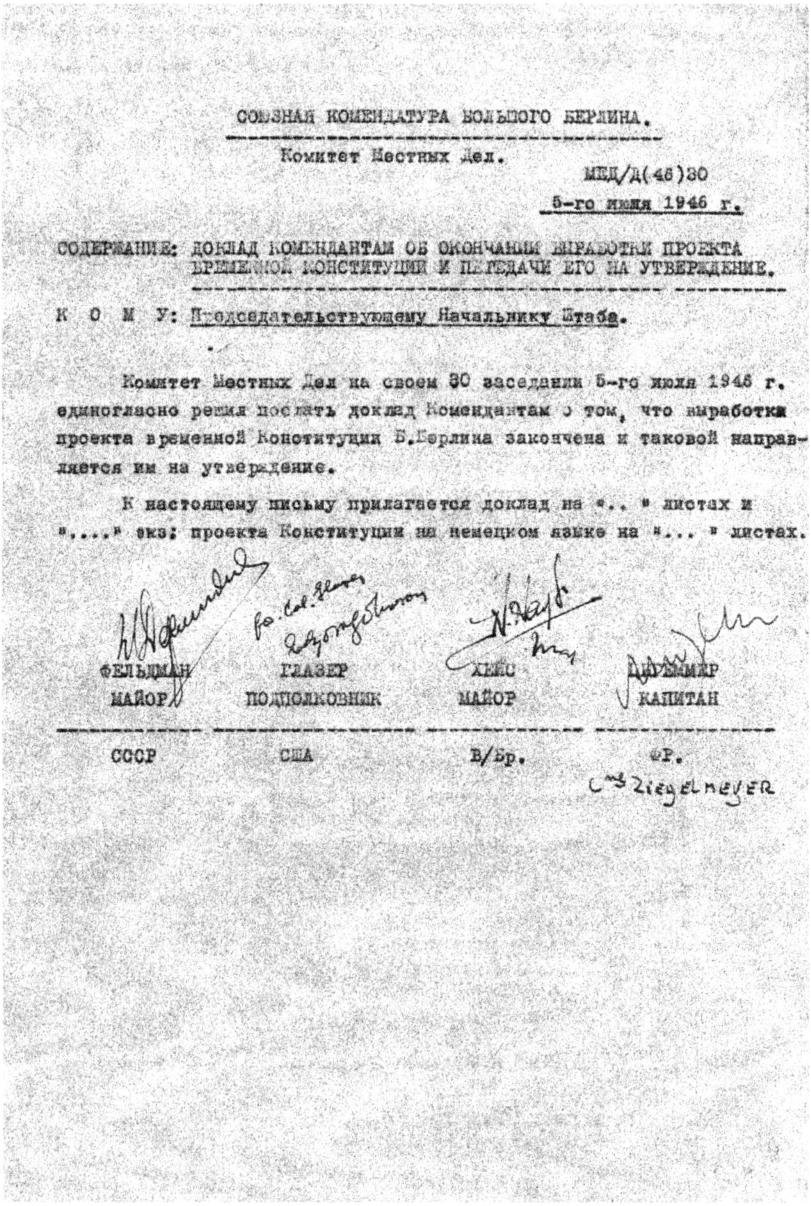

СОЮЗНАЯ КОМЕНДАТУРА БОЛЬШОГО БЕРЛИНА.

Комитет Местных Дел.

МЕД/Д(46)30

5-го июля 1946 г.

СОДЕРЖАНИЕ: ДОКЛАД КОМЕНДАНТАМ ОБ ОКОНЧАНИИ ВЫРАБОТКИ ПРОЕКТА ВРЕМЕННОЙ КОНСТИТУЦИИ И ПЕРЕДАЧИ ЕГО НА УТВЕРЖДЕНИЕ.

К О М У: Председательствующему Начальнику Штаба.

Комитет Местных Дел на своем 30 заседании 5-го июля 1946 г. единогласно решил послать доклад Комендантам о том, что выработка проекта временной Конституции Б.Берлина закончена и таковой направляется им на утверждение.

К настоящему письму прилагается доклад на «.. » листах и «...» экз; проекта Конституции на немецком языке на «... » листах.

ФЕЛЬДМАН	ГЛАЗЕР	ХЕЙС	ЦИГЕЛЬМАЙР
МАЙОР	ПОДПОЛКОВНИК	МАЙОР	КАПИТАН
СССР	США	В/Бр.	ФР.

Abb. 70 *Bericht des Local Government Committee, Allied Kommandatura Berlin, über den Entwurf einer vorläufigen Berliner Verfassung, 5. Juli 1946, unterzeichnet haben (von links): Major Iossif Moissejewitsch Feldman (Sowjetunion), Edgar N. Johnson für Lieutenant Colonel Louis Glaser (USA), Major Harold Hays (Großbritannien) und Capitaine Jean Victor Ziegelmeyer (Frankreich).*

The National Archives, Kew, Richmond, Surrey, Großbritannien, Allied Kommandatura: Directives, Minutes and Papers, FO 1112/377

TEMPORARY CONSTITUTION OF BERLIN

To provide for the situation arising after the collapse of the national-socialist regime, and the occupation by the Allied Powers, and in continuation of the constitutional right, according to the City Statutes of 30 May, 1853, to the Law on the formation of a new Municipality Berlin of 27 April, 1920, and the Law on the preliminary regulation of various problems of the municipal constitutional right of the City of Berlin of 30 March, 1931, Berlin receives the following

CONSTITUTION

Chapter I: GENERAL PROVISIONS

Article 1

(1) Greater Berlin is the exclusively established Public Territorial Corporation for the Territory of the Municipality of Berlin.

(2) Greater Berlin has to fulfil all the public duties in its district in accordance with this Constitution.

(3) Greater Berlin bears the Arms and Flag with the Bear. Particulars hereof will be laid down in a special Order.

Article 2

(1) The whole of the German citizens of Greater-Berlin express their will through their elected representative bodies.

(2) All citizens of Greater Berlin are, within the framework of the effective laws, of equal status independent of Race, Sex, Confession and extent of Property owned.

(3) The representative bodies are the Stadtverordnetenversammlung and the Magistrat.

Article 3

(1) The Stadtverordnetenversammlung is constituted on ground of general, equal, direct, and secret election by the inhabitants of Berlin, who are entitled to vote according to the principles of proportional representation.

(2) The members of the Magistrat will be elected by the Stadtverordnetenversammlung for the period of the election term. All political parties composing the Stadtverordnetenversammlung

11

Abb. 71 *Vorläufige Verfassung von Groß-Berlin vom 13. August 1946, englischsprachige Fassung, erste Seite des Textes aus einer Broschüre, printed by Printing and Stationery Service, Control Commission for Germany (BE), Berlin.*
Freundlicherweise zur Verfügung gestellt von Anthony J. Glaser, Bethesda, Maryland, USA

23. August 1946

An die
Alliierte Kommandantur von Berlin

Berlin - Dahlem
Kaiserswertherstr. 8/10

Meine hochverehrten Herren Kommandanten!

Die Übermittlung der " Vorläufigen Verfassung von
Gross - Berlin " ist mir ein willkommener Anlass, Ihnen
im Namen des Magistrats und in meinem eigenen Namen den
besonderen Dank der Stadt und der Bevölkerung von Berlin
für das grosse Vertrauen auszusprechen, das Sie damit
zur demokratischen Gesinnung Berlins bewiesen haben.

Wir betrachten die von der Alliierten Kommandantur
redigierte Vorläufige Verfassung als eine wichtige Unterstützung, die Sie der Berliner Bevölkerung in ihren
Bemühungen um eine wahrhaft demokratische Gestaltung ihrer
Zukunft gewährt haben.

Ich bin gewiss, dass die Bevölkerung von Berlin dieses
Vertrauen als eine Verpflichtung empfinden wird, allseit
die völkerversöhnenden Grundsätze der Demokratie zum
Fundament ihres politischen Glaubens zu machen.

Mit dem Ausdruck vorzüglicher Hochachtung
Ihr sehr ergebener

Abb. 72 *Nach Übermittlung der*
Vorläufigen Verfassung von Groß-Berlin mit BK/O (46) 326:
Dankschreiben von Oberbürgermeister Arthur Werner
an die Stadtkommandanten, 23. August 1946.
Landesarchiv Berlin, C Rep. 101 (Magistrat von Berlin, Oberbürgermeister), Nr. 65

ALLIED KOMMANDATURA BERLIN
16-18, Kaiserswerther Str.

31 August 1946

SUBJECT: Letter of Commendation

TO : Local Government Committee,
Allied Kommandatura Berlin:

US   Lt. Colonel Louis Glaser
Dr. E. N. Johnson
Mr. P. G. Artzrouni

BR   Commander Athelstane Doelberg
Major Harold Hays
Mr. Bernard Francis Emmerson
Capt. John Archibald Robert
Miss Emma Grace Gibson

FR   Capt. Jean Victor Ziegelmayer
Lt. Claude Ampoulange
Lt. Georges Dmitrieff
Lt. Antoine Gaspoercic

USSR Lt. Colonel Alexander Zozulya
Major Feldman
Lt. Yurovsky
Lt. Rojko

    The Commandants of the Allied Kommandatura Berlin are aware of the long, arduous hours that the Local Government Committee has labored in formulating and drafting the Constitution of the City of Berlin and the instructions to the Magistrat concerning the "Electoral Procedure of Berlin". The members of the Local Government Committee have given unstintingly of their time, and have drawn deeply upon their professional knowledge and experience to complete this important and difficult task assigned them by the Commandants. The completed document on the "Electoral Procedure of Berlin" is a testimonial to the patience and devotion to duty shown by all members of this Committee in reconciling divergent points of view and thereby producing a sound document.

Abb. 73 und Abb. 74 *Dankschreiben der Stadtkommandanten an das Local Government Committee, Allied Kommandatura Berlin, 31. August 1946.*
Anthony J. Glaser, Bethesda, Maryland, USA

The superior and practical work of the Local Government Committee in producing this document affords an example that all other Committees of the Allied Kommandatura Berlin may well emulate.

The Commandants commend the members of the Local Government Committee individually and collectively for their work in the successful completion of this highly important task.

C. E. RYAN	E. P. NARES	Charles LANCON	A. G. KOTIKOV
Brig. General	Maj.Gen.CBE MC	Gen. de Brig.	Maj. General
US Commandant	BR Commandant	FR Commandant	USSR Commandant

Abb. 75 *Dankschreiben von General Frank A. Keating an Edgar N. Johnson, 5. Juli 1946.*
Candice E. und Thomas R. Johnson, Denver, Colorado, USA

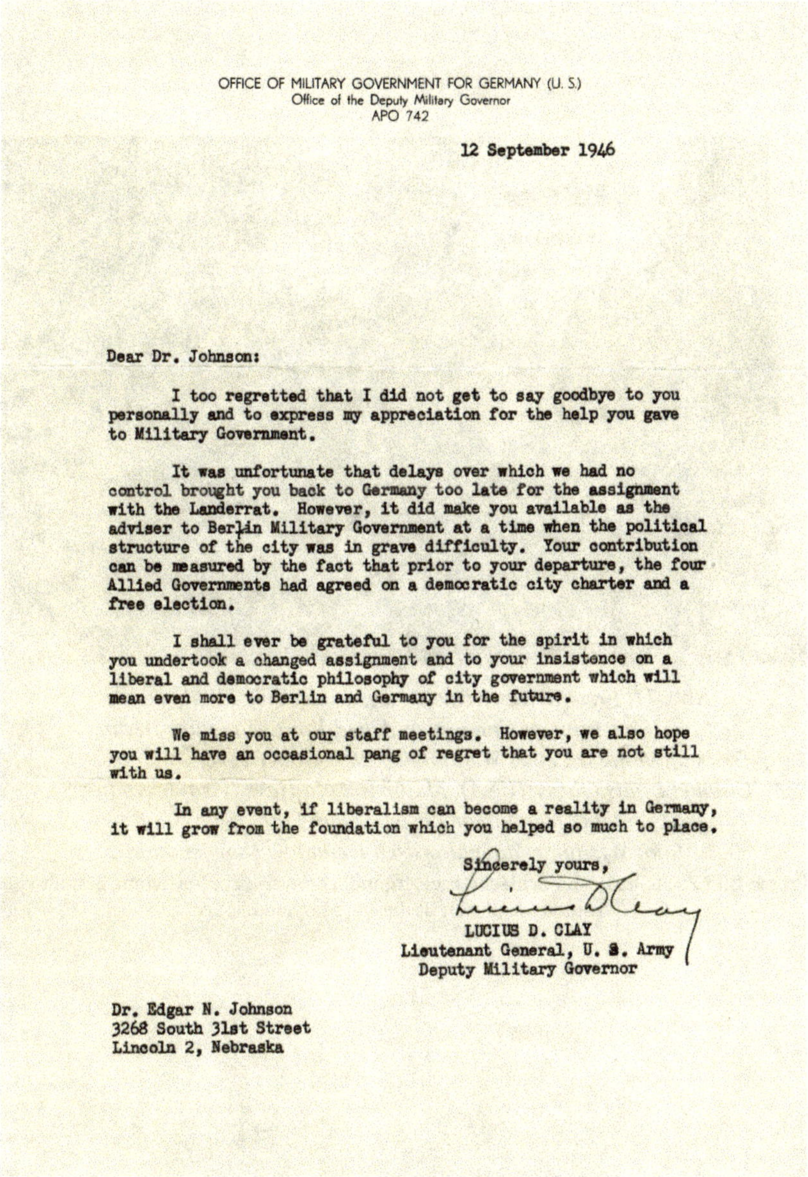

OFFICE OF MILITARY GOVERNMENT FOR GERMANY (U. S.)
Office of the Deputy Military Governor
APO 742

12 September 1946

Dear Dr. Johnson:

I too regretted that I did not get to say goodbye to you personally and to express my appreciation for the help you gave to Military Government.

It was unfortunate that delays over which we had no control brought you back to Germany too late for the assignment with the Länderrat. However, it did make you available as the adviser to Berlin Military Government at a time when the political structure of the city was in grave difficulty. Your contribution can be measured by the fact that prior to your departure, the four Allied Governments had agreed on a democratic city charter and a free election.

I shall ever be grateful to you for the spirit in which you undertook a changed assignment and to your insistence on a liberal and democratic philosophy of city government which will mean even more to Berlin and Germany in the future.

We miss you at our staff meetings. However, we also hope you will have an occasional pang of regret that you are not still with us.

In any event, if liberalism can become a reality in Germany, it will grow from the foundation which you helped so much to place.

Sincerely yours,

LUCIUS D. CLAY
Lieutenant General, U. S. Army
Deputy Military Governor

Dr. Edgar N. Johnson
3268 South 31st Street
Lincoln 2, Nebraska

Abb. 76 *Dankschreiben von General Lucius D. Clay an Edgar N. Johnson, 12. September 1946.*
The University of Chicago Library, Special Collections Research Center, Chicago, Illinois, USA, Edgar N. Johnson Papers

Abb. 77 *Erste Berliner Nachkriegswahlen, die Mitglieder des Local Government Committee, Allied Kommandatura Berlin, beim Verlassen eines Wahllokals, 20. Oktober 1946, von links: Colonel Louis Glaser (USA), Major Harold Hays (Großbritannien), Capitaine Jean Victor Ziegelmeyer (Frankreich) und Major Wladimir Michailowitsch Demidow (Sowjetunion).*
Presse Bild Zscheile, Berlin-Schlachtensee, freundlicherweise zur Verfügung gestellt von Anthony J. Glaser, Bethesda, Maryland, USA

Bildanhang 419

Abb. 78 *Stimmzettel zur Wahl der Stadtverordneten am 20. Oktober 1946.*
Landesarchiv Berlin, C Rep. 102 (Magistrat von Berlin,
Abteilung Verwaltung und Personalpolitik), Nr. 163

Abb. 79 *Anna Engelhorn,*
1927/1928 Edgar N. Johnsons Pensionswirtin in München,
Aufnahme aus den 1920er-Jahren.
Dieter Loew, Basel, Schweiz

Abb. 80 *Otto Suhr,*
August 1946–1947 Generalsekretär (davor geschäftsführender Generalsekretär)
der neu organisierten Berliner SPD,
Aufnahme aus dem Jahre 1946.
Archiv der sozialen Demokratie der Friedrich-Ebert-Stiftung, Bonn-Bad Godesberg

Abb. 81 *Franz Neumann,
April 1946–1958 Vorsitzender der Berliner SPD,
Aufnahme aus dem Jahre 1946.*
Pressebildagentur Schirner/Deutsches Historisches Museum, Berlin

Abb. 82 *Vereinigungsparteitag von KPD und SPD im Admiralspalast, Friedrichstraße 101/102, Berlin-Mitte, 21. April 1946, vorn von links: Max Fechner, Wilhelm Pieck, Otto Grotewohl und Walter Ulbricht.*
Landesarchiv Berlin, F Rep. 290 (Allgemeine Fotosammlung), Nr. 74142

Abb. 83 *Friedrich Haas, März–Dezember 1946 kommissarischer Stadtkämmerer, Aufnahme aus dem Jahre 1946.*
Landesarchiv Berlin/Alois Bankhardt, F Rep. 290 (Allgemeine Fotosammlung), Nr. 88477

Dr. Friedrich H a a s
Mitglied des Magistrats und
Kämmerer von Groß-Berlin
- - -

Berlin C 2, den 30.Dez.1946.
Neues Stadthaus, Parochialstr.
1-3
Privatanschrift: Bln.-Dahlem,
Löhleinstr.27

Lieber Herr J o h n s o n !

Herzlichen Dank für Ihre werten Zeilen, die ich im Oktober erhalten habe. Mit Hilfe von Mr.Biel bin ich bereits zweimal in Süddeutschland gewesen. Das letzte Mal nahm ich an einer interzonalen Tagung von Finanzfachleuten in der französischen Zone teil.

Die Arbeit ist hier vor wie nach den Wahlen in steigendem Tempo weitergegangen. Die Schwierigkeiten haben nicht abgenommen. Die vorläufige Verfassung, an der Sie so großen Anteil hatten, ist am 13.August 1946 veröffentlicht und am Wahltag, am 20.Oktober, in Kraft getreten. Inzwischen ist der neue Magistrat gewählt und hat zum größten Teil seine Tätigkeit aufgenommen. Der Wechsel vom alten, von den Besatzungsmächten eingesetzten zum neuen, von den Bürgern gewählten war nicht einfach. Wir befinden uns zur Zeit noch im Übergangsstadium.

Ich selbst wurde im Dezember zum Mitglied des neuen Magistrats, und zwar als Leiter der Rechts- und Verfassungsabteilung gewählt und auch von den Besatzungsmächten bestätigt. Da jedoch für meinen Nachfolger in der Finanzabteilung Schwierigkeiten eintraten, mußte ich am 19.Dezember wieder die Leitung der Finanzabteilung übernehmen. Ich bin nunmehr

also

Abb. 84 und Abb. 85 *Schreiben von Friedrich Haas an Edgar N. Johnson, 30. Dezember 1946.*
The University of Chicago Library, Special Collections Research Center, Chicago, Illinois, USA, Edgar N. Johnson Papers

also der auch in der vorläufigen Verfassung erwähnte Kämmerer von Groß-Berlin und daher gezwungen, die verfassungsrechtlichen Fragen nur noch nebenbei behandeln zu können. Augenblicklich benutze ich die Tage um Weihnachten und Neujahr, um den Ihnen angekündigten Kommentar zur vorläufigen Verfassung zu schreiben. Ich hoffe, mit dem Entwurf Mitte Januar fertig zu sein. Sobald er gedruckt ist, werde ich Ihnen ein Stück zugehen lassen. Daß ich bei der Erläuterung der vorläufigen Verfassung beinahe bei jedem Wort an unsere freundliche und offene Aussprache denke, brauche ich wohl nicht besonders zu betonen. Die Stunden und Tage unseres Kennenlernens und Zusammenarbeitens für eine größere, in die Zukunft weisende gemeinsame Sache bleiben mir unvergessen.

In der Hoffnung, Ihnen bald den Kommentar übermitteln zu können, verbleibt mit den ergebensten Grüßen für ein erfolgreiches Jahr 1947 auch an Ihre werte Frau

Ihr

Abb. 86 *Edgar N. Johnsons „Studierhütte"
in den Rocky Mountains im US-Bundesstaat Colorado,
wo sich die Briefe an seine Ehefrau fanden,
Aufnahme aus dem Jahre 2012.*
Candice E. und Thomas R. Johnson, Denver, Colorado, USA

Abkürzungsverzeichnis

AB	Artium Baccalaureus (Bachelor of Arts)
Abb.	Abbildung
ACA	Allied Control Authority
ACDP	Archiv für Christlich-Demokratische Politik
ACSP	Archiv für Christlich-Soziale Politik
AFP	Agence France-Presse
AG	Aktiengesellschaft
AGO	Adjutant General's Office
a. m.	ante meridiem
AMG	American Military Government
Anm.	Anmerkung
Antifa	Antifaschismus
AOF	Archives de l'Occupation Française
APO	Army Post Office
Art.	Artikel
Aug.	August
BA	Bachelor of Arts
BAB	Branchen-Adreßbücher
BArch	Bundesarchiv
BASC	Berlin Air Safety Center
BCS	Bachelor of Commercial Science
BD	Bachelor of Divinity; Berlin District
Bd.	Band
Bde.	Bände
BE	Bachelor of Engineering; British Element
bearb.	bearbeitet
betr.	betroffen
BICO	Bipartite Control Office
BKC/M	Berlin Kommandatura Commandants/Minutes of meeting
BKD/M	Berlin Kommandatura Deputy Commandants/Minutes of meeting
BK/O; BK/Ord.	Berlin Kommandatura/Order
Bl.	Blatt
BMus	Bachelor of Music
BS; BSc	Bachelor of Science
BS in Ed	Bachelor of Science in Education
BVG	Berliner Verkehrsbetriebe
BWV	Bachwerkeverzeichnis
bzw.	beziehungsweise
ca.	circa
CAF	Clerical, Administrative, and Fiscal Service

Capt.	Captain
C. A. R.	Children of the American Revolution
CARE	Cooperative for American Remittances to Europe
CC	Control Council
C-C	Coca-Cola
CCG (BE)	Control Commission for Germany (British Element)
CDU	Christlich-Demokratische Union
CI	Civil Internment
CIA; C. I. A.	Central Intelligence Agency
CID	Criminal Investigation Department
Cie.	Compagnie
CIO	Congress of Industrial Organizations
cm	Zentimeter
Co.	Compagnie; Company
c/o	care of
Col.	Colonel
Cols.	Colonels
Com.	Committee
CORC/M	Coordinating Committee/Minutes of meeting
CSU	Christlich-Soziale Union
D. A. R.	Daughters of the American Revolution
D. C.	District of Columbia
D day; D-day; D-Day	Day day; Day-day; Day-Day
DDR	Deutsche Demokratische Republik
DDr.	Doktor Doktor
ders.	derselbe
DFD	Demokratischer Frauenbund Deutschlands
d. h.	das heißt
DIAC	Directorate of Internal Affairs and Communications
DIAC/CAC/M	Directorate of Internal Affairs and Communications/Civil Administration Committee/Minutes of meeting
DLitt	Doctor Litterarum (Doctor of Letters)
Dok.	Dokument
DOMG	Director, Office of Military Government
dpa	Deutsche Presse-Agentur
DPOL/M	Political Directorate/Minutes of meeting
DPs	Displaced Persons
Dr.	Doctor; Doktor
Dr. jur.	Doctor juris (Doktor der Rechtswissenschaft)
Dr. med. h. c.	Doctor medicinae honoris causa (Doktor der Medizin ehrenhalber)
Dr. oec. publ.	Doctor oeconomiae publicae (Doktor der Staatswissenschaften)
Dr. phil.	Doctor philosophiae (Doktor der Philosophie)
Dr. rer. pol.	Doctor rerum politicarum (Doktor der Staatswissenschaften)

Drs.	Doctores
EAC; E. A. C.	European Advisory Commission
ebd.	ebenda
ECA	Economic Cooperation Administration
EdD	Educationis Doctor (Doctor of Education)
e. g.	exempli gratia
eigentl.	eigentlich
eingel.	eingeleitet
E-Mail	Electronic Mail
erg.	ergänzt
erl.	erläutert
erw.	erweitert
ET	European Theater
et al.	et alii
etc.	et cetera
EUCOM	European Command
e. V.	eingetragener Verein
f.	folgende; folgendes
FDGB	Freier Deutscher Gewerkschaftsbund
FDJ	Freie Deutsche Jugend
Febr.	February
Fi	Fieseler
FO	Foreign Office
geb.	geboren; geborene
Gebr.	Gebrüder
gen.	genannt
Gen.	General
gesch.	geschiedene
gest.	gestorben
Gestapo	Geheime Staatspolizei
GFCC	Groupe Français du Conseil de Contrôle
GI; G. I.	Government Issue
GIs; GI's	Government Issues
GMFB	Gouvernement Militaire Français de Berlin
GPU	Gossudarstwennoje Polititscheskoje Uprawlenije
GStA PK	Geheimes Staatsarchiv Preußischer Kulturbesitz
ha	Hektar
HA	Hauptabteilung
Halbbd.	Halbband
HICOG	High Commissioner for Germany
HICOG-BE	High Commissioner for Germany-Berlin
Hon.	Honourable
hrsg.	herausgegeben

Hrsg.	Herausgeber
IA + C	Internal Affairs and Communications
ID	Identification
i. e.	id est
IfZ	Institut für Zeitgeschichte
Inc.	Incorporated
IWM	Imperial War Museum
Jg.	Jahrgang
Jr.	Junior
km	Kilometer
Komintern	Kommunistische Internationale
KPD	Kommunistische Partei Deutschlands
KZ	Konzentrationslager
LAB	Landesarchiv Berlin
LAZ	Landesarchiv Berlin, Abteilung Zeitgeschichte
LDP	Liberal-Demokratische Partei Deutschlands
LG/M	Local Government/Minutes of meeting
Lieut. Col.	Lieutenant Colonel
LLB	Legum Baccalaureus (Bachelor of Laws)
LLD	Legum Doctor (Doctor of Laws)
LOC GOV/R	Local Government/Report
LRGS	Sammlung der Länderratsgesetze
Lt.	Lieutenant
Lt. Cols.	Lieutenant Colonels
m	Meter
MA	Master of Arts
Maj. Gen.	Major General
MBA	Master of Business Administration
MBE	Member of the Order of the British Empire
MD	Medicinae Doctor (Doctor of Medicine)
MdB	Mitglied des Bundestages
MdL	Mitglied des Landtages
MdR	Mitglied des Reichstages
MGBD	Military Government, Berlin District
MGBTB	Military Government British Troops Berlin
Mil. Gov.	Military Government
MLS	Master of Library Science
MoMA	Museum of Modern Art
MP; M. P.	Military Police; Military Police officer
M + P	Miller & Paine
MPL	Master of Patent Law
MP's; M. P.'s	Military Police officers

Mr.	Mister
MRP	Mouvement Républicain Populaire
Mrs.	Mistress
NAM	National Association of Manufacturers
NARA	National Archives and Records Administration
NATO	North Atlantic Treaty Organization
Nazi	Nationalsozialist
Nazis	Nationalsozialisten
n. Chr.	nach Christus
neubearb.	neubearbeitet
NKVD; NKWD	Narodny Komissariat Vnutrennikh Del; Narodny Komissariat Wnutrennich Del
no.; No.	numero; Numero
Nr.	Nummer
NS	Nationalsozialismus
NSDAP	Nationalsozialistische Deutsche Arbeiterpartei
NW; N. W.	Northwest
NY; N. Y.	New York
od.	oder
o. D.	ohne Datum
OdF	Opfer des Faschismus
Ok; OK; O. K.	okay
OLCB	Office of Land Commissioner for Bavaria
OLCH	Office of Land Commissioner for Hesse
OMGBD; OMG BD	Office of Military Government, Berlin District
OMGBS	Office of Military Government, Berlin Sector
OMGBY	Office of Military Government, Bavaria
OMGGH	Office of Military Government, Greater Hesse
OMGHE	Office of Military Government, Hesse
Omgus; OMGUS	Office of Military Government for Germany (US)
OMGUSZ	Office of Military Government (US Zone)
OMGWB	Office of Military Government, Württemberg-Baden
o. O.	ohne Ort
o. O. und J.	ohne Ort und Jahr
op.	opus
OSS; O. S. S.	Office of Strategic Services
O. T.	Organisation Todt
para	paragraph
PCF	Parti Communiste Français
PDS	Partei des Demokratischen Sozialismus
PhB	Philosophiae Baccalaureus (Bachelor of Philosophy)
PhD; Ph. D.	Philosophiae Doctor (Doctor of Philosophy)
pm; p. m.	post meridiem
PM	Postmaster

POE	Port of Embarkation
POLAD	Political Adviser
POW	Prisoner of War
Prof.	Professor
P. S.	Post Scriptum
PTA	Parent Teacher Association
PW	Prisoner of War
PW's	Prisoners of War
PX	Post Exchange
PX's	Post Exchanges
R + A	Research and Analysis Branch
Rep.	Repositur
Rev.	Reverend
RG	Record Group
RGCO	Regional Government Coordinating Office
S.	Seite
SAPMO-BArch	Stiftung Archiv der Parteien und Massenorganisationen der DDR im Bundesarchiv
SBZ	Sowjetische Besatzungszone
SD's	Social Democrats
s. e.	southeast
SED	Sozialistische Einheitspartei Deutschlands
SEP	Sozialistische Einheitspartei
Sept.	September
SFIO	Section Française de l'Internationale Ouvrière
Sgt.	Sergeant
SHAEF	Supreme Headquarters, Allied Expeditionary Forces
SLUGA	Special Legal Unit – Germany/Austria
S + M	Schmoller & Mueller
SMAD	Sowjetische Militäradministration in Deutschland
Sp.	Spalte
SPD	Sozialdemokratische Partei Deutschlands
Sr.	Senior
SS	Steam Ship
St.	Saint; Sankt
StAB	Staatsarchiv Bremen
SW	Southwest
t	Tonne
TNA	The National Archives
T. O.	Table of Organization
u.	und
u. a.	und andere; unter anderem
überarb.	überarbeitet

UChicago	University of Chicago
UCLA	University of California, Los Angeles
UdSSR	Union der Sozialistischen Sowjetrepubliken
ugs.	umgangssprachlich
UK	United Kingdom
UN	United Nations
UNESCO	United Nations Educational, Scientific and Cultural Organization
Uni	Universität
UNL	University of Nebraska-Lincoln
UNO	United Nations Organization
UNRRA	United Nations Relief and Rehabilitation Administration
U. of C.	University of Chicago
urspr.	ursprünglich
US; U. S.	United States
USA	United States of America
USAFI	United States Armed Forces Institute
USAMHI	United States Army Military History Institute
USAT	United States Army Transport
USFA	United States Forces Austria
USGCC	United States Group, Control Council
USPD	Unabhängige Sozialdemokratische Partei Deutschlands
USS	United States Ship
USSR	Union of Soviet Socialist Republics
UW-Madison	University of Wisconsin-Madison
V 1; V-1	Vergeltungswaffe 1
V 2; V-2	Vergeltungswaffe 2
VBK	Verwaltungsbezirk
v. Chr.	vor Christus
VdN	Verfolgte des Naziregimes
V-E	Victory-in-Europe
verh.	verheiratete
verw.	verwitwete
vgl.	vergleiche
VIP	Very Important Person
VIPs	Very Important Persons
viz.	videlicet
Vol.	Volume
V-Waffen	Vergeltungswaffen
Wac; WAC	Women's Army Corps; Member of the Women's Army Corps
Wacs	Members of the Women's Army Corps
Waves; WAVES	Women Accepted for Volunteer Emergency Service

WHS	Wisconsin Historical Society
WKP(B)	Wsessojusnaja Kommunistitscheskaja Partija (Bolschewiki)
WPA	Works Progress Administration; Works Projects Administration
WSW	West-Southwest
z. B.	zum Beispiel
zit.	zitiert

Quellen- und Literaturverzeichnis

1. Ungedruckte Quellen

Archivalien

Archiv des Instituts für Zeitgeschichte (IfZ), München
OMGUS-Akten (Mikrofiche-Reproduktion).
OMGUS – Staff Conferences (Protokollkopien), Fg 12/3-5.

Archiv für Christlich-Demokratische Politik (ACDP) der Konrad-Adenauer-Stiftung, Sankt Augustin
Landesverband Berlin, 03-012-032/1.

Archiv für Christlich-Soziale Politik (ACSP) der Hanns-Seidel-Stiftung, München
Nachlass Josef Müller.

Archives de l'Occupation Française (AOF) en Allemagne et en Autriche, Ministère des Affaires Etrangères, Colmar, Frankreich
Services Français à Berlin: Gouvernement Militaire Français de Berlin (GMFB), Groupe Français du Conseil de Contrôle (GFCC).

Bundesarchiv (BArch), Koblenz
Allied Control Authority, Office of Records and Archives, Z 46.
Länderrat des amerikanischen Besatzungsgebietes, 1945–49, Z 1.
Nachlass Friedrich Glum, N 1457.
Office of Military Government for Germany (U. S.) (OMGUS), 1944–49, Z 45 F.

Geheimes Staatsarchiv Preußischer Kulturbesitz (GStA PK), Berlin
Personalakte Käthe Bungert, I. HA, Rep. 178 (Generaldirektion der Staatsarchive), Nr. 1404.
Personalakte Ernst Posner, I. HA, Rep. 178 (Generaldirektion der Staatsarchive), Nr. 1627.

Imperial War Museum (IWM) Duxford, Cambridgeshire, Großbritannien
Lieutenant Colonel Harold Hays MBE Collection.

Landesarchiv Berlin (LAB)
Amtsgericht Charlottenburg – Handelsregister, A Rep. 342-02.
Einwohnermeldeamt Berlin, B Rep. 021.
Hauptausschuss „Opfer des Faschismus" (OdF)/Referat Verfolgte des Naziregimes (VdN), C Rep. 118-01.
Kommunistische Partei Deutschlands (KPD) – Bezirksorganisation Groß-Berlin, C Rep. 900-01.
Landesleitung Berlin der SED, C Rep. 901.
Landesverwaltungsamt Berlin, B Rep. 080.
Magistrat von Berlin, Abteilung Verwaltung und Personalpolitik, C Rep. 102.
Magistrat von Berlin, Abteilung Volksbildung, C Rep. 120.
Nachlass Otto Suhr, E Rep. 200-17.
Nachlass Arthur Werner, E Rep. 300-09.
Office of Military Government, Berlin Sector (OMGBS), B Rep. 036-01.
Quellensammlung zur Berliner Zeitgeschichte (LAZ-Sammlung), F Rep. 280.

Rechtsanwaltskammer Berlin, B Rep. 068.
Sammlung Amerikanische Behörden in Berlin, F Rep. 037.
Sozialdemokratische Partei Deutschlands (SPD) – Bezirksorganisation Berlin (1945/46), C Rep. 900-02.

National Archives and Records Administration (NARA), College Park, Maryland, USA
Records of the Office of Strategic Services, Record Group 226.

Staatsarchiv Bremen (StAB)
Bd. 2 der Hafenverkehrsbücher Bremerhaven, Überseehäfen und Columbuskaje – Seeschifffahrt, 4,72/2-57.

Stiftung Archiv der Parteien und Massenorganisationen der DDR im Bundesarchiv (SAPMO-BArch), Berlin
Nachlass Otto Grotewohl, NY 4090.

The National Archives (TNA), Kew, Richmond, Surrey, Großbritannien
Allied Kommandatura: Directives, Minutes and Papers.
Control Commission for Germany (British Element), CCG (BE).

The University of Chicago (UChicago) Library, Special Collections Research Center, Chicago, Illinois, USA
Edgar N. Johnson Papers.

Union College, Schaffer Library, Special Collections, Schenectady, New York, USA
Unterlagen zu William J. Anderson.

University of California, Los Angeles (UCLA), Charles E. Young Research Library, Department of Special Collections, Los Angeles, California, USA
Eugene N. Anderson Papers, Collection 2074.

University of Nebraska-Lincoln (UNL) Libraries, Archives & Special Collections, Lincoln, Nebraska, USA
Biographical File of Edgar N. Johnson, RG/52-01, Box 134.
Bulletins & Catalogs (University, General), RG/00-07.

University of Strathclyde Archives, Glasgow, Großbritannien
Seven Chapters of Miette Dernbach's (née Hardy) Family Biography, T-MIN/31.

University of Wisconsin-Madison (UW-Madison) Archives, Madison, Wisconsin, USA
Department of History, Faculty Personnel Files.

US Army Military History Institute (USAMHI), Carlisle, Pennsylvania, USA
Frank L. Howley Papers.

Wisconsin Historical Society (WHS) Archives, Madison, Wisconsin, USA
Roswell P. Rosengren Papers.

Materialien aus Privatbesitz

Glaser, Anthony J., Bethesda, Maryland, USA
Unterlagen aus dem Nachlass Louis Glaser.

Johnson, Candice E. und Thomas R., Denver, Colorado, USA
Unterlagen aus dem Nachlass Edgar N. Johnson.

Loew, Dieter, Basel, Schweiz
Erinnerungen von Marcus Löw-Suter

E-Mails und Schreiben

Anderson Jr., Eugene N., E-Mails vom 23. Juni 2007, 3. Juli 2007, 17. Juli 2007 und 30. Juli 2007.

Anderson, James E., E-Mails vom 30. Mai 2008 und 24. Februar 2013.

Baldner, Thomas, E-Mails vom 20. September 2010 und 21. September 2010.

Cherdel, Jean-Yves, E-Mail vom 2. Dezember 2013.

Davis, Lisa F., Acting Executive Director, Medieval Academy of America, E-Mail vom 29. Mai 2013.

Dutilh-von Schmidt Seidlitz, Hedda, Schreiben vom 19. Oktober 2010.

Gailey III, Charles K., E-Mails vom 26. Oktober 2009 und 2. November 2009.

Gailey, Christine W., E-Mails vom 25. Oktober 2009 und 26. Oktober 2009.

Gailey, Timothy H., E-Mail vom 29. Juli 2011.

Gass, Geoffrey A., E-Mail vom 30. Dezember 2009.

Glaser, Anthony J., E-Mails vom 22. August 2009, 27. September 2009 und 23. Oktober 2012.

Grady, Sister Mary Rita, Archivist, Regis College Archives, E-Mail vom 25. April 2013.

Imperial War Museum Duxford, Department of Documents, E-Mail vom 30. Juni 2009.

Johnson, Candice E. und Thomas R., E-Mails vom 4. Mai 2007, 16. Dezember 2007, 24. Mai 2010, 1. Juni 2010, 24. April 2013, 14. Juni 2013 und 18. Oktober 2013.

Loomis, Kelly, E-Mail vom 14. Juni 2012.

Marburger Universitätsmuseum, E-Mail vom 29. Mai 2009.

McLean, Jack, E-Mail vom 16. Juli 2008.

Murie, Alison G., E-Mails vom 10. Januar 2010 und 15. Januar 2010.

National Archives and Records Administration, Schreiben vom 21. Dezember 2010.

Oppenheimer, Wolfgang, Schreiben vom 10. Januar 2012.

Schertz, Georg, E-Mail vom 26. Juni 2007.

Schuyler, Philip V. R., E-Mails vom 8. Februar 2008 und 6. März 2008.

Stadtarchiv München, Schreiben vom 4. August 2009, E-Mail vom 26. März 2010.

The Royal Engineers Museum, E-Mail vom 24. Juni 2009.

Treece, Will, Friends Historical Library Intern, Swarthmore College, E-Mail vom 6. Juli 2009.

Wimmer, Ulrich, Richter am Kammergericht, E-Mail vom 6. November 2012.

Wolf, Dieter, Leiter des Museums und Stadtarchivs der Stadt Butzbach, E-Mails vom 12. Juli 2007 und 9. Dezember 2011.

Wolford, Claire A., Graduate Assistant, New York University Archives, E-Mail vom 11. April 2013.

Mündlich befragte Personen

Baldner, Thomas, Telefongespräch am 29. April 2009.

Gailey, Timothy H., Interview am 10. August 2011 in Berlin.

Heller, Aribert, Telefongespräch am 5. Januar 2010.

Impekoven, Holger, Telefongespräch am 16. Oktober 2013.

Johnson, Candice E. und Thomas R., Interview am 13. September 2012 in Berlin.

Wepper, Angela, Telefongespräch am 18. Juni 2009.

2. Gedruckte Quellen und Literatur

Akten zur Vorgeschichte der Bundesrepublik Deutschland 1945–1949, Bd. 1: September 1945–Dezember 1946, bearb. von Walter Vogel/Christoph Weisz, München und Wien 1976.
Allert, Tilman: Der deutsche Gruß. Geschichte einer unheilvollen Geste, Frankfurt am Main 2005.
Amtliches Fernsprechbuch für den Bezirk der Reichspostdirektion Berlin, 1941.
Ausstellung Ewald Vetter, Walther-Rathenau-Saal, Rathaus-Wedding (Altbau), Berlin 65, Müllerstraße 146/147, 7.10.–11.11.75, Katalog zur Ausstellung des Kunstamts Wedding, Berlin 1975.
BAB Straßenführer durch Berlin mit allen Änderungen nach dem neuesten Stand, 1. Jg. 1946.
Backer, John H.: Die deutschen Jahre des Generals Clay. Der Weg zur Bundesrepublik 1945–1949, München 1983.
Bajohr, Frank: Gauleiter in Hamburg. Zur Person und Tätigkeit Karl Kaufmanns, in: Vierteljahrshefte für Zeitgeschichte, 43. Jg. 1995, S. 267–295.
Balkow-Gölitzer, Harry/Rüdiger Reitmeier/Bettina Biedermann/Jörg Riedel: Prominente in Berlin-Wannsee und ihre Geschichten, hrsg. von Burkhardt Sonnenstuhl, Berlin 2006.
Bauer, A./J. Carpentier: Répertoire des Artistes d'Alsace des XIXe et XXe siècles. Peintres – Sculpteurs – Graveurs – Dessinateurs, V–Z, Straßburg 1991.

Bavendamm, Gundula (Hrsg.): Amerikaner in Hessen. Eine besondere Beziehung im Wandel der Zeit, Hanau 2008.
Becker, Josef/Theo Stammen/Peter Waldmann (Hrsg.): Vorgeschichte der Bundesrepublik Deutschland. Zwischen Kapitulation und Grundgesetz (= Uni-Taschenbücher 854), München 1979.
Befehle des Obersten Chefs der Sowjetischen Militärverwaltung in Deutschland. Aus dem Stab der Sowjetischen Militärverwaltung in Deutschland, Sammelheft 1: 1945, Berlin 1946.
Benjamin Franklin. Sein Leben von ihm selbst erzählt, Berlin 1946.
Bergsträsser, Ludwig: Befreiung, Besatzung, Neubeginn. Tagebuch des Darmstädter Regierungspräsidenten 1945–1948, hrsg. von Walter Mühlhausen (= Biographische Quellen zur deutschen Geschichte nach 1945, Bd. 5), München 1987.
Bering, Henrik: Outpost Berlin. The History of the American Military Forces in Berlin 1945–1994, Chicago, Berlin, Tokio und Moskau 1995.
Berlin. Kampf um Freiheit und Selbstverwaltung 1945–1946, hrsg. im Auftrage des Senats von Berlin (= Schriftenreihe zur Berliner Zeitgeschichte, Bd. 1), 2., erg. und erw. Auflage, Berlin 1961.
Berlin. Quellen und Dokumente 1945–1951, hrsg. im Auftrage des Senats von Berlin, bearb. durch Hans J. Reichhardt/Hanns U. Treutler/Albrecht Lampe (= Schriftenreihe zur Berliner Zeitgeschichte, Bd. 4/1. und 2. Halbbd.), Berlin 1964.
Berlin Handbuch. Das Lexikon der Bundeshauptstadt, hrsg. vom Presse- und Informationsamt des Landes Berlin, Berlin 1992.
Berlin in Zahlen 1947. Taschenbuch, Hrsg.: Hauptamt für Statistik, Berlin 1949.
Berlin Observer, 1946.
Berlin und seine Bauten, bearb. und hrsg. vom Architekten-Verein zu Berlin und der Vereinigung Berliner Architekten. III. Bd.: Privatbauten, Berlin 1896.
Berliner Adreßbuch, 1920–1943.
Berliner Zeitung, 1946.
Biografisches Handbuch der Berliner Stadtverordneten und Abgeordneten 1946–1963, im Auftrag des Präsidenten des Abgeordnetenhauses von Berlin bearb. von Werner Breunig/Andreas Herbst, mit einer Einleitung von Siegfried Heimann (= Schriftenreihe des Landesarchivs Berlin, Bd. 14), Berlin 2011.
Biographic Register of the Department of State, 1944/1945/1949.
Biographical Register of the Officers and Graduates of the U. S. Military Academy at West Point, New York, 1920–1930/1930–1940/1940–1950.
Biographisches Handbuch der deutschsprachigen Emigration nach 1933/International Biographical Dictionary of Central European Emigrés 1933–1945, hrsg. vom Institut für Zeitgeschichte, München, und von der Research Foundation for Jewish Immigration, Inc., New York, unter der Gesamtleitung von Werner Röder/Herbert A. Strauss, Bd. I–III, München, New York, London und Paris 1980/1983.
Blixen, Tania: Sieben phantastische Geschichten, Stuttgart 1979.
Boyens, Armin: Die Kirchenpolitik der amerikanischen Besatzungsmacht in Deutschland von 1944 bis 1946, in: Kirchen in der Nachkriegszeit. Vier zeitgeschichtliche Beiträge von Armin Boyens/Martin Greschat/Rudolf von Thadden/Paolo Pombeni (= Arbeiten zur kirchlichen Zeitgeschichte, Reihe B: Darstellungen, Bd. 8), Göttingen 1979, S. 7–99.
Brandeis University Bulletin, 1958–1959/1963–1964.
Braunfels, Sigrid: Skulptur und Architektur des Wasserspiels. Die Brunnen Adolf von Hildebrands, München und Berlin 2005.
Breunig, Werner: Verfassunggebung in Berlin 1945–1950 (= Beiträge zur Politischen Wissenschaft, Bd. 58), Berlin 1990.
Breunig, Werner: Berlin 1945/46. Vom Kriegsende bis zum parlamentarischen Neubeginn, in: „Berlin kommt wieder". Die Nachkriegsjahre 1945/46 (= Ausstellungskataloge des Landesarchivs Berlin, 16), Berlin 2005, S. 7–43.

Breunig, Werner: „Berlin kommt wieder". Die Nachkriegsjahre 1945/46, in: Museums-Journal, Nr. III, 19. Jg., Juli 2005, S. 89 f.

Breunig, Werner: Der parlamentarische Neubeginn. Die Konstituierung der Stadtverordnetenversammlung von Groß-Berlin am 26. November 1946, in: Berlin in Geschichte und Gegenwart. Jahrbuch des Landesarchivs Berlin 2011, S. 213–235.

Buckow, Anjana: Zwischen Propaganda und Realpolitik. Die USA und der sowjetisch besetzte Teil Deutschlands 1945–1955 (= USA-Studien, Bd. 13), Stuttgart 2003.

Chalou, George C. (Hrsg.): The Secrets War. The Office of Strategic Services in World War II, Washington, D. C., 1992.

Charles, Roland W.: Troopships of World War II, with a foreword by Major General Edmond H. Leavey, Washington, D. C., 1947.

Chicago Daily Tribune, 1946.

Clay, Lucius D.: Entscheidung in Deutschland, Frankfurt am Main 1950.

Das erste Jahr. Berlin im Neuaufbau. Ein Rechenschaftsbericht des Magistrats der Stadt Berlin, hrsg. im Auftrage des Magistrats der Stadt Berlin, Berlin 1946.

Das Jahr 1945 und das Kino, Berlin 1995.

Das Nationalkomitee „Freies Deutschland" und der Bund Deutscher Offiziere, hrsg. von Gerd R. Ueberschär (Die Zeit des Nationalsozialismus. Eine Buchreihe), Frankfurt am Main 1995.

Das Volk, 1946.

Davis, Luckett V.: Louis, Joe, in: American National Biography, Bd. 13, New York und Oxford 1999, S. 942–944.

Der Berliner, 1946.

Der Kurier, 1946.

Der Länderrat des amerikanischen Besatzungsgebietes, hrsg. im Auftrag der Ministerpräsidenten von Bayern, Hessen, Württemberg-Baden und des Präsidenten des Senats der Freien Hansestadt Bremen vom Direktorium des Länderrats, zusammengestellt von Lia Härtel, ehemalige Archivarin beim Länderrat, Stuttgart und Köln 1951.

Der Morgen, 1946.

Der Sozialdemokrat, 1946.

Der Tagesspiegel, 1946.

Dettmar, Werner: Die Zerstörung Kassels im Oktober 1943. Eine Dokumentation, Fuldabrück 1983.

Deutschland unter alliierter Besatzung 1945–1949/55, hrsg. von Wolfgang Benz, Berlin 1999.

Die Entstehung der Verfassung von Berlin. Eine Dokumentation, im Auftrag des Präsidenten des Abgeordnetenhauses von Berlin hrsg. von Hans J. Reichhardt unter Mitarbeit von Werner Breunig/Josephine Gabler, 2 Bde., Berlin und New York 1990.

Die Neue Zeitung, 1946/1947.

Die Sitzungsprotokolle des Magistrats der Stadt Berlin 1945/46. Teil I: 1945, bearb. und eingel. von Dieter Hanauske (= Schriftenreihe des Landesarchivs Berlin, Bd. 2/I), Berlin 1995.

Die Sitzungsprotokolle des Magistrats der Stadt Berlin 1945/46. Teil II: 1946, bearb. und eingel. von Dieter Hanauske (= Schriftenreihe des Landesarchivs Berlin, Bd. 2/II), Berlin 1999.

Die UdSSR und die deutsche Frage 1941–1948. Dokumente aus dem Archiv für Außenpolitik der Russischen Föderation, bearb. und hrsg. von Jochen P. Laufer/Georgij P. Kynin unter Mitarbeit von Viktor Knoll, Bd. 2: 9. Mai 1945 bis 3. Oktober 1946, Berlin 2004.

Die UdSSR und die deutsche Frage 1941–1948. Dokumente aus dem Archiv für Außenpolitik der Russischen Föderation, bearb. und hrsg. von Jochen P. Laufer/Georgij P.

Kynin unter Mitarbeit von Viktor Knoll, Bd. 3: 6. Oktober 1946 bis 15. Juni 1948, Berlin 2004.

Die Vier Mächte in Berlin. Beiträge zur Politik der Alliierten in der besetzten Stadt, hrsg. von Michael Bienert/Uwe Schaper/Andrea Theissen unter Mitarbeit von Werner Breunig (= Schriftenreihe des Landesarchivs Berlin, Bd. 9), Berlin 2007.

Dinesen, Isak: Seven Gothic Tales (Penguin Modern Classics), London u. a. 1988.

Dinter, Andreas: Berlin in Trümmern. Ernährungslage und medizinische Versorgung der Bevölkerung Berlins nach dem II. Weltkrieg (= Geschichte[n] der Medizin, Bd. 1), Berlin 1999.

Dokumente zur Berlin-Frage 1944–1966, mit einem Vorwort des Regierenden Bürgermeisters von Berlin, hrsg. vom Forschungsinstitut der Deutschen Gesellschaft für Auswärtige Politik e.V., Bonn, in Zusammenarbeit mit dem Senat von Berlin (= Schriften des Forschungsinstituts der Deutschen Gesellschaft für Auswärtige Politik e.V., Bonn, Reihe: Internationale Politik und Wirtschaft, Bd. 52/I), 4. Auflage, München 1987.

Dorn, Walter L.: Inspektionsreisen in der US-Zone. Notizen, Denkschriften und Erinnerungen aus dem Nachlaß übersetzt und hrsg. von Lutz Niethammer (= Schriftenreihe der Vierteljahrshefte für Zeitgeschichte, Nr. 26), Stuttgart 1973.

Dornberger, Walter: Peenemünde. Die Geschichte der V-Waffen, mit einem Geleitwort von Eberhard Rees, Huntsville/Alabama, Eßlingen 1981.

Dulles, John Foster: Thoughts on Soviet Foreign Policy and What To Do About It, in: Life vom 3. Juni 1946, S. 112–126 (Part I), und vom 10. Juni 1946, S. 118–130 (Part II).

Dulles, John Foster: Gedanken über die Sowjet-Außenpolitik und was dazu zu tun ist, der Zeitschrift „Life" entnommen, Hamburg 1947.

Dzuback, Mary Ann: Robert M. Hutchins. Portrait of an Educator, Chicago und London 1991.

Eakin-Thimme, Gabriela Ann: Geschichte im Exil. Deutschsprachige Historiker nach 1933 (= Forum deutsche Geschichte, 8), München 2005.

Eisenhauer, Gregor: Ingeborg von Streletzky. Geb. 1916. Es war keine gütige Fee, es war harte Arbeit und unbarmherzige Dressur, in: Der Tagesspiegel vom 25. November 2011, S. 12.

Engel, Helmut: Villen und Landhäuser, fotografiert von Wolfgang Reuss (= Meisterwerke Berliner Baukunst, Bd. I), Berlin 2001.

Erd, Rainer (Hrsg.): Reform und Resignation. Gespräche über Franz L. Neumann (= edition suhrkamp 1239, Neue Folge Bd. 239), Frankfurt am Main 1985.

Esche-Braunfels, Sigrid: Adolf von Hildebrand (1847–1921), Berlin 1993.

Fait, Barbara: „In einer Atmosphäre von Freiheit". Die Rolle der Amerikaner bei der Verfassunggebung in den Ländern der US-Zone 1946, in: Vierteljahrshefte für Zeitgeschichte, 33. Jg. 1985, S. 420–455.

Fait, Barbara: Demokratische Erneuerung unter dem Sternenbanner. Amerikanische Kontrolle und Verfassunggebung in Bayern 1946 (= Beiträge zur Geschichte des Parlamentarismus und der politischen Parteien, Bd. 114), Düsseldorf 1998.

Fichter, Michael: Besatzungsmacht und Gewerkschaften. Zur Entwicklung und Anwendung der US-Gewerkschaftspolitik in Deutschland 1944–1948 (= Schriften des Zentralinstituts für sozialwissenschaftliche Forschung der Freien Universität Berlin, Bd. 40), Opladen 1982.

Fippel, Günter: Demokratische Gegner und Willküropfer von Besatzungsmacht und SED in Sachsenhausen (1946 bis 1950). Das sowjetische Speziallager Sachsenhausen – Teil des Stalinschen Lagerimperiums, unter Mitarbeit von Paul Radicke, mit einem einführenden Essay von Klaus-Dieter Müller, Herausgabe und Redaktion: Klaus-Dieter Müller/Mike Schmeitzner, Leipzig 2008, S. 122.

Fischer, Rolf: Hermann Lüdemann und die deutsche Demokratie, Neumünster 2006.

Flechtheim, Ossip K.: Die Anpassung der SPD: 1914, 1933 und 1959, in: Politologie und Soziologie. Otto Stammer zum 65. Geburtstag, hrsg. von Jürgen Fijalkowski, Köln und Opladen 1965, S. 182–202.
Franklin, Benjamin: The Autobiography, with an introduction by Daniel Aaron, New York 1990.
Franklin, Benjamin: Autobiographie, mit einem Nachwort von Klaus Harpprecht (= Beck'sche Reihe, 1510), 2. Auflage, München 2010.
Führe, Dorothea: Die französische Besatzungspolitik in Berlin von 1945 bis 1949. Déprussianisation und Décentralisation, Berlin 2001.
25 Jahre Theater in Berlin. Theaterpremieren 1945–1970, mit einem Vorwort von Friedrich Luft, hrsg. im Auftrage des Senats von Berlin, bearb. durch Hans J. Reichhardt/ Joachim Drogmann/Helmut Rosenthal/Hanns U. Treutler (= Schriftenreihe zur Berliner Zeitgeschichte, Bd. 7), Berlin 1972.
Füssl, Karl-Heinz: Die Umerziehung der Deutschen. Jugend und Schule unter den Siegermächten des Zweiten Weltkriegs 1945–1955 (Sammlung Schöningh zur Geschichte und Gegenwart), 2. Auflage, Paderborn, München, Wien und Zürich 1995.

Gaiba, Francesca: The Origins of Simultaneous Interpretation. The Nuremberg Trial (Perspectives on Translation), Ottawa 1998.
Gartendenkmale in Berlin: Privatgärten, bearb. von Katrin Lesser, mit einer Einführung von Klaus-Henning von Krosigk und Beiträgen von Josef Batzhuber et al. (= Beiträge zur Denkmalpflege in Berlin, 21), Petersberg 2005.
Geheimdienstkrieg gegen Deutschland. Subversion, Propaganda und politische Planungen des amerikanischen Geheimdienstes im Zweiten Weltkrieg, hrsg. von Jürgen Heideking/Christof Mauch (Sammlung Vandenhoeck), Göttingen 1993.
Germer, Karl J.: Von Grotewohl bis Brandt. Ein dokumentarischer Bericht über die SPD in den ersten Nachkriegsjahren, Landshut 1974.
Geschichtswissenschaft in Berlin im 19. und 20. Jahrhundert. Persönlichkeiten und Institutionen, hrsg. von Reimer Hansen/Wolfgang Ribbe (= Veröffentlichungen der Historischen Kommission zu Berlin, Bd. 82; Publikationen der Sektion für die Geschichte Berlins), Berlin und New York 1992.
Gesetz über die Bildung einer neuen Stadtgemeinde Berlin vom 27. April 1920, in: Preußische Gesetzsammlung, 1920, S. 123–150.
Gesetz über die vorläufige Regelung verschiedener Punkte des Gemeindeverfassungsrechts für die Hauptstadt Berlin vom 30. März 1931, in: Preußische Gesetzsammlung, 1931, S. 39–44.
Giesecke, Dagmar: Ernst Maximilian Posner. Eine skizzenhafte Biographie, Diplomarbeit Fachhochschule Potsdam, Fachbereich Archiv – Bibliothek – Dokumentation, 1996.
Gilbert, Felix: Lehrjahre im alten Europa. Erinnerungen 1905–1945, Berlin 1989.
Gimbel, John: Amerikanische Besatzungspolitik in Deutschland 1945–1949, Frankfurt am Main 1971.
Glum, Friedrich: Die Organisation der Riesenstadt. Die Verfassungen von Paris, London, New York, Wien und Berlin. Aus Anlaß des Entwurfs der Staatsregierung über die Bildung einer Stadt Groß-Berlin, Berlin 1920.
Glum, Friedrich: Zwischen Wissenschaft, Wirtschaft und Politik. Erlebtes und Erdachtes in vier Reichen, Bonn 1964.
Gniffke, Erich W.: Jahre mit Ulbricht, mit einem Vorwort von Herbert Wehner, Köln 1966 (Reprint 1990).
Graml, Hermann: Die Alliierten und die Teilung Deutschlands. Konflikte und Entscheidungen 1941–1948, Frankfurt am Main 1985.
Grathwol, Robert P./Donita M. Moorhus: American Forces in Berlin 1945–1994. Cold War Outpost, Washington, D. C., 1994.
Grathwol, Roger P./Donita M. Moorhus: Berlin and the American Military. A Cold War Chronicle, edited by Gareth L. Steen, New York und London 1999.

Grebner, Susanne: Der Telegraf. Entstehung einer SPD-nahen Lizenzzeitung in Berlin 1946 bis 1950 (= Kommunikationsgeschichte, Bd. 13), Münster, Hamburg und London 2002.

Hanauske, Dieter: „... als leuchtendes Signal für ganz Deutschland". Der Berliner Magistrat von 1945/46 als „antifaschistisch-demokratisches" Musterbeispiel?, in: Berlin in Geschichte und Gegenwart. Jahrbuch des Landesarchivs Berlin 1999, S. 145-183.
Hanauske, Dieter: „Ein ehrlicher Mann, aber etwas naiv". Arthur Werner – Berliner Oberbürgermeister von 1945/46, in: Der Bär von Berlin. Jahrbuch 2002 des Vereins für die Geschichte Berlins, S. 131-160.
Hansen, Reimer: Neuer Name in historischer Tradition. Von der Friedrich-Wilhelms- zur Humboldt-Universität 1945-1949, in: Berlin in Geschichte und Gegenwart. Jahrbuch des Landesarchivs Berlin 2009, S. 349-375.
Heiss, Hans/Gustav Pfeifer (Hrsg.): Südtirol – Stunde Null? Kriegsende 1945-1946 (= Veröffentlichungen des Südtiroler Landesarchivs, Bd. 10), Innsbruck, Wien und München 2000.
Henke, Klaus-Dietmar: Die amerikanische Besetzung Deutschlands (= Quellen und Darstellungen zur Zeitgeschichte, Bd. 27), München 1995.
Henning, Eckart/Marion Kazemi: Dahlem – Domäne der Wissenschaft. Ein Spaziergang zu den Berliner Instituten der Kaiser-Wilhelm-/Max-Planck-Gesellschaft im „deutschen Oxford" (= Veröffentlichungen aus dem Archiv der Max-Planck-Gesellschaft, Bd. 16/I), 4., erw. und aktualisierte Auflage, Berlin 2009.
Hinz, Gerhard: Ernst Walz †, in: Ruperto-Carola. Zeitschrift der Vereinigung der Freunde der Studentenschaft der Universität Heidelberg e. V., Juni 1967, S. 46f.
Hirtenbriefe und Ansprachen zu Gesellschaft und Politik 1945-1949, bearb. von Wolfgang Löhr (= Dokumente deutscher Bischöfe, Bd. I), Würzburg 1985.
Horizont, 1946.
Howley, Frank: Berlin Command, New York 1950.
Hurwitz, Harold: Die politische Kultur der Bevölkerung und der Neubeginn konservativer Politik (= Demokratie und Antikommunismus in Berlin nach 1945, Bd. I), Köln 1983.
Hurwitz, Harold/Klaus Sühl: Autoritäre Tradierung und Demokratiepotential in der sozialdemokratischen Arbeiterbewegung (= Demokratie und Antikommunismus in Berlin nach 1945, Bd. II), Köln 1984.
Hurwitz, Harold: Die Eintracht der Siegermächte und die Orientierungsnot der Deutschen 1945-1946 (= Demokratie und Antikommunismus in Berlin nach 1945, Bd. III), Köln 1984.
Hurwitz, Harold, unter Mitarbeit von Andreas Büning/Johannes-Berthold Hohmann/ Klaus Sühl/Ingolore Mensch-Khan: Die Anfänge des Widerstands, Teil 1: Führungsanspruch und Isolation der Sozialdemokraten (= Demokratie und Antikommunismus in Berlin nach 1945, Bd. IV), Köln 1990.
Hurwitz, Harold, unter Mitarbeit von Andreas Büning/Johannes-Berthold Hohmann/ Klaus Sühl/Ingolore Mensch-Khan: Die Anfänge des Widerstands, Teil 2: Zwischen Selbsttäuschung und Zivilcourage: Der Fusionskampf (= Demokratie und Antikommunismus in Berlin nach 1945, Bd. IV), Köln 1990.
Hurwitz, Harold, unter Mitarbeit von Ursula Böhme/Andreas Malycha: Die Stalinisierung der SED. Zum Verlust von Freiräumen und sozialdemokratischer Identität in den Vorständen 1946-1949 (= Schriften des Zentralinstituts für sozialwissenschaftliche Forschung der Freien Universität Berlin, Bd. 79), Opladen 1997.

Impekoven, Holger: Die Alexander von Humboldt-Stiftung und das Ausländerstudium in Deutschland 1925-1945. Von der „geräuschlosen Propaganda" zur Ausbildung der „geistigen Wehr" des „Neuen Europa" (= Internationale Beziehungen. Theorie und Geschichte, Bd. 9), Göttingen 2013.

Internationaler Militärgerichtshof Nürnberg (Hrsg.): Der Prozeß gegen die Hauptkriegsverbrecher vor dem Internationalen Militärgerichtshof, Nürnberg 14. November 1945–1. Oktober 1946, Bd. XX: Verhandlungsniederschriften 30. Juli 1946–10. August 1946, Nürnberg 1948.

Jeschonnek, Friedrich/Dieter Riedel/William Durie: Alliierte in Berlin 1945–1994. Ein Handbuch zur Geschichte der militärischen Präsenz der Westmächte, Berlin 2002.
Johnson, Edgar N.: The American Occupation of Austria, in: Nebraska History, Vol. 26, 1945, S. 201–210.
Johnson, Edgar N./John Dean Bickford: The Contemplated Anglo-German Alliance: 1890–1901, in: Political Science Quarterly, Vol. 42, No. 1 (März 1927), S. 1–57.
Jordan, Karl: Rezension von: Edgar Nathaniel Johnson, The Secular Activities of the German Episcopate 919–1024, Lincoln, Nebraska, 1932, in: Deutsche Literaturzeitung, 1933, Heft 50, Sp. 2378–2380.

Kahn, Arthur D.: Experiment in Occupation. Witness to the Turnabout. Anti-Nazi War to Cold War 1944–1946, University Park, Pennsylvania, 2004.
Katalog der Grossen Berliner Kunst-Ausstellung 1908, Berlin, Stuttgart und Leipzig 1908.
Katz, Barry M.: Foreign Intelligence. Research and Analysis in the Office of Strategic Services 1942–1945, Cambridge, Massachusetts, und London 1989.
Keesing's Archiv der Gegenwart, XV.–XVII. Jg., 1945–1947.
Keiderling, Gerhard: Die Alliierte Kommandantur der Stadt Berlin. Von der EAC 1944/45 bis zum Ende der Viermächteverwaltung 1948, in: Jahrbuch für Geschichte, Bd. 35 (1987), S. 565–615.
Kemp, Kathryn W.: God's Capitalist. Asa Candler of Coca-Cola, Macon, Georgia, 2002.
Knappen, Marshall: And call it peace, Chicago 1947.
Knoll, Robert E.: Prairie University. A History of the University of Nebraska, Lincoln, Nebraska, 1995.
Kohl, Ulrike: Die Präsidenten der Kaiser-Wilhelm-Gesellschaft im Nationalsozialismus. Max Planck, Carl Bosch und Albert Vögler zwischen Wissenschaft und Macht (= Pallas Athene. Beiträge zur Universitäts- und Wissenschaftsgeschichte, Bd. 5), Stuttgart 2002.
Königseder, Angelika: Flucht nach Berlin. Jüdische Displaced Persons 1945–1948 (= Reihe Dokumente – Texte – Materialien. Veröffentlicht vom Zentrum für Antisemitismusforschung der Technischen Universität Berlin, Bd. 27), Berlin 1998.
Koop, Volker: Besetzt. Französische Besatzungspolitik in Deutschland. Berlin 2005.
Koop, Volker: Besetzt. Amerikanische Besatzungspolitik in Deutschland. Berlin 2006.
Koop, Volker: Besetzt. Britische Besatzungspolitik in Deutschland. Berlin 2007.
Koop, Volker: Besetzt. Sowjetische Besatzungspolitik in Deutschland. Berlin 2008.
Köpf, Peter: Die Mommsens. Von 1848 bis heute – die Geschichte einer Familie ist die Geschichte der Deutschen, Hamburg, Leipzig und Wien 2004.
Kraus, Elisabeth: Ministerien für das ganze Deutschland? Der Alliierte Kontrollrat und die Frage gesamtdeutscher Zentralverwaltungen (= Studien zur Zeitgeschichte, Bd. 37), München 1990.
Krieger, Wolfgang: General Lucius D. Clay und die amerikanische Deutschlandpolitik 1945–1949 (= Forschungen und Quellen zur Zeitgeschichte, Bd. 10), Stuttgart 1987.
Krüger, Ingo: Landhäuser und Villen in Berlin & Potsdam. Nr. 3: Großer Wannsee, Colonie Alsen, Villa Liebermann, Bremen 2005.
Krumholz, Walter, unter Mitarbeit von Wilhelm Lutze/Oskar Kruß/Richard Höpfner u. a.: Berlin-ABC, Berlin und München 1969.

Lange, Gunter: Otto Suhr. Im Schatten von Ernst Reuter und Willy Brandt. Eine Biographie (Reihe Praktische Demokratie), Bonn 1994.

Latour, Conrad F./Thilo Vogelsang: Okkupation und Wiederaufbau. Die Tätigkeit der Militärregierung in der amerikanischen Besatzungszone Deutschlands 1944–1947 (Studien zur Zeitgeschichte), Stuttgart 1973.
Leesch, Wolfgang: Die deutschen Archivare 1500–1945, Bd. 2: Biographisches Lexikon, München, London, New York und Paris 1992.
Lehmann, Bernhard: Katholische Kirche und Besatzungsmacht in Bayern 1945–1949 im Spiegel der OMGUS-Akten (= Miscellanea Bavarica Monacensia. Dissertationen zur Bayerischen Landes- und Münchner Stadtgeschichte, Bd. 153), München 1994.
Leonhard, Wolfgang: Die Revolution entläßt ihre Kinder, 8. Auflage, München 1985.
Leonhard, Wolfgang: Meine Geschichte der DDR, 2. Auflage, Berlin 2007.
Leuerer, Thomas: Die Stationierung amerikanischer Streitkräfte in Deutschland. Militärgemeinden der U. S. Army in Deutschland seit 1945 als ziviles Element der Stationierungspolitik der Vereinigten Staaten (= Politik und Gesellschaft. Würzburger Universitätsschriften, Bd. 6), Würzburg 1997.
Life, 1946.
Lill, Rudolf: Südtirol in der Zeit des Nationalismus, Konstanz 2002.
Lotz, François, avec la collaboration de Joseph Fuchs/Léon Kieffer/René Metz: Artistes-Peintres Alsaciens de jadis et de naguère (1880–1982), Kaysersberg 1987.
Ludwig-Maximilians-Universität München. Verzeichnis der Vorlesungen Winter-Halbjahr 1927/28, München 1927.

Maginnis, John J.: Military Government Journal. Normandy to Berlin, Hrsg.: Robert A. Hart, Amherst, Massachusetts, 1971.
Mai, Gunther: Der Alliierte Kontrollrat in Deutschland 1945–1948. Alliierte Einheit – deutsche Teilung? (= Quellen und Darstellungen zur Zeitgeschichte, Bd. 37), München 1995.
Marquardt-Bigman, Petra: Amerikanische Geheimdienstanalysen über Deutschland 1942–1949 (= Studien zur Zeitgeschichte, Bd. 45), München 1995.
Mauch, Christof: Schattenkrieg gegen Hitler. Das Dritte Reich im Visier der amerikanischen Geheimdienste 1941–1945, Stuttgart 1999.
Mitchell, Americus: Mitchell and Related Families, Kilmarnock, Virginia, 1984.
Mommsen, Wolfgang A.: Ernst Posner, Mittler zwischen deutschem und amerikanischem Archivwesen. Zu seinem 75. Geburtstag, in: Der Archivar, Jg. 20, 1967, Heft 3, Sp. 217–230.
Müller, Tim B.: Die gelehrten Krieger und die Rockefeller-Revolution. Intellektuelle zwischen Geheimdienst, Neuer Linken und dem Entwurf einer neuen Ideengeschichte, in: Geschichte und Gesellschaft, Heft 2007/33,2, S. 198–227.
Murphy, Robert: Diplomat among Warriors, Garden City, New York, 1964.

Nebraska State Journal, 1946.
Neiman, Gilbert: Lazarus Laughs, in: Accent. A Quarterly of New Literature, Vol. 6, No. 1 (Herbst 1945), S. 13–22.
Nevada State Journal, 1946.
New York Herald Tribune, European Edition, 1946.

Oberreuter, Heinrich/Jürgen Weber (Hrsg.): Freundliche Feinde? Die Alliierten und die Demokratiegründung in Deutschland (= Akademiebeiträge zur politischen Bildung, Bd. 29), München und Landsberg am Lech 1996.
Office of Military Government U. S. Berlin District (Hrsg.): Six Months Report 4 July 1945–3 January 1946, Berlin 1946.
Office of Military Government U. S. Berlin District (Hrsg.): Six Months Report 4 January–3 July 1946, Berlin 1946.
Office of Military Government Berlin Sector (Hrsg.): Six Months Report 4 July 1946 to 1 January 1947, Berlin 1947.

Office of Military Government U. S. Sector, Berlin (Hrsg.): A Four Year Report July 1, 1945–September 1, 1949, Berlin 1949.
Official Army Register, 1945/1946/1947.
OMGUS-Handbuch. Die amerikanische Militärregierung in Deutschland 1945–1949, hrsg. von Christoph Weisz (= Quellen und Darstellungen zur Zeitgeschichte, Bd. 35), München 1994.
OMGUS Observer, 1946.
Otto, Martin: Ulrich Biel (1907–1996) – graue Eminenz der (West-)Berliner Politik. Eine erste biografische Annäherung, in: Berlin in Geschichte und Gegenwart. Jahrbuch des Landesarchivs Berlin 2011, S. 285-304.

Padover, S. K./L. F. Gittler/P. R. Sweet: The Political Situation in Aachen, in: Propaganda in War and Crisis. Materials for American Policy, edited with an introduction by Daniel Lerner, New York 1951 (Reprint 1972), S. 434-456.
Panton, Kenneth J.: Historical Dictionary of London (= Historical Dictionaries of Cities of the World, No. 11), Lanham, Maryland, und London 2001.
Personenstand der Ludwig-Maximilians-Universität München. Winter-Halbjahr 1927/28, München 1928.
Pfetsch, Frank R.: Die Verfassungspolitik der westlichen Besatzungsmächte in den Ländern nach 1945. Oktroyierte Systemübertragung oder eigenständiger demokratischer Neubeginn?, in: Aus Politik und Zeitgeschichte. Beilage zur Wochenzeitung Das Parlament, 22/1986, S. 3-17.
Pfetsch, Frank R., unter Mitarbeit von Werner Breunig/Wolfgang Kringe: Ursprünge der Zweiten Republik. Prozesse der Verfassungsgebung in den Westzonen und in der Bundesrepublik, Opladen 1990.
Pollock, James K.: Besatzung und Staatsaufbau nach 1945. Occupation Diary and Private Correspondence 1945-1948, hrsg. von Ingrid Krüger-Bulcke (= Biographische Quellen zur deutschen Geschichte nach 1945, Bd. 14), München 1994.
Poltorak, Arkadi: Nürnberger Epilog, 5. Auflage, Berlin 1988.
Protokoll des Vereinigungsparteitages der Sozialdemokratischen Partei Deutschlands (SPD) und der Kommunistischen Partei Deutschlands (KPD) am 21. und 22. April 1946 in der Staatsoper „Admiralspalast" in Berlin, Berlin 1946.

Rathkolb, Oliver (Hrsg.): Gesellschaft und Politik am Beginn der Zweiten Republik. Vertrauliche Berichte der US-Militäradministration aus Österreich 1945 in englischer Originalfassung, Wien, Köln und Graz 1985.
Register of the Department of State, 1946/1948/1950.
Reichsgesetzblatt, Teil I, 1933.
Reif, Janin/Horst Schumacher/Lothar Uebel: Schwanenwerder. Ein Inselparadies in Berlin, Berlin 2000.
Reno Evening Gazette, 1946.
Rhein-Neckar-Zeitung, 1946.
Ribbe, Wolfgang: Berlin 1945–2000. Grundzüge der Stadtgeschichte (= Kleine Schriftenreihe der Historischen Kommission zu Berlin, Heft 6), Berlin 2002.
Robichon, Jacques/J. V. Ziegelmeyer: L'affaire de Berlin 1945–1959 (L'air du temps), 9. Auflage, Paris 1959.
Rodnick, David: Postwar Germans. An Anthropologist's Account, New Haven, Connecticut, 1948.
Rupieper, Hermann-Josef: Die Wurzeln der westdeutschen Nachkriegsdemokratie. Der amerikanische Beitrag 1945-1952, Opladen 1993.

Sammlung der Länderratsgesetze (LRGS), o. O. und J.
SBZ-Handbuch. Staatliche Verwaltungen, Parteien, gesellschaftliche Organisationen und ihre Führungskräfte in der Sowjetischen Besatzungszone Deutschlands 1945–1949, im Auftrag des Arbeitsbereiches Geschichte und Politik der DDR an der Universität

Mannheim und des Instituts für Zeitgeschichte München hrsg. von Martin Broszat/ Hermann Weber, München 1990.
Schertz, Georg: Schwanenwerder. Eine Insel im Spiegelbild der Geschichte, in: Berlin in Geschichte und Gegenwart. Jahrbuch des Landesarchivs Berlin 2005, S. 209-223.
Scheurig, Bodo: Verräter oder Patrioten. Das Nationalkomitee „Freies Deutschland" und der Bund Deutscher Offiziere in der Sowjetunion 1943-1945, Berlin und Frankfurt am Main 1993.
Schivelbusch, Wolfgang: Vor dem Vorhang. Das geistige Berlin 1945-1948, München und Wien 1995.
Schmidt, Klaus: Die Brandnacht. Dokumente von der Zerstörung Darmstadts am 11. September 1944, 3. Auflage, Darmstadt 1964.
Schmidt, Wolfgang: Vom Feind zum Partner. Amerikanische Deutschlandpolitik von 1944 bis 1949, Bonn 1996.
Schnakenberg, Ulrich: Democracy-building. Britische Einwirkungen auf die Entstehung der Verfassungen Nordwestdeutschlands 1945-1952 (= Veröffentlichungen der Historischen Kommission für Niedersachsen und Bremen, 237), Hannover 2007.
Scholz, Friedrich: Berlin und seine Justiz. Die Geschichte des Kammergerichtsbezirks 1945 bis 1980, Berlin und New York 1982.
Schwarz, Max: MdR. Biographisches Handbuch der Reichstage, Hannover 1965.
Semler, Daniel: Brigitte Helm. Der Vamp des deutschen Films, München 2008.
SMAD-Handbuch. Die Sowjetische Militäradministration in Deutschland 1945-1949, im Auftrag der Gemeinsamen Kommission zur Erforschung der neuesten Geschichte der deutsch-russischen Beziehungen hrsg. von Horst Möller/Alexandr O. Tschubarjan in Zusammenarbeit mit Wladimir P. Koslow/Sergei W. Mironienko/Hartmut Weber, München 2009.
Smith, Bradley F.: The Shadow Warriors. O. S. S. and the Origins of the C. I. A., New York 1983.
Smith, Jean E.: Der Weg ins Dilemma. Preisgabe und Verteidigung der Stadt Berlin, Berlin 1965.
Smith, Jean E.: Lucius D. Clay. An American Life, New York 1990.
Sonnenstuhl, Burkhardt (Hrsg.): Prominente in Berlin-Wannsee und ihre Geschichten, Berlin 2006.
Spandauer Volksblatt, 1946.
Speculum, 1946.
Spencer, K. A.: Flycatcher. Memoirs of an amateur entomologist, The Hague 1992.
Städte-Ordnung für die sechs östlichen Provinzen der Preußischen Monarchie vom 30. Mai 1853, in: Gesetz-Sammlung für die Königlichen Preußischen Staaten, 1853, S. 261-290.
Stadtoberhäupter. Biographien Berliner Bürgermeister im 19. und 20. Jahrhundert, hrsg. von Wolfgang Ribbe (= Berlinische Lebensbilder, Bd. 7), Berlin 1992.
Steger, Bernd: General Clays Stabskonferenzen und die Organisation der amerikanischen Militärregierung in Deutschland. Die „Clay-Minutes" als historische Quelle, in: Vierteljahrshefte für Zeitgeschichte, 27. Jg. 1979, S. 113-130.
Steininger, Rolf: Südtirol im 20. Jahrhundert. Vom Leben und Überleben einer Minderheit, Innsbruck und Wien 1997.
Stiefel, Ernst C./Frank Mecklenburg: Deutsche Juristen im amerikanischen Exil (1933-1950), Tübingen 1991.
Stuttgarter Zeitung, 1946.
Suhr, Susanne: Biographische Einleitung, in: Otto Suhr. Eine Auswahl aus Reden und Schriften, mit einer biographischen Einleitung von Susanne Suhr, Geleitwort von Ernst Fraenkel, Tübingen 1967, S. 3-50.

Tägliche Rundschau, 1946.
Telegraf, 1946.

Tent, James F.: Mission on the Rhine. Reeducation and Denazification in American-Occupied Germany, Chicago und London 1982.
The American Historical Review, 1919/1942/1946.
The American Journal of Sociology, 1921.
The Atlanta Constitution, 1923.
The Berlin Sentinel, 1945.
The Christian Science Monitor, 1946.
The Grooper, 1946.
The New York Times, 1919/1922/1923/1924/1943/1945/1946.
The Papers of General Lucius D. Clay. Germany 1945–1949, Vol. One, edited by Jean Edward Smith, a Publication of the Institute of German Studies at Indiana University supported by the Volkswagen Foundation, Bloomington und London 1974.
The Stars and Stripes, European Edition, 1946.
The Washington Post, 1946/1952/1988.
Thompson, James Westfall/Edgar Nathaniel Johnson: An Introduction to Medieval Europe 300–1500, New York 1937.

Um ein antifaschistisch-demokratisches Deutschland. Dokumente aus den Jahren 1945–1949, Hrsg.: Ministerium für Auswärtige Angelegenheiten der DDR/Ministerium für Auswärtige Angelegenheiten der UdSSR, Berlin 1968.
UNRRA. The History of the United Nations Relief and Rehabilitation Administration, prepared by a special staff under the direction of George Woodbridge, Vol. I, New York 1950.

Views and Facts of Berlin. As seen through the eyes of the American soldier and intended for the folks and friends at home, o. O. und J.
Vorläufige Verfassung von Groß-Berlin, erl. von Dr. Haas, Kämmerer von Groß-Berlin, 4., neubearb. Auflage, Berlin 1947.
Vorwärts, 1946.

Waibel, Dieter: Von der wohlwollenden Despotie zur Herrschaft des Rechts. Entwicklungsstufen der amerikanischen Besatzung Deutschlands 1944–1949 (= Beiträge zur Rechtsgeschichte des 20. Jahrhunderts, 15), Tübingen 1996.
Weber, Hermann/Andreas Herbst: Deutsche Kommunisten. Biographisches Handbuch 1918 bis 1945, 2., überarb. und stark erw. Auflage, Berlin 2008.
Welt und Wort. Literarische Monatsschrift, 1946.
Weniger, Kay: Das große Personenlexikon des Films, Dritter Bd.: F-H, Berlin 2001.
Who's who in CIA. Ein biographisches Nachschlagewerk über 3000 Mitarbeiter der zivilen und militärischen Geheimdienstzweige der USA in 120 Staaten, hrsg. von Julius Mader, Berlin 1968.
Willoughby, John: Remaking the Conquering Heroes. The Social and Geopolitical Impact of the Post-War American Occupation of Germany, New York und Basingstoke 2001.
Winks, Robin W.: Cloak & Gown. Scholars in the Secret War 1939–1961, New York 1987.
Wistrich, Robert: Wer war wer im Dritten Reich. Anhänger, Mitläufer, Gegner aus Politik, Wirtschaft, Militär, Kunst und Wissenschaft, München 1983.

Ziegler, Donald J.: Prelude to Democracy. A Study of Proportional Representation and the Heritage of Weimar Germany 1871–1920 (= University of Nebraska Studies, New Series No. 20), Lincoln, Nebraska, 1958.
Ziemke, Earl F.: The U. S. Army in the Occupation of Germany 1944–1946 (Army Historical Series), Washington, D. C., 1975.
Zur Archäologie der Demokratie in Deutschland. Analysen politischer Emigranten im amerikanischen Geheimdienst, Bd. 1: 1943–1945, hrsg. von Alfons Söllner, Frankfurt am Main 1982.

Zur Archäologie der Demokratie in Deutschland, Bd. 2: Analysen von politischen Emigranten im amerikanischen Außenministerium 1946–1949, hrsg. von Alfons Söllner, Frankfurt am Main 1986.

3. Internet

http://bombsight.org/#15/51.5050/-0.0900.
http://history.fas.harvard.edu/news/?p=258.
http://vimeo.com/12266425.
http://web.utk.edu/~csws/interviews/alexander2.pdf.
http://ww2.debello.ca/balkans/transylvania/index.html.
http://www.americanacademy.de/home/about-us/hans-arnhold-center/.
http://www.berlinbrats.org/pdfs/46Guide.pdf.
http://www.cityofjerseycity.org/hague/index.shtml.
http://www.culver.org/about-culver/introduction/history-a-traditions/overview.
http://www.dar.org/natsociety/history.cfm.
http://www.digam.net/einfuehrung.php?lput=632&.
http://www.frick.org/.
http://www.fr-online.de/zeitgeschichte/internierungslager-mit-eigener-zeitung-und-universitaet,1477344,2802516.html.
http://www.gallagher.com/ww2/chapter11.html.
http://www.gwu.edu/~erpapers/myday/displaydoc.cfm?_y=1946&_f=md000267.
http://www.history.navy.mil/danfs/g4/george_w_goethals.htm.
http://www.history.navy.mil/photos/sh-civil/civsh-g/gen-goet.htm.
http://www.hollandamerica.com/news/NewsRelease.action?newsReleaseId=593.
http://www.ibdb.com/production.php?id=1751.
http://www.ibdb.com/production.php?id=1773.
http://www.lib.uchicago.edu/e/scrc/findingaids/view.php?eadid=ICU.SPCL.ENJOHNSON.
http://www.lib.utexas.edu/taro/utcah/02351/cah-02351.html.
http://www.medievalacademy.org/.
http://www.moma.org/.
http://www.norwayheritage.com/p_ship.asp?sh=mont6.
http://www.skylighters.org/special/cigcamps/.
http://www.sonnenberg-verein.de/.
http://www.theberlinobserver.com/archive/1946V2/V2_N13_Mar_30.pdf.
http://www.usarmygermany.com/School_Comd/USAREUR_SchoolCommand.htm.
http://www.zzf-pdm.de/site/mid__2870/ModeID__0/EhPageID__303/369/default.aspx.
https://my.tennessee.edu/pls/portal/docs/PAGE/WAR/WAR_SOCIETY/ORAL/INTERVIEW_LISTING/INT_ALEXANDERR.PDF.

Personenregister

Abbink, John 287
Achaz *siehe* Duisberg, Carl Ludwig
Adams, Henry 6
Adcock, Clarence L. 67, 101, 103, 106, 109, 142, 219, 323, 329
Adler, Julius O. 178
Alcorn, Robert H. 11
Alden, John R. 279, 288, 298
Alexander, Harley B. 38
Alexander, Richard T. 34, 295
Alexander Jr., Richard T. 295
Anders, Peter 263 f.
Anderson, Albin T. 298
Anderson, Edith B. 89 f.
Anderson, Eugene N. 12, 37–39, 57, 63, 66, 70, 73, 75–77, 84, 92, 105, 116, 133 f., 233, 291, 306, 313
Anderson Jr., Eugene N. 5, 10, 37–39, 63, 66, 73, 75–77, 128
Anderson, James 88
Anderson, James E. 89
Anderson, Julia F. 88
Anderson, Pauline R. 66, 73, 75–77, 80, 84, 116, 133 f., 291, 306
Anderson, William J. 87–89, 92, 336
Anouilh, Jean 82
Armstrong, Mary H. 71
Armstrong, Sinclair W. 71, 145
Arnhold (Familie) 217
Arnhold, Hans 24, 144, 216 f., 340
Arnold, Thurman W. 126
Ashton, John Pennington 225 f., 249, 408

Babcock, William T. 235, 244
Bach, Johann Sebastian 99, 178 f., 301
Baginski, Maximilian 252
Baird (Administrative Officer) 306
Baldner (Familie) 130, 251
Baldner, Angelika 130, 173, 251
Baldner, Charlotte 129, 147, 173, 185, 339
Baldner, Lutz 130, 173, 251
Baldner, Max 26, 51, 129 f., 147, 173, 185, 240, 251, 339, 402 f.
Baldner, Monika 130
Baldner, Thomas 129–131, 147, 251, 403
Baldwin, Dwight H. 211
Bankhardt, Alois 423
Barbour, Philip L. 406
Barker, Ray W. 19, 24, 44–48, 122–125, 132, 139, 141–146, 153–155, 158, 161 f., 164, 166–169, 171, 175–180, 186 f., 189 f., 197–203, 219, 285, 288, 349, 382 f., 385 f., 400

Barlach, Ernst 184
Barnes, Elmer E. 145, 385
Bartók, Béla 184
Basoco, Doris 302 f.
Basoco, Miguel A. 185, 302 f.
Bauer, Carl H. 158
Bauer, Else 158
Baumgartner, Joseph 326
Beam, Jacob D. 84
Beckhart, Benjamin H. 287
Beethoven, Ludwig van 14, 129, 183, 185, 281, 318, 352
Benton, Thomas H. 99
Benton, William B. 77 f.
Berger, Erna 263, 282, 300
Bergsträsser, Ludwig 3, 29 f., 318 f.
Bersarin, Nikolai Erastowitsch 343
Bible, Dana X. 111
Bickford, Alice D. 331
Bickford, John D. 6 f., 100, 331
Biel, Ulrich E. 125, 235
Biklen, Mildred L. C. 294
Blixen, Karen 97
Bond, Charles C. 157
Boothe, Clare *siehe* Luce, Clare Boothe
Borter (Military Government Officer, Karlsruhe) 102
Bose, Henry H. 328
Boser, Petronella 264
Bouchel, Onezima de 90 f.
Boucher, Chauncey S. 231 f.
Bowers, Claude G. 243
Brahms, Johannes 14, 183
Brandt, Günter 227 f.
Breuhaus de Groot, Fritz August 158
Brown, Mrs. (Emily L. Johnsons Haushaltshilfe) 171, 261
Bruchollerie, Monique de la 281
Buchanan, Scott M. 332
Burgess, Randolph 287
Burnham, Lee H. 345
Bush, Henry C. S. 122, 170
Butler, Hugh A. 33, 269, 272, 276
Byler, Arthur W. 303
Byrnes, James F. 78, 210

Cäcilia (Heilige) 283
Candler, Asa G. 90 f.
Carlucci, Orazio R. 285
Caruso, Enrico 285
Casals, Pablo 147
Case, Mr. 81

Celibidache, Sergiu 281, 300
Chard, Robert H. 66f.
Chase, Warren M. 212
Chatham, Mrs. (Overseas Branch, Department of War) 66
Cherdel, Françoise 157
Cherdel, Jean-Yves 157
Cherdel, Marie 157
Cherdel, René 156f.
Chopin, Frédéric 312
Churchill, Winston 266
Clay, Lucius D. 1, 5, 16–19, 21, 27–29, 34f., 44f., 48f., 53f., 66f., 82, 104–109, 111, 113–115, 117, 123f., 126, 132, 138–140, 142f., 148–150, 152, 158, 163f., 166, 168, 178, 186f., 189, 199, 201f., 206, 210, 217–219, 238, 245–247, 251, 253–258, 260, 262, 273, 278, 280, 285, 289f., 293, 297f., 303, 306, 308, 313f., 323, 329, 334, 379–381, 417
Clay, Marjorie McK. 262, 292
Cleere, Roy 304
Clementi, Muzio 221
Clive, John L. 372
Conrad, G. Bryan 114
Cornell, Katharine 82
Creighton, Cuthbert 182
Creighton, Louise 181
Creighton, Mandell 181
Creighton, Thomas Richmond Mandell 181f.
Culver, Henry H. 5
Cunningham Jr., H. Francis 331

Dalada, Daniil Sergejewitsch 156
Davies, Godfrey 6
Davis, Lisa F. 10
Dawson, Marguerite 321
Dawson, William W. 30, 320f., 327
Delahaye, Ina 196, 229
Delahaye, J. V. 196
Demidow, Wladimir Michailowitsch 418
Dernbach, Miette *siehe* Hardy, Miette
Dernbach-Mayen, Joseph 216
Dinesen, Isak *siehe* Blixen, Karen
Dollard, William A. S. 167, 181f.
Donneck (Edgar N. Johnsons Sekretärin) 157, 203, 329
Doren, Carl Van 332
Doren, Mark Van 332
Dorn, Walter L. 6, 12, 15, 19, 67, 74, 103–106, 108f., 122–124, 141–143, 145, 167, 218, 224f., 232f., 235f., 238, 240f., 268, 275, 298, 308, 329, 380
Douglas-Hamilton, Douglas, 14. Herzog von Hamilton 323
Dowd, David L. 231, 272, 298

Draper Jr., William H. 113
Dratwin, Michail Iwanowitsch 246f.
Drew, Marian P. 68
Duisberg, Carl 112
Duisberg, Carl Ludwig 112
Dulles, John Foster 331
Durand, Dana B. 146
Dutilh-von Schmidt Seidlitz, Hedda 158, 400
Dvořák, Antonín Leopold 173, 251

Eberle, Rosalie 172, 315
Echols, Oliver P. 105, 113
Eisenberg, Robert 226
Eisenhower, Dwight D. 118, 140, 251f.
Eitner, Lorenz 13
Engelhorn, Anna 7f., 14, 31, 324–326, 420
Engelhorn, Hedwig 325
Engelhorn, Karl 7, 324
Erhardt, John G. 14, 125, 301, 331
Ernst, Fritz 30
Esch-Marowski, Barbara 394, 396, 401f.
Evans, Maurice 82

Fahy, Charles H. 125, 139
Faulhaber, Michael von 31, 94, 311f.
Fechner, Max 163, 192, 348, 423
Feldman, Iossif Moissejewitsch 229f., 249, 252, 269f., 286, 293, 297, 354, 408, 410f.
Ferguson, Wallace K. 38f.
Feuermann, Emanuel 129
Fischer, Edwin 284
Fling, Fred M. 249f.
Floyd, Emily L. *siehe* Johnson, Emily L.
Fontaine (französischer Vertreter, Alliierte Kontrollbehörde für Deutschland) 120
Forrest (amerikanischer Dolmetscher) 120
Fraenkel, Ernst 64
Francais, Jean 157
Franck, César 99
Franco, Francisco 275
Frank, Karl C. 284
Franklin, Benjamin 3, 25, 36f., 243, 248, 250, 255f., 258, 276, 280, 407
Frantz, Ray W. 93, 221, 244, 248, 253, 257, 264f., 269
Freisler, Roland 119
Frick, Henry C. 83
Frick, Wilhelm 324
Fromson, Howard A. 254
Funk, Walther 25, 45, 144, 164, 167, 217, 313, 339f.
Furtwängler, Wilhelm 127

Gailey Jr., Charles K. 18, 105f., 108f., 111–113, 117f., 120f., 124–127, 136, 143, 381

Gailey III, Charles K.   111 f., 381
Gailey, Christine W.   108, 111
Gailey, John Bruce   112
Gailey, Margaret A.   112
Gailey, Timothy H.   112, 126
Galantiere, Lewis   82
Gannett, Frank E.   178
Gass (Familie)   221, 274
Gass, Alison E.   27, 232, 290, 307
Gass, Geoffrey A.   274
Gass, Sherlock B.   274, 290, 332
Gaulle, Charles de   309
Gaylord, Robert   287
Germer, Edith   183
Germer Jr., Karl J.   182
Geschke, Ottomar   160
Gewehr, Wesley M.   232 f.
Gigli, Beniamino   285
Gilbert, Felix   12, 65, 227, 372
Ginsburg, Michael S.   93
Gittler, Lewis F.   157
Glaser, Anthony J.   2, 24, 125, 155, 262, 305, 388, 410, 412, 414, 418
Glaser, Louis   2, 22, 24, 45, 125, 155, 157 f., 187, 190, 195 f., 214 f., 219, 229, 235, 243, 245, 250, 262-264, 266 f., 278, 281, 286-288, 301, 305, 328 f., 388 f., 400, 410 f., 418
Glaser, Marguerite K.   196, 262, 328
Glassford, William A.   168
Glière, Reinhold   300
Glum (Familie)   283
Glum, Christine   284
Glum, Elisabeth   283
Glum, Friedrich   2, 23, 102, 282 f.
Glum, Hildebrand   284
Glum, Michael   284
Glum, Peter   284
Glum, Ursula   284
Goebbels, Joseph   8, 112
Goethals, George W.   82
Goethe, Johann Wolfgang von   240, 347
Gomułka, Władysław   151
Good, Paul F.   277
Goodman, Benny   282
Göring, Hermann   136, 240, 313, 323
Gouin, Félix   242
Grady, Mary Rita   40
Graves, Helena Clarissa   182
Gray, Cecil W.   331
Gray, Glenn W.   231, 279 f., 288, 298, 320
Greenfield, Kent R.   69
Greindl, Josef   263 f.
Griswold, Dwight P.   33, 269, 272
Grotewohl, Otto   47, 161-163, 192, 204, 235 f., 238, 240, 348, 351-353, 423

Grovert, Robert E.   145
Gründgens, Gustaf   241
Günter, Heinrich   7
Gusev, Fedor Tarasovič   13
Gustavson, Reuben G.   34, 232, 277, 329

Haas, Charlotte   35, 309
Haas, Friedrich   23, 35 f., 53, 227, 309 f., 356, 423 f.
Hague, Frank   285
Hall (britischer Vertreter, Alliierte Kontrollbehörde für Deutschland)   120
Hamilton (Familie)   274
Hamilton, Cliff S.   274
Hamlin, Emmons   211
Hancock, Ernest W.   74, 159, 187, 189
Hardy, Marcel   24, 216, 340
Hardy, Miette   216
Harnack, Adolf von   104
Harper, Robert W.   213
Harrington, Davis O.   87
Harrington, Margaret M.   87
Harrington, Nancy L.   87
Harris, Joel Chandler   265
Hartmann, Richard   271
Hays, Harold   2 f., 22, 225 f., 229 f., 249, 269 f., 286, 328 f., 355, 410 f., 418
Heasty Jr., Charles F.   104
Heath, Donald R.   32, 84, 122 f., 132, 138, 146, 168, 182 f., 212-214, 230, 235, 247, 252, 262, 282, 292, 301, 313
Heath Jr., Donald R.   301
Heath, Louise B.   252, 292, 301, 313
Heller, Aribert   127
Heller, Erich   126 f.
Heller, Helene   126 f.
Heller, William F.   273
Helm, Brigitte   117, 404
Henschel, Georg   223
Henssel, Karl Heinz   25, 243, 250
Herman (amerikanischer Sergeant)   317
Herwarth von Bittenfeld, Hans-Heinrich   327
Herzogenberg, Elisabeth von   283
Herzogenberg, Heinrich von   283
Heß, Rudolf   323
Hildebrand (Familie)   283
Hildebrand, Adolf von   283
Hildebrand, Frieda   283
Hildebrand, Otto   283
Hilldring, John H.   66, 105, 313, 330
Hinde, William Robert Norris   156, 196
Hirth, Ernst   324
Hitler, Adolf   112, 119, 136, 154, 184, 293, 316, 323, 334
Hoegner, Wilhelm   31, 54, 94, 188, 326

Hoffmann, Helmut 403
Holborn, Hajo 12, 71
Hölderlin, Friedrich 184
Holzman, Robert A. 385
Hoover, Glenn E. 87, 336
Hopkins, Robert E. 244
Howe, John P. 77 f.
Howley, Edith 328 f.
Howley, Frank L. 22, 34, 39, 45, 123, 146, 156, 171, 195, 199, 215, 292, 308, 328 f., 387, 402
Hutchins, Robert M. 332
Huth Jr., Carl F. 6, 8, 126
Huxley, Aldous 93

Ickes, Harold L. 78
Impekoven, Holger 6 f.
Ingrams, William Harold 120
Iwanow, Nikolai Wassiljewitsch 230, 234, 242, 252

Jackson, Robert H. 228
James II., König von England, Schottland und Irland 226
Jendretzky, Hans 204, 348
Joachimsen, Paul 7
Johnson (Familie) 27, 39 f., 127, 290
Johnson, Candice E. 1, 2 f., 7 f., 10–12, 16, 26–30, 32, 36, 70, 72, 82, 85, 87, 107, 128, 159, 172, 174 f., 185, 187, 193, 199, 204, 210 f., 214, 220–222, 231, 239, 243 f., 253, 256, 261 f., 268, 272, 277 f., 288 f., 299, 301–303, 307, 311, 313, 315, 319, 326, 328, 365–371, 376–378, 391, 396, 405–407, 416, 426
Johnson, Emily L. 1 f., 6, 10–15, 17, 26–28, 32, 38–41, 43 f., 66, 73, 76, 83, 85, 90, 95 f., 100, 102, 107, 118, 121, 127, 133, 140, 150, 160, 165 f., 172, 174 f., 177, 179 f., 185, 188 f., 193, 199, 205, 207, 210 f., 214, 220–222, 231 f., 237, 239, 244, 246, 248, 253, 256 f., 261 f., 264 f., 268 f., 272, 275, 277–279, 289 f., 296 f., 299, 301, 305, 307, 312 f., 359, 367–369, 376–378
Johnson, Frank E. 5, 72, 75, 171, 174, 180, 202, 206, 215, 291, 295, 306, 331
Johnson, Jack 90
Johnson, John F. 10, 13, 26 f., 38 f., 51, 68, 70, 73, 79, 85, 95, 107, 112, 121, 128, 138, 140, 143, 147 f., 150, 159, 166, 172, 179 f., 187–189, 204, 207, 215, 220 f., 245 f., 253, 256, 260 f., 265, 273 f., 277, 289, 299, 301, 303 f., 307, 312, 314, 332 f., 367 f., 378
Johnson, Lucille 72 f., 291
Johnson, Mabel A. 5, 215

Johnson, Mildred H. *siehe* Williams, Mildred H.
Johnson, Norman D. 27, 72 f., 174, 215, 291, 295 f.
Johnson, Samuel 146
Johnson, Thomas R. 2 f., 8, 10–13, 15 f., 26–30, 32 f., 36, 39–41, 68, 70, 72 f., 79, 82, 85, 95, 107, 112, 116, 121, 138, 140, 143, 148, 150, 159, 166, 172, 174–176, 179, 185, 187–189, 193, 199, 204, 210 f., 214–216, 220–222, 231, 239, 243–246, 253, 256, 261 f., 265, 268, 272, 274, 277 f., 288 f., 297, 299, 301–304, 307, 311–313, 315, 319, 326, 328, 333, 365–371, 376–378, 391, 396, 405–407, 416, 426
Jones, Lawrence McC. 111
Joranson, Einar 6
Jordan, Karl 8
Joublanc, Joseph C. 345
Joyce, James 112
Jurr, Gerhard 171, 200

Kammermeier, Wilhelm 171, 200
Karl der Große 141 f.
Kasatkin (sowjetischer Hauptmann) 355
Kasprzycki, Matthew J. 345
Katz, Barry M. 372
Kaufmann, Karl 324
Kazewa, Eugenia 229
Keating, Frank A. 19, 28, 48, 54, 189, 200–202, 213, 245, 250–255, 266 f., 270 f., 275, 286, 292 f., 297, 301, 303–305, 308, 312, 329, 384 f., 416
Keenan, Joseph D. 256
Kennedy, John F. 66
Kern, Katharina 204
Kidd, Coburn B. 232
King, Alfred Hazell 146
Kirchheimer, Otto 64
Kissinger, Henry 32
Klett, Arnulf 149
Klingler, Karl 129
Knappen, Marshall M. 84, 94, 105 f., 108, 113, 124, 142
Knoll, Robert E. 38
Kodály, Zoltán 184
Koeltz, Louis Marie 246–248
Kollwitz, Käthe 184
Kotikow, Alexandr Georgijewitsch 176, 191, 197, 199, 204, 266, 270 f., 304 f., 352, 359, 383
Kramer (Sekretärin) 120
Kramer, Abe 222 f., 233, 270
Krieger, Leonard 65
Kristeller, Friedrich 145
Krüger, Karl 223

Krutch, Joseph W. 145 f.
Kunheim, Hugo 117
Kunheim, Pieter 117

Laiou (Familie) 40
Laiou, Angeliki 40
Lancaster, Lane W. 244
Lancaster, Mary 244, 261
Lancaster, Mary B. 244
Lançon, Charles J. M. 153 f., 383
Landin, Harold W. 320
Lang, Fritz 117
Leber, Annedore 136
Leber, Julius 136
Leber, Katharina 136
Leber, Matthias 136
Lee, Mabel 146 f.
Legal, Ernst 264
Lehmann, Paul 7, 45
Lemmer, Ernst 131 f.
Lenin, Wladimir Iljitsch 191, 343
Lesser, Moritz Ernst 117
Lewin (sowjetischer Leutnant) 181
Lhévinne, Rosina 39
Lichtenstein, Walter 126, 232
Lincoln, Abraham 39
Lindemann, Leopold 129
Lippmann, Walter 271 f.
List, Carroll Glenn 221
List, Eugene 221
Loew, Dieter 7 f., 420
Loomis, John J. 133
Loomis, Kelly 132
Loomis, Virginia P. *siehe* Pettit, Virginia M.
Lothrop, Harriett M. 90
Louis, Joe 90
Löw-Suter, Marcus 7 f.
Löwenthal, Hermann 300, 353
Luce, Clare Boothe 179
Luce, Henry R. 178 f.
Lüdemann, Hermann 264
Luther, Martin 132

MacArthur, Douglas 79
MacDonald, John C. 385
MacNeill, John P. 266
Madden, J. Warren 126
Marcuse, Herbert 12 f., 40, 64
Maria II., Königin von England, Schottland und Irland 226
Markgraf, Paul 153, 343
Maron, Karl 52, 310, 343
Marshall (Familie) 278
Marshall, Leon S. 278 f.
Mason, Henry 211
Mauldin, William H. 110

Mauleon (französischer Vertreter, Alliierte Kontrollbehörde für Deutschland) 120
McCarthy, Joseph R. 33, 38, 63
McClintic, Guthrie 82
McClure, Robert A. 114, 127, 149
McGehee, Daniel R. 200 f.
McLaughlin, Kathleen 170, 230
McLean Jr., Donald H. 126, 164
McLean, Jack 164
McNarney, Joseph T. 114, 140, 212, 258
McSherry, Frank J. 114
Meade, Frank C. 113, 127
Meinecke, Friedrich 65, 71, 227
Melchior, Hedwig 134 f.
Mercer, James Sidney 87
Mercer, Margaret V. 87
Meredith, Burgess 110
Meyer, Vincent 174
Meyer-Wendeborn, Willi 324
Middleton, Dr. (Military Government British Troops Berlin) 181
Mikołajczyk, Stanisław 151
Milburn, Bryan L. 104, 108, 113, 115, 201, 256, 303
Milne, Alan A. 312
Mitchell Jr., Americus 200 f., 211, 255
Mitchum, Robert 110
Molotow, Wjatscheslaw Michailowitsch 210, 293
Mommsen, Konrad 226 f.
Mommsen, Theodor 227
Mommsen, Theodor Ernst 227
Moore, Burton E. 172
Moore, Hanna E. 172, 315 f.
Morell, Theodor 112
Morgan, Albert C. 169, 172
Morgen, Ernst von 130
Morgen, Margarethe von 130
Morris, Brewster H. 165, 170, 178, 182, 236, 240, 258, 329
Mosely, Philip E. 13
Mozart, Wolfgang Amadeus 251, 263, 282
Muccio, John J. 123, 212, 329
Müller, Josef 31, 327, 342
Muller, Walter J. 32, 326, 379
Murie, Alison G. *siehe* Gass, Alison E.
Murphy, Robert D. 21, 44, 84, 106, 109, 113 f., 117, 121 f., 138–141, 143 f., 163, 166, 168, 170, 200–202, 213 f., 292, 329, 380
Murr, Wilhelm 321
Mussolini, Benito 209
Muthesius, Eckart 216

Nares, Eric Paytherus 153 f., 196, 383
Neumann, Franz 182 f., 256, 422

Neumann, Franz L. 11–13, 34, 64, 135, 183, 193f., 219, 256
Neumann, Karl August 263
Neville, Glenn T. 178
Newman, James R. 28, 320, 379
Novalis 184
Nye, Wilbur S. 168f.

Oldfather (Familie) 273
Oldfather, Charles Henry 5–9, 36, 68f., 77, 92f., 202, 205–207, 219f., 231, 245, 272f., 279, 288f., 298
Oldfather, Margaret K. 273
Olsen, C. Arild 252
Oncken, Hermann 7, 45
Oppenheim, Franz 144
Oppenheimer, Clara 8
Oppenheimer, Clemens 8
Oppenheimer, Fritz E. 217f.
Oppenheimer, Wolfgang 7f.
Osóbka-Morawski, Edward 151
Ostrowski, Otto 264
Otzen, Johannes 144

Paddock, Albert W. 244
Padover, Saul K. 127, 157
Panin, Alexei Wassiljewitsch 270
Pape, Wesley F. 267
Papen, Franz von 323
Parkman, Henry C. 105f.
Patton Jr., George S. 94
Pauley, Edwin W. 78
Pawling, George F. 345
Peterson, Wilma 132
Pettit, Virginia M. 132f.
Pfeiffer, Anton 327
Phenix, Elizabeth Q. 109
Pieck, Arthur 343
Pieck, Wilhelm 52, 162f., 191, 204, 258, 268, 343, 348, 352f., 423
Pirtle, James J. 333
Platow, Thomas 402, 404
Pollock, James K. 16–18, 27, 30, 43, 48, 54, 68, 103–106, 108f., 113f., 141, 202, 206, 245, 260, 262, 293, 298, 321, 379
Posner, Ernst 133
Posner, Katharina 80, 133
Post, Gaines 10, 65
Preysing-Lichtenegg-Moos, Konrad Graf von 311f.
Prokofjew, Sergei Sergejewitsch 300
Proust, Marcel 112
Puccini, Giacomo 311

Raeder, Erich 228, 323
Ranke, Leopold von 182

Rathkolb, Oliver 4, 13
Rausch, Adolf 30
Raysor, Ellen D. 95
Raysor, Thomas M. 95
Redmann, Albert 24f., 216, 340
Reed, Philip D. 287
Reinhardt, Max 240
Rembrandt 184
Renner, Karl 14
Reuter, Ernst 264
Rheinstein, Max 51, 93, 128f., 131, 147, 184, 251, 336, 339
Ribbentrop, Joachim von 323
Richmond, Clarence 282f.
Riddleberger, James W. 84, 138, 330
Ries, Henry 392
Robertson, Sir Brian Hubert 246f., 258
Rodnick, David 224f.
Rodnick, Elizabeth A. 224f.
Rogers, George H. 273
Rogers, Margarete H. 273, 312
Roosevelt, Anna Eleanor 85
Roosevelt, Franklin D. 85, 201
Roosevelt, Theodore 78
Rosendale, David 317
Rosengren, Erik L. 262
Rosengren, Roswell P. 120, 262
Rosenlof, George W. 332
Rosenman, Samuel I. 201
Rosenwald, Henry (Heinz) M. 101
Rosenzweig (amerikanischer Captain) 67, 81, 83
Ross, Ethel P. 11
Russell, William F. 295

Sabo, John A. 345
Saint-Saëns, Camille 264
Sanow, Artur 28, 36, 157, 174, 178, 194, 203, 207f., 223, 233, 239, 254, 284, 308, 312, 314, 316–318, 327–329, 395, 397
Sattler, Carl 102, 104
Scammon, Richard M. 321
Schacht, Hjalmar 228, 324
Schaper, Uwe 4
Scherff, Julius 300, 353
Schertz, Georg 361
Schevill, Ferdinand 6, 9
Schicht, Johann Heinrich 144f.
Schipa, Tito 285
Schkwarin, Alexei Iwanowitsch 119
Schmidt, Bob 297
Schmidt, Herbert 160, 221, 273, 303
Schmidt, Karl 263
Schmitt, Bernadotte E. 6f.
Scholz, Arno 194, 227
Schönberg, Arnold 129

Personenregister

Schorske, Carl E. 372
Schostakowitsch, Dmitri Dmitrijewitsch 300
Schryver, Elliott W. 372
Schubert, Franz 14, 27, 183, 251, 264, 282, 290
Schukow, Georgi Konstantinowitsch 343, 357
Schumacher, Kurt 190, 213
Schumann, Robert 264, 282
Schünemann, Georg 129
Schütz, Gert 404
Schuyler, Cortlandt V. R. 96
Schuyler, Philip V. R. 96
Schuyler, Wynona C. 87, 96
Schwabacher, Adolph 145
Schweitzer, Jürgen 111
Scott, Arthur P. 8
Seifried, Josef 327
Sellers, James L. 231f., 239, 245, 260, 274, 279, 288, 298
Sellers, Nell K. 239, 274
Senning, John P. 93
Shakespeare, William 82
Sheehan, William R. 29, 318f.
Shumate, Roger V. 320
Siegfried, André 201
Smirnow, Dmitri Iwanowitsch 146, 153-155, 351f.
Smith (amerikanischer Major) 66f., 81f., 86
Soldatow, W. G. 119
Sooter (Bekannter von Edgar N. Johnson) 299
Sophokles 82
Sosulja, Alexandr Michailowitsch 286, 294, 305, 355, 410
Speer, Albert 112
Spencer, Kenneth Angus 196, 286f., 294
Stalin, Iossif Wissarianowitsch 151, 192
Stassen, Harold E. 272
Stayer, Morrison C. 113f.
Steere, Anna W. 146f.
Steere, Loyd V. 124, 146f., 158, 168, 329-331
Steinmetz, Charles P. 89
Steinway, Henry E. 75
Steinweg, Heinrich Engelhard *siehe* Steinway, Henry E.
Stepanek, Natasha 307
Stepanek, Olga F. 257, 307
Stepanek, Orin 257, 276, 307
Stephens, Thomas M. 317
Sternberger, Dolf 30
Sternheim, Carl 240
Still, Bayrd 39

Stradivari, Antonio 185
Strang, Sir William 213
Strauß, Meta 194
Strauss, Richard 14
Streich, Rita 263
Streicher, Julius 323
Streletzky, Ingeborg von 201
Strucksberg, Georg 266, 271
Sudakow, A. N. 181
Suhr, Otto 20, 53, 193-195, 256, 308, 351, 421
Suhr, Susanne 193f.
Swart, Hugo 310
Sweet, Paul R. 70, 92, 127, 157, 200, 231, 272f., 277, 331
Swoboda, Leo A. 156f.

Taylor, John W. 34, 113, 124, 142, 252, 295
Taylor, Katherine W. 252
Taylor, Maxwell D. 201
Telschow, Ernst 102
Thayer, Charles W. 168, 170, 331
Thompson, James W. 6, 8, 126
Thompson Jr., Llewellyn E. 151
Tolstoi, Lew 182
Tolstoi, Lew Nikolajewitsch 182
Treece, Will 68
Trivers, Howard 284, 288
Truman, Harry S. 78, 201, 266
Truscott Jr., Lucian K. 94
Tschaikowsky, Peter Iljitsch 281

Ulbricht, Walter 2, 52, 191, 258, 343, 348, 423
Umberto, Kronprinz von Italien 212
Utter, Marvin E. 133

Vedeler, Harold C. 68-70, 75, 77, 92, 122, 263, 284, 291, 298, 306, 313
Vedeler, Marguerite C. 68, 70, 75, 79, 291, 306
Vetter, Ewald 184, 403

Wagner, Richard 264
Wallace, Henry A. 201
Walstrom, Hannah 74, 215, 291, 306, 331
Walton, Stephen 329
Washington, George 217
Wason, Robert R. 287
Weber, Alfred 30
Weber, Helene 26, 302
Weber, Marianne 31
Weber, Max 31
Wegscheider, Hans 324
Weidenreich, Peter *siehe* Wyden, Peter H.
Weigert, Oscar 64

Weisenborn, Günther 26, 302
Wellman, William A. 110
Wells, Roger H. 120, 235
Wepper, Angela 130
Werkmeister, Lucyle T. 316
Werkmeister, William H. 316
Werner, Arthur 154, 191, 233, 310, 343, 413
Werts, Leo R. 140
Wiesner, Jean H. 109
Wiesner, Louis A. 64, 84, 109, 122 f., 329
Wilhelm III. von Oranien, König von England, Schottland und Irland 226
Williams, David G. 74 f., 291
Williams, David H. 74
Williams, Kirsten D. 74
Williams, Mildred H. 7, 74 f., 100, 215, 291, 306, 331
Williams, William G. 74
Williamson, Francis T. 69
Wilson, Anna W. *siehe* Steere, Anna W.
Wilson, Woodrow 249
Wimberly, Lowry C. 276

Wimmer, Ulrich 119
Winnacker, Rudolph A. 69, 77, 92
Winnecke, Anna *siehe* Engelhorn, Anna
Winnecke, August 7, 324
Winnecke, Hedwig 324
Winning, Charles D. 30, 320 f.
Winning, Freda G. 321
Winzer, Otto 343
Wolf, Dieter 314, 316
Wolff, Erich J. 14
Wolford, Claire A. 39
Woods, Sam E. 201
Wyden, Peter H. 170

Yorck von Wartenburg, Paul Graf 251

Zernick, Helmut 183
Ziegelmeyer, Jean Victor 248 f., 270, 286, 355, 408, 410 f., 418
Ziegelmeyer, Jeanne 358
Ziegelmeyer, Joseph 357
Ziegler, Donald J. 38
Zumwinkel, Essie 215, 231, 289, 304